Marc David Baer is professor of International History at the London School of Economics and Political Science. He is the author of five books, including *Honored by the Glory of Islam: Conversion* and *Conquest in Ottoman Europe*, which won the Albert Hourani Prize. He lives in Lo

Praise for *The (*

'A compellingly readable account of one of the great world empires from its origins in thirteenth century to modern times... Blending the sacred and the profane, the social and the political, the sublime and the absurd, Baer brings his subject to life in rich vignettes. An outstanding book' Eugene Rogan, author of *The Fall of the Ottomans*

'A scintillating and brilliantly panoramic account of the history of the Ottoman empire, from its genesis to its dissolution ... It challenges and transforms how we think of 'East' and 'West,' 'Enlightenment,' and 'modernity,' and directly confronts the horrors as well as the achievements of Ottoman rule' Peter Sarris, University of Cambridge

'A fuller, fresher view of the dynasty that ruled an empire for 500 years and helped shape the West ... A major achievement' Anthony Sattin, *The Spectator*

'[Baer's] enlightening forays into the side alleys of Ottoman history make this book very enjoyable ... splendid' *Literary Review*

'Forceful history' *New Yorker*

'Baer's colourful, readable book is informed by all the newest research on his massive subject. In showing how an epic of universal empire, conquest and toleration turned into the drama of nationalism, crisis, and genocide, he gives us not only an expansive history of the Ottomans, but an expanded history of Europe' James McDougall, University of Oxford

'Provocative and engaging, this book is a refreshing new study of the Ottoman Empire and its legacy . . . Populated by vivid characters and descriptions of events this book is well-paced, rich and beautifully executed. Essential reading not only for those interested in the history of the Middle East, but also for those interested more broadly in the history of Europe, the history of Empire and the politics of genocide' Katherine Pangonis, author of *Queens of Jerusalem*

'[A] fascinating, thought-provoking book that wears its learning lightly. It asks us not only to rethink the Ottomans, but also to consider what exactly constitutes being European' Roger Crowley, *Aspects of History*

'An epic, sweeping history of the Ottoman Empire . . . It's absolutely fabulous' Alex Churchill, History Hack podcast

'A thrilling history of one of the world's largest empires' *All About History*

'Expertly captures the undercurrents of Ottoman history . . . There's no study more masterful' *Library Journal*

THE OTTOMANS

Khans, Caesars, and Caliphs

MARC DAVID BAER

LONDON

First published in Great Britain in 2021 by Basic Books UK
An imprint of John Murray Press
An Hachette UK company

This paperback edition published in 2022

8

Maps drawn by Rodney Paull

A CIP catalogue record for this title is available from the British Library

Paperback ISBN 9781473695740
eBook ISBN 9781473695726

Printed and bound in Great Britain by Clays Ltd, Elcograf S.p.A.

John Murray Press policy is to use papers that are natural, renewable and
recyclable products and made from wood grown in sustainable forests.
The logging and manufacturing processes are expected to conform to the
environmental regulations of the country of origin.

Basic Books UK
Carmelite House
50 Victoria Embankment
London EC4Y 0DZ

www.basicbooks.uk

The authorised representative in the EEA is Hachette Ireland, 8 Castlecourt
Centre, Dublin 15, D15 XTP3, Ireland (email: info@hbgi.ie)

CONTENTS

AUTHOR'S NOTE

To make the book accessible to the general reader, Ottoman and Turkish names have been rendered in modern Turkish spelling, and non-English terms have been translated into English. Those Arabic, Ottoman, and Turkish words generally known in English, such as *pasha*, *sheikh*, and the like, are presented in their English forms.

The Turkish letters and their pronunciation are as follows:

c as *j* in John
ç as *ch* in church
ğ is silent; it lengthens the preceding vowel
ı as *i* in cousin
ş as *sh* in ship

Istanbul or Constantinople? Despite the fact that the name Constantinople was used by the Ottomans themselves, it is convention to call the Byzantine city of Constantinople by that name only until the Ottoman conquest in 1453, and thereafter to use the name Istanbul, which derives from the Greek *stin poli* (to the city), the name officially given to the city only after the fall of the empire and the birth of the Turkish Republic in 1923. This book follows that convention.

Because the Ottomans used the term 'Anatolia' to refer to Southwest Asia/Asia Minor, this is the term used in this book.

Likewise, the region often referred to as the Balkans—but which the Ottomans called Rûmeli (land of the Romans)—is rendered as 'Rûm'. The approximate English translation of this is Southeastern Europe, the term most often used in this book.

To Esra, Azize, and Firuze

Where are the valiant princes of whom I have told?
Those who said 'The world is mine'?
Doom has taken them, earth has hidden them.
Who inherits this transient world,
The world to which people come, from which they go,
The world whose latter end is death?

The Book of Dede Korkut, medieval epic

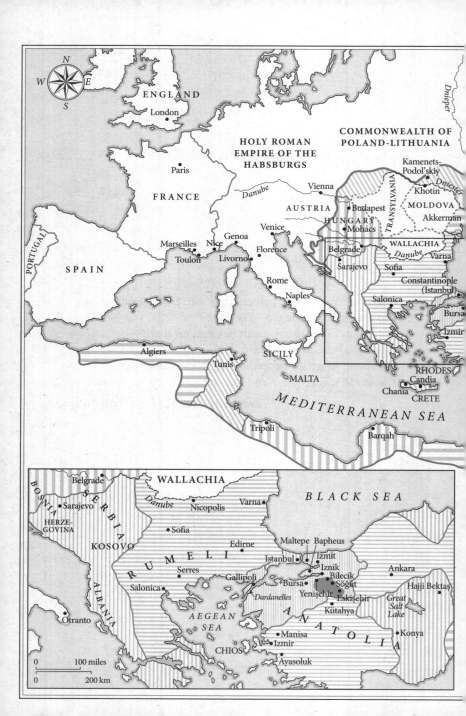

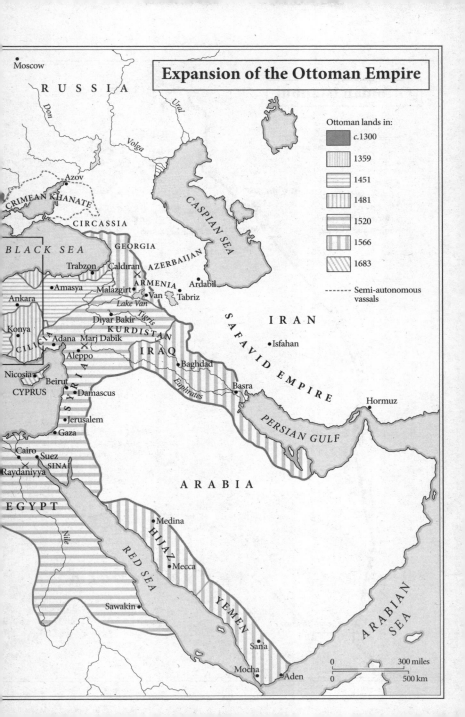

Expansion of the Ottoman Empire

Ottoman lands in:

- c.1300
- 1359
- 1451
- 1481
- 1520
- 1566
- 1683

-------- Semi-autonomous vassals

Moscow

RUSSIA

Don

Ural

Volga

Azov

CRIMEAN KHANATE

CIRCASSIA

CASPIAN SEA

BLACK SEA

GEORGIA

Trabzon

Çaldıran

AZERBAIJAN

ARMENIA

Ardabil

IRAN

Amasya

Malazgirt

Van

Tabriz

Ankara

Lake Van

SAFAVID EMPIRE

Isfahan

Konya

Diyar Bakir

Tigris

KURDISTAN

CILICIA

Adana

Marj Dabik

IRAQ

Aleppo

Baghdad

Nicosia

SYRIA

Beirut

Damascus

Euphrates

Basra

Hormuz

CYPRUS

Jerusalem

PERSIAN GULF

Gaza

Cairo

Suez

SINAI

Raydaniyya

EGYPT

ARABIA

Nile

Medina

HIJAZ

RED SEA

Mecca

Sawakin

YEMEN

ARABIAN SEA

Sana

Mocha

Aden

0   300 miles

0   500 km

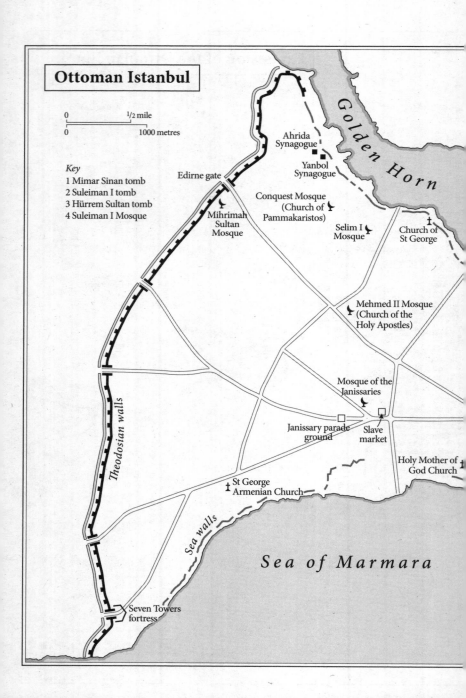

Ottoman Istanbul

0   1/2 mile
0   1000 metres

Key
1 Mimar Sinan tomb
2 Suleiman I tomb
3 Hürrem Sultan tomb
4 Suleiman I Mosque

Golden Horn

Ahrida
Synagogue

Yanbol
Synagogue

Edirne gate

Conquest Mosque
(Church of
Pammakaristos)

Selim I
Mosque

Church of
St George

Mihrimah
Sultan
Mosque

Mehmed II Mosque
(Church of the
Holy Apostles)

Theodosian walls

Mosque of the
Janissaries

Janissary parade
ground

Slave
market

Holy Mother of
God Church

St George
Armenian Church

Sea walls

Sea of Marmara

Seven Towers
fortress

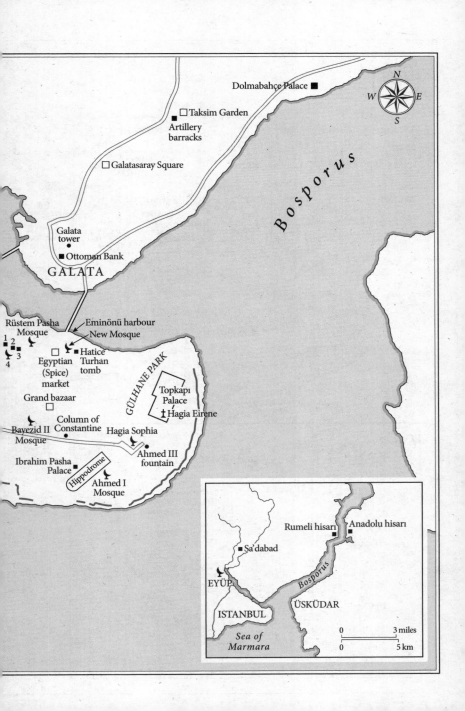

Dolmabahçe Palace ■

□ Taksim Garden
■ Artillery
barracks

□ Galatasaray Square

B o s p o r u s

N
W   E
S

Galata
tower •
■ Ottoman Bank
GALATA

Rüstem Pasha
Mosque
1 2
■ ■
🕌 □ ■ Hatice
4 3 □ Turhan
Egyptian tomb
(Spice)
market

Eminönü harbour
New Mosque

Grand bazaar
□

GÜLHANE PARK

Topkapı
Palace
✝ Hagia Eirene

Column of
Constantine
Bayezid II
Mosque

Hagia Sophia
🕌
• Ahmed III
fountain

Ibrahim Pasha
Palace ■
Hippodrome
• Ahmed I
Mosque

Rumeli hisarı ■   ■ Anadolu hisarı

■ Sa'dabad

🕌
EYÜP

Bosporus

İSTANBUL   **ÜSKÜDAR**

*Sea of
Marmara*

0   3 miles
0   5 km

The Ottoman Empire after 1878

Ottoman Empire

RUSSIAN EMPIRE

CASPIAN SEA

GEORGIA

AZERBAIJAN

Batum
Kars
Sarıkamış
ARMENIA
Aras
Trabzon
Erzurum
Doğubayezid
Erzincan
Van
Urmia
Sivas
Dersim
Elazığ
Bitlis
Hakkari
Malatya
Diyar Bakir
Urfa
Ras al-Ayn
Mosul

IRAN

Isfahan

Tigris

Aleppo
Deir ez-Zor
Baghdad
Beirut
Euphrates
Kut
Damascus
Basra
Jerusalem

PERSIAN GULF

Medina

HIJAZ

RED SEA

EGYPT
(British occup. 1882;
indep. 1922)

Mecca

YEMEN

ARABIAN SEA

| 0 | | 300 miles |
| 0 | | 500 km |

INTRODUCTION

The White Castle

HISTORIANS ARE KNOWN for their love of maps, which illuminate not only the physical contours of their geographic subjects but also the ambitious mindsets of their makers. Over two decades ago, I was conducting research in the Topkapı Palace Library in Istanbul for my first book. Off-limits to the hordes of tourists that inundated the palace grounds six days a week, the small library was refreshingly quiet. Located in the former prayer space of a diminutive red-brick mosque built by Mehmed II in the fifteenth century, the library is lined with brilliant blue tiles with intricate green and red floral patterns. A small panel depicts the Ka'ba at Mecca, the black, cube-shaped shrine that is Islam's holiest place. Containing one reading table for researchers and another facing it for staff to watch over them, the room was freezing cold in winter, lacking heat and often electricity. To write or type on a laptop, researchers had to wear thin leather gloves or winter gloves with the fingers cut off. In summer it was cloyingly hot, humid, and dark, the windows shuttered to block out the sunlight, the dust, and the noise.

The reading room offered one ray of hope, for its internal door led to one of the richest manuscript collections in the world, a place only the library staff were allowed to enter. But one had to come prepared. One could not ask to see just any valuable work from the past, such as, say, something in Armenian, Greek, or Hebrew from Mehmed II's personal library. Scholars were required to declare their research interests well in advance and have them approved by the Turkish Foreign Ministry, Interior Ministry, and Culture Ministry. One could not simply change research topic midtrip. What I usually read were seventeenth-century Ottoman chronicles. Some came in dark-red leather bindings, sometimes frayed or bug eaten, written on paper with a background of marbled swirls, the script accentuated in gold-leaf lettering. What a novelist once wrote about another library is true of that reading room: 'Books and silence filled the room, and a wonderful rich smell of leather bindings, yellowing paper, mould, a strange hint of seaweed and old glue, of wisdom, secrets and dust'.[1]

Although I experienced an acute case of document jealousy whenever the researchers near me were given a golden illuminated Seljuk Qur'an or a sixteenth-century copy of Ferdowsi's Persian *Book of Kings*, each scintillating with their brilliantly painted miniatures, nothing was as remarkable as what I saw once thanks to a Japanese television crew filming a documentary on Asian seafaring. One day, I opened the five-hundred-year-old intricately carved mosque door to view the surviving segment of Piri Reis's famous early sixteenth-century world map depicting Spain and West Africa, the Atlantic Ocean, the Caribbean, and the South American coastline, bathed in bright artificial light.

The white-gloved Turkish librarians unrolled it, spreading its gazelle-skin parchment out in the small room, revealing its precious, colourful detail inch by inch to the appreciative camera crew. At his own initiative, Piri Reis of Gallipoli, a former corsair and future Ottoman navy admiral, had drawn one of the earliest surviving maps of the coastline of the New World. He based it on Christopher Columbus's original, which is lost, and even interviewed a crew member from Columbus's voyages. To produce for the sultan one of the most complete and accurate maps in the world, Piri Reis had consulted ancient Ptolemaic, medieval Arab, and contemporary Portuguese and Spanish maps. Imagining themselves as rulers of a universal empire and rivalling the Portuguese in the battle for the seas from Egypt to Indonesia, the Ottomans were interested in keeping up with the latest Western European discoveries. Why weren't these connections better known in the West today? Had the Ottomans participated in what is known as the Age of Discovery? What role did they play in European and Asian history?

Like its language, the Ottoman Empire (ca. 1288–1922) was not simply Turkish. Nor was it made up only of Muslims. It was not a Turkish empire. Like the Roman Empire, it was a multiethnic, multilingual, multiracial, multireligious empire that stretched across Europe, Africa, and Asia. It incorporated part of the territory the Romans had ruled. As early as 1352 and as late as the dawn of the First World War, the Ottoman dynasty controlled parts of Southeastern Europe, and at its height it governed almost a quarter of Europe's land area. From 1402 to 1453, the Byzantine city of Adrianople (today Edirne, Turkey), located on the Southeastern European territory of Thrace, functioned as the second seat of the Ottoman dynasty. Constantinople, the capital of the Eastern Roman Empire—or Byzantium, remembered as the Byzantine Empire—served as the Ottoman capital for nearly five centuries, beginning with its conquest in 1453. It was not given the new name of Istanbul until 1930, seven years after the establishment of the Turkish Republic amid the ruins of the empire. If for nearly five hundred years the Ottoman Empire had straddled East and West, Asia and Europe, why had its dual nature been forgotten? Had accepted ideas about it changed?

THE WHITE CASTLE

Sometimes it takes a novel to help us understand the true nature of a thing. Nobel Prize–winning Turkish novelist Orhan Pamuk's

The White Castle weaves a tale of identity swapping that questions the received wisdom about East and West, the Ottoman Empire, and the rest of Europe. Set in the seventeenth century, at the height of Ottoman confidence and territorial expansion, the book begins with an Ottoman Muslim astrologer known as Hoja being given custody of an Italian slave in Istanbul. The slave, a young, un-named scholar who bears an uncanny resemblance to Hoja, had been captured by pirates and sold in the Istanbul slave market. The narrator, whom we believe at this point to be the Italian, de-clares the resemblance between himself and his new custodian to be eerie. Upon first sight, he thinks he is looking at himself. Eager to learn about the scientific and intellectual advances in Western Europe, Hoja promises to free his doppelgänger once the Italian has taught him everything he knows, from astronomy to medi-cine. What he really wants, however, is to understand everything about his lookalike, seeking an answer to the question 'Why am I what I am'?[2]

Hoja and the slave spend months sitting opposite each other, writing down all their recollections in an effort to discover the character of the other. At first, Hoja is incapable of answering the question of who he is, other than by declaring what he is not. The slave insists that Hoja write about his faults: 'He had his neg-ative sides like everyone else, and if he delved into them he would find his true self'. By writing about his own faults, Hoja would come to understand how others have become who they are. The slave, who hopes to gain his freedom by turning the tables and proving himself superior to his master, believes that, through this process of self-reflection and faultfinding, Hoja might find him-self as contemptible as his slave. What they end up with instead is a sort of equality. Standing next to each other, gazing into the mirror, they see how the two of them are in fact one and the same. Hoja decides that they will switch identities and places. He will take up the slave's life in Venice, and the slave will take up his in Istanbul.[3]

Using their combined scientific knowledge, Hoja and his slave create an incredible new weapon, which is used by the Ottoman army at the siege of the novel's namesake white castle in Poland. The pure white castle set against the background of a black forest, however, is 'beautiful and unattainable'. Stuck in a swamp, the weapon fails. Disgraced and fearing for his life, Hoja sets off for Venice in the guise of the Italian slave, while his Italian double takes up Hoja's life as an Ottoman scholar.[4] Because people the world over are so similar to one another, it seems, they can easily switch places.

While the reader is led to believe that the two men exchange lives at the white castle, by the end of the novel one cannot determine who is narrator, who is master, who is slave, or even whether master and slave are the same person. Through his doubled character Hoja, Pamuk asks the reader to consider where the boundary between East and West lies, and whether Muslim and Christian— the Ottoman Empire and the rest of Europe—are so different after all. As the Italian declares of his Turkish doppelgänger in the end, 'I loved him with the stupid revulsion and stupid joy of knowing myself'.[5]

Like Pamuk's novel, *The Ottomans* demonstrates that the Ottoman Empire is not, as it is usually perceived, unrelated to Europe. The Ottomans ruled over an empire that was partly in Asia but also partly in Europe. It was a European empire that remains an integral part of European culture and history. By this I do not mean that the Ottomans are a part of European history because they occupied Europeans' territory and minds—causing fear and distrust, curiosity and admiration.[6] This is not a book about the place of the Ottomans in European political thought. This is a book that asks the reader to look at Europe—both as an idea and as a geography—as a whole, to conceptualise a Europe that is not merely Christian. Imagine, if you will, a Europe that is Europe whether it is ruled by Christians or by Muslims. Imagine that the boundary of Europe did not end at the walls of Vienna—the edge of the Holy Roman Empire, the scene of two failed Ottoman sieges. How then might we define Europe, and who might we include as rightfully belonging to it?

It is conventional to interpret the Ottoman conquest of Constantinople in 1453 as a severing of the eastern lands of the Roman Empire (the Byzantine Empire) from Europe.[7] But does European territory cease belonging to Europe when it is ruled by Muslims? According to the Ottomans, their advance into Europe meant that they were the inheritors of Byzantium and were thus to be considered the new Romans. These Muslim rulers of Europe saw themselves as the rightful inheritors of Rome, not by virtue of the incorporation of territory alone but because of their vision of building a universal empire. The Ottomans have been referred to as Europe's Muslim emperors and caliphs as often as they have been seen as the Middle East's caesars and 'the Romans of the Muslim world'.[8] Why not refer to them simply as Romans? Arabs, Persians, Indians, and Turks referred to the Ottoman rulers as caesars and their dominion as the Roman Empire, and, beginning with the Ottoman conquest of Constantinople, some Western European writers did too. Some posited that the Ottomans were descendants of the Trojans. Others worried about the legitimacy of Ottoman claims to the inheritance of Roman rights. One sixteenth-century papal advisor noted that the sultan 'often says that the Empire of Rome and of the whole of the West belongs to him by right, as he is the legitimate successor of the Emperor Constantine, who transferred the empire to Constantinople'.[9] Why have we forgotten what Europeans thought five hundred years ago?

In fact, the Ottomans have been treated as poorly as the Byzantines. Both the Ottoman Empire and the Byzantine Empire—whose legacy the Ottoman dynasty inherited and whose capital city it made its own—were long-lasting, centralised empires that to this day stand outside the standard Western narratives about the formation of Europe.[10] Both are held up to later, Western European benchmarks of development and history such as the Renaissance and Reformation and found lacking. Think of what comes to mind when we use the term 'Byzantine' today: medieval, backward, Oriental, exotic, religiously distinct, and unfathomable due to the hurdle of language and orthography. Because the religiosity of both empires has been overemphasised, their secular aspects are less often investigated. At a certain point in both their histories they have been portrayed as decadent, corrupt, and in a state of irrevocable decline. Both the Byzantines and the Ottomans have been depicted predominantly in the negative as the antithesis of the West.

But when we consider how these empires thought of themselves, we realise how false these views are. Both empires saw themselves as the heirs to Rome and claimed Europeanness. The Ottomans called their Southeastern European provinces Rûmeli (land of the Romans). Rûm was the Turkish way of saying Rome, the core territory of the Byzantine Empire in the Balkans and western Anatolia.[11] This view of the Ottomans as insiders raises the question of who owns or inherits an empire, who a civilisation, who a continent? What do we count or discount as historical continuity? Who bears historical responsibility for what? What happens when both history and responsibility are shared?

The histories of the Byzantines and the Ottomans are subject to the nationalist and religious agendas of their modern-day counterparts—the Byzantines to the Greeks, the Ottomans to the Turks. Today, these agendas are tied to visions of restoring history formerly belonging to 'their' empire, such as when Turkish 'neo-Ottomanism' glorifies former conquests and denies former atrocities. History is used for political ends whenever Greek donors endow university chairs in ancient, Byzantine, and modern Hellenic or Greek studies that ignore that the Ottomans ruled what is today Greece for over five hundred years, or when the Turkish Republic endows chairs in Ottoman studies that gloss over the significant inheritance of Byzantine and Greek peoples, institutions, and attitudes. The way we remember the past would look quite different if we instead referred to both the Byzantines and the Ottomans as Romans, which is how they viewed themselves.

Acknowledging the Ottoman dynasty as part of European history allows us to see that the Ottomans were not separate from the Roman Empire and did not seek to be, but rather claimed to inherit universal rule over that former empire. They did not evolve in parallel with Europe; their story is the unacknowledged part of the story the West tells about itself.

The Ottomans actually partook in many aspects of European religious and political development long attributed to Western Europeans alone. Recognition of this shared history of dynasties and societies in the whole of Europe emerges when we focus on the Eurasian empire of the Ottomans. Rather than being an attempt to prove that the Ottomans measure up to Eurocentric standards, acknowledging their role in European history causes us to expand the meaning of that history and rewrite its basic concepts and frameworks—things such as the Renaissance, the Age of Discovery, the Reformation, the Enlightenment, and the Scientific Revolution, as well as the meaning of millenarianism and messianism, sexuality and pleasure, absolutism and limited government, slavery and Orientalism, and world war.

OTTOMAN PATHWAYS TO TOLERANCE, SECULARISM, MODERNITY, AND GENOCIDE

Viewing the history of the Ottomans as part and parcel of European history allows us to understand the origins and meaning of concepts and practices such as religious tolerance, secularism, modernity, and even genocide in a different light. We recognise that they began with Muslim Europeans. The conventional claim of European history that Europeans first had to figure out how to live with people of different religions only in the sixteenth century, due exclusively to the Reformation and Counter-Reformation, begins to seem improbable. In that story, only then was the concept of tolerance first debated and became a reality of daily life.[12] Tolerance, modernity, and secularism emerged for the first time, we are told, in Western Europe only after the 'wars of religion' that raged roughly from 1550 to 1650. The first concrete steps were supposedly taken with the signing of the Peace of Westphalia in 1648, a series of treaties that instituted the principle of tolerance of religious minorities. From 1650 to 1700, Europe entered what is celebrated as the Enlightenment, symbolised by John Locke's seminal essay of 1689, 'A Letter Concerning Toleration', which opened the way towards a live-and-let-live approach to religious difference and the secular, modern age. With more and more intellectuals promoting tolerance, some enlightened European rulers began to institute it in the eighteenth century.

But the historical record demonstrates that the principles and practices of toleration had already been established at the onset of Ottoman rule in Southeastern Europe in the fourteenth century, a fact made especially visible in Constantinople after the Ottoman conquest of that Byzantine city in 1453. Ottoman religious tolerance was based upon Islamic precedent already introduced to Europe in eighth-century Muslim Spain, and upon nomadic, pre-Islamic Mongol antecedents from the Eurasian steppe—that crossroads of Europe and Asia out of which the Ottomans grew. While full toleration did not exist in medieval Christian Europe, it did exist in medieval Islamic Europe, including in Ottoman domains. Ottoman tolerance is European tolerance.

Why, then, aren't the Ottomans conventionally included in the history of religious tolerance in Europe? By the time Western Europeans first encountered questions about how to live together, the Ottomans had already figured out the answers to them. These included what rights and privileges each religious group would have, where different groups would worship, how they would pay for the upkeep of their religious community (including its houses of worship and schools), how charity would be raised and distributed, whether people from different groups could inter-marry, where they could live, how they could interact socially and economically, how holidays would be celebrated in public, and how each religious group would be governed and its relation to the government.[13] In the view of one mid-seventeenth-century English writer, Ottoman toleration of many religions was pref-erable to the violent enforcing of one, as occurred in Christian Europe.[14] Religious civil wars and persecution of those with dis-senting beliefs actually continued in Catholic- and Protestant-majority areas of Europe into the eighteenth century.

While Christian Europeans have laid claim to originating the institutions of secularism in the seventeenth century, the Otto-mans had for centuries been subordinating religious authority to imperial authority and had made secular law equivalent in force to religious law, surpassing any other European or Islamic polity in this regard. They even institutionalised practices that clearly violated Islamic law and custom in favour of secular law. Why is this not part of the story we tell about when modernity and secu-larism began?

Although the Ottoman Empire embraced tolerance, religious conversion was vital to its success. The Ottoman dynasty empha-sised religious change beginning at the top. In Ottoman Turkish, the only terms for 'conversion' denote conversion to Islam. Con-version can go in only one direction; there is no term other than 'apostasy' for when a Muslim becomes a Christian or a Jew. One cannot say, 'A Muslim converted to Christianity'. Accordingly, apostates were executed. Tolerance is not the same as celebrat-ing diversity, coexistence, equality, multiculturalism, or mutual acceptance.[15] To tolerate means 'to suffer, endure, or put up with something objectionable'.[16] The tolerating party considers its own religion to be true and the tolerated groups' religious claims to be false. John Locke famously refused to include Catholics in his conception of tolerance. Tolerance is in fact the expression of a power relationship. Its presence or absence can be wielded as a warning or a threat against a vulnerable group. Tolerance is a state of inequality where the powerful party, such as the ruler, determines whether a less powerful group may exist and to what extent members of that group may be allowed to express their difference. A ruler or regime may discriminate against a group while at the same time tolerating its members being different from the members of the ruling elite. This was how Ottoman tolerance functioned in terms of class, gender, and religious difference.[17]

In the Ottoman Empire, certain groups—women, Christians and Jews, slaves—were legally subordinate to others—men, Muslims, the free. All religions were not deemed equally valid. Some groups were proscribed, such as Shi'is (Muslims who believe their leader must be a descendant of the Prophet Muhammad and his family), dissident Muslim groups, and Buddhists. Ottoman society was plural, and individuals could at times change groups or positions of power, yet each group had a fixed place within the hierarchy based on class, gender, and religion.

In practice, tolerance of diversity meant creating an empire that was built on the maintenance of difference. The Ottomans did not seek to make all subjects into Muslims or even into Ottomans, the members of the ruling elite. Rather, they fostered institutions—such as the patriarchates, the spiritual offices and jurisdictions of the Armenian and Greek church leaders—that allowed Christians and Jews to go about their personal lives, enjoying cultural, religious, and linguistic rights without much interference or limitation.

Yet at the same time, religious conversion was used as a means of integration into the Ottoman Empire's highly stratified social fabric. The empire recruited its elite from the cream of the crop of conquered peoples, especially their youth and women, thereby ensuring the dynasty's greatness and the subject peoples' subordination. Conquered Christian and Muslim royalty, military and religious leaders, and commoners were all incorporated into the imperial project from the beginning. The Ottoman dynasty

intermarried with European royal houses, including the Byzantine and Serbian—yet another reason to include this Muslim
imperial family within European history. As cruel, unjust, and
violent as it was, especially for women, slavery allowed individuals to be incorporated into the elite levels of society when women
joined the harem and boys were inducted into the administration
and military. Christians were made into members of the Ottoman
ruling elite through cooperation, subordination, or conversion.
Like other empires in history, the Ottomans oversaw large-scale
demographic change through conversion of the ruled population.
What are today the countries of Bosnia, Bulgaria, Greece, Hungary, Serbia, and Turkey underwent massive religious conversion
in the Ottoman centuries. Christians and to a lesser extent Jews became Muslims, and the landscape was Islamised to a great extent,
the most important churches replaced by mosques, seminaries by
madrasas (Islamic colleges), convents by Sufi (mystic) lodges.

Although such regimes as the Mamluk Sultanate of Egypt
(1250–1517) relied on converted slave soldiers, from whose ranks
arose the sultan, the Ottoman Empire relied mainly on converts
to make up key elements of its ruling family dynasty, administration, and military, converting massive numbers of people in
the process over its first three centuries. It defined membership
in essential ranks of the elite class by religious conversion and
continually changed its interpretation of its religion. As the as-
tute seventeenth-century English resident of the Ottoman Empire Sir Paul Rycaut observed, 'No people in the World have ever
been more open to receive all sorts of Nations to them, than they',
and 'the *English* call it Naturalisation, the *French* Enfranchise-
ment, and the *Turks* [Ottomans] call it Becoming a Believer'.[18] It
truly was an empire of conversion, fostering extensive population
change while tolerating the existence of religious groups at vari-
ance with the ruler's religion—nearly until its tragic end.

Tolerance and intolerance were not opposites.[19] Tolerance, discrimination, and persecution always went together. At the same

time that social and legal hierarchies preserved the peace for centuries, discrimination and division were a fact of daily life and opportunities. For centuries, the Ottomans were open to receiving every type of person as a Muslim, whatever his or her language or background, whether a slave, a commoner, or a member of the elite. But then, in later years, the Ottomans turned away from incorporating diversity and tried to save the empire by remaking it first into an Ottoman Muslim polity and later a more Turkish one. The consequence was that tolerance—such as it was—was replaced by ethnic cleansing and genocide, leading ultimately to the dynasty's demise.

In the late nineteenth century, a group of intellectuals in the Ottoman Empire merged European Enlightenment thought and Islam, resulting in compelling experiments with constitutionalism and parliamentary democracy. These efforts failed, however, leading to mass bloodshed, including massacres of tens of thousands of Armenians in the 1890s and in 1909, and the Armenian genocide of 1915. Along with earlier Ottoman religious toleration, why isn't this genocide considered a part of European history? The fact that German generals and soldiers assisted the Ottomans in committing mass murder during the First World War does make it part of European history. But more importantly, accepting the Ottomans as a European empire allows us to recognise the Armenian genocide as the first genocide committed by a European empire in Europe, one that began in Istanbul. Viewing the Ottomans as part of European history does not mean the Ottoman contribution was always positive. The story of the Ottoman dynasty and its empire that is told in these pages seeks neither to glorify the house of Osman nor to condemn it, but to present all that makes it both different and surprisingly familiar for the general reader.

1

THE BEGINNING
Gazi Osman and Orhan

T HE OTTOMAN STORY begins at the end of the thirteenth century, with one group of Turkic peoples among many. Turks and Mongols had dominated the political landscape of West Asia since the eleventh century. Osman (reigned ca. 1288–ca. 1324), the eponymous founder of the Ottoman dynasty, was one of the Muslim Turkic nomadic horsemen who migrated to Christian-majority Anatolia (the Asian part of modern-day Turkey). He was part of the wave of western migration of Turkic herdsmen with their sheep and horses that was part of the expansion of the great Mongol Empire from East and Central Asia. With a motley crew of mounted nomadic warriors—armed with bows, arrows, and swords—Muslim Sufis (mystics), Christian brothers-in-arms, and allied princes, Osman battled Christians and Turks alike in north-west Anatolia, established a small chieftaincy, and bequeathed it to his son Orhan, who greatly expanded it.

Turcoman, or Turkish groups of Central Asian origin, sought grazing land on the marches, unhindered by empires, sultanates, and principalities. The Turcoman established chieftaincies on the borderlands between the Orthodox Christian Byzantine Empire to the west and the Turkic and Mongol empires to the east. The Muslim-Turkic Great Seljuk Empire (1037–1118) defeated the Byzantines at Malazgirt (Manzikert) near Lake Van in 1071, opening the eastern end of the central plateau of Anatolia to unhindered Turcoman migration. The rout of the Byzantine army and their emperor in an ambush in a mountain pass at Myriokephalon in 1176 by the Great Seljuk Empire's successor in Anatolia, the Seljuk Sultanate of Rûm (1077–1307), opened the western end. Having been weakened by the Fourth Crusade in 1204, the Byzantines could do little to stop them. The Latin Christians captured Constantinople from their Greek Orthodox Christian rivals during the Fourth Crusade and held it for over fifty years, resulting in the partitioning of the Byzantine Empire. The Mongols paid them little heed, having no interest in western Anatolia. The Mongol defeat of the Seljuk Sultanate of Rûm in 1243 at Köse Dağ in northeastern Anatolia, which made the Seljuks as well as the Armenian Kingdom of Cilicia into tribute-paying vassals, sent larger waves of Turcoman herdsmen and their animals westward.

The religiously tolerant and eclectic Mongol Empire, the largest contiguous land empire in the history of the world, controlled most of Eurasia at the time—save the westernmost part of the landmass, or Europe. Its eastern half was the empire of the Great Khans (the Yuan dynasty of China, 1206–1368). Its western half was divided into three realms, whose leaders converted from shamanism or Buddhism to Islam. The Kipchak Khanate or Golden Horde (1224–1391), north of the Caspian and Black Seas, included Kiev and Moscow. The Chagatai Khanate (1227–1358) in the centre in Transoxania, included Samarkand in today's Uzbekistan. And the Ilkhanate Khanate (1255–1353) in the south, based in Persia, contained the cities of Bukhara, Baghdad, and Tabriz, and controlled what is today Afghanistan, Iran, Iraq, Turkmenistan, and most of Anatolia.

The first generation of Ilkhanids, who plundered Baghdad and ended the storied Abbasid Caliphate of Harun al-Rashid in Iraq and Iran in 1258, were originally heavy-drinking adherents of Tibetan Buddhism who favoured the Chinese arts and employed

Christian ambassadors and Jewish government ministers.[1] But in 1295, under the former Buddhist Ghazan Khan, they converted to Islam. Smashing Buddhist temples in their capital of Tabriz, the Ilkhanids became some of the greatest benefactors of Islamic art, architecture, and literature.[2] Although they continued to build towers of severed heads as grand spectacle to dishonour their enemies and instil fear in the survivors, they also constructed some of the most monumental and beautiful mosques the world has ever seen, glazed in brilliant blue tile.[3]

An Ilkhanate vassal state, the Seljuk Sultanate of Rûm, based in Iconium (Konya) in southwestern Anatolia, ruled part of eastern Anatolia. The Greek Kingdom of Trebizond on the Black Sea was to the north, the Armenian Kingdom of Cilicia on the Mediterranean Sea to the south, and various Arab and Kurdish principalities were peppered throughout Anatolia. To the far west stood the Byzantine Empire—based in Constantinople and the seat of the Orthodox Church—which still ruled part of western Anatolia.

In the thirteenth century, the majority of the population of Anatolia was Christian, mainly Armenian or Greek. A sizeable minority was made up of Muslim Turcoman, who had brought Islam to Anatolia from the east. Not all of the Turkic migrants were Muslim, however. Some Turcoman were Buddhist, Manichean (believing in a cosmic struggle between dark and light), or Nestorian Christian (uniquely denying that Christ's human and divine natures are united in a single person). Some still followed the Central Asian custom of exposing corpses to the open air until they were pure and could be buried.[4] A minority of Jews lived in urban centres. Most Muslims, the other demographic minority, were new to their faith. The Turkic peoples of the Central Asian steppe had originally been shaman, following ecstatic religious figures who communicated with the spirits through trances. But as they had migrated west, they had become Buddhist, Jewish, Manichean, Nestorian Christian, Taoist, and Zoroastrian. The preaching and alleged miracle working of Muslim spiritualists known as Sufis travelling along the Silk Road compelled others to become Muslim.

Anatolia at the time was an unstable patchwork controlled by Mongol forces, Armenian kingdoms, Byzantine Greek princes and governors, and other Turcoman, Arab, and Kurdish principalities, frequently at war.

At the far southwestern tip of Asia and the western end of the Silk Road, on the frontier between Christian Byzantium to the west and the Islamic Seljuk Sultanate of Rûm in the east, more than a dozen Turkic Muslim principalities emerged and disappeared between the eleventh and sixteenth centuries. Most are forgotten today. The only principality we remember is the one that lasted the longest, the Osmanlı, named after Osman. The drama and tragedy of the Ottoman dynasty begins as the curtain rises on this nomadic warrior.

OSMAN, THE FIRST CHIEFTAIN

According to the story the Ottomans would tell centuries later about their origins, Osman's grandfather was Suleiman Shah. After Suleiman Shah was swept away along with his horse by the mighty Euphrates river in northern Syria, his sons, including one named Ertuğrul, travelled northeast along the route of the same river and settled in northeastern Anatolia in the regions of Erzincan, Erzurum, and Sürmeli Çukur (today Iğdır, Turkey). Ertuğrul had three sons. One was named Osman. With their hundreds of nomad tents, Ertuğrul and his followers perpetually sought the most suitable land for their clan and hardy animals. Wishing to go raiding in that part of land that had fallen under the sovereignty of a vassal of the Mongol khan of the Ilkhanate Empire, the Seljuk Sultanate of Rûm, Ertuğrul asked Sultan Ala al-Din for permanent grazing grounds on which to build a homeland.[5] We do not know whether it was Sultan Ala al-Din I, or II, or III, or whether it was the middle of the thirteenth or the late thirteenth century. It is much more likely that Ertuğrul and his sons were actually part of the mass wave of migrants moving with or ahead of the Mongol irruption in the east and were not connected to the Seljuks.[6]

The Ottomans would later claim that Ertuğrul and his sons had been sent by the Seljuks westward, passing through Ankara to settle in Söğüt in northwestern Anatolia.[7] Söğüt is located in a valley at the foot of rolling hills fifty kilometres northwest of the ancient city of Dorylaeum (today's Eskişehir). Centuries later, Ottoman chroniclers remembered Söğüt being located between Osman's first two conquests, what they termed the Christian castles of Bilecik (thirty kilometres to the north) and Karaca Hisar (outside Eskişehir). But Karaca Hisar was actually in the hands of their rival Turcoman Muslim principality, the Germiyan.[8]

When Ertuğrul died and his tomb was erected in Söğüt, Osman succeeded him in that frontier town, although we do not know in what capacity, holding what title, or ruling in whose name. We know that Seljuks battled Mongols. Since the majority of the Mongol armies were made up of Turkic horse nomads, this meant Turks fought Turks. Much later, after the Mongols were no longer present in Anatolia, yet while multiple Sunni Muslim Turkic rivals abounded, Ottoman chroniclers searched for a way to distinguish their ancestors. They concocted a bizarre story of emasculating the enemy to turn the Ottomans into the legitimate heirs of the Seljuks, thereby distancing themselves from the Mongols and Ghazan Khan, to whom Osman actually owed his liege.[9] They related that one field of battle was known as 'the Plain of Testicles' because the victorious Seljuks cut the testicles off the defeated Mongol troops, sewed the skins together, covered them with felt, and made tent awnings out of them.[10]

NOMADISM

The use of tents reminds us that the Ottomans originated among a nomadic people. The Ottoman Empire first took root in that region of Anatolia most resembling the steppes of Central Asia. The great central plateau of Anatolia, which rises to one thousand metres and has the great salt lake Tuz Gölü at its centre, is a semi-arid steppe grassland characterised by warm, dry summers and very cold winters. It receives little rainfall, has very few forests, provides little water or wood, and is largely unsuitable for cultivation. Ringed by mountain ranges and surrounded on three sides by coastlands and their ancient Byzantine and Armenian cities, ports, and agrarian regions, the central plateau offered ideal conditions for the nomad. Befitting his Turco-Mongol background, Osman is described in the Ottoman chronicles as having lived a nomadic lifestyle.[11] He migrated with his herds of horses, oxen, goats, and sheep annually between summer and winter pastures, the former in the hills, the latter in the valleys.

Nomadic men such as Osman relied on strong, independent women who played leadership roles or provided much of the labour that sustained their lifestyle. Arabs travelling on the steppe in Central Asia to the Kipchak Khanate were surprised by the respect shown to women by the Turkic peoples, their freedom and near equality to men. The women did not veil themselves as Arab women did.[12] Mongol women played an open role in politics. Each Friday after the midday prayer, the khan—who had declared Islam his religion upon coming to power in 1313—held a public audience in a tent together with his four khatun (the royal wives, one of whom was a Byzantine princess), who sat on either side of him. In full view of the assembled public and without the use of any screen or veils, when the senior khatun entered the tent, the khan walked to the entrance to meet her, saluted her, took her by the hand, and sat down only after she had taken her seat on the divan.[13] While we do not learn as much about the ordinary women in Osman's principality, such as whether they took part in raids or not, we do know that they milked the animals to make cheese, butter, and cream, and that they wove their hair into the elaborate-yet-durable round felt tents in which they lived and the carpets upon which they sat.

The presence of horses attests to the fact that Osman and his supporters fought as nomads do. Their travelling camps included ironmongers who made their swords, daggers, and axe heads, along with their cauldrons for cooking stews, which were suspended by chains over fire. Osman's first battle recorded in contemporary sources in the region occurred in 1301 or 1302 against the Byzantines at Bapheus on the southern shore of the Sea of Marmara close to Nicea (İznik), over eighty kilometres north of Söğüt. Having inherited Mongol military tactics with a force of lightly armed archers mounted on horseback, Osman and his men engaged in guerrilla warfare. Utilising their mobility, speed, and ability to travel long distances, their stratagems were ambushes and surprise attacks—seizing roads, villages, and the countryside, raiding Byzantine forces at night, and retreating to forests and mountains when pursued.[14] Under Osman, they were unable to launch lengthy sieges and take large, heavily guarded forts and cities. Accordingly, they acquired little territory of their own.

DEVIANT DERVISHES: GOD'S UNRULY FRIENDS

From the beginning, the Ottoman dynasty relied on Muslims to give it their spiritual blessing, while using Islam to cultivate loyalty to the leaders and dynasty, to strengthen the bonds among its followers and supporters, and to motivate and mobilise them against its enemies. Yet in every era, radical Muslims and their ideas also served as a potentially destabilising, rebellious force that threatened to overthrow the dynasty.

Many of the Muslims in Osman's sphere were Sufis, or mystics. Sufis were not a separate Islamic sect, but Sunni or Shi'i spiritualists. Marked by the master-disciple relationship and ceremonies of initiation such as girding of swords, Islam in Anatolia often took on a Sufi dimension. Sufi beliefs were expressed in unique rituals, such as whirling to music or repeating God's ninety-nine names.

Sufis kept a genealogy of teachers linking the order's founder back in a chain of transmission to Ali—the Prophet Muhammad's cousin and husband of Fatima, Muhammad's daughter—with whom Muhammad had reportedly shared esoteric teachings. Sufis erected tombs for their founding saints, which became pilgrimage sites, and, alongside them, hostels. There, Sufis lived, prayed, and offered hospitality to a public whose hearts were opened through ecstatic worship, bellies were filled in Sufi soup kitchens, and minds were attracted to the associations of like-minded spiritualists. Many believed in the Sufis' preaching and eclectic beliefs and accepted the stories of their moral purity, ordeals endured, marvels performed, and miracles ascribed.[15]

We need to go back to the Sufis' religious background before going any further. Sufism was foundational to the spread, expression, and interpretation of Islam from its earliest centuries. It was fundamental to the Ottoman understanding and practice of the religion. A couple of generations before Osman, in the early thirteenth century, a Muslim from Spain named Ibn Arabi had compiled the most comprehensive synthesis of Sufi thought, enumerating the individual paths to God.[16] After migrating to the Middle East, Ibn Arabi travelled widely in Arabia, Syria, and Anatolia, developing his ideas. Composing a practical guide to obtaining spiritual enlightenment, he defined the stages and terms institutionalised in Sufi orders and provided a blueprint for how to advance along the path to becoming a Sufi.

Ibn Arabi introduced four revolutionary concepts concerning the relationship of people to God that were to have a major impact on Ottoman political and religious history. The concept of the 'poles of the universe' posits four figures who are the true deputies of God. They are the centre of the universe, the mirror of God, and the pivot of the world, ruling through their seven secret deputies and the heads of the Sufi associations, God's visible representatives.[17] 'Saints' are those who are close to God; in other words, they are God's friends. The theory of 'the unity of being' or the oneness of existence holds that nothing exists other than God. All that exists is therefore a manifestation of the attributes of God, God's ninety-nine names. The 'perfect human' is the perfect Sufi saint who knows God totally, whose spiritual authority is total, but whose identity is secret. These electrifying concepts about the hierarchy of men ruling the universe would offer charismatic Sufis the opportunity to stake politico-religious claims—including to their own messiahship, obviating the need to obey the sultan—and foment revolution. Over the centuries, individual Sufi sheikhs in Ottoman lands would convince their followers to revolt against political authorities by claiming that God had spoken to them and deputised them, as poles of the universe, to establish justice in the world by overthrowing the oppressive, illegitimate Ottoman dynasty.[18]

While Ibn Arabi's concepts were potentially rebellious, another contemporary Sufi leader, Mevlana ('Our Master') Rûmi, and his followers pursued the love of God following the example of Muhammad within Sunni Islam and Islamic law. Based in Seljuk Konya, in south central Anatolia, Rûmi and his followers focused on the inner meaning and intention behind religious acts and rituals rather than on the deeds themselves. They valued spiritual experience rather than mere book knowledge. The Mevlevi Sufi order established by the conformist majority of his followers was thus politically quietist. It numbered Seljuk sultans among its patrons and members, and they offered royal patronage and protection in exchange for spiritual blessings.[19]

Rûmi's masterpiece, *The Spiritual Couplets*, injected Islam with ecstatic expressions of love. It opened a path for men's ritualised gazing at young boys as the expression of absolute beauty and male-male devotion. For some men, such ecstasy was part of a culture of man-boy love. Rûmi depicted himself as having been impregnated by the spirit of his older soul mate, Şams al-Tabrizi.[20] Preaching to Christians, Jews, and newly Islamised Turcoman, Rûmi argued that neither language nor words was important.

What mattered was 'intent and rapture', for 'Love's folk live beyond religious borders'.[21]

Some of the most important Muslims in Osman's circle were another type of Sufi, referred to as deviant dervishes for their blatant transgression of social norms. While Rûmi's ideas called for his followers to obey rulers and the law, the followers of Hajji Bektaş were religiously transgressive and politically suspect.[22] Believing themselves to have overcome the ego and to have 'died', the dervishes who surrounded Hajji Bektaş lived in absolute poverty, bereft of proper food, shelter, or clothing. Reflecting the views of Ibn Arabi that God was present in all creatures and that they themselves were saints, they refused to comply with social and legal norms.

Hajji Bektaş was a contemporary of Rûmi (and, like Ibn Arabi, lived before Osman). Like Rûmi, Hajji Bektaş migrated to Anatolia from northeastern Iran. Especially popular among the Turcoman of central Anatolia, Hajji Bektaş and his followers were rivals of the Mevlevis. Rûmi condemned the Bektaşis for not following the way of Muhammad and Islamic law.[23] Hajji Bektaş traced his spiritual lineage to Baba İlyas-i Horasani. A Turcoman self-proclaimed messenger of God from Khurasan, Horasani united the poor and nomads, Turcoman and Kurds, together with deviant dervishes in a utopian, revolutionary movement opposed to the Seljuk upper class and the Mevlevi order.[24] After Horasani died, other deviant dervishes continued his movement, lurking as a potential threat.[25]

Hajji Bektaş claimed to be the recipient of the teachings of the Qur'an from Muhammad, who taught him the literal meaning, and Ali, who revealed to him its secret meaning.[26] At Hajji Bektaş's shrine in the town named after him in central Anatolia, five hundred kilometres east of Söğüt, a banner declares him a 'saint' or 'friend of God' who is also the reincarnation of Ali.

Hajji Bektaş allegedly worked miracles: curing the sick and the infertile, multiplying food, resurrecting the dead, and taking the form of animals or birds. According to his followers, Hajji Bektaş was celibate yet his woman disciple Kadıncık Ana gave birth to three sons after being impregnated by drinking his used ablution water.[27] He is said to have migrated to Anatolia by taking the form of a pigeon and flying from Khurasan. He converted many people to Islam, making them into his disciples. He lived as an ascetic and frequently withdrew to caves and mountains for forty-day periods of seclusion before settling permanently in a cell that became his dervish lodge and mausoleum. The tomb, with its telltale dome consisting of a pyramidal roof built on an octagonal base, was built by a Mongolian princess and decorated by Greek craftsmen in the late thirteenth to early fourteenth centuries.[28]

The Bektaşis and numerous deviant dervish groups whose names we will encounter again and again—the Abdals, Haydaris, Kalenderis, and Torlaks—combined asceticism with anarchy. They withdrew from society while keeping one foot within it, conspicuously mocking its social customs. Arising at the same time as the mendicant Franciscan and Dominican orders in Western Europe, they practised asceticism through begging, homelessness, and wandering, settling temporarily in the wilderness or in cemeteries, refusing to work, rejecting marriage and sexual reproduction, and cultivating poor health, including through self-harm. The latter practices were manifestations of the philosophy of disregarding the human body and killing the ego before one's death and return to God.

Deviant dervishes deliberately practised abhorrent behaviour to make their open renunciation of society and social norms complete. They were not recluses. They were nonconformists who aimed to shock their metaphorical parents, namely, other Sufis. The deviant dervishes attracted men who had broken their social bonds: adolescents who had broken ties with their parents, students who had been disaffected by their teachers, cavalrymen who had broken with their masters, upper-class youth who had dropped out of society, and the young offspring of respected Sufis, military commanders, elites, rulers, and royalty who were rebelling against their fathers.

These nihilist dervishes refused to pray and fast, two of the obligatory practices common to Sunni and Shi'i Islam, or to engage in any other religious obligations. They went about stark naked or with a few leaves covering their private parts, symbolising Adam's fig leaf. Some wore loincloths or woolen sacks, furs, or animal hides. They went barefoot. Contravening Muslim male practice, which held that hairlessness was affiliated with a lack of honour and status, some shaved their hair, eyebrows, beard, and moustache. A smooth face, they argued, symbolised their readiness to face the divine without need of veils. Along with their outlandish outfits, they marked their bodies in shocking ways: wearing iron rings, metal earrings, neck collars, bracelets, anklets, and genital piercings.

Especially outrageous were those who wore their cloaks open to expose the iron rings hung on their pierced penises. Some sported tattoos of Ali's sword, the name of Ali, or snakes. They carried strange paraphernalia: hatchets, clubs, bones, and horns. All groups openly consumed marijuana and hashish and were frequently intoxicated and screaming. The wine-drinking dervishes also displayed this ecstatic tendency. Like other Sufis, they enjoyed music and dance, but to an extreme. They were notorious for their large, public gatherings where they played tambourines, drums, and horns, sang loudly, and danced ecstatically, chanting to God. Some included young boys in their retinue, referred to as boy dancers or hashish servers. Their enemies accused them of sodomy and bestiality. A group of itinerant women Sufis, called the Sisters of Rûm, were also well-known in that era in Anatolia.

Gazing at young boys, being impregnated by spirits, shaving the hair, piercing the genitals, engaging in self harm, taking drugs, and dancing in ecstasy: in the thirteenth century and early fourteenth century, Islam could be interpreted and practiced in ways that are unrecognisable to Muslims today. Turkic chieftains such as Osman—for whom Sufis were crucial for providing approval for his rule and propagating Islam in his domains—were anything but narrow-minded. They had an ecumenical understanding of who was a Muslim that included perfect humans, poles of the universe, and saints and messiahs who took animal form and flew like birds. Osman's success was based in part on his ability to mobilise a variety of Islamic groups to join his side without trying to reconcile their differences, let alone judge whether they were 'true' Muslims or not.

CONQUEST AND DIVINE FAVOUR

The very first Ottoman chroniclers linked the royal house to Sufis, both to the conformist orders and to the orders of deviant dervishes. Even the spiritual biography of Hajji Bektaş claims that the deviant dervish had announced that God's sanction would be removed from the Seljuks and transferred to Ertuğrul, Osman's father.[29] Hajji Bektaş's followers believed that, due to his proximity to God, he had the power to intercede in the transmission of secular authority.

A century and a half after his death, Osman's followers narrated the politically useful story of how Osman stayed one night at the home of Sheikh Edebali, a Sufi connected to radical Turcoman streams of mysticism. Osman's host was a disciple of Horasani, the militant proselytiser who, as the voice of the Turcoman nomads, had led a Sufi revolt in Anatolia against the Seljuks, the aristocracy, and the urban Sufi orders. The connection established between Osman and the sheikh, however, was more in the Mevlevi than the Bektaşi fashion, as Osman was symbolically 'impregnated' by the holy man. As he slept, Osman saw in his dream that the moon rose out of Sheikh Edebali's chest and sank in his own. Then a tree grew from Osman's navel, its shade covering the whole world. In its shade there were mountains with streams issuing from them. People drank from these streams, used them to water their gardens, and built flowing fountains.[30] When he awoke, Osman recounted his dream to the sheikh. The sheikh responded, 'Osman, my son! Sovereignty has been granted to you and your descendants', and he gave his daughter Malhun to be Osman's bride.

As we are meant to see in this dream, Osman's future success was predicted by a Sufi sheikh, into whose family he would marry. In addition to the Islamic Sufi elements, his dream contains the Mongol shamanistic natural elements of mountain, shady tree, and flowing stream.[31] God allegedly favoured the Ottomans, as revealed through the holy man's interpretation of Osman's dream. But this dream is not that of a thirteenth-century pastoralist. It is the dream reflecting the perspective of a fifteenth-century agriculturalist ex-nomad society that had settled down. The product of the sentiments of the later chronicler Aşıkpaşazade (died 1484), the dream predicted the Ottomans' transition after Osman from nomadism to sedentary empire.[32]

'HOLY WAR' AND CONVERSION TO ISLAM

Fifteenth-century Ottoman chroniclers remembered theirs and the preceding centuries as an era of 'holy war' between Christians and Muslims. The oldest extant narrative account of the Ottoman dynasty, *History of the Kings of the Ottoman Lineage and Their Gaza Against the Infidels*, from the beginning of the fifteenth century, depicts the early Ottoman rulers as *gazis* (holy warriors, mujahideen) battling infidels.[33] Its author's vision for the dynasty is clear: in contrast to the Mongols, who oppressed people, the Ottoman cause was just because they were waging *gaza* (holy war, jihad) against the infidel.[34] The author's sense of justice offers a genocidal vision: the Ottomans and their warriors would eradicate every last enemy man and boy and enslave all women and girls.

A passage from this first chronicle dedicated to the Ottomans is instructive here. The Seljuk sultan had sent some men 'to kill the [Christian] infidel' in the west. But because the Mongols were attacking Seljuk realms further east, the sultan withdrew to Konya, leaving Ertuğrul to continue the battle against the Christians.[35] When Ertuğrul passed away in the mid or late thirteenth century, his son Osman carried on as before in his place.[36] This 'great gazi' sent his soldiers in every direction to 'kill the infidel'. The sword-wielding gazi warrior is referred to as 'an instrument of the true religion [Islam]', who serves God by 'cleansing this land of the filth of polytheism [Christianity]'.

While 'gaza' denoted holy war against infidel Christianity and 'gazi' meant holy warrior, the very same *History of the Kings of the Ottoman Lineage and Their Gaza Against the Infidels* offers a much more complex world than that merely divided by a Christian/Muslim split. Gaza was also used to describe warfare against Turcoman Muslim princes, the same princes who commonly referred to themselves as gazis battling infidels in God's name.[37] Gazi fought against gazi, Turkic Muslim slayed Turkic Muslim. Anyone in Osman's ever-expanding path westward in northwestern Anatolia—no matter the religion or ethnic origin—was on the wrong side and deserving of a punishing raid. Osman fought as often against some of the other nearly two dozen Turcoman Muslim principalities in Anatolia—especially the Germiyan based in Kütahya, around one hundred kilometres south of Söğüt—as he did against Byzantines. And he fought with the Tatars, Turco-Mongols who were probably Buddhists at that point.

Indeed, Osman had better relations with a Greek warrior and friend named Beardless Michael, a local prince or ruler, than with the Turcoman Muslim Germiyan and even with members of his own family. Osman shot his uncle Dündar with an arrow, killing the relative whom some had wanted to be leader when Ertuğrul had passed away.[38] Beardless Michael, described by an Ottoman chronicler as Osman's 'very close friend', remained a Christian fighting together with Osman for a decade and a half before converting to Islam in 1304.[39] During that time, whenever Osman went on a raid, Beardless Michael was always with him. Most of Osman's retainers were Christians as well.

In the case of Beardless Michael, the term gazi denoted a warrior fighting on the frontier for Osman's side—a side that included coreligionists as well as people from other religions—against the enemy of the moment, who may have been from another religion or, more often than not, a coreligionist.[40] Byzantine frontier troops were very similar to their Turcoman counterparts, and they, too, allied with and warred against Muslims. Gaza was thus not holy war—except when it was. And gazis were not holy warriors—except when they were. It was only for later chroniclers that they became incontrovertibly holy Muslim warriors fighting against Christians on God's path.

In the fourteenth and fifteenth centuries, Christians, including Christian Turks, also served without converting to Islam in important administrative and military positions as warriors, cavalrymen, land-grant holders, auxiliary troops, and village security forces.[41] In many places, Christians made up the majority of Ottoman troops.

What mattered in this early era was ability and service, not religion. Osman's band of gazis illustrates well William Shakespeare's immortal lines in *Henry V*: 'We few, we happy few, we band of brothers. / For he today that sheds his blood with me / Shall be my brother'.[42] The first Ottomans were migrant warriors who, bound by ties of personal loyalty, raided neighbouring communities. Over time, those leading and fighting for that increasingly settled confederacy would have to become Muslim, and the paramount value of that conglomerate would be Islam. It is for this reason that the chronicles penned one and two centuries later retrospectively emphasised their having been holy warriors for Islam.

Osman gained legitimacy through conquest, through gaza. In the earliest accounts of the Ottomans, including the first

chronicles composed at the end of the fifteenth century and beginning of the sixteenth century, when he conquered Christian
castles and territories, he had all men and boys put to the sword
and treated the women and girls as captives. He gave their houses
to immigrating Turcoman. He had their churches converted
to mosques.

His rule was based on Mongol and Sunni Islamic precedent.
The Mongols had demonstrated that might made right, that political legitimacy in a Muslim-majority society arose from power
alone. It did not stem from religious principles, such as heredity.
Heredity was the Shi'i interpretation, which accepts as leader only
a descendant of Ali. In contrast, beginning with the Mongols, any
ruler of a Muslim-majority society could demand subjects' liege
simply because he was in power, even if that power was obtained
by force. Osman did not become a leader because he had a royal
pedigree, or by being a descendant of Muhammad. Most certain
is that his legitimacy was based on conquest.

Osman and his band of mounted archers raided to take captives and booty: 'Some took gold and silver, some took horses;
Some took their choice of the maidens'.[43] Osman bestowed the
spoils of his raids—booty, women and child captives, villages, and
estates—on his gazis, attracting ever more warriors to his side.
During Osman's time, he and his supporters did not have the skills
to conquer large Byzantine strongholds such as İznik and Bursa,
the latter located one hundred twenty kilometres west of Söğüt.
Osman and his men conquered smaller Byzantine castles within
eighty kilometres to the west or northwest that lay in their path
to Bursa, including İnegöl, whose Greek prince harassed Osman's
semiannual migration to his summer and winter pastures.[44]

Osman also resorted to various ruses. To take the castle of
Bilecik, he feigned friendship with its Greek prince. Invited to
the Christian's wedding, he hid warriors among wedding gifts of
knotted carpets, flatweaves, and sheep sent with trains of oxen.
Other gazis were dressed as women. One supposes they drew

veils over their moustaches. While not as impressive as the giant wooden Trojan Horse, this deceit allowed Osman and his men to take Bilecik by surprise and behead its tipsy Greek prince. They abducted the Christian princess bride, Asporça, and Osman married her to his young son, Orhan.[45]

After over thirty years of raiding, Osman's forces eventually became effective at mounting sieges of large towns by controlling the countryside and starving their enemy into submission.[46] In 1326, after Osman's death, Beardless Michael and Orhan (reigned 1324–1362) conquered the great Byzantine citadel of Bursa in this fashion, which would be remembered as the first Ottoman seat of the dynasty. Minting coins there in his own name, Orhan aimed to demonstrate that the Ottomans had finally shaken off all traces of vassalage to the Ilkhanids.[47] Yet like his father, whose corpse Orhan disinterred in Söğüt and reburied in Bursa, he still paid tribute to the Mongols—in his case, until at least 1350.[48] The conquest of Bursa was a great windfall for the gazis, who took 'much silver and gold', slaves and servants 'fair and silver-breasted'.[49] Orhan gave wealth away to his gazis, who became very rich.

According to Arab traveller Ibn Battuta, Bursa was 'a great city with fine bazaars and broad streets, surrounded by orchards and running springs'. Orhan—who introduced his wife to visitors, sharing, as he did, the culture of his Central Asian ancestors—was 'the greatest of the kings of the Turcomans and the richest in wealth, lands, and military forces'.[50] He possessed nearly a hundred fortresses, devoting most of his time to making the rounds of them. It was said that he never stayed for a month in any town, fighting continually. He compared favourably to his Turcoman competitors: the prince of Balıkesir was reportedly 'a worthless person', its people 'good-for-nothings' who could not even bother to build a roof for their new mosque. Orhan, in contrast, built the first Ottoman Islamic college in a ruined and near-deserted İznik in 1331, when that city's remaining Byzantine defenders finally surrendered following a two-year siege.

Even if İznik had been left largely uninhabited by warfare, the Ottomans soon found themselves ruling over large populations of Greeks. How did the Greeks view them and their conquests? The archbishop of Byzantine Thessalonike (modern Salonica, or Thessaloniki, Greece), Gregory Palamas, fell captive to the Ottomans in 1355 when his ship was captured near Gallipoli. A theologian and mystic, he was posthumously named a saint by the Greek Orthodox Church. Referring to Muslims as 'barbarians' and 'infidels', he wrote after his capture that the Ottomans lived 'by their bows and swords, rejoicing in enslavement, murder, raiding, looting, wantonness, adultery, sodomy. And not only do they indulge in such practices, but (O madness!) they think that God approves of them'.[51] He engaged in tense theological debates at Orhan's court in Bursa and elsewhere with Sufis, but was beaten by one of them. During another heated conversation with an imam, Christians told Palamas to be silent so as not to provoke rising Muslim ire.

In some towns, Greeks wanted to know why God had abandoned them. Palamas saw churches converted to mosques and large numbers of Greeks who had converted to Islam out of desperation. But in others, he met Greeks who served the Ottomans and large flourishing Greek populations that were tolerated by the new rulers. Orhan's physician was a Greek, and the ruler took an interest in Muslim-Christian theological debates. The Muslims Palamas encountered asked him why he did not believe in their Prophet (Muhammad) when they believed in his (Jesus).[52] Rather than being an example of 'religious syncretism' reconciling Jesus with Muhammad, this was a proselytization tactic. To Christians, Jesus is not a prophet, but a messiah. This messianism is what distinguishes Christianity from other religions. Accepting Muhammad as a prophet makes one a Muslim. This is the tenet that distinguishes Islam from other religions. Palamas noted that the zealous Sufis attached to Orhan's court spread Islam among the conquered Greeks.

FROM OSMAN TO ORHAN

When Osman died in 1324, his son Orhan and his followers allegedly discovered that he owned but the possessions of a simple nomadic pastoralist and raider.[53] They counted one caftan, one suit of armour, and one mess kit containing a saltcellar and a spoon rack. Turks ate stews and yoghurt: stews cooked from millet and meat cut into small morsels, washed down with curdled mare's milk, like the Mongols drank. We know that Osman owned one pair of high boots, several herds of horses, several herds of sheep, and several pairs of saddle blankets. He possessed no books, no luxuries, no silver or gold, and no religious items or prayer mats.

The Ottoman chroniclers idealised Osman's simplicity and nomadic lifestyle. But in fact, Söğüt—where the Ottomans later claimed Osman's father Ertuğrul had first settled and battled against Christians—was a border zone in northwestern Anatolia located on the fringe of the central plateau. The much richer agricultural land and urban settlements to the north and northwest offered greener pastures. These attracted the Ottomans, leading to their rapid settling soon after Osman's death.[54] When enumerating his estate, Osman's successors also counted the land he had conquered, which represented the most significant legacy he bequeathed to them and to his immediate successor, Orhan.[55] Osman's confederacy of warriors was the only Turcoman Muslim principality in western Anatolia that would become a world power in later centuries. Every kingdom from England to China would come to know the name of this dynasty and fear or respect it. To what did it owe its success?

2

THE SULTAN AND
HIS CONVERTED SLAVES
Murad I

F ROM 1301 TO 1401, the Ottoman dynasty experienced a remarkable transformation. In 1301, Osman first waged successful battle against the Byzantines. At the time, the Ottomans
were one small Turkic principality among many. But by 1401, a
century later, that small principality had followed a uniquely fortunate trajectory to become an ever-expanding sultanate knock-
ing at Constantinople's door. How did the Ottomans succeed?
By luck and by material, economic, and social factors, surely. But
above all, the policies taken by Murad I—the first sultan, who established Janissaries (the corps of converted military slaves) and
fratricide as a succession policy—led to their rise. Ottoman tolerance of diversity meant creating an empire that was built upon the
maintenance of hierarchies and difference, thereby ensuring the
dynasty's greatness and the subject peoples' subordination.

EXPLAINING OTTOMAN SUCCESS

A number of explanations have been put forward for the Ottomans' early achievements. According to the Ottoman tradition

and conventional history writing about the dynasty, the gazi or holy warrior spirit was the key. Historians today favour instead the confluence of a number of factors. The Ottomans were lucky. The Seljuk Sultanate of Rûm collapsed by 1300, just as Osman was taking his four castles. The Ilkhanate Khanate collapsed in the 1350s, just as Orhan was expanding his principality. The two main eastern threats to Ottoman survival vanished at the right time. Human agency—the ability of individuals to shape their own destiny—also played a role. The dynasty owed its success in part to Osman's political acumen.[1] He understood well whom to treat as enemies and whom as friends, and when to make friends into enemies and vice versa.

Material factors also played a role. These include the human material with which Osman had to work, the fortuitous location of his principality, and the desperate political and economic situation of the Byzantines. The Byzantine Empire at the time was split internally, its territory shrinking. This division invited outsiders into the empire's internal politics. The independent, coastal Aegean Turkic principalities benefited from trade with Venice and Genoa. Yet their location meant they faced crusaders (including the Knights Hospitaller), corsairs, and constant war without commanding the sea. In the 1340s, they were devastated by the bubonic plague epidemic known as the Black Death.[2] By contrast, Osman's inland, nomadic principality was protected from human and epidemiological coastal depredations yet located on commercial routes at the edge of the frontier between empires. Osman's Mongol overlords paid his principality little heed, as they were busy crushing only those large Turcoman principalities nearest them in eastern Anatolia. It was in this way that the Ottomans escaped the wrath of larger, more dangerous foes.

The Ottomans also benefited from the fact that during the twelfth and thirteenth centuries, Anatolia had been transformed by a boom in international trade with Southwest and East Asia and with the Byzantine Empire. This was thanks in large part

to the Seljuk Sultanate of Rûm, which had developed and beau-
tified urban areas, built a network of caravanserais (inns for
long-distance travellers) crisscrossing the land north to south
and east to west, dug dozens of silver mines for many mints producing coins of exceedingly high purity, and expanded ports on
the Mediterranean at Antalya and on the Black Sea at Sinope.[3]
The Ottomans established themselves at the fortuitous location
astride the Constantinople-to-Konya and Constantinople-to-
Iran-and-China trade routes. And they were situated at the cusp
of the divide between the sown and the barren, the agricultural
and the pastoral lands. Their position allowed them to move location and transition to being settled agriculturalists whenever
they faced environmental disruptions on their home soil, whether
flood or famine.[4]

Social factors also played their part in the dynasty's rise. Osman constructed a set of alliances to increase his sphere of influence. He intermarried with local sheikhs and Christians, ably
manipulating the many shifting alliances. There is also the military element. Osman constantly sent his men on raids, benefiting
from the restless energies of highly motivated nomads and adventurers, thereby adding fuel to the materialist explanation. Success
attracted ever more raiders bringing fame and riches, which he
distributed to his ever-growing body of followers. Osman's success attracted merchants and commoners, as he had a reputation
for being just and generous. They provided a material basis for
launching more raids.[5] Warfare meant profit in women, slaves,
wealth, and land, fuelling further expansion. After conquest, the
Ottomans took slaves from the conquered population and converted them to Islam, while allowing most other subjects to carry
on their lives in villages and cities, tolerating their religious differences and seeing them as a source of tax revenue.

Further decisions would provide the tools for transform-
ing confederation into empire. The first was turning away from
the Mongol practice of appanage, dividing the ruler's dominion

equally among his sons.[6] The Ottomans favoured unigeniture, in which one son takes over rule of the entire principality.[7] Orhan succeeded his father in a smooth transition. Osman may have granted him landholdings on the frontier, where he could act autonomously, then given him command of his army, and, finally, designated him as his successor. Or, according to the nostalgic accounts penned in very different circumstances centuries later, Orhan became leader when his brother Ala al-Din, thanks to the intervention of a council of dervishes acting as mediator, peacefully agreed to retire to a quiet life of mystical contemplation.[8] Just as Mongol rulers based their authority on descent from Genghis Khan and on the personal loyalty sworn by their followers, so, too, did Ottoman authority arise from a man being a descendant of Osman surrounded by followers pledging their fealty. Not able to claim descent from Muhammad, Genghis Khan, or both, the Ottomans found themselves at a disadvantage.

In this first phase of the dynasty's history, which lasted approximately three centuries, Ottomans believed that fortune (*devlet*) and power were bestowed upon the sultan. Devlet was one necessary condition for his rule. The other was *saltanat* (sovereignty, or sultanate). Invested with these two qualities, his duty was to promote justice, stability, obedience, a hierarchical social order, and conquest.[9] In these centuries, the sultan was a normal Muslim man, to be sure, but one considered to be graced with more rank than any other person—a person who embodied the dynasty. The following chapters will have a personality-centred approach to the dynasty because this was the type of regime that existed in this period.

ORHAN: CHRISTIANS AND SUFIS IN THE EXPANDING REALM

Orhan's capture of the wealthy, ancient city of Bursa in northwest Anatolia in 1326 and its rich agricultural hinterlands had greatly enriched his supporters, leading to changed cultural practices. Like Osman, Orhan was depicted by later chroniclers as a migratory nomad who preferred sleeping in a tent and spending summers in the countryside on a verdant mountain where he fed his flock. But by the time of the capture of Bursa, he was less nomad warrior and more Byzantine prince. He and his court in Bursa loved their Greek wine.[10]

When the Ottomans fought the Byzantines at the Battle of Pelakanon on the northern shore of the Sea of Marmara (today Maltepe, Istanbul) in 1329, the Byzantines retreated after their emperor Andronicus III (reigned 1328–1341) was wounded. Orhan realised that sending hundreds of mounted archers at the enemy was only one way to fight. Mounted archers depended on having sufficient pastureland and water for a large number of horses to serve as remounts. This was not sustainable in the built-up and cultivated regions into which the Ottomans were moving. This battle was the last time the Ottomans relied solely on such steppe nomad tactics. Like the Byzantines, they would have to turn to infantry tactics as well. Pelakanon would be the Byzantines' last attempt to take back lands from the Ottomans, whose turn to an elite infantry would prove a brilliant and significant decision.[11]

Orhan expanded Osman's territory from Asia into Europe. He followed his father's practices of fighting against Muslim and Christian alike while forging alliances, including through marriage, with the ever-disunited Byzantines. The Byzantines were wracked by civil war, and Turkish mercenaries were hired to do battle on both sides of the many intra-Byzantine disputes. Byzantine emperor John VI Kantakouzenos gave his daughter Theodora in marriage to Orhan in 1346 in exchange for Ottoman troops coming to aid his side in the Byzantine civil war.[12] Theodora remained a Christian and did not convert. Their son Halil was betrothed to Irene, daughter of John VI's son, Matthew.[13] Because of such marriages and other trysts, Ottoman princes were born of Byzantine as well as Armenian, Serbian, and other Christian mothers.

The Byzantine context was crucial for understanding how the Ottomans won over the Christian peoples they conquered. Owing to years of warfare, instability, and disruption, Byzantine governors and bishops lost contact with their subjects and coreligionists. Increasingly impoverished local priests had to find ways to accommodate their new overlords, the Ottomans, to ensure the survival of Christianity. This was a Sisyphean task. As they conquered Byzantine lands, the Ottomans also took over the farms, fields, flocks, cities, and towns, converting their most prominent buildings and seizing their revenues and bestowing them instead upon Muslims. Many churches became mosques, and many seminaries and monasteries became madrasas (Islamic colleges).[14] As the Ottomans settled into and remade Byzantine and Armenian castles, cities, towns, and territories as their own, they converted the main church of each into the main mosque. Yet their intention was not to abolish Christianity and Judaism: they allowed other churches and synagogues to remain.

The Ottomans oversaw the conversion of both peoples and landscapes. Muslims adopted and renamed Christian sacred groves and springs, festivals, saints, tombs, shrines, and other sacred sites.[15] They built caravanserais, hospitals, soup kitchens, fountains, and Sufi lodges, providing material and spiritual sustenance to the conquered Armenians and Greeks. At Hajji Bektaş's complex in central Anatolia, the Sufis served hot stews to large numbers of guests from enormous black cauldrons.

The entire spectrum of Muslim denominations and Sufi associations coexisted in Orhan's realm and in the neighbouring Turcoman principalities, all of which served to spread Islam. Orhan endowed a mosque complex in Bursa imitating Seljuk style that also functioned as a Sufi lodge. The earliest extant Ottoman document, witnessed by male and female members of the dynasty, is a deed written in Persian in 1324 for another dervish lodge that Orhan endowed. In it, he refers to himself as the 'Champion of the Faith' and to his father Osman as the 'Glory of the Faith'.[16]

The Ottomans allowed deviant dervishes in Anatolia and on the frontier zone between the Muslim and Byzantine territories to proselytise among Christians. Sufis played a central role in the Ottoman military forces. The miracles of saints were repeated orally or recorded in popular books narrating their heroic deeds. One of Ibn Arabi's main disciples preached in Bursa. Deviant dervishes even engaged in Sufi rituals in the Byzantine imperial palace in Constantinople. A Byzantine historian related Christian irritation about the noisy singing, dancing, drunken Sufis crying out odes to Muhammad at the court of Orhan's father-in-law and ally John VI Kantakouzenos.[17]

The Ottomans managed their subject peoples wisely, incorporating conquered leaders as part of the machinery of their rule. They used the churches' ecclesiastical hierarchies primarily as tax farms for cash income derived from the churches' holdings and followers. They made the church leaders their revenue collectors, granting individuals the right to take their positions as hierarchs in return for yearly payments to the administration.[18] The Ottomans also gained intermediaries in helping them rule over new populations in the more practical local bishops, who cooperated with the Ottomans in order to remain in their churches. The Ottomans integrated the church and its functionaries into their administrative structure, utilising Christians in the growing bureaucracy. Early Ottoman tax records were often recorded in Greek. So, too, were diplomatic records, as they employed Greeks as envoys and had many dealings with Byzantines and other Europeans. The Ottomans even gave some Christians land grants without compelling them to convert—all while proselytising Islam to Christian subjects.

The incorporation of the leaders of the Armenian Apostolic and Greek Orthodox churches was but one example of the way the Ottomans transformed preexisting local hierarchies into hierarchies that served their own expanding principality. Their success lay in harnessing the power of local leaders for their own political project. They did the same by marrying Christian princesses, and by allowing Christian knights to retain their arms and men and Christian nobles to retain their lands without having to convert to Islam. The Ottomans then enfolded these Christians within their political system to create new hierarchies, with the Muslim ruling elite above them and the Ottoman ruler on top. And over time, the Christian elite became Muslim.

Often, as in the case of Beardless Michael, Osman's Greek comrade in arms who took some fifteen years to become a Muslim, the Ottomans first collaborated with the local elite and then integrated them through voluntary conversion. The local elite gradually became Ottomans (and Muslims). The Ottomans were outsiders who made themselves into insiders. They were foreigners who became local with the help of conquered local elites who eventually became the agents of their own Ottomanisation and Islamisation. Local Christians and Jews embraced, accommodated, or resisted the Ottomans. But not all became Muslim: Christians would remain the numerical majority of Ottoman subjects for several centuries.

MURAD I: THE SULTAN AND HIS SLAVE SOLDIERS

Osman's nomad confederation had been small and landlocked. He conquered no cities, but agricultural lands provided the Ottomans' livelihood. Orhan, his son and successor, expanded the urban and rural territory drastically, especially to the west, northwest, and northeast, including both coasts of the Sea of Marmara and land on the Aegean and Black Sea coasts as well. Ottoman expansion was facilitated by the fact that the Byzantines also suffered from disease and natural disaster. The spread of the Black Death in the 1340s depopulated Constantinople and other cities and coastal settlements of the Byzantine Empire.[19] The 1354 earthquake that destroyed the city walls of Gallipoli and other towns outside Constantinople allowed Orhan's forces to cross the

42   THE OTTOMANS

Dardanelles and continue their advance into Europe, the first Ottoman foothold there. Orhan made his son and heir, Murad, the governor-general of his Southeastern European province. Under the leadership of Murad I, the Ottomans took Adrianople (Edirne) in Thrace in 1369 and made it the second seat of the dynasty, in addition to Bursa.

Murad I is memorialised in much later Ottoman chronicles as a gazi warrior and miracle-working saint. In European histories, he is remembered for having been cut down in battle on the Field of Blackbirds in Kosovo in 1389. Despite the fact that the Serbs lost their King Lazar and the Ottomans won the battle, the event is commemorated to this day in Serbia. The Ottoman victory led to nearly five hundred years of Ottoman rule over the Serbs. But even with these conquests, Murad I made a more significant mark on Ottoman history by instituting policies that contributed to the Ottoman dynasty's long-term staying power and success. He changed titular customs, elite recruitment, and succession practices.

Murad I organised the first Janissary (*yeni çeri*, literally, 'new army' or 'new soldiers') units from prisoners of war taken in battle in Christian-ruled regions. Like the deviant dervishes, the Janissaries shaved their heads, but they also sported horseshoe moustaches. The ruler needed a loyal following, and these slaves were the answer. They were deemed more trustworthy than native Turkish Muslims, who served competing principalities and might come from rival powerful families. To paraphrase one Byzantine observer, because the Ottoman ruler rewarded the circumcised and converted goatherds, shepherds, cowherds, and swineherds and treated them like his own sons, they did not hesitate to sacrifice their lives for him.[20] So as not to lose the 'glory to which they had been raised by chance, they sustain superhuman suffering in time of battle and consequently win the victory'. Having a diverse pool of recruits also ensured that Murad I would have linguistic and cultural knowledge of the newly incorporated territories, crucial for maintaining rule over them. With such an army, the ruler was able to conduct major battles and engage in long sieges.

At the same time, Murad I introduced into the Ottoman territories the Byzantine and Seljuk land-grant and slave-soldier systems. Rather than rely on nomad archers, Murad I used the nonhereditary land grant (*timar*) to fund a stable cavalry force. The ruler granted to resident cavalrymen landholders (*sipahi*), Christian and Muslim, the tax revenues from goods produced on the land by the peasants in exchange for having to muster and lead cavalry troops in imperial military campaigns and local policing. In the words of a later Ottoman chronicler looking back nostalgically at the dynasty's first centuries, when a land grant fell vacant, it was granted to a brave man who was useful with a sword and had already 'cut off heads in battles'.[21]

As can be seen in the coins minted in his name, Murad I was the first head of the Ottoman dynasty to style himself as sultan, the secular civil and military leader. His predecessors Osman and Orhan had claimed only to be chiefs (*bey*). The name 'sultan' symbolises the Ottoman transition from tents to towns, from nomad archers to infantry, from Osman's introduction of the first market tax to managing long-distance trade, large heterogenous populations, agricultural and financial surpluses, and a more sophisticated administration. Accompanying all these changes was an attendant increase in the documentation of land grants, military rolls, revenues, and expenses. The Ottoman rulers continued to spend winters and summers in different places, reflecting their nomadic background. They still patronised both the deviant dervishes and the Islamic scholars from the east. But it is during the reign of Murad I that the Ottoman chieftaincy became the Ottoman sultanate. This was significant, for it marked a change of consciousness. The Ottoman leader had been a minor player with limited regional aspirations. Now he was a sovereign in his own right, with bolder claims. The dynasty began to imagine itself as an empire and to lay the foundations for future success and expansion.

MANPOWER AND SUCCESSION:
FROM MURAD I TO BAYEZID I

Murad I's innovation was the institutionalisation of the Collection (*devşirme*). The Collection was a child levy on Christian subjects of the sultan, in which one in forty eight-to-eighteen-year-old Christian boys were taken from each judicial district in Southeastern Europe and Anatolia to the seat of the sultan, which at that time was Edirne.[22] There, they were circumcised and converted to Islam and trained as leading officials and palace servants or elite soldiers of the sultanate.

The main reason the Ottomans relied on this method of recruitment was that they wished to replace the local Muslim aristocracy with a new and completely loyal class of servants devoted to their patron, the sultan. In theory, according to the Ottoman 'Laws of the Janissaries', while Turks 'would abuse the privilege' if recruited as servants of the sultans, when 'Christian children accept Islam, they become zealous in the faith and enemies of their relatives'.[23] As early as the ninth century, Muslim-majority Arab empires had relied on just these types of foreign slave soldiers and commanders, usually Turks recently converted to Islam, who, despite their slave status, possessed high social rank. The Ottoman Turks employed Christians converted to Islam. In principle, these young men—torn from their parents and ancestral lands at an impressionable age and made to forget their native tongue and religion—were to be given the opportunity to rise in station. Given the best education and seeing how advancement rested on merit alone, they would be motivated to strive to reach the highest possible position. The aim was that they should remain always devoted to the dynasty and the empire that had brought them from a life of obscurity in a remote village to a privileged position at the heart of power.

The Ottoman elite was formed not only of converts to Islam, however. The Christian elite had been the first group to be incorporated into the Ottoman politico-military hierarchy. In the first centuries of Ottoman rule, Christian nobles and military gentry did not have to immediately convert in order to maintain their landholding rights and administrative and military positions.[24] The Ottomans were most concerned during this period with accommodating them and making them into vassals. In the fifteenth century, Albanian, Bulgarian, Greek, and Serbian Christians would hold nonhereditary military land grants and maintain their religion without converting. As late as the mid-sixteenth century, Christians would hold such prebends in eastern Anatolia and Hungary.[25] Yet in the sixteenth century, Christian nobles, royalty, and military aristocrats gradually converted to Islam in order to maintain their privileged economic, social, and political position.[26] They viewed conversion as a means of retaining their property, position, status, and power, as a way to ally against older enemies with the new regional power, or as a path for identifying with their conquerors.

While the motivation for the Collection was clear, its legal justification was murky. According to long-standing Islamic law and custom, a Muslim ruler was not permitted to enslave Muslims nor take into captivity his own Christian subjects and forcibly convert them to Islam. Christians ruled by Muslim sovereigns were supposed to be a protected people, whose lives and property were secure. Although Muslims were to be excepted from enslavement, the Ottomans recruited Westerners and Europeans such as Bosnian Muslims through the Collection, whereas Eastern Muslims—Arabs, Iranians, Kurds, and Turks—were excluded from the levy. They recruited their Christian subjects, but excluded Roma and Sinti—'Gypsies' who may have been Christian or Muslim or of another religion—and Jews. From the standpoint of Islamic law, these practices were illegal.

Affirming pre-Islamic custom, the Qur'an assigned part of the booty taken in war, including captured persons, to the military leader, the Prophet Muhammad.[27] The Ottoman ruler may have modelled his practice on that of the Prophet. But this would only apply to captives taken immediately after military conquest. Another possibility is that the Ottomans favoured an interpretation of the law that excluded recruiting peoples who were Christian or Jewish at the time of Muhammad in the seventh century. As much of Ottoman-ruled Southeastern Europe was not Christianised until after the seventh century, the Ottomans may have believed themselves justified in recruiting them as slaves. But this would not be true for Anatolia. There was no escaping the fact that taking boys from the subject population was a legally dubious innovation.

Whatever the justification for the Collection, hundreds of thousands of Albanians, Bosnians, Bulgarians, Croats, Greeks, Serbs, and others were made into recruits. In 1429, Murad II was presented with a treatise that boasted that 'every year more or less fifty thousand male and female infidels are taken from the abode of war [enemy territory] as captives; those become Muslim, and their progeny join the rank of the faithful'.[28] A memoir written by a Serb Janissary who had served in the Ottoman military from 1456 to 1463 and had participated in the siege of Belgrade and an early sixteenth-century Ottoman document that served as a template for the levy both referred to the taking of children from one in every forty households.[29] According to an Ottoman chronicler, by the end of the sixteenth century, more than two hundred thousand Christian youth had been made into Muslim servants of the sultan in this fashion.[30] This was conversion and acculturation of Christian youth to Islam on an unprecedented scale.

When we look at the family histories of some prominent men in the empire, we realise that some Christians may have been eager to enrol their children in the Collection as a way of attaining higher status. Apparently, they calculated that if their sons were to rise to grand vizier—the chief minister and advisor to the sultan, carrying out military and administrative duties—the family and village would be rewarded and protected. But it is hard to ignore the emotional anguish of these children's parents and imagine that the child levy was just another tax that Ottoman subjects agreed to pay in return for peace and security. It was in fact a harsh measure, which most Christian families sought to avoid.[31] Typical is a sermon concerning 'the carrying off of the children' by the Ottomans from 1395. Isidore Glabas, the metropolitan of Thessalonike, cried out that he went nearly mad upon seeing 'a child, whom he had begotten and raised . . . carried off by the hands of foreigners, suddenly and by force, and forced to change over to alien customs and to become a vessel of barbaric garb, speech, impiety, and other contaminations, all in a moment'.[32] Christians feared and hated the practice. The Ottomans recognised this fact. They added pledges to many capitulation agreements with the rulers of principalities that had surrendered not to enslave their children and make Muslims of them, nor to enrol them in the Janissaries. A sixteenth-century Ottoman miniature depicts a crowd watching boys being registered to be taken away from a Southeastern European town by Ottoman officials. The unknown Muslim artist, who may have been a Collection recruit, included an upset woman and a young child clinging to her.

According to modern international legal concepts, the Collection was an act of genocide. Article II of the 1948 Convention on the Prevention and Punishment of the Crime of Genocide defines genocide as 'any of the following acts committed with intent to destroy, in whole or in part, a national, ethnical, racial or religious group, as such' including 'forcibly transferring children of the group to another group'.[33] As brutal as it was, this was Murad I's answer to the question of how to create loyal soldiers and administrators.

Murad I also solved the problem of dynastic succession in a cruel way. As noted earlier, in the Seljuk Sultanate of Rûm, rulers had followed Mongol practice by dividing the lands of the empire among their sons. The Ottomans retained an echo of this custom. Beginning with Murad I, the sultan sent his sons and their mothers to provincial governates in the annexed former capitals of their rivals in Anatolia, where they reproduced in miniature the royal court. The sons remained under the sultan's control, however, rather than establishing independent rule, as in the Turco-Mongol tradition. But in a stark break from this tradition, Murad I established the pitiless sultanic practice of murdering all one's brothers and uncles—and often all one's male relatives, no matter their age—upon coming to power. Fratricide was meant to ensure that the ruler had no familial rivals. The practice was codified in the mid-fifteenth century in the Ottoman law code attributed to Mehmed II. It stated, 'To whichever of my sons the Sultanate shall be granted, he should kill his brothers to ensure the good order of the world. The majority of the religious class has declared this permissible'.[34]

The practice was justified on the grounds that it was preferable to harm an individual than to harm the public.[35] According to this logic, if a sultan did not murder his male relatives, power would be fragmented and political authority would be weakened, leading to social disorder. In the opinion of the most influential sixteenth-century Ottoman jurist, just as an army cannot have two commanders in chief, two lions cannot share a single den, and two swords cannot be placed in a single scabbard, two sultans cannot rule the same territory. Since the emperor was the head and the empire his body, it was not appropriate for this body to be two-headed. Therefore, to prevent the dangerous situation where several sovereigns existed in the same kingdom, legitimate candidates to the throne had to be eliminated.[36] The practice of fratricide was intended as a means to safeguard the peace and unity of the dynasty and its empire. Rather than perceiving a sultan who murdered his male relatives, including infants, as a murderer of the innocents, Ottoman religious scholars and chroniclers depicted him as their redeemer, cutting off the many-headed hydra of division.[37]

The sultan's sons would be groomed to rule by training as governors and army commanders in the provinces until the father's demise, at which time they would race to the capital. The victorious one assured his rule either by having slain his brothers in battle or by executing them after his enthronement. Such an arrangement was little different from the internecine warfare to obtain the thrones of Western Europe at the time, such as the Wars of the Roses in England. The difference with the Ottomans was that the bloodshed was systematised and legalised.

BAYEZID I: FOLLOWING MURAD I'S PRECEDENT

During the Battle of the Field of Blackbirds in Kosovo on 15 June 1389, a Serb had approached Murad I, feigning a desire to kiss the sultan's hand in obeisance. Bowing while holding his battle helmet before him in one hand, the Serbian assassin had hidden his dagger in his other hand behind his back. Murad I's commanders quickly erected a tent around the fallen sultan's corpse. They captured the Serbian king Lazar and his son, Stephen, and brought them to the same tent. After showing them the corpse of Murad I, they thrashed them without mercy, 'as if they were curs'. They beheaded King Lazar but spared Stephen to serve as an Ottoman vassal. Murad I's only sons, Bayezid and Yakub, had also taken part in the battle, each leading a wing of the army. Bayezid I (reigned 1389–1402) received the oath of allegiance in his father's place in the same tent, now piling up with corpses of dead kings. Another body would fall there. The new sultan's men, without revealing Murad I's death, called Yakub to the same tent. Saying, 'Come, your father wants you', they killed the superfluous son, as Murad I had stipulated.[38]

Bayezid I became the first Ottoman ruler to have his brother murdered upon his becoming head of the dynasty. He was also the first to call himself not only sultan, but the sultan of Rûm— the sultan of Rome. He had cast his eyes on the Roman realm of Byzantium. By 1390, his troops had annexed the entire west coast of Anatolia, expanded maritime trade with Venice and Genoa, and made the Byzantine emperor in Constantinople his vassal. He insisted that an Islamic magistrate be appointed to adjudicate disputes among the Muslims residing in Constantinople so that they would not be forced to appear before a Christian judge.[39] In 1394, after conquering Black Sea ports, Macedonia, Albania, Thessaly, the Bulgarian capital, and Thessalonike, Bayezid I began the first Ottoman siege of Constantinople, the ancient walled Byzantine capital surrounded on three sides by water. By that point, the Ottomans were capable of building siege towers to scale high walls, mining tunnels to collapse them, and enforcing blockades to cut off the enemy even by sea.[40] Walls were tumbling from above and below.

Bayezid I's fortunes rose higher when he led tens of thousands of Ottoman fighters to victory over a similar number of crusaders led by King Sigismund of Hungary at Nicopolis (today Nikopol, Bulgaria) on the banks of the Danube in September 1396. Although Bayezid I still relied heavily on lightly armed cavalry, the 'servants' of the sultan, his Collection recruits, made all the difference. The Ottomans drew the overconfident Christian knights into a trap and encircled them. The Ottomans then pounced upon their heavily armed English, Flemish, French, Hungarian, and Italian opponents 'with much clamour and blaring of trumpets'.[41] It was no contest. The Janissaries felled the crusaders' horses and 'slaughtered' the dismounted French and Hungarian knights, hacking them to death with axes and flanged maces. A contingent of Serbian cavalry led by Bayezid I's brother-in-law and vassal, Stephen Lazarević—whose sister Maria had been made the sultan's wife after her father, King Lazar, was slain in the Battle of the Field of Blackbirds—finished off those crusaders who fled, sealing the victory with their arrows and swords. Sinking like stones, some crusaders drowned after throwing themselves into the mighty river to escape. Ottoman swords beheaded thousands of captured knights, one by one. The young men were spared, only to be enslaved. The ransoming of these captives led to the first diplomatic relations between the Ottomans and France. One of the last Crusades launched against the Ottomans had failed.

With the dynasty's western frontier secured, Bayezid I turned east. The move would have fatal consequences. In 1402, at the height of his power and territorial expansion, having defeated Turcoman principalities, including the Karamanids at Konya, and pushed his forces into the Black Sea region at Sivas, Malatya in eastern Anatolia, and Erzincan in northeastern Anatolia, with his army and administration racing ahead in top gear, Bayezid I faced an unexpected yet fatal threat from the east: Tamerlane, a Central Asian Turkish general and sultan who claimed Mongol descent and whom Turks know as Timur Lenk (Timur the Lame), because he limped. His appearance on the Anatolian stage takes us into the next phase of Ottoman history. In the preceding hundred years, thanks to various interrelated forces ranging from luck to wise decisions to thoroughgoing policies, the Ottoman dynasty under Osman I, Orhan I, Murad I, and Bayezid I had gone from success to success. But now it would almost cease to exist.

3

RESURRECTING THE DYNASTY
Bayezid I, Mehmed I, and Murad II

A T THE BEGINNING of the fifteenth century, the Ottoman dynasty faced two vastly different enemies. In 1402, a massive nomad army ravished its domains from east to west. And in 1416, a deviant dervish set off uprisings within Ottoman society. The two might seem to have little in common, but both Tamerlane and Sheikh Bedreddin drew on popular discontent with the Ottoman family's lack of religiosity. Add to this a decade-long interregnum that was sandwiched between the two, from 1402 to 1413, and the whole thing spelled near disaster. Two of the same forces that had brought the Ottoman dynasty to power—its Turco-Mongol heritage and its Sufi, or mystical, version of Islam—threatened now to destroy it.

Bayezid I was not much of a model Muslim. Or a model ruler for that matter. He set siege to Constantinople unsuccessfully for eight years (1394–1402) from Anadolu Hisarı, his fort complex on the Asian side of the Bosporus. He had defeated the Western crusaders at Nicopolis in 1396, but he had a miserable reputation among Christians and Muslims alike. Known as an alcoholic who did not attend mosque, Bayezid I was barred from giving testimony at Bursa's Islamic law court, an unusually censorious limit to be imposed upon a sultan.[1] This meant foregoing the spiritual blessings of Muslims and the ability to use the religion to promote loyalty to the dynasty, to unite followers and supporters, and to urge them to fight against its enemies.

A story circulated that catalogues his main vice. When completing the massive Great Mosque in Bursa in the final years of the fourteenth century, Bayezid I asked the pious Sufi sheikh Emir Sultan if everything about it was in order. Emir Sultan cleverly told him that one thing was missing: he should add taverns to the mosque so that he and his boon companions would have a reason to visit. Byzantine emperor Manuel II Paleologus also complained about Bayezid I's drinking. Serving as his vassal and accompanying him on military campaigns in Anatolia in 1391, the Byzantine ruler complained that he could not keep up with his counterpart's daily partying, the excessive drinking, 'the flocks of flute players, the choruses of singers, the tribes of dancers, the clang of cymbals, and the senseless laughter after the strong wine. Is it possible for those who suffer all this not to have their minds dulled?'[2]

TAMERLANE: THREAT FROM WITHOUT

As if a divine punishment, in 1402 Timur Lenk's armies appeared in the east. His reputation for plundering and massacre circulating before his armies arrived, Timur terrorised resisting populations by reviving the practice of constructing towers of thousands of severed heads to dishonour the defeated enemy and serve as a warning to all who would oppose him.[3] Timur considered himself the inheritor of the empire of Genghis Khan. Emerging to rule the lands of the former Chagatai Khanate in Central Asia (today's Uzbekistan) in 1370, Timur conquered the former Ilkhanid lands of Iran and Iraq further west in the 1380s. As Osman was formerly an Ilkhanid vassal, Timur reasoned that Bayezid I was supposed to be his vassal as well, but the Ottoman sultan refused to recognise Timur as overlord. That meant war when Timur—after campaigns in Central Asia and South Asia in the 1390s, including the sacks of Moscow and Delhi—returned to Anatolia at the beginning of the fifteenth century.

At the Battle of Ankara, in central Anatolia on 28 July 1402, Timur commanded an army twice as large as that of the Ottomans. Timur's estimated 150,000 soldiers included a number of Turcoman chiefs defeated by the Ottomans and seeking revenge, and, according to a German eyewitness, dozens of elephants launching 'Greek fire' at the Ottoman troops.[4] Bayezid I's army was made up of Janissaries, soldiers of the Turcoman chieftains it had incorporated, and a contingent of Serbs led by his brother-in-law and vassal, Stephen Lazarević. While the Janissaries and Serbs remained loyal, much of the rest of the Ottoman army switched sides or fled, and Bayezid I was captured. Several fifteenth- and sixteenth-century Ottoman chronicles narrate that Timur imprisoned Bayezid I in an iron cage, where out of despair the sultan committed suicide by consuming poison he kept in the collet of his jewelled ring.[5]

English writer Christopher Marlowe increased the drama of these events by making Bayezid I and his wife Maria the slaves of Timur, who kept them in a cage and made the sultan his throne's footstool.[6] When the Ottoman sultan kills himself by bashing his head against the bars, his wife does the same, much like a Turkish *Romeo and Juliet*.[7] Marlowe's blood-soaked play, *Tamburlaine the Great* (1587), became very popular in England.[8] Its villain, Timur—who declares, 'I that am termed the scourge and wrath of God / The only fear and terror of the world' (act 3, scene 2)—burns the Qur'an and declares himself greater than any god.

In fact, Tamerlane may not have incinerated any Qur'ans, but he just about destroyed the newly established empire. He nearly returned it to the political state it had been in under Osman: a Turcoman principality under probable Mongol suzerainty. Instead of Osman in vassalage to the Ilkhanid leader Ghazan Khan, it was now whoever came out on top among Bayezid I's sons in vassalage to Timur.

Timur and his army spent nearly a year pillaging and looting in Anatolia as far west as the citadel of İzmir. It was allegedly Sheikh Emir Sultan and his hundreds of dervishes, rather than Bayezid I's soldiers, who saved Bursa from Timur's armies. Although Timur re-parcelled out the empire to the various Turcoman principalities whose lands the Ottomans had absorbed, he never crossed into Southeastern Europe. Nor did he wipe out the dynasty. Gathering the remaining Mongols in Anatolia, who had lived as nomads there since the mid-thirteenth century, Timur's armies had returned to Central Asia by 1404, where Timur died before he could invade Ming China. After they left, Bayezid I's four sons—Mehmed (Muhammad), Musa (Moses), Isa (Jesus), and Suleiman (Solomon)—would spend over a decade battling for the throne and the remaining Ottoman territories.

SHEIKH BEDREDDIN: THREAT FROM WITHIN

In the middle of the interregnum, the remaining Ottoman domains were convulsed by the greatest rebellion the empire had ever seen. The rebellion was led by deviant dervishes. In every era, radical Sufis were a potential threat to the dynasty.

To the sheikh's supporters—including his Afro-Ottoman grandson, Halil son of Ismail, who composed a glowing biography after his deceased grandfather allegedly appeared to him in a dream—Sheikh Bedreddin was a descendant of the Seljuk dynasty, an esteemed Muslim scholar, and a miracle-working Sufi who could allegedly bring the dead back to life.[9] They considered him an ascetic and a saint who came from an important gazi, or warrior, family.

Sheikh Bedreddin, born Mahmud, was half-Greek and half-Turkish. His father, Israil, was a Muslim gazi raider who captured the fortress of Simavna (the Byzantine town of Ammovounon) near Edirne and took the Christian prince's daughter (who subsequently converted to Islam and adopted the name Melek) for his wife. They made the castle church their home, where Mahmud, the future Sheikh Bedreddin, was born around 1359, as the Ottomans were first raiding into Southeastern Europe.

After his father's death, Mahmud began a life of Islamic learning. As a jurist in Cairo, he won the favour of the reigning Mamluk sultan Barquq. Barquq presented him with an Ethiopian slave woman, who gave birth to Ismail, the father of the author of the Sufi's life story. In Egypt, Mahmud became famous for his Qur'anic commentaries. It was also in Egypt that he became a Sufi, after having ecstatic experiences of God. Mahmud studied with a deviant dervish master in Cairo and accepted Ibn Arabi's concepts of the poles of the universe, the unity of being (the idea that God manifests God's self in everything in the universe), sainthood, and the existence of perfect humans. Contravening traditional Islamic views, Mahmud argued that there was no hell or paradise, no Day of Judgement or resurrection after death, and that the world is eternal and not created.

According to the vivid biography written by his grandson, Mahmud was committed to his Sufi order and to his sheikh, whose place he would take. He continuously fasted and remained in seclusion for three months, allegedly without food or drink. He endured seven forty-day periods of seclusion, reportedly only inhaling the steam of warm milk and licking salt. Only then was he deemed ready to become the successor to his master and spiritual guide.

Homesick, he left for Rûm in 1400. As he passed through Syria and Anatolia, Muslims offered to establish Sufi lodges for him so that he would stay in their town and be their spiritual guide. In Konya, the centre of the Karaman principality, Mahmud, now known as Sheikh Bedreddin, won over the Karamanid ruler with his rapturous Sufi performance of a mystical recitation of God's unity. The ruler took an oath of allegiance to the sheikh as his Sufi guide. Sheikh Bedreddin also won the allegiance of the rulers and much of the populace of the Germiyan and Aydın principalities, old Ottoman rivals, becoming their spiritual guide.

Along the way, Sheikh Bedreddin passed through many Anatolian towns where he demonstrated his alleged miracle-working powers and gained a wide following among deviant dervishes, townsmen and women, peasants, Christians, and Jews. Börklüce Mustafa, a Christian convert, became his disciple in the western Anatolian town of Tire, the former capital of the Aydın principality. A Jewish convert named Torlak Hu Kemal also began to follow him. After the sheikh allegedly appeared to the leader of the İzmiroğlu principality in a dream, he and his followers also became the Sufi's disciples.

According to the enthusiastic biography written by Sheikh Bedreddin's grandson, priests on the island of Chios also allegedly implored him to visit them to demonstrate his miracles, requesting that he reveal the secrets of the messiah. They gave him many presents and kissed the earth before him, inviting him to join them as a monk. They were apparently convinced he was Jesus returned. Day and night, Sheikh Bedreddin engaged in mystical recitation of God's oneness, winning over the priests. The sheikh's rapture reportedly converted many to Islam. Both in Bursa and Edirne, where he spent seven years in the early 1400s withdrawn into Sufi seclusion, many Muslims swore an oath of allegiance to him and became his disciples—including many women, even his own mother, Melek. When one of the priests he had converted on Chios came to visit him in Edirne, he emerged from his seclusion so as to convert the rest of the man's family to Islam and to bless the union of the sheikh's son and the former priest's niece in marriage. In this way, the sheikh's grandchildren continued the process of Christian integration with Muslims. But following this one reappearance, he returned to his pious seclusion, allegedly subsisting on the occasional boiled turnip. It is implied that his main form of subsistence was an edible marijuana paste.

It was at this time that the empire was shattered by the interregnum following Bayezid I's ignominious death at the hands of Timur. In 1410, the sheikh allegedly appeared to Musa Çelebi, one of Bayezid I's four sons and one of the claimants to the Ottoman throne, in a dream in the guise of his imam. The sheikh, who had not left seclusion for seven years other than to render his daily prayers in the mosque, accepted Musa's subsequent offer to become chief military judge of the province of Southeastern Europe. Musa Çelebi would rely on the support of regional disaffected gazis who had opposed Bayezid I's centralising tendencies and his replacement of them with his own slave servants. Musa's choice in appointing Sheikh Bedreddin to the important office of chief military judge was shrewd, as the sheikh was himself descended from gazis.

MEHMED I: ANNIHILATING
THE DEVIANT DERVISHES

Unfortunately for Sheikh Bedreddin, Musa Çelebi lost the contest for the sultanate. Without recounting the numerous schemes, betrayals, and crossings back and forth across the Bosporus, the sudden appearance of pretenders to the throne, or the battles among the brothers, suffice it to say that, in 1413, twenty-four-year-old Mehmed Çelebi and his army of Byzantine, Serbian, Tatar, and Turcoman forces managed to best the others and to defeat and kill Musa Çelebi in battle near Sofia. Mounting the Ottoman throne—which was a long, cushioned, golden and jewelled divan rather than a high-backed coronation chair as in England—and receiving the oath of allegiance from religious officials and viziers, the conqueror reigned as Mehmed I from 1413 to 1421. His aim was to reunite the empire as it had been under his father. He sent the sheikh and his family, including his grandson Halil son of Ismail, into house arrest in İznik.

Yet shortly thereafter, two rebellions in Sheikh Bedreddin's name convulsed the territories the sultan held so tenuously. These rebellions were inspired by the speculative mysticism of Ibn Arabi. They sounded the grievances and fired the ecstatic dreams of the disgruntled supporters of the losing side in the Ottoman civil war—deviant dervishes, nomads, and gazis—together with those of Christians and Jews newly converted to Islam. To counter the popularity of the sheikh, Mehmed Çelebi's court immediately commissioned a florid religious work that referred to the sultan as the divinely assisted, long-awaited redeemer, who brings justice and joy to the world.[10] It did not produce the desired effect.

From İznik in 1416, the sheikh sent Börklüce Mustafa, a Christian converted to Islam and disciple, as his deputy to lead thousands of Christian and Muslim followers in rebellion in his name on the west coast of Anatolia near İzmir. At the same time, his Jewish convert to Islam and disciple Torlak Hu Kemal incited a revolt in Tire, in the same Aegean region, going on the march with thousands of harp-, drum- and tambourine-playing deviant dervishes.

Börklüce Mustafa appeared in the mountains on the Stylarion (Karaburun) peninsula opposite the Aegean island of Chios. He preached to other Muslims that 'they must own no property' and 'decreed that, with the exception of women, everything must be shared in common—provisions, clothing, yokes of beasts, and fields'.[11] He preached this faith in proto-communism not only to Muslims but also to Christians, commoner and clergy alike. He declared they were all Sufis worshipping the same God. A Cretan monk believed that the Jesus-like sheikh could walk on water, crossing from the Anatolian mainland to the island of Samos to appear next to him as a monk. Börklüce was a deviant dervish, probably a Kalenderi or Torlak. His disciples wore 'only simple tunics, their uncovered heads shaved bald, and their feet without sandals'.[12]

Whether they feared his proto-communism or believed he was leading Muslims to convert to Christianity, Ottoman forces marched against Börklüce Mustafa. They were led by a Christian convert to Islam made governor, the son of the last Bulgarian ruler, Fat John III (reigned 1371–1393), whose sister had entered Murad I's harem. But he and his soldiers were massacred by the sheikh's many supporters on the peninsula, who, according to a Byzantine historian, revered Börklüce 'as one greater than a prophet'.[13]

The Ottomans sent the governor of the neighbouring province to attack, but most of his men were also massacred by the peasant revolutionaries. Finally, Mehmed I sent his main fighting force against the sheikh, led by Grand Vizier Bayezid Pasha and twelve-year-old Prince Murad and supplemented by soldiers from several provinces. According to the same Byzantine historian, suffering huge losses, the Ottoman forces 'mercilessly struck down everyone in sight, the old as well as infants, men, and women; in a word, they massacred everyone, regardless of age, as they advanced to the mountain defended by the dervishes'.[14]

After offering much resistance, the peasants and their leader were arrested, put in chains, and brought to a marketplace on the mainland. Despite being tortured, Börklüce Mustafa refused to recant his beliefs. Ottoman historians alleged that his followers changed the Islamic credo from 'There is no God but God, and Muhammad is God's messenger' to 'There is no God but God, and Börklüce Mustafa is God's messenger', thereby justifying his execution.[15] Because he was originally a Christian, in an act of symbolic violence, they crucified him in a town long associated with Christianity and the Bible. Sitting him on a camel with his hands nailed to a wooden cross, they paraded him through the centre of Ayasoluk (today called Selçuk), two kilometres from the ancient Greek town of Ephesus, which boasts the alleged final home of Mary mother of Jesus. Because Börklüce's disciples refused to renounce their teacher's doctrine, they were all slaughtered before his eyes, their 'bare necks split like pomegranates'.[16] Bayezid Pasha and Prince Murad continued the bloodletting by killing all deviant dervishes they encountered.

Meanwhile, at around the same time, Sheikh Bedreddin escaped house arrest in İznik and travelled to Southeastern Europe, where he fomented rebellion among like-minded Sufis, nomads,

Turcoman, and Christians in Bulgaria. Attracting Muslim and Christian men and women to his side—commoners, members of the elite, and many rivals to the Ottomans—Sheikh Bedreddin took refuge with an Ottoman enemy, the Christian prince of Wallachia. His disciples came out in rebellion in the sheikh's name at Crazy Forest (Dobruja in today's Bulgaria), where he visited Sufi Sarı Saltuk's lodge, a Kalenderi deviant dervish centre. Many who gathered around him and offered him gifts had been favoured by him while he had been chief military judge.

With large-scale rebellions convulsing his domain, Sultan Mehmed I decided to act mercilessly towards the sheikh. After Ottoman forces had crucified Börklüce Mustafa and hanged Torlak Hu Kemal in Manisa, Mehmed I sent two hundred men to arrest Sheikh Bedreddin. They brought him to the Macedonian town of Siroz (Serres, Greece) soon after Mehmed I had hanged a false pretender to the throne who had marched on Edirne and had had his name read at Friday prayers in place of the sultan's.

Sultan Mehmed I asked for a fatwa, a legal opinion from a competent authority, concerning the legitimacy of executing Sheikh Bedreddin. The Islamic expert he called upon was the Persian scholar Mevlana Haydar. Ottoman court culture in that era was heavily influenced by deviant dervishes and Persian Muslims. The inscriptions in Mehmed I's beautiful Green Mosque in Bursa, named after its stunning blue-green tilework designed by artists from Tabriz (in modern-day Iran), include references to Ali, more common in Shi'i Islam, and Persian poetry, along with the sayings of Muhammad rather than Qur'anic verses.[17]

According to the fatwa Mevlana Haydar gave, killing the sheikh was deemed lawful, but taking his property was not.[18] This was the penalty in Islamic law for a rebel. He was sentenced to hang for the crime of sedition, an affront to the sultan's authority. What mattered was loyalty, not theology. His was not the first Ottoman 'blasphemy' trial, because he was not given the punishment for an apostate, which required execution *and* confiscation of property.

To produce the greatest spectacle, Sheikh Bedreddin was hanged
stark naked from a tree. As narrated by a twentieth-century Turkish poet, 'The slippery rope wrapped like a nimble snake around
his thin neck beneath his long white beard'.[19] 'Swinging on a bare
branch, wet with rain', his corpse was left to rot in the marketplace of Siroz in 1416.[20] It was rumoured that his disciples took
the corpse down and buried it in a secret location. Disciples of
Sheikh Bedreddin remained in Southeastern Europe, ready to
outrage conservative Muslims or hatch another rebellion.[21]

Ottoman chroniclers deprecated his followers by claiming that
'although these Sufis say "we are dervishes of God", they are not
dervishes'.[22] 'Although the rotten Sufi's tongue says "God", his
heart says "gold and silver and silver coin"'.[23] They justified the
bloodbath by asserting that Sheikh Bedreddin and his disciples
had been motivated by evil: 'Satan, the accursed, whispered evil
doubts and sins in his ear and won him over'.[24] Börklüce Mustafa's
bare-headed deviant dervishes were alleged to have seduced the
commoners to engage in unlawful acts, just as Torlak Hu Kemal
and his Torlaks were said to have called the people to sedition
and to have given permission for animal pleasures. The sheikh
had supposedly issued fatwas permitting wine drinking, ecstatic
whirling, lascivious dancing to music, and pederasty.[25]

MEHMED I AND MURAD II:
RESURRECTING AND EXPANDING THE EMPIRE

In reality, what had frightened the dynasty the most, causing its
supporters to exaggerate the sins of Sheikh Bedreddin and his disciples, was the fact that the sheikh had managed to foment several
popular, nonsectarian peasant rebellions—the only premodern
movements in Ottoman history that brought together Christians,
Jews, and Muslims in a common cause against the empire. In the
words of a modern Turkish communist poet,

The ten thousand heretic comrades of Börklüce Mustafa—
Turkish peasants from Aydın,
Greek sailors from Chios,
and Jewish artisans—
plunged like ten thousand axes into the enemy forest.
Their standards red and green,
Their shields inlaid, their ranks of bronze helmets
were broken to smithereens;
as day turned to evening in the driving rain,
of the ten thousand only two thousand remained.

Ten thousand sacrificed eight thousand
to be able to sing with one voice
and to pull the nets all together from the sea,
all together to forge the iron like lace,
to plough the earth all together,
to be able to eat honey-filled figs all together,
and to be able to say:
everywhere,
all together
we will share everything but the cheek of the beloved![26]

All that the Ottomans had constructed over the past century had been threatened by the uprisings of Sheikh Bedreddin and his disciples. Turning away from earlier foundational visions and the groups that propelled the rise of the dynasty to power in the thirteenth and fourteenth centuries, namely the gazi 'holy warriors', caused tensions that increased support for rebellions. These rebellions illustrated the clash between interpretations of Islam and what happens when the electrifying ideas of Ibn Arabi are acted upon. That Börklüce Mustafa was originally a Christian and Torlak Hu Kemal a Jew demonstrates the unexpected outcomes of Islamic conversion.[27]

Everything the Ottomans had built since their founding had been shattered by the steppe cavalry archers of the nomad conqueror Timur and betrayed by those Ottoman subjects opposed to Bayezid I who deserted the sultan to join them. At the time, Ottoman failures seemed to suggest that the reliance on slave soldiers and not gazis had been a fatal error. But after Timur, sedentary gunpowder empires, including that of the reborn Ottomans, would gradually rise to power, making a standing army vital.[28]

The determining factors in the continued existence of the empire were the powerful interests that wanted it put back together. Along with the remaining members of the dynasty itself who had been spared by Timur, these included those who held land grants (cavalry and Christian families in Southeastern Europe) and the servants of the sultan who had been recruited through the Collection (Janissaries and administrators). Given their interest in reviving the dynasty, it seemed unlikely that such leading figures would return the revitalised empire to its mystical and warrior roots. They would instead attempt to rein in the centrifugal force of the deviant dervishes, who in 1416 had proven themselves too much of a threat to the survival of the empire.

Mehmed I resurrected most of the territories of the empire prior to being crushed by his own horse in an accident in Edirne in 1421. According to two Ottoman chroniclers, several days after his death, his viziers came up with a macabre ruse to calm the palace and make his Janissary commanders believe the sultan was still alive until they were able to put a new ruler on the throne. The sultan's Persian physician propped up Mehmed I's corpse and had a page stand behind it, using the deceased's own hand to stroke his beard. Continuing the ploy, the physician begged the assembled to leave and let the sultan recover his health. Convinced or not, thus chastised, they left the (deceased) sultan in peace.[29]

They hid Mehmed I's corpse for forty-one days until his nineteen-year-old son and designated successor Murad II (reigned 1421–1444, 1446–1451) could be enthroned in Bursa.[30] He expanded the empire further, but only after defeating two Mustafas. The first Mustafa was Mehmed I's brother, who had proclaimed himself sultan in Edirne. During battle between the opposing armies of nephew and uncle near Bursa, Mustafa fled but was captured and killed. Then Murad II had to contend with the army of his thirteen-year-old brother, Mustafa, who besieged Bursa. After the two sides fought outside İznik, Murad II's forces captured his younger brother and strangled him.

Murad II reconquered Thessalonike in 1430 after an eight-year siege. The Ottomans sacked the city, converted churches to mosques, and enslaved much of the population. Despite taking the Byzantines' second city and dominating Southeastern Europe and Northwest Asia, however, Murad II's territory was split in two at its centre by Byzantine Constantinople, which controlled the Bosporus straits. He also faced powerful enemies to the west, especially the Kingdom of Hungary, and to the east, including the Turcoman principality of Karaman. Should the Hungarians and Karamanids launch a simultaneous, two-pronged military invasion while the Byzantines and their Venetian allies blockaded the narrow waterway, hindering the sultan's armies from crossing between Europe and Asia, it could spell the end of the Ottoman dynasty. Such a nightmare scenario was almost realised by the Crusade of Varna of 1444, a Crusade not fought in the Middle East, but in Southeastern Europe. The battle was one of the major turning points in fifteenth-century European and Asian history.

No matter that each side formulated this as a 'holy war' against 'infidels', the Crusade or gaza was not simply a battle between Muslims and Christians. The crusaders had Muslim allies and the Ottomans had Christian support. The main crusader protagonists were Pope Eugenius IV, the Byzantine emperor John VIII, and the king of Hungary Vladislav I (who was also Władysław III of Poland), along with others such as the Burgundian Knights aiming to retaliate for the debacle at Nicopolis half a century earlier. Venice's rival, the Genoese, based in their enclave in Pera—the walled, hilly district marked by the well-known stone tower built in the mid-fourteenth century, facing Constantinople across the Golden Horn—and assisted the Ottomans, who faced formidable enemies.

Murad II's opponents had a military advantage. The Kingdom of Hungary, led in the field by King Vladislav and the ruler of Transylvania, John Hunyadi, were able to deploy more troops than the Ottomans. More significant was their technological edge. The Hungarians employed the wagenburg tactic, a 'mobile fortification, with cannon mounted on carts', and utilised armour that Ottoman weapons could not penetrate.[31] In one skirmish, Ottoman infantry shot John Hunyadi's horse out from under him, and he 'crashed to the ground with his horse and weapons, like a dog falling off the roof of a bazaar'.[32] But because he was 'clad in pure iron', the Ottomans could not kill him, and he was able to escape. In many battles, whether the Ottomans used arrows or arquebuses, the Hungarians were able to retreat to their wagenburgs, firing cannons and arquebuses in return. The Ottomans succeeded in stopping the Hungarians at Zlatitsa Pass in Bulgaria, but could not defeat them.

Murad II realised peace was necessary.[33] With the assistance of his Serbian wife, Mara, the daughter of his vassal George Branković, Murad II concluded a ten-year truce with Hungary in summer 1444.

John VIII, the Byzantine emperor, did not give up hope to save his kingdom from the Ottomans, however. Promising a simultaneous Hungarian attack from the west (despite the truce), and a blockade of the Bosporus straits, which would hinder the sultan's advance from Europe, the emperor spurred the Karamanids to attack from the east that same year.[34] Although the Karamanids launched an offensive, their leader capitulated without battling Murad II's forces.[35]

Believing that the Ottoman Empire was secure in the west and east, with a European truce and Asian peace restored, the forty-one-year-old sultan surprised his court by abdicating the throne, the first Ottoman leader to do so.[36] To this day, we are not sure why he made this decision. Twenty-three years earlier, he had chosen to have his accession ceremony in the Grand Mosque of Bursa, where he girded the sword of, or was invested with the cloak of, a Sufi sheikh, as if becoming initiated as his disciple.[37] Perhaps, tiring of the trappings of power in this world, he wished to retire to contemplate the afterlife in a dervish lodge. Murad II also had a reputation for being a heavy wine drinker. The oldest extant line written in Turkish by an Ottoman ruler—'Cupbearer bring, bring here again [what is left over from] yesterday's wine'—reads like the pleading of an alcoholic.[38] As he went off to spend his days in mystical retreat, or in his cups, Ottoman rule passed to his twelve-year-old son, Mehmed II (reigned 1444–1446, 1451–1481), who was enthroned in Edirne.

But the peace was short-lived. Due to pressure from Polish knights and the papal legate, who absolved him of having to honour his commitment, the Hungarian king quickly abjured his agreement with the sultan and resumed the war.[39]

Viziers implored Murad II, who was in Anatolia at the time, to return to the throne in Edirne to perform his duty as gazi. He grudgingly agreed.[40] Fearing imminent Hungarian occupation, the Ottomans felled large trees to block the probable path of the Hungarian army and dug a moat around Edirne, evacuating the countryside and ordering civilians to take refuge in the citadel.[41] Such scenes of impending doom spurred the appearance of an apocalyptic Muslim scholar in the city preaching faith in Jesus. To quell this internal upheaval, Ottoman authorities executed him and tortured his many followers.[42]

To participate in the campaign against the Hungarian army with the Anatolian army, Murad II had to cross the straits. But by October 1444, the Venetians and others had blockaded the Bosporus. The only way to overcome this was to place Ottoman artillery on both shores, 'so that cannon on either side should be able to kiss each other', providing cover for the sultan and his army to cross safely to the European side.[43] Part of his army managed to cross further south of Constantinople at Gallipoli and set up the battlements on the European shore. The sultan used Genoese cannoneers to set up artillery on the Asian bank. The Byzantines launched two giant ships loaded with arquebuses into the Bosporus, but Ottoman cannon balls burst into one of the ships, turning its hull to matchsticks and sinking it, and tore a huge hole in the other.[44] Crossing on Genoese boats procured for the occasion, the sultan and his troops landed safely in Europe.

Prince Mehmed, although 'still a fresh rose', impudently demanded to lead the campaign against the Hungarians while his father defended Edirne, the seat of the sultan.[45] Murad II admonished him to do as he told him, and to defend Edirne and say his prayers.[46]

As tens of thousands of Hungarian soldiers swept across Southeastern Europe, the Ottoman defenders, male and female, were praised for their manliness—firing their cannons, arquebuses, lances, and arrows from their castles—but because the Hungarians wore armour of steel, Ottoman swords, axes, clubs, and maces were useless.[47] As Hungarian forces burned Ottoman citadels, some defenders threw themselves to their deaths. At one castle, the victorious Hungarians threw the Ottoman defenders from the castle into the moat, and any that survived were cut down by arrows before they could stand.[48] The Hungarians moved ever closer to their goal of seizing Edirne.

On 10 November 1444, the two sides met in battle at Varna on the coast of the Black Sea. The Hungarians took to the field blaring trumpets, as the Ottomans went into battle accompanied by thundering kettledrums.[49] Murad II and his Janissaries and infantry soldiers took up a position at the centre rear, stationed on a mountain, his Southeastern European cavalry to his left and his Anatolian cavalry to his right.[50]

The battle began with a loud clamour. One 'could hear stabbing, and, above all, blows ringing out from both the armies', as 'arrows began to fly like grasshoppers from out of the grass'.[51] The Hungarians decimated the Anatolian wing of the cavalry and killed their commander. Because the Hungarians were 'clad from head to toe in iron', Ottoman swords could not make a dent in them, so those on the Southeastern European wing used their axes, maces, and clubs to bash their opponents, but after fighting for a while, they fled the battlefield.[52] Without cavalry, Murad II and his Janissaries were left alone at the centre to fight. Battling with few men, including his palace pages, it was a bloodbath, where 'heads and legs, fingers and fingernails, axes and hammers, arrows and lances, shields and weapons poured on the battlefield like a carpenter's chippings'.[53]

According to a Greek chronicler, Hungarian king Vladislav was killed 'as a result of his stupidity'.[54] Ignoring the ruler of Transylvania Hunyadi's advice to wait for reinforcements, the king waded into battle, where a Janissary knocked him off his horse with a mace and other Janissaries hacked him to pieces with their axes.[55] They 'cut off his head and hoisted it on a lance'.[56] Hungarian knights fell all around him 'like autumn leaves'.[57] The Southeastern European Ottoman cavalry then returned to rout the Christian knights. Thousands of crusaders were annihilated. The anonymous Ottoman author of the account of the battle proclaimed:

> So lie his slaughtered enemies,
> Each one's body lies there headless.
> The valleys are so full of them
> That no one can find a way through.
> Corpses are so swimming in blood
> That whoever sees them goes out of his mind.[58]

The victorious Ottomans executed captives over the age of twenty by sword and enslaved the 'fresh-faced lads'.[59] Murad II kept some captured Hungarian knights alive, sending them to Muslim rulers—the Mamluks, the khan of the Crimea, and the

Karamanids—to be paraded in humiliation.[60] A group of these captive knights caused a great tumult in Cairo, as they were mounted on horseback and outfitted with armour 'and bowl-like helmets on their heads'.[61] Some of them allegedly converted to Islam.[62]

With the victory, Ottoman control of Southeastern Europe was total. The Ottomans ruled as far west as the borderlands of Serbia and Albania and as far north as the Danube. Murad II then again retired, placing Mehmed back on the throne. But a Janissary rebellion in Edirne in 1446 precipitated Murad's final years in power. Murad II again took his throne away from his son.

Newly back in power, Murad II was approached by the disciples of a militant Shi'i Sufi, Sheikh Junayd (died 1460). Sheikh Junayd was a descendant of Safi al-Din (died 1334), a contemporary of Osman, who had been exiled from Ardabil (in northwestern Iran) by the Turcoman Karakoyunlu ruler Jahanshah (died 1467). The Sufi sought refuge in Ottoman domains, requesting Murad II grant him a landholding. He was refused based on the premise that 'two emperors cannot sit on the same throne'.[63] So instead, Junayd built a following among Ottoman Turcoman rivals in central and eastern Anatolia after being granted protection for a short period by the Karamanids at Konya. At the beginning of the sixteenth century, his grandson, Ismail, would establish the Ottoman's greatest military and religious rival, the Safavid dynasty based in Iran, which fomented massive revolts in Ottoman territories.

The appearance of another Sufi was an omen of misfortune. One day in 1451, while Murad II was riding his horse in the environs of Edirne, a dervish blocked his path as he crossed a bridge. The Sufi told him his death was near; he must repent and ask God's forgiveness. When the sultan returned to the palace after the ride, he followed the Sufi's instructions, then complained, 'I have a headache'. He lay in bed three days and then passed away. His viziers kept the news secret and hid the corpse for nearly two weeks until nineteen-year-old Mehmed II arrived in Edirne, where he could again accede to the throne.[64] Complying with the custom of fratricide, he had his only brother, one-year-old Little Ahmed, put to death.[65] Not wishing to be demoted a third time, he aimed high. This time he wished to do what many Arab and Turkish rulers before him had failed to do over the course of the previous seven hundred years: he wished to conquer Constantinople.

4

CONQUERING
THE SECOND ROME
Mehmed II

THE CONVENTIONAL CLAIM of European history is that secularism, tolerance, and modernity began in Europe with the
signing of the Peace of Westphalia in 1648. That series of treaties
ended the Christian European wars of religion and instituted the
principle of tolerance of religious minorities. But nearly two hundred years earlier, after the Ottoman conquest of Constantinople
in 1453, melancholy conqueror and resolute leader Mehmed II
institutionalised the principles and practices of toleration that
had begun the century before under his predecessors. Mehmed II
made decisions that left their mark on Ottoman and world history. He conquered Constantinople and then sought to legitimise
his victory and rule over it by appealing to Muslims and Christians alike. He called himself caesar and claimed the inheritance
of Rome, appropriating the monuments of Constantinople's greatest ancient rulers, Constantine and Justinian.[1] He rebuilt the city
not only as the centre of the Ottoman dynasty and the heart of his
new imperial administration formed out of converts, but also as a
multireligious metropolis. How did he do it?

THE SIEGE AND CONQUEST OF CONSTANTINOPLE

By the time twenty-year-old Mehmed II launched the siege of Constantinople, the great Byzantine capital was no longer the envy of the world. Once it had boasted half a million inhabitants and had been one of the wealthiest cities in the world. But by 1452, its population thinned by waves of plague, it may have had a paltry fifty thousand people within its walls.[2] It was protected on three sides by water and on the fourth side by massive land walls thirty metres high and ten metres deep that had stood for a thousand years. But seen in the larger scope of things, Constantinople was but a small island of Byzantium marooned in the middle of an Ottoman sea.

Determined to capture Constantinople, Mehmed II played a leading role in the siege, making a number of brilliant tactical decisions. He first ordered the construction of Rumeli Hisarı, a new fortress five kilometres north of the city on a steep, rocky slope on the European side of the narrowest point of the Bosporus (merely seven hundred metres across), opposite Anadolu Hisarı, a fourteenth-century Ottoman fortress on the Asian side. Anadolu Hisarı had been constructed by Mehmed II's grandfather, Bayezid I, in readiness for his failed eight-year attempt to take Constantinople at the turn of the fifteenth century.

Realising that the fortress was an omen of the destruction of the Christian city and ruin of the Byzantine Empire, the inhabitants of the last island of a once mighty kingdom 'trembled in their deep distress'.[3] The wild hillside, previously covered in large swaths of lilac-coloured Judas trees, soon boasted a triple-towered stone fortress. Mehmed II is said to have personally participated in its rapid construction. The fortress was raised in less than four months.

By August 1452, Constantinople's access to the Black Sea was cut off. Reflecting this turn of events, the Ottomans named the fortress Boğazkesen, which means 'Cutter of the Straits', or more literally, 'Throat-Cutter'. In Greek, it translates as 'Decapitator'.[4] Mehmed II ordered that any ship attempting to pass the fortress would have to stop, and any ship disobeying would be sunk. A Venetian ship, the first vessel attempting to pass through to deliver goods to the now besieged Constantinople, was sunk by the Ottomans' massive and accurate cannons. Its crew was brought ashore and decapitated, and its captain impaled 'by a stake through the anus'.[5]

Although he had cut off access to the Black Sea side of the Bosporus strait and was using his navy in the Marmara Sea to bombard the sea walls, Mehmed II still faced the problem of not being able to get his ships close enough to attack the inner city. For the Byzantines had constructed a giant chain, which they used as a seemingly impenetrable floating gate, to block access to the Golden Horn, the waterway that led inland to the city's harbour. So confident were the Byzantines that the city was safe from Ottoman naval attack that they left the walls along the Golden Horn unguarded. But Mehmed II had a plan. In April 1453, he ordered his men to lay down giant beams greased with animal fat leading inland from the Bosporus to the Golden Horn. Five dozen ships were fastened to long cables and pulled along these glide ways up the steep hill and across land by the hands of thousands of soldiers from the Bosporus to the Genoese colony—marked by its tower and numerous Catholic churches—and then downhill to the Golden Horn. It made for an unbelievable sight, 'ships borne along on the mainland as if sailing on the sea, with their crews and their sails'.[6] Seeing the Ottoman warships lying at anchor in the Golden Horn, the Byzantine defenders were stupefied. Bad portents—icons dropped at religious processions, flash floods and torrential hail, a dense fog that signalled the divine presence abandoning the city—terrified them further.[7]

Attacking by land and sea, Ottoman forces surrounded the city and outnumbered the city's defenders more than ten to one. Well over one hundred thousand Ottoman soldiers—Muslims, Christians converted to Islam, and those who remained Christians—faced six or seven thousand Byzantine and allied defenders, including Catalans, Genoese, and Venetians. The Byzantines managed to survive another month, but by May the city's fate had been sealed. Mehmed II had ordered the building of a pontoon bridge across the Golden Horn, which the Byzantines could not destroy. To destroy the city's land walls in the west, Mehmed II had also ordered the construction of one of the largest cannons the world had ever seen. Cast by a Christian renegade from Hungary, the cannon would allow Ottoman forces to break through.[8] It marked the first time the Ottomans used gunpowder technology to bring down a besieged city's walls.

The Ottomans' final assault began before dawn and lasted until late morning on 29 May 1453. The bronze cannon's innovative gunpowder-filled metal cannon balls tore holes through the ancient land walls with a 'blast and crash like thunder from the heavens' whose 'piercing air-rending sound' could be heard over ten miles away and whose sudden shock was allegedly so powerful that it left unsuspecting men speechless and caused pregnant women to abort.[9] Having rent the walls thanks to the unrelenting bombardment, Mehmed II's army entered the city on the fifty-fourth day of the siege. Such gunpowder weapons would soon be adopted across Western Europe. The Byzantine emperor, Constantine XI Paleologus, died in that last battle, his corpse reportedly identified by its purple shoes.

Byzantine and Ottoman historians concur about what followed. Mehmed II allowed his soldiers one day's rampage and free plunder. They gave no quarter to commoner or nobility, raping women, maidens, nuns, and 'beautiful young boys'.[10] They murdered or enslaved the survivors of the siege and conquest. They looted and pillaged, desecrated churches and tombs—disinterring corpses in the search for gold—plundered the Byzantines' riches, destroyed their icons, and burned their holy books.[11] Indeed, 'there was good booty and plunder. Gold and silver and jewels and fine stuffs. . . . They enslaved the infidels of the city and the gazis embraced [raped] their beloved women and girls'.[12] As the Ottomans boasted, 'Every tent [of the sultan's army] was heaven, filled with boys and girls, the sexual servants of paradise, each a stately beauty, a cypress, from which shoots spring, [offering] a juicy peach' (that is, a wet, lover's kiss).[13]

As the conquering soldiers overran the city, thousands of Christians sought refuge in the Church of Divine Wisdom (Hagia Sophia), believing in a prophecy. A sword-wielding angel would descend to the thirty-five metre, fourth-century Column of Constantine standing at the heart of Constantinople on its main thoroughfare and hand the weapon to a common man, who would single-handedly avenge the Greeks, causing the Ottomans to flee while cutting them down and driving them from Byzantium.[14] The angel failed to arrive on cue.

Ottoman soldiers reached the church, broke down the locked doors, and took the thousands of Christians inside captive. 'Who can describe the wailing and the cries of the babes, the mothers' tearful screams and the fathers' lamentations?'[15] The most common soldier 'sought the most tender maiden. The lovely nun, who heretofore belonged only to the one God, was now seized and bound by another master. The rapine caused the tugging and pulling of braids of hair, the exposure of bosoms and breasts, and outstretched arms'.

And then Mehmed II cut the rape short. He rode through the Edirne Gate at the western edge of Constantinople. When he saw 'what a large number had been killed, and the ruin of the buildings, and the wholesale ruin and destruction of the City, he was filled with compassion and repented not a little'. As his eyes filled with tears, he cried, 'What a city we have given over to plunder and destruction!'[16] He rode through the city on a white horse to the glorious sixth-century Church of Divine Wisdom. The Hagia Sophia was not only the seat of the Greek Orthodox Church but the largest building in the world, with the most magnificent, highest dome ever built. Mehmed II dismounted from his horse and entered. He ascended to the dome to gaze upon the conquered city. Those accompanying him exclaimed, 'If you seek Paradise, Oh you Sufi, the topmost heaven is Hagia Sophia'.[17]

Mehmed II examined the 'strange and wondrous' icons, frescoes, and mosaics that decorated the church, 'mounting as Jesus the spirit of God ascended to the fourth sphere of heaven'. As he looked down upon the ruined buildings, 'he thought of the impermanence and instability of this world, and of its ultimate destruction'. In sadness, he recited an ancient Persian verse from the thirteenth-century poet Saadi about the transitory and unstable nature of power: 'The spider is curtain-bearer in the palace of Chosroes [an ancient Persian Shah] / The owl sounds the relief in the castle of Afrasiyab [Samarkand]'.[18] Life is short, and even in moments of triumph a leader must remember his own mortality.

Along with such melancholy, was there also love among the ruins for Mehmed II?[19] After the conquest, the sultan offered Lukas Notaras, the high admiral and grand duke of Constantinople, the opportunity to serve as leader to the remaining Greeks in the city. But while drunk at a banquet, he also demanded that Notaras give him his beautiful youngest son, a fourteen-year-old beardless youth. Mehmed II may have wanted to have the young man join his wine-drinking soirees to serve as the object of love poetry, and eventually have him converted to Islam and trained in the palace to join either his bureaucracy or his elite infantry regiment, the Janissaries. Mehmed II had other Byzantine nobles executed, and 'from among their wives and children, he selected the beautiful maidens and handsome boys, and entrusted them to the watchful care of the Chief Eunuch'.[20]

Immediately after the conquest, a history written to flatter Mehmed II describes how he had taken his share of the human spoils, including 'beautiful virgins' and 'the handsomest boys, some of whom he even bought from the soldiers'.[21] He appointed some of the scions of nobility to serve as his bodyguards 'and to be constantly near him', and others to serve as his palace pages, boys who 'were indeed of signal physical beauty' and 'splendid physique'.[22] The same Ottoman phrase 'palace pages' was used to describe the 'loveable catamite boys' at Bayezid I's court who 'served' the sultan.[23] Perhaps one day Notaras's youngest son would serve the sultan as grand vizier, the head of his government.

With the Notaras father deployed as head of the Christians and the son a loyal servant trained in his palace, Mehmed II would ensure control over the Christian population, maintain the loyalty of an important Byzantine family, and gain a handsome young man at his side. But it was not to be. Notaras refused to surrender his child to the conqueror, reportedly protesting, 'It is not our custom to hand over my own child to be despoiled by him. It would be far better for me if the executioner were sent to take my head'. And this Mehmed II did. He responded by having Notaras and his sons killed in this fashion.[24]

Mehmed II did, however, use the conquest to gain legitimacy among Muslims and Christians alike. Ever since the third quarter of the seventh century, Muslim empires had sent armies to capture Constantinople. But none had never succeeded. Seeking Islamic legitimacy, Mehmed II made sure the hadith—the saying attributed to Muhammad, 'Constantinople will be conquered. Blessed is the commander who will conquer it, and blessed are his troops'—would be inscribed in Arabic at the entrance to his imperial mosque complex in the centre of the historic peninsula.

During the siege, Mehmed II was accompanied by his spiritual advisor, a Sufi named Sheikh Akşemseddin, who claimed that, in a village outside the land walls on the Golden Horn, he had rediscovered the tomb of Ayyub al-Ansari, a companion of Muhammad sent to conquer Constantinople in the late seventh century. The alleged finding of the tomb linked Mehmed II to Islam's Prophet and contributed further to his Islamic legitimacy. After the conquest, at that location he built a mosque and proper tomb for al-Ansari, which became a pilgrimage site for Muslims. As the city's holiest mosque, it became the place where future sultans would perform the ceremony of 'girding the sword', the equivalent of a coronation, embracing a sword that had allegedly belonged to Muhammad.

Rather than seeing his exploit as merely an Islamic conquest, however, Mehmed II cultivated awareness of his connection to the Roman legacy. In the words of Mehmed II's Greek counsellor George Amiroutzes, writing to the sultan over a dozen years after the conquest, 'No one doubts that you are the Emperor of the Romans. Whoever holds by right the centre of the Empire is the Emperor and the centre of the Roman Empire is Constantinople'.[25] Mehmed II's chroniclers, Greek and Ottoman, placed him in a long line of great leaders including the Macedonian Alexander the Great and the Roman Julius Caesar. They compared the conquest of Constantinople to those of Troy, Babylon, Carthage, Rome, and Jerusalem. Addressing the sultan, one panegyrist wondered whether the comparatively petty deeds of others were better known because they had been carried out by Greeks in Greek history, while Mehmed II's vast accomplishments, comparable to those of Alexander the Great, would not be passed on to posterity in Greek.[26] The sultan's historian depicted Mehmed II as aiming to rule the world in emulation of the Alexanders and Pompeys and caesars and other famous kings and generals.[27] This historian wrote in Greek to inform not only Greeks of Mehmed II's deeds but all of Western Europe, even those who inhabited the British Isles.[28]

To flatter him, the same Greek author depicted the sultan as a great general and a wise philosopher king. Mehmed II may have had great physical power and energy, but that alone did not make him a ruler worthy of respect. His wisdom and his knowledge of history aided his ability to rule, for he studied the philosophies and histories of the Arabs, Ottomans, and Greeks.[29]

A Venetian visitor concurred, describing Mehmed II as being 'as eager for fame as Alexander of Macedonia. Daily he has Roman and other historical works read to him' by an Italian. Keen to expand his domains, he made a great effort to 'learn the geography of Italy', including 'where the Pope is and that of the Emperor, and how many kingdoms there are in Europe'. He possessed a map of Europe, as he was most interested in 'the geography of the world and of military affairs'. Most frightening for the observer was how the sultan stated that 'the times have changed and declared that he will advance from East to West as in former times the Westerners advanced into the Orient. There must, he says, be only one empire, one faith, and one sovereignty in the world'.[30] To build this universal vision of one world religion, there was no place more worthy than Constantinople.

REBUILDING THE CITY, CREATING THE EMPIRE OF DIFFERENCE

No sooner had he conquered the city than Mehmed II set about rebuilding it. He converted its greatest church, Hagia Sophia, into a mosque by adding a single minaret, but he did not cover up all the mosaics and frescoes inside the church. Muslims could still see winged angels with mysterious faces soaring above them as they prayed. Nearby Hagia Eirene (Church of Holy Peace), the first church built in Constantinople, however, was converted into an arsenal and incorporated within the New Palace (Topkapı Palace) grounds. The hilltop imperial Christ the Almighty (Saint Saviour Pantocrator) monastery and church became the city's first Islamic college.

The first Ottoman chroniclers writing about Mehmed II's reign wished to see the fall of Constantinople as the conquest of a Christian city and the erection of a Muslim city in its place. They envisioned a city full of mosques, madrasas, and Sufi lodges, of Muslims pious and ascetic, referring to Constantinople as Islambol, 'full of Islam'.[31] Other writers offered a unidimensional account of good, pious Muslims shouting, 'Allahu Akbar' (God is most great) and fighting on God's side against evil, impious Christian infidels, who are inevitably defeated in battle and are killed or surrender and then humbled for the glory of Islam. Devoting two folios to the marvellous dome of Hagia Sophia and ten folios to the reconstruction of the city, one chronicler devoted only one sentence to the mention of the sultan's having transported 'captives from the lands of the infidels which he conquered by sword and settled them around Constantinople'.[32] He was more interested in narrating how Mehmed II had made Constantinople into a Muslim city with mosques and madrasas, Sufi lodges, and a mausoleum and mosque for Ayyub al-Ansari, the 'patron saint' of the Muslim city.[33] He mentioned Ottoman Muslims arriving voluntarily to take possession of abandoned homes and properties.[34]

In point of fact, Mehmed II did not choose to remake Constantinople as a purely Muslim city. Because the city was taken by force, its defenders, the Greeks, should have been barred from the city, as in Thessalonike. After its nadir in the immediate aftermath of conquest, however, the Greek population of Constantinople increased thanks to Mehmed II's policies.[35] The sultan sent commands to every corner of the empire that as many Christians, Muslims, and Jews as possible should be forcibly deported there.[36] Following the conquest, Mehmed II ordered the deportation of all of Thessalonike's Greek Jews to Istanbul. Due to these forced relocations, approximately twenty-five years after the conquest Istanbul's depleted population had grown by 50 percent to around eighty thousand. Sixty percent of the population was Muslim, 20 percent Greek Orthodox, 11 percent Jewish, 5 percent Armenian, and 3 percent Italian.[37] Across the Golden Horn lay Pera and Galata, the former Genoese colony with which the Ottomans had long engaged in trade, and which had surrendered to the conquerors a couple of days after the city fell in 1453. Galata's population was 39 percent Greek Orthodox, 35 percent Muslim, 22 percent Italian (mainly Genoese), and 4 percent Armenian.[38]

The new migrants needed new homes and new markets. Mehmed II constructed the first component market areas of what would become the Grand Bazaar, which would grow over the ensuing centuries into a sprawling covered market comprising dozens of streets and thousands of stalls. There, Arab, Armenian, Genoese, Greek, Jewish, Turkish, and Venetian merchants sold precious luxury goods including jewels, gold, and silver, and textiles such as silks, leather goods, and carpets. It was an entrepôt befitting a wealthy city open to the world.

The many migrants also needed new places of worship and congregation: churches, mosques, and synagogues; fountains, taverns, hospices, Sufi lodges, inns, and public bath houses; Islamic colleges and universities. These, too, were constructed, even though the city had been conquered by force. In such a situation, according to Islamic precedent, no new Christian or Jewish houses of worship should have been permitted to be built. But they were.

To rule over all these new migrants, deportees, and the diverse population that remained after the conquest, Mehmed II institutionalised the toleration Ottomans had been practising de facto for over a century in Southeastern Europe. This was at least a century before religious minorities were tolerated in Western and Central Europe. In the first decade after the conquest, Mehmed II appointed leaders for the recognised religions of the Ottoman Empire—Sunni Islam, Greek Orthodoxy, Judaism, and Armenian Christianity (the Apostolic Church)—in the imperial capital. In the eighteenth and nineteenth centuries, these leaders' jurisdiction would extend to include all members of their respective religions in the empire. Members of these religions were permitted to live according to their own system of beliefs and practices. Muslim, Christian, and Jewish leaders were granted the privilege of restricted administrative, fiscal, and legal powers to regulate their members' private and spiritual affairs. They oversaw judicial courts, judges, jails, and policing agents adjudicating personal law (marriage, divorce, and inheritance), as well as schools and seminaries, hospitals, cemeteries, and houses of worship. In the following centuries, the Greeks, Jews, and Armenians were even allowed to set up printing presses in the city, before Muslims were permitted to operate their own. They were expected in return to raise taxes to fund their own religious institutions and to pay for the privilege. Such tolerance of diversity was an expression of the Ottomans' Turco-Mongol and Islamic heritages, out of which they created an empire built upon the maintenance of difference. The Ottomans did not aim to make all subjects into Muslims, or even into Ottomans—that is, the members of the ruling elite. Rather, they established institutions that allowed members of tolerated religions to pursue their religious and personal lives with minimal interference.

Mehmed II appointed a mufti, a specialist in Islamic law. He relied on the Byzantine rabbi Moses Capsali as a mediator with Jews in the city.[39] He also tapped an Armenian he knew, the metropolitan of Bursa, Hovakim, to be the first Armenian patriarchate in the city, so as to rival the catholicates in Echmiadzin in Armenia and Sis in Cilicia.[40] As Greek patriarch, he named a man he could trust: the anti-papist George Scholarios, also known as Gennadios, who opposed the union of the Catholic Church with the Orthodox Church. He could be counted on not to support a Crusade to liberate the city.[41]

The fact that the patriarchs (and indeed, all church officials) were appointed by the sultan and that a synod could only affirm his choice demonstrated the awesome powers assumed by the Ottoman ruler within this system of tolerance and secular control of the religious hierarchy. The patriarch would refer to the sultan as the 'legal emperor' with the right to intervene in church affairs, a right that previously had been given to the Byzantine emperor.[42]

Whereas in the former Byzantine Empire the emperor, as head of the church, had had the authority to appoint and dismiss the

Greek patriarch, the Muslim sultan assumed this duty because he was head of the government. The Greek and Armenian patriarchs were given limited jurisdiction over church offices in the imperial capital and surrounding regions, restricted control of church properties, nonexclusive authority in family law, and the ability to collect taxes from Christians.[43] The patriarchs serving as designated tax collectors simplified the taxation of their members and ensured Christian loyalty. This system was also practical, in that it eased the otherwise onerous task of ruling over diverse populations, making it easier to locate cooperative partners who would collect taxes and share in the responsibility of rule as part and parcel of society. Greek, Armenian, and Jewish law courts were not separate and autonomous, but were instead an integral part of the Ottoman system of law.

But tolerance is built on hierarchies, and in the religious hierarchy of the empire, Islam was supreme. Tolerance is the expression of an unequal power relation. The sultan and not the patriarchs had the authority to decide to what extent the visible remains of the city's Christian past would endure. Mehmed II dreamed of erecting his own monumental imperial mosque and palace complex at the centre of Constantinople. To build his mosque in 1463, he demolished the Church of the Holy Apostles, which held the tombs of Byzantine emperors since Constantine and housed the Greek patriarchate that he had established less than a decade earlier.[44] The second church to serve as the patriarchate, Pammakaristos, would be converted to a mosque called 'Conquest' a century later.[45] Mehmed II's mosque complex combined a royal congregational house of prayer, a dynastic monument, the premier educational institutions in the empire, and a new residential and commercial area. This first palace, which would come to be referred to as the Old Palace, became the primary residence of the women and young children of the dynasty. Located at the centre of the city, he found it unsatisfactory.

TOPKAPI PALACE: CENTRE OF AN
ADMINISTRATION DOMINATED BY CONVERTS

For a palatial centre of his power, Mehmed II was drawn instead to the isolated hill at the tip of the peninsula, the site of the former Byzantine acropolis, extending into where the Bosporus strait spills into the Marmara Sea.[46] There, between 1459 and 1478, he constructed his second palace, the exclusively male New Palace, or Topkapı (Cannon Ball Gate) Palace. The palace's ornate inscription on the outermost Imperial Gate (Bab-ı Hümayun) refers to Mehmed II in the tripartite fashion befitting his and his empire's nature: in the Turco-Mongol style as 'khan' and 'sultan', in the Islamic style as 'the shadow of God', and as the ruler of Asia and Europe as sovereign 'of the two continents' and the two seas [the Mediterranean and the Black Sea]'.

Topkapı Palace bore all the hallmarks of the Ottoman's tripartite heritage: Byzantine-Roman, Turco-Mongol, and Muslim.[47] The outermost court of the palace contained the former church of Hagia Eirene converted into an arsenal. Like his Seljuk predecessors, the sultan conferred much administrative and military authority on his deputies, called viziers, and so his New Palace was divided into an outer palace complex for relations with the outside world, and an inner complex that included the precinct where he resided without his family. Mehmed II housed his family in the harem, or private quarters, of the Old Palace in the centre of the city.

Mehmed II set in motion the process, realised in the next century, of making the office of the sultanate into a more secluded and less public role, more like a caesar than a frontier gazi. Topkapı Palace comprised a series of connected courts arranged in hierarchical fashion, each space more restricted in access and smaller than the preceding one. The unseen yet all-seeing sultan was situated at its symbolic core, the many features and functions of palace design revolving around him.[48] Yet, in a gesture to his Turco-Mongolian heritage, Mehmed II also made sure to include ample space in the palace gardens for a sport pitch with an attached tiled pavilion from which he could enjoy a good game of Mongolian polo, a feature that would not be out of place in Central Asia. A series of single-story buildings given precise functions was like a Turco-Mongol military tent camp—in which the tents of the soldiers were set up around the tent of the khan at the centre—in stone form.[49]

Although the palace grounds contained a number of mosques, Topkapı was built next to Hagia Sophia, which was used as the imperial Friday mosque. The first courtyard, accessed by the Imperial Gate, was open to everyone. It contained a hospital, the imperial mint, a bakery, and the former Hagia Eirene, used as an armoury. Passing through the Middle Gate or Gate of Salutation (Bab-üs Selâm), one reached the second courtyard, the location of the treasury and the divan, the meeting place of the imperial council. The first and second courtyards were thus devoted to public ceremonies and administration. At the opposite end of the second courtyard was the Gate of Felicity (Bab-üs Saadet), where the sultan sat when presiding over ceremonies. After Mehmed II's reign, most enthronements were held at this gate.

During an enthronement, the sultan sat on the gold divan throne before the Gate of Felicity, accompanied by the acclamations and prayers of a palace herald. The viziers, army commanders, and leaders of the Muslim religious class bowed, knelt, or prostrated before the seated sovereign. One by one, they kissed either the tips of his fingers, his feet, the hem of his robe, the foot of the throne, the carpet placed before it, or even the ground before him, offering their oath of allegiance and wishes of good fortune.[50] The oath of allegiance had both an Islamic and a Turco-Mongol precedent. In the Ottoman case, it expressed the proper relation between the master (the sultan) and his servants. An accession gratuity would be distributed to the army, including the

Janissaries, to ensure a smooth and peaceful transition from one sultan to the next. A cannon salute would sound to inform the residents of the city that a new ruler had taken over, and town criers would share at the public squares the news, which would also be announced from minarets. Coins would be minted in the new sultan's name. Preferably held on a Friday, the enthronement would be followed by communal prayers at the nearby Hagia Sophia, where the sermon would be read in the sultan's name.[51]

Only the highest officials in the land and foreign ambassadors could pass through the Gate of Felicity. The Chamber of Petitions, the external throne room, was located just on its other side, in the third courtyard. Within the third courtyard, the gate itself was flanked by the dormitories and schools of the pages in training for palace service, a male harem. The third and fourth courtyards thus made up the inner palace, hosting the sultan and the youth being trained for imperial service. The fourth courtyard contained gardens, pools, and pavilions, and the residence of the sultan's private physician. Mehmed II's privy physician was an Italian Jew, Giacomo of Gaeta, who converted to Islam and became known as Hekim Yakub Pasha.[52]

The Collection of children was institutionalised with the building of the schools in Topkapı Palace. An Ottoman decree from 1493 commanded those conducting the levy to take boys except those who 'show signs of reaching puberty or [who] have begun to grow a beard'.[53] When the levied boys arrived in Istanbul as a tribute tax imposed on Christian subjects, they were circumcised. The 'children of superior beauty' were taken into inner palace service.[54] Their superior moral qualities were allegedly revealed by the pseudoscience of physiognomy, which deduced which boys had 'the sign of felicity on their foreheads' as determined by the eunuch who was the agha ('lord' or 'master', a ranking servant of the imperial household) of the Gate of Felicity.[55] After a number of years of education in the palace, those in this first, privileged group—the pretty palace pages—again passed through a selection process in which those with the best moral character and physique were chosen for further physical, spiritual, and cultural education. They would become the leading administrators of the empire.

Those with 'the mark of evil and rebellion in the part of the forehead between the middle and the temple', however, would not be taken into inner palace service, for they would be susceptible to being 'seditious, tyrannical, and egotistical and destroy the peasantry with the flame of oppression, burning them'.[56] Rather than obtain administrative positions, they would become soldiers. The majority of boys were thus not taken into palace training as pages but were sent to Turkish farms in Anatolia en route to becoming Janissaries. They engaged in difficult physical labour for seven or eight years, becoming accustomed to hardship, learning Turkish, and studying Islam after having been circumcised and converted to the faith. Following this, the young men were called back to the imperial capital, where they served as a labour force in the palace stables, kitchens, and gardens, or in apprenticeships at the arsenal or mosque construction sites, or with the military (army or navy) before finally being enrolled in the elite infantry unit of the Janissaries, one of the army's two main fighting forces (the other being the provincial cavalry).

The presence of the pages in the innermost courtyard of the palace illustrates Mehmed II's preference for creating a new Ottoman class in place of the Turcoman gazi warriors who had been instrumental in the dynasty's rise to power. Mehmed II refused to 'respectfully stand up at the sound of martial music as a sign of readiness for gaza'.[57] This defiance was a concrete manifestation of his new strategy of rule, which entrusted his bureaucracy and army to Christian boys who were converted to Islam and raised in the palace schools. The important law code attributed to him confirmed this practice, signalling a turning away from the gazi ethos towards a bureaucratic empire.

Mehmed II's code of law set out the ranks and duties of officials, such as the eunuchs in charge of the different spheres of the court, the military judges, the financial secretary or treasurer, and the chancellor. It elaborated the functioning of the palace system, including the imperial council, which met after 1470 in the newly completed council chamber in the second courtyard of Topkapı Palace. The council, presided over by the grand vizier, met four days a week to advise the sultan on political and military matters, issue decrees in his name, make promotions and appointments, and act as a law court for the most serious crimes, especially those committed by the sultan's servants. Its executive officers included three or more top viziers, the two military judges (*kadıasker*) of Rûmeli (Southeastern Europe) and Anatolia, one or more treasurers, and a chancellor. Mehmed II's code of law detailed court etiquette, including proper facial hair and turban material and size: the higher and finer the turban, the more exalted one's rank. As the sultan's deputy, the grand vizier was granted political and executive authority and replaced the sultan as the man responsible for the day-to-day affairs of administration and in leading troops to battle. The grand vizier, and no longer the sultan, presided over the imperial council and served as army commander. The sultan thereafter would become less gazi and more caesar.

After the conquest, Sultan Mehmed II had ordered the dismissal and execution of veteran grand vizier Çandarlıoğlu Halil Pasha, who unlike the lesser viziers had advocated peace with the Byzantines and had counselled against the conquest of Constantinople. His Anatolian Muslim family had provided viziers to the dynasty for two centuries. He was replaced by the convert Mahmud Pasha (in office 1455–1474, executed 1474). This change marked the beginning of the end of the power of great Muslim families and the creation of a new meritocracy of converts trained in the palace and entrusted with many important positions. Sultan Mehmed II's subjugation of most of Southeastern Europe in the latter part of his reign secured this source of manpower. Converts recruited through the Collection would henceforth serve in the highest office in the administration, the grand vizierate, and

make up the Janissary corps. Thereafter, the leading administrators of the empire, especially the grand vizier, would usually not
be Turkish Muslims. In the fifteenth century, they would often be
the converted offspring of conquered Christian dynasties, including Byzantine.

With his new, elevated status and an aloof relationship with
the outside world, Mehmed II withdrew into an envelope of silence within the palace. He spent most of his time at the centre
of the series of increasingly secluded courtyards that culminated
in the inaccessible royal residence housing the sultan and his boy
pages, while his family lived at the Old Palace.[58] The outcome
was the consolidation of the new ruling class. The New Palace,
Topkapı, was the centre of the administration and of ritualised,
Byzantine-style pomp and ceremony, where orchestrated ritual
movement marked the passage from one carefully guarded formal station and courtyard to the next, expressing the new hierarchy of empire.

The dynasty's transition from a principality based on Ottoman gazis to an empire based on meritocracy and converts did
not go smoothly, however. Elite Byzantine families remained in
the city and still held positions of power—some while remaining
Christians, others after converting to Islam.[59] Many of the grand
viziers between 1453 and 1515 would be from elite Greek families, including the nephew of the defeated Byzantine emperor
Constantine XI Paleologus.[60] As late as the end of the sixteenth
century, descendants of Byzantine royalty held key financial
positions.[61] Tensions following the conquest centred on the rise
of this Christian-convert administrative class, the appointing of
Christians—especially Byzantine nobles who were members of
the Paleologon dynasty—and Jews to positions of authority, and
the allocation of revenues and landholdings to them. The rise to
power of Collection recruits and individual Christians and Jews
was accompanied by the decreased power of born Muslims, especially Sufis, nomads, frontier warriors, and even members of the

religious class. The latter were infuriated by Mehmed II's abolishment of the endowments that had funded religious institutions. Mehmed II's new silver coin, taxation, extension of imperial control over the lands of wealthy families, and expansion of tax farming were all unpopular.[62]

Seeing the writing on the wall that these changes were permanent, gazis protested when in 1457 Mehmed II ordered an assault on Belgrade. The gazis said that when the city was captured, they would have to plough the land.[63] They did not want to be settled agriculturalists, tied to the land and controlled by others. They wanted to wage constant war and live from plunder and booty. They sought to pin their frustrations on others. That the assault was led by converted Byzantine noble and grand vizier Mehmed Pasha Angelović (in office 1455–1468) contributed to their sense of alienation.[64]

Viziers of Christian and Jewish origin and Jewish tax farmers were vilified in historical accounts written after Mehmed II's death by those representing the interests of the mystics and frontier warriors whose power and privilege had been limited by Mehmed II. They expressed resentment of the financial favours given to Greeks settled by Mehmed II in Istanbul, which resulted in some Christians or converted Christians rising to positions of wealth and power. Sufis' wrath targeted the sultan's confidant, the converted Byzantine noble Grand Vizier Rûm Mehmed Pasha, who was blamed for convincing Mehmed II to impose policies benefiting Christians and harming Muslims.[65] The most prominent author among these writers was outraged by the new financial policies imposed by the vizier, which meant that he had to pay rent on the mansions and shops he had acquired after the conquest, contrary to Mehmed II's original decree that any Muslim who voluntarily settled in the city would be allowed to own abandoned Christian or Jewish property.[66]

Writers also cast their aspersion on Jews, focusing in particular on Mehmed II's converted Jewish physician and later boon

companion and vizier, Hekim Yakub Pasha. The same Muslim
author who sided with Sufis and gazis and castigated viziers of
Christian origin claimed that, supposedly, prior to Hekim Yakub,
sultans had never assigned public office to Jews 'because they
considered them corrupters of morals'. But when Hekim Yakub
became vizier, 'however many greedy Jews there are, they all meddled in the Sultan's business'. Further, 'Until he came, administrators were not hanged'.[67] The author was referring to the Jewish
tax farmer Yakub son of Israel, who was executed in 1472. When
Mehmed II died in 1481, the Janissaries blamed Hekim Yakub
Pasha—he was alleged to have been paid by Venice to poison the
sultan—and went on a rampage in Istanbul, looting Jewish and
Christian homes in the city, attacking the mansions of the wealthy
and government officials, and decapitating the grand vizier and
plundering his palace.[68] What this burst of violence meant was
that the interplay between integrating a new elite through conversion and the resulting tensions of this multireligious metropolis
would have to be managed.

FIRST CONSTANTINOPLE, THEN ROME?

As of 1453, one of the greatest cities of Christendom was in Muslim hands. Unlike so many Arab and Turkish rulers before him,
Mehmed II had succeeded in conquering Constantinople. But was
it enough in his eyes? As he was completing his new palace in
1480, the sultan sent his navy to attack the Knights Hospitaller
of Saint John on the island of Rhodes and their ally the Kingdom
of Naples. The siege of Rhodes failed, but the fleet conquered the
fortress of Otranto on the Italian mainland. After holding it for a
year, however, it was relinquished without further territorial gain.
The sultan had to content himself with being the ruler of the Second Rome, not the first.

Emperor and caesar. Khan and sultan. The Ottoman dynasty
bore all the hallmarks of its Byzantine, Mongol-Turkish, and

Muslim heritage, a Eurasian amalgam that lasted more than five hundred years. With their conquest of the Second Rome, the Ottomans became more like the Byzantines, claiming authority as successors to the Eastern Roman Empire, taking on an imperial ideology, seeing themselves as the inheritors of Rome, and adapting its architectural models. Like the Byzantine ruler before him, the Ottoman ruler called himself emperor and Roman caesar, with new horizons of power. The Byzantine emperor had been 'God's regent' on earth, and the Ottoman ruler was 'God's shadow on earth'. Both appointed the leader of the ruling religious institution. After conquering Constantinople, Ottoman architecture, especially its mosques, always emulated the magnificent domed Byzantine Church of Divine Wisdom, the Hagia Sophia.

The Ottomans had become less like the Mongols. In 1478, for the first time, Mongol khans—in this case the Tatar khans of the Crimea, the descendants of Genghis Khan—acknowledged Ottoman suzerainty, rather than the reverse.[69] The Ottomans established dominion over most of Anatolia by utilising artillery to decimate the Karamanids, one of the last of the Turcoman principalities, centred at Konya in the south, and the White Sheep (Akkoyunlu), the last of the Turcoman-nomad armies in the east, who had failed to obtain promised Venetian firearms.[70]

But like the Mongols, the Ottomans based their authority on the personal loyalty of their followers, borrowing their concepts of secular law and forms of military organisation, utilising gunpowder and cavalry. Genghis Khan had pronounced rules and regulations as well as set penalties for crimes; each decree was recorded and consulted and enacted by future rulers.[71] Secular law came into being as the result of decisions made by the khan. Intended as more than merely the decrees of individual rulers, this dynastic law, the law of the ruling family, was binding so long as that family remained in power.[72] Ottoman sultans also pronounced decrees that became the law of the land. The first Ottoman law code is attributed to Mehmed II.

As the Mongol rulers had before him, Mehmed II—who called himself, among other things, 'khan' like a Mongol leader—allowed for religious privileges among the conquered population. Genghis Khan had opposed bigotry and the preference of one 'superior' faith over another because he was the adherent of no religion. He had 'honoured and respected the learned and pious of every sect'. His children and grandchildren had chosen different faiths, while others in his retinue followed the religions of their forefathers or none at all. No matter what religion they confessed, they adhered to Genghis Khan's secular law, which did not distinguish between sects.[73] At the Mongol court, the wives of the khan practised different religions than he, including Christianity. So, too, had the Christian princesses who lived as wives or concubines or mothers of sultans in the Seljuk harem been allowed to remain Christian. They had practised Christian rites in the harem's chapels presided over by priests and had baptised their children, including future sultans, who were also circumcised according to Islamic custom.[74] Many Seljuk rulers had spoken Greek with their wives, mothers, and daughters. This reflected the fact that until puberty they had been raised by their mothers in the harem where Greek women and Orthodox Christianity predominated. Many Seljuk sultans were half-Greek and half-Turkish.

But unlike the Mongols and the Seljuks, the large proportion of Christian women of the Ottoman harem were converted to Islam and taught to speak Turkish. The Ottomans tolerated differences, but they were not indifferent to them. They ranked religions according to a hierarchy: superior (Sunni Islam), tolerated (Christianity and Judaism), and ostensibly prohibited (Shi'i Islam, paganism, and atheism). Less religiously tolerant than the Mongols, and shedding their nomad ethos, the Ottomans became ever more European. They consolidated a new ruling class composed mostly of converted Christians. Their territory was the same as the Byzantine Empire when it had controlled much of Southeastern Europe and Anatolia. They made the Orthodox patriarch and church an arm of Ottoman power, laying the groundwork for the expansion of Orthodox Christianity at the expense of the Catholic Church in the Mediterranean and Southeastern Europe.[75]

The conquest of Constantinople made the Ottoman enterprise into a truly European empire, opening much of Southeastern Europe to further conquest. With Constantinople's capture, the Ottomans ended Byzantine rule, declared themselves the inheritors of ancient Rome, and rebuilt the city. Mehmed II's programme for the transformation of Constantinople—including the conversion of Byzantine churches, monasteries, and palaces, and the construction of Topkapı Palace as the new centre of administration—led to a new, Islamised cityscape. As the Ottomans revitalised the 'dead centre of a dead empire', whose revival was fed by repopulating the city with Christians, Jews, and Muslims from their ever-expanding empire, the Islamic world gained an imperial centre to match and even surpass Christendom in its wealth, size, and magnificence.[76]

The city was the beating heart of an Islamic power that was superior to the West prior to the modern West's rise to global predominance. And, as we shall see, with a ruler who patronised Italian artists, attracted the admiration of his Western European peers, collected the wisdom of the ancients and his contemporaries in multiple languages in his personal library, and strengthened diplomatic and economic relations with the rest of Europe, Istanbul was anything but cut off from the exciting developments of the Renaissance.

5

A RENAISSANCE PRINCE
Mehmed II

A PORTRAIT OF MEHMED II, painted in 1480 by the Venetian Renaissance master Gentile Bellini, is on display in the Renaissance collection at the Victoria and Albert Museum in London. The portrait is similar to other Renaissance works, including the same artist's 1501 portrait of Leonardo Loredan, the doge of Venice, which stares at Mehmed II's portrait from the other side of the same room. Bellini depicted the Ottoman sultan as he did any other Renaissance figure. He framed Mehmed II in a classic, columned arch. He painted the portrait realistically and in three-quarter view, not shying from depicting Mehmed II's aquiline nose. Although Ottoman rulers generally wore turbans rather than crowns, the artist added three golden crowns in the background, symbolising Mehmed II as the ruler of the Byzantine Empire in the west (Constantinople) and in the east (Trebizond) and as the monarch of Asia. The question is, does the painting belong in this room?

Many have claimed that it is an exaggeration to rank Mehmed II among contemporary Renaissance rulers.[1] Even though he gathered Greek and Italian scholars at his court, ordered the Greek patriarch to write a treatise explaining Christianity, commissioned a map of the world, made great effort to learn the wisdom of the ancients, had Ptolemy's *Geographia* translated, filled his library with Greek and Latin works, and established the Ottoman tradition of sultanic portraiture when he brought Bellini from Venice, his contemporaries in the rest of Europe saw him as a Muslim whose interest in the West arose only from his desire to conquer it. Were they right?

When Mehmed II conquered Constantinople, the conversion from Eurasian nomad to Renaissance prince was complete. Once a pastoral and nomadic shepherd, the Ottoman ruler had become the settled leader of a huge bureaucratic undertaking.[2] Beginning with Mehmed II, Ottoman rulers perceived themselves as caesars, the inheritors of ancient Rome, and world conquerors of the stature of Alexander the Great. Mehmed II was as keen to collect the wisdom of the West as that of the East. He collected books in Arabic, Armenian, Greek (Homer's *Iliad*), Hebrew (Maimonides's *Guide for the Perplexed*), Persian, and other languages for his library, including classical works such as Arrian's *Anabasis* and *Indica*, the main sources about Alexander the Great's life.[3] The sultan's library contained the books looted from the Byzantine emperors' libraries, as well as works he ordered on contemporary European siege engines and artillery. He read classical literature, geography, cosmography, astronomy, and history. He favoured art and literature from Muslim-majority societies—though not Qur'anic commentaries and the like—especially heroic fiction, such as the chivalric romance of the Arab hero Antar; works on Sufism, law, medicine, philosophy, and music; and illustrated albums.[4]

He was as eager to recruit Greek scholars from the defeated Byzantine Empire as Persian scholars from the Central Asian and Turkic empires. Upon conquering the last Byzantine stronghold in the Black Sea port of Trebizond (Trabzon) in 1461, Mehmed II brought a Greek counsellor to his court, the philosopher George Amiroutzes. Amiroutzes was a cousin of convert-Greek grand vizier Mehmed Pasha Angelović, with whom he negotiated the surrender of the city.[5] After its submission, the city's main church,

also called Hagia Sophia like its namesake in Istanbul, was converted to the central mosque and Anatolian Muslims were forced
to settle in the city. In later years, Trabzon's Greek population was
deported to Istanbul.[6]

Amiroutzes was master of the philosophy of the Peripatetics
and Stoics. Mehmed II spent much time conversing with Amiroutzes about the wisdom of the ancient Greeks.[7] At the sultan's command, the philosopher created for him a world map, replete with
labels in Arabic, based on the separate maps in Ptolemy's *Geographia*.[8] After defeating the Turcoman White Sheep confederacy
in eastern Anatolia in 1473, Mehmed II brought Giyas al-Din of
Isfahan, the head of the White Sheep chancery, or office of public
records, to his court.[9]

More significant was Mehmed II's attraction of the celebrated
astronomer Ali Kuşçu from Samarkand, who became professor of
astronomy and keeper of the observatory attached to Hagia Sophia in Istanbul. The star tables he had compiled in Central Asia
transformed Ottoman astronomy and made their way to the Polish scholar Nicolaus Copernicus and the Danish scholar and imperial court astronomer to the Habsburg emperor, Tycho Brahe.
These tables were later formulated by Johannes Kepler (died 1630)
at the court of the Holy Roman emperor into the laws of planetary
motion, revolutionising European astronomy and contributing to
the Scientific Revolution.

Mehmed II was a typical Renaissance patron of the arts, having
his portrait made by one of the greatest of Renaissance painters
and commissioning medallions with his image, also on display
in the Renaissance rooms at the Victoria and Albert. He commissioned a medallion of himself made by Lorenzo de' Medici's
sculptor, Bertoldo di Giovanni, which depicts him as a heroic figure standing triumphant on a chariot. He reportedly had Bellini
make him a view of Venice. Leonardo da Vinci sketched a plan
for a bridge over the Golden Horn and may have visited Istanbul. Mehmed II decorated his palace with wall paintings made by

other Italian artists. He had Bellini paint him an image of the virgin and child. He amassed a large and strange collection of Christian relics, including the corpse of Isaiah, complete with beard, hair, and ears.[10] He collected ancient and Byzantine statuary.

Mehmed II owned and commissioned many Renaissance works of art and literature. He contacted various Italian rulers, among them the king of Naples and the Medicis in Florence, to send their court artists to him, including painters, sculptors, and medallion casters. Along with the Bellini portrait of the Ottoman ruler, a similar portrait, likely created by an Ottoman artist trained by an Italian at the court in Istanbul and long attributed to Nakkaş Sinan Bey, also bears evidence of Renaissance style, as it depicts a three-quarter, realistic profile of Mehmed II's visage. What makes it unique is that the artist added the sultan's full body in sitting position, rather than merely the upper body. Thereafter, sultans' bodies would be depicted in this fashion, an outcome of the Italian-Ottoman artistic exchange at Mehmed II's court.[11]

THE OTTOMANS AS THE ANTITHESIS OF RENAISSANCE EUROPE

We usually do not think of Mehmed II when we think of the Renaissance. What comes to mind instead are the Medici family ruling Florence; Dante Alighieri's *Divine Comedy* (1321); Filippo Brunelleschi's cathedral dome in Florence (1436); Leonardo da Vinci's paintings *The Last Supper* (1495–1498) and *Mona Lisa* (1503–1506); Niccolò Machiavelli's *The Prince* (1513); and Michelangelo's sculpture of David (1501–1504) and Sistine Chapel ceiling (1508–1512) in the Vatican. Generally understood as the revival of classical culture and learning in fifteenth- and sixteenth-century Western Europe, the Renaissance is not thought to have encompassed the Ottomans and their empire.

If we think of the Ottomans and the Renaissance at all, it is with a negative association based on two myths. The first myth is

that the Renaissance was sparked in Italy by the arrival of Greek
humanists fleeing Constantinople in 1453 after it fell to the Ottomans. But there are new views about the Muslim and Jewish role
in the European Renaissance. We now know that until the fifteenth century, cultural exchange between the Muslim-majority
regions and Western Europe was extremely one-sided.[12] Muslims
found little to learn from Western Europe, while Western Europeans absorbed knowledge from Muslims, which led to the growth
of their own cultures. Ancient Greek culture and learning—
including history, philosophy, medicine, chemistry, mathematics,
and astronomy—were actually preserved by being translated into
Arabic or Syriac and improved upon with new commentaries by
Christian, Jewish, and Muslim thinkers originating in Middle
Eastern Islamic empires such as the Abbasid Caliphate in Baghdad in the eighth, ninth, and tenth centuries.

In the twelfth, thirteenth, and fourteenth centuries, this hu-
manistic worldview and knowledge was then transmitted to
Christian Europe through Islamic Spain and Sicily when it was
translated from Arabic into Hebrew and Latin. The *Divine Comedy*'s section entitled 'Inferno' demonstrates that Dante was familiar with Islamic narratives of Muhammad's ascent to paradise
and used it as a framing device for this work. Thus, the European
Renaissance has its roots in Islamic Spain and the Arab world.
The Renaissance raised Western Europe to the cultural level of
Muslim-majority societies by incorporating the achievements of
Eurasian, especially Islamic, societies.[13] Importantly, the Islamic
world in general and the Ottomans in particular had never been
cut off from ancient knowledge as had Western Europeans. They
had never needed to rediscover the wisdom of the ancients and
catch up as the other Europeans had.

The second myth about the European Renaissance is that the
Ottoman conquest of Constantinople closed traditional sea routes
to India and China, causing Europeans to innovate. This then
sparked the Age of Discovery in the fifteenth to mid-seventeenth

centuries, leading eventually to Western world hegemony. But the Ottomans did not close off the spice trade in the Mediterranean. They connected Europe to the Red Sea and the East African and South Asian trade routes. Far from cutting off the Mediterranean, the conquest of Constantinople actually led to greatly increased trade between the Ottomans and Venice and Florence, including materials such as Murano glass and bronze, the latter for casting medallions and cannons. European powers such as the Portuguese relied on Muslims in their naval expeditions as navigators, and in the East they simply tapped into preexisting Arab-Islamic commercial networks. The Ottomans launched their own commercial-imperial seaborne empire in the Red Sea, the Persian Gulf, and the Indian Ocean, and sent naval expeditions as far as Indonesia. The Ottomans were very much seen as an integral part of Europe in terms of both diplomacy and commerce. The French and English obtained silks and cotton through the Ottoman Empire, and the Ottomans exchanged ambassadors and made commercial treaties with European powers.

The sources of these myths are easy to locate. The Greek humanists' response to the conquest of Constantinople in 1453 shaped Western perception of the Ottomans. Arriving in the Latin west, these Byzantine immigrants played a key role as mediators and translators of prejudice against the Ottomans, despite the 1054 schism between the Orthodox and Roman Catholic churches, whose failure to unite facilitated the fall of the Second Rome to Mehmed II.[14] Byzantine immigrants worked as teachers and translators of ancient Greek learning for humanists in Italy, using their positions to gain support against the Ottomans and encourage the sense of a West-East, Europe-Asia divide. Latin hostility towards the Orthodox Greeks decreased, and a new philhellenism was linked to anti-Ottomanism. What these humanists added to medieval religious hostility towards Muslims—which had long existed in the West, witness the Crusades—was a secular, cultural, and political frame for animosity. Some still couched

the conflict in religious terms—seeing the Ottomans as God's
scourge and blaming their own moral failings for the disaster—or
interpreted the loss in apocalyptic terms. Or they saw Muslims as
potential converts: countless Western European sources declared
Mehmed II to be on the verge of converting to Christianity. Crusader imagery and motivation were still present.

Hoping to inspire Christian leaders to take up arms against
the Ottomans, the Byzantine immigrants used classical rhetoric
and ancient models to frame the contemporary situation. Already before the conquest of Constantinople, Italian humanists
had likened the advance into Southeastern Europe of the 'uncivilised' Ottomans—who were supposedly hostile to learning
and culture—to the 'barbarian' Goths and Vandals who sacked
Rome in the fifth and sixth centuries and caused the decline of
Roman civilisation.[15] The sack of Rome and the ensuing plunge
into a dark age was brought up more frequently following the
conquest of Constantinople. Utilising and reinterpreting classical
texts, borrowing their myths and historical concepts, Byzantine
humanists who fled to Italy resurrected cultural prejudices that
the 'civilised West' held against the 'barbarian East'.[16]

Formerly conceived as ancient Greece, the West now became
Christian Europe. The East, formerly understood as ancient Persia
or the Trojans, became the Ottoman Empire. Byzantine intellectuals deployed the sharp distinction between Greece and Asia made
by Herodotus in his analysis of the Greco-Persian Wars of the fifth
century BCE.[17] They utilised Aristotle's depiction of Greeks as a
noble people facing the menace of barbarians from without. They
made the Ottomans into Asians, outsiders who did not belong in
Europe. They conceived of a dichotomy between the supposedly
uncultivated peoples of the 'Orient'—who lacked morality, letters,
arts, and sciences and who wantonly destroyed books—and the
superior peoples inhabiting the 'Occident'. A humanist and future
pope called the conquest of Constantinople and the looting of its
libraries 'a second death for Homer and a second destruction of

Plato'.[18] Even Erasmus of Rotterdam referred to the Turks as 'a barbarous race'.[19] The idea that the (Persian, Asian, Eastern) Turks were inferior barbarians who had destroyed a superior (Greek, European, Western) civilisation—burning its books, which were the storehouse of ancient learning—would be repeated time and again by European writers in the ensuing centuries.

For their part, at this stage in their history, the Ottomans were not immune to this way of thinking. When Mehmed II visited the presumed site of Troy in 1462, he declared that he had avenged the injustices inflicted on the Trojans and the East by the West.[20] Yet the more common Ottoman way of seeing the world was not an East-versus-West binary. Rather, the Ottomans preferred to see themselves uniting East and West, just as their empire integrated Asia and Europe. Most of Mehmed II's chroniclers made this claim about the sultan.

Alongside the Greek humanists, another group that was influential in shaping Western European opinion about the Ottomans was the ambassadors of the Republic of Venice who served in the empire. Members of the cultured elite, they were also immersed in humanist thought. Upon his return to Venice following a tenure in Istanbul, each ambassador gave a lengthy, ceremonial speech reporting his observations at a public session of the senate. Their speeches were not only popular among Venetians—from the early sixteenth century they were translated and circulated to chanceries across Europe, thus widening their impact.

For the first three-quarters of the sixteenth century, the Venetian ambassadorial reports reveal fascination, admiration, and respect for their Ottoman opponents, as well as an aversion and perceived threat.[21] During this period, Venice controlled islands and ports across the Mediterranean, including those in Crete and Cyprus, and fought three wars against the Ottomans (1499–1503, 1537–1540, and 1570–1573). Its ambassadors perceived the Ottoman Empire as wealthy and powerful, its subjects as obedient. It was a society where all servants of the sultan supposedly acted 'of a single will for the public good', devoted to their emperor.[22] The centre was a machine 'in which every part had its place'. Each subordinate part, be it in the administration or military, was 'measured, ordered, named, and situated in a strict configuration' and absolutely deferential to the authority of the sovereign.[23]

The ambassadors depicted the Ottomans as the antithesis of the West, the opposite of what the Venetians presumed their republic to be—a free, enlightened polity. They were especially repulsed by the chaotic transfer of power from one ruler to the next. They abhorred the absence of a hereditary aristocracy that could check what they thought was the absolute power of the ruler over his subjects. By the late sixteenth century and in the wake of the Venetians' defeat in the third Venetian-Ottoman War—which saw the Ottomans conquer Cyprus, where monthslong sieges of Nicosia and Famagusta were followed by the killing and enslavement of thousands of Christians, who were banished from living within the conquered cities' walls—what these reports constructed was an image of Ottoman rulers as oppressive, violent, and arbitrary 'Oriental despots'. The Venetians saw their own polity as Plato's Republic ruled by sages, where liberty and nobility were core principles. The Ottoman dynasty, by contrast, led 'a government or republic of slaves', a republic of fear.[24] This negative way of perceiving the Ottoman dynasty was taken up by Western European Christian thinkers who expanded the meaning of despotism, describing not only the administrators and soldiers of the sultan as slaves, but the entire subject population. As a consequence, the theory of despotism in Western political thought was based on what was perceived as the Ottoman model.[25]

A final major source of Western European antipathy towards the Ottomans was the Habsburg court of the Holy Roman Empire. As the Ottomans' premier rival in the Mediterranean and Central Europe, the Habsburgs—whose progenitor King Rudolf was a contemporary of Osman—produced much propaganda against their enemy in the form of cartography, history writing, and even the decorative arts. The best example of the latter is a series of tapestries Charles V (reigned 1519–1556) commissioned in 1546 to commemorate his capture of Tunis from the Ottomans in 1535, illustrating his view of himself as valiant crusader and defender of the Christian faith. The panels portray the Ottomans as a massive, menacing, violent, and well-armed threat. Completed in 1554, the twelve magnificent panels of *The Conquest of Tunis* measure six-hundred square metres when hung side by side and are the most significant set of tapestries the Habsburgs commissioned.[26] They were displayed at all major Habsburg court festivals, religious ceremonies, and official events. During Charles V's reign, the tapestries were hung in the reception rooms of the Brussels Palace and then Alcázar Palace in Madrid, alongside those of his sister, Mary of Hungary—governor of the Netherlands (1531–1555), whose husband, Louis, had been slain by the Ottomans in the Battle of Mohács (1526)—and his son, Philip II (reigned 1556–1598). Smaller replicas were also produced and distributed to other Habsburg palaces across Europe. The valuable tapestries depicting the fall of the Ottoman heathens in gold, silk, and wool were displayed so often that in the eighteenth century a less expensive replica set was ordered to be displayed in their place, so as to conserve the precious originals.

RENAISSANCE EUROPEANS ADMIRE AND ARE FASCINATED BY THE OTTOMANS

Despite their generalised antipathy towards the Ottomans, sixteenth-century European intellectuals and statesmen could not help but express admiration for Ottoman military success, for the discipline and obedience of the sultan's troops, and for his clever statecraft. Analysing the strengths and weaknesses of different government systems, they considered whether Christian-ruled polities should adopt Ottoman practices, if only to defend their lands and defeat their rival.[27] One late-sixteenth-century writer

went so far as to promote raising Christian boys into a holy militia to battle the Ottomans, a kind of Roman Catholic Janissary
corps.[28] The origins of such 'reason of state' thinking have been
traced to Niccolò Machiavelli. Dedicating his work to Lorenzo de'
Medici, Machiavelli notes in *The Prince* how difficult it would be
to conquer the Ottoman Empire because of its system of government. He writes that, unlike kingdoms such as France, where the
king rules together with the noble class, in the Ottoman Empire
there is only one lord—the ruler—and all others are his servants,
whom he appoints as he wills. As a result, Machiavelli argues, it is
difficult to conquer Ottoman territory, as the invader cannot side
with any errant, treasonous nobles, as would exist in a kingdom
like France. The sultan's ministers, being all slaves and servants,
cannot be easily bribed, and one can expect little advantage from
them when they have been bribed, as they have no base of support
among the populace. As a result, whosoever attacks the Ottomans
will face a united people and will have to rely more on his own
strength than on the rebellion of Ottoman subjects.[29]

The Englishman Richard Knolles, author of *The General History of the Turks* (1603), displayed admiration, envy, horror, and
fascination with Ottoman wealth, splendour, and military might.
Knolles used Marlowe's description of Timur to refer to the Ottomans in general as 'the present terror of the world' and Mehmed II
in particular as a bloodthirsty, cruel tyrant responsible for the
death of nearly a million people. What the Bellini portrait hinted
at was exaggerated by the Englishman: Knolles claimed that the
sultan was hideously ugly, his face marred by a nose so crooked
and sharp it nearly touched his upper lip. Yet he also spoke highly
of the same Ottoman ruler. He admits that Mehmed II had notable intellectual qualities.[30] Knolles declared Mehmed II to be 'of a
very sharp and apprehensive wit, learned . . . especially in astronomy' and able to 'speak Greek, Latin, Arabic, Chaldee [Syriac?],
and Persian', a man who 'delighted much in reading of histories,
and the lives of worthy men, especially the lives of Alexander the

Great and of Julius Caesar, whom he proposed to himself as examples to follow'.

The English were fascinated by the Ottomans and other Muslim kingdoms. Nearly five dozen plays featuring Turks, North Africans, and Persians were staged in London between 1576 and 1603, forty of them between 1588 and 1599, when England was negotiating an anti-Spanish alliance with Morocco and sending its first ambassadors and merchants to Istanbul.[31] The Ottomans play significant roles in the works of Christopher Marlowe. Marlowe's blood-soaked play *Tamburlaine the Great*, featuring the humiliating death of Bayezid I, was a smash hit. In *The Jew of Malta*, written in 1589–1590, Marlowe conjures an anti-Christian Muslim-Jewish alliance among the evil Jewish merchant Barabas, his Turkish slave Ithamore, and the Ottoman troops besieging the island. In this play, the Jew and Muslim are united in their malicious hatred for Christians.

In *Richard II* (1597), William Shakespeare imagined England as isolated from the world.[32] Yet Shakespeare's view is belied by how internationally connected England was in his day. Just as London was peopled by foreigners, so, too, are his plays, and it is for this reason that he included Muslim characters in some. Among these are the villain Aaron the Moor in *Titus Andronicus* (1594) and the virtuous prince of Morocco, who claims to have defeated the Ottomans in battle, in *The Merchant of Venice* (1600). When, from 1600 to 1601, a large Moroccan entourage visited London to conclude an anti-Catholic, anti-Spanish alliance, they were seen by thousands of Londoners, including Shakespeare.[33]

The first Arab ambassador to Queen Elizabeth I (reigned 1558–1603), Abd al-Wahid bin Muhammad al-Annuri, may have been the model for Shakespeare's *Othello* (1604). Ottomans, Venetians, and Moroccans all have a part in this play dominated by the tragic hero Othello, a baptised North African Muslim mercenary general in the service of Venice. Othello is charged with commanding the defence of the Venetian island of Cyprus from

Ottoman attack. When Othello is first introduced by name, he is addressed as 'valiant Othello, we must straight employ you against the general enemy Ottoman'.[34] But by the end of the play, after the Ottoman navy has been scattered by a storm and Cyprus saved—contradicting the real event, in which the Ottomans conquered the island in 1571—Othello 'turns Turk', reverting to the stereotypical, cruel, bloodthirsty Ottoman, murdering his Christian lover Desdemona and then killing himself.

Were we to list all the terms Shakespeare associates with the Turk in his play, they would read thusly: cruel, jealous, lustful, violent, aggressive, merciless, faithless, lawless, damned, circumcised, murderous, adulterous, whoring, wrathful, seductive, polygamous, libertine, black devil, destructive energy, despot, tyrant, ally of Satan, enemy, sodomy, castration, and unnaturalness.[35] The Shakespearean English theatregoer would imagine him or herself to be the opposite of all these terms. But at the same time, they wished to be like the Turks—to be as successful, rich, and powerful as them. The Turks had what the English wanted. They wanted their goods.

RENAISSANCE EUROPEANS TRADE AND BUILD ALLIANCES WITH THE OTTOMANS

Even as English playwrights such as Shakespeare depicted 'the Turks' (along with 'the Moors', the Black North African Muslims) as angry, lustful pagans or evil sinners, the English Crown and merchant companies pursued ever increasing diplomatic and trade relations with Muslim empires when it suited their interests.[36] The Ottomans were considered an integral part of the balance of power within Europe during the Renaissance period, as they had been since their rupture into Southeastern Europe in the fourteenth century. Since medieval times, the Ottomans had allied with one European Christian kingdom after another against other Christian rulers, beginning with the Byzantines and Serbs.

Prior to that, they had forged alliances with Christian princes in Anatolia. Renaissance-era Ottoman-European alliances were simply a continuation of a much longer history of accords. Both Christians and Muslims often became 'allies with the infidel'.[37] While European powers were motivated to use an alliance with the Ottomans to threaten their enemies with the might of the most powerful empire in Europe, the Ottomans sought alliances to defeat their main rivals, as well as to divide Europe, ensuring it did not unite against them.

Together with political alliances and dynastic need, another motivating factor pushing Western Europe and the Ottoman Empire together was trade. Western Europeans such as the English and French engaged in commerce with the Ottomans as junior partners, having been granted capitulations in the form of favourable trading privileges and legal autonomy. Opening embassies in the Ottoman Empire, these Western Europeans were allowed to have their own postal system, law courts, and churches, and the right to protect their subjects. The Ottomans became the largest trading partner of Western Europe in the Renaissance era, paving the way for Western European global expansion. Seeking allies against enemy Spain, Elizabeth I established close diplomatic and trade relations with Muslim powers, including the Ottomans, to whom England sent its first ambassador in 1583. Had it not been for Moroccan sugar, she would have kept her teeth.[38]

The Ottomans did not perceive the other European powers to be their equals. In the first flurry of diplomatic exchanges and correspondence between England and the Ottoman Empire at the end of the sixteenth century, the Ottoman ruler Murad III (reigned 1574–1595) was

> the monarch of the lands, the exalter of the empire, the Khan of the seven climes at this auspicious conjunction and the fortunate lord of the four corners of the earth, the emperor of the regions of Rûm [Southeastern Europe] and Persia and Hungary, of the

lands of the Tatars and Wallachians and Russians, of the Turks
and Arabs and Moldavia, of the dominions of Karamania and
Abyssinia and the Kipchak steppes, of the eastern climes and of
Cawazir [Iraq] and Shirvan, of the western climes and of Algeria
and Kairouan [Tunisia], the padishah bearing the crown of the
lands of Hind and Sind and Baghdad, of the Franks and Croa-
tians and Belgrade, possessor of the crown of his [eleven] predecessors, Sultan son of Sultan . . . the Shadow of God, the protector
of faith and state, Khan Murad.[39]

In contrast, Elizabeth I is referred to as merely 'the pride of the
virtuous Christian women, the chosen of the honoured ladies in
the Messiah's nation, the supreme mediatrix of the Nazarene sect'
and queen of England.[40]

Elizabeth's father, Henry VIII (reigned 1509–1547), enjoyed
dressing like the sultan, complete with turban, and Islamic fashions were the rage at his court, from clothing to rugs.[41] The jewels
and fabrics Elizabeth wore in the famous *Rainbow Portrait* make
her look like an Ottoman sultana. What is considered Tudor dress
is actually Ottoman style, as seen in portraits on display at Hampton Court Palace. One of the portraits there is of a European
woman in Persian attire.[42] It is not a coincidence.

Attracted by the allure of adventure and opportunities for employment, social mobility, and advancement, hundreds of common English, Irish, Scottish, Welsh and other Christian European
men travelled to Ottoman and other Muslim-majority lands such
as Algiers, Morocco, and Tunis.[43] There they lived as sailors, ship
captains, slavers, soldiers, pirates, and merchants, many in the
service of Muslim sovereigns. Thousands of other Europeans
were captured on the high seas and spent years as slaves in captivity, forced to serve in Muslim militaries. Many acculturated and
converted to Islam in the process and were circumcised, married,
and remained in North Africa or the Ottoman Empire. At the
same time, Muslims were not just characters on the English stage.

Hundreds of Muslim men appeared in southern England and Wales, as traders, pirates, ambassadors—the first Ottoman emissary was seen by thousands of Londoners bearing lions, horses, and 'unicorn horns'—servants of dukes, or prisoners captured at sea.[44] England exchanged Muslim captives it held for English captives jailed by Morocco and the Ottoman Empire as often as it traded goods. A few of the Muslims appearing in England became Anglicans.

A GLOBAL RENAISSANCE

Contrary to the inherited view, the Renaissance was not a strictly Christian European affair, for it was undergirded by economic, diplomatic, intellectual, and cultural interaction with Muslim-majority societies. When we add the Ottomans to the Renaissance as it is traditionally understood, we see it as the global phenomenon that it was. The revival of ancient knowledge was a process that occurred not sui generis in fifteenth-century Florence, but connected to an older and ongoing phenomenon, a diffusion of knowledge travelling from East to West, from eighth-century Baghdad, to twelfth-century Cordoba, to fifteenth-century Florence and Constantinople.[45] How indeed did Filippo Brunelleschi, a goldsmith with no formal architectural training, manage to create the most sublime monument of the Renaissance?[46] Perhaps because the Ilkhanid khan Öljeitü's turquoise-blue, double-shell, domed mausoleum, built at the beginning of the fourteenth century at Sultaniye in Iran, anticipated Brunelleschi's double-shell, domed cathedral in Florence by a century. It may in fact have been its inspiration.

So, too, can we accept that Ottoman sultan Mehmed II was as much a Renaissance prince as were François I of France (reigned 1515–1547) and Charles V of the Holy Roman Empire. The curators at Henry VIII's Hampton Court Palace outside London choose to display portraits of these two men as the English king's

contemporary rivals. What is missing is the portrait of the Ottoman sultan that the Tudor elite owned.

Contrary to conventional wisdom, too, the Ottomans did not
play a negative role in the Renaissance, blocking cultural, diplomatic, and economic exchange across the Mediterranean. Instead,
sultans were Renaissance princes, employing the same artists to
paint their portraits, sharing the same history and heritage, and
engaging in cross-confessional military and political alliances.
Admired and envied, the Ottomans stimulated classic European
political thought, including promulgation of an imagined division between East and West that continues to this day.

For the Ottomans, however, no matter Sultan Mehmed II's
cultural relations or references, the exchange with Renaissance
Italy was to be brief. An effigy of Mehmed II was reportedly borne
atop his coffin during his funeral procession from Topkapı Palace to his mosque in 1481. If so, it was an allusion to the funeral
march of Constantine the Great, founder of Constantinople. It
meant that Mehmed II saw himself as the heir of the Romans.[47]
But Mehmed II's pious successor, Bayezid II (reigned 1481–1512),
was opposed to human depictions in art. He sold the Christian
relics his father had collected—as well as the palace frescoes and
paintings he had commissioned, including Bellini's portrait—in
the bazaars of the city.[48] The latter eventually found its way to
London.

Bayezid II may have turned away from being a patron of Renaissance art, but he found himself in the thick of European politics due to his family troubles. Bayezid II's fight for the throne
with his own brother and his fear of this and other threats compelled the dynasty to record its history for the first time, nearly
two centuries after its establishment.

6

A PIOUS LEADER FACES ENEMIES AT HOME AND ABROAD

Bayezid II

F ACING MULTIPLE THREATS, Bayezid II sought to legitimate the dynasty's rule with both sword and pen. Because sultans were judged by the success of their military campaigns, the sanctity of their spiritual patrons, and the greatness of their forebears, Bayezid II did what no other sultan had done before him: he was the first Ottoman sovereign to commission historical accounts of the rise of the Ottomans. Attempting to defend his throne against the claims of his exiled brother Cem and those of the Sunni Mamluk dynasty in Egypt, deviant dervish rebellions and assassins, and the new Shi'i Turkic Safavid dynasty based in Iran, Bayezid II commissioned comprehensive histories in both Ottoman Turkish and Persian. The purpose of these works was to ensure loyalty to the sultan and dynasty amid the destabilising calls to rebel from other Muslims. He hoped these histories would serve as propaganda to strengthen the bonds among the dynasty's followers and supporters, and to mobilise them against their dangerous enemies. To shore up his spiritual authority, the sultan had himself proclaimed a saint, or friend of God. To ensure his political authority, the histories placed the Ottomans firmly within their

Turco-Mongol heritage, proclaiming the Oğuz Turks of Central
Asia as their ancestors.

BROTHER CEM: BAYEZID II
AND THE STRUGGLE FOR SUCCESSION

When forty-nine-year-old Mehmed II passed away unexpectedly for unknown reasons—he had long suffered from gout, the
painful, disabling, arthritic 'disease of kings'—in 1481, viziers
were unable to keep the death a secret until his successor was
enthroned. Without a master to obey, the Janissaries rioted in
Istanbul. During the ensuing political chaos, the sultan's corpse
was forgotten in the palace for two weeks, and according to the
chief halberdier, stank tremendously before it was finally buried.[1] Mehmed II's grandson Korkud, the son of oldest son Prince
Bayezid, was enthroned temporarily to quell the violence.[2] Supported by the Janissaries and the Sufis, to whom he promised the
return of their endowments seized by Mehmed II, Prince Bayezid
raced from his princely governate in Amasya in northern Anatolia to reach Istanbul before his younger brother Cem, who was
governor in the central Anatolian city of Konya.

Upon Bayezid II's accession in Istanbul, Cem—supported by
the Turcoman in Karaman, central Anatolia, where he had been
governor—proclaimed himself as sultan in the first Ottoman capital of Bursa, where he had the Friday prayers read in his name
and minted coins, again in his own name—the classic claims
of Muslim sovereignty.[3] He offered his brother a split kingdom,
as in the Mongol empires. Cem would rule the Asian provinces
from Bursa, and Bayezid could rule the European provinces from
Istanbul. Bayezid refused and defeated Cem's forces near Bursa
soon after. Cem fled to Adana in southern Anatolia, a buffer state
between the Ottoman and Mamluk empires, and then to Mamluk territory, which encompassed southeastern Anatolia, Syria,
Egypt, and the Hijaz (in modern-day Saudi Arabia).

From Cairo, Cem took the pilgrimage to Mecca, one of the very rare instances when a member of the dynasty went on the hajj. No reigning sultan ever did. The Mamluks, the remnants of the old Turkic Muslim Anatolian Karamanid dynasty, and even the Hungarians wanted Cem to lead the battle against the Ottomans at the head of their own armies. They saw the enemy of their enemy as their ally. After further failed military forays into central Anatolia, in 1482 Cem journeyed to the island of Rhodes, held by the Order of the Knights of the Hospital of Saint John of Jerusalem, known as the Knights Hospitaller. Mehmed II's Greek-convert fleet commander, Mesih (Christ) Pasha, had failed to conquer it only two years earlier. Never, it seemed, was there a more favourable time for Christian Europe to stop the Ottomans' westward advance.

But jealousy and rivalry between the pope and the competing kingdoms of Europe made united action impossible. So long as Cem lived and rallied opponents to his side, however, he cast a shadow of doubt over Bayezid II's reign. Bayezid II feared that he and his brother were repeating the internecine struggle of the interregnum less than a century earlier. While Cem drew support from alienated frontier warriors, Bayezid II killed Cem's sons and followers and made a deal with the Knights Hospitaller of Rhodes. Using a man named Hussein, a Greek convert to Islam from a prominent Byzantine family, as his trusted ambassador, Bayezid II negotiated a deal by which the knights would keep Cem in custody in exchange for an annual payment.[4] But the knights sent Cem to France in 1483, where they also kept him as a prisoner. Cem had expected to travel from there to Hungary, where he would lead an army against his brother, not be kept under house arrest in a castle tower.

In 1489, in exchange for keeping Cem in his kingdom, the king of France was offered the Church of the Holy Sepulchre in Jerusalem, in the event that the Ottomans seized the city from the Mamluks. The lance that had pierced Jesus, other relics, and

a large payment were also part of the deal.[5] But concurrent negotiations between the Knights Hospitaller and Pope Innocent VIII
(papacy 1484–1492) led instead to Cem being sent to Rome to remain in the custody of the pope.

Despite the Ottomans paying the costs of Cem's upkeep, Pope
Innocent VIII's successor, Alexander VI, wished to place Cem at
the head of a papal Crusade. But this was not to be. French king
Charles VIII (reigned 1483–1495) invaded the Italian peninsula
in 1495 just as Pope Alexander VI was seeking help from the Ottomans against the invaders. Charles VIII claimed it as a first
step in his own Crusade, but it also came to no avail. Charles
VIII captured Rome and reclaimed Cem, who died shortly after
in Naples.[6] In 1499, the corpse was finally sent to the Ottoman
Empire for burial in the persimmon tree–dotted royal cemetery
in Bursa.

All the while, the Ottomans had engaged in diplomacy with
the relevant European powers to keep the claimant to the throne
away from the empire. To accomplish this aim, Bayezid II pledged
not to attack Rome or Rhodes and offered payments for the pope
keeping Cem under house arrest. Both sides kept to their agreement, and war and Crusade were avoided. All these efforts served
to engage the Ottomans ever more directly with Christian Europe, confirming that the Ottomans were an essential element
in Renaissance diplomacy and making Ottoman figures part of
European Renaissance culture, including Cem, who was depicted
as a Renaissance prince. Cem appeared in paintings and in Bal-
dassare Castiglione's *The Book of the Courtier* (1528)—a popular
advice book for Renaissance court life, published in many languages—which demonstrated that the Ottomans were considered
part of a Europe-wide court culture. Until he died, Cem remained
a danger, as Muslim and Christian powers rallied around him
against the empire, threatening to lead their armies in battle
against the Ottomans.

SUNNI SULTANS OF THE MAMLUK EMPIRE

One of Cem's allies against his brother had been the rival dynasty based in Cairo. The Mamluks challenged the Ottomans for control over eastern Anatolia and northern Syria. The Mamluks' boast of being the custodians of the two holy shrines of Mecca and Medina, as well as of Jerusalem, and the protectors of the Abbasid caliphs mocked Ottoman claims of being the leading Islamic power. The caliphs were descendants of the members of the Abbasid dynasty who had survived the Mongol sacking of Baghdad in 1258. Residing in Mamluk Cairo, the Sunni caliph was the successor to Muhammad and the four rightly guided caliphs (Abu Bakr, Umar, Uthman, and Ali) and thus theoretically the supreme head of the Sunni Muslim community.

Capturing Egypt and its rich agrarian lands and profitable commercial artery of the Red Sea, connecting Europe to the spices and textiles of South Asia and China, would be a great windfall. Mehmed II had died while embarking on a campaign against the Mamluks to conquer Aleppo and Syria in 1481. Bayezid II picked up where he had left off, attempting alternately to destroy the Mamluks and to keep them at bay through the Dulkadır, Mamluk clients who were sometimes their ally and at other times their enemy. Bayezid II waged war against the Mamluks from 1485 to 1491, gaining little territory despite naval and land campaigns.[7] The two sides ultimately made peace, the Ottomans acknowledging Mamluk control over Syria and southeastern Anatolia.

DEVIANT DERVISH REBELS AND ASSASSINS

It was not only Mamluk control of the holiest sites in Sunni Islam that challenged Bayezid II's claims to being the most important Muslim leader. A number of charismatic religious leaders claimed they had a right to rule in place of the sultan in that era. Ibn Arabi's development and propagation of key mystical concepts had firmly taken hold. Especially significant during Bayezid II's reign was Ibn Arabi's notion that there is one living figure who is the pole of the universe. This idea produced a challenge to Bayezid II's authority. The pole was allegedly the one person in each epoch who is proximate to God—literally the centre of the universe and pivot as well. The entire heavens turned about the pole, and God was supposedly manifest in him. Believers in poles and their deputies need not bear allegiance to a political authority such as a sultan. Instead, in their view, the existence of the pole necessitated that everyone, ruler and ruled, had to consult him, since all actions in the world took place with the pole's knowledge and initiative. He was the support upon which everything in the world depended, to whom everyone must bear liege as the only legitimate spiritual and political authority.

According to this view, there were three other pillars and seven substitutes who ranked beneath the pole and through whom God preserves the universe. Ranking below the pole as deputies, deviant dervishes participated in the preservation of the world order by immersing themselves in the love of God and reaching out to help the oppressed and powerless to restore order and justice over and against their oppressors. Their oppressors included worldly rulers such as Bayezid II.

To counter the rising threat of deviant Sufis, Bayezid II promoted an image of himself as a pious sheikh. His Sufi leanings were of the quietist variety. He permitted Istanbul's first Mevlevi lodge to be built on the site of a Byzantine monastery and refurbished the Konya shrine to the namesake of the Mevlevi, Rûmi, whose followers included members of the elite. Bayezid II also assumed the title of a saint, or friend of God, which was the designation of deviant dervish Hajji Bektaş, a figure revered by the Janissaries and whose shrine the sultan made sure to visit. Turning to writing, Bayezid II had his own 'miracles' and 'wondrous deeds' recorded in an ecstatic life story recited to the public. But the deviant dervishes refused to accept Bayezid II's authority.

These included the followers of Otman Baba. Otman Baba took the ideas of three earlier deviant dervishes—Barak Baba, Kaygusuz Abdal, and Sultan Şüca—and propagated them among the Abdals of Rûm, the outlandish and extreme shaven and near-naked deviant dervishes who had been present since Osman's reign. Beardless Barak Baba (died 1308) of Tokat in Anatolia traced his spiritual descent from Hajji Bektaş and Baba İlyas-i Horasani and wandered from place to place naked save for a loin-cloth.[8] Allegedly able to communicate with animals, he attached buffalo horns to his turban. His hundreds of narcotic-taking disciples played tambourines and drums as he engaged in animal-like dance movements and wailed like a monkey. He was nicknamed 'Hairy Dog' because he swallowed a morsel spit out by his master, Sarı Saltuk, a 'dragon-slaying' dervish and gazi proselytiser of Islam in Europe.[9] Kaygusuz Abdal dressed in a fur cloak, shaved his moustache, beard, eyebrows, and hair, and enjoyed hashish.[10] His contemporary, holy man Sultan Şüca, also shaved his facial hair, went around naked, and spent winters in a cave.

Otman Baba was an ascetic wanderer who likened money to faeces. He drank used bath water, proclaiming that, since everything was a manifestation of God, everything was pure—an echo of Ibn Arabi's unity of being concept. Claiming to be the reincarnation of Adam, Moses, Jesus, Muhammad, Ali, and Hajji Bektaş, or even God, he had a close relationship with Mehmed II while at the same time denouncing mainstream Sufis and the religious class.[11] Mehmed II allegedly accepted Otman Baba as the 'true' (spiritual) sultan.[12] Otman Baba's followers believed that he was the pole of the universe in that age and that his disciples ranked just below him as his deputies.

In 1492, one of Otman Baba's Kalenderi (also called Torlak) disciples attempted to assassinate Bayezid II while he was on a military campaign in Albania. Bayezid II responded brutally. He ordered the torture and execution of Otman Baba's followers and deviant dervishes in the Edirne region and a hunt for them in

Southeastern Europe, deporting them en masse to Anatolia, where they looked for another radical leader. They soon found one.

SHI'I TURCOMAN SAFAVID DYNASTY IN IRAN

Bayezid II's most dangerous enemy was Shi'i shah Ismail I (reigned 1501–1524), who founded the Safavid dynasty in Tabriz (Iranian Azerbaijan) in 1501. The Safavids had undergone their own religious conversion and political transformation from Sunnis to Shi'i dervishes. Sheikh Junayd had transformed the thirteenth-century Sunni Sufi Safavi order at Ardabil (Iran), founded by Sheikh Safi al-Din, into a movement of radical mystic Shi'ism in eastern Anatolia and Azerbaijan. He organised the order's zealous followers into a military force made up of Kurds and Turcoman known as the Red Heads, named for their headgear. When Shah Ismail I was enthroned in Tabriz in 1501, he demanded their devotion in exactly the same way the head of a Sufi order demands devotion from his disciples. The Red Heads cried, 'God has come'. Ismail I depicted himself as both the perfect Sufi spiritual leader and the Persian God-king. Writing poetry in Turkish, he proclaimed himself 'God's mystery', the son of Muhammad's daughter Fatima and son-in-law and cousin Ali, and even God.[13] The Red Heads saw Ismail I as their saviour. They spread the Safavid call in Ottoman domains in Anatolia, where many former supporters of the recently defeated White Sheep confederation joined them.

Shah Ismail I proclaimed himself the emperor of the world and the perfect spiritual guide. His soldiers were his disciples, willing to be martyrs for their new king. How could Bayezid II challenge that? He could battle him with propaganda or warfare. He preferred the former. He was terrified lest Ismail I become a latter-day Timur. The Safavids drew their strength from many Kurds and Turcoman living in the Ottoman Empire. Both Bayezid II and Ismail I competed for the claim to sovereignty among the same Muslims in eastern Anatolia.

Until the end of his reign, Bayezid II faced Safavid-supported apocalyptic rebellions in Anatolia, whose firebrands believed the end-time had come. The largest was that of a disciple of Shah Ismail I named Shahkulu in 1511, who, like Sheikh Bedreddin, led a revolt that gained widespread support not only among radical Sufis—the deviant dervishes—but also among Kurdish and Turcoman cavalrymen and other disaffected men of high station. The revolt convulsed much of Anatolia in bloodshed. Instead of referring to Shahkulu as 'the slave of the shah', the literal meaning of his name, the Ottomans labelled him 'the slave of Satan'. Shahkulu claimed to be God, Muhammad, and the redeemer. The apocalyptic movement was crushed with a great amount of bloodletting near Kayseri in central Anatolia, not too far from Hajji Bektaş's dervish lodge and mausoleum. But half a dozen more such messianic revolts would convulse the land until the end of the sixteenth century.[14]

The initial clash between Ottomans and Safavids was not, however, a struggle between Sunnis and Shi'is, or between Sufis and 'orthodox' Muslims. Bayezid II supported some Sufi orders, such as the Halveti, which had spread first in Amasya province, where Bayezid had governed as a prince. Much of Sufism in that age in both Ottoman and Safavid domains was characterised by devotion to Ali, the cousin and son-in-law of Muhammad. Today this reverence would be considered a characteristic of Shi'ism alone. Just as the Red Heads were disciples of the Safavid order, the Janissaries were referred to as the corps of the Bektaşis. Both Red Heads and Bektaşis assigned primary dedication to a 'divine' Ali, as they elevated sainthood over prophethood. They venerated Ali, whom they considered to possess secret, divine knowledge. They also believed in the transmigration of souls and in Ibn Arabi and Sheikh Bedreddin's concepts of the unity of being, and desperately waited for the return of the Mehdi, the redeemer.[15]

The Safavid dynasty posed a clear and present danger to the Ottoman dynasty. After crushing the White Sheep federation of

Turcoman tribes centred in Tabriz in 1501, the Safavids controlled the provinces of Diyar Bakir and northern Iraq and the cities of Erzincan and Erzurum. The founder of the dynasty and first leader, Shah Ismail I had several strategic advantages. He was head of a Sufi order. As the grandson of White Sheep ruler Hasan the Tall, who had married Sheikh Junayd's sister, he was related to the White Sheep Turcoman dynasty, which had until recently ruled eastern Anatolia, Iraq, and western Iran (Azerbaijan). Because his grandfather had also married a Byzantine princess, he was also related to the Byzantine dynasty. Rather than being an Iranian, Shah Ismail I was yet another revolutionary Greco-Turk. The Safavids thus had both religious and political legitimacy on their side. They were Sufi masters demanding total obedience from their disciples. They were inheritors of the throne of an eastern Anatolia Turcoman dynasty through a matrilineal line (which would be disputed by other claimants), as well as that of the Byzantines, whose final days of rule had been in Trabzon. In contrast, the Ottomans had no legitimacy or authority to rule Anatolia, other than by might. And they were not the strongest Turcoman power, either.

Turkish speaking and at one with the Ali-devoted Turcoman religious culture of eastern Anatolia, the Safavids controlled the upper Euphrates, which was crisscrossed by the major trade routes linking Iran to Southwest Asia and the international entrepôt of Aleppo, terminus of the Silk Road. From this position, they controlled the export of silk produced in Iran, particularly the route passing from Tabriz to Van to Bitlis to Diyar Bakir to Aleppo. As long as Aleppo lay in Mamluk hands or those of its allies, the Safavids controlled the trade from eastern Anatolia and northern Iraq to the Mediterranean. As a rich source of revenue as well as the symbol of wealth and prosperity, the Ottoman silk industry, centred in Bursa, was crucial to the economy of both empires. The Safavids threatened to put this industry in a precarious position.

WRITING THE HISTORY OF THE DYNASTY

Facing all these grave religious, political, and economic threats, with internal opponents linked with external enemies, alternative candidates for the throne, and competing models for rule—such as the divine Sufi sheikh and gazi, the Safavid shah—Bayezid II responded with military and diplomatic weapons when he had to. But he also responded with pen and ink. The writing of history was consonant with imperial ambitions. Sovereigns were judged both by the success of their military campaigns and by the greatness of the works composed in their honour—their cultural capital. Patronising literature made a ruler appear worthy of his sultanate. Bayezid II's court encouraged or employed writers to glorify him and his dynasty, to increase his prestige and assert his claims. While these men may not have been official historians, they nevertheless backed the dynasty. Whether gazis, Sufis, or learned Persian men of state, they were lavishly rewarded for presenting pleasing chronicles to Bayezid II's court.[16]

The Ottomans had been constantly changing their understanding of who they were and what mattered to them. It was not until the fifteenth century, the second of their more than six centuries in power, that the Ottomans decided to commission writers to record the dynasty's exploits for posterity. And when they did so, all writers seemed to be in agreement. They accepted the class system, with the sultan at its apex. They assumed it natural that the Ottoman dynasty had a right to rule, that succession should pass from the sultan to one of his sons, and that their subjects should unquestionably bear them liege. None tried to connect the royal family to Muhammad's lineage or to Genghis Khan's. Such claims could be easily disproved. Instead, they all agreed that the Ottomans had descended from the Turkic Oğuz tribe of western Central Asia and were the successors of the Seljuks of Rûm.

The earliest accounts of the Ottomans, dedicated to but not commissioned by the dynasty, however, had referred to Osman's forefathers and the Oğuz as travelling companions on the road to gaza, holy war. These accounts said they were comrades in arms and did not claim that Osman's father, Ertuğrul, was a descendant of the Oğuz.[17] By the reign of Murad II, however, when Timur's heir Shahrukh demanded like his father that the Ottomans recognise his suzerainty, the Ottomans refused and created a genealogy making Ertuğrul a leader of the Oğuz. The motivation was to proclaim their descent was not any way inferior to that of Timur. They owed no one their liege, certainly not the Mongols. If Ertuğrul was sent to Anatolia by a Seljuk sultan, and later named as the successor of the last Seljuk sultan before that empire collapsed, then the Ottomans were their legitimate political heirs. It was at this time that the first *Chronicles of the Ottoman Dynasty*, which included the Seljuk succession story, appeared, and the stories that make up *The Book of Dede Korkut*, which narrates the exploits of the Oğuz, were first written down.[18]

According to *The Book of Dede Korkut*, the Oğuz were a people whose main value was manliness, a trait that both men and women could possess. Manliness was bravery, not turning in flight from the enemy. A boy would not be named until he cut off heads and spilled blood.[19] The ideal wife rose before the husband, mounted his horse, and brought him some heads before he reached the enemy.[20] Brave, manly warriors on horseback who believed the best horses were sired by a supernatural stallion, the Oğuz wore golden earrings and sported moustaches.[21] Their march was accompanied by the sound of war drums and kettle drums and horns and pipes. They carried horse-tail banners and standards, wooing maidens or mates through their displays of valour. For entertainment, they watched bulls wrestle camels, or men wrestle bulls. They went hunting and hawking. They were honest, heroic, falcon-like warrior chieftains, steppe nomads who lived in tented encampments. Their felt tents lay over a wooden frame in the shape of a beehive, with golden-framed smoke holes.[22] They herded tens of thousands of sheep, goats, and camels, and rode

Arabian horses. They hunted and fought with strong bows, lances, maces, spears, and swords.

To feast, they ate mutton stew and slaughtered horses, red camels, white and black sheep, and cattle. They also sacrificed them to give thanks. They drank fermented mare's milk, as well as strong wine. They ate garlic and meat roasted on the spit, milk, cheese, cream, yoghurt, and a salty yoghurt drink from their herds. Enormous dogs and slingshot-wielding young boys drove the animals across the steppe. They were ever-wary of grey wolves, although they venerated them. The Oğuz migrated between the valleys in winter and mountains in summer, seeking pastures with their tents and their livestock. They sought the shade of trees and cool streams in the summer, threatened by drought. At their gatherings, the nobles drank red wine from golden goblets served by slave girls.

The historical and genealogical effort, including choosing the Oğuz as ancestors and making themselves the legal successors of the Seljuks, was part of a propaganda war against competing Turcoman empires and principalities in Anatolia, Central Asia, Iran, and the Arabic-speaking region. The Dulkadır, Black Sheep (Karakoyunlu), Karamanids, and White Sheep were all battling for control of eastern Anatolia and proclaiming their own illustrious descent, real and fictitious, from Central Asian khans. Many of these rivals also claimed descent from the Oğuz. The Ottoman circulation of genealogies during the reign of Murad II showing that they were descended from 'the senior son of the senior son of Oğuz Khan' was an obvious effort to make them the most legitimate Turkic dynasty in the region.[23] It would answer a need to explain who the Ottomans were and how descent and political appointment brought them to power. And it would silence rival claims to the throne.

Hardly confident, the Ottomans still found a need to explain what had happened after Timur's invasion in 1402 and during the interregnum, including the insurrection of Sheikh Bedreddin. The volume of history writing increased during Bayezid II's reign.

Bayezid II sought to articulate a new imperial consciousness, in both simple Turkish and sophisticated Persian, to improve the image of his predecessor and father, Mehmed II, in the face of negative reactions to his harsh policies and to validate his own claims against his rivals for the Ottoman throne. Mehmed II's building of a more unified, centralised empire—turning away from the gazi holy warriors and towards the Ottoman-trained Christian recruits, the Janissaries—had strained the populace with its unending military campaigns and consequent unending demand for new fiscal sources.

Upon returning from the military campaign of 1484–1485 in Southeastern Europe and his conquests of the Moldovan Black Sea ports of Kilia and Akkerman, which Mehmed II had been unable to take, Bayezid II ordered the collecting and recording of oral histories about the dynasty and the writing of new general histories of the Ottomans in Turkish.[24] The effort continued until the first decade of the sixteenth century. The Kurdish former chancellor of the White Sheep was ordered by Bayezid II to compose an elegant history in Persian.[25] Bayezid II desperately needed to recapture the loyalty of disaffected members of the elite by recalling the great deeds of the dynasty and his place in it. Bayezid II's policies differed greatly from Mehmed II's—he returned foundations and landholdings seized by his father to their owners while promoting a more pious image—and he wished to put the best spin on them.[26]

Above all, these works demonstrate that what mattered was loyalty to the dynasty. The accounts express a lingering fear about the threat of deviant dervishes. They are haunted by the rebellions of Sheikh Bedreddin during the interregnum at the beginning of the fifteenth century, which they narrate in great detail. When the Safavids suddenly emerged on the Ottoman eastern frontier a century later, Ottoman writers began to refer to Sheikh Bedreddin and his disciples as Shi'is and Red Heads, an allusion to the contemporary followers of Shah Ismail I.[27] Sheikh Bedreddin had revolted in unstable regions recently retaken by the Ottomans. In the sixteenth century, the Ottomans feared the Safavids would do the same, and they faced revolts in border regions as well as in their heartland provinces.

BAYEZID II'S FATAL THREAT: HIS OWN SON, SELIM

Despite his efforts by sword and pen, Bayezid II was incapable of defending the dynasty from its internal and external enemies. Bayezid II may have considered himself a saint on par with Ibn Arabi and Sheikh Bedreddin, but even greater claims and deeds awaited his youngest son and successor, Selim. Selim I (reigned 1512–1520) is uniquely depicted in contemporary portraiture with a large golden hoop earring and handlebar moustache, but no beard. He looks like a Janissary. This may not be coincidental. Based in the princely governorship of remote Trabzon, Selim had faced the brunt of Safavid incursions. He had gained a great reputation among military men for his confrontations with the Safavids, slaving raids, and successful battles to the northeast in the Caucasus against Christian Georgia. A panegyric account of his 1508 Caucasus invasion boasts that the raid netted large numbers of enslaved women, girls, and boys. It takes pride in mass rape as collective violence:

> Into the possession of the gazis, the guides of the gaza, the army of mail-clad warriors, came gratuitously beautiful, graceful and rosebud-mouthed creatures, and elegantly-walking, cypress-statured, rose-scented idols. Many jasmine-complexioned girls were taken, girls who imparted gladness and whose beauty was a delight. [They were] fairy-faced and houri-featured [virgins of paradise], with curling locks and with ambergris-fragrant ringlets. The inside of the camp became full of [these] fairies, like a sky full of moons, suns and Jupiters.[28]

Selim rewarded his supporters with authorisation to violate girls, wage combat, and pillage. But what he wanted for himself was the sultanate.

In 1511 he deposited his teenage son Suleiman in his governorship in Kefe (Caffa, today Feodosia), the great slaving port in the Crimea, the peninsula jutting out into the Black Sea. Crimean Tatar raids into Eastern Europe and the northern Caucasus may have netted two million slaves between 1500 and 1700, a number comparable to the Atlantic slave trade in the same era.[29] From the Crimea, Selim travelled with his army by sea to Akkerman in Southeastern Europe.

From there they marched on Edirne, where Bayezid II and his court had settled due to a massive earthquake in Istanbul two years earlier. The natural disaster rained stones from the city's towers on terrified people who scrambled to escape and had even thrown down 'lofty minarets, which touched the heavenly sphere'.[30] Bayezid II consented to Selim's demands for a governorship nearer Istanbul—which was Selim's ruse to be nearer than his brothers to the imperial capital when the elderly sultan died—and also declared he would not abdicate for his favourite son, Ahmed. Unappeased, Selim readied his army for battle near Çorlu, midway between Edirne and Istanbul, against the imperial army led by his father, who, because of his advanced age, sat in a carriage rather than saddled a horse. Despite his brave reputation, when the battle commenced and the battlefield was choked with the smoke of cannon fire, Selim 'slackened the bow of war immediately. He did not draw a sharp sword against his father'. He fled the battlefield and returned to Kefe.[31]

Aware of these events, Prince Ahmed marched on Istanbul from southwestern Anatolia with his army so that Bayezid II would declare him sultan. But when he reached the imperial capital, the Janissaries rebelled, for they favoured Selim. They considered Ahmed 'effeminate', a man devoted to pleasure, drinking, and music, his only desire 'to kiss the mouths of rosebud-lipped beauties and to clasp the waists of those whose tall figures resemble cypresses'.[32] And in contrast with his elderly and ill sixty-year-old father, Selim had a reputation for being eager to take action against the Ottomans' enemies, especially the Safavids. With the Janissaries preventing him from entering Istanbul, Ahmed retreated and Selim returned with his army. While Ottoman chronicles insist that Bayezid II voluntarily abdicated, in reality, Selim I deposed his father.[33] He declared, 'I can no longer restrain myself, my father is senile and allowing the empire to fall into ruins'.[34] In April 1512, after forcing Bayezid II to abdicate, Selim I was enthroned in his place. He sent his father in the imperial carriage from Istanbul to retirement in pleasant Dimetoka (today Didymoteicho, Greece), south of Edirne. But Bayezid II never made it. Suspicions are that Selim I had him poisoned en route.

Over the course of the next year, Selim I faced rival claims to the throne from his brothers, princes Ahmed and Korkud. Leaving his eighteen-year-old son Suleiman in the palace in Istanbul, in case he fell in battle, Selim I crossed Anatolia with his army, hunting his brothers and their supporters. Midforties Korkud was found hiding in a cave outside Manisa near the Aegean coast and strangled. Ahmed was also strangled after being defeated in battle by Selim I at Yenişehir, east of Bursa. Their sons were executed, in accordance with Ottoman law.

Despite his mercilessness, Selim I's brief reign was to inspire messianic claims typical of the Reformation era. Such claims would lead to similar sectarian splits in Islam as those rocking Western Christianity.

7

MAGNIFICENCE

From Selim I to the First Ottoman Caliph,
Suleiman I

T HE SIXTEENTH CENTURY was marked by a clash of religious
claims. This was not a clash between Christianity and Islam.
Instead, what rocked the empires of Europe and Asia was an internal sectarian conflict over the right to make the same competing claim. Rulers West and East perceived themselves as the
single, universal political ruler and head of a universal religion.
At the same time, just as Christian Europeans fought among
themselves with pen and sword for the right to call themselves
'the church', Muslims, too, fought over who deserved to claim the
mantle of leader of the Muslim faith based on correct fulfilment
of the Prophet's legacy.

In the sixteenth century, the dominant view among Christians
and Muslims was that an apocalyptic battle between the forces
of good and evil would usher in an age of peace. And just as the
church in the West split into three during the Reformation, also
referred to as the age of confessionalisation, so, too, did the chasm
between Sunni and Shi'i Muslims—established already at the out-
set of Islamic history in the seventh century, when Muslims differed over who had a right to lead the Muslim community after

the death of Muhammad—deepen as the Ottomans affirmed their Sunnism and the Safavids their Shi'ism in unprecedented ways. Selim I would engage in an apocalyptic battle with Ismail I of Iran, the Safavid ruler, whom he defeated. Then he conquered Mamluk Egypt and took the holy cities of Mecca, Medina, and Jerusalem. Selim I's son and successor, Suleiman I, faced Charles V, Holy Roman emperor, in a battle to be the inheritor of Rome. Like Charles V, he would face internal strife from rival religious claimants to his power. As claimant to the Holy Roman Empire, Suleiman I would have a helmetlike crown made that combined European Christian imperial and papal regalia. He would also assist the Protestants in the Reformation. The tenth sultan born at the turn of the tenth Islamic era, Suleiman I was the 'Master of the Auspicious Conjunction', the expected universal ruler. He was the first sultan to call himself caliph.

The broad similarities and crucial differences between Christian European and Ottoman historical religious developments would play out on a sweeping scale through the spiritual, political, and military contests between Selim I and Ismail I of the Safavid Empire and between Suleiman I and Charles V of the Habsburg Holy Roman Empire.

SELIM I AND ISMAIL I: SUFIS AND SAINTS

Taking up where his father Bayezid II had left off, Selim I commanded the wittiest minds in his chancery to compose a suitably insulting letter to Safavid shah Ismail I. In the pugnacious letter, Selim I proclaimed that the 'obligation of extirpation, extermination, and expulsion of evil innovation must be the aim of our exalted aspiration'.[1] Selim I referred to himself as the wise Solomon and the eminent Alexander. He styled himself the 'slayer of the wicked and the infidel, guardian of the noble and the pious; the gazi, the defender of the faith' and 'standard-bearer of justice and righteousness'. He claimed Shah Ismail I was a wicked infidel who introduced evil innovations and had to be eradicated. Selim I addressed his opponent as a mere prince, 'the possessor of the land of tyranny and perversion, the captain of the vicious, the chief of the malicious', usurping and malevolent, 'the peer of Cain'. Selim I proclaimed himself 'the instrument of divine will'. He accused his Safavid rival of oppressing and massacring Sunni Muslims in Iran, of undermining Islam, of not prohibiting what is prohibited nor allowing what is permitted, but promoting adultery and fornication, shedding the blood of the innocent, eating and drinking that which is forbidden, and denigrating the Qur'an.

Consequently, Selim I considered an Ottoman assault on the Safavids legitimate. He was eager that 'the thunder of our avenging mace shall dash out the muddled brains of the enemies of the faith as rations for the lion-hearted gazis'. Such a terrible fate would not await the Safavids, Selim I promised, if they ceased oppressing their subjects, repented and returned to the path of Sunni Islam, and submitted to Ottoman rule. Failing that, with God's assistance, he would 'crown the head of every gallows tree with the head of a crown-wearing Sufi [Red Heads] and clear that faction from the face of the earth'.

Shah Ismail I responded nonchalantly and sarcastically with an 'affectionate' and 'friendly' letter, written with 'good will', mocking Selim I by repeating many of the Ottoman ruler's self-proclaimed titles, making fun of his sending such a letter, and taking much 'enjoyment and pleasure' from the 'boldness and vigour' of its contents.[2] He proclaimed that he was baffled why Selim I appeared so angry, when the Ottomans and Safavids had had good relations in the past when Selim was governor at Trabzon. He imagined that domestic political problems compelled his new rival to act this way, and that the attacks were the 'fabrications of the opium-clouded minds' of his bureaucrats. Despite the light tone, Shah Ismail I stated correctly that support for the Safavids was widespread in Anatolia, implying that he could provoke armed uprisings at any time. Due to Selim I's threats, the shah began preparing his armies for war.

Drawing upon the same theme of Turcoman warrior mysticism that had risen in support of Sheikh Bedreddin's multiple rebellions in 1416 that nearly overthrew the dynasty, Shah Ismail I declared himself the Persian deified God-king, the perfect Sufi spiritual guide, the awaited redeemer, the occulted twelfth Shi'i imam, and even God. Writing poetry in Turkish, addressing himself to the Janissaries and other Ottoman military forces, Shah Ismail I declared that 'Gazis say Allah, Gazis I am the faith of the Shah. Come before me bow down to me, Gazis I am the faith of the Shah'.[3] Writing under the pen name 'the Sinner', Shah Ismail I called himself 'the mystery of God' and a prophet, the successor to Muhammad. He styled himself as the living Elijah and Jesus, as well as the Alexander of his age and the commander of the gazis. In his eyes, he was the one who had turned away from the Sunnis, whom he labelled 'polytheists', 'hypocrites', and 'the damned'. He declared himself the son of Fatima and Ali, the master of the twelve Shi'i imams, and the sixth imam, Jafer as-Sadiq, the one who avenged the murder of Ali's son Hussein. Finally, Ismail I asserted that he was the spiritual-political-military leader of the Safavid Sufi order and the Safavid dynasty. How could the new sultan Selim I respond to such heady claims?

The clashes between Selim I and Ismail I would set the stage for over a hundred years of conflict that would cause divisions between Sunnis and Shi'is to sharpen and propel the Ottomans towards conquering the Muslim holy cities of Mecca, Medina, and Jerusalem.

For all of these reasons, Shah Ismail I posed a direct threat to the Ottomans, challenging the loyalty of their troops. He led an upstart, formidable rival empire on their border. His soldiers were recruited from among Ottoman Turcoman devotees, and they venerated the shah as God's incarnation, as the reincarnation of prophets and ancient Iranian kings, and as a perfect Sufi saint. Shah Ismail I's fanatic followers in eastern Anatolia, the Red Heads, drew a large following. On either side, the Ottoman deviant dervishes known as Bektaşis, the Janissaries, and the Safavid Red Heads believed in the manifestation of God in humans, Ali's divinity and supremacy as the ultimate warrior, and his reincarnation in later men. Yet the crucial difference was that the Bektaşis believed Ali to have been reincarnated in Hajji Bektaş, the saint of the Janissaries. The Red Heads believed Ali was reincarnated in Shah Ismail I.[4]

By propagating Shi'i Islam, Shah Ismail I was challenging the Sunni Ottoman sultan's claim to lead Muslims. Lacking a genealogy leading back to Muhammad, the Ottomans had no claim to religious authority or hereditary Islamic legitimacy. They could not boast as the Safavids did, tracing their descent allegedly back to Muhammad through Ali, the Prophet's cousin and son-in-law. Believing as Shi'is that Muhammad had proclaimed Ali his successor, the Safavids presented themselves as Ali's descendants with the legitimate right to rule Muslim-majority lands. This meant that all other claimants to power, including the Ottomans, were usurpers. It was a popular idea in Anatolia, where many awaited the appearance of the twelfth imam, the occulted successor to Ali, to serve as leader.[5] Shah Ismail I declared that he was the awaited one.

The Ottomans' only claim to legitimacy was their might, and even that was being undermined by Shah Ismail I's declarations that he was the most virile, manly warrior. Safavid supporters fomented uprisings across Ottoman Anatolia, assisted by Red Head guerrillas. These rebellions gained many supporters, turning Anatolia, from Antalya to Sivas, into a landscape of rivers of blood and floods of fire. The upheaval had ended the reign of Bayezid II, deposed by his youngest son Selim, then governor in Trabzon and supported by the Janissaries, who accused his father of being too reluctant to shed blood.[6]

Selim I was sanctioned in his policy of war, not surprisingly, by the Ottoman chief military judge (*kadıasker*) of Rûmeli—the highest-ranking Islamic legal authority at that time—whom he had appointed. The short, blond military judge, Sarıgörez Efendi, declared that the Safavid leader Ismail I and his soldiers, the Red Heads, had ceased to be Muslims.[7] He gave the legal opinion that those who killed the Red Heads were the greatest gazis and those killed by them the greatest martyrs. In another fatwa, he opined that the Red Heads were neither Shi'is nor Muslims, but infidels, a worthy target of 'holy warfare'. They allegedly violated religious law by engaging in pederasty, allowing what was forbidden, and changing the direction of prayer from Mecca to Ardabil in Iran, the location of the shrine of their founding sheikh. The fatwas accused the Safavids of denigrating the Qur'an and the hadith of the Prophet, cursing the first three Sunni caliphs—Abu Bakr, Umar, and Uthman—destroying mosques, and desecrating the graves of Sunnis. In general, they accused the Safavids of oppression, tyranny, and spreading their 'false religion'. Most egregious: the Safavids dared to overthrow the Ottoman dynasty. In short, they were accused of attempting to destroy Islam. Because of all of this, the military judge opined that it was a duty incumbent on the Muslim believer to wage war against them and kill them.[8]

War between the two rival rulers came in summer 1514. First, Selim I attempted to cut off the Safavid economy from Europe by expelling Persian merchants from the Ottoman silk centre of Bursa in northwest Anatolia and prohibiting Persian silk imports and exports passing through the empire. In March 1514, Selim I's forces numbering more than one hundred thousand troops set out from Edirne on a nearly 1,800-kilometre march across Anatolia. To gain further spiritual sanction for the war, Selim I visited the tomb of the deviant dervish Seyyid Gazi in the town of the same name in northwestern Anatolia and gave alms to the Sufis collected there.[9] In the north-central Anatolian towns of Amasya, Tokat, Samsun, Sivas, and Yozgat, they beheaded tens of thousands of Red Heads, each of whom had been registered by name by officials sent out before the army arrived.[10] Selim I's exhausted troops were nearing mutiny after the five-month journey, when finally on 23 August in the blazing heat of summer they met Shah Ismail's warriors northeast of Lake Van on the plain of Çaldıran.

Selim I's ten thousand musket-armed Janissaries—whose weapons roared like thunderbolts and spit fire like lightning— several hundred cannons, and ninety thousand troops claimed victory on the battlefield against Shah Ismail I's seventy-five thousand Turcoman cavalry archers.[11] It seems that the Safavids did not possess a single firearm. The Ottomans stopped the Shi'i juggernaut and proceeded to occupy the Safavid capital of Tabriz in northwestern Iran, centre of the Persian silk trade. Just as Osman had abducted the bride of the Christian prince of Bilecik and married her to his son Orhan, Selim I captured Shah Ismail I's favourite wife, Taçlu Khatun, and gave her in marriage to his military judge of Anatolia.[12] After his troops had plundered the city, raping women, boys, and girls, Selim I and his army began the long journey home, taking Tabriz's leading artists, craftsmen, merchants, and poets with them.

The battle was a major turning point for both dynasties, ending the possibility of a Safavid conquest of Anatolia and disappointing Shah Ismail I's followers. They could not believe that a divine being could be defeated. Yet he survived, fleeing further east into Iran. The Ottomans may have had the military technology for victory on the battlefield, but they could not hold on to Tabriz, over 1,800 kilometres from Istanbul. They were unable to maintain such a long supply line in winter. They could not expand further to the east.

After the battle of Çaldıran and the defeat of Shah Ismail I, Sunni Kurdish princes and tribal leaders threw in their lot one by one with the Ottomans. A crucial role was played by the Kurdish historian and advisor to the sultan Idris-i Bidlisi, who helped convince them to rebel against the remaining Safavid overlords. The people of Diyar Bakir, a city encircled by five to six kilometres of Byzantine black-basalt walls, rose up and killed or expelled

the local Safavid forces and declared their obedience to Sultan Selim I. Safavid commanders, however, besieged the city again for a
year before the Ottomans were able to defeat them and claim it as
part of the empire in September 1515.[13] Much of Kurdistan then
came under Ottoman control.

Also in 1515, the Ottomans defeated and annexed Dulkadır
principality, a Mamluk client and buffer state lying in southeastern Anatolia and northern Syria between the two empires. Selim
I sent the severed head of its last ruler, Ala al-Dawla, and those of
his sons and vizier to the septuagenarian Mamluk sultan Qansuh Al-Ghawri (reigned 1501–1516), in Cairo.[14] The conquest and
gruesome parcel was cause for war between Selim I and the Mamluk Empire.

The east pacified militarily, Selim I's religious scholars justified war against fellow Sunni Muslims on the specious grounds
that their aiding the 'infidel' Shah Ismail I had turned them into
infidels themselves. So, the sultan turned against the Mamluks in
the south. Again, the Ottomans used gunpowder weapons (cannons and muskets) to defeat a Muslim rival armed with swords,
bows, and arrows—the weapons of aristocrats and men of leisure
who looked down on the musket, which any untrained soldier
could use.

In the sweltering heat of summer, in August 1516, Selim I and
his army advanced on Aleppo in northern Syria, the great entrepôt at the end of the Silk Road defended by a mighty citadel. At
Marj Dabik, forty kilometres north of the Mamluk city, the two
armies met. The Ottoman force was composed of at least sixty
thousand men, mainly cavalry positioned on either flank, and
the elite Janissary infantry armed with firearms and the sultan
at the strongly fortified centre, fitted with hundreds of gun carts
bearing cannons.[15] They met a Mamluk army composed of twenty
thousand cavalry and Bedouin Arabs. Despite being surrounded
by forty descendants of the Prophet Muhammad 'bearing cop-
ies of the Qur'an on their heads', according to a contemporary

Arab historian, and assorted Sufi sheikhs and the caliph, Mamluk sultan Qansuh Al-Ghawri was killed, the seventy-five-year-old's head presented to Selim I, and his army defeated.[16] Arquebuses had defeated arrows again. The Mamluks' refusal to use artillery on the battlefield spelled their doom. The Janissary corps defeated an army that, in order to hold on to its elite status, paid the price of not adapting to change. Soon after, the Ottomans began a global arms-trade business, supplying their allies in Africa, Central Asia, South Asia, and Southeast Asia with firearms, as their enemies, the Safavids, sought arms from Western Europe.[17]

The Aleppines threw in their lot with the victorious Ottomans without further battle. So, too, did the inhabitants of the rest of the cities of Syria, including Damascus and Jerusalem, where Selim I visited the Mevlevi Sufi lodge, as the Ottoman army swept south without facing armed resistance. Local Muslims complained, however, of the Ottomans' strange Sufi religious practices.

After an easy victory over regrouped Mamluk forces at Gaza in December 1516, the Ottoman military faced Egypt unimpeded. In January 1517, Selim I and his forces—including fifteen thousand camels transporting thirty thousand water pouches for his thirsty troops—cut across the sand dunes of the Sinai Desert.[18] According to the chronicles, they defeated the Mamluk army in twenty minutes at Raydaniyya outside Cairo.[19] Although the Mamluk position was defended by artillery pieces that were cast in Cairo and transported to the fort over the previous decade, the weapons were so large they were practically immobile.[20] The Ottomans had simply bypassed their fortified position and overwhelmed the defenders with superior firepower. But Selim I and his army faced much resistance from Mamluks along with other troops who did not hesitate to use handguns to defend Cairo, a city as large as if not larger than Istanbul.[21] After repeated street fighting and skirmishes in and around the city, ending in the beheading of thousands of Mamluks, only in April was Selim I able to capture and kill the last Mamluk-leader-turned-guerrilla-fighter, Tuman

Bey. His death made into a spectacle, Tuman Bey was hanged at the ornate, eleventh-century, twin-minaret Zuwayla Gate, the site of executions and the departure point of the pilgrim caravan to Mecca. The sharif of Mecca, the city's religious leader, sent Selim I the keys of Mecca and Medina.[22] The Ottomans would effectively rule what we now term the Middle East until 1917.

In conquering the Mamluk Empire, the Ottomans gained control over the eastern Mediterranean as far west as Barqah (in today's Libya) and Egypt—a rich, populous, strategic, agriculture-producing province, with outlets to the Red Sea, including Sawakin in Sudan, and to the Indian Ocean. Having added Syria and Egypt to his domains, Selim I gave the dynasty sizable new populations of Greek Orthodox and Jewish subjects, but more important, prepared the ground for the empire to have a Muslim demographic majority for the first time, along with custodianship of the two holy shrines of Mecca and Medina and control over the hajj routes and the caliph, whom Selim I had captured at the battle of Marj Dabik and brought to Cairo.

A contemporary Egyptian chronicler compared the Ottoman conquest of Cairo and the subsequent three days of looting and massacres of Mamluks to the pagan Mongol conquest of Baghdad in 1258, which had ended the Abbasid Caliphate.[23] He depicted an alcohol-drinking Selim I as cruel, bloodthirsty, and a pederast, and his soldiers who occupied Cairo as hashish addicts who drank alcohol, assaulted women and boys in the streets, did not fast during Ramadan, did not even pray, and desecrated Muslim shrines and sanctuaries.[24] Capturing the caliph, however, gave Selim I and the Ottoman dynasty elevated Islamic authority.

Selim I did not proclaim himself the caliph. He dispatched the caliph, Al-Mutawakkil, descendant of the members of the Abbasid dynasty who had survived the Mongol sacking of Baghdad and taken refuge with the Mamluks, from Cairo to Istanbul.[25] Along with the caliph and Christian, Jewish, and Muslim artisans, merchants, and government officials, he also shipped the holy relics of

Muhammad there, which the Ottomans encased in gold and precious jewels. These included his mantle, battle standard, sword,
bow, beard hair, a tooth, and a footprint, as well as the mantle and
prayer mat of his daughter and wife of Ali, Fatima. The holy loot
included the swords of Muhammad's companions, the cooking
pot of Abraham, Joseph's robe, Moses's staff, and King David's
sword for good measure. The Ottomans also kept relics from John
the Baptist taken in their conquests. They included pieces of bone
from John's right hand—which he used to baptise Jesus—placed
inside a realistic golden right arm, as well as a large piece of his
skull. All of these items are displayed today in the Pavilion of the
Holy Mantle and Holy Relics at Topkapı Palace Museum, where a
reader chants the Qur'an.

The Ottomans were not alone in collecting sacred relics and
believing in their power. A similar Habsburg collection includes
gilded reliquaries containing pieces of the loincloth of Jesus, pieces
of wood from Jesus's manger, and pieces of the cross on which he
was crucified. The Habsburgs collected bits of the tablecloth from
the Last Supper, as well as fragments of the robe of John the Baptist and one of the saint's teeth.[26]

As with Selim I and Ismail I's claims and counterclaims, in
the sixteenth century urgent millenarian expectation—the idea
that there would be an apocalyptic battle between the forces of
good and evil in which good would triumph, ushering in an age of
peace—was the shared ideology in European and Asian empires,
both Christian and Muslim. It was the rationale for imperial expansion from the Tagus on the Iberian Peninsula to the Ganges
in the Indian subcontinent, from Habsburg Central Europe to Ottoman and Safavid Southwest Asia to Mughal South Asia.[27] Such
prognostications were not the preserve of the famous Nostrada-
mus, French author of a popular mid-sixteenth-century book of
prophecies, alone.

Apocalypticism was the common coin of imperialism in Europe and Asia. Dom Manuel of Portugal (reigned 1495–1521), Holy

Roman Emperor Charles V, Suleiman I, Safavid shah Tahmasp I (reigned 1524–1576), Mughal emperor Jalal al-Din Muhammad Akbar I (reigned 1556–1605), and the men serving them saw signs and wonders that they believed were omens of their destiny in leading a universal empire. The world was swept by millenarian expectations. Muslims expected the *mujaddid*—the renewer of religion of his age, reformer of the world—or the *mahdi*—the awaited one whose appearance would announce the end-time and the Day of Judgement—to appear in the Muslim year AH 1000, which corresponds to CE 1591–1592.

It is conventional wisdom that Selim I and Ottoman religious authorities presented him as the defender of Sunni Islam in his encounter with the Shi'i Safavid Ismail I. Often overlooked is the fact that after conquering Syria and Egypt, Selim I was described in his own law code as a messianic leader, 'succoured by God', 'world conqueror', 'the master of the conjunction', and 'the Shadow of God'.[28] He was called the renewer of religion of his age, the tenth century of the Muslim calendar.[29] Muslims from outside the empire called him the 'messiah of the last age' and a 'divine force'.[30] Mirroring the language of Shah Ismail I, Selim I also referred to his servants and soldiers as his disciples and spiritual followers, as if he were head of a Sufi order, as the Safavid leader was. The Ottoman-Safavid conflict was at least partly motivated by competing claims about who the messianic ruler was. Ottoman messianism may not have been as extreme as that of the Safavids, but it was every bit as real.

In keeping with this religious vision, when visiting Damascus on his return from Egypt, Selim I found and restored the dilapidated tomb of the Spanish Sufi Ibn Arabi. It is an event similar to Mehmed II (or rather, his Sufi spiritual advisor) finding the tomb of Muhammad's companion Ayyub al-Ansari prior to the conquest of Constantinople. Selim I converted Ibn Arabi's tomb into a site for pilgrimage, as if fulfilling the alleged predictions of the saint that Selim I would discover and rehabilitate his tomb.

Selim I did not take the hajj to Mecca and Medina. No Ottoman sultan ever did. He found what he needed in Damascus, the place where Muslims believe Jesus will descend at the end-time.[31] It is where, Ibn Arabi claimed, in 1229 Muhammad gave him the complete text of *The Bezels of Wisdom*, a work recorded for his limited group of initiates that explicates the themes of saint-hood, the unity of being, and the perfect human, the critical link between humans and God.[32] The perfect human was a saint or 'friend of God', a spiritual pole of the epoch who leads humanity to salvation. As the awaited world restorer, the perfect human was the eschatological redeemer who would appear at the end of time to revive religion and prepare the ground for the arrival of the Qur'anic Jesus in Damascus, the harbinger of the final hour. Ibn Arabi claimed himself as one such perfect human. Selim I's supporters believed he was one too.

Ibn Arabi's ideas were controversial and spawned a backlash in the Arabic-speaking region where the Ottomans had just asserted their rule. Ibn Arabi had been accused of espousing political ambitions in his time. But for messianic political ambitions, Selim I would be surpassed by his only son and uncontested successor, Suleiman I.

SULEIMAN I AND CHARLES V: UNIVERSAL RULE AT AN AUSPICIOUS CONJUNCTION

Suleiman I (reigned 1520–1566) became ruler at the age of twenty-five upon the sudden death from unknown causes of his nearly fifty-year-old charismatic father as he travelled from Edirne to Istanbul in 1520. An Ottoman chronicler writing at the end of the sixteenth century related the incredible tale of what happened next, as told to him by his father, who was a confidant of Selim I. In order to promote a pious image of Selim I, the writer narrates how, apparently, when Selim I's three physicians were washing his corpse for burial, twice the dead man covered his penis with his right hand. So amazed were the doctors by his posthumous act of modesty that they immediately declared 'God is great!' and rendered their prayers.[33] Selim I's corpse was then temporarily buried beneath his tent, as his nervous viziers waited for Suleiman to arrive in Istanbul to be enthroned, whereafter they could unbury the cadaver, transport it to the imperial capital, and publicly entomb it.[34]

Once enthroned, Suleiman I built upon the foundations laid by his predecessors. Along with his father, these included Murad I, who established the Janissaries based on the child levy of Collection recruits, and Mehmed II, who was credited with issuing the law code that established the centralised administration that organised the religious class. Mehmed II had added the title 'Roman caesar' to those of 'sultan', 'emperor', and 'khan', thereby integrating Christian, Islamic, Persian, and Turco-Mongol ruling traditions. Referred to as the 'Master of the Auspicious Conjunction', Suleiman I would top even his grandfather. This lofty title derives from the fact that he was the tenth sultan, born at the turn of the tenth Islamic era, and thus the expected universal ruler, proved by a reading of the heavens.[35]

Despite his fortuitous beginnings as a youth referred to as 'Master of the Auspicious Conjunction', when Suleiman I and his childhood pal and favourite palace page Ibrahim arrived in Istanbul to take the throne, the viziers and pashas who remained from Selim I's administration refused to follow the orders of the unproven leader who had not participated in any of his father's military campaigns. Nor would they listen to Ibrahim, a man appointed to high-level administrative and military positions without any previous government experience. Those early years were marked by the sultan's inexperience, struggles at court, and tensions in the administration.

To prove himself, Suleiman I turned to the battlefield. He led his armies and navies to Central European and Mediterranean theatres of war that were strategically important, aiming to succeed where his predecessors had failed. The first targets were Belgrade and Rhodes.

At first, Suleiman I intended to march on Buda and defeat the powerful Hungarian king in battle. Leading the army in person, he changed plans and besieged the important citadel of Belgrade, also controlled by the Hungarians, which lay on the route to the Hungarian capital.[36] In August 1521, after a monthlong siege of the massive, ancient fortress on the Danube, whose defence force numbered only in the hundreds, the Ottomans used land and sea forces to take the strategic city that neither Murad II nor Mehmed II had been able to conquer. The victory rendered Hungary ripe for the taking the next time the Ottomans attacked.

In the next campaign season the following spring, Suleiman I's army and navy began an attack on the seemingly impenetrable fortress of Rhodes, which Mehmed II had been unable to seize despite a two-month siege. Even Selim I had abandoned an attempt to storm it.[37] But driven by public opinion that demanded he do something about the reported ill-treatment of several thousand Muslim pilgrims captured at sea and used as slave labourers expanding the fortifications on the island, Suleiman I decided to campaign in person to expel the Knights Hospitaller.[38]

That summer of 1522, with a fleet of as many as 250 ships at his disposal to attack and blockade the island, Suleiman I crossed the turquoise waters separating Marmaris on the coast of Anatolia from Rhodes.[39] He watched the progress of the long and difficult siege from the island's highest point, the site of the ancient acropolis. Employing Christian conscripts as sappers, the Ottomans mined under the citadel walls as part of their efforts. Despite seeing the walls crumbling from below, being ripped apart from above—bombed from siege towers and platforms—or blasted by cannons, the defenders resisted repeated attacks that autumn.[40] Even though they were vastly outnumbered—the order's Grand Master Philippe Villiers de l'Isle Adam had only six hundred knights and sixteen thousand men at his disposal against a force estimated to be one hundred thousand soldiers—the Knights Hospitaller caused the Ottomans heavy losses over the course of five months.[41] Nevertheless, the Ottomans seemed to have an inexhaustible supply of gunpowder. Offered favourable terms of surrender, the knights finally capitulated on Christmas Eve 1522.

Acting like a chivalrous Renaissance prince, Suleiman I allowed the grand master and his surviving Knights Hospitaller and thousands of civilians to leave the island unharmed. But he prohibited Christians from living within the city walls and sent Spanish Jews to settle in their place. He converted the churches to mosques on Christmas Day and put to death the son and grandson of Mehmed II's fugitive son Cem, cousins who had converted to Christianity on the island.[42]

Following these battles, his renown assured and his coffers filled, Suleiman I faced the problem of how to express the reasons for his astounding wealth, political power, and military success. To say he owed his favoured position to the success of his father and grandfather would not do. As with the Roman emperor Augustus, the answer was—following Mediterranean, Christian, Jewish, Roman, Persian, and Islamic precedent—to treat him like a god and use divine terms for him. Accordingly, in the preamble to the new law code for Egypt bearing the sultan's seal and signature promulgated in 1525, Suleiman I is referred to as 'holy', the 'expected one', 'the emperor of the time', the 'ruler of the spiritual world, sultan of the celestial throne, possessor of the moral qualities of the prophets, saint above all saints, whose face resembles the shining sun'.[43]

Having conquered the last independent Catholic island in the eastern Mediterranean with great difficulty, Suleiman I then surprised himself with the relatively easy overthrow of the once mighty kingdom of Hungary. He accomplished this in only two hours at the rain-soaked, swampy Battle of Mohács in August 1526, where King Louis II of Hungary drowned in the Danube while fleeing.[44] As with the previous two military efforts, the Ottomans had the advantage of superior numbers: Ottoman soldiers out-numbered their opponents at the battle in southern Hungary by two or three to one. But the key factor in all of these successes was a technological one. To prepare for the Mohács campaign, the sultan's armouries were ordered to make tens of thousands of car-bines, hundreds of small guns, and large mortars.[45] Crossing two raging, swollen rivers on pontoon bridges, the Ottoman army had the expertise to transport large numbers of troops and heavy artil-lery to the battlefield.[46] Just as the use of artillery on the field had given the Ottomans victory over the Safavid and Mamluk cavalry, so, too, at Mohács did thousands of musket-bearing Janissaries and hundreds of canons give the Ottomans the upper hand over the heavily armoured Hungarian horsemen. After the victory, Suleiman I and his forces marched to the Hungarian capital of Buda, which they looted and burned to the ground, save the royal palace.[47] An independent Kingdom of Hungary no longer existed. Next, they hoped, was the turn of the Holy Roman Empire.

Three years later in 1529, Suleiman I launched a brief siege of the Habsburg capital of Vienna. After first retaking Buda, which had been occupied by the army of Charles V's brother, Archduke Ferdinand of Austria, Ottoman forces pressed on, despite the campaign season having ended. They were doomed from the on-set by adverse weather. Heavy rains caused floods and swollen riv-ers, which forced the drained Ottoman troops to leave their heavy weapons behind. The sultan's own chroniclers recorded 'snow from evening until noon next day', 'much loss of horses and men in swamps', 'many die of hunger'—so ran the account of the bleak march.[48] Slowed by rain and flooded rivers, lacking in provisions, and running out of time, Suleiman I did not arrive before Vienna until the end of September, where he faced a well-garrisoned city. The appearance of Suleiman I at the walls of Vienna nevertheless struck terror in the hearts of Christian Europe.

The Ottomans besieged Vienna with 120,000 soldiers, the majority of whom were land-grant holders, tied to their land

and available for only a limited campaign season from spring to autumn. The siege was defeated as much by the rainy autumn weather, floods, overextended supply lines, and transportation difficulties as by defence works and the tactics of the besieged. In the middle of October, the sultan called off the siege.

While gunpowder weapons could usually blow away medieval walls, it took the besieger a long time to transport the right weapons.[49] Three to four months travel time from Istanbul, some 1,500 kilometres, was the limit of Ottoman strategic capabilities—they could raid but had not been able to hold Tabriz. And when the Ottomans advanced, the Habsburgs did not offer pitched battle, but retreated to their earthworks and small forts, retarding the Ottoman advance. Vienna's glorious Ringstrasse, with its wedding-cake nineteenth-century buildings, marks the former wall protecting Vienna. The Ottoman defeat is remembered and celebrated in Austria to this day.

Engaged in a struggle for universal dominion, Suleiman I promoted an identity for himself as the earth's single monarch and last world emperor before the final judgement. Battling Safavid shah Tahmasp in the east and Holy Roman Emperor Charles V in the west over the Roman inheritance, Suleiman I aimed to unite East and West under one monarch and one religion by conquering Vienna, Rome, Baghdad, and Tabriz throughout the late 1520s and early 1530s. Suleiman I was unique from his imperial contemporaries in this way. While he wanted to be Holy Roman emperor, Charles V did not challenge Suleiman I to be leader of the Muslims of the world. Nor did Tahmasp wish to rule the West.

During the first two-thirds of his reign, from the 1520s to the 1540s, Suleiman I engaged in a religious dual with the Safavids in the east and with the Habsburgs in the west, propagating millenarian aspirations about himself. He claimed to be a leader who possessed sanctity and ruled with divine mandate, amalgamating temporal and spiritual authority to impose justice and prosperity in the last stage of history. According to an eschatological prophecy written in poetic form for use as a public address, Suleiman I was a man whose divinity surpassed even that of the Sufi sheikh Ibn Arabi.[50] He was allegedly the seat of saintly authority, the messianic ruler, invincible hero, renewer of religion, redeemer, saintly pole of the universe, and universal ruler who would impose a single world religion.[51]

Such messianic terms were also used to describe Suleiman I by his grand viziers, Ibrahim Pasha (in office 1523–1536) and Lutfi Pasha (in office 1539–1541). The same types of claims were made in the works of Sufi leaders with whom Suleiman I associated, who belonged to an order that saw God in man and believed there were poles of the universe. Sheikh Pir Ali Alaeddin Aksarayı (died 1528) met with Suleiman I and declared him the redeemer. Seyyid Lokman, an Iranian Turcoman and official court historian, wrote that Suleiman I was one of 'the perfect humans'.[52]

In the palace, mystics engaged in apocalyptic prognostication. Suleiman I's court was keen on astrology, magic, the interpretation of dreams, and prophecies both ancient and new.[53] The most popular prophecy was written by a Sufi indebted to the work of Ibn Arabi who had instructed Sheikh Bedreddin and who had a close relationship to Murad II.[54] It circulated at court, including in pocket-size versions, in the early sixteenth century. Predicting that the world would soon end and that the last universal ruler would arise in the tenth Islamic century from within the Ottoman dynasty, the prophecy's object was understood to be none other than Suleiman I. For three decades, the sultan employed a geomancer who had fled the Safavid court after the death of Shah Ismail I.[55] Calling Suleiman I the last world conqueror, the master of the age, and pole of poles, he claimed that God was speaking through him. He proclaimed that an invisible army of angels, prophets, and saints accompanied Suleiman I into battle.[56] A writer of a history of Suleiman I's reign around 1530 claimed that the army of saints had actually been seen at the Battle of Mohács.[57]

In precisely the same imperial and religious vein as Suleiman I, Charles V, who had recently been crowned Holy Roman emperor in Bologna by Pope Clement VII and had been met with shouts of 'Caesar', inherited Spain, Italy, Austria, the Netherlands, Sicily, and Germany and defeated France. He claimed to be the successor to Julius Caesar and Augustus—the emperor and world ruler, the reviver of ancient Rome, which he sacked. Would Charles V reunite Christendom and be the new Charlemagne?

Motivated by the same conviction that *he* was the rightful inheritor of Roman rule and biblical revelation, Suleiman I, to face this rival, donned an astonishing four-crowned golden helmet, a composite of European Christian imperial and papal regalia symbolising the four biblical kingdoms prophesied by Daniel. Topped by a plumed aigrette, the crowned helmet was created by Venetian artisans in 1532, another example of the global Renaissance.[58] An astonishing work of craftmanship, the helmet, obtained by Grand Vizier Ibrahim Pasha for his sultan, was decorated with fifty diamonds, forty-nine pearls, forty-seven rubies, twenty-seven emeralds, and a large turquoise.[59] Although such an item was foreign to Islamic kingship customs, the helmet formed part of a set of ceremonial objects, including a sceptre and a golden throne, for use by the Muslim sovereign.[60]

Just as Charles V had done only three years earlier with a similar crown in Vienna, Suleiman I wore or displayed the crowned helmet on his march through Belgrade en route to Vienna, passing under classical, Roman-style triumphal arches. Mimicking the ceremonial political language of Charles V following his coronation, Suleiman I also rode with his imperial helmet on a horse richly adorned in jewels under a brocade canopy with flags embroidered in jewels. Meeting Habsburg ambassadors in his tent, he sat on the golden throne and displayed the helmet, which the ambassadors assumed to be his imperial crown.[61] News of the sensational crown spread in Western Europe, not only through ambassadorial reports but also in pamphlets, folksongs, and prints. It seemed there were two caesars.

As he was attempting to conquer Vienna with his crowned helmet, which incorporated a papal tiara as well, Suleiman I planned to attack Italy and Austria by land and sea so as to conquer Rome and claim the title of Holy Roman emperor. The crowned helmet—which had the appearance of the plumed helmets Muslims imagined ancient monarchs wore—was also referred to as the crown of Alexander the Great.[62] The bejewelled mirror that came with it was believed to be the ancient ruler's mirror that reflected the whole world, proof of his universal sovereignty. Some in Western Europe seemed convinced. The Frenchman Jean Bodin, one of the major political theorists of the sixteenth century, ridiculed Habsburg universal pretensions in favour of the Ottomans'. In his view, the Ottomans had the greater claim to Roman inheritance because they ruled more Roman territories: 'If there is anywhere in the world any majesty of empire and of true monarchy, it must radiate from the Sultan'. This was because 'he owns the richest parts of Asia, Africa, and Europe, and he rules far and wide over the entire Mediterranean and all but a few of its islands. Moreover, in armed forces and strength he is such that he alone is the equal of almost all the princes'.[63]

CONTRIBUTING TO THE REFORMATION IN CENTRAL EUROPE

As part of his war against the Catholic Habsburgs, Suleiman I sided with their internal enemies, and the rebels' response was enthusiastic. Protestants argued that it would be better to be ruled by Muslims than by Catholics. They preferred the sultan to the pope.[64]

The Ottoman threat to the Habsburgs contributed to the success of the Protestant Reformation and the rise and establishment of Protestantism in Europe. The proponents of the new churches found themselves able to use fear of the powerful Ottoman Empire as a bargaining chip in exchange for the granting of concessions by European Catholic powers. Martin Luther declared the Ottomans to be the instrument of divine punishment against the church, the 'scourge of God'.[65] As Erasmus before him, he railed against wars against the Muslim enemy in favour of reforming Christian belief and practice first. His famous *Ninety-Five Theses* (1517) included his protest against the granting of church indulgences to finance wars against the Ottomans. Time and again, from the 1520s to the 1540s, when the Ottomans threatened the territory of the Holy Roman Empire, Protestants gave their political cooperation to Catholics only in return for religious concessions.[66] The Ottoman threat enabled them to consolidate their gains.

The Ottomans armed Morisco (Muslims converted to Catholicism) rebels in Habsburg Spain; encouraged ties between Moroccans and Moriscos, as well as between Protestants and Moroccans; organised Mediterranean naval support of uprisings; allied themselves with Calvinists in Hungary; and sent secret agents promising military aid to Lutherans in the Habsburg-ruled Netherlands and German-speaking lands who were against the pope and the Holy Roman Empire.[67] Protestant soldiers reportedly claimed it would be better to fight for the 'Unbaptised Turk', Sultan Suleiman I, than for the 'Baptised Turk', Emperor Charles V.[68] Such siding of Protestant Christians with the Muslim sultan damaged Charles V's ability to recreate a European spiritual monarchy, with territorial repercussions. Suleiman I informed the Protestants that Muslims shared their iconoclasm and opposition to the pope. In 1555, Lutherans obtained official recognition, in part as a result of Holy Roman emperors having been more concerned with fighting the Ottomans in Hungary than with attending to internal German affairs.

Charles V was more focused on conquering the Italian peninsula than on handling the strife at home in Germany. And his younger brother Ferdinand, whom he established in Germany while he campaigned, was more engaged in defending Hungary and his Hungarian inheritance from the Ottomans. In 1526, the pope refused to call a council to debate on reforms. But when the nobles declared that they would not send forces against the Ottomans until such a council met, Ferdinand agreed to a diet in the town of Speyer, at which an edict outlawing Martin Luther and his writings was temporarily suspended. The upshot of this delay was that the anti-Catholic Christians were able to establish Lutheranism in Germany in exchange for sending troops to fight the Ottomans. Suleiman I's armies conquered central Hungary and made Transylvania into a vassal land—cannons beating cavalry again—following the Battle of Mohács in 1526.

In 1530, the Diet of Augsburg proclaimed a death sentence for the Lutherans. But the Holy Roman Empire was still threatened by the Ottomans in Hungary, and this grave threat was its primary concern. In 1532, Charles V accepted Lutheran support against the Ottomans in return for guaranteeing the existence of Lutheranism until a council could be convened. The pope refused to convene the council, and by 1540 Lutherans had secured far-reaching guarantees. Lutheranism had to be tolerated due to the international situation. Suleiman I's Ottoman forces had taken control of central Hungary, and his ally François I of France, Charles V's archrival for control of Christian Europe, was attacking Italy. Not until 1546 could the Holy Roman Empire attempt to put the Lutheran movement down, but by then the split between Lutherans and Catholics had become irreconcilable and was finally acknowledged in 1555 with the Peace of Augsburg. The growth and eventual acceptance of Lutheranism in Germany is attributed in part to the aspirations of Ottoman imperialism.[69]

The Protestant Church struck root in Hungary for one primary reason. With the use of Counter-Reformation tactics designed to enforce religious conformity and political centralisation, the Habsburgs had estranged many Hungarians to such an extent that they preferred Ottoman rule.[70] And with Ottoman rule, they

opted for Protestantism as well as Islam. By 1550, the majority of
the Christians in the now Ottoman province of Buda and the vassal land of Transylvania had converted from Catholicism to Protestantism or Islam.[71] A dazzling, golden, bejewelled, orb-shaped
crown would be made by Sultan Ahmed I (reigned 1603–1617) for
the Hungarian Stefan Bocskay, who led a Calvinist revolt in upper Hungary against Habsburg rule. Bocskay was rewarded by the
Ottomans by being crowned in Pest in 1605 as the ruler of Hungary. He may not have lasted long in power, dying suddenly the
next year from illness, but the crown made of gold and precious
stones—including alternating bands of rubies, emeralds, pearls,
and opals topped with a gigantic oval emerald in place of a cross—
is still on display in the Imperial Treasury in Vienna.

A RENEWED THREAT FROM
DEVIANT DERVISHES

Although he sided with religious rebels in the Habsburg Empire,
Suleiman I still faced competition for his spiritual role and the
source of the dynasty's legitimacy within his own empire. He faced
large-scale, violent rebellions in central Anatolia from deviant dervishes, such as that led in 1527 by the Sufi Kalender Çelebi, heir
of Hajji Bektaş and leader of his shrine in central Anatolia, whose
supporters destroyed the first army sent to defeat it. His devotees
raised their banners and beat their kettledrums and blew their
horns in support. A Bektaşi poet proclaimed, 'O Ottoman! This
world will not be left to you. Do not assume that Son of the Shah
will not avenge this blood on you'.[72] Kalender Çelebi was killed by
Ottoman forces, ending his rebellion, and the shrine of Hajji Bektaş
was closed for nearly three decades. Also in 1527, Istanbul-trained
scholar Molla Kabiz preached that the Qur'an was not superior to
nor did it supersede the Torah and Gospel, but was rather dependent upon them. He also taught that Jesus was superior to Muhammad.[73] Molla Kabiz refused to recant and was publicly executed.[74]

Two years later, the same fate was met by the boy sheikh İsmail Maşuki. Maşuki was a member of a deviant dervish order that followed the teaching of Emir the Cutler, who died in 1476. Like the Sufi Baba Tükles, who had converted a Mongol ruler, Emir the Cutler had allegedly emerged unharmed after dancing into a fire, only his robe singed.[75] Maşuki had developed a considerable following by claiming that man was eternal and that everything made illicit in Islamic law was licit, including drinking alcohol. He proclaimed that because they were exceedingly enjoyable, adultery and sodomy were not forbidden but encouraged. He preached that the five pillars of Sunni practice—the five daily prayers, fasting during Ramadan, the pilgrimage to Mecca, alms giving, and profession of the faith—were not necessary for the enlightened to follow. In his view, there was no Day of Judgement but there was reincarnation. Souls migrated from one person to another. Man creates himself. In short, everyone is God. For these shocking proclamations, already espoused by Sheikh Bedreddin, he and twelve of his disciples were beheaded in 1529 before a great crowd that had gathered at the Hippodrome in Istanbul to see the bodily punishment meted out to one who challenged conventionally held truths.[76]

In 1561, the Ottomans executed the deviant Bosnian dervish Sheikh Hamza Bali for claiming to be the pole of the universe. Only Suleiman I was allowed to make such a spiritual claim. A follower of Hamza Bali would assassinate the grand vizier in revenge, probably intending to kill Sheikhulislam Ebussuud Efendi, who had issued the legal opinion permitting Hamza Bali's execution. Writers in the sultan's circle proclaimed Suleiman I as the pole. They declared that political success required saintliness and that, as the saint of saints, the sultan was sovereign in both worlds. His eschatological role was to be the last world emperor before the end-time. This was not a matter of theological orthodoxy. It was the assignation of the locus of all radical spiritual claims, whether made by Savafid Shi'is or by Ottoman Sunnis, to their proper place—the body of Suleiman I.

Unlike in Christian Europe—where church councils determined orthodoxy, condemned nonconforming beliefs as heresies, and persecuted the dissenters as heretics—in the Ottoman Empire such views were seen as challenges to the sultan's spiritual and political authority. Suleiman I opposed those who disputed his religious authority as the Sufi perfect man, the redeemer and renewer of the age. Two of the three trials against Sufi dissenters during this period—that of Molla Kabiz and İsmail Maşuki—occurred during the first twenty years of Suleiman I's reign, when propaganda at court was anything but what we would today recognise as normative Sunni Islam. The Sufi executed in the third trial, Hamza Bali, was seen as a threat in part for the support he enjoyed among the Janissaries—whose devotion, like the Shi'is, focused on Muhammad's son-in-law Ali. Likewise, Suleiman I implemented a number of practices that had been engaged in earlier by Mehmed II as part of bureaucratisation, expansion, empire building, and centralisation that were not an imposition of orthodoxy.

AN ISLAMIC REFORMATION?

In addition to the ubiquitous use of millenarian claims in both East and West, the sixteenth century was characterised by a challenge to the right to call oneself a true believer. Following the Reformation, Christianity in Western and Central Europe split into the Catholic, Lutheran, and Calvinist churches. As religious rivals pursuing common strategies and goals, each church promoted piety and individual spirituality, the internalisation of church teachings, the drawing of dichotomies between faiths, and the quest for uniform orthodoxy. They utilised violence to ensure religious homogeneity in the territories they ruled. Book burnings, inquisitions, heresy trials, the persecution of dissenters, and the burning of 'witches' were frequent and vicious. Most of the latter victims were women, usually old, poor, and widowed or single—women not considered to be controlled by a man and thus not conforming to male standards of female behaviour.

Just as the church in the West split into three denominations during the Reformation, so, too, did the chasm between Sunni and Shi'i Muslims deepen in the same era. Selim I's attacks on Shah Ismail I are similar to the aspersions Martin Luther cast on the Catholic Church. As Selim I condemned Shi'i 'temporary marriage' as adultery and fornication, Luther excoriated monks and clergy in Rome for their mistresses and prostitutes. The Sunni-Shi'i split was rooted in Islamic history in the seventh century following Muhammad's death. They debated who had the right to rule the community: men chosen by consensus or members of Muhammad's family, the latter calling themselves the *shi'at* Ali (partisans of Ali). That sectarian split became more pronounced in the sixteenth century, catalysed by the Safavid threat and attracting the support of Turcoman in Ottoman Anatolia, with the Ottomans affirming their Sunnism in unprecedented ways. Suleiman I ordered a mosque to be built in every Muslim village in the empire, which was meant to centralise as well as Islamise and stamp out pro-Safavid or deviant-dervish alternative interpretations of Islam. Such alternative interpretations were demonstrated partly through the forcible sorting out of the two denominations through conversion, deportation, war, banishment, and massacre. Ottoman historians boasted about how Selim I massacred tens of thousands of Shi'ites, a bloodbath that was similar to the Saint Bartholomew's Day massacre of 1572, in which Catholics in France slaughtered thousands of Protestants (called Huguenots) and mutilated their corpses.[77]

For their part, the Safavids butchered large numbers of Sunnis while compelling the wholescale conversion of Iran's Muslim population from Sunnism to Shi'ism under Shah Ismail I and his successors in the sixteenth century. To effect this change, the

Safavids also brought in Shi'i scholars from Ottoman territories
such as Lebanon, who were conversant in both interpretations of
the faith, to help define and police the boundaries of Shi'i belief.
Soon the Shi'i call to prayer, which includes the line, 'I testify Ali
is the friend of God, I testify Ali is proof of God', rang out from
minarets three times a day across the Safavid Empire.

Yet in the same century, the Janissaries repeatedly marched off
into battle against the Shi'i Safavids while extolling Shi'i propaganda. Their standards were emblazoned with the phrases 'saint'
or 'friend of God', 'Hajji Bektaş is the manifestation of the divine
light of Ali', and 'There is no one as valiant as Ali, there is no
sword of God other than Ali's sword'. They vowed to avenge the
seventh-century killing of their 'shah', Ali's son Hussein, at Kar-
bala in Iraq. The same banners declared, 'Long live my Sultan,
may he reign for a 1000 years'. What mattered, once again, was
loyalty, not ideological purity, as in Reformation Christian Europe. The Janissaries were never made into normative Sunni Muslims, yet the explicit expression of the rival faith was permitted at
the centre of empire. Whereas in Reformation Europe the religion
of the ruler became the religion of the subjects, in the Ottoman
Empire authorities tolerated a significant community of Shi'is
in Lebanon.

But to understand this age of confessionalisation and how the
great empires of Europe and Asia participated in it, it is worth
bearing in mind that the Islamic institution of the caliphate was
not the same as the Christian institution of the papacy. Because
they were more concerned with public behaviour than private
belief, Muslims lacked institutions with which to pronounce and
repress 'heresy', such as the Inquisition, or to discipline authority
and institutions of 'orthodoxy'.

The Ottoman imperial council did hear cases of subjects ut-
tering abominable statements about Islam. Yet, it was no Inquisi-
tional authority, as most trials were concerned with treason and
social upheaval. The authorities could pardon the offending party

if he pledged political allegiance. It would therefore be a mistake to use the terms 'orthodox', 'heterodox', and 'heresy' in the absence of institutions with authority to pronounce true religion and punish those who did not follow it. Although the distinction between Sunni and Shi'i sharpened during this period, what mattered was not confessional divide—as in the split between Calvinist, Catholic, and Lutheran in Christian Europe—but allegiance to a dynasty.

As for loyalty to the ideal that the Ottoman sultan was the messiah, one group surpassed all others in the fervency and tenacity of this belief. Jews who had migrated to the Ottoman Empire from Spain and Portugal following their forced conversion to Catholicism or expulsion perceived Ottoman sultans as carrying out God's plan for them. The ingathering of European Jews in the sultan's domains would lead Jews East and West to place the Ottoman sultan at the centre of their apocalyptic drama.

In the first seven chapters, the reader has encountered a narrative of the Ottoman dynasty from its origins at the turn of the fourteenth century through to the middle of the sixteenth century. At this point, we will break the narrative flow in order to devote the next five chapters to exploring several major themes that emerged, before returning to the story of the changes faced by the dynasty at the end of the sixteenth century. The themes are the ingathering of Jews, Jewish utopian views of the empire, and ecstatic, messianic depictions of the sultan; the development of the Ottomans as a maritime power and their participation in the Age of Discovery; the unique Ottoman way as expressed in class structure, law, culture, and ideology; the role of women and eunuchs in the palace and dynastic politics; and the culture of same-sex desire.

8

SULTANIC SAVIOURS

MUSLIMS WERE NOT the only Ottoman subjects who viewed sultans as God-sent messiahs. So, too, did Jews.[1] Massacred, forcibly converted, and expelled from every medieval kingdom in Christian Europe, including England, Jews found refuge in the Ottoman Empire. Following their forced departure from Spain in 1492 and from Portugal in 1497, as many as one hundred thousand Spanish and Portuguese Jews, as well as a large number of conversos (Iberian Jews compelled to convert to Catholicism) migrated to the Ottoman Empire. There, conversos found that they were able to return to Judaism, which was a crime punishable by death in Western Europe. Jews were amazed to discover that they were relatively free to openly practice Judaism in the Ottoman Empire, unlike almost anywhere else in contemporary Europe. Thanks in part to the Ottomans, for much of history Jews have had a positive image of Muslims. Equally astounding was the fact that individual Jews rose to important positions at the Ottoman court.

Between 1453 and 1600, Jews served the dynasty as privy physicians, diplomats, translators, advisors, spies, and ladies-in-waiting to the harem and were given licence to conduct trade as international bankers. Prominent Jews included the illustrious physicians and diplomatic agents Joseph (born in 1450 in Granada) and Moses Hamon. The Portuguese converso and international merchant

Doña Gracia Mendes Nasi headed one of the greatest family businesses in Western Europe. Forcibly converted to Catholicism and then persecuted for being secret Jews, she and members of her family, including her nephew, João Miguez, migrated to the Ottoman Empire in order to return to their ancestral Judaism, bringing their wealth and connections with them. Miguez, who would become the duke of Naxos, also served the Ottoman court as a diplomatic agent. A relative of Gracia Mendes and Miguez, the Portuguese Jew Don Alvaro Mendes (Salomon ibn Yaesh), would serve as counsellor to Murad III and helped establish close relations between England and the Ottoman Empire, both eager to counter Philip II of Spain. Physician, advisor, diplomatic agent, and international merchant Salomon ben Natan Eskenazi would become the trusted advisor of Grand Vizier Sokollu Mehmed Pasha and official envoy of the sultan to Venice and the Habsburgs.[2]

The prominence of such Jews at court and the fact that after 1517 the Ottomans controlled the Holy Land meant that Jews could make pilgrimage to or settle in Jerusalem. This raised Jews' messianic expectations. Used to brutal treatment at the hands of Christians, Jews across the Mediterranean were grateful for this reception and wrote ecstatic accounts of the Ottomans.

Messianic desires and an emotional state of gratefulness compelled Jews in the fifteenth, sixteenth, and seventeenth centuries to be exceptionally loyal to the Ottoman sultans, who at that time ruled one of the only kingdoms in the world that permitted them to be Jews. This shaped a utopian image of the Ottomans and their sultan. Jews saw the Ottoman sultan as a personification of the empire, depicting him in messianic terms as God's rod, the one who fulfils God's plan in the world by smiting the Jews' Christian oppressors. They also credited him for gathering the Jewish diaspora from across the Mediterranean, conquering Jerusalem, and enabling Jews to settle in the Holy Land. In their view, these all served as signs and wonders, omens for the beginning of the messianic age and the redemption of the Jews.

Rabbi Elijah ben Elkanah Capsali of Candia (Iráklion, on Venetian Crete), wrote ecstatically of Mehmed II, Bayezid II, Selim I, and Suleiman I. He saw them as redeemers of the Jews, players in the cosmic drama between the forces of good and evil that preceded the advent of the messiah.[3] While Greeks lamented how 'all things turned to evil. What and how and why? Because of our sins!', non-Greek Jews had the opposite reaction to the fall of Constantinople and the Byzantine Empire.[4] The sultans were 'messengers of God' who punished 'wicked' nations and gathered the exiled Jews.[5] Capsali claimed that God had promised Osman, the founder of the Ottoman Empire, 'a kingdom as hard as iron'. This is a reference to the fourth kingdom of the vision of Daniel in the Bible, the last before the redemption to attack the Jews' oppressors.[6] That is why God brought the Turks from a faraway land, blessed them, and made the Ottomans great and powerful.[7] The Turk 'is the rod' of God's wrath with which 'God punishes the different nations'.[8] Having punished Byzantine Constantinople, God made Ottoman Istanbul flourish as a reward to the sultan, who had carried out God's will.[9] Jews looked to Suleiman I with hope, for he was the tenth Ottoman sultan, and, as the Torah predicts, 'every tenth one shall be holy to God' and 'in his days Judah shall be delivered and Israel shall dwell secure' and 'a redeemer shall come to Zion'.[10]

Imbued with such millenarian expectations, Solomon Molho—the former Diego Pires, a Portuguese converso who had returned to Judaism in the Ottoman Empire, where he studied Kabbalah (Jewish mysticism)—proclaimed himself as the messiah around 1525. In Regensburg, Bavaria, he had an audience with Holy Roman Emperor Charles V. The meeting did not go well, and Molho was turned over to the Inquisition. He was burned at the stake in 1532.

As messianic views continued to be kindled, subsequent Jewish writers expressed ecstatic gratefulness to the sultans. One of them was Portuguese converso Samuel Usque. Usque, an ardent follower of Solomon Molho, believed his group's suffering marked the end of history. The great comfort was that all these travails were foretold by the prophets, and that as the prophecies of evil were verified, so should Jews trust that the prophecies of good would also be fulfilled. Writing to fellow exiles, he argued that conversos suffered because the millennium was at hand, after which a new age would dawn and their misfortunes would end.[11] Like the nations around them, Jews, he argued, had sinned and become idolatrous. For this they had been punished by God. If they repented, God would forgive them. If they returned to Judaism and God, their misfortunes would end. Usque interpreted the expulsions from Christian Europe as fulfilments of biblical prophecies, which meant that once all the conversos returned to Judaism, redemption of the Jews would be at hand.[12]

Usque argued that the Ottoman Empire was the greatest consolation for the persecution of Jewry.[13] He compared the Ottoman Empire to the Red Sea, across which the Israelites had fled to safety from the pharaohs of Egypt. According to him, the Ottoman Empire 'is like a broad and expansive sea which our Lord has opened with the rod of His mercy, as Moses did for you in the Exodus from Egypt, so that the swells of your present misfortunes, which relentlessly pursue you in all the kingdoms of Europe like the infinite multitude of Egyptians, might cease and be consumed by it'. In the Ottoman Empire 'the gates of liberty are always wide open for you that you may fully practice your Judaism'.[14] Jews were allowed to embrace their former faith and abandon the rites they had been forced to adopt.

Other writers continued the inter-Jewish dialogue, praising the Ottomans in emotional, messianic terms. Joseph ben Joshua ha-Kohen was born in France, the son of expelled Castilian Spanish Jews. His family was subsequently expelled from Provence, and he spent most of his life in Genoa, where he also faced expulsion decrees. He aimed to prove that Christians were being punished by the Ottomans for the calamities to which they subjected

Jews and that redemption was at hand.[15] He described Mehmed II as 'a scourge and breaker of the uncircumcised' [the Christians].[16] In describing Suleiman I's reign, ha-Kohen argued that the messianic age was approaching and that the Ottoman and Habsburg dynasties represented the forces of good and evil. The world war between these empires meant that the prophecy of Ezekiel—in which the enemies of the Jews would be defeated and the Temple restored—was being realised.

For ha-Kohen, God had awakened the sultan's soul to rebuild the walls of Jerusalem, predicting the messiah would come in his lifetime. Suleiman I rebuilt the walls of the Old City of Jerusalem. The walls include Jaffa and Damascus Gates, as well as the sealed Golden Gate, or Gate of Mercy, located on the eastern side of the Temple Mount. According to Jews, this was the door through which the messiah would come. According to Christians, the messiah had already come through this door in the person of Jesus.

Along with these Mediterranean Jews, Ottoman Jews such as Samuel de Medina—chief rabbi of Salonica, Macedonia, and scion of a Castilian family—also believed God caused Mehmed II to besiege Istanbul and allowed him to capture it.

In messianic expectation, Doña Gracia Mendes Nasi settled former conversos returned to Judaism in the Holy Land. She paid for the construction of public works, housing, and a synagogue in Tiberias. She had mulberry trees planted to jump-start the silk industry and imported merino sheep to be raised for their high-quality wool. Gracia Mendes planned to move to Tiberias, close to the main Kabbalist centre of Safed, due to feverish expectations about the onset of the messianic era, but she passed away in 1569 before doing so.[17]

Her nephew João Miguez played a more significant role in the Ottoman Empire. Having worked as Gracia Mendes's agent and representative in Western Europe, Miguez migrated to Istanbul and returned to Judaism, becoming known as Don Joseph Nasi.[18]

Unlike his aunt, Joseph Nasi was able to enter royal circles, specifically that of Prince Selim, who became Selim II upon Suleiman I's death in 1566.

During Selim II's reign (1566–1574), Joseph Nasi, whose commercial agents in Western Europe proved useful for gathering intelligence for the Ottomans, quickly rose at court as an advisor and diplomat. Throughout the 1560s, he negotiated treaties with Poland, the Habsburgs, and France, and promoted rebellions by Protestants in the Netherlands and by Moriscos—Spanish Muslims converted to Catholicism—in Spain. He allegedly convinced the sultan to launch the successful conquest of Venetian Cyprus in 1571. In return, he was named duke of Naxos and the rest of the Cyclades, a group of recently annexed former Venetian islands in the south Aegean Sea. His wife, Gracia Jr., was named the duchess of Naxos.[19] He was granted extensive tax farms, as well as the monopoly on the regional wine trade. Contemporary Western European accounts of this Jewish man's alleged desire to be 'king of Cyprus' made him the scapegoat for Ottoman failures during the Age of Discovery. But the fact that other Europeans considered the Ottomans a decisive sea power during the era is significant. For the Age of Discovery was also a time of critical successes for the Ottoman Empire.

9

THE OTTOMAN AGE
OF DISCOVERY

B OTH THE OTTOMAN conquest of Constantinople in 1453 and
the defeat and conquest of the territories of the Mamluk Empire in 1516–1517, including the Middle East, by Selim I made the
Ottomans into a naval power with a worldwide vision. Selim I's
conquests doubled the size of the empire and set it on the path
for having a Muslim majority in the following centuries. Selim I's
successor, Suleiman I, proclaimed himself the caliph, the universal protector of the entire Muslim-ruled world, the defender of
Sunni Muslims from the Mediterranean to the Indian Ocean.
Advances in military and naval technology—firearms, artillery,
and ocean-sailing vessels—allowed the Ottomans to project
their power and control oceangoing trade to Southeast Asia. All
of this led to a cultural florescence, a rediscovery of overlooked
ancient knowledge, the launching of curious Ottoman travellers,
the translations of Western works, and the production of new
Ottoman maps, atlases, and geographical treatises. If such developments are the major determinants of whether an empire partook in the Age of Discovery, then there was an Ottoman Age
of Discovery.[1]

The Ottomans did not possess a land empire only. From the
fifteenth century, theirs was also a seaborne empire. Thanks in

part to the influx after 1492 of refugee European Jews and their knowledge of geography, technology, military developments, and politics, and because of the continued use of converts in key positions, the Ottoman maritime empire emerged in the same century as that of the Portuguese.[2] Beginning with the reign of Mehmed II, sultans referred to themselves as 'Lord of the two seas and two continents'. The sultans were the rulers of the Mediterranean and Black Seas, Europe and Asia. From Egypt to Indonesia, the Ottomans rivalled the Portuguese in the battle for the seas and played a major role in international trade. Why, then, are the Ottomans not included as major participants in the European Age of Discovery?[3] Ottoman writers of the time confute such an exclusion.

Sea captain (or *reis*) Seydi Ali—the author of *The Mirror of Countries* (1560), which was based on his travels through India, Afghanistan, Uzbekistan, and Iran—explains how in 1552 he was appointed Ottoman admiral of the Egyptian fleet. He had 'always been very fond of the sea, had taken part in the expedition against Rhodes under Sultan Suleiman I, and had since had a share in almost all engagements, both by land and by sea'. He had 'fought under Barbarossa Hayreddin Pasha, Sinan Pasha, and other captains, and had cruised about on the Western [Mediterranean] sea' such that he 'knew every nook and corner of it'. Seydi Ali 'had written several books on astronomy, nautical science, and other matters bearing upon navigation'. His 'father and grandfather, since the conquest of Constantinople, had had charge of the arsenal at Galata; they had both been eminent in their profession, and their skill had come down to me as an heirloom'.[4] Seydi Ali was a typical explorer of that era.

The Age of Discovery is conventionally understood as the sixteenth-century European maritime exploration and mastery of the sea that served as the basis for the expansion of global European influence.[5] In the accepted story, Muslim powers such as the Ottomans are depicted as obstacles to Western European domination, obstacles to the Europeans' 'natural path of expansion' into Africa and the Middle East.[6] When we think of what immediately preceded the Age of Discovery, we imagine the Portuguese and Spanish—and later the Dutch, English, and French—not as being engaged in world trade, but as existing first in a period of relative geographic and intellectual isolation limited to the North Atlantic and the Mediterranean. Incongruously, they possessed a decisively bold political and religious legitimating ideology that allowed them to imagine conquering the world. This boldness was manifested in the Treaty of Tordesillas of 1494, in which the Spanish and Portuguese divided up the extra-European world between them, despite not even controlling one part of it. As they launched their voyages of discovery, there followed rapid and significant technological advances—particularly in firearms and oceangoing vessels, which were combined into formidable warships as they put cannons onboard carracks. Curiosity gave rise to cultural and intellectual transformation, the blossoming of scholarly and artistic achievements—especially in cartography, geography, and classical studies—and an interest in the outside world and their ability to control it.[7]

One might be tempted to imagine the brief period of Ottoman control over Morocco and the entire North African littoral during the reign of Murad III as comparable to the European Age of Discovery. Had the Ottomans remained in power there, they might well have expanded down the west coast of Africa. This was uncharted territory for the Ottomans, in some ways as foreign to them as the New World was to the Western European powers. A better comparison, however, lies with the Ottomans' economic and naval expansion into the Indian Ocean basin.[8] Given their lack of development of oceangoing vessels and the Europeans' comparative advantage, it is easy to disparage the idea that the Ottomans experienced maritime expansion in this age. But the Ottomans actively participated in the Age of Discovery in the sixteenth century.

CONTROLLING THE MEDITERRANEAN SEA

Following Mehmed II's conquest of Constantinople—won in part by a clever use of naval power in the Golden Horn—the sultan utilised the Italian and Greek expertise at hand to improve Ottoman naval might. He invested in building an arsenal and shipyard in Istanbul that helped him gain control of the Black Sea by expelling the Genoese. He acquired Byzantine manuscripts of Ptolemy's world map *Geographia*, commissioned the Byzantine George Amiroutzes of Trabzon to provide a translation into Turkish, and gathered contemporary Italian versions of the same work.[9] His naval abilities were limited, however, and the Ottomans failed to take Rhodes in 1480. His son and successor, Bayezid II, expanded the Ottoman navy, recruiting Aegean corsair captains like Piri Reis.[10]

Bayezid II ordered the construction of what an Ottoman chronicler called 'ships agile as sea serpents' to challenge the Venetians in the eastern Mediterranean (including the Aegean and the Adriatic).[11] It worked. By 1499, just as the Portuguese reached the western coast of India, the Ottomans controlled much of the eastern Mediterranean.[12] At the turn of the sixteenth century, Bayezid II commanded the repairing of the fleet, the building of hundreds of new, better ships, the mobilisation of tens of thousands of oarsmen and sailors, and the manufacture of cannons to be used especially in the Mediterranean and Aegean Seas and, towards the end of his reign, in the Red Sea and Indian Ocean.[13]

Like Dom Henrique 'Henry the Navigator' of Portugal, Mehmed II's grandson, Selim I, laid the groundwork for maritime empire.[14] During Selim I's reign, the first original Ottoman geographical works appeared, such as *The Book of Cathay*, an account of a voyage from the Safavid Empire to China, written by merchant Ali Akbar in 1516.[15] Western European sources would not analyse Chinese society to this extent for another century. After Selim I destroyed his former ally against the Portuguese and the Safavids, the Mamluk Empire, and annexed Egypt and Syria, the Ottomans—assisted by the Mamluk fleet at Suez and headed by Selman Reis—controlled most of the eastern Mediterranean and expanded into the Red Sea along the coast of Arabia, the Persian Gulf, and the Indian Ocean.[16] Thereafter, Ottomans devised new taxation policies to extract profits from the trade that passed through these regions, stationing commercial agents across them and even organising trade convoys. Yet it would be an exaggeration to claim they established monopolies like the Portuguese.

The Ottomans were focused not only on the East. They also kept an eye on the Mediterranean. Suleiman I expanded Ottoman naval power against pockets of resistance in the Mediterranean, notably at the island of Rhodes in 1522. In the end, Suleiman I was able to starve the Knights Hospitaller into submission, agreeing to let the surviving knights depart unharmed. They resettled on the island of Malta, given to them for the symbolic rent of one falcon per year by Charles V.[17]

The Ottoman conquering of ports including Tunis in North Africa (1534), which was retaken by Charles V the following year, was the beginning of a fifty-year struggle with the Habsburgs for control of the western Mediterranean. The Knights Hospitaller would remain a thorn in the Ottoman side at Malta, and Suleiman I came to regret not having slaughtered them all.

In the early sixteenth century, as France and the Holy Roman Empire competed for dominion of European Christendom, they and the Ottoman Empire also sought control of the Mediterranean and the Italian peninsula, to which all had dynastic claims, both real and imagined. Suleiman I found the king of France, François I, amenable in the 1540s to an alliance against his brother-in-law and rival, Charles V, king of Spain and Holy Roman emperor. Charles V castigated the alliance as outside the bounds of accepted diplomatic practice because François I had made common cause with an infidel, a Muslim ruler.[18]

Many Europeans found it hard to imagine France asking for Ottoman help against another Catholic power. They forgot about how Christians had been making alliances with the Ottomans since the fourteenth century—Orthodox Christians such as the Byzantines and Serbs, and Catholics such as the Genoese and Venetians. The French were not dissuaded. They needed a powerful counterforce against the Habsburg threat. François I's defenders argued that making an alliance with the Ottomans did not harm 'his title and honour of "Most Christian"'.[19] While many Christian rulers who supported Emperor Charles V made a fuss that King François I sought and received Ottoman help, his supporters asserted that 'against an enemy one may make arrows of all wood'.[20] François I nursed the pain of having been passed over as Holy Roman emperor in favour of Charles V in 1519. Six years later, before his alliance with the Ottomans, the French king had suffered ignominious defeat at the Battle of Pavia in Italy and was taken prisoner by the Habsburg emperor. He imagined that, together with the assistance of the Ottoman army and navy, he could defeat the Habsburgs and become the premier Christian power.[21]

The alliance would allow the Ottomans to divide Europe, if not conquer the Habsburgs, their most powerful enemy. The Ottomans hardly viewed the French as their equals, however. In a written exchange between the two rulers, Suleiman I referred to himself as 'Sultan of Sultans, king of kings, the Shadow of God who bestows the crown to the monarchs on earth, the supreme ruler of the White [Mediterranean] and Black Seas, Rumelia [Southeastern Europe] and Anatolia, Persia, Damascus, and Aleppo, Egypt, Mecca and Medina, Jerusalem, and all of the Arab dominions, and Yemen, and the Sultan the supreme king of many nations'.[22] He refers to King François as 'the governor of the French province'.

In 1543, Suleiman I sent the Ottoman fleet led by the red-bearded, formidable Hayreddin Barbarossa Pasha to assist François I against the Habsburgs. Barbarossa was a man born to a Muslim father and Greek mother on the island of Lesbos.[23] He served various Muslim North African kingdoms as a corsair before conquering Algiers for Selim I and becoming its governor. In 1533, he was appointed grand admiral. In 1537, the Ottomans and French planned to launch joint naval attacks against Italy, but they were unable to coordinate their campaigns.[24] Six years later, France requested the Ottomans send their fleet to wage war against coastal Habsburg territory. In summer 1543, Barbarossa arrived in Marseilles with 150 ships and as many as thirty thousand men.[25] François I desired a joint Franco-Ottoman naval siege of Nice. What is remembered in France today about that failed assault on the city—then a port ruled by the duke of Savoy, Charles V's ally—is only the myth about a local washerwoman, Catherine Ségurane, who allegedly led local resistance, wiping her bottom with a captured Ottoman banner, 'which made them flee'.[26] She was made patron saint of the city. Every year the Niçois celebrate Saint Catherine's Day on 25 November.

After the assault on Nice, the Ottoman navy wintered in the French port of Toulon. Most of its population was compelled to abandon the city to the Muslim sailors.[27] Until the French Revolution at the end of the eighteenth century, a painting of the Ottoman fleet in the city's harbour hung in Toulon's town hall. The caption thanked the Ottomans for coming to assist the French.[28] However, François I, who had money enough to appoint Leonardo da Vinci as his premier painter, engineer, and architect, failed to live up to his side of the agreement with the sultan to provision the Ottoman fleet and pay its sailors.[29] Plans for a joint campaign against Genoa were not carried out either, although in the summer of 1544 the French supported Ottoman attacks on the Italian coast as the Ottoman fleet was returning to Istanbul.[30] When the fleet arrived home, the Ottomans learned that François I had signed a peace treaty with Charles V. But as an example of shifting European alliances, Pope Paul IV (in office 1555–1559) proposed a Crusade against the Habsburgs, including a joint French-Ottoman attack on Naples and Sicily.[31] 'The Turks [Ottomans] will not fail us!' he proclaimed, although the plans came to nought.[32]

Benefiting from Spain's expulsion of its Muslims, the Ottomans utilised the Moriscos—Muslims converted to Catholicism who remained in Spain—as spies and agents. They encouraged uprisings in Spain by supplying firearms and ammunition, co-ordinating the Morisco attacks with their own naval campaigns in North Africa.[33] The Ottomans facilitated contacts between Moriscos and Moroccans and encouraged them to unite with Protestants in the Habsburg Netherlands against their oppressive overlords. Recognising that the Ottomans tolerated religious minorities whereas their own emperor did not, anti-Habsburg rebels in the Netherlands promoted the slogan 'Rather Turkish than Popish', even minting the motto on crescent-bedecked coins in the 1570s.[34] Whether actualised or not, the threat of Ottoman support of Morisco and Protestant rebellion in that era—Selim II and the Dutch prince William I of Orange sent secret envoys to each other's courts to discuss such plans—diverted Habsburg forces and helped the Ottomans accomplish their military aims.[35]

CONTROLLING THE PERSIAN GULF AND STAKING CLAIMS TO THE INDIAN OCEAN AND BEYOND

By 1510 the Ottomans were sending naval forces to assist the Mamluks in keeping the Portuguese at bay in the Red Sea and Indian Ocean, building and manning a fleet at Suez.[36] Throughout the sixteenth century, beginning in the 1530s during the reign of Suleiman I, as they battled the Habsburgs for control of the Western Mediterranean and the North African coast, the Ottomans also attempted to expel the Portuguese from the region stretching from the Red Sea to the Persian Gulf and Indian Ocean.[37] This led to repeated unsuccessful attempts to capture the strategic Strait of Hormuz, which controls the entrance to the Persian Gulf; the island of Bahrain, jutting into the Persian Gulf from Arabia; and Diu, Gujarat, on the northwest coast of what is today India. The

Ottomans annexed Eritrea (1557) and southern Egypt, threatening the Portuguese naval base in Mozambique. Ottoman navies attacked Portuguese shipping as far away as Bengal and sent firearms and special forces to assist Muslim rulers and would-be rulers and promote uprisings from East Africa to Southeast Asia. They used their navies to conquer and control commercial entrepôts and maritime choke points. They sent tax and trade officials throughout the region to maximise customs revenues. They regularly escorted large numbers of imperial-owned ships importing spices from Southeast and South Asia to Egypt. They used the newfound wealth to fill the coffers of Ottoman provinces. South Asia witnessed the growth of Ottoman Muslim merchant communities.

To gain knowledge about their new maritime regions, Suleiman I's Greek-convert grand vizier and very close childhood friend Ibrahim Pasha (in office 1523–1536) commissioned two works. The first was authored by Piri Reis, the former pirate and navigator, commander of the Ottoman fleet at Suez, and admiral of the Indian Ocean fleet. At his own initiative in 1513, Piri Reis drew one of the earliest surviving maps of the coastline of the New World based on Christopher Columbus's map, and he presented it to Selim I in Cairo after he had conquered Egypt.[38] Importantly, the main focus of his map was the part depicting the Mediterranean and Indian Ocean, which Selim I may have used by detaching it from the part depicting the Western Hemisphere. The section containing the Eastern Hemisphere no longer survives. But the existence of the map demonstrates that the Ottomans were interested in the latest Western European discoveries and imagined themselves as rulers of a universal empire. Ibrahim Pasha also obtained the Portuguese court's official chart of Ferdinand Magellan's discoveries (1519).

Aiming to convince Suleiman I to expand Ottoman forces in the Indian Ocean, Ibrahim Pasha authorised Piri Reis to compose the *Book of the Sea* (1526), the greatest work of Ottoman cartography. It is a comprehensive atlas and navigational guide to the Mediterranean, the Red Sea, and Indian Ocean basin that includes the voyages of Vasco da Gama (died 1524) in these areas, Christopher Columbus's 'discoveries', and an explanation of the latest technological developments. Ibrahim Pasha also instructed Matrakçı Nasuh to compose the *Description of the Stages of Sultan Suleiman Khan's Campaign in the Two Iraqs* (1537), following the progress of Suleiman I from Istanbul to Baghdad in 1533–1536. It is an illustrated account mapping and describing the new territories, focusing on ports and fortresses, marking distances between halting stations, and distinguishing between friend and foe. Its geographical and topographical information and description of the principal buildings of each city is as valuable as Piri Reis's *Book of the Sea*, which showed coastal towns and features. It also celebrates the expansion of Ottoman rule. Nasuh refers to Suleiman I as master of the seven climes, as was Alexander the Great. Suleiman I's chronicler, Kemalpashazade, author of the *Chronicles of the Ottoman Dynasty* (begun in 1502), also referred to the ruler as 'majestic Sultan of sea and land, issuer of edicts for the seven climes, whose awe-inspiring voice penetrates the six corners of the world and commands the attention of all humankind'.

The Ottomans launched their biggest ever fleet in the Indian Ocean in 1538. It was one of the most massive armadas appearing in that ocean since Ming China's expeditions to the coast of East Africa at the beginning of the fifteenth century, led by the Muslim court eunuch and commander Cheng Ho.[39] The Ottoman armada besieged the important port of Diu in Gujarat, India, which, like other ports in the region, had a sizeable community of resident Ottoman Muslim traders with their own head merchant. The siege may have failed in part due to disagreements with the Ottomans' disparate allies, an assembly of Muslims from East Africa, South Asia, and Southeast Asia. But more significant was that, as a consequence of that campaign and after failed earlier attempts in the 1520s, the Ottomans were able to take Aden and Mocha and establish Yemen as a province. This gave them a stable base in the Arabian Sea and a direct link from Istanbul to Egypt through the Red Sea.[40]

The Ottoman governor of Yemen would carry the title admiral of the Indian Ocean; the Ottoman fleet at Suez would be renamed the Indian armada and its commander admiral of the Indies.[41] With their arsenal and shipyard at Suez, Egypt, the Ottomans attempted to build a canal connecting the Red Sea and the Nile (1531–1532). After 1538, the Ottomans were also able to establish rule over Surat, replacing Diu as the main port for trade between the Red Sea and Gujarat. Around 1540, Albanian-born grand vizier Lutfi Pasha advised Suleiman I that although many previous sultans had ruled the land, few had ruled the sea. It was time to overcome Christian Europeans in naval warfare.

Having occupied Tabriz and taken Baghdad in 1534, the Ottomans conquered Basra near the head of the Persian Gulf in Iraq in 1546. Their aims were to take the Strait of Hormuz, the narrow gateway between the Gulf of Oman and the entire Persian Gulf, and to attack the Portuguese in India. From there, they would be able to launch naval expeditions to South Asia. They even planned to send troops and artillery from Egypt to the sultan of Aceh in Sumatra in Southeast Asia. The purpose was to help that Muslim ruler gain control of the Malacca Strait and thus cut off Portuguese access to the spice trade in Southeast Asia and hinder their vessels travelling to China and Japan.

In 1552, Ottoman forces led by nonagenarian Piri Reis sacked Muscat in Oman and besieged the Strait of Hormuz, but without success. Having failed to attack the secondary target of Bahrain and contrary to orders, Piri Reis returned to Suez with the booty and captives gained in the campaign, having abandoned his fleet at Basra. He was arrested and executed for the crime.[42] Two years later, the Ottoman fleet of Seydi Ali Reis was ambushed and defeated by the Portuguese off the coast of Muscat. Nevertheless, Ottoman Muslim merchants and commercial agents were dispersed across all the major ports of the region including Cairo, Aden, Mocha, Jidda, Suez, Massawa, Diu, and Goa, filling Ottoman coffers and dwarfing the levels of trade achieved in Mamluk Egypt and by their Portuguese rivals.

Despite setbacks, elements of the Ottoman administration still retained big naval dreams. One of the most notable was a Serbian Collection recruit, Grand Vizier Sokollu Mehmed Pasha (assassinated in 1579 by a deviant dervish), who counted his father-in-law, Selim II, as well as the sultana (the sultan's wife, descended from Venetian nobles), Jewish courtiers, Venetian ambassadors, and members of the Ottoman Greek elite among his private circle.[43] Sokollu Mehmed Pasha sent artillery experts to Aceh and other agents throughout the Indian Basin to incite rebellion against the Portuguese. By the end of the 1560s, under Suleiman I's successor, Selim II, the grand vizier found that a number of Muslim rulers and factions in the region apparently wished for their territories to be annexed to the imperial domains, including Aceh, Gujarat, and the Maldives. Even Calicut in Kerala and Ceylon (Sri Lanka) desired to be made part of the Ottoman realm and their leaders to convert to Islam.[44] A major expedition to Sumatra to make these dreams a reality was prepared in 1567 but averted due to rebellion in Yemen.[45] The Ottomans sent hundreds of musketeers to fight as guerrillas on the side of Morisco rebels in Andalusia, Spain.[46]

With Sultan Selim II being less interested in matters of state, it was Sokollu Mehmed Pasha who took the lead. As part of a broad vision of connecting Muslims across Eurasia, Sokollu Mehmed Pasha in 1568 planned to build a canal connecting the Mediterranean and Suez to improve efforts against the Portuguese in India. In 1569 he proposed another, linking the Don and Volga rivers in southern Russia.[47] The canal would connect the Black Sea to the Caspian Sea and allow Ottoman fleets to attack Russia and the Safavids. It would also facilitate the trade and pilgrimage of Sunni Muslims from Central Asia threatened by Russian advancement in the Volga basin, the Caucasus, and the Black Sea region, and,

Fifteenth-century miniature of
a horseman drawing his bow
Credit: Topkapı Palace Museum,
Istanbul/Bridgeman Images

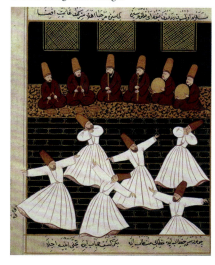

Seventeenth-century depiction
of Mevlevi Sufis
Credit: Bridgeman Images

Sixteenth-century depiction of
deviant dervishes
Credit: Heinrich Hendrowski,
Maler des kaiserlichen
Gesandten Bartholomäus Pezzen
in Istanbul, *Bilder aus dem
türkischen Volksleben*, Prague,
um 1600, ms. Vienna, Austrian
National Library, Sammlung
von Handschriften und alten
Drucken, Codex Vindobonensis
8626, fol. 107a

Ottoman miniature of the devşirme youth levy (1558)
Credit: Suleymânnâme, Ms. Hazine 1517, folio 31 verso, Topkapı Palace Museum, Istanbul/Bridgeman Images

Assassination of Murad I at the Battle of Kosovo in 1389 (1584)
Credit: Lokman, *Hünernâme*, Ms. Hazine 1523, folio 7, Topkapı Palace Museum, Istanbul/Bridgeman Images

Bayezid I routs the Crusaders at the Battle of Nicopolis in 1396 (1584)
Credit: Lokman, *Hünernâme*/Worcester Art Museum, Worcester, USA/ Bridgeman Images

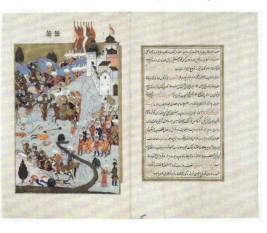

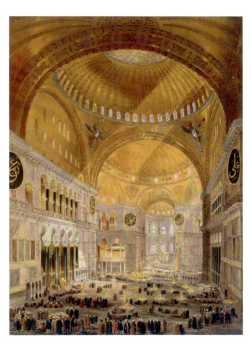

Coloured lithograph of Hagia Sophia, with Byzantine angels visible (1852)
Credit: colour lithograph by Louis Haghe/Bridgeman Images

Gentile Bellini portrait of Mehmed II (1480)
Credit: The National Gallery, London/ Bridgeman Images

Renaissance fresco in which Cem Sultan appears, wearing a white turban and looking directly at the painter
Credit: Pinturicchio, 'Pope Pius II at Ancona' (1503–1508), Piccolomini Library, Siena Cathedral, Siena, Italy/Bridgeman Images

The enthronement of Selim I
Credit: Lokman, *Hünernâme*, Ms. Hazine 1523, folio 201a, Topkapı Palace Museum, Istanbul/Bridgeman Images

Safavid depiction of the Battle of Çaldıran of 1514
Credit: fresco in Chehel Sotoun, Isfahan, Iran/imageBROKER/Alamy Stock Photo

Miniature depicting
Jesus carried by
two angels from the
minaret of the mosque
of Damascus
Credit: Lokman, *Zübdetu'
Tevarih* (1583), Topkapı
Palace Museum, Istanbul/
Bridgeman Images

Suleiman I's four-crowned helmet
Credit: engraving by Agostino Veneziano (Agostino dei Musi) (1535), Metropolitan Museum of Art, New York, 42.41.1, public domain

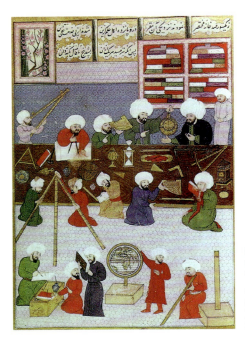

Scholars at work in the observatory of Takiyyüddin Mehmed
Credit: 'Ala ad-Din Mansur Shirazi, *Şâh-nâme*, written in honour of Sultan Murad III/ Bridgeman Images

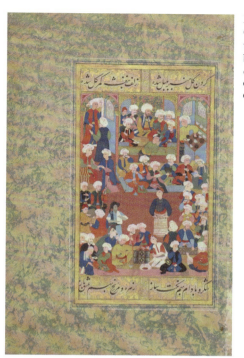

Miniature depicting an Ottoman coffeehouse. Note the boy dancer and many beardless beloveds.

Surviving portion of Piri Reis map (1513). Spain and West Africa are on the upper right. The coast of Brazil is on the lower left.

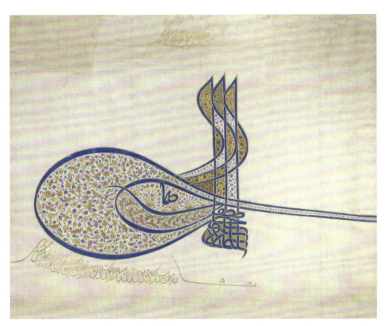

The imperial cipher (*tughra*) of Suleiman I. It reads, 'Suleiman Shah, son of Selim Shah, the ever-victorious Khan'. Drawn in blue and gold ink on paper.
Credit: The Metropolitan Museum of Art, New York, public domain

An elderly Suleiman I
Credit: miniature by Nigari,
Topkapı Palace Museum,
Istanbul/Bridgeman Images

in a sense, link them to India. With so much happening in the eastern hemisphere, it would make little sense for the Ottomans to have any interest in the West. Ottoman works analysing the Spanish conquest of the New World, such as Hasan al-Su'udi's *History of the West Indies* (1582), focused more on Ottoman strategy regarding the Portuguese in the Indian Ocean than on the Americas, and on the necessity of digging a Suez canal.[48]

FAILURES AND SUCCESSES

But neither the Suez canal nor the Don-Volga canal was realised. The failure of Sokollu Mehmed Pasha's global plans for the region stretching from Western Europe to Southeast Asia is blamed by contemporary historians on a Jewish 'culprit', Joseph Nasi.[49] Nasi is fingered for daring to propose focusing on the Mediterranean and conquering Venetian Cyprus instead. Cyprus had been a Venetian colony for nearly a century. Validated by a legal opinion from his *sheikhulislam*, Selim II in 1570 broke the peace treaty with Venice and launched an assault on the island in the eastern Mediterranean. To finance the campaign, the sultan confiscated Ottoman church lands and then made their owners buy them back at considerable profit to the imperial treasury.[50] Ottoman forces captured Nicosia in the centre of the island in 1570 and Famagusta on the east coast following a nearly yearlong siege in 1571. The victory caused a Christian alliance calling itself 'the Holy League' made up of Venice, Spain, the Knights Hospitaller, and the pope to send ships to confront the Ottomans.

Commanded by Don John of Austria, the Holy League navy met the Ottoman fleet in the Gulf of Corinth near the island of Nafpaktos (Lepanto). Involving nearly five hundred ships of war, the Battle of Lepanto on 7 October 1571 was one of the biggest naval battles to have ever taken place in the Mediterranean. The Christian forces included not only hundreds of armed warships but half a dozen large galleys fitted out with very large cannons.

The Ottoman fleet at Lepanto did not possess any of the larger ships with heavy cannons and was routed.[51] The Holy League was able to sink 200 of the Ottomans' 230 vessels.[52] It was a massacre at close quarters, turning the sea red. Over fifty thousand seamen were lost. Grand Vizier Sokollu Mehmed Pasha responded defiantly to the Venetian representative in Istanbul with a hairy metaphor: 'A cut off arm does not grow back, but a shaved beard regrows stronger than before'.[53] That winter, he rebuilt the navy and used diplomacy to undermine the Christian coalition raised against the Ottomans. In 1573, Venice surrendered Cyprus to the Ottomans. The next year, the Ottomans conquered Tunis.

By the end of the sixteenth century, most of North Africa—including Algiers, Tripoli, and Tunis—was nominally under Ottoman control. There were failures, however, such as the 1565 siege of the Knights Hospitaller on Malta, who despite Ottoman efforts were able to control traffic in the western Mediterranean. There were setbacks, such as the Battle of Lepanto, memorialised everywhere in Western Europe as a victory, including in a massive early seventeenth-century Italian painting on display at the foot of the main staircase at Ham House outside London.[54] But thanks to their century of seaborne activity, the Ottomans had reached the peak of their global political power and prosperity. The Muslim Friday sermon was now read in the Ottoman sultan's name from the Horn of Africa to Southeast Asia, and perhaps even in China. Ottoman spies, merchants, and soldiers operated from North Africa to Indonesia. The Ottoman-Habsburg battle for control of the western Mediterranean ended with a truce in 1580. Peace and prosperity were at hand.[55]

Muslims had achieved the same level of technical advances as the Portuguese and had succeeded in holding them back, making them merely one of many empires engaged in the global trade of the Indian Ocean.[56] The Ottomans had incorporated the latest Western European knowledge in maps depicting the entire, connected globe, including a separate landmass which they, too, called the New World.[57] The Ottomans had reached the extent of their naval expansion, and the Age of Discovery was over. Why should they venture west across the Atlantic Ocean? They had already achieved much in the East.

A GLOBAL AGE OF DISCOVERY

Many stereotypes about Muslims have been used to answer the question of why, despite their wealth and splendour and advanced military technology, the Ottomans (and Muslim kingdoms more generally) never 'discovered' the Americas. Or why they were never bold enough to venture west into the unknown world. Did they have no vision for world hegemony like other empires?

As a civilisational indictment, the Ottomans and other Islamic empires were assumed to be insular. The Ottomans were described by an influential modern Turkish historian as impervious to change, 'self-satisfied, inward-looking and closed to outside influences'.[58] To be 'inward-looking' was to lack intellectual curiosity about the 'other', to be adverse to change and progress, to be 'anti-modern'. The Ottomans allegedly 'never fully broke away from the values and outlook of Near Eastern culture, sanctified' by Islamic law, 'and never wished to understand the mentality' that had allowed Western European empires to rise. While European Christians sought to describe the Ottomans in objective terms, it was said, the Ottomans, 'convinced of their own religious and political superiority, closed their eyes to the outside world'. In 1580, the observatory in Istanbul, built in 1577 by the chief astrologer, astronomer Takiyyüddin Mehmed—which was considered no less advanced than the most modern in Europe— was blamed by the sheikhulislam for an outbreak of plague and razed. This fact was adduced in support of the conclusion that this meant a 'clear victory of religious fanaticism over the rational sciences'—a spectacular accusation to be inferred from one event.[59]

In this interpretation, Islam supposedly held the Ottomans back from venturing across oceans. Religion was used to explain how the West rose to global hegemony and colonised Muslim-majority societies. To explain the Ottomans' alleged lack of interest in other societies, some posited that Islam was so conservative that it hindered progress, capitalism, and the use of the printing press, and that it kept Muslims from benefiting from European scientific developments. The Ottomans were depicted as little more than warriors from Central Asia. Any adoption of Western knowledge was trivial and had no effect on their core Islamic beliefs.

Like the Romans, they were alleged to have had no interest in venturing to sea. Muslims played no role in international trade, the story went, as they apparently felt repugnance for commerce and left it in the hands of Christians and Jews or even foreigners instead. They could construct only a land-based empire grounded in an agricultural economy, not a maritime empire like that of the superior Greeks, which was based on control of commercial entrepôts and trade in commodities.

Muslims also allegedly viewed Christian Europe as 'an outer darkness of barbarism and unbelief, from which the sun-lit world of Islam had little to fear and less to learn'.[60] Although Western Europeans had long been curious about the Ottomans, the Ottomans were alleged to lack a reciprocal interest in Western European developments and ignored what was happening there, seeing even political and economic changes as irrelevant.[61] They only 'found it necessary from time to time to collect and compile some information, but until the end of the eighteenth century their information was usually superficial, often inaccurate, and almost always out of date'.[62] What kept them back was an alleged feeling of superiority, when they were anything but: 'Masked by the imposing military might of the Ottoman Empire, the peoples of Islam continued until the dawn of the modern age to cherish the conviction of the immeasurable and immutable superiority of their own civilisation to all others'.[63]

But such stereotypes are easily countered. Ottoman society was open to newcomers. For example, there was a constant stream of Western European Jews who brought to the empire new geographical and medical knowledge and translated many important works while holding positions at court from the fifteenth through the seventeenth centuries. The fact that Hebrew printing presses thrived in the Ottoman Empire in the fifteenth century is also overlooked, as if Jews were not part of Ottoman society. Islamic religion and culture did not hinder cross-cultural trade. Ottoman trade was not solely in the hands of its Christian and Jewish subjects. Ottoman Muslims traded in lands not ruled by Muslims. From the fourteenth century, Turkish merchants appeared in Byzantine Constantinople. By the fifteenth century they were engaged in international commerce in Ancona and Venice. In the sixteenth century Ottoman Muslim merchants operated in South Asia and Java. There were so many Muslim merchants in Venice in the late sixteenth century that, fearing how they were 'leading boys away, keeping company with Christian women', authorities constructed an inn to house them and laws to regulate their residency in the Venetian Republic.[64] Venice, which introduced the Jewish ghetto to Europe, was also the only city with a Muslim residential compound, the Fondaco dei Turchi, a former palazzo on the Grand Canal that included a mosque.[65]

No Ottoman religious authority hindered Ottoman subjects—neither elite nor commoner—from international trade or trading with foreigners. They did not fear 'cultural contamination' from interaction with Christians—or Hindus or Buddhists for that matter. On the contrary, Ottoman authorities regularly intervened with foreign rulers to assist and protect their subjects—Christian, Jewish, and Muslim—who traded abroad and complained of being arrested or of having their goods confiscated by local authorities.

Rather than being inward looking and conservative, Ottoman merchants like those trading in Venice introduced products and innovations that had profound effects on Ottoman cultural, economic, and social life. New innovations included changing commercial practices, agricultural activity (cultivating tobacco), culinary habits (consuming tomato paste), leisure activities (card games), and personal items (watches, clocks, eyeglasses).[66] Coffee—first brewed by Ethiopians and then consumed by Sufis in Yemen in the fifteenth century—became a global commodity in the sixteenth century after the Ottomans conquered the region, exporting the bean from the port of Mocha. The first coffeehouses opened in Mecca, Cairo, Damascus, Aleppo and then in Istanbul in the midst of the sixteenth-century seaborne expansion.[67] None other than the Ottoman grand admiral Hayreddin Barbarossa Pasha added a coffee chamber to his home in Istanbul, where 'sugary sherbets and musky coffee flowed like rivers' at his banquets.[68] One can gain a sense—or earthy smell—of the intoxicating, innovative effect of coffee by visiting the sweetest-smelling corner of Istanbul today, in the same neighbourhood where the first coffeehouse in the city was established in the mid-sixteenth century. The coffee roaster is located in the bustling alley just outside the western entrance of the Egyptian or Spice Market, where such new consumer products as coffee would have been sold. Why would the Islamic empires need to journey west when the richest and greatest states at the time were all located in the Mediterranean and the East? Intent on promoting a triumphant vision of Western hegemony, such views fail to consider the rest of the story.

The Age of Discovery was in fact an accident. Seeking to take over trade with the East, the Western European empires ended up lost in the Americas, a mishap that would fortuitously serve as a windfall funding their rise to power. From the Western European point of view, the Muslim kingdoms were an obstacle. Rather than take the direct route across the Mediterranean and Red Sea and then through the Indian Ocean to the Malabar Coast of India, centre of the world spice trade, Vasco da Gama travelled all the way down the west coast of Africa, around the cape, and then up the east coast in 1497 because the Ottomans and the Mamluk

Empire in Egypt controlled the eastern Mediterranean trade. He aimed to find a passage to India to break their monopoly. Lacking the necessary maritime knowledge, da Gama hired an Arab or Gujarati navigator in Kenya to pilot him and his crew to India. When they arrived in Calicut the next year, they were met at first by South Asians astonished that the Europeans did not know Arabic. They sent for Castilian- and Genoese-speaking Muslim Tunisians residing in Calicut who asked them what in the devil they were doing there and why they had travelled so far.[69] Da Gama was astounded, for he never imagined he would hear his language spoken so far from Portugal. He replied that he was seeking cinnamon (spices) and Christians.

When Christopher Columbus sailed west across the Atlantic Ocean in 1492, he was searching for a new route to India that bypassed the Mamluk-controlled eastern Mediterranean, and so made sure to take a translator who spoke Arabic. Columbus wrote in a letter addressed to the king and queen of Spain, 'In this present year 1492, after Your Highnesses completed the war against the Muslims who ruled in Europe'—whom he refers to as 'the enemies of the false doctrine of Muhammad'—and 'after having expelled all the Jews out of your realms and dominions . . . Your Highnesses in this same month of January commanded me to set out with a sufficient armada to the said regions of India' to 'convert the people there to our Holy Faith'.[70]

Columbus envisioned a crusading plan to gain the assistance of powerful monarchs in the East—who reportedly desired to become Christian—and together take Jerusalem, which at that time was controlled by the Mamluks, for Christendom.[71] Filled with messianic hopes, he carried a popular book of prognostication with him, and would later write his own. Approaching Cuba, he compared the silhouette of a mountain to a mosque. Judaism and Islam haunted Columbus's imagination. As Columbus knew then, 1492 witnessed interrelated events—the expulsion of the Jews, the defeat and subjugation of Granada (the last Muslim kingdom in

Spain), and the colonisation of the Americas. The latter led to the genocide of the native population and importation of African slaves to exploit the continent's wealth for Spain's enrichment.

The Spanish Christian war against Spanish Jews and Spanish Muslims to 'purify' the peninsula went hand in hand with the voyages to the Americas. Columbus's voyages were financed by confiscated Jewish and Muslim wealth. Columbus could not depart from Cádiz; he had to settle for the port of Palos (today called Palos de la Frontera) because the shipping lanes were filled with tens of thousands of fleeing Jews. They fled first to North Africa (Morocco mainly) or to Italy, and the majority continued on to the Ottoman Empire, where they reestablished their lives in the ports of Salonica (today Thessaloniki, Greece) and Istanbul. After facing burnings of holy books and forced conversions, like the Jews, the Spanish Muslims were also given the choice of baptism or expulsion. The last Muslims in Spain would be expelled over a century later, between 1609 and 1614.

Muslim ghosts haunt Spanish history. Miguel de Cervantes, who believed it would be better to die in battle than not to have fought for God and king, was wounded by the Ottomans at the Battle of Lepanto. Several years later, he was captured at sea and enslaved in Algiers. After his release he gained fame through his novel *Don Quixote* (1605–1615), a fundamental text in the Western literary canon, written as the last Muslims were expelled from Spain. Cervantes's conceit is that the history of Don Quixote he relates is a relic of the former Spanish Muslim culture, for it is from an old Arabic book written by a fictional Muslim historian found in the market in Toledo and translated by a Moor into Castilian.[72] Santiago Matamoros, Saint James the Moor-Slayer, became the patron saint of Spain after the Muslims were expelled. In churches throughout Spain, such as at Córdoba, one can view statues of him astride a horse whose hooves are crushing the heads of Muslims.

The Muslims, too, fled to North Africa and then to the Ottoman Empire, taking up abode in the very same neighbourhoods in Istanbul as the Jews, especially in Galata, where a Catholic church was converted into the 'Arab Mosque'. Just as the Jews and Muslims of Spain were subjected to forced conversion, massacre, and expulsion, so, too, would the native peoples in the Spanish colonies of the Americas face forced conversion, massacre, and genocide. But, along with the story of how fleeing Jewish, converso, and Muslim European refugees found shelter in the Ottoman Empire, becoming valued subjects in their new home—something unimaginable in the Europe they left behind—these tragic elements of the story are dropped from the triumphant version of the Age of Discovery.

Western expansion occurred overseas as Portugal, Spain, and then France, the Netherlands, and England conquered territory in the 'unknown' Atlantic world. The Ottomans, by contrast, conquered territory in the 'known' world of Europe and Asia. Despite setbacks, in a little over a century from the conquest of Constantinople the Ottomans grew into a maritime power, partly by incorporating Christian renegades into the highest ranks of their navy. Controlling sea lanes, the Ottomans enlarged their coffers by tapping into the rich vein of trade in spices and silk. Acting as custodian of the most holy Islamic pilgrimage sites, they gained legitimacy among Muslims.

At the beginning of the sixteenth century, the Portuguese aimed to control shipping routes in and out of the Red Sea, establish a monopoly over the spice trade in the Indian Ocean, defeat Mamluk Egypt, and take Jerusalem for Christendom. But it was the Ottomans who accomplished most of these goals, recapturing the third-holiest Muslim city for Islam.[73] In the sixteenth century the Ottomans became a commercial maritime power nearly comparable with Portugal and Spain. From the beginning, the Ottomans deployed an innovative, monetised political and economic system in these regions, utilising tax farms and paying officials in cash, instead of in land grants.[74] The Ottomans never established a monopoly over the spice trade, nor did they ever aim to do so.[75]

We could believe in the triumphant, dramatic narrative of Western European intellectual and cultural superiority giving rise to a curiosity to venture into the world and the subsequent oceanic voyages, discoveries, construction of colonial empires, and deserved global dominion. We could view Muslims as outsiders or hindrances to this effort, or as passive recipients of enlightened European rule. Or we can add the Ottomans to the Age of Discovery as an expanding, seaborne empire, making new discoveries of its own, growing its territory manyfold, and reaching the pinnacle of wealth and splendour.

Should we believe the Portuguese admiral Afonso de Albuquerque, duke of Goa, who reported to his king in 1513 that even the rumour of the Portuguese navy coming caused Mamluk and then Ottoman ships to vanish, deserting the Red Sea? Or should we accept the claim of Ottoman admiral Selman Reis, who reported to his government in 1525 that the Ottoman navy in the Red Sea, whose ships resembled fire-breathing dragons, was so powerful that none but those who saw the ships could believe it nor describe them, that their very existence meant the inevitable annihilation of the Portuguese navy? We were formerly inclined only to accept the first; now we may also consider the second. Both are exaggerated and display the same mindset.

In his *The Mirror of Countries*, while narrating his visit to the court of the Mughal emperor Humayun in the 1550s, the Ottoman admiral Seydi Ali relates what he had learned about China. He had been told in the Gujarati port of Surat by Ottoman Muslims that in China, diverse Muslim worshippers desired to have the Friday sermon read in the name of their own rulers. But Ottoman Muslim worshippers appealed to the khan of China, declaring that only their emperor was the custodian of Mecca and Medina. The khan, who was not a Muslim, agreed, decreeing that the sermon could be read only in the name of the Ottoman sultan. The Ottoman dynasty was apparently recognised as the suzerain of all Muslim communities stretching from Istanbul to China. Impressed by the story, the Mughal emperor addressed Sultan Suleiman I as 'Caliph of the World'.[76] Such a title would not have been bestowed had it not been for Ottoman efforts establishing themselves as a seaborne empire in the Age of Discovery.

10

NO WAY LIKE THE 'OTTOMAN WAY'

I N JUST TWO and a half centuries, from the turn of the four-teenth century to the middle of the sixteenth century, the Ot-toman dynasty had progressed from nomadic chieftains to settled princes to rulers of a globe-girdling empire that stretched from Algeria in the western Mediterranean through the Middle East, and even had influence on the Indian Ocean basin to Sumatra. By the middle of the sixteenth century, the Ottomans had asserted their own vision of empire. One artefact from that century conveys what the dynasty had become.

The British Museum in London owns an outstanding example of the 'caliph of the world' Suleiman I's calligraphic seal, the *tughra*. The imperial monogram reads, 'Suleiman Shah, son of Selim Shah, the ever-victorious Khan'.[1] The rest of the document is missing, but the fact that the cipher itself has a height of 45.5 cm and a width of 61.5 cm means that it was part of a very large scroll. Written in interlocking Arabic letters in cobalt blue and gold ink, forming a three-dimensional, glittering whole, it is a stunning work of art and expression of power.

Like gold-tipped Ottoman battle standards, the seal has three blue lines rising on the right, ending in loops filled in with gold. They are held up by a base made of the name 'Suleiman'. Wrapped with curling lines forming an aigrette, the three vertical lines in turn form the base for a giant, battle-helmet-shaped blue loop, racing off to the left. A short, curved dagger leads out to the right. Bold, energetic, swirling, whirling circles and cords of gold and blue flowers fill in the loops and lines. Split palmettes, carnations, lotuses, pomegranates, tulips, roses, and hyacinths dance across the interior of the tughra, forming a spiralling, golden nautilus shell.

The nautilus is the symbol of expansion. Nautilus shell, flowers, dagger, battle helmet, aigrette, battle standard, and gold, the cipher is the concise, beautiful expression of a confident military power and sophisticated culture. It resembles musical notes written in priceless, golden letters. The sultan, represented by the letters of his name, encircles myriad flowers representing the diverse parts and peoples of his kingdom, all under his control, the conductor of a grand orchestra.

The cipher is the symbol of what it meant to be an Ottoman in the sixteenth century, the special characteristics that defined the ruling class, why their armies were so successful, and what their sources of manpower were. Converting enemies into cogs in their military machine, the Ottoman rulers expanded their territory fast, conquering much of the former Roman Empire, their success enabled by their unique political organisation. Central to their distinctive imperial vision and way of life was their use of conversion-based meritocracy as a way to absorb and integrate enemies, an imperial feature esteemed by European observers.

This 'Ottoman Way', first described by a diplomat from the Holy Roman Empire, was articulated in class structure, language, law, culture, and ideology. Society was divided into the *askeri* (the military and the sultan's salaried servants or holders of fiefs), *reaya* (commoners and tax-paying subjects), and slave classes. A centrepiece of the system was the *timar*, a land grant allowing the holder to keep the revenue on the goods produced on that land in exchange for the responsibility of raising a mounted military force to serve the sultan when called to battle. The empire was also based on a gendered religious hierarchy of long-standing Islamic precedent, wherein Muslims were favoured over Christians and Jews, men were advantaged over women, and the free were privileged over slaves. Westerners (Rûmis or Romans) were preferred to easterners. Yet the social order was flexible. Christians and Jews could become Muslim; slaves could be freed. Women could rise in station, especially through dynastic marriage or becoming childbearing concubines to the sultan. The Ottomans created a new language, a composite of Arabic, Persian, and Turkish grammar and vocabulary, written in modified Persian script. This was the language of administration and culture, especially poetry. The Ottoman Way was also expressed in law, as chancellor Celalzade Mustafa and head of the religious establishment Sheikhulislam Ebussuud Efendi harmonised secular law (*kanun*), based on custom and sultanic decree, and religious law (Sharia) so as to fit the empire's aims. It was another example of how the Ottomans had long subordinated religious authority to imperial authority and had made secular law equivalent in force to religious law. Ottoman culture was expressed in textile and ceramic art and mosque architecture by Collection recruits in court workshops, including the great architect Sinan, famous for his mosques built for Suleiman I and Selim II.

Ottoman ideology in that age rested on several pillars. One was a meritocracy that balanced and properly utilised the diverse human resources at the empire's disposal. That in turn reflected how the Ottomans created an 'empire of difference' that tolerated, rather than sought to erase, diversity—as realised, for example, by granting Armenians, Greeks, Jews, and Muslims their own law courts, judges, and the ability to adjudicate marriage, divorce, inheritance, and so on according to their own religion.[2] A third pillar was projecting Ottoman power and might both in Muslim-majority Eurasia and in Christian Europe, best articulated by Suleiman I's mosque built on the highest hill in Istanbul.

The magnificent structure expresses Ottoman wealth, power, piety, and harmony.

CONVERSION AS INTEGRATION: FORGING KEY ELEMENTS OF THE RULING ELITE THROUGH MERITOCRACY

The Ottomans rose to world prominence in part due to their unique way of forging an elite through conversion to Islam. Visiting foreign dignitaries remarked upon the praiseworthy qualities of Ottoman society, composing favourable accounts of the Ottomans in order to critique their own societies and exaggerating the positive aspects of the Ottoman administration and military so as to galvanise other European powers to meet the Ottoman threat.

Ogier Ghiselin de Busbecq (in office 1555–1562), the Holy Roman Empire's ambassador to the Ottoman court, praised the rival empire for being a meritocracy where no man 'owed his dignity to anything but his personal merits and bravery; no one is distinguished from the rest by his birth, and honour is paid to each man according to the nature of the duty and offices which he discharges'.[3] Each man was rewarded according to what he deserved, and government positions were filled by men suited for them. Every subject of the sultan had the opportunity to rise to the top. Busbecq found that the sultan's highest officeholders were often men of the lowest birth—shepherds and herdsmen. Because the Ottomans valued good training and hard work rather than high birth, Busbecq concluded, they succeeded in everything and expanded the boundaries of their dominion day by day.[4]

Visiting the court of Suleiman I when thousands of cavalrymen and Janissaries were present, Busbecq gushed as he looked upon all the turbaned heads wrapped in bright white silk. He was dazzled by the brilliance of gold and silver, silk and satin, later describing it as the most beautiful spectacle he had ever seen. The assembly was the sultan's cipher in human form. Yet despite the display of luxury, he found modesty, too, as every man had the same form of dress despite being different in rank, with no wasteful frippery. What impressed the ambassador the most in that great crowd of soldiers was their absolute silence and discipline. The thousands of Janissaries stood so motionless that he thought they were statues until they all bowed to him simultaneously.

While allowing for the fact that Busbecq used his praise of the Ottomans as a way to criticise the perceived faults of his own society and thus to shame it, he described the idealised Ottoman Way, which was so different from what prevailed in the rest of Europe. While there the elite was made up of blue blood—local, noble families—the Ottomans created much of their own elite from deracinated slaves. The Ottoman Way was grounded in the creation of a loyal class of administrators and soldiers through the Collection, the system in which boys were recruited in conquered territories, brought to the imperial centre, converted to Islam, trained in the palace, and given positions based on their natural abilities.

Busbecq did not realise it, but girls were also recruited in this fashion from conquered territories to be made into Ottomans in the palace. Converted Christian princesses and slaves became the leading women of the royal family. Girls were brought to the imperial centre—first to the Old Palace after 1453, and then from the mid-sixteenth century to the women's harem in Topkapı Palace—converted to Islam, and educated. They followed a system of apprenticeship, promotion, and ranks. The recruited slave women were taught literacy, how to be Muslim, and to sing, dance, play musical instruments, tell stories, and embroider. Converted slaves taught to forget their past competed with each other to rise in the ranks and serve the dynasty.

Just as European eunuchs strictly policed every aspect of the pages' lives in the sultan's palace, so, too, did African eunuchs enforce a strict code of conduct over the women recruits in the harem. Many of these women were married to pages when they left the palace, or to administrators. If they became concubines to the sultan, they could give birth to princes, raising their sons in the provinces and readying them for the day when they, too, would sit on the throne.

This elaborate system of recruitment shows how the Ottomans, unlike their Western European rivals—so intent on 'purifying' their realms of all religious minorities—viewed the people they ruled as potential cogs in the machine. Their diverse subject peoples were raw material that could be perfected to serve the needs of the empire as it dissolved and integrated formerly powerful dynasties. By the sixteenth century, the palace recruits were most often converted sons of Christian peasants—first mainly of Greek and Bosnian origin, then of Albanian, and later of Circassian, Abkhazian, and Georgian background, raised in the palace to be a loyal corps of soldiers and statesmen without ties to existing nobility.

The system was not as perfect as Busbecq described.[5] Recruits remembered their homelands. Sokollu Mehmed Pasha, a grand vizier born in Bosnia of Serbian origin, would build the famous bridge over the Drina river in Višegrad and restored the Serbian Patriarchate of Peć.[6] Recruits retained their languages and dress. They maintained relations with family members, ensuring that relatives also rose in the administration or military. There was vicious competition between recruits from Southeastern Europe (Albania and Bosnia) and those from the Caucasus (Abkhazia, Circassia, and Georgia). There was also rivalry between Albanian and Bosnian factions in the administration and military. A Bosnian-origin intellectual depicted Albanians as rebellious, cowardly, stubborn, ignorant, violent, and ugly.[7] Such group competition created ethnic stereotypes: Albanians were impulsively violent, Abkhaz were masturbating simpletons, and Circassians were filthy thieves. The Collection was established to hinder men of the same origins from going beyond expressions of solidarity to foment rebellion, from becoming more loyal to their ethnic group than to the sultan.

Istanbul during Suleiman I's reign became one of the largest cities in Europe, with as many as 350,000 inhabitants, one-third of whom were Christian.[8] As noted earlier, Suleiman I welcomed Jews and Muslims who had been forcibly converted to Catholicism in Spain; they settled in the same neighbourhood in Galata as the Roman Catholics.[9] Each district in Istanbul took on a particular ethno-religious character, although most neighbourhoods had diverse populations. There were no ghettoes as in Christian Europe. By the end of the seventeenth century, Istanbul had an estimated population of half a million, including 210,000 Christians and 40,000 Jews.[10]

Thus Istanbul was a microcosm of the empire, a veritable alphabet of diversity: Abkhaz, Albanian, Arab, Armenian, Ashkenazi, and Austrian; Bosnian and Bulgarian; Catalan, Circassian, Cordovan, Crimean, and Croatian; Dalmatian; Egyptian; French; Georgian, German, and Greek; Hungarian; Indian, Iranian, Iraqi, and Italian; Jewish; Karaite and Kurdish; Laz; Macedonian and Moldovan; Palestinian, Polish, and Portuguese; Ragusan, Roma, Romaniot, and Russian; Sephardic, Serbian, Sicilian, Spanish, Sudanese, and Syrian; Tatar, Turcoman, and Turkish; Uzbek; Venetian and Vlach; Wallachian and Western European; Yemeni; and Zaza. And for O, there were the Ottomans, who transcended all national and ethnic categories.

IMPERIAL SYNTHESIS:
SECULAR LAW AND ISLAMIC LAW

The sheikhulislam—formerly the mufti of Istanbul, the leading jurisconsult—gave legal opinions on juridical questions concerning conformity of political decisions with Islamic law. Under Ebussuud Efendi, who held the position under Suleiman I and Selim II, the sheikhulislam became the head of the entire religious hierarchy, making all pedagogical and judicial appointments. He was like a Christian patriarch. Nothing like it had been seen in

Islamic history. Just as the grand vizier was the sultan's deputy executing political authority for him, the sheikhulislam was his deputy executing religious authority in his name. The sheikhulislam made all nominations to religious posts, appointed judgeships, and sat atop a system of promotion. The mufti of Istanbul had been an independent figure, but the sheikhulislam was made part of the imperial administration, head of the religious class.

Religious law became an arm of sultanic power, legitimising practices or actions that violated Islamic law. The Collection should not have been allowed, as it entailed enslaving the ruler's subjects and forcibly converting them to Islam. Likewise, the slave status of the ruling class, not merely the soldiers, was also unusual.

Ebussuud Efendi declared that rent-producing properties endowed with cash, a moveable good, were licit, contrary to the view of practically any other Muslim scholar. The interest paid the salaries of preachers and filled the pockets of the endower, which should have been illegal due to the prohibition on interest. Ebussuud Efendi rationalised that it was customary practice, as it was by then the prevailing mode of endowment, and that it was good for prosperity, although it was rare before the Ottoman age.[11] The sheikhulislam found legal grounds to permit the launch of the siege of Cyprus in 1570, which violated a peace treaty to which the Ottomans had agreed. He justified the massacres of Shi'is and Yazidis in eastern Anatolia on the grounds that they were unbelievers.[12] He legalised taxes on wine and pork. He manufactured legal fictions to allow Jews to build or repair their houses of worship that by the usual interpretation of Islamic law should have been destroyed. This was yet another example of the sheikhulislam creating the legal basis for imperial rule, even when it went against Islamic law and custom.

Suleiman I ordered Sheikhulislam Ebussuud Efendi and Chancellor Celalzade Mustafa to align Islamic law and secular canon law. Ebussuud Efendi centralised the religious institution as Celalzade Mustafa bureaucratised the civil administration. Through the laws and regulations enacted under Celalzade Mustafa's supervision, the basic institutions of the imperial system received final form and were systematically applied. This entailed collecting and codifying canon law codes to compile a comprehensive and coherent body of legislation. The aim was to establish consistency in principle and resolve conflicts of practice as the 'sheikhulislam of canon law'.[13] The legitimisation of dynastic law was a central element in the consolidation of the empire and its bureaucracy. Suleiman I began to be referred to as 'the lawgiver'.

Christian Europeans may have developed secular institutions in the seventeenth century, but as we see during the reign of Suleiman I, the Ottomans had already made religious authority secondary to sultanic authority and had made secular law equivalent in force to religious law. They were ahead of all other Christian and Islamic polities in this regard. But sultans remained vigorous proponents of Islam.

SULEIMAN I'S PIETY: A MOSQUE
BEFITTING THE FIRST OTTOMAN CALIPH

At the end of Suleiman I's reign, the emperor turned to a life of religious devotion. By that point, the Ottomans had unified administration, aesthetic taste, and secular and religious expression, and had fashioned them in their own unique way. Their robes of honour, monumental mosques, carpets, ceramics used in public banquets, and the sultan's cipher all projected the image the Ottomans desired: they were grand, yet devout. The Suleimaniye Mosque complex, built in Istanbul from 1550 to 1557, displays a mature architectural synthesis, decorated with the best products of the imperial workshops.

Just as Holy Roman Emperor Charles V ended his days retired in a monastery, by 1550, thirty years into his reign, Suleiman I turned away from ecstatic messianic claims and apocalypticism—as well as from his former appreciation for sumptuous textiles,

gold, jewels, wine, and music—and turned instead to piety.[14] The
sultan opposed the importation of luxury goods and the use of
ornament. Thereafter dressing modestly and no longer practising
goldsmithing, Suleiman I opposed figural images and the display of jewels and gilding on religious architecture. The melancholy sultan ordered musical instruments destroyed, stripped his
private apartments of all luxury, and began to wear only green
woolen vests, as Muhammad reportedly had. The tapestry depicting Charles V went into storage. According to the Habsburg
ambassador, the sultan's expression in 1555 was 'anything but
smiling, and has a sternness which, although sad, is full of majesty'.[15] The Treaty of Amasya that same year ended the ruinous
struggle with the Safavids, providing a stable eastern frontier and
dampening the likelihood of Shi'i-inspired deviant dervish uprisings in the realm. The last years of Suleiman I's reign were increasingly shaped by the Sunni-Shi'i split, when his court turned from
ecstatic belief in the end-time and Day of Judgement to a Sunnism
we would recognise today. From the 1540s, Suleiman I considered
himself sultan and caliph, which would be the standard title for
Ottoman rulers thereafter.[16]

The Safavids also converted from religious extremists and ecstatic believers in the impending end of history to Shi'is recognisable to their descendants today. Suleiman I's contemporary Shah
Tahmasp—son and successor to Shah Ismail I and a great painter
and calligrapher—also spent the end of his reign in pious contemplation following the establishment of peaceful relations with the
Ottomans.

From 1550, standardised Ottoman fashions emerged. The
royal textile workshop made its own ceremonial robes. A new,
non-figural floral Ottoman ceramic industry came into being, its
workshops in the hands of Collection recruits. Palace-trained recruits produced the distinct imperial Ottoman artistic and architectural style. The centralised Ottoman system produced its own
masters from within. Beginning in 1538, the chief architect was

Sinan, an Armenian Collection recruit from Kayseri in central Anatolia. Collection recruits in the service of Suleiman I created Ottoman designs, distinct from Persian, Turcoman, and European precedents, that would be the model for future generations, especially in mosque building. Taste was not imported but spread outward throughout the domains of the empire from the centre.

Suleiman I's turn towards Sunni piety was best articulated in his mosque complex. The magnificent structure expresses Ottoman wealth, power, and religiosity. He constructed it as a crown for the city, capping its highest hill. Rising after the signing of peace treaties with the Habsburgs (1547) and Safavids (1555), appearing as a sign of Sunni Islam's apparent victory over Catholicism and Shi'ism, the mosque is grave, austere, and imperial.[17] Replete with a soaring dome, it propagated the magnificence of Suleiman I and his dynasty.

The monumental Suleimaniye complex is a grand city within the city, where a Sunni Muslim could fulfil his social, religious, educational, economic, and bodily purposes—to pray, study, learn, heal, sleep, eat, drink, relieve himself, bathe, trade, and shop. It has Suleiman I's mosque at its centre, surrounded by a tomb for the sultan and one for his wife, Hürrem Sultan (died 1558), as well as another for its architect, Sinan. The other buildings include law schools, a medical school, a school for studying the sayings of Muhammad, a Qur'an school for children, a hospital, a hostel, a soup kitchen, a public bath, fountains, latrines, a caravanserai, and shops. From the grassy knoll beside the mosque, one looks down upon the Bosporus, green-grey as a moss-covered ship's iron. The sultan's mosque complex provided for all of his Muslim subjects' spiritual and physical needs for posterity, reflecting the idea that the sultan is the star at the centre of the Ottoman universe.

The mosque complex was given Sunni Islamic as well as biblical meaning. Suleiman I's mausoleum is similar to the Dome of the Rock in Jerusalem, which stands atop Solomon's Temple

(Suleiman I was called 'the Solomon of the age').[18] The mosque was modelled on Hagia Sophia, which had been built as the 'new Solomonic temple', its first builder, the emperor Justinian, declaring, 'Solomon, I have surpassed you'![19] Just as Justinian brought marble columns from the Temple of Jupiter in Baalbek to build the Hagia Sophia, so, too, did Suleiman I ship a column from the same place, which Muslims referred to as a palace Solomon made for the Queen of Sheba. While the mosque connected Suleiman I to his biblical namesake, its inscriptions likened the four columns that support the central dome to the four Sunni caliphs— Abu Bakr, Umar, Uthman, and Ali (the first three cursed by Shi'i Muslims)—and the mosque itself as the Ka'ba, the Muslims' most sacred site on earth.[20] A piece of the Ka'ba's black stone was set into the gate of the sultan's tomb.

The mosque's inscriptions also promote an imperial Sunni Islam. The foundation's inscription, composed by Ebussuud Efendi, articulates the sultan's God-given right to rule, his role as defender of Sunni Islam and Islamic law, and his position as a just ruler declaring and codifying secular law. It declares that the mosque is the site for continual public prayer, reflecting the emphasis in the second part of Suleiman I's reign on conformity to normative Sunni Islam, replacing his earlier eschatological beliefs. The rest of the mosque inscriptions, which all come from the Qur'an, refer to the ritual duties required of Sunni Muslims.[21] 'There is no God save God and Muhammad is God's messenger', the Sunni profession of faith, is inscribed on the main entrance to the mosque's courtyard.

Ottoman mosques built prior to the conquest of Constantinople boasted inscriptions not only from the Qur'an but also from the sayings of Muhammad and Persian poetry, and had many references to Ali, the pivot upon whom Shi'i Islam is based. But the Suleimaniye Mosque is arranged so as to condemn Shi'ism and the Safavids as false and to promote normative Sunni Islam as the true faith, enforced by the caliph and lawgiver, Suleiman I.

Travelling to campaign against the Safavids in 1534 and 1548, Suleiman I had visited the shrines of deviant dervishes in Anatolia.[22] At the shrine of Seyyid Gazi in northwest Anatolia, Suleiman I visited the tomb, giving alms to the barefoot, half-naked, tattooed itinerant dervishes with self-inflicted burn wounds and shaved heads. He spoke with men 'chained with iron chains like hunted lions, fastened with yokes on their necks like camels, and wearing nose-rings', some of whom were intoxicated by hashish.[23] A decade later, Suleiman I turned against such Sufis and their practices, taking their shrines away from them.

During the later years of Suleiman I's reign, when his mosque complex was constructed, Sufi lodges were converted into madrasas and the sultan promoted the empire's centrally controlled religious class and normative Sunni Islam at the expense of the Islam of deviant dervishes, including the persistent followers of Sheikh Bedreddin. The Janissaries also tried to distance themselves from the practices of deviant Sufis, such as we see in a petition to Suleiman I in the mid-1550s, proclaiming, 'Unlike the Janissaries of old times, we do not indulge in wine, women and young boys'. Instead, 'we perform our canonical prayers five times a day and constantly pray for you'.[24]

The Bektaşis, with whom the Janissaries had been intimately linked since the age of Murad I, were also transformed in this era from a deviant dervish group to a reputable Sufi order. At the beginning of the sixteenth century, Bektaşis shaved their hair and beards, were devoted to Ali and his sons Hasan and Hussein, dressed in felt, and travelled about chanting prayers, banging drums and tambourines, and claiming to be saints. They wore caps symbolising heads, as they were 'beheaded dead people', meaning that they had already killed their egos.[25] But by the mid-sixteenth century the group had transformed themselves into a mainstream Sufi order that absorbed other deviant dervish groups—Kalenderis (or Torlaks), Haydaris, and Abdals of Rûm—who had openly articulated Shi'i beliefs, as well as their lodges and their tombs. While other groups of dervishes were pressured to disappear, the Bektaşis thrived because they were tied to the Janissaries, who saw Hajji Bektaş as their patron saint.[26] As a way to gain control of the radical Sufis in the realm, the dynasty had incorporated the Bektaşis into a key imperial institution—its military elite.

The Mevlevis, by contrast, had been attached to the political elite from the beginning. They were politically passive and dependent on Ottoman patronage. The sheikhulislam approved every sheikh chosen by the head of the order: the grand çelebi in Konya, a descendant of Rûmi who girded the sultan at enthronements. Suleiman I built a hall for whirling meditation and a mosque at the Mevlevi complex in Konya, and a marble sarcophagus for Rûmi. The sultan's Sunni piety allowed only for the toleration of obedient dervishes.

SULEIMAN I: GOD'S SHADOW ON EARTH

For Friday prayers, Suleiman I paraded through the streets of Istanbul to his mosque, preceded by thousands of silent, marching Janissaries, administrative officials on horseback, and good-looking palace pages. All along the route, massive crowds bowed their heads in grave silence when seeing the normally hidden sultan. According to an eyewitness, the French ambassador to Istanbul, 'a single glance from [the sultan], as from Medusa, would transform men into marble or silent fish, for they hold the very firm opinion that their lord is the shadow and the breath of God on earth'.[27] The only sound heard was that of horse hooves hitting cobblestone streets. The day before, the sultan's horse would be held aloft by ropes and denied food, so as to guarantee it would trot carefully, with a measured gait.

Like his intricate imperial cipher, Suleiman I's mosque, built of material and by craftsmen assembled from diverse parts of his realm, was the expression of wealth and power. It demonstrated his control over vast territories and peoples, the spoils acquired through victorious military campaigns, and his ability to command it all in the name of religion and empire. Court ceremony demanded complete silence when the sultan appeared in public. The sultan and those around him used a unique sign language to express their wishes and commands. In the presence of thousands of troops and officials, silence conveyed the status of the ruler, leaving foreign visitors in awe of his apparently complete power over his servants.

Ambassador Busbecq, who witnessed a silent and disciplined assembly of Janissaries gathered before the sultan, warned Charles V that his empire had much to fear from the Ottomans. He depicted their enemy as having all the resources of a powerful empire, its strength unbroken, its soldiery experienced in warfare, its army unified and disciplined.[28] The Habsburgs, by contrast, were weak and lacked spirit. Their army was neither hardy nor well trained. Their soldiers were disobedient, and the officers were greedy, without discipline, reckless, drunk, and debauched. For Busbecq, worst of all, the Ottomans were accustomed to victory, while the Habsburgs were used to defeat. He trembled to think what the future would bring when he compared the Ottoman system with his own.

But Busbecq's European compatriots paid little heed. They were more interested in gossip about the sultan's personal life. They were especially curious about the women of the harem. Long misunderstood, the institution of the harem, how it developed, and the women and eunuchs of the palace deserve closer scrutiny. Within the empire's social hierarchies, gender, too, could be a path to social mobility—and a source of upheaval when those social hierarchies were overturned, particularly in the home of the sultan. It was events in Suleiman's private life that caused him to turn to piety in the second half of his reign.

HAREM MEANS HOME

O TTOMAN HISTORY WAS not made by men alone. The politics of reproduction played a crucial role in Ottoman history. To understand this, however, we must reassess our notions of what politics and the political are. Normally one speaks of politics as being played out in public. The private realm is excluded from consideration. But the distinction between public and private is not helpful here. If *harem* means "home" and that home is the home of the sultan and his family, then the private is most assuredly political, for decisions made in his home had repercussions for the entire empire.[1] The women in the harem were educated and politically ambitious. Far from being a purely domestic space, the harem was a political centre filled with powerful women, reflecting the Ottomans' Turco-Mongol heritage. Pre-Islamic Turcoman society, as depicted in folk epics—many of which are devoted to manly warriors—contains many stories of women who were also fearsome combatants, swift horse riders, and political players. The Ottoman harem was anything but the lascivious fantasyland depicted in the West. The majority of its inhabitants had no sexual relations with the sultan. It was more akin to a convent, with rigid rules of behaviour based on notions of sexual propriety, all with the aim of ensuring the continuity of the dynasty.

The politics of reproduction in the Ottoman Empire passed through different stages.[2] In the fourteenth and fifteenth centuries, the Ottoman sultans usually married Christian (especially Greek and Serbian) and Muslim (Central Asian and Turcoman) princesses. This was a means of forging political alliances or dissolving conquered dynasties. But rather than allowing the sultan to produce offspring with his wives, the dynasty preferred him to have an unlimited number of Christian and Muslim concubines for childbearing purposes. The aim was to prevent entangling alliances with formerly or potentially powerful families. By the mid-fifteenth century, sultans no longer even entered into childless marriages. For whereas married, free Muslim women had the right to children and sexual satisfaction from their husband, concubines, who were legally slaves, had no such rights. As in the Seljuk harem, the dynasty adopted a 'one mother, one son' policy. A concubine who had given birth to a male heir was no longer allowed to be a sexual partner of the sultan. Or, at least, if she was still intimate with the sultan, she was required to use birth control—usually intravaginal suppositories made of herbs, spices, and plant essences—and abortion to ensure no more children. Roles of royal consort and mother were distinguished. The mother of a sultan's son and other post-sexual women, including the *valide sultan* (mother of the sultan), had the highest status in the harem.

From the mid-fourteenth century to the end of the sixteenth century, the mother and son, when he reached the age of eighteen, were sent to a princely apprenticeship in Amasya, Konya, Kütahya, or Manisa, former capitals of vanquished rival Muslim principalities and dynasties, where the prince served as governor and commander, learning the arts of war and governance under his mother's tutelage. It was a reflection of the Mongol legacy, in which senior women commanded soldiers in war, although the prince was also assigned an administrator as tutor. The role of the Ottoman mother was not as impressive as that of her Safavid counterparts, who went to war, although not without tragedy—one of Shah Ismail I's wives was captured by Selim I in 1514 and given as booty to one of his officers. Upon the news of the death of his father, the sultan, the prince and his mother raced to Istanbul to proclaim him as the next ruler. The son who defeated his other brothers in combat or outmanoeuvred them to be the first proclaimed as sultan rose to the top. His mother was determined to ensure this happened. Until the end of the sixteenth century, succession was accompanied by fratricide. Upon being enthroned, the new sultan killed all potential rival male claimants—brothers, nephews, cousins, and uncles—wiping out all branches of the dynasty that were not his own. Sultans were not above having unfavoured sons murdered to allow an easier succession for their favourite. The Ottomans maintained the Mongol tradition of giving all sons equal claim to sovereignty, while utilising fratricide to ensure that the ruler, once enthroned, went unchallenged. A new phase began, however, with the life of Suleiman I's love, Hürrem Sultan.

SULEIMAN I'S TWO LOVES IN THE PALACE: HÜRREM SULTAN AND IBRAHIM PASHA

Europeans were fascinated by the woman they knew as Roxelana, 'the maiden from Ruthenia' in western Ukraine, then part of the Commonwealth of Poland-Lithuania.[3] A bronze statue of her stands in Rohatyn, Ukraine, allegedly her birthplace, where everyone in her family, including her priest father, was supposedly killed by Muslim slave raiders. The teenager was seized by Crimean Tatar slavers, who were given the monopoly in slave trading after Mehmed II conquered Constantinople. Their raids into Poland, Ukraine, and Russia netted millions of slaves, a huge source of tax revenue for the Ottomans. Roxelana, like the others, was subject to physical abuse, marched on foot in chains from her homeland to the Crimean peninsula, and was sent by boat to

Istanbul, centre of the east Mediterranean slave trade. Many of these captives converted to Islam during the journey to Istanbul, hoping it might improve their plight.[4]

Arriving in Istanbul, Roxelana faced a gender-segregated world. Passing a virginity check, she was purchased at the slave market for the harem, perhaps a 'gift' given to Suleiman I at his enthronement in 1520. After converting her to Islam, the Ottomans knew her by her Muslim name, Hürrem. Just as the Ottomans entrusted their administration and military elite to deracinated slave boys, so, too, did they entrust their royal family to slave girls. They only trusted those they could raise themselves to be absolutely loyal to serving the dynasty and its interests.

At that time, the harem—the home of royal women, concubines, and children—was located in the Old Palace in the centre of Istanbul, which was also the school for female slaves being instructed to become Ottomans. The sultan, his administration, and male recruits educated for the bureaucracy and military lived in the New Palace, Topkapı Palace, at the tip of the peninsula. Eunuchs, considered neither male nor female, served in both palaces. Princesses were married to men of state. These were unions of elite women and men, all of whom began as humble slaves. Hürrem was sent to the Old Palace. As the slave of the sultan, she would be freed after he died if she bore him a child.

Haseki sultan (favourite concubines) like herself were given only one sexual-political role. No matter how many daughters she bore, once a concubine bore a male child to a prince or sultan she was no longer allowed sexual relations with the father. One concubine, one son. Her duty was to train the son to rule and to do everything in her power to place him on the throne. For if he did not become sultan, he would be killed and she would be retired from sexual and political life. The way to become sultan was to defeat all the other princes in battle upon the demise of their father. Once victorious, the new sultan would have all his remaining male relatives put to death.

But Suleiman I kept calling Hürrem to his bed. She kept bearing sons. Mehmed in 1521. Selim in 1524. Bayezid in 1525.[5] In 1525, the Janissaries rebelled and trashed the Jewish Quarter as well as Grand Vizier Ibrahim Pasha's residence, signs of their anger towards the sultan, as Suleiman I had gone against two centuries of customary practice. In their view, he spent too much time hunting and with Hürrem, rather than waging war and acquiring human and material booty.

Already in 1515 before he became sultan, Suleiman I's previous favourite concubine, Mahidevran, had given birth to his son and presumed successor, the popular Mustafa, who was supported by the Janissaries. But Hürrem Sultan overcame that disadvantage by breaking precedent and marrying the sultan in 1534. Their union was celebrated publicly two years later in a lavish spectacle complete with marching giraffes.[6] It was the first sultanic marriage in nearly a century. This meant that Suleiman I had freed her. To free her and then have sex without marrying her would have been considered adultery. In another break with precedent, Hürrem Sultan then moved from the Old Palace, residence and school for royal women slaves and their children, to the all-male Topkapı Palace, royal residence, seat of Ottoman power and government, and training ground for male slaves.

Other than the concubines who had temporarily stayed in a suite of rooms known as the Hall of Maidens to sleep with the sultan, she was the first woman to reside in Topkapı Palace. The women's harem thereafter became a key Ottoman institution within the palace. The harem was located alongside the second and third courts, with access, to those so privileged, from either court. As it developed over the centuries, it would contain mosques, baths, pools, courtyards, gardens, a throne room, the privy chamber (private bedroom) of the sultan, and the apartments of his wives and concubines. What was new in Hürrem's time was that royal women went from being segregated in another palace across town to residing at the literal and symbolic innermost core of Ottoman political power and exalted authority, formerly a privilege for men alone, with its own male harem of palace pages. The imperial harem, with its separate male and female halves, became the centre of the dynasty and empire. This had been the practice in the palace of the Byzantine emperor, where the *gynaeceum* served as the female apartments, as well as in the palace of the Seljuk Sultanate of Rûm, a Mongol vassal.

Hürrem Sultan became one of Suleiman I's most trusted advisors. Many, such as the Janissaries, opposed her rise. They referred to her as an evil sorceress who had bewitched the sultan. Otherwise, why would he agree to these changes that upended the social hierarchy? Why would he forsake his favoured son Mustafa and his mother, Mahidevran, governing in Manisa, when Hürrem did not accompany her sons to the provinces when they turned eighteen?

Observers were also concerned about Suleiman I's other love, Ibrahim Pasha, whose trajectory in many ways paralleled Hürrem Sultan's rise to power. Just as her life story puts a face to the idea of the harem, so, too, does Ibrahim Pasha's biography allow us to see the individual journey of a male slave from obscurity to towering influence.

The pages of the school in Topkapı Palace were the beloved boys of the sultan's court. Sultans preferred garden parties with pleasant, witty, refined conversation with their gentlemen-in-waiting—and beautiful boys—accompanied by wine, music, and recitations of poetry. Love defined the relationship between the sultan and his patronage-dependent courtiers as well; these less powerful men tried to win his favour in the way a lover tries to gain the attention of his beloved. They submitted to a capricious tyrant and gained their desires through flattery as supplicants to the dominant master. The sultan was the ultimate beloved whom everyone was trying to woo.[7] At the same time, the sultan's male servants were his slaves, recruited from his Christian subjects, captured as prisoners of war, or purchased abroad. The women of his harem were likewise his Christian-born slaves. Suleiman I is remembered for his passion for two of his slaves: for his beloved Ibrahim when the sultan was a hot-blooded youth, and for his beloved Hürrem when he was mature. He was a man dominated by his passions and his loves.

Handsome Ibrahim was the Greek slave who entered palace service and became young Prince Suleiman's intimate friend and companion. Ibrahim Pasha is referred to as 'the favourite' for good reason.[8] He was born a Venetian subject in Parga, opposite Corfu, on the coast of Epirus in northwest Greece. Captured as a young boy and sold into slavery to the household of a wealthy military official, Ibrahim was presented as a gift to Prince Suleiman, who was the same age. Like Hoja and his slave in *The White Castle*, Suleiman and Ibrahim became inseparable; they were like one person.[9] When Suleiman acceded to the throne in 1520, he appointed Ibrahim chief of the sultan's privy chamber, guaranteeing him the most intimate access to the most powerful man in the realm. It was reported that they slept together in the same bed.[10]

The following year, appropriating the Roman imperial past by revitalising Istanbul's ceremonial core, the sultan built Ibrahim Pasha a sumptuous palace on the ancient Hippodrome, Istanbul's main forum just outside the Hagia Sophia and Topkapı Palace. The large public space became the new site of dynastic celebrations, including Ibrahim Pasha's two-week-long marriage festival in 1524, replete with the captured tents of the foreign rulers the Ottomans had defeated in combat. He wedded a bride name Muhsine from one of the wealthiest families in the city. Her grandfather was a convert to Islam who had established the first lodge of Rûmi's Mevlevi order of Sufis in the capital.[11] Yet despite being married and residing in his own palace, Ibrahim sometimes spent the night with Suleiman I at Topkapı Palace. The sultan could sleep at Ibrahim Pasha's lodgings as well.

Like the sultan, Ibrahim Pasha was devoted to beloved boys. A poet poked fun of his devotion with the couplet, 'It's not clear who is ruled and who rules these days / It's a wedding feast, so who is dancing and who plays?'[12] Although ostensibly concerning a boyfriend of Ibrahim Pasha's, the poem implies that Suleiman I was under Ibrahim Pasha's spell. Perhaps this was because Ibrahim Pasha even had a private room in the harem, contrary to normal practice.[13] His presence muddied the architectural and hierarchical distinctions between the inner and outer sections of the palace and among the inhabitants. Ibrahim Pasha, who had had poets executed for accusing him of not being a true Muslim, eventually seemed to overshadow the sultan.

In 1523, following Suleiman I's successful campaigns against Belgrade and Rhodes, Ibrahim Pasha was appointed grand vizier and governor general of Southeastern Europe, despite being only about thirty years old and lacking in actual military experience. Tongues wagged at this unprecedented promotion straight from palace service to the two highest offices of the state. It offended the more experienced Ahmed Pasha—who had expected the promotions but was appointed governor of Egypt instead—and made other courtiers wonder what was going on. In spring 1524, Ibrahim's marriage was celebrated in a lavish ceremony sponsored and attended by the sultan on the Hippodrome. That autumn, Ibrahim Pasha set out for Egypt to repress the revolt of Ahmed Pasha, the one whose rightful position as grand vizier he had usurped. The campaign was successful.

Celalzade Mustafa's law code for Egypt the next year promoted Suleiman I as military commander, lawgiver, and the shadow of God on earth. Suleiman I was depicted as the divinely appointed, saintly, prophetic ruler spreading God's justice through conquest and promulgation of a harmonised secular canon and Islamic law with the assistance of Ibrahim Pasha, his deputy.[14] In the preamble, which describes the grand vizier as the absolutist sultan's alter ego, Ibrahim Pasha speaks in first person, referring to himself as 'Asaf [King Solomon's legendary vizier] in purity, Plato in wisdom, Aristotle in expertise, Galen in faithfulness'.[15] Thus the grand vizier's arrogance knew no bounds.[16] Putting his trust in his cocky yet beloved boyhood friend, Suleiman I appointed Ibrahim Pasha field marshal of the 1526 Hungary campaign, the 1529 campaign to Vienna, and, three years later, the war against the Safavids. After wintering at Aleppo, Ibrahim Pasha occupied Tabriz in August 1534, where the sultan joined him. Together they took Baghdad in December. The sultan and the grand vizier arrived back at Istanbul in 1536, and during the next month Ibrahim led negotiations with the French ambassador about the capitulations, granting French merchants trading privileges.

Despite, or perhaps because of, all his successes on military and diplomatic fronts, Ibrahim Pasha was suddenly executed on Suleiman I's orders during the Ides of March in 1536. After no hint that he was no longer the sultan's favourite, Ibrahim was strangled in his sleep in his bedroom in the harem of Topkapı Palace after having earlier broken the Ramadan fast with Suleiman I. The man who had been the sultan's 'breath and heart' was buried in an obscure grave.[17]

The sultan could promote his inexperienced converted male favourite whom he passionately loved to the highest office in government, bestow upon him an extraordinary income and a magnificent palace to go with it, and even pay for his wedding. He could also murder this slave arbitrarily and without trial to show who was master. Ibrahim Pasha's ruin coincided with the rise of Suleiman I's other love, Hürrem, during his mature years.

But rather than castigating the sultan's Rasputin-like advisor, Haydar, a geomancer whose yearly predictions the sultan kept close in his private bedroom, or Suleiman I himself, most blamed Hürrem Sultan for Ibrahim Pasha's astonishing fall.[18] It is possible that she had a role in it, jealous of Suleiman I's affections for his childhood friend and former chief falconer about whom much gossip was spread. Why, they asked, was Ibrahim Pasha allowed to sleep in Topkapı Palace, despite being a grown man? The sultan was supposed to be the only adult male resident aside from the palace pages. Their relations were considered too intimate for two grown men. Before Ibrahim's murder, Ferhad Pasha—Suleiman I's sister Beyhan's husband—had called him Suleiman I's 'whore'.[19] They seem to have violated the convention that powerful men could desire only beardless youths, not other powerful men. Hürrem was worried that Suleiman I loved Ibrahim Pasha more than her. He appeared to have not one, but two favourites.

Suleiman I was devastated when his eldest son by Hürrem, Mehmed, died of plague aged twenty-two in 1543. He cried for hours, refusing to part from the coffin, not allowing it to be buried. This grave loss was part of the reason he turned pious. Suleiman I's decision to execute his eldest son by Mahidevran, Mustafa, a decade later is therefore surprising. Had he forgotten how painful it was to bury his own children? Ottoman historians blamed Hürrem for being so influential in the sultan's life that she convinced him that thirty-eight-year-old Mustafa was plotting with the Janissaries to murder Grand Vizier Rüstem Pasha (Hürrem's son-in-law through his marriage to her daughter, Mihrimah) and depose Suleiman I in favour of the popular and capable Mustafa. Suleiman I called Mustafa to his tent outside Konya and had him strangled in 1553; his corpse was then thrown outside. Mustafa's only son was also strangled. Suleiman I feared a repeat of what had happened to his grandfather: Selim I had forced Bayezid II to abdicate in Istanbul, was enthroned in his place, and was suspected of having his father poisoned as he journeyed to his retirement. Suleiman I never recovered from his decision to have Mustafa killed. He became religious, reserved, and melancholy.

People were outraged and blamed Hürrem (and Rüstem Pasha, who had forged a treasonous correspondence between Mustafa and the Safavid shah Tahmasp). Rüstem Pasha was dismissed from his post as grand vizier after nearly a decade in office. Some brave voices, however, blamed the sultan. The poet Nisayi of the imperial harem—a woman in the retinue of Mustafa's mother, Mahidevran—wrote a scathing poem castigating the sultan for being tyrannical, unjust, and lacking compassion: 'You allowed the words of a Russian witch into your ears / Deluded by tricks and deceit, you did the bidding of that spiteful hag / You slaughtered that swaying cypress, fruit of life's orchard / What has the merciless Monarch of the World done to Sultan Mustafa?'[20] Her poem averred that the people held the sultan in contempt and cursed the sheikhulislam who approved the execution. But despite his execution of his favourite vizier (Ibrahim Pasha), his execution of his favourite son (Mustafa), the killing of another son (the thirty-six-year-old Bayezid was assassinated in Safavid Iran, where he had fled after defeat on the battlefield against his brother Selim in 1559), and the execution of a number of grandsons (the sons of Mustafa and Bayezid) and three brothers-in-law, Suleiman I continued to enjoy a glowing reputation among his people and still today among modern historians. His faults were placed at the foot of Hürrem. Hürrem was helped again when Rüstem Pasha's replacement in 1553, Kara Ahmed Pasha, husband of Suleiman I's sister Fatma, was executed in 1555 on trumped-up charges, and Rüstem Pasha called back to the grand vizierate.

Suleiman I died of unknown causes aged sixty-five while waging a campaign in Hungary on the night of 6–7 September 1566. In order not to allow a break in dynastic continuity as manifested in the physical presence of the sultan, the Ottomans did not hold public funerary prayers for a deceased sultan until a new one had been enthroned. The problem was that Suleiman I's only surviving son, Selim, was far away in Kütahya, in northwest Anatolia. Urgent dispatches were secretly conveyed to him to rush to Istanbul. In the meantime, the Ottoman leaders had to do something to preserve the corpse. Suleiman I's body was ritually washed according to Muslim custom. The corpse was heavily perfumed with musk and ambergris, wrapped in waxed bandages, and temporarily buried beneath his tent before the walls of Szigetvár.[21] The fortress soon surrendered to the Ottomans. Grand Vizier Sokollu Mehmed Pasha, who had succeeded Rüstem Pasha after his death in 1561, had to pretend the sultan was still alive so that false claim-ants to the throne would not arise and the Janissaries would not rebel in Hungary or in Istanbul. To continue the subterfuge, he administered the empire on behalf of the deceased sultan, whose death he kept secret. He pretended to consult him orally and in writing, composing responses in the sultan's handwriting.[22]

Three weeks later, forty-two-year-old Selim mounted the throne at the Gate of Felicity in Topkapı Palace and became Sultan Selim II (reigned 1566–1574). His reign began on a sublime, reli-gious note. At his accession, the viziers and leaders of the Muslim religious class gave their oath of allegiance to him as caliph, the leader of all Sunni Muslims. As his father, Suleiman I, had adopted the caliphal title midway through his reign, Selim II was the first sultan to receive such a loyalty pledge at his enthronement.[23] From that moment, Ottoman sultans were sultan-caliphs. He was also the first to take a pilgrimage to the tomb of Muhammad's com-panion Ayyub al-Ansari in Eyüp on the Golden Horn as part of his accession rituals.[24] The waterborne procession to the holy tomb and great military procession afterward displayed the new dynas-tic leader to the public. Selim II then continued his journey to-wards Hungary—as his father's corpse travelled towards Istanbul.

Six weeks after his death, Suleiman I's corpse was disinterred for the journey to Istanbul. According to an Ottoman chroni-cler, one of the palace pages who had accompanied the sultan to Hungary, the secret of the sultan's passing was still kept from his troops. A stand-in 'white-faced, hawk-nosed' Bosnian palace page 'with a sparse beard and a bandaged neck, and an appearance of ill-health' sat in the sultan's carriage and waved to the soldiers on their return march.[25] It was only in Belgrade, forty-eight days after Suleiman I's death, that public funeral prayers for the sultan were recited and Selim II received the oath of allegiance from the army commanders as the new head of the dynasty.

At last, the procession of Suleiman I's coffin, topped by a giant turban and followed by the deceased's riderless horses, reached the cemetery behind his mosque in Istanbul. As a tent was erected above, he was buried in the earth. Once he was interred, the tent was replaced by a domed, octagonal mausoleum illuminated by stained-glass windows framed in arches of red and white stone resting on pillars. Its walls are lined in exquisite panels of emerald-green and turquoise İznik tile and alternating bands of red and green marble. Although it is a palatial monument for an earthly king, the tomb's Qur'anic verses remind humans to be humble, for it is God's throne that encompasses the heavens and earth. Eight years had passed since Suleiman I's wife Hürrem had been laid to rest in her adjacent, smaller tomb.

Hürrem's son, Selim II, was generally disinterested in ruling and empowered his grand vizier, Sokollu Mehmed Pasha, to make most decisions. Selim II is credited with the conquest of Cyprus in 1571 and of Tunis in 1574. But he was a corpulent glutton who could barely saddle a horse, an important sign of a sultan's power and majesty. Foreigners and Ottomans observed that he was devoted to wine, women, and boys and neglected to attend mosque in favour of poetry gatherings.[26] That the polyamorous and beautiful widowed poet Hubbi Hatun was a royal confidant attracted additional opprobrium.[27] Selim II tried to improve his image by having the master architect Sinan construct the finest of all Ottoman mosques, the Selimiye in Edirne (1575). He vowed to give up drinking and partying.[28] But at age fifty, he died after a fall in the bath. Ottoman writers lamented that had the capable Mustafa been allowed to rule, the empire would have continued its grand adventure in capable hands.

OTTOMAN SULTANAS, BYZANTINE EMPRESSES, AND MONGOL KHATUNS: THE POLITICAL ROLE OF ROYAL WOMEN

Ottoman royal women played important roles in the political life of their empire, but they were less significant than Byzantine empresses, Mongol khatuns, and Christian European queens. Much of Ottoman court ceremony and life reflected earlier practices. Byzantine women had been influential and even exercised power at court for over a thousand years, sometimes ruling as empress. The empress was not necessarily the wife of the emperor, but could be his sister, mother, or daughter. Because of the Christian emphasis on monogamy, imperial widows often refused to remarry and retained their position at court. The structure of the Byzantine court—like that at the future Topkapı Palace—was one reason for their influence.[29] The empress had her own quarters, staffed by her own eunuchs, who held posts parallel to the emperor's staff. She and her courtiers arranged royal marriages, burials, and enthronements, organising the female part of court ceremony. She gave birth to the heirs of the empire in the purple chamber in her quarters. Being 'born in the purple' was used for seven centuries to guarantee and legitimate imperial authority.[30] Another reason for the empress's influence was that Byzantine royal women were financially independent. Unlike in Islam, Byzantine law ensured that daughters inherited equally as sons. They had an income and owned and managed properties.[31] They became great patrons of the arts and of monumental buildings, such as churches and monasteries.

Both Ottoman and Byzantine princesses were wed for the purpose of political alliance. In the early centuries, the Ottomans married foreign princesses who almost never bore children, because that role was for slave concubines whose loyalty to the dynasty would not be doubted. In contrast, the Byzantines sent their princesses to marry foreign rulers. The aim was to build alliances and serve as ambassadors for the dynasty.[32] Such women maintained their own retinue, including priests, and spread Orthodox Christianity in other lands. Byzantine emperor Michael VIII's (reigned 1261–1282) daughter Maria was sent to Persia to marry the Mongol Ilkhanid ruler. In Persia she promoted Christianity, including the building of a church.[33] When her husband died, she returned to Constantinople, where an ancient church was renamed Saint Mary of the Mongols in her honour. Today it is the only still-functioning Byzantine church in Istanbul, where she became patron of the Chora Monastery. Ottoman princesses, however, did not marry Christian rulers as part of marriage alliances meant to serve diplomacy and improve or maintain foreign relations. They were wed for the purpose of alliance in the early centuries to Muslim rivals.[34] In later centuries, Ottoman women from the palace, themselves slaves from foreign lands, wed administrators who came from the Collection, the viziers.

Ottoman women never ruled the empire as empresses as Byzantine women had. Nor were they khatuns equal to khans, as in the Mongol Empire. They never served on the battlefield as their Turco-Mongol predecessors had. Genghis Khan was successful thanks to his mother's role as a warrior in battle. Sorkoktani Beki—the mother of the fourth Mongol khan Möngke, the fifth khan Kubilai, and Khan Hülegü, founder of the Ilkhanids—also trained her children.[35] An Arab traveller in Central Asia noted how 'remarkable was the respect shown to women by the Turks, for they hold a more dignified position than the men'.[36] When the Mongol Golden Horde khan issued a decree, he reported, it said, 'By command of the Sultan and the Khatuns'. In Ottoman İznik, the traveller was welcomed not by the sultan but by Orhan's wife, a woman who also commanded the soldiers in the newly conquered yet deserted city.[37]

Compared with these predecessors, Ottoman women had less power after the conquest of Constantinople. Although they had an important role, it should nevertheless not be exaggerated to counter Western images of the harem as orgy rooms for lascivious Oriental tyrants. Women played an important part in reproducing the dynasty, in politics in the palace, and in spreading the good and pious name of the Ottoman dynasty. Beginning with Hürrem Sultan in the sixteenth century, royal women sponsored mosques in Istanbul. Although the chief harem eunuch served as overseer of royal foundations, some royal women provided funds for monumental public works across the empire. Hürrem Sultan endowed mosques, madrasas, public baths, soup kitchens, hospitals, primary schools, bakeries, public toilets, inns, and pilgrim hostels in Mecca, Medina, and Jerusalem (just as Helena, mother of Byzantine emperor Constantine, had sponsored public works in that city), as well as Edirne and Istanbul. The neighbourhood in Istanbul where Hürrem Sultan's mosque foundation was located is still named Haseki—the favourite—after her.

Suleiman I's only surviving daughter and close confidant, Mihrimah, who was never considered eligible to rule because she was a woman, sponsored two mosques in Istanbul. The first appeared in the 1540s in the east, on the Asian side, in the heart of Üsküdar. The second was built in the 1560s in the far west at Edirne Gate, where the conquering Mehmed II had entered the city in 1453. From the latter's minaret, one can get the best views over the red-tiled roofs of the old city surrounded by seas of aquamarine, as the Renaissance tower sways disturbingly in the breeze.

Royal women sponsored lavish public ceremonies. The fifty-day circumcision festival of Prince Mehmed (the future Mehmed III) in summer 1582 on the Hippodrome was perhaps the largest public spectacle the dynasty ever produced. The people of Istanbul were feted with dancing boys—'of lovely countenance and smelling of musk; a tall cypress and moon face, sweet tongued and slender waisted'—bears, fireworks, and feasts.[38] Each parading group of bearded tradesmen masters included a troupe of their boy beloveds, their apprentices. The eroticism of the youth and the bonds between men and boys were openly displayed. Unlike their Byzantine or Mongol predecessors, Ottoman royal women remained invisible. They watched the spectacles from behind screens or latticed windows. Crowds were instructed to look away when their royal carriages passed, although their doors and windows were screened.

Leading Ottoman ladies were diplomats, exchanging letters and gifts with foreign rulers and their representatives in Istanbul. By the sixteenth century, they never did so in person. This was a far cry from Turco-Mongol practice, where a khan sent his mother as emissary to foreign courts. Mehmed II received White Sheep sultan Hasan the Tall's mother, Sara Khatun, to negotiate peace on her son's behalf. Cem, son of Mehmed II, sent an aunt to his brother Bayezid to negotiate the division of the empire between them. In the sixteenth century, Ottoman royal women corresponded by pen. When foreign queens and regents sought to curry favour with the Ottomans, they did so through the sultanas. Hürrem Sultan corresponded with Sultanim, sister of Shah Tahmasp—who gave Persian carpets to cover the floor of Suleiman I's mosque—as well as with male and female members of the Polish royal family. Nurbanu Sultan, who was valide sultan (mother of the sultan) from 1574 to 1583, was the daughter of a Venetian family. She corresponded with the Venetians and with Catherine de' Medici (mother of three successive kings in France) and appears to have hindered an Ottoman invasion of Venetian Crete. Safiye Sultan (valide sultan 1595–1603) exchanged letters and gifts with England's Elizabeth I, who sent her a jewelled portrait of herself. These women promoted good international relations.

CONNECTING SULTANAS TO THE WORLD: JEWISH LADIES-IN-WAITING AT THE PALACE

As the significance of palace women grew in the sixteenth century, so, too, did that of their ladies-in-waiting. Both caused resentment. By the end of the sixteenth century, contemporaries mistook the rise in importance of palace women for corruption of power. Tensions over the increased power of royal women—especially that of the valide sultan—led to the creation of scapegoats. The 'Jewish

dame'—Jewish ladies-in-waiting in service to various sultanas—
became the sign of a world turned upside down. It mattered that
the lady-in-waiting was both a woman and Jewish.

Jewish women served as ladies-in-waiting to the harem
throughout the fifteenth and sixteenth centuries. In the early
sixteenth century, Strongilah, a Karaite Jew—a member of the
Jewish sect that accepts only the Torah, but not the Talmud (the
corpus of Jewish law), as binding—served Hafsa Sultan, Suleiman I's mother. Strongilah converted to Islam at the end of her
life, during Suleiman I's reign, becoming Fatma. Around the time
of her death, the Spanish Jewish lady-in-waiting Esther Handali
began to serve the harem. She served Nurbanu Sultan, the favourite of Selim II and later the valide sultan of Murad III, from 1566
to 1595. Esther was followed by several others, including an Italian Jew, Esperanza Malki, who served Safiye Sultan, the favourite
of Murad III and mother of Mehmed III (reigned 1595–1603).

Having gained the confidence of the various sultanas, these
Jewish women functioned as mediators between the harem and
the outside world. They exchanged gems, jewellery, and other
valuables with foreign leaders and their representatives as part of
diplomatic relations, becoming very wealthy and influential. They
passed information about the dynasty to foreign ambassadors
in exchange for valuable silks for the sultana. A letter sent from
Safiye Sultan to the English queen Elizabeth I in 1599 mentioned
how she had entrusted the lady-in-waiting to give the British ambassador a crown of rubies and diamonds for the queen. The lady-
in-waiting also relayed important political messages from the
valide sultan.[39]

Later that same year the lady-in-waiting Esperanza Malki
wrote a personal letter in Italian to Queen Elizabeth I. Malki declared that Elizabeth's 'power and greatness' attracted even those
who were not English to wish to serve her, including the Jewish
lady-in-waiting.[40] After mentioning the gifts the valide sultan had
sent the queen, including the crown of gems, she confided that

beautiful and flattering silk and wool cloths were more dear to the valide sultan than jewels.[41] Noting that the ruler of England was a woman like her, she was not embarrassed to request that the queen send a gift of rare distilled waters for the face and perfumed oils for the hands, which she would personally deliver to the valide sultan. Being articles for ladies, she did not wish them to pass through men's hands.

Elizabeth I must have been surprised to be addressed by a Jew with such confidence and intimacy. Her kingdom had banished the People of the Book in 1290. That the Ottomans not only tolerated their existence in their kingdom but employed them in the palace and as go-betweens with foreign ambassadors and rulers must have been a surprising discovery. The English had established relations with the Ottomans only a decade earlier. Elizabeth I's private physician was a Portuguese converso, Roderigo Lopez, but he was legally a Christian. Old prejudices remained: he was drawn and quartered for allegedly plotting to poison Elizabeth I on behalf of the Spanish in 1594.[42] Like Lopez, Malki would suffer a grim fate.

On a Friday at the end of March 1600, when Grand Vizier Ibrahim Pasha returned from campaign, thousands of outraged cavalry troops stormed his palace in Istanbul demanding lucrative tax allocations. They claimed they were owed them in place of the less profitable ones they regularly received.[43] They asked whether they had been distributed to the women and eunuchs in the palace, complaining that the coins with which they had been paid were worthless.[44] They rushed to Sheikhulislam Sunullah Efendi, demanding to know whether the food they had purchased with the worthless silver coins given to them as their salary was halal, ritually approved. He responded that it was not. 'The Jewish hag lady-in-waiting farms the customs revenue', they replied. 'She is the one who gives us these counterfeit coins—they belong to her! We will kill her', the cavalrymen declared, requesting a fatwa approving her execution. The sheikhulislam responded that Islamic law did not permit her killing. At worst she could be expelled from the city.[45] He told them to record their wishes in a petition that he would pass on to the sultan, who would then issue an imperial decree. This response only emboldened the cavalry troops in their rebelliousness.

The next morning at the crack of dawn, a great mob went to the gate of Deputy Grand Vizier Halil Pasha's palace, demanding the 'lady-in-waiting hag'. When she was found in her home in the Jewish Quarter and brought out, they mounted her on a pack-horse and brought her to the gate of the pasha's palace. No sooner had she dismounted than the impatient cavalrymen drew their daggers and 'cut her to pieces' according to an Ottoman chronicler. They tied a rope to one of her feet and dragged the 'carcass' to the Hippodrome. They 'cut off the accursed one's hand, which was the appendage of bribery, and cut out her vulva, nailing them to the doors of those conceited ones who obtained their posts by means of that accursed woman'.[46]

The English traveller John Sanderson confirmed the grisly details. He added that dogs devoured all save her 'bones, sinews of her legs, and soles of her feet'. Sultan Mehmed III watched the lynching. The cavalrymen paraded her head on a pike through the city. They also carried 'her shameful part; also many small pieces of her flesh, which the Turks, Janissaries, and others carried about tied in little packets, showing to the Jews and others, and in derision said: "Behold the whore's flesh"'. He saw a slice of her passing by his home in Galata.[47]

The next day, the mob again went to the gate of the pasha's palace, demanding that her children and other relatives be brought forth immediately, lest they start a bigger riot.[48] When her older son was brought out, they hacked him limb from limb with their daggers, 'showing no mercy'. They dragged the 'carcass' to the Hippodrome, placing it next to what remained of his mother's 'carcass'.[49] There, they accepted her younger son's conversion to Islam, sparing his life, on condition that he promised to pay the treasury the revenues held by his mother as tax farms. What remained of the lady-in-waiting and her son's bodies was cremated because 'the disgusting carcasses of the accursed ones were prey to the dogs for many days on the Hippodrome, creating an abominable stench, which annoyed Muslims'.[50] Islam and Judaism generally view cremation as an abomination.

The treatment of the lady-in-waiting and her son was shocking to Muslims and Jews alike. Recoiling from the 'shameful' way the lady-in-waiting had been killed, a horrified Safiye Sultan declared to her son, Mehmed III, 'If her execution was necessary, did it have to be carried out like this? She could have been [sewn into a sack and] thrown into the sea. The execution in such a way of a woman so closely connected to the harem is damaging to the integrity' of the empire.[51]

The mob had mutilated her corpse and that of her son to make a point: those who violated the gendered religious hierarchy of society would be publicly humiliated. Confirming that the rise to power and influence of a Jewish woman had upset the social order, immediately following these events the sultan issued a decree imposing clothing and employment restrictions on Jews.[52] Jews were no longer allowed to wear fine garments and had to wear a red cap. They were no longer permitted to be tax farmers. Such measures were a way of ensuring that Jews were barred from becoming rich and lording it over Muslims. Dressed in a coloured cap and clothes befitting their lower station, they would ever be identifiable as Jews. The tensions created by the development of the harem institution, which had inverted both gender and religious hierarchies, had ended in a rebellion against the lady-in-waiting, resolvable only by the hierarchies' restoration and her demise.

Jews served as ladies-in-waiting, physicians, advisors, bankers, spies, and diplomats during the Ottoman Jewish 'golden age' from the conquest of Istanbul in 1453 to a generation beyond the death of Sultan Suleiman I in 1566. Both Jewish men and women were entrusted with intimate advisory roles and sensitive diplomatic missions. This demonstrated the level of trust sultans, the various sultanas, and members of the elite placed in them. But this is not what the Ottoman chroniclers remembered. Jewish usefulness and loyalty went unmentioned in their chronicles. Their preferred figure was that of the untrustworthy Jew, and they expressed relief when Jews in prominent positions were replaced by Muslims. Moses Hamon's rise to prominence as privy physician to Suleiman I was criticised. Upon Hamon's death an author celebrated how 'the Sultan's court was purified of the filth of his existence'.[53] He was depicted as a source of danger because he transgressed the social order.

Rather than focusing on the positive roles of the Jewish physician Moses Hamon or the philanthropist Doña Gracia Mendes Nasi, Ottoman history writers' attention was drawn to figures who betrayed the dynasty's trust. Ottoman descriptions of the rise and fall of the 'Jewish dame'—Malki, the Jewish figure most often mentioned in Ottoman histories from the sixteenth through the eighteenth centuries—reflected their displeasure and discomfort that Jews and women were ever given such distinguished roles in the first place. They preferred men to women and Muslims to Jews in positions of power.

EUNUCHS IN THE PALACE

Along with women, including ladies-in-waiting, another important group that rose to influence in the palace and in Ottoman politics by the end of the sixteenth century were the castrated male eunuchs. Especially significant were the harem eunuchs, members of the sultan's household responsible for guarding the women and children of the royal family. Like their Byzantine and Seljuk predecessors, Ottoman rulers had utilised slaves and eunuchs in their entourage from the beginning. Establishing a dervish lodge in 1324, Orhan awarded stewardship of the endowment to a freed slave and eunuch. In Topkapı Palace, the chief harem eunuch was responsible for the education of young Ottoman princes and the women of the harem, and played a role in making and unmaking grand viziers, a role usually filled by the sultan's son-in-law.

Eunuchs became especially noticeable in Ottoman politics after the conquest of Constantinople. By the end of the sixteenth century, the Ottomans employed one thousand eunuchs in Topkapı Palace, divided into two groups.[54] Men who originated in Central Europe, especially Hungary, or the Caucasus, especially Georgia and Circassia, guarded the threshold in front of the sultan's audience chamber, located between the second and third courts of the palace. This group resided with the palace pages in the palace school in the third court. They were responsible for guarding the men of the palace, including the sultan. Men of East African, especially Ethiopian and Sudanese, origin guarded the women of the palace and the harem, and resided within it. Nowhere else was there such a concentration of Afro-Ottomans, and their presence attracted the horror and fascination of European Christian observers.

Despite the lack of such terms in Ottoman Turkish, the head eunuchs of both groups are referred to by Westerners as the 'chief black eunuch' and 'chief white eunuch'. Their official titles were agha (lord) of the Abode of Felicity (the harem) and agha of the Gate of Felicity (the third palace gate), respectively. We have no explanation for why the dynasty chose men of African origin to guard the royal family while deploying men of Caucasian origin to guard the palace recruits and sultan. The Ottoman conquest of Egypt gave the dynasty further access to the African slave trade and to Mamluk Egyptian precedent. Mamluk Egypt, a dynasty ruled entirely by Turkic or Circassian slaves, assigned eunuchs to guard Muhammad's tomb and mosque in Medina and gave them control of administering endowments in Mecca and Medina. The Ottomans continued these traditions.

Other aspects of the eunuchs of the palace drew the attention of Ottomans and foreigners alike. Like the youth recruited for the

Collection, the eunuchs were acquired as slaves of Christian origin, whether from East Africa, Central Europe, or the Caucasus. Their enslavement again raises the question of the legality of the act. They were often recruited from regions ruled by the Ottomans, which should have exempted these Orthodox Ethiopian, Coptic, Catholic, Apostolic Armenian, or Orthodox Christians from enslavement.

Castration also violated Islamic law as understood and practised in that period. To circumvent this, the Ottomans usually had Christian physicians carry out the operation, whether Armenians in the Caucasus or Copts in Sudan. But castrations were also carried out in Topkapı Palace, where in that period there were no Christian physicians.[55] African eunuchs typically lost both their testicles and penis, whereas Caucasian or Central European eunuchs had only the testicles removed. We do not know the reasons for these different procedures. It appears that the Ottomans followed Mamluk precedent for the castration of African eunuchs and Byzantine practice for European eunuchs. Removal of the penis would prevent the African eunuchs from having sexual relations with the women and children they were entrusted to guard. Enemies of the African-origin eunuchs at the Ottoman court criticised their alleged practice of saving their private parts to be buried with them when they died.[56]

The castration process had profound physical repercussions for these men. The smell of urine accompanied them, which may be the reason why they had their own mosque at Topkapı Palace.[57] They carried quills in their turbans to be used as catheters, which, along with incontinence, may have been the source of their smell and unhygienic reputation. Castrated prior to puberty, their bones did not develop properly. They often suffered from osteoporosis, causing them to stoop and have skeletal deformities, including very long arms and legs. Hormonal imbalance conspired to make them unusually thin or very fat. With fingers reaching nearly to their knees, skin that wrinkled beginning at a young age, unusually large faces that remained beardless, very high-pitched voices, and lives that stretched into their eighties and nineties, eunuchs were an unmistakable feature of the palace.

No matter his strange appearance and other defining characteristics, the chief harem eunuch became an indispensable power holder in the palace and beyond. He served like a Western European lady-in-waiting, as the mediator between the royal women—the concubines and valide sultan—and the rest of the administration. The chief harem eunuch became the sultan's main companion beginning with the reign of Murad III, the first sultan to leave the privy chamber (his private bedroom) and the young men in the third court to live in the harem, where he built a lavish bedchamber. His royal bed was guarded by elderly women, rather than young palace pages. Murad III also transferred the supervision of all lucrative foundations of Mecca and Medina from the agha of the Gate of Felicity, who supervised the palace pages, to the chief harem eunuch.[58] As chief treasurer of the harem and then administrator of the endowments in Arabia, as well as his own investments in Yemeni coffee, Murad III's chief harem eunuch controlled great wealth. As patron of libraries, mosques, and colleges, he was an empire-wide benefactor of Sunni Islam. As chief tomb eunuch at the Prophet's tomb in Medina, he sealed his reputation as a wealthy, powerful, Sunni Muslim Ottoman dignitary controlling the revenues from the two holy shrines and serving as the palace's trusted set of eyes and ears.

Despite bearing names such as Hyacinth and Sweet Basil, these dignified men—permitted to ride white horses during their lives and buried in the cemetery at Eyüp, the holiest Muslim shrine in Istanbul—were referred to on their tombstones as virtuous, noble, pious, generous, and learned men whose destiny was paradise. Their lives illustrate how far a person of humble African or Christian origins could rise in the Ottoman order of things.[59]

Their names also provide another insight into Ottoman culture. Significantly, the name Hyacinth was a moniker for the hair of the beloved. For along with eunuchs, another unmistakable presence in Ottoman society from the beginning was that of the boy beloved. The fact that mature men had boy lovers means that the Ottomans were quintessentially European. Exploring this theme as it relates to boy beloveds remains integral to showing that the Ottomans participated in European history, which requires us to rewrite and broaden our understanding of what being European means—expanding it to include being both Roman and Muslim.

BEARDED MEN AND
BEARDLESS YOUTHS

T HE HAREM INSTITUTION may have distinguished Ottoman
society from Christian Europe, albeit not as it was imagined
as a playground for a lustful sultan. Although the Byzantines had
also employed eunuchs in the palace, the fact that the harem was
guarded by castrated males from Africa caused the European
imagination to run wild. Yet in important ways, sexuality in the
Ottoman Empire and the rest of Renaissance Europe was comparable. A shared culture of man-boy love, which drew on ancient
Greek and Roman precedent, encompassed Europe in London,
Florence, Venice, Rome, and Istanbul. Homosexual desire was
seen as the domain not of a numerical minority but of all men, a
building block of culture, especially in the military and schools.[1]
And it went all the way to the top of society. Mehmed II described
in a poem the young male Christian object of his sexual desire:

> I saw an angel, a sun face
> or this world's moon.
> Black hyacinth curls,
> smoky sighs of lovers.
> An alluring cypress,
> clad in black, like the moon

> *in night, or the Franks [Western Europeans]*
> *whom his beauty rules.*
> *If your heart is not bound*
> *in the knot of his heathen belt,*
> *you're no true believer,*
> *but a lost soul among lovers.*
> *His lips give life anew*
> *to those whom his glances kill*
> *just so, for that giver of life*
> *follows the way of Jesus.*
> *Avnî [Mehmed II's pen name], have no doubt,*
> *that beauty will one day be tame*
> *for you are ruler of Constantinople.*[2]

Mehmed II was not alone in his affections. His writing reflects that of the Sufi Rûmi, recorded two centuries earlier. Rûmi was spiritually transformed by his passionate relationship with his elder Şams al-Tabrizi, another Sufi from the east. Rûmi called Şams 'heart-stealer' and 'soul's beloved' for whom his heart burst with ecstasy.[3] He praised his 'beauteous face', 'bewitching narcissi [eyes]', 'brow of hyacinth', and his lips, which were as 'rubies sweet to taste'. After Şams left him, an anguished Rûmi referred to him as a 'gorgeous heartbreaker', a 'heartthrob', and 'luscious bough of rosebuds'. He lamented how bitter it was to be separated 'from such sugary lips'.

A chaste reading interprets such verses as symbolising humans held captive by worldly illusions. The lover is spellbound, contemplating the beauty of God. Rûmi's love for and devotion to Şams is seen as a model of his love of God.[4] The Sufi practice of gazing at young boys is interpreted as a window onto human contemplation of God's beauty. Rûmi's biographers go out of their way to deny that the writers of homoerotic verse engaged in physical love. Perhaps. Just as verses written about earthly profane love may be seen as metaphors for the human love for God, so, too, may poems articulating human love for God be seen as metaphors for earthly profane love. In a world before sexual preferences constituted an identity, where men who desired other males were not considered members of a biologically determined, distinctive subculture with a fixed nature, the verses written by Rûmi dedicated to Şams al-Tabrizi were erotic love poetry, the ecstatic expression of one younger man's love for an older one.

The socially acceptable practice of men drinking wine and adoring and having sexual relations with beardless youths, who were the inspiration for lyric love poetry, was common practice in England, Italy, and the Ottoman Empire, as well as in contemporary Iran. A character in Richard Barnfield's *The Affectionate Shepherd* (1594) declares, 'If it be sin to love a sweet-faced boy, / Whose amber locks trust up in golden trammels / Dangle adown his lovely cheeks with joy, / When pearl and flowers his fair hair enamels; / If it be sin to love a lovely lad, / Oh then sin I, for whom my soul is sad'.[5] In the Ottoman Empire, Sufis and the male urban elite saw beautiful boys as objects of desire.

Regarding sexuality in Renaissance Europe and the contemporary Muslim-majority world, what mattered was age and stage of life, not gender. What was important was one's place in the social order, not one's social identity. Distinctions were drawn between adult men who loved boys (which was acceptable), the boys themselves (who once they matured could love only boys, not other men), and adult men (between whom sexual relations were not socially acceptable). Once one's beard grew, one could no longer be an object of anyone's same-sex affection.

Of consequence was life stage. A young man would be considered desirable, a passive object of affection and sexual penetration indistinguishable from a woman, and expected to attract male admirers. When he matured and married, he would in turn become the lover of young male beaus. Over the course of their lives, men would be both the lover and beloved of another man. Sexuality was conceived as a power relation, not an identity. The penetrator was considered strong and dominant. Anyone who could be dominated and penetrated, be it a girl, boy, or woman, could be the object of sexual desire and was accordingly considered weak and inferior.[6]

Mature men desired beardless youths or women, both of whom they described in verse, although most poetry concerned boys. Poets who were attracted to women rather than boys were described as peculiar. Androgyny was a feature of Ottoman literature. As the sixteenth-century poet Azizi writes in a couplet, 'Those who concentrate on pleasure / Grant male and female equal measure'.[7] Yet poems were mostly addressed by men to youths. According to a Qajar Iranian, the beloved is inevitably described as 'rose-faced, silver-bodied, cypress-statured, narcissus-eyed, coquettish, with sugar lips, wine bearers with tulip cheeks, moon-faced, Venus-shaped, with crescent eyebrows, magic eyes, black-scented hair, and crystalline chin folds, and full of games and coquettishness'.[8] Female and male beloveds had the same characteristics. The ideal beautiful woman's 'body is a swaying cypress, her hair a hyacinth, her moles are like peppercorns, her cheek a rose, her lip like wine' and her face 'a shining moon'.[9] At the same time, a beautiful boy 'has a cypress body, a tulip cheek, a rosebud lip, an apple chin, a moon face and a crescent brow', and his moles 'are like peppercorns, his hair like the hyacinth'.

From the sixteenth through eighteenth centuries, Ottoman poets authored collections of poetry dedicated to beloved shop boys. These 'city thrillers' were works dedicated to the beautiful boys of a particular city, including Belgrade, Bursa, Edirne, Istanbul, and Rize in the eastern Black Sea region. A book dedicated to the beautiful boys of Edirne was composed in honour of the visit of Bayezid II. Along with the apprentices working in the bazaar, the boys included theology students, sons of callers to prayer, sons of Qur'an reciters, and young Janissaries. Of the nearly fifty extant collections devoted to the beauties of a city, only one describes women. Sixteenth-century Ottoman writers found that work to be the anomaly and considered it strange because it did not describe beloved boys.[10] Of the poet, an author wrote disparagingly, 'He was a lover of women, but then only God is without fault'.

Galata, the former Genoese colony across the Golden Horn from Istanbul—a district known for its Christian, Jewish, and Italian inhabitants and taverns—was described as a place of pleasure, where Muslim men went to enjoy wine and Christian boy beloveds: 'For wine and beloved [boys] it is without peer'. But 'Adviser, don't bar the reveller from wine saying it's forbidden / The fatwa [legal opinion] in hand says the law of Jesus makes it licit'.[11] Fatwas were posed in the sixteenth century asking whether it was permissible for a beautiful boy to pray in the front row of a mosque, or whether he should be forbidden, for his prostrations would excite the men standing behind him. A poet urged libertines to 'take your glass in the direction of Galata / He who wishes to see Europe in Ottoman lands / Let him ever cross to see that city of two beauties / Pious one, should you see those Frankish [Western European] boys but once / You would never cast an eye on the houris [the maidens promised to believers] in paradise'.[12] Ottoman taverns were similar to English molly houses. In both places, elite men drank and cavorted with lower-class boy lovers.

Before the nineteenth century, the view of the medical sciences in the Ottoman Empire and in Safavid and Qajar Iran (founded in 1785) was not based on the two-sex model, but instead viewed women as biologically imperfect men.[13] Because men and women were not understood as opposites, same-sex relations were not considered to go against nature. Moreover, it was believed that both men and women produced semen, although women's was assumed to be inferior. Both thus possessed analogous powers of procreation and needed to discharge it, causing men and women to desire sexual intercourse equally. Moreover, female orgasm was understood to be critical to conception.[14] Physicians wrote manuals instructing men how to pleasure women sexually, on efficacious aphrodisiacs, and on the various types of contraception.

Men believed women had an insatiable sexual appetite that they were unable to control. Based on a saying of Muhammad, men envisioned every part of a woman as being a private sexual part. They used this view to legitimise men's control over women, keeping them covered, veiled, and away from unrelated men. According to this view, if men did not segregate women, they would want to have sex with any man they ran across, whether the man was willing or not.

Although inconceivable to most Ottoman men, there were women who loved women and pleasured them. Poet Crazy Brother (Deli Birader) Gazali was an Islamic scholar, law professor, Sufi, bathhouse owner, and pornographer. He aimed to entertain his readers when he wrote about the 'famous dildo women' in large Ottoman cities who dressed as men, rode horses like cavalrymen, and 'strap[ped] dildos about their hips, oil[ed] them with almond oil, and set about the business in the usual manner, working away dildoing the cunt' of elite women.[15]

Sex manuals were written or translated for Ottoman princes and sultans. On the orders of Selim I in 1519, *Restoration of the Old Man to Youth Through the Power of Libido/Intercourse*, for example, was translated from the Arabic and expanded. The same work was translated by the disaffected Ottoman bureaucrat Mustafa Ali as *The Carnal Souls' Comfort* (1569) for Prince Mehmed, two years old at the time, who became Mehmed III a quarter of a century later.[16]

Sexuality was openly visible in the sexually charged plays of the Ottoman shadow theatre.[17] The shadow theatre was most likely an export from Egypt brought back to Istanbul by Selim I after his defeat of the Mamluks in the sixteenth century. Commonly called Karagöz, after the main character, the shadow plays were performed in the palace, in coffeehouses, and to large crowds during festivities such as circumcision feasts, marriages, and the nightly fast breaking during the month of Ramadan. Cartoonish puppets made out of coloured, translucent camel leather were held by long sticks by a puppeteer, who projected their images onto a screen by means of lit candles or lanterns and played the roles of all characters, male and female. These comic and carnivalesque shows mocked, parodied, and critiqued society and its morals, showing a world full of lusty lawlessness and freedom. Men and women were sexually libidinous and promiscuous, always looking to ensnare others for pleasure. Men chased after boy dancers dressed as women. Women also chased after women. No one attempted to maintain their virtue, save their soul, or fight off Satan's temptations, and women were not inferior to men. The main female character in all plays was an unabashed flirt on the lookout for sex, literally turning tricks. Women were bare breasted. The main character, Karagöz, was depicted with an enormous, moveable phallus.

Collections of sexually explicit poems, jokes, and stories were common in the sixteenth century. Crazy Brother (Deli Birader) Gazali composed *The Expeller of Sorrows and Remover of Worries* (ca. 1483–1511). It contains a hilarious imagined debate fought between virile 'pederasts' and weak 'fornicators'. The work includes odes to the anus and to the vagina.[18] The 'boy lovers' win and convert the 'women lovers' to their view: 'When he was done, the boy stood up and farted several times on the sheikh's exhausted head. He said, "Oh what pleasure you gave me!" and left. Then the leader of the pederasts came forward. Putting his arm around the former sheikh of fornicators' neck, he said, "Now you are one of us and on our team"'.

This text, copied in manuscript and circulated until the nineteenth century, was written for a potential heir to the throne, Prince Korkud (died 1513), son of Bayezid II, when the prince was governor of Manisa. Gazali, professor at an Islamic college in Bursa, wrote the text at the request of one of Korkud's courtiers. It was meant to be both morally instructive and humorous. The chapters concern the sexual objects of mature men: 'The Benefits of Marriage and Sexual Intercourse' (mostly revealing the drawbacks to marriage); 'War Between the Pederasts and the Fornicators'; 'How to Enjoy the Company of Boys'; 'How to Enjoy the Company of Girls'; 'Masturbation, Nocturnal Emissions, and Bestiality'; 'The Passive Homosexuals'; 'The Pimps'.[19] The chapter 'How to Enjoy the Company of Boys', which is the only chapter to contain a discussion of sexual positions, is longer than 'How to Enjoy the Company of Girls' or the chapter concerning sexual intercourse with one's wife. In fact, the chapter on loving boys is by far the longest of the text.

The author depicted women as having more passion than men, and thus their insatiable sexual yearning posed a threat. Young boys and young girls, on the other hand, posed no danger. They were easily taken for a small gift, easily satisfied because they had the lowest expectations—having sex for a few coins, with money for a bath after—and gave the most pleasure. They were 'fresh', and their orifices were 'tight'.[20] Married women with children were the worst possible sexual partners for obvious reasons according to this type of classification.

The disgruntled sixteenth-century Ottoman historian and bureaucrat Mustafa Ali, who expressed his love for wine and beautiful boys in his youth and old age, wrote in a similar vein in his work *Etiquette of Salons*.[21] A chapter is entitled, 'Describing the Smooth-Cheeked Boys Ready for Pleasure'. He wrote that in his era, 'the popularity of beardless youth, smooth-cheeked boys, and well-behaved lads, whose sweet beauty is apparent', exceeded the popularity of beautiful women.[22] The reason was that while a female beloved had to be concealed for fear of malicious gossip, keeping company with a young man was connected to acceptable sociability. A relationship between males could be enjoyed either secretly or openly. Beardless youths were available to their middle-aged masters as friends and lovers, whether on military campaign or at home. Their relation could be enjoyed in public, unlike that between a man and a woman, who could not be companions.[23] Inherent to this patriarchal vision was a disparaging view of women, seen neither as friends nor companions, but as intellectual inferiors. Women could offer only physical satisfaction, which was denigrated as worldly but necessary for procreation. Same-sex relations, by contrast, with an intellectually equal but socially inferior male friend and beloved, were supposedly heavenly, satisfying metaphysical and spiritual needs.

Mustafa Ali also provided a sexual ethnography of boys from different nations. Looking down on easterners (Arabs and Turks), the Bosnian-origin writer praised the 'large, thick-lipped slave boys of Bosnia [who] are always amenable to service'. Beardless Kurds were 'faultless and constrained to be amiable and abundantly obedient in whatever is proposed to them' and they dyed themselves 'below the waist with henna'. Those who desired 'the famously fair of face and wish fervently to be serviced by silver-bodied cypresses, tall of stature and elegantly moving' turned to the boy dancers of Southeastern Europe, or the Circassians, or the 'musky, delectable Croats from among the Janissaries'. Albanians stole the heart of their lovers, but they were 'impertinent and obstinate'. Georgians and Russians were also available 'for erotic pleasures'. Mustafa Ali quoted a poem from *The Expeller of Sorrows and Remover of Worries*, which he commented upon favourably: 'The following is famous for its originality, so much so that reading it compares with orgasm: "It opens like a smiling rose, O anus, / And closes a rosebud-lip in wonder, O anus! / The vagina is a house built in a narrow place like the crotch, / But, it is in a plaza to play boccia ball, O anus!"'[24]

The sexual encounters between men and youths—whether bathhouse attendants, waiters in taverns and coffeeshops, apprentices to tradesmen, Sufi novices, or servants to soldiers on campaign—were always meant to be based on an unequal power and status relationship. The relationship was predicated on dominance and submission. It was entered into in exchange for money, wine, and favours. The boys were not supposed to take any sexual pleasure in the encounter. Violence and force were also often used—described in Ottoman legal discussions of rape of boys and women and literary accounts of older men taking advantage of boys when they passed out from drinking too much wine. In one story in Gazali's pornographic work meant to entertain, a beautiful boy drinks too much wine, passes out, and is raped by numerous men while unconscious. When he awakes, he states, 'The wine would be just dandy—if only it weren't such a pain in the butt'.[25] His gang rape was supposed to be funny.

Mustafa Ali saw sexual danger lurking at the heart of empire, like worms devouring an apple from within. In the first chapter in his book *Etiquette of Salons*, entitled 'About the Situation in the Palaces of the Sultans and About the Boy Servants in the Harem', Mustafa Ali imagined that in the past only boys with good morals, as observable from their physiognomy, were recruited to serve in the palace. Yet in his day, those who served the sultan were allegedly 'impudent converts who rush about madly in the service of shameless lowlife types', people who had 'mingled with hooligans of the city-boy class', and 'those notorious for going to taverns and being sold [for sex]'.[26] Such sexual adventurers, he argued, were a danger to the royal family and should not be servants of the sultan. He perceived the rewarding of positions to such people as a main cause of what he thought was Ottoman decline.

The topic of decline occupied many of the best Ottoman minds of this era, minds fearful that the Ottoman Way that had made the empire great was being abandoned. Mustafa Ali was one of the keenest observers of the transformations that rocked the late sixteenth- and early seventeenth-century empire. To understand them, we must turn to Ali's life and analysis of the source of Ottoman greatness and how he saw that greatness threatened.

It is at this point that we can return to a chronological account of the dynasty and its empire from the late sixteenth century. The next four chapters examine transformations in the succession to the sultanate and the role of the sultan; the rise of royal women in politics; changes to military, administrative, and palace recruitment; the breakdown of class distinctions; the Ottoman military losing its edge over other imperial armies; and the impact of these developments on Ottoman ideology. Intellectuals were compelled to critique the changes they saw occurring. Sultans mounted tragic attempts to take back power.

13

BEING OTTOMAN, BEING ROMAN

From Murad III to Osman II

A T THE END of the sixteenth century, Murad III (reigned 1574–1595) sat on the Ottoman throne. The oldest son of his father Selim II, Murad was the only son sent to a provincial governate. The others were kept in the palace. Thus prepared to rule, Murad was called to reign in Istanbul when his father passed away in December 1574. At the insistence of the sultan's widow, the favourite Nurbanu Sultan, Selim II's corpse was kept on ice in the palace until his son could arrive from Manisa in western Anatolia for his enthronement.[1] Only then could the father be publicly buried. Murad's journey to Istanbul was not auspicious. He boarded a small galley meant for transporting grain waiting for him at the port of Mudanya. The sea was so rough that the future sultan became violently sick.[2] After an exhausted Murad arrived at the palace, his accession was free of conflict, although following the law he ordered the palace mutes—court servants whose disability ensured their trustworthiness—to execute all five of his younger brothers.

His dynasty appeared to rule the most expansive, most influential, strongest, wealthiest, most strategic, and most politically powerful empire in Europe, indeed, anywhere in the world, save China.[3] Its realm extended from Algiers in the west to Budapest in the north to Yemen in the south to Basra on the Persian Gulf in the east. These territories contained some of the largest, most important commercial cities on the planet, including Aleppo, Bursa, Cairo, Damascus, and Dubrovnik, and some of the most venerable, such as Baghdad, Jerusalem, and Salonica. Curiosity, vitality, and creativity characterised Ottoman culture. In Istanbul some of the greatest minds of the day worked at the new observatory. In Edirne in 1575, master architect Sinan completed Murad III's predecessor Selim II's mosque, his most sublime work. An Ottoman-Habsburg truce was signed in 1580. What was there to be worried about?

Mustafa Ali saw plenty that bothered him. Ali was born in 1541 to a father who was (most likely) a freed slave and Bosnian Christian who had converted to Islam and a mother who came from a family of conservative, regime-supporting Nakşibendi Sufi sheikhs.[4] Reflecting his own background, Ali boasted that the ideal Ottoman emerged from the mingling of the three pillars of Ottoman inheritance: Byzantine-Roman, Turco-Mongol, and Islamic. He argued that the Rûmis (those from Southeastern Europe and northwestern Anatolia), who traced their descent to Turks and Mongols, were notable for their Muslim piety and faith. He also praised the fact that most Rûmis were of mixed ethnic origins and descended from converts to Islam. In his words, their genealogy was 'traced to a filthy infidel'.[5] Despite using such a pejorative adjective, he described the union of Christians and Muslims as the grafting of different fruit trees. The fruit of their union offered the best qualities of their ancestors, 'either in physical beauty, or in spiritual wisdom'. He argued that the Ottoman dynasty had created a new governing class that had acquired optimal physical, intellectual, and moral qualities through a process of deracination, conversion, education, and Ottomanisation.[6] The 'true Ottomans' were these converts who knew that the Ottoman Way rested on a multiracial and multiethnic foundation.[7]

His vision was of a synthesis of East and West, Muslim and Christian. Yet his was not the multiculturalism we know of today.

He preferred westerners (Rûmis) to easterners (mainly referring to
Iranians, Iran beginning in Kurdish Diyar Bakir).[8] Ali, like other
Ottomans, differentiated between the 'homeland' of Rûm on the
one hand, and Iran and the lands of the Arabs on the other. He
argued that certain ethnicities were not suited for administrative
positions. Given too much power and wealth, they turned uppity,
fomenting rebellion.[9] He singled out for opprobrium 'obstinate'
and 'perfidious' Kurds and 'malicious' and 'mischievous' Turcoman nomads.

After training for a career as a religious scholar in Istanbul, in
1560 Ali became a chancery secretary to Suleiman I's son, prince
Selim, who would become Selim II, in Konya. Failing to win the
favour of Suleiman I, he also did not gain the patronage of Selim II
or his successor Murad III. Over the course of a forty-year career,
other than a two-year stint as secretary of the Janissary corps and
registrar of the imperial council in Istanbul, Ali bounced around
in provincial postings as chancery secretary, registrar of land
grants, and finance director in Syria, Iraq, and Anatolia. He was
often dismissed from his posts and suffered unemployment, at
one point having to sell all his possessions to avoid starving. In
1597 he begged Murad III's successor, Mehmed III, for the chan-
cellorship or a governor-generalship, which was denied. Instead,
in 1599 he was appointed to a position in Jidda, the port of Mecca,
where he passed away the next year.[10]

What this précis of his life shows is that Mustafa Ali was often stuck in provincial postings and repeatedly passed over for
promotion, never obtaining his career goal. Those around him to
whom he felt superior were promoted because they had the right
connections. These ignoramuses became rich, while he sank further into debt. He had to take out loans to augment his unfulfilling
job. He noted sarcastically that wealthy merchants with business
in India sat up all night counting their money.[11] He contemplated
migrating to India, where he felt that learned men such as himself,

now unable to attain high-level administrative positions at the empire's centre, would be valued.[12]

The frustrated man felt he deserved a high position in the administration in the capital, but none was forthcoming. Foreigners from the east had infiltrated the country. They entered the system undeservedly and advanced, while he—a true son of the land— was ignored. Women and Afro-Ottoman eunuchs at the centre of power made administrative decisions. He did not see their rise to importance as the consequence of developments within the dynasty's culture and administrative practices, which had led to power being concentrated in the harem. He saw it as a symbol of Ottoman 'corruption' and a turn away from meritocracy.

According to Mustafa Ali, the sultan preferred Iranians—a broad term meaning easterners, which included Arabs, Iranians, Kurds, and Turcoman—to novice palace recruits from Southeastern Europe and northwestern Anatolia or the scions of local educated families such as himself. He complained that this meant that, as foreign commoners were appointed to important positions, deserving locals such as himself were ignored.[13] For three centuries, the empire had recruited military slaves from Rûm to serve as its elite class of administrators and fighting forces. Freeborn Muslims from Rûm, Romans, dominated its religious class. Mustafa Ali argued that such human material made the most loyal, exemplary servants. Maintaining this system of recruitment and the class system separating the ruling, military class from commoners made the Ottomans admirable. He claimed that the Ottoman Way was predicated on 'Rûminess' (being Roman) and palace recruitment and education, as established by Ottoman secular law and custom.[14]

Angry, disappointed, resentful, and fearful, Ali penned *Counsel for Sultans* in 1581 when he was forty-one and the Ottoman Empire was about to enter its fourth century. Ali's book set in motion an idea about imperial decline that would persist for centuries. The meritocratic Ottoman Way—predicated on conversion, palace education, and secular law—had produced what was most excellent about Ottomanness: its Romanness. In creating a new governing class of deracinated, mixed-ethnic, convert-origin recruits, the Ottoman dynasty had taken the best people available and combined them into the progenitors of a powerful empire. Now, as losers in the seismic socioeconomic transformations that were changing the social contract between ruler and ruled, the empire's critics searched for an explanation of what they perceived to be decline. *Counsel for Sultans* was thus a declaration of a crisis, real and imagined. It focused on the imbalance among the component groups of the empire, the ascent of a new social class identified by wealth rather than merit, and the distrust of new criteria for high office.[15] Ottoman decline became such a powerful explanatory lens that even the nearly concurrent Ottoman and English regicides of the seventeenth century—a first for both regimes, representing a shift in the balance of power—would be interpreted very differently by modern historians.

AFTER SULEIMAN I:
THE 'SULTANATE OF WOMEN'

What angered Mustafa Ali was what he perceived as the total abandonment of racialised class distinctions. Wealthy Kurds and Turks were being awarded government positions, he claimed, despite the fact they 'do not have the capability and qualifications enough' to be given power and authority, and will 'never be fit' to govern 'and to distinguish right from wrong'. Giving them arms, horses, and military kit was enough for them. Going beyond this was incomprehensible, something he termed dangerous and evil. He disparaged their native trustworthiness, loyalty, and fitness to rule themselves. If only, he argued, sultans would study what history teaches, then they would see the errors of the present.[16] But he was wrong to place his hopes in the sultanate.

After Suleiman I's passing in 1566, the Ottomans entered a new phase in the politics of reproduction. A sedentary as opposed to warrior sultanate arose, alongside the rise to influence of the women of the harem. Seniority became the new law of succession rather than military victory and fratricide. It made succession an automatic procedure. Facilitated by the fact that the successor also resided in the palace, enthronements became quick and easy. But they did not end subsequent political crises or violence. From the end of the sixteenth century, we witness an era once referred to derogatorily as the 'sultanate of women', in which the mother of the sultan (valide sultan), a post-sexual woman, was more influential than the sultan. She controlled the imperial household, transmitted political values, and protected and preserved the dynasty.

Correlated with the rise of the valide sultan was a decreased emphasis upon the sultan being a gazi and waging jihad, or war against the Christian powers.[17] Martial abilities had been of great importance to Ottoman sultans from the 1280s to 1453, especially the leading of troops in gaza, a prerequisite for maintaining their power, according to the Ottoman history writers. But, after the conquest of Constantinople in 1453, the Ottoman Empire was no longer a frontier-oriented realm whose motivating drive was warfare and territorial expansion. Instead, it became a bureaucratic, sedentary empire. Ever since Mehmed II had refused to stand at the sound of martial music, the primary component of a sultan's identity was less gazi and more emperor.[18]

The abolishing of this custom symbolised how the imperatives of rule had changed during the transition of the sultan from the head warrior of a frontier principality to the ruler of an empire that spanned continents yet marginalised warriors. The lives of sultans had been marked by mobility, the childhood of sultans by a princely governate. Living in small towns in Anatolia, future sultans were taught the arts of war and governance. Once a sultan died, his sons raced to the capital to be enthroned, battling and ultimately killing their brothers in the process.

Murad III's oldest son and successor, Mehmed III, was the last prince sent out to train in the provinces. He was also the last to enforce the law of fratricide at his accession, having all nineteen of his brothers, including infants, strangled with a silken bowstring when he became sultan.[19] This extreme act of fratricide alarmed the sultan's subjects outside the palace walls: according to an Ottoman chronicler, 'the sound of wailing for the fate of these innocent people rose to Heaven'.[20] Mehmed III's father, Murad III, had such an unsatiable sexual appetite that he bedded virgins and widows without discrimination, and produced over one hundred children during his reign.[21] He allegedly had been so driven by lust that he did not heed secular law, which would have prevented his having so many male children, who were, in the words of an Ottoman intellectual, 'cruelly and wastefully' killed at a young age when he died.[22] His twenty-seven daughters, seven pregnant concubines, and numerous other concubines were sent with their eunuchs and servants to the Old Palace, as Mehmed III's mother, concubines, and children took their place in the harem at Topkapı Palace.[23]

Mehmed III's rise to power left a deep scar on the palace. Thereafter the throne would pass from prince to prince, brother to brother, in descending order of age. Upon Mehmed III's death in the palace, his thirteen-year-old son Ahmed I (reigned 1603–1617) was immediately enthroned, and he became the first sultan to be circumcised after becoming the ruler.[24] Contrary to his predecessors, he was young and lacked military or administrative experience. To acquire legitimacy in the eyes of his army commanders, he was the first to ritually gird a sword—likely that of Osman I— as part of the accession ceremonies.[25] He also spared the life of his younger brother, Mustafa. He was confined in a part of the palace harem near the apartments of the valide sultan. Sealed from the outside world, the princely suite was dubbed 'the cage' in later centuries. In 1617, when Ahmed I passed away at the age of twenty-seven, he became the first sultan to be succeeded by his brother; twenty-six-year-old Mustafa became Mustafa I (reigned

1617–1618, 1622–1623).[26] Seniority had by then replaced fratricide as the Ottoman method of succession. Ahmed I's eldest son, the thirteen-year-old Osman, was allowed to live.

By then, the male head of the Ottoman dynasty was more sedentary than mobile, more often engaged in ceremony than battle. And when on the rare occasion they were compelled to head the imperial army, sedentary sultans with weak constitutions did not last long. Ahmed I built a stunning, six-minaret mosque, popularly referred to as the Blue Mosque due to its exquisite interior blue tilework, on the Hippodrome to celebrate the final suppression of rebellion in Anatolia. But he was no martial leader. As a Venetian contemporary noted, he had been happier in his garden in Topkapı than where wolves prowled.[27]

Beginning at the turn of the seventeenth century, rather than fighting for or actively claiming the throne, sultans were more often than not placed passively on it, sometimes even against their will. Primogeniture—the right of the firstborn son to inheritance—ensured that princes, compelled now to live deep in the palace in the harem, spent their entire childhood surrounded by eunuchs, boys, and women, gaining knowledge neither of how to lead troops in battle nor of the proper forms of statecraft.

Without a childhood spent training in male virtues and the cultivation of manliness, they had little chance to develop into 'virtuous men', as understood in that era. While mercifully left alive, Ottoman princes were politically neutralised in the palace, hermetically sealed off from the world, confined and condemned to a life of isolation. They waited for death or a chance to rule without having been prepared for the position. For some sultans, the only sword they would ever unsheathe was the ceremonial one that accompanied their accession. This was reflected in art, as it became conventional for miniaturists to depict the sultan on the throne and not on horseback leading a military campaign.[28] In the seventeenth century, it was expected that the sultan would be a pacific figure.[29]

The sultan had been removed from the operations of government. The executive had shifted from the harem and palace to the grand vizier. Because he no longer administered the empire nor led gaza, the sultan withdrew from subjects and servants and from public view. Since ordinary speech was considered undignified for sultans to use, they communicated by sign language. Unable even to speak in public, the sultan became out of touch with ordinary people as well as administrators and the military, and he was visible only on rare, carefully staged processions through the capital. The sultan had become a showpiece and, like an icon, sat silently immobile on his throne wearing a three-foot turban. He appeared to be aloof, secluded, and as sublime as a Byzantine or Persian emperor. He had been reduced to a legitimating figure with merely symbolic, ceremonial functions.

Residing in the palace, sultans spent the dynasty's wealth but not the empire's. The two treasuries had been separated. Under these circumstances in which the dynasty and the empire became distinct yet connected entities, loyalty was owed to the dynasty and not to individual sultans, who became far less significant figures than they had been in the past. Although the empire still earned its legitimacy from its affiliation with the dynasty, the royal household was separated from the empire's administration. Sultans reigned, but others ruled. New centres of power arose, in part due to a revolution in socioeconomic relations.

A CLIMATE OF REBELLION

From the mid-sixteenth century, the central administration attempted to limit the power of the military elite. But rather than reduce the role of the cavalry or reorganise the Janissary infantry—particularly to reduce the expense of maintaining the latter—the administration began to hire additional salaried troops in the provinces from among commoners. These foot soldiers armed with muskets were used by commanders in imperial campaigns against the Habsburgs and the Safavids. The armies of Christian Europe especially had seen benefit in equipping their infantry with the latest types of firearms.[30] The diffusion of firearms had lasting societal effects in the Ottoman Empire. Whether they deserted or returned from a usually unsuccessful military campaign, provincial foot soldiers kept their weapons. Armed young men with no future and raised expectations spelled trouble.

At the same time, provincial governors in Anatolia and the Arabic-speaking regions enlisted musketeers as mercenaries for their private armies. These men terrorised the countryside as bands of outlaws.[31] Anatolia and Syria were rent by rebellion and brigandry for decades.

International commerce and money changing caused cash to flow into the empire, which allowed rebel leaders who engaged in these new sources of wealth, like imperial army commanders and regional governors, to hire mercenaries equipped with firearms.[32] These rebels had made great fortunes and were able to use their wealth to buy their way into political power, bribing their way into office.[33] They were more like rogue clients who wanted their piece of the pie. Some demanded to join the professional army of the Janissaries and enter the military class, which meant becoming Ottomans. Their desire was to be in and not out, to be included as part of the system with a secure and privileged place in the Ottoman order.[34] They were met with a mix of reward and punishment. Competing for local power, other rebels were awarded governorships by the administration in Istanbul.[35]

This upheaval was fed by climate change, as it coincided with the extreme cold of the Little Ice Age. Huge snowstorms closed roads for months at a time and caused roofs to collapse, while the Golden Horn froze over.[36] The unprecedented weather conditions caused severe drought and crop failure that led to food shortages, famine, disease, and massive population movement.[37] Facing terrible conditions, peasants fled the countryside for urban areas, causing the depopulation of rural areas and increasing pressure on the remaining commoners to produce foodstuffs and pay taxes. Provincial rebellion by peasants and local military leaders led to the increased stationing of provincial Janissary garrisons, which became new power centres. The number of firearm-bearing Janissaries tripled, whereas that of cavalrymen halved. The Janissaries were paid a salary by the central treasury, but the cavalry earned their income from provincial landholdings, which were far less productive due to the crop failure and population flight. The cavalrymen were no longer the largest component of the Ottoman army; they were overtaken by the Janissaries just as the Collection, the system of recruiting and converting children, fell into abeyance along with its system of rigorous training. Although the Collection ceased in the mid-seventeenth century, large numbers of new converts to Islam in such places as Crete and the Trabzon region joined the military and immediately fought against their former coreligionists.[38] Religious change still provided Christians an avenue of integration and social mobility in the empire.

New power centres also emerged in the capital, where there was the rise of grand vizier households such as that of the Köprülü family. The Köprülüs produced influential statesmen from the mid-seventeenth century through the beginning of the eighteenth century. The growth in political power of vizier households, like the appearance of powerful provincial rebel leaders and governors, coincided with a turn away from the military land-grant system that financed the cavalrymen and towards the monetisation of landholding. This included the expansion of tax farming, which was previously limited to imperial enterprises such as mines. Tax farming in its agricultural form turned out to be harmful both to the central treasury and to the subjects of the sultan. Required to provide an agreed amount of revenue to the imperial treasury each year, tax farmers—whether Christian, Muslim, or Jewish, and appointed by the administration in Istanbul—exploited the peasants to maximise their revenues, demanding a much greater yearly amount than obliged and pocketing the difference. To

carve out their own power centre in the provinces with these ex-
tra funds, the tax farmers raised armies of mercenaries that challenged central authority.

With Istanbul losing its monopoly over the ability to collect
revenues and control those assigned to extract them—it could no
longer simply remove land-grant holders from office as before,
as they were protected by their patrons, the vizier households—
peasants resorted to resistance, including flight and rebellion.
They could not easily transition from tax in-kind to cash payment. Tax farmers and new mini-dynasties in the provinces were
difficult to dislodge. As land grants were converted by their holders into private property and placed out of reach of Istanbul, the
regime increasingly had to rely on tax farmers who provided the
material basis for the new power holders and the nouveau riche.
The nouveau riche included Christian and Muslim provincial
notables (*ayan*) whose wealth was based on 'land-holding, trade,
money-lending and tax farming'.[39] Oriented towards the market, tax farmers, merchants, and provincial governors sold their
goods illegally abroad rather than earning income for the imperial treasury.[40]

The dynasty lost not only revenue but also its ability to enforce
a major economic policy—the provisioning of Istanbul. The seat
of the dynasty was a vast, hungry mouth, fed by the goods produced in the far-flung empire. Yet at the turn of the seventeenth
century, İzmir (Smyrna) on the Aegean coast rapidly expanded.[41]
It became a cog in the machine of world commerce, especially
fulfilling Western European (Dutch and English) demand for cotton by sidestepping Ottoman restrictions on exports of all goods.
Rather than send their surplus to Istanbul for fixed prices, local
Armenian, Greek, Jewish, and Muslim merchants realised large
profits by diverting regional agricultural products to İzmir and
selling them abroad instead. What this meant was that the regime could no longer control domestic prices, markets, or social
stability. Price controls and interference in the market had been

essential components of Ottoman policy, crucial to maintaining social hierarchies. With prices no longer set by central authority, others benefited, including commoners and merchants. To hinder the distribution of surplus outside its control, the regime wanted the economy to be subsumed under the traditional, centrally controlled political power structure, where all decisions were made in Istanbul, not the provinces. But Istanbul could no longer direct foreign or domestic trade. Nor could it hinder the rise of a merchant class and the emergence of new paths to social mobility.[42]

In the idealised economic and class system, capital was to be accumulated by the elite for the consumption of luxury goods and the establishment of their own patronage networks. These networks of relations were modelled on the sultanic household, where the sultan was the patron. Goods flowed at fair prices yet were controlled by the central government so there were no shortages. Social status was guaranteed—each class was kept in its place—and the commoners flourished. Yet by 1600, as capital flowed outside the rigidly policed social boundaries, a nouveau riche class including Christians, Jews, and Muslims emerged, along with increased use of cash in the economy. Pay overtook patronage. This became especially clear for the landholdings granted by the central government. Social contracts changed as the cavalry funded by land grants passed away. Other changing social contracts were between the sultan and the commoners, and between the sultan and the military class—the designated mediators of the sultan's authority. Istanbul trained a military elite and sent it out to the provinces to control the empire. But with the rise of a monetised economy and new powers, including tax farmers and merchants, this ruling military and political elite lost its formerly secure place. What was required was for the dynasty to acknowledge the claims of the ruling elite to be the sole holders of power and wealth. But the regime decided to circumvent this by hiring commoners as soldiers, allowing peasants a share of the privileges of the elite, precipitating a clash. The military class, including the administration, resisted having to share its financial and ruling privileges with commoners.

By the seventeenth century, it was easy for Christian commoners to join the military class through conversion to Islam. This avenue had not been as open in earlier centuries when the government had relied more on restricted members of professional troops, Collection Janissaries in particular, and less on volunteers and irregular troops. Consequently, in this era, facing decreased distinction of membership, the first major Janissary revolts occurred. Their rebelliousness was accompanied by an excessive growth in their numbers caused by an opening of their ranks beyond Collection recruits. There were so many of them that the sultan could not confine the Janissaries to their barracks as bachelors, so they lived in urban areas, married, and joined guilds. Rather than remaining an elite, on-call force, these new Janissaries compelled actual guild masters to make them partners, sharing in their profits, opening shops where they wished, and selling goods at the prices they desired. In general, these Janissaries flouted guild regulations. Beholden to their families and businesses, their loyalty was less to the sultan and more to their own financial status. Yet they still expected regular payment of their salaries from the treasury. When their payments were delayed, or when they were paid in debased coinage such as in 1589, they rebelled, joined by the merchants with whom they had become entangled.

OTTOMAN OBSERVERS OF OTTOMAN DECLINE

Following decades of peace, renewed, decades-long wars against the Habsburgs and Safavids between 1578 and 1618, combined with changes in the key administrative institutions including the sultanate, led to a perception of decline among members of those same ruling institutions. This in turn led to a growth in political analysis and calls for reform in how the empire was governed and by whom. Searching for remedies to cure the body politic, many argued for turning the clock back to a romanticised 'golden age' with a strong sultan as unopposed military leader, along the lines of a caesar.

Beginning in the late sixteenth century, in order to 'save' the empire, Ottoman intellectuals began to analyse the birth of Ottoman decline, what had caused it, and how it could be reversed. In an inscription on a citadel in Moldova, Suleiman I had once boasted of his own sultanship: 'I am God's slave and Sultan of this world. By the grace of God I am head of Muhammad's community. God's might and Muhammad's miracles are my companions. I am Suleiman, in whose name the Friday sermon is read in Mecca and Medina. In Baghdad I am the Shah, in Byzantine realms the Caesar, and in Egypt, the Sultan; who sends his fleets to the seas of Europe, North Africa, and India. I am the Sultan who took the crown and throne of Hungary and granted them to a humble slave'.[43] It was against this template—conquest, wealth, Islamic piety—that all future sultans would be judged.

Despite Suleiman I's claims, the Ottomans did not destroy the Habsburgs or Safavids. Nor did they take the capitals of Vienna or Tabriz (more than temporarily) or Isfahan, let alone Venice or the seat of the pope in Rome. After Suleiman I, the Ottomans waged long, costly, and ultimately fruitless campaigns. The Ottomans fought the Safavids in the Caucasus under Murad III from 1578 to 1590, and during the entire reign of Ahmed I from 1603 to 1618. Murad III, Mehmed III, and Ahmed I waged continuous campaigns against the Habsburgs in Central Europe from 1593 to 1606. The Ottomans lost their former military superiority, not least in gunpowder technology.

After the reign of Safavid shah Tahmasp ended when he was poisoned in 1576 during a dispute with the Red Heads over who would inherit his throne, the Ottoman rival entered a decade of political chaos. The Red Heads, not the dynasty, were in charge. To reign in these ecstatic warriors, Shah Tahmasp had begun to recruit Christian slaves from the Caucasus to be trained as a central army. After his death, Tahmasp's younger son Ismail II acceded to the throne, but he was murdered a year later by the Red Heads and replaced by Tahmasp's only other son by a Turkish concubine, Muhammad Khudabanda. Stability returned only with the ascension of Shah Abbas I (reigned 1588–1629). Abbas I—who was brought to power in a Red Head coup—aimed to end the Red Heads' political and military domination. The Safavids turned fully away, like the Ottomans, from a primary reliance on nomadic warriors and put their trust in a loyal standing army made up of converted Christian military slaves from Georgia and Circassia supplied with artillery and paid salaries by a central treasury. The Safavids became again a formidable enemy of the Ottomans as they expanded to their greatest territorial extent and prosperity during Abbas I's reign. They constructed the majestic and massive Royal Square complex—with its bazaar, gardens, palace decorated with colourful frescoes depicting battles against Ottomans, and stunning blue-tiled mosques—in the new capital of Isfahan. Their textile, carpet, and silk industries flourished. These were all symbols of the Safavid resurgence.

In 1603, Shah Abbas I retook Tabriz (held temporarily by the Ottomans); Yerevan, Armenia, after a nine-month siege; and Kars and Van in eastern Anatolia. In 1605, he pushed the Ottomans out of much of the Caucasus and Azerbaijan, including Tbilisi, Georgia. By 1606, the Ottomans had lost all gains in the east made in the wars against the Safavids between 1578 and 1590. In 1624, Abbas I seized Baghdad, held by the Ottomans for nearly a century. Only after Shah Abbas I died were the Ottomans able to retake the revered Arab city on the Tigris.

Such military defeats were seen as a symptom of systemic problems. Ottoman intellectuals railed against favouritism in political appointments, what they perceived as moral decline and financial corruption, the breakdown of class hierarchies, the withdrawal of the sultan from day-to-day decision-making and his reduction to a ceremonial figurehead, and, especially, the

rise in power and influence of the women of the harem, including the awarding of the revenues of provincial landholdings to
royal ladies.[44]

By the end of the sixteenth century there existed an elite of
religious scholars, the military, and the bureaucracy that was the
product of Suleiman I's reign.[45] This intellectual elite was self-
conscious of its identity, its privileged place, and its history. Members saw themselves as bearers and articulators of the meritocratic
Ottoman Way.[46] Addressing political tracts to the sultan, the authors of critical works painted an ideal image of the empire at
work, partly based on their own grievances. Writing polemical
works in defence of the interests of their class and to express frus-
tration about their own failure to acquire the power and privilege
they believed they deserved, these authors analysed the causes of
the imperial system's transformation and prescribed remedies.
They aimed to restore the idealised practices of the past, the age
of Mehmed II, Selim I, or Suleiman I, and focused on what they
perceived to be institutional failure, injustice, and social disruptions. Intellectuals saw canon law (kanun, secular law)—on par
with Islamic law (Sharia, religious law)—as a symbol embodying
the Ottoman commitment to justice, the very basis of its political legitimacy.[47] Promoting secular (canon) and sacred (Islamic
law) justice, they equated injustice with imperial failure. These
authors complained of secular law not being followed, custom being violated, the erosion of elite orders, corruption, and military
inefficiency borne of the military class having been 'infiltrated' by
commoners and 'foreigners'.[48]

From the end of the sixteenth century to the early eighteenth
century, Mustafa Ali was joined by a number of other elitist, grip-
ing, misogynist, prejudiced, prudish, xenophobic Ottoman intellectuals who waxed nostalgic for Suleiman I's reign.[49] Writers of
his type sought in vain to control social mobility, especially entry
into the privileged, ruling elite. They perceived social disruption

and administrative disorder everywhere, blaming this state of affairs on royal women having power over men and the fact that princesses, eunuchs, and 'foreigners' rather than cavalrymen were being given large land grants. They raged against 'accursed', 'traitorous' Jews holding positions at court while Sunni Muslims were supposedly viewed with scorn.[50] They blamed the sultan: '"The fish stinks from the head" they say; the head of all this woe is known'.[51] They perceived an imperial household overrun by 'Turks, Gypsies, Jews, people without religion or faith, cutpurses and city riff-raff'. The Janissaries had become crowded with 'townsmen, Turks, Gypsies, Tats [an Iranian group], Lazes [a Black Sea people], muleteers, camel-drivers, porters', and highway robbers.[52]

These intellectuals longed for a powerful, resolute man of the sword to lead a political elite built on meritocracy. They idealised a time when cavalry fought for God and not pleasure, when society was ruled by Islamic law and not greed, as in the new monetised economy, which expanded the membership of the elite and witnessed the rise of new social groups. To rectify these problems, they advocated that the sultan become again a real man of the sword, not a ceremonial figure withdrawn from battle and decision-making.[53] One tragic figure would take their advice but pay the consequences.

THE FIRST REGICIDE: THE KILLING OF OSMAN II

These tirades were the manifestation of a public sphere where the elite debated the course of the empire, pronouncing harsh criticisms after a sultan passed away and offering detailed policy proposals for change.[54] But this discourse should not be exaggerated. There was no free speech in that era, and words considered treasonous or blasphemous caused many an execution. Nor did these intellectuals form an organised opposition. Not many were bold enough to go so far as to question the right of the Ottoman dynasty to rule or the legitimacy of its form of government. Most desired to save the empire on its own terms.

But the grumbling intellectuals were on to something. The empire was changing, if not in ways they liked. If we acknowledge their biased view and personal stake as the losers in the transformation, we can still use their laments and prescriptions for change to decipher how a new state of government was coming into being.

We should not call this 'decline'. If there was political decline in the empire, it came much later than with the death of Suleiman I. The empire lasted 356 years beyond his death, representing a very long decline. So long, in fact, that it lasted over half the empire's lifetime. The term 'transformation' or the phrase 'crisis and change' might be preferable to 'decline' and 'stagnation'. The former terms have none of the negative, moralistic baggage of the latter. But that is just wordplay.

In 1618, Mustafa I became the second sultan in the dynasty's history to be deposed (Bayezid II was the first). He was also the first to be unseated by machinations at court rather than by the Janissaries. The architect of his downfall after only three months in power was the chief harem eunuch, Mustafa Agha—another sign of the weakened sultanate.[55] Mustafa I was declared mentally unfit to rule and sequestered in the princely apartments in the harem. According to an Ottoman chronicler, the 'weak-mindedness and deranged nature' of the sultan was obvious, and his strange deeds had become the subject of gossip. In public he repeatedly gesticulated as if he were throwing gold pieces at fish in the sea, suggesting that he reenacted the enthronement ceremonies, including scattering coins to the Janissaries, which must have traumatised him.[56]

He was replaced by his fourteen-year-old nephew, Osman II (reigned 1618–1622), the first firstborn Ottoman prince since 1453 to be born in Istanbul.[57] All previous firstborns had been born in provincial capitals where their fathers served as governors and trained for the sultanate. Those days were over. The only aspect of provincial training reflected in Osman II's early life was his love of horses, horse riding, and hunting. He buried his favourite horse in the grounds of one of the palaces and erected a tombstone for it.[58]

Osman II aimed to return power to the sultanate. And he was in a hurry. At only the age of sixteen he led a military campaign in person on the northernmost march ever undertaken by the Ottoman army.[59] Before he left Istanbul, he had his eldest brother, Mehmed, strangled, lest he launch a coup in his absence.[60] The 1621 campaign against the Commonwealth of Poland-Lithuania at the crucial citadel of Khotin, Ukraine—on the banks of the Dniester river, at the border between the Ottoman vassal Moldova and the opposing Polish-Lithuanian empire—ended in a draw, however. A draw was a failure for the sultan, who had hoped for a quick, spectacular victory.[61] Returning to the Ottoman capital at the beginning of the next year, Osman II sought to retake the reins from jurists and soldiers who had not performed well and recentralise political power in his hands. He aimed to abolish the Janissary corps and replace it with a new army equipped with muskets recruited from Arab, Druze, and Kurdish Muslim mercenaries, as well as peasants and nomads from Anatolia and Syria. He appointed as grand vizier a provincial governor who had raised his own mercenary army, another example of the concurrent monetisation of the economy and rise of new regional political forces.[62] Osman II wanted to relocate the Ottoman capital to Damascus, Syria, so as to make the empire more Middle Eastern than European, more Eastern than Western. He even planned to take the hajj to Mecca, which no sultan had ever done. Jurists and soldiers alike opposed his eastward journey and the threat of a new army that would replace the old. A new stage in the development of the dynasty had been reached.

Sultans had become symbolic shadows of power whose deposition and killing was licit according to legal scholars. The spring day Osman II was to set off to raise his new mercenary army, en route to the pilgrimage and moving the imperial capital, became his last in power. On 18 May 1622, rumours that the sultan was also taking the imperial treasury to pay the new troops and planning to abolish the established military elites' salaries and landholdings motivated the Janissaries and cavalry to riot jointly in Istanbul.[63] After gaining support from the sheikhulislam, they demanded the execution of the chief harem eunuch Suleiman Agha (successor of Mustafa Agha), whom they blamed for these plans. The sultan dismissed his grand vizier instead, and the next day a greater crowd consisting of Janissaries, cavalrymen, and jurists gathered at the Hippodrome. They presented a petition to the sheikhulislam demanding even more heads. According to the contemporary account of a Jewish palace physician, several thousand rebels 'crashed suddenly on the palace like ocean waves'.[64] The sultan was unresponsive to the demands to turn over the chief harem eunuch. At that point, the crowd made its decision to depose him.

Several Janissaries scaled the roof of the palace and, using axes, broke through the lead-covered dome of the room in the harem where the deposed Mustafa I, who had preceded Osman II on the throne, was hidden. They descended on improvised ropes made of curtains. Killing several harem eunuchs who fired arrows at them, they entered the sultan's bedroom and looted his treasury. After finding Suleiman Agha, they took him outside and 'with over three hundred sword blows riddled his corpse with holes'.[65] They found Mustafa I in a small, padlocked room with two servants, emaciated as no one had remembered to provide food or water during the past days of tumult.[66] He requested a sip of water from his saviours. The grand vizier was found hiding elsewhere in the city and killed.

The rebels located Sultan Osman II taking refuge in the home of the Janissary commander, whom they murdered. As a sign of his humiliation, Osman II was not permitted to wear a turban.

Treating him worse than an ordinary person, the soldiers marched him to the mosque of the Janissary barracks near the mosque of Mehmed II in the centre of the peninsula. From the palace they also brought Mustafa I and the mother of the sultan, who spoke to the throng assembled in the mosque with her face veiled. Unfortunately, her name was not recorded for posterity. The bare-headed sultan wanted a turban and to speak to the crowd too, but neither was he given a head covering nor did anyone want to hear from him. He promised the crowd gold and silver and valuable cloaks but they paid no heed, as the rebels had decided to kill him. Twice the rebel leader Davud Pasha, who was selected to be the new grand vizier by Mustafa I's mother, had the chief armourer try to put a noose around Osman II's neck to strangle him, but the sultan pushed him away. The mob shouted insults at him and spat in his face. He became petrified seeing the reaction of the angry crowd.[67]

While the mother of the sultan and Mustafa I returned in the imperial carriage to Topkapı Palace so the latter could be enthroned for a second time, the deposed Sultan Osman II was dumped unceremoniously outside the mosque in a market wagon. According to the Jewish palace physician, the sultan 'who previously slept on a feather bed was made to sit on a stack of hay'.[68] Acting on the order of Grand Vizier Davud Pasha, Janissaries and cavalrymen escorted Osman II to the royal dungeon in the Seven Towers fortress.[69] An immense crowd followed the common wagon all the way to Seven Towers, jeering at the former sultan and reaching into the vehicle to assault him. Imprisonment at that dungeon, located on the Sea of Marmara at the southwesternmost corner of Istanbul, was a death sentence.

On Friday, 20 May, they murdered him. According to a contemporary Ottoman historian, the chief armourer put the oiled noose used for executions around his neck. Because the eighteen-year-old Osman II courageously resisted, attacking his guards with a wild fury, a cavalry commander named Kalender 'squeezed his testicles and exhausted him until he gave up his soul'.[70] The chief armourer then cut off Osman II's ear and brought it to the mother of the sultan as proof of the death of her son's rival. Treating Osman II as a criminal, perhaps they cut off his nose as well. As the historian concludes, no ruler of the Ottoman dynasty had ever been treated with such contempt. Princes had been killed for centuries according to the law of fratricide—though not in this humiliating manner—but never a sultan.[71]

Davud Pasha's grand vizierate only lasted a few weeks. In little over half a year, the three men responsible for the killing of Osman II—Davud Pasha, the chief armourer, and the cavalry commander Kalender (whose name, perhaps not coincidentally, is the same term used for a type of deviant dervish)—were arrested and killed by strangling or having their throats slit. Kalender's corpse was not buried, but thrown in the Bosporus, 'like that of a dead dog'.[72] A year later, Mustafa I was deposed again, as his already poor mental health, manifested in his strange speech and gestures, had worsened. Yet the mother of the sultan intervened to ensure he was not executed.

What these episodes demonstrate is that by this moment in Ottoman history, the dynasty had entered a new phase. From the time of Osman I, power and fortune (*devlet*) and the sultanate had inhered in the sultan. By the beginning of the seventeenth century, as made concrete with the enthronement and deposition of Mustafa I, as well as the deposition and murder of Osman II, devlet meant the dynasty, the whole Ottoman family. Allegiance and loyalty were due to the dynasty and the sultanate, no matter the qualities of the individual sultan.

Previously the sultanate and the man holding that position were seen as one. The sultan was a mere mortal but one who embodied the dynasty. The death of the sultan was a real crisis. His death seemed to mean the dynasty had temporarily ended. But by this point in time the sultan had two natures. The sultan's body, unlike in the rest of Europe, was not considered sacred, and once deposed could be treated worse than any other. Killing the sultan did not mean ending the dynasty. It was the man, not the sultanate, whose time on earth had ended. Another man could be chosen to rule in his stead, guaranteeing dynastic continuity.[73] The Ottoman dynasty had become a different kind of regime. For this reason, the following chapters will focus more on the family dynasty and the royal women than on the sultan.

A SHIFT TOWARDS LIMITED GOVERNMENT

The first regicide in Ottoman history—carried out in horrible fashion and sandwiched between the two dethronements of Mustafa I—forever altered the bonds between the sultan and his subjects. Thereafter his power was limited, constrained by the law as interpreted by jurists, who, though appointed by the sultan to rule in his name, acted independently to limit his power. They curbed the sultan's power when they legitimated the actions of the Janissary corps, who, once a crucial cog in the centralised administration, now served as a check on the authority of the central government. The sultan's subjects were no longer his servants and slaves. He was theirs. In the two centuries following Osman II's dethronement and murder, seven of fourteen sultans were deposed. Rather than being outsiders ill-deserving of a share in power or a say in who was fit to rule, the Janissaries and jurists who deposed these sultans were expressing the will of—if not all, then a larger segment of—the people than when only the royal family decided who should rule.

What the authors and actors of this time were in fact witnessing was a new polity, a limited government centred on the Janissaries, who represented a sector of the common people or at least the urban Muslim population.[74] We do not know if the Janissaries of this time were a sort of a political party representing the will of the people, because we do not know whether they had a group consciousness or mentality. One wonders how popular they were among the guilds when they forced merchants to pay 'tribute'. It is debatable whether the Janissaries 'spoke for' the Christians and Jews of urban areas or for the majority of Ottoman subjects, the peasantry. Nevertheless, they and the jurists were one of the two groups compelling a new polity. In contrast to previous centuries when slaves rose in the social hierarchy to dominate the administration and military, in the new polity any free Muslim male could join the ruling elite and rise in the government hierarchy.[75]

Introduced by the rebellions of military men and the legal reasoning of jurists, limited government may have sowed the seeds for democracy, even if they were never fully reaped. The Janissaries were neither political reactionaries nor economic conservatives. Due to their often primary role as merchants rather than soldiers, the Janissaries supported the transition to a market economy. Sometimes they acted as a collective representing the interests of Muslim merchants and artisans. At other times, merchants revolted in Istanbul with the jurists on their side. Islamic law did not hinder a monetary economy and limited government. Earlier jurists had already legitimised the use of cash to endow public foundations such as mosques and the ability to profit from interest. Jurists allied with the merchant class defended tax farming and cash endowments, interpreting the law in opposition to absolutist government. The same jurists backed rebellious Janissaries by legitimising the deposition and enthronement of sultans. They brought the sultanate under legal supervision, using Islamic law to counter secular canon law. The reins of power were no longer in the hands of the sultans. They were held by the Janissaries and jurists.

The actions of Janissaries and jurists in turn led to the creation of a form of polity more civil than military. The social uprisings that they led began to curtail the unlimited authority of the sultan in the old order. They helped build the foundation for a state apparatus differentiated from the person of the ruler, one of the key features of modernity. Modernity was not something Western, imposed by outsiders on the Ottoman Empire at a later time. Developments East and West are related, as the Ottoman Empire was part of Europe and Europe was part of Eurasia.

This fact was noticed by well-informed Western European writers. Luigi Ferdinando Marsigli was a Bolognese intellectual who had lived in Istanbul but then served in the Habsburg military, became an Ottoman prisoner of war, was released, took part in the negotiations for the Treaty of Karlowitz of 1699, and led the Habsburg commission mapping the boundary between the two empires. In his treatise on the Ottoman military, he noted that the Ottoman despotism of the age of Suleiman I had long since ended, as Janissaries dethroned sultans, imprisoned or killed them, and enthroned others in their place when backed by the authority of the jurists. For in this new era, sultanic rule was dependent on 'the consent of both Estates, the judicial one and the military one'.[76] Exaggerating, he called it a 'democracy'.[77]

In the world's oldest democracy, England, Charles I was the first (and only) king to be executed. He had come to the throne in 1625 and immediately wrangled with Parliament over the limits to their respective powers. Charles I dismissed Parliament in 1629 and ruled without it until 1640. But he was forced to bring Parliament back to raise money for war against Scotland, and the legislature refused, presenting instead a long list of grievances against him. Charles I responded by attempting to arrest the leaders of Parliament. This led to eight years of civil war between the supporters of Parliament and the king, the forces of the former claiming victory. Charles I was found guilty of treason and beheaded in public before Banqueting House in the centre of London in 1649. Thereafter, for almost a dozen years, Oliver Cromwell ruled an English Republic, but in 1660 Charles II was restored to the throne.

Some of the political developments in England were shared by the Ottoman Empire. The killing of Osman II is thus yet another example of the Ottomans partaking in European historical developments. In both Istanbul and London, the regicides of the seventeenth century compelled a turn away from a system of government in which rulers had unlimited authority and towards a new system of limited monarchy. The murder of Osman II was the onset of a period of limited government in which royal authority was diminished and the institution of government was made distinct from the person of the sultan.

Events East and West could occur at the same time, but it did not mean they were coterminous or that distinct societies were on the same trajectory. At the time the English had a long-standing Parliament and the Ottomans had not yet established theirs. Unlike the English, the Ottomans did not temporarily establish a republic, nor promulgate a Bill of Rights as the English did, leading to a constitutional monarchy. What was analogous was how the affairs of Ottoman government were now in the hands of the grand vizier, whose role was similar to that of a prime minister. His office was located outside the palace grounds.

While conventional European history views the 1649 execution of Charles I as ushering in the modern era, the 1622 killing of Osman II twenty-seven years earlier—the first regicide in Ottoman history—was as earthshaking a political event. What was happening in the Ottoman Empire should be compared with how similar events in England were viewed by historians.[78] Thereafter in the Ottoman Empire, three generations of jurists from the same family would sanction deposing and even executing sultans.[79] It was the start of a new age, a shift in the balance of power wherein the high authority of the ruler was challenged and lost.

THE DEMAND FOR A MANLY SULTAN

The revolts of Janissaries and jurists may have ushered in a new political era, yet supporters of the old order promoted the return of a determined sultan as the solution to the real and imagined crises of the era. Mustafa Naima of Aleppo, son of a Janissary who served as official court 'annalist', suggested remedies for saving the empire.[80] Naima was influenced by the Tunisian thinker Ibn Khaldun, whose ideas Ottoman intellectual circles found relevant in the sixteenth, seventeenth, and eighteenth centuries.[81] Ibn Khaldun argued that empires pass through five inevitable stages. Ottoman thinkers desperately tried to determine where theirs fell on the spectrum—beginning with the heroic age and passing through stages of consolidation, confidence and security, contentment or surfeit and decline, and finally disintegration—and what they could do about it. Naima believed that the Ottomans had reached the penultimate stage. He sought measures to restore the dynasty and empire to an earlier stage of historical development.

Ibn Khaldun also became popular because he employed ideas already familiar to Ottoman thinkers, as expressed by jurist Kınalızade Ali, who propagated the older Persian and Greek theory of the 'circle of justice':

> There can be no royal authority without the military.
> There can be no military without wealth.
> The subjects produce the wealth.
> Justice preserves the subjects' loyalty to the sovereign.
> Justice requires harmony in the world.
> The world is a garden, its walls are the state.
> Islamic law orders the state.
> There is no support for Islamic law except through royal
> authority.[82]

Justice was embodied in dynastic secular law that was harmonised with Islamic law. Justice legitimised Ottoman rule. Considering the ideas of Ibn Khaldun and Kınalızade, the practical-minded Naima advocated remedies for regenerating the empire. They included the balancing of expenses and income, ending the practice of delaying payments to salaried officials, making all military corps full strength, giving military security to peasants, and

making the land prosperous. The final recommendation was that
the sultan should be cheerful, which would create affection, causing all to be loyal to him. The greatest good, Naima argued, was
having a strong sultan.

We have heard this before. Again and again, intellectuals had
argued that all that was needed to right the wrongs they perceived
was the rise to power of a decisive, manly, gazi sultan. But Osman II tried to be this, and he was deposed and killed. Would the
return of a warrior-sultan be enough? Was it too late to reverse the
socioeconomic changes the intellectuals such as Mustafa Ali so
despised? Who would dare aim to make the sultanate once more
the centre of Ottoman power? Osman II would not be the last
such attempt at imperial relevance by a sultan gazi.

RETURN OF THE GAZI
Mehmed IV

B Y THE EARLY seventeenth century, the Ottoman sultanate had greatly declined in prestige. Sultans had been relegated to a sedentary, ceremonial role. They were dominated by valide sultans who, as the only indispensable members of the dynasty, were the de facto rulers behind the scenes at Topkapı Palace. Sultans were also overshadowed by grand viziers—it was they who made the day-to-day decisions of government and led military campaigns.

Because they were dispensable, seventeenth-century sultans were the first and only Ottoman rulers to be executed. Osman II had attempted to break this pathetic mould and make himself into a warrior-sultan who engaged in battle with the Christian enemy and left the palace in order to appear as a living person, not just a figurehead, to his subjects. But his efforts were resisted violently and he paid the ultimate price.

To seventeenth-century Ottoman historians, manliness and male virtue were central in the making and unmaking of sultans.[1] Prior to the modern era, Ottoman writers, like writers in the rest of Europe, did not distinguish between masculinity and femininity. Instead, in Renaissance Europe and the Ottoman Empire, authors judged people by their male or female virtues and performance of gendered positions. In the Ottoman Empire, manliness was defined by bravery and courage proven on the battlefield—labelled interchangeably gaza or jihad. To understand what this meant for Ottoman sultans, we only need consider the reigns of Ibrahim I (reigned 1640–1648) and Mehmed IV (reigned 1648–1687).

IBRAHIM I: THE SECOND SULTAN TO BE EXECUTED

Following Mustafa I's second deposition, when he was sent to the harem to while away the rest of his days in 1623, Ahmed I's eldest surviving son, the eleven-year-old Murad, replaced him as Murad IV (reigned 1623–1640) on the throne. Murad IV was overshadowed for the first ten years of his reign by his regent, favourite of Ahmed I and mother of the sultan Kösem Sultan. In these years, the Ottomans lost Baghdad to the Safavids in 1624 and Murad IV failed to take it back in 1630. He managed to reconquer Yerevan, Armenia, in 1635 and retook Baghdad in 1638. After the first conquest, he had his brothers Bayezid and Suleiman put to death; after the second, it was the turn of his brother Kasım.[2] To commemorate his military feats, he built the stunningly beautiful, octagonal, blue-tiled Baghdad and Yerevan pleasure pavilions in the fourth courtyard at Topkapı Palace. Following Murad IV's victory over the Safavids, in 1639 the two rival empires agreed to the Treaty of Zuhab (a town on the Iraq-Iran frontier), which ended over a century of warfare started by Selim I's defeat of Ismail I at Çaldıran. But within a year of leading his army on campaign, Murad IV died of complications from gout—he was overweight and a heavy drinker—at the age of twenty-nine.[3] One chronicler noted with irony that he passed away in the same chamber where he had had his brother Kasım put to death.[4] Since Mustafa I, his uncle, had recently passed away, and Murad IV had already had his three other brothers killed, the only one who could inherit the throne was the single living male Ottoman heir, his younger brother Ibrahim.

Ottoman chroniclers declared that Ibrahim I displayed none of the expected male virtues. They condemned him for his alleged lack of manliness as displayed by his inability to control himself or the women of the harem, with whom he spent an inordinate amount of his time.[5] As in the rest of contemporary Europe, these virtues included self-discipline; subduing the passions; not being consumed by a drive for luxury, ease, sensuality, and pleasure; and control over others in the household, particularly women. These were features apparently lacking in Ibrahim I, which led to his demise. Like young men in early modern England, he was criticised for lust and idleness—allegedly the outcomes of the absence of self-mastery, the defining feature of manliness. Ottoman chroniclers depicted a topsy-turvy world where female royals made decisions for the sultan and represented the dynasty, while a sultan without virtue sat on the throne.

Ibrahim I was told to procreate lest the dynasty become extinct, and he was accordingly presented many concubines for this purpose.[6] But on the other hand, he was criticised for being over-indulgent in fulfilling his own desires. He was unable to make it appear as if he could successfully combine procreation and a reasonable enjoyment of sexual relations. One Ottoman writer wrote fancifully that in Transylvania he saw frescoes in the great hall of an elaborate fifteenth-century Hungarian palace. The master painter had predicted the main affairs of each sultanic reign. According to the writer, two centuries earlier the painter had anticipated that Sultan Ibrahim I 'would be martyred holding his penis in his hand'.[7] As evident in this evocative image, contemporaries viewed the problem to be Ibrahim I's lack of self-control and intimacy with women. Desiring to please them, he became ensnared in the trap of enjoyment that led to his death.

According to his enemies, Ibrahim I's alleged lack of male virtue led to moral, political, and financial corruption. Ibrahim I

allegedly spent most of his life in the 'prison' of the harem, surrounded by women.[8] To observers, this was detrimental to his
ability to be a manly ruler. They linked state affairs going astray
with women dominating the sultanate. Men were supposed to
dominate politics.[9] One author longed for a nonexistent strong
and powerful royal man who would put women in their place. Yet
this need could not be fulfilled by Ibrahim I, especially considering his behaviour when facing the crisis of being the last living
Ottoman male, the last male descendant of Osman.

Ibrahim I's lack of male virtue was blamed for economic crises
as well. The influence of royal women had direct financial consequences at a precarious time. Women allegedly were in charge of
a bribery scheme buying and selling government positions, which
ruined the empire's finances. Thanks to the generosity of the leading men of state, rather than supporting one favourite concubine
(haseki sultan) as was customary, Ibrahim I had numerous concubines and *eight* favourites. Supposedly due to these expenditures
for maintaining so many women, 'there was excessive waste and
squandering inside and outside' the palace; 'revenues coming to
the treasury were limited, the salaries of the Sultan's servants were
not being given, and all suffered straitened circumstances and
poverty' so that Ibrahim's favourite females could live the high
life.[10] Royal women were accused of sometimes awarding land
grants to themselves, rather than to men, which was only the tip
of the financial-impropriety iceberg. The sultan bankrupted the
leading men of state with his unceasing demands for expensive
sable fur. Several Janissary commanders claimed they possessed
only gunpowder and bullets and not furs or perfume. There were
rumours that Ibrahim I braided his beard with diamonds and
wore diamonds on the soles of his shoes.

Palace women were enriched at the Janissaries' expense as
Ibrahim I gave the most lucrative landholdings to his favourites.
In the eyes of Ottoman chroniclers, he had to be dethroned in
order to protect male privilege. The rule of men was referred to

as the law of the land. Men's satisfaction and prosperity mattered
more than those of women.

Misogynistic writers favoured the logic of 'reasonable and legal'
proposals of 'rational men' to the 'anger and wrath' of the valide
sultan.[11] Ibrahim I's heeding of his female companions' desires
was responsible for turning gender relations upside down and destroying the empire.[12] Lacking manliness and male virtue, Ibrahim I's frivolous disposition led to his associating with women. In
wasting his sperm, the man who was supposed to be leading the
dynasty and empire also squandered his symbolic and economic
capital. Lost to his multiple favourites, he could not even choose
who was best. Gender politics and the proper gendered hierarchy
of royal men and women were at work in the minds of those who
opposed the man who 'disgraced the honour of the Sultanate', and
of those who justified his overthrow and execution.[13]

MEHMED IV: BOY SULTAN TO MANLY SULTAN

In summer 1648, Janissaries, jurists (including Sheikhulislam
Karaçelebizade), and a big crowd referred to by some Ottoman
chroniclers as 'the public' (representing the will of the people)
marched to the third gate, the Gate of Felicity, of Topkapı Palace,
site of enthronements. They demanded the dethronement of Ibrahim I and the enthronement of his oldest son, Prince Mehmed, in
his place. At the anteroom to the third gate, Kösem Sultan—the
spouse of (deceased) Ahmed I, the mother of (deceased) Murad IV
and of Ibrahim I, and the grandmother of Prince Mehmed—
upbraided the rebels for agreeing to whatever Ibrahim I had desired, stating, 'Now you want to replace him with a small child.
What an evil plan this is. This crime of sedition is your doing'.[14]

She demanded to know how a seven-year-old could be king.
They told her that legal opinions had been issued declaring that it
was not permissible to allow a buffoon to rule. When an unrea-
sonable man is the sovereign, he cannot be persuaded to follow a

rational path and causes great harm to the realm. When a child sits on the throne he does not actually govern; his viziers do. They debated for hours until the soldiers lost patience and demanded that if the mother of the sultan did not surrender the prince they would storm the harem and forcibly take him. After assenting to their setting up the emerald throne before the gate, the valide sultan 'tucked up her skirts in fury' and went inside to get the prince. Some time later, with 'apparent distress and hatred in her face' she brought the boy out, asking, 'Is this what you want?'[15] Karaçelebizade set him on the throne. All the ministers took their oath of allegiance to their new child leader, Mehmed IV. But, so the little boy would not be frightened, the hundreds of Janissaries with their oversized moustaches and high caps were kept from taking the oath. After the excitement, the new emperor took a nap guarded by harem eunuchs.[16]

Battle raged on the Hippodrome (the city's main plaza, located just outside the palace) between the Janissaries, who supported Mehmed IV, and the cavalrymen, who backed Ibrahim I. The outcome was predictable. It was as when Ottoman forces battled the Safavids or the Mamluks: Janissary long rifles defeated swords and arrows every time. It was a massacre. The surviving cavalrymen took refuge inside Sultan Ahmed I's mosque (the Blue Mosque), but the Janissaries showed no mercy. Their bullets 'rained down on' the cavalrymen as they were murdered before the pulpit and prayer niche.[17] Prayers were not said over the dead, whose bodies were dumped into the Sea of Marmara.[18]

One of the first imperial decrees issued in the name of the boy sultan declared that Ibrahim I, living under house arrest, was stirring insurrection with the assistance of his loyal followers, including harem eunuchs and palace guards, some of whom wished to reenthrone him.[19] Jurists and Janissaries asked the sheikhulislam for a legal opinion about whether it was permissible to have him executed to prevent further rebellion, utilising the same logic used to defend fratricide. Karaçelebizade consented. Kösem

Sultan, weeping while praying before the mantle of the Prophet, responded to the decision by asking, 'Who gave this man the evil eye'?[20] Learning of his fate, which was to be the same as that of his older brother Osman II, wearing a skullcap and holding a Qur'an in his hand, Ibrahim I wailed, 'Why will you kill me? This is God's book, you tyrants, what authority permits you to murder me?'[21] Three weeks after Ibrahim I was dethroned, a reluctant executioner strangled the thirty-five-year-old former sultan with an oiled lasso.[22]

Ibrahim I was the second sultan to be killed in a generation. If a sultan's right to rule was justified by his being a war leader, little kept sultans on the throne in the seventeenth century, when they were no longer warrior-kings.

Mehmed IV became sultan at the age of seven, before he had even been circumcised. Predictably, during his minority little Mehmed IV wilted into the background, overshadowed by royal women. Initially, the most significant of these was Kösem Sultan. This wealthy woman built the largest commercial building in Istanbul and served as regent at the beginning of three sultans' reigns.

Ottoman women serving as regent during a sultan's minority is comparable to the practice in the rest of Europe, where women royals frequently held a regency. Nevertheless, the political authority of Ottoman royal women should not be exaggerated. Sovereignty may have been held by the entire dynastic family, but women never ruled as sultana, a Western word denoting the royal women surrounding the sultan: mothers, wives, and consorts. They may have exercised power, but they did not hold it. Elsewhere in Europe it was different. England had Mary I (reigned 1553–1558), Elizabeth I (reigned 1558–1603), and Anne Stuart (reigned 1702–1714). Mary Stuart (reigned 1542–1587) was monarch of Scotland. Queen Christina (reigned 1632–1654) was sovereign of Sweden. Maria Theresa of Austria (reigned 1740–1780) ruled Habsburg territories in Central Europe; she was also empress by marriage. Russian women monarchs included Elizabeth Petrovna (reigned 1741–1762) and Catherine II (reigned 1762–1796). The Ottomans had Kösem Sultan.

Kösem Sultan was regent after Mehmed IV's enthronement. While the grand vizier was responsible for day-to-day imperial affairs and leading the empire in war, the valide sultan and chief eunuch, who had access to men and women in the dynasty, ran the household and palace. With the decreased importance of the sultan and the increased role of Ottoman royal women, at the beginning of Mehmed IV's reign, when the boy was enthroned as a child, Kösem Sultan and Mehmed IV's mother, Hatice Turhan Sultan, competed to be the boy's regent. The former won the initial contest. The two women continued to struggle for power in the palace, along with the chief eunuch of the harem.

A weak sultanate and constant struggle between the valide sultan, the grand vizier, and the chief eunuch meant the Janissaries were a powerful faction at court.[23] They were able to make or unmake sultans at will. They revolted nine times during the first eight years of Mehmed IV's reign, and the grand vizier spent much of his time in office attempting to rein in this elite military force. Although by this time there was no longer any need for the sultan to display manly virtues, that did not mean that all members of the elite were pleased with the influence of the Janissaries at the sultan's expense, or with the rise of the valide sultan and the chief eunuch. Some pined for a return of the sultan's display of male virtue and expression of manliness through warfare. The display of such virtues could serve as a rallying cry for those alienated by the rise of these new power holders.

In 1651, palace guards backing Mehmed IV's young mother, Hatice Turhan Sultan, strangled the seventy-year-old Kösem Sultan, perhaps with her own plaits. Thereafter, Hatice Turhan—who had been given as a gift to Kösem as a newly converted Russian captive—served as Mehmed IV's regent. The valide sultan always stood by his side. She was present when Mehmed IV met with the grand vizier, asking questions or responding to Mehmed IV's questions.[24] She stopped at nothing to ensure she led the dynasty and became the one charged with the well-being of its name. Writs of the grand viziers customarily addressed to the sultan were directed to his mother the regent instead. The valide sultan was the real decision-maker and de facto ruler of the dynasty.[25] Even when the sultan was twelve, his mother proclaimed, 'My lion is still a child'.[26]

Hatice Turhan was opposed by many due to her young age. Female elders were respected and given greater freedom, as they were beyond their childbearing years. Young women, by contrast, were not considered mature enough to be able to control themselves and to concentrate on non-sexual, important matters. To gain prestige and promote a pious image, Hatice Turhan endowed the New Mosque (Yeni Cami) in Istanbul. It included the largest royal tomb complex—with the catafalque of its sponsor taking pride of place—and the nearby Egyptian Bazaar.[27] She paid for the repair of two fortresses on Gallipoli, the peninsula on the Aegean Sea and Dardanelles guarding the entrance to the Sea of Marmara and Istanbul, and built mosques, schools, public baths, barracks, shops, and markets for them.[28] Beginning in 1656, Hatice Turhan's power was challenged by the first of many men of the Köprülü family in palace service. Mehmed Köprülü served as grand vizier until 1661. His five years in office were marked by cruelty and repression, as well as fiscal austerity. He even had the Greek Orthodox patriarch Parthenios III executed in 1657.

But the real challenge to Hatice Turhan's power came from her son. Unexpectedly, when he entered his twenties in 1663, Mehmed IV attempted to break free from being overshadowed by women regents and grand viziers alike.[29] At twenty-two, he turned his back on the harem in Istanbul and moved to the old Ottoman frontier warrior capital of Edirne. He aimed to return to an earlier model of a pious, mobile, virtuous, manly, holy-warrior sultan waging military campaigns in Europe. For the two decades after he moved to Edirne, he employed an official chronicler and a number of writers of conquest books. They promoted the message that he was no sedentary sultan idly sitting by in a bureaucratic empire. His writers depicted him constantly on horseback, hunting, throwing the javelin, and waging military campaigns with equal vigour. He enjoyed watching the local oil-wrestling festival where, accompanied by drum and horn, men wearing only trousers made of buffalo hide, their skin glistening with a mixture of olive oil and water, attempted the nearly impossible task of gaining purchase on their slippery opponents and pinning them to the ground. Like an oil wrestler, Mehmed IV was depicted as manly, strong, tanned, and rough, a big man with a solid chest, thick arms, wide hands, and broad shoulders.[30] Responding to the gendered critiques of his father, Ibrahim I, Mehmed IV's chroniclers promoted the view that the sultan was a mobile gazi who had broken out of the harem cage in Topkapı Palace and now spent most of his reign motivated by religious zeal to bring war to the Christian enemy throughout Central and Eastern Europe and the Mediterranean.[31]

Depicted as having recaptured male power from women, Mehmed IV evoked an earlier age when sultans were manly military leaders. This calls to mind one of the competing models of male virtue in medieval Western Europe, that of the knight, whose claim to manliness was based on the fundamental measures of courage displayed in battle against other men and dominance over women. Unlike his father, too busy indulging in non-martial pursuits in the harem, Mehmed IV was considered an earthy, rough, simple leader more comfortable on horseback than sitting on a throne. And far from being presented as a sedate font of peace and reconciliation, the peripatetic Mehmed IV was depicted as eagerly promoting war and overseeing battle. Unlike most other seventeenth-century sultans, he pursued conquest. His armies penetrated enemy territory with swords and missiles, sold the wives of the enemy into slavery, and replaced the signs of their existence (churches) with those of the conqueror (mosques) to demonstrate potency.

In 1666, Mehmed IV relaunched his father's earlier campaign for Crete, one of the largest islands in the Mediterranean. Over twenty years earlier, the partly successful effort had begun under Ibrahim I, whose red-brick, pink-domed mosque crowns the island's windswept, hilltop fortress of Rethymno, located in between Chania and Candia on the north coast of the island. Ibrahim I had been able to conquer several of Crete's cities, but not the entire island.

Under Mehmed IV, the Ottomans successfully captured the entire island by taking its last stronghold, the seemingly impregnable fortress of Candia (Iráklion) in 1669. The sultan did not want to be like his father, who had waged an inconclusive eight-year military campaign for Crete before he was deposed. Mehmed IV's honour was on the line. The sultan challenged the grand vizier to take up the campaign for Crete and said he would personally join the battle, 'preferring to suffer hardship on the path of God', according to one of his conquest book chroniclers.[32] Mehmed IV employed the metaphor of sexual impotence, tying victory to the empire's honour and by extension to his own, for he sought to prove his potency on the battlefield: he told his grand vizier that prolonging the siege would render the empire 'impotent'.[33] During the campaign, he called his army to discipline, bravery, and virility, stating that it would bring shame upon Islamic zeal should his army just 'pull out'.[34]

Mehmed IV's jihad was successful 'because of the zeal, patience, virility, and bravery in battle', according to the author of the island's conquest book.[35] This then led to gendered transformations of the island's buildings. Tall bell towers became minarets. Churches were converted into mosques or public baths. In an act of symbolic violence, a nunnery, an abode of virginal Christian women devoted to a peaceful life of prayer, was converted into a Janissary barracks. It became the quarters of converted Christian men who dedicated their lives to waging war on behalf of an Islamic empire.[36]

Mehmed IV played a direct role in battle, making his presence known and even determining when his forces should fire their cannons. When he arrived before a citadel, Mehmed IV often sent a message to its defenders to turn it over without a fight. If the citadel was taken by force, he would annihilate them.[37] On one occasion, the defenders responded to the sultan by saying, 'Other than the builder, no hand had ever touched the citadel since the day it was built. It is a virgin citadel. Because of this, we prefer to spill our blood [like a virgin who has never been touched]'. On the sultan's command, Ottoman forces bombed the citadel to pieces.

Mehmed IV wanted his legacy to be as a warrior for the faith. His writers responded. Mehmed IV was 'the hero who defeats and destroys the enemy'.[38] Like Osman II, he dared invade Poland twice in person, in 1672 and 1673, launching an arduous campaign in a distant land untouched by 'the hooves of the horses of the gazis'.[39] Mehmed IV was 'the high-flying royal falcon'.[40] This apt imagery, in contrast to the images used when he was a minor, is that of a focused, driven, active, vigorous, powerful, swift, deadly, and ruthless attacker. The falcon sultan swooped down upon his prey, joined by his soldiers, also described as falcons attacking 'the nest of polytheist [Catholic] crows'.[41]

Writers emphasised Mehmed IV's subduing of women vicariously through his warriors' feats of sexual possession and conquest. The 'white castle' of Kameniçe (Kamenets-Podolskiy), the Carpathian fortress perched on a lofty rock in Orhan Pamuk's novel of the same name, was 'an impregnable citadel' located in the southeast corner of Poland (today Ukraine) bordering the northern region of Moldova, the key to Poland and Ukraine.[42] But it stood no chance, being attacked by thousands of manly braves who staked their lives for the cause of gaza.[43] When the warriors beheld the city within the citadel, they felt a sense of wonder and disgust. Accordingly, they converted those areas into 'places of beauty of the gazis' and 'places of worldly pleasure of the believers'. The term 'places of beauty' also means the bride's apartment where the virgin unveils herself for the first time to her husband.

CONVERTING CHRISTIANS AND JEWS, ISLAMISING ISTANBUL

Along with military campaigns, Mehmed IV also sought to burnish a glorious image by Islamising territory and converting his subjects to Islam. In all of the conquered territories, Mehmed IV ordered the great churches be converted to mosques. He also personally converted people. Mehmed IV was constantly on the move in Southeastern Europe. He engaged in massive, Mongol-style hunting parties for which he forced thousands of Christian and Jewish peasants to serve as his drovers, flushing the game towards him as he waited on horseback with arrows, axes, blades, and bullets.[44] During these occasions, thousands converted to Islam in his presence when he either compelled them to change religion or facilitated their doing so at conversion ceremonies.

John Covel, the chaplain to the English ambassador, was a guest at the two-week-long circumcision festivities of princes Ahmed and Mustafa at Edirne in 1675, where thousands of boys and men were circumcised amid musicians and jugglers present to divert their attention. Covel observed that he saw many hundreds of the two thousand 'cut' [circumcised], and the Ottomans, rather than hinder his seeing, made way for him. There were many 'of riper yeares, especially renegades that turn'd Turks'. He saw 'an old man which they reported to be 53 yeares old, cut'. He also saw a twenty-year-old Russian who 'came to the tent skipping and rejoicing excessively; yet, in cutting he frowned (as many of riper ages doe)'. Covel concluded, 'There were at least 200 proselytes made in these 13 days. It is our shame, for I believe all Europe have not gained so many Turkes to us these 200 years'.[45] In fact, so many Christian and Jewish men, women, and children converted to Islam before Mehmed IV in the 1660s and 1670s that in 1676 he was compelled to order the compilation of 'The Statute of the New Muslim' to stipulate correct procedure to follow.[46]

Mehmed IV, along with his mother Hatice Turhan Sultan and Grand Vizier Fazıl Ahmed Pasha (in office 1661–1676), also endured the worst conflagration Istanbul had experienced—which they would use to similar ends.[47]

It was already a typical hot, humid, dusty Istanbul summer day on 24 July 1660 when a young man's tobacco smoking set off a fire that within forty-eight hours reduced two-thirds of the city to ash and suffocated with smoke or burned alive forty thousand inhabitants.[48] The fire began in a straw store near Firewood Gate in the city's harbour of Eminönü. The flames quickly jumped to adjacent timber stores and engulfed them. Thanks to the prevailing Poyraz winds, the fire raced across Istanbul, whose building stock consisted of nearly adjoining timbered structures located on narrow streets in dense neighbourhoods. Fire patrols were useless against an army of flames that 'split into divisions, and every single division spread to a different district'.[49] The spires of the four minarets of Suleiman I's mosque burned like candles. Even mansions and palaces were incinerated as the soot and smoke turned day to night and flames illuminated what was supposed to be the dark night. Seeking escape from death, hundreds of thousands of terrified Istanbulites, 'naked and weeping, barefoot and bareheaded', crowded into the open space of the Hippodrome.[50]

Scapegoats were sought. Was it divine punishment because religious scholars violated Islamic law? Was it brought down by merchants who cheated their customers? Was it caused by the insubordination of slaves to masters, soldiers to officers? Or was it because Istanbulites did nothing other than engage in adultery, fornication, sodomy, and pederasty?[51] What good could come from this suffering?

Following the massive fire in July 1660, the dynasty and viziers made the decision to Islamise the area from the walls of Topkapı Palace in the east all the way to the centre of the peninsula in the west, as well as the heart of Galata, across the Golden Horn from Istanbul, which had burned in another fire in April. An imperial decree expelled Jews from a wide swath of Istanbul so that they would not rebuild their homes, houses of worship, and shops. This included the harbour area of Eminönü, Istanbul's main port and commercial district and home to most of the city's Jewish population, where Hatice Turhan Sultan had decided to build her New Mosque.[52] The plots of land on which synagogues and Jewish-owned homes had burned and the properties the congregations possessed accrued to the state treasury and became state-owned land, sold to Muslims at auction. Among the synagogues was one built by Jews who had migrated from Aragon, Spain, less than two centuries earlier. Whereas since the conquest in 1453 Ottoman authorities had contravened Islamic law by allowing new synagogues and churches to be built and old ones to be rebuilt, after the fire in July 1660 they applied the letter of the law, prohibiting reconstruction of destroyed houses of worship.

An imperial decree copied into the Istanbul Islamic law court register reveals that a year later authorities also razed and destroyed nearly two dozen churches that had been rebuilt after the fires of April and July and seized their property for redistribution to Muslims.[53] At a time when the Ottomans were at war with the Habsburgs, it is no coincidence that Catholics in the city—who were allowed to build churches only in Galata, across the Golden Horn from Istanbul—were most affected by the loss of churches, some of which would be replaced by mosques. A scribe at the Islamic law court wrote a hadith, a saying attributed to Muhammad, in the margin of an entry recording the appropriation by Muslims of formerly Christian property: 'God builds a home in Paradise for the one who builds a mosque for God on earth'. These policies illustrate how tolerance is a power relation. Tolerance can be given, and it can be taken away. The fire was used to usher in an Islamisation rebuilding campaign across the city.

Those who constructed the New Mosque compared the banishment of Jews from Eminönü with Muhammad's banishment of the Jewish tribe of Banu Nadir from Medina in the seventh century by choosing the Qur'anic chapter 'Exile' (or 'Banishment', al-Hashr, 59) to adorn the gallery level near the royal lodge.[54] 'Exile' narrates how God cast unbelieving Jews out of the city of believers. And, in what could be seen as a reference to recent events, the chapter warns that in the world to come those Jews will be punished in hellfire.

Writers praised Mehmed IV and emphasised the sultan's engagement in a pursuit—gaza—that only royal men could pursue. Hatice Turhan's Islamisation of a Jewish neighbourhood in Istanbul through the construction of a mosque complex was depicted as a conquest of infidel land.[55] This was a far cry from the way royal women had been depicted earlier. With a gazi warrior on the throne and male privilege restored, it was again acceptable to praise the religious piety of a valide sultan. And in an era when gaza was emphasised, it was natural to compare the conversion of the sacred geography of Istanbul to jihad.

Islamising space in the imperial capital nearest Topkapı Palace, Mehmed IV's court also converted Jews in his inner circle. A number of well-known Jews were compelled to convert to Islam before the sultan or valide sultan at court in the 1660s. Hatice Turhan offered the prominent Jews nearest the sultan, especially the staff of privy physicians, the non-choice of converting to Islam or losing their coveted palace positions. Jewish physicians in earlier centuries had occasionally converted and become chief physicians while in palace service. In the seventeenth century the practice became the norm. The sultan's court did not maintain its sixteenth-century attitude, which had allowed Jews to treat the sultan as head physician without converting.[56] When this attitude changed, so did Jews' ability to function in office as Jews.

Jews had had a privileged position with the royal family and resided mainly in the heart of the city. By the end of the 1660s, the geographic position of the Jews reflected their fall from importance. Most Jews in Istanbul by then resided on the Golden Horn and the Bosporus, and those who remained in the most important palace positions were now Muslims.[57]

Following the fire and construction of the New Mosque and the compulsory conversion of physicians, the political position of Jews had become so weak that none could intervene to change the decision to banish them from much of the peninsula of Istanbul. Those Jews who remained best positioned in the palace were involved in their own struggle to retain their posts. The son of a Jewish tailor who learned medicine from Jewish doctors was quickly replaced by a madrasa-trained Muslim. Coinciding with the rise of the wealthy Greek lay elite known as the Phanariots, named after the Istanbul district of Fener (Phanar), where the Orthodox patriarchate was located, Greeks became the predominant group practising medicine in the palace.[58] Whereas a century earlier Jewish physicians had treated the sultan and were trusted by him to serve as translators and negotiate international treaties, by the late seventeenth century this role had been taken by Christian physicians.[59] If there had ever been a Jewish 'golden age' in the Ottoman Empire, it was over.

Coming to power when Janissaries and jurists were the kingmakers, deposing and executing sultans, including his own father, Mehmed IV and his supporters were determined to reclaim the central role of the dynasty and its male head by displaying manliness through military campaigning and espousing Islam. Wherever he appeared, Mehmed IV was a convert maker. Embodying the empire of conversion, he brought thousands of Christians and Jews to Islam: Jewish palace physicians, Christian peasants recruited for his massive hunting trips, members of ambassadorial retinues, prisoners of war, war-weary civilians, and individuals brought to his palace in other circumstances. One of these was Sabbatai Zevi, a Jewish messiah whose followers believed he would become sultan and make Mehmed IV his personal slave. Sabbatai Zevi's messianic uprising is significant for the history of the dynasty because it reminds us how in every age deviant dervishes (even including, as in this case, Jewish mystics) fomented popular uprisings and posed a powerful threat to the Ottomans. Mehmed IV's response to Sabbatai Zevi's claims also shows how the dynasty's and Ottoman elite's approach to Islam had changed over the centuries.

15

A JEWISH MESSIAH IN
THE OTTOMAN PALACE

THE RELIGIOUS PIETY and propagation of Islam by Mehmed IV and his court was the culmination of spiritual trends begun a century and a half earlier. Between 1501 and 1566 the Sunni-Shi'i divide sharpened, exacerbated by the clash between the Ottomans and Safavids, which accompanied empire building and the incorporation of the religious class into the administration. Following these processes, we witness in the period from 1566 to 1683 a turn of many Ottoman Muslims to Islamic fundamentalism. Sunni Muslim religious zealotry was manifested in promotion of public piety. This came from the top down, from administrative elites and members of the dynasty, as well as from below, from popular movements culminating with the Kadızadeli reform movement in the sixteenth- and seventeenth-century Ottoman Empire. The Kadızadeli Muslim reformists were named after the early seventeenth-century preacher Kadızade Mehmed of Balıkesir, in northwestern Anatolia, who had begun his spiritual life as a Sufi but turned against the Sufi way. His followers promoted a return to what they considered the true faith practised by the first Muslims in seventh-century Medina, shorn of corrupting innovations. The Kadızadelis promoted a modern, rational religion pruned of magic, superstition, miracles, and mediators between humans and God. Their aim was to create a brotherhood of all believers, without distinction between those who supposedly were blessed by proximity to God and those who were not. As in the rest of contemporary Europe, pietism and political power were linked as the Kadızadelis found friends at court, at first during the reign of Murad IV, but especially during the reign of Mehmed IV.

The Kadızadeli reformist preacher movement was led by men who saw themselves as performing the Qur'anic injunction to 'command the good and forbid evil'. They promoted Sunni Islam and condemned those Muslims, especially some groups of Sufis, they found deviating from it. They attacked the ideas of Ibn Arabi: while Sufis called him 'the First Sheikh', Kadızadelis deemed him 'the Worst Sheikh'.[1] They promoted a crackdown on mystics gazing at young boys and public worship, especially ceremonies accompanied by dancing and music. They were opposed to pleasure—music, dancing, consumption of addictive substances—and aimed to ensure that Muslim men conducted their prayers, lived modestly, and did not gamble. Following a large fire in Istanbul in 1633, which they considered God's punishment for widespread immorality, the Kadızadelis convinced Murad IV to demolish the coffeehouses, where mature men met their boy lovers. According to an Iranian visitor to the city, in each coffeehouse 'a number of delicate and pretty youths are seated who have tresses and moles that are snares, and who act as magnets to attract hearts'.[2] The Kadızadelis also wanted the sultan to ban the consumption by Muslims of wine, opium, and tobacco. The reason was that Janissaries, stoked up on wine or coffee, abducted naked women from bathhouses, consumed tobacco in mosques, harassed men, bloodied a lot of noses, and, according to a contemporary Ottoman observer, 'hastily, yet openly engaged in fornication and sodomy' on street corners.[3] Such a libertine atmosphere led to the angry backlash of these puritans.

The Kadızadelis condemned the widespread practice of payment for religious services and pious foundations to establish mosques endowed with cash, since the practice appeared to condone usury, which is forbidden in Islam. They asked why the dynasty had built a mosque with six minarets—Ahmed I's mosque on the Hippodrome, popularly known as the Blue Mosque—the same number as possessed by the Great Mosque in Mecca, to which a seventh was added. The Kadızadeli preachers chased prostitutes and single women out of neighbourhoods, closed brothels, railed against beardless youths in general and those accompanying the Janissaries on military campaigns in particular, and ensured Muslim women did not have sexual relations with Christians and Jews.[4]

In this context, at noon on Friday, 28 June 1680, hundreds of thousands of people crowded into the Hippodrome to stone to death a Muslim woman accused of having committed adultery with an infidel and to witness the beheading of the Jew who was alleged to be her lover.[5] They had violated the gendered social hierarchy of Ottoman society. They broke the law prohibiting Christian or Jewish men from having sex with Muslim women. These accusations guaranteed that their punishment would be administered to the body in a public spectacle. Sultan Mehmed IV attended the double execution in person, watching the spectacular sight from the veranda of Suleiman I's grand vizier Ibrahim Pasha's palace. Mehmed IV offered the man conversion to Islam, permitting him to die swiftly and with dignity by decapitation. The woman, the wife of a Janissary, was treated much worse, despite her proclamations of innocence. 'Wailing and lamenting' the accused adulteress cried, 'They have slandered me. I am innocent and have committed no sin. For the sake of the princes, do not kill me, release me!'[6] But the sultan did not allow her to be freed. She was buried in a pit up to her waist in front of an ancient spiral column with three intertwined serpent heads. After her brother cast the first stone, the crowd joined in to punish her in this cruel fashion. Her bloody corpse reminded one writer of *keşkek*, a stew made of wheat boiled with meat.

Along with a focus on putting women in their place, the Kadızadelis and the activist Muslim elite—including members of the dynasty and administration—promoted conversion to Islam. They were given an opportunity to do so by the messianic movement of Sabbatai Zevi in 1665, the greatest Jewish messianic movement after that of Jesus. This movement broke out in the Ottoman Empire, and Jews all over Europe would be swept up in it. Within the royal palace, Mehmed IV, his preacher Vani Mehmed, his mother Hatice Turhan, and Grand Vizier Fazıl Ahmed Pasha—who ironically died of alcoholism—all experienced a revival of their faith. This intensification of religious fervour turned belief in a purified and reformed Islam into political policy. They attempted to transform the way Muslims practised their religion, spurring the conversion of other Muslims to their puritanical interpretation of Islam. Outlawing certain Sufi orders and practices—banning public whirling ceremonies, closing their lodges, destroying their shrines, exiling their leaders, and decapitating those deemed deviant dervishes—they sought to root out what they considered illegitimate practices among Muslims.

The dynasty's campaign to cool religious ecstasy, tear down places where euphoric spiritual exercises were performed, and eradicate what they considered illicit practices coincided with the outbreak of Sabbatai Zevi's movement. The movement aimed to revolutionise Jewish life and convert Jews to Sabbatai Zevi's understanding of God's prophecy.[7] Prophecies concerning the imminent arrival of the messiah, long current in Mediterranean and Ottoman Jewish circles, convinced many Jews that Sabbatai Zevi was the awaited one.[8] Just as Ottoman history is part of Europe's history, Ottoman history and Jewish history are one.

SABBATAI ZEVI: THE RENEWED THREAT OF A SOUTHEASTERN EUROPEAN SPIRITUALIST

Jews had read the Ottoman conquest of Constantinople, the smiting of traditional Jewish enemies both Catholic and Byzantine, and the taking of the Land of Israel in millenarian ways—as the beginning of the end-time and the arrival of the messianic era. The speculations of Kabbalists in the Ottoman-ruled Holy Land, especially in the hilltop town of Safed in the upper Galilee, one of Judaism's four holy cities, furthered messianic expectations among Jews. Those descended from the Jews and conversos expelled from Spain and Portugal, in particular, believed Sabbatai Zevi would dethrone the sultan and crown himself king.

Just as Sheikh Bedreddin was a Southeastern European spiritualist who was half-Greek and half-Turkish, Sabbatai Zevi was born in the Aegean port city of İzmir in 1626 to a Greek Jewish family originating in Southeastern Europe. His parents had immigrated to İzmir, the region where the disciples of Sheikh Bedreddin, Börklüce Mustafa, and Torlak Hu Kemal had preached their version of proto-communism and universal brotherhood and sisterhood at the beginning of the fifteenth century. İzmir was a relatively new city in the seventeenth century, a rough-and-tumble town of Armenians, Jews, Muslims, Orthodox Christians, English, French, and Dutch that rivalled Istanbul as an international entrepôt.[9] In this bold, heterogeneous environment where Western European hope for the imminent Day of Judgement mixed with ecstatic Sufism, the charismatic Sabbatai Zevi began at the age of eighteen to lead his own group of students of Kabbalah. He behaved mercurially, passing from ecstasy to melancholy and back again. Because of his strange powers and magical and ascetic practices, he became the spiritual guide for many Jews. They believed that the messiah would appear in the year 1648.[10]

In that year Sabbatai Zevi pronounced the never-to-be-spoken holy name of God (the tetragrammaton) and engaged in other scandalous practices, including proclaiming himself the messiah. The rabbis of İzmir banned everyone from having contact with him. He left İzmir and travelled to Ottoman cities with large Jewish populations, including Salonica (today Thessaloniki, Greece), the only Ottoman city with a Jewish majority. Salonica at the time was one of the most important centres of Jewish learning and Kabbalah. But Sabbatai Zevi's outrageous acts in Salonica caused him again to be banished. He travelled to Istanbul in 1658. There, too, his blasphemy, offences against tradition, strange acts, and pronouncing licit what the rabbis proclaimed illicit compelled him to flee the wrath of the rabbis. But he also attracted the attention of like-minded mystics, for he behaved like a deviant dervish. No one had forgotten Börklüce Mustafa and Torlak Hu Kemal's insurrections in the Aegean region. The heavy suffering of the Jews during the great fire in Istanbul in 1660 allegedly pleased Sabbatai Zevi because he saw it as an act of God calling Jews to repent.[11]

In 1662, Sabbatai Zevi travelled to Jerusalem. There he found Jews in financial and spiritual despair because the Ottoman government had levied extraordinary taxes on them to help finance the campaign for Crete. The leaders of the community sent Sabbatai Zevi to Egypt to raise funds for their survival. While in Egypt, in 1664 he married Sarah, an orphan of the 1648–1649 massacres of tens of thousands of Jews during a Cossack and Ukrainian peasant uprising against Polish rule in Ukraine. Raised a Catholic in a Polish convent, she had become a fortune-teller and prostitute and had lived in Amsterdam as well as Livorno, Italy. Most significant, she had proclaimed she would one day marry the messiah. That day had come.

On Sabbatai Zevi's return to Jerusalem in April 1665, he met the well-known Kabbalist Nathan of Gaza. Nathan was a miracle-working, charismatic man of God, similar to a Sufi sheikh.[12] Nathan told him he had seen a revelation in which Sabbatai Zevi was enthroned as the messiah. He was the first to recognise Sabbatai Zevi's messianic claims. He predicted that Sabbatai Zevi would peacefully take authority from the sultan and, through his hymns and prayers, all kings would submit to him. Wherever he turned to conquer, he would take the sultan with him as his 'personal slave'.[13] He expected the sultan to set his own 'crown' on Sabbatai Zevi's head and give him the Land of Israel.

As a result, Sabbatai Zevi revealed himself as the messiah in May 1665 in Gaza. Nathan dispatched letters to Western European and Ottoman Jewry informing them of the acts of this allegedly miracle-working messiah. His missives led to widespread acceptance of Sabbatai Zevi's divine role because Jews at the time were accustomed to claims of prophecy and expected no less. Sabbatai Zevi mattered not only to Jews. Some Christians and Muslims became his disciples. His movement attracted the excited attention of Christian Europe, much of which, including England, was witnessing its own spiritual upheaval.

In the cities of the Ottoman Empire, thousands of frenzied women and girls prophesied that Sabbatai Zevi was the messiah. They described visions of him enthroned in the clouds with a crown on his head, visits from Moses, or wondrous lights and angels.[14] Their ecstatic prophecies, similar to those of converso women and girls in the wake of the expulsion, convinced many to believe Sabbatai Zevi's messianic claims. By the seventeenth century, Ottoman Jewish communities were dominated by former Iberian conversos and Sephardic Jews, especially in İzmir, Sabbatai Zevi's hometown, where he had close relations with them.

With roots in the messianism of Iberian Jews forcibly converted to Catholicism, Sabbatianism was perhaps also influenced by contemporary Christian millenarianism (Anabaptists, Mennonites, Quakers) and Bektaşi Sufism, which included women among its acolytes. All of this readied Sabbatianism for the acceptance of female prophecy and agency. Another factor was the prominent role converso women had played in secretly preserving Judaism at home in Western Europe, as public practice of Judaism, a male sphere of activity, was forbidden.[15] For the first time,

women became central to the observation of Judaism. The prophecies of Sabbatai Zevi's wife Sarah, foretelling her destiny to be the
messiah's bride, also played a key role in the movement.

One of the reasons Sabbatian messianism was such a threat to
Jews and Muslims alike was that it envisioned and partially realised a class and gender revolution in Judaism. It offered a radical
departure in understandings of female spirituality.[16] In traditional
Judaism, as in Islam, Catholicism, and Orthodox Christianity,
women are exempted from ritual obligations and excluded from
all institutions promoting the religion's intellectual and spiritual
aims. Sabbatianism's emphasis on faith rather than on commandments incumbent only upon men offered Jewish women their
first opportunity to partake in religious life as equals, even as
celibate holy virgins, for they were no longer viewed as merely
material beings.

Sabbatianism offered a continuous and ever-radicalising egalitarian agenda.[17] The plan began with Sabbatai Zevi's pledge to
annul the original sin and abrogate Eve's curse—the pain of child-
birth and subservience to men.[18] This meant the emancipation of
women. Women were liberated from physical suffering and inferiority. They were free to engage in spiritual pursuits. Teaching
women and all other people the secret doctrines of Jewish mysticism and its key texts, traditionally taught only to adepts who had
reached the age of forty or the appropriate spiritual readiness, was
a concrete expression of this pledge.[19]

Sabbatianism was revolutionary, egalitarian, and libertine.[20]
Just like the Islam promoted for centuries by deviant dervishes, it
also adopted antinomianism, the belief that faith, not adherence
to moral law, is necessary for salvation. If there was no primordial
sin, then all the old understandings of what was good and what
was evil were also obsolete, including sexual prohibitions. Sabbatai Zevi abolished them. His movement used women's bodies to
purposely transgress tradition by violating commandments, especially those regarding sexual purity and marriage, engagement

in sexual intercourse during menstruation, incest, and sexual libertinism, including ritualised orgies. Openly performing acts that Jews were forbidden to commit, which were largely centred on the body, also established parity of the sexes and gave women a central role in religious life. The promotion of previously prohibited sexual relations—especially adultery—offered women, particularly prophetesses, an active role.

Sabbatianism placed sole emphasis on personal faith in the messiah rather than compliance with Jewish ritual. It was seen by its opponents as sexual depravity and evoked a violent response that delegitimised any public display of female spirituality. Because women were seen as lacking in self-control, female spirituality was equated with unbridled sexuality and stimulated the construction of impermeable gender barriers in Orthodox Judaism.[21] As in Islam, the view that every part of a woman was a private sexual part necessitated their covering.

Especially among women, Sabbatai Zevi's following continued to surge. He received a ban from frightened rabbis in Jerusalem and was expelled from the city in May 1665. He returned to his birthplace of İzmir where, in December, he publicly showed himself while ecstatic after a period of seclusion and melancholy by storming the city's Portuguese Synagogue with hundreds of his supporters, breaking the door down with an axe. He led a prayer service, during which he proclaimed the coming of the redeemer and messianic king.[22] He called women to the reading of the Torah, an exclusively male honour, another manifestation of his promise to liberate women.[23]

When Sabbatai Zevi had resided in Istanbul eight years earlier, Jews had shown him little interest and Ottoman authorities paid him no attention.[24] But in 1666, many Jews in Istanbul welcomed his mission with enthusiasm, and authorities treated him as a real danger. The messianic age was proclaimed in İzmir one month prior to the first Friday prayers in the New Mosque in Istanbul. The New Mosque symbolised how much the city had been transformed since Sabbatai Zevi's leave-taking in 1659. As a result of Hatice Turhan's building programme, it was a dramatically different city. Before 1660, one approaching Eminönü would have seen a skyline dominated by multistorey Jewish apartments. The presence of the New Mosque on the waterfront proclaimed that profound changes had occurred.

Many Jews greeted him ecstatically as a redeemer. Jews had suffered greatly over the previous five years. They lived in crowded conditions on the fringes of the city, having recently faced a horrible fire, plague, and much death, the transformation of properties that had once housed synagogues into an imperial mosque complex, the loss of ancient synagogues of diverse rites, and expulsion from the heart of the city on pain of death and prohibition of their return.[25]

Alerted by Jews opposed to Sabbatai Zevi, Ottoman officials became concerned when he announced himself to be king of the world, delegated the kingdoms of all empires to his followers, and declared through these actions that Ottoman rule was illegitimate.[26] The Ottomans were at the time trying to subdue the last Venetian bastion in Crete. They could not tolerate instability in the empire, especially from one attempting to convert others to a competing vision of the true interpretation of God's desire and claiming that his authority superseded that of the sultan. While Sultan Mehmed IV was urging the grand vizier to conquer the citadel in Crete as part of a jihad against accursed infidels, a Jew had appeared within the empire claiming to be a prophet and had acquired a large, potentially threatening following.[27] The dynasty feared it again was facing a large-scale deviant dervish insurrection.

Because they believed that the end of days had arrived, Jews engaged in purifying rituals and special prayers to mark the age, inciting a fervent response from Jews in the lands beyond the frontiers of the Ottoman Empire and as far away as Morocco, Yemen, and Germany. Jewish businesswoman Glückel of Hameln related how the Jews of her German town were ecstatic when they received the good news from İzmir that the messiah had arrived. The Sephardi, descendants of the Jews expelled from Spain and Portugal, dressed in their finery and danced en route to their synagogue, where they read the news out loud. Straightaway, according to Glückel, 'many sold their houses and lands and all their possessions, for any day they hoped to be redeemed'.[28] Her father-in-law abandoned everything and journeyed to Hamburg, expecting to set sail for the Land of Israel, waiting for the sign that it was time to depart.

In February 1666, Sabbatai Zevi was arrested and imprisoned after his boat was intercepted by authorities en route to Istanbul.[29] Jews in Istanbul flocked to the dungeon where he was held. They had no need to sell their property and pack because the messiah would replace the sultan on his throne in that city and reward them with the wealth of Christians and Muslims.[30]

Because large crowds gathered where Sabbatai Zevi was first incarcerated, in April he was banished to Hatice Turhan's fortress on the European side of the Dardanelles. But the Ottoman authorities treated him leniently—perhaps because his Janissary guards were Bektaşi Sufis—allowing him to receive many pilgrims, some of whom believed him to be divine. He continued to instruct his followers from prison. He abolished the fast on the ninth of the Hebrew month of Av, the date Jews commemorate the destruction of the First and Second Temple, ordering Jews to instead celebrate a festival on that day for the dawning of the messianic age. That day would have to be deferred. Glückel of Hameln's father-in-law waited in vain. Glückel expressed the disappointment that Jews 'were like a woman who sits in labour and suffers mighty pangs, and thinks once her suffering is over she shall be blessed with a child; but it was only hearkening after a wind'.[31]

For nearly two decades, Sabbatai Zevi had built a spiritual movement that grew in fits and starts until it dramatically snowballed into a force that threatened to topple the sultan. But

ultimately, in 1666, Mehmed IV, who had turned away from ecstatic Sufism towards a fundamentalist, pietist approach to Islam,
cracked down on these ecstatic spiritualists and demanded to see
their leader.

Perhaps incited to action by complaints from Sabbatai Zevi's
Jewish enemies, in September 1666 Mehmed IV ordered the Jewish spiritualist to be interrogated beneath his gaze in Edirne by
the members of the imperial council.[32] These included the sultan's
preacher, Vani Mehmed, and Grand Vizier Fazıl Ahmed Pasha's
deputy, Mustafa Pasha, a man much experienced in facilitating
conversion to Islam. Also present was Sheikhulislam Minkarizade
Yahya Efendi, who had issued a fatwa permitting pressured conversion to Islam. A Muslim official could say, 'Be a Muslim', and
compel a Christian or Jew to convert.[33]

As messianic terminology and expectation no longer held cur-
rency at court, the sultan's chronicler narrated instead how Jews
believed Sabbatai Zevi to be a prophet, causing social corruption
and disturbance of the peace.[34] Sabbatai Zevi was seen as a deviant dervish, but Mehmed IV and his court stifled such radical
Sufis, especially those who considered themselves prophets or
messiahs. Rumours reaching the sultan's ears included how Sabbatai Zevi allegedly performed miracles. Unlike his predecessors,
Mehmed IV did not believe in miracle-working saints. There was
only one way to test if the Jewish spiritualist had divine powers.
The sultan's council demanded Sabbatai Zevi remove his cloak so
that imperial archers could use him as target practice with arrows tipped with fire. Sabbatai Zevi was given another choice. The
Jewish messiah could become a Muslim. Mehmed IV compelled
Sabbatai Zevi to change religion and become his servant at court.

He was given an honorary position in the palace, bathed in
the bath of the palace pages, and given Muslim dress. The sultan's preacher, Vani Mehmed, instructed him in Kadızadeli
tenets of Islam. His wife, Sarah, who converted to Islam with him
and was renamed Fatma, was given an usher position. Unlike

Börklüce Mustafa—the fifteenth-century Christian convert to Islam and fellow deviant dervish who also allegedly proclaimed himself a prophet, raised a large following, and caused social disorder in the same region where Sabbatai Zevi had begun his messianic agitations—the Jewish Sufi was not crucified.

Making powerful religious figures and rebels into servants of the sultan was seen as a sign of the victory of purified, rationalised Islam over the ecstatic excesses of deviant dervishes and Jews who appeared as radical Sufis. Despite Sabbatai Zevi's promises to make the sultan his slave, his messianic movement culminated in Jewish conversion to Islam. The Kadızadeli reform movement that promoted a rational religion preferred by the sultan prevailed over the competing ecstatic movement of the Jewish mystic. It was assumed that the converted would serve as a model of religious transformation and bring others to the sultan's form of religiosity.[35]

For Mehmed IV, humbling Sabbatai Zevi by making him a Muslim and keeping him near as a reminder of his conversion would serve to remind others of the truth of Islam. If even a Jewish man who proclaimed himself a prophet could accept Muhammad as the Prophet, who could resist it? And if he was rewarded for his decision with a palace position and the most sumptuous garments forbidden to be worn by Christians and Jews, who could not see the rewards accruing to those who converted and joined what the dynasty considered the superior religion?

After his conversion, Sabbatai Zevi cruised the streets of Edirne from 1666 to 1672 with a large retinue of turban-wearing Jewish converts to Islam, preaching in synagogues to gain more converts.[36] Accompanied by Vani Mehmed's men, Sabbatai Zevi encouraged Jews to become Muslim, and the royal preacher gave out white turbans, converting them at his residence. Sabbatai Zevi invited rabbis to debate with him in the imperial audience hall in the palace in Edirne as the sultan and his preacher observed. Many Jews converted before the grand vizier.[37] It appeared that the sultan had successfully transformed a force of disorder and sedition into a proselytiser for the truth.

Ostensibly a Muslim after his conversion, Sabbatai Zevi also continued to engage in practices of his own that merged Kabbalah, the Jewish mystical tradition, and Sufism. For that reason, he was banished to remote Ülgün (Ulcinj), a town on the southern Adriatic coast of Montenegro, in 1673. After his death in 1676, his followers went underground, coalescing in Ottoman Salonica, one of the only cities in the world with a Jewish majority, where they prospered for centuries.

In the view of his supporters, Mehmed IV had restored the strong sultanate by being a manly, pious gazi converting people and places across Europe. The empire had survived a great test, triumphed even, but Mehmed IV's coming attempt to conquer Vienna would lead to disastrous consequences for himself and the pious preachers he supported.

THE SECOND SIEGE OF VIENNA AND THE SWEET WATERS OF EUROPE

From Mehmed IV to Ahmed III

A T THE HEIGHT of his power, having survived the Jewish upheaval at home that reminded him of a deviant dervish uprising, Mehmed IV and his armies would conquer much territory in Europe. After the conquest of Crete in 1669, the Ottomans launched numerous successful campaigns on the mainland. Mehmed IV participated in person in the first of these campaigns, that against the Commonwealth of Poland-Lithuania in 1672, conquering the fabled 'white castle' in Kameniçe (unlike in the novel of the same name, in which the Ottoman siege is unsuccessful), the key to Poland and Ukraine. A second campaign against the same kingdom was launched the following year, as well as a successful campaign against the Russian Empire in 1678. Through these campaigns, the Ottoman Empire was propelled to its greatest northernmost expansion. In 1681, the Ottomans signed their first treaty with Russia, which brought two decades of peace. Yet it sowed the seeds of future crises, with Russia claiming to be protector of Orthodox Christians in the empire.

In Central Europe, the Ottomans supported a Calvinist noble and military leader named Imre Thököly, who was as opposed to the Habsburgs as he was to their Catholicism. In 1682 the Ottomans made him their vassal, the king of central Hungary. With such an ally, Mehmed IV was confident he could launch a campaign to conquer Vienna, located 1,500 kilometres to the northwest of Constantinople. The Habsburg capital was deemed the mythical 'golden apple'. So confident was he of his impending triumphal horseback ride through the city that Mehmed IV summoned his fortysomething-year-old younger brother Suleiman from the harem at Topkapı Palace in April 1683, when he and his army set out from Edirne. He took his sons Ahmed and Mustafa as well as their mother, his favourite concubine Rabia Gülnüş, along on the journey as far as Belgrade, more than halfway to Vienna, to show them to his Ottoman subjects. Mehmed IV broke with prevailing tradition and gave his future successors a belated lesson in being a gazi.

Mehmed IV could have learned from the mistakes made by Suleiman I over a century and a half earlier. A major campaign that far from Istanbul was a harsh test of Ottoman capabilities.[1] The commander confronted the serious problems of provisioning his troops and transporting them along roads and across streams and mighty rivers to the battlefield. Most war matériel had to be carried overland on animals. Winter weather typically arrived early in Southeastern Europe.

As a legitimating call to holy war, in Belgrade Mehmed IV handed the black wool banner of Muhammad the Prophet to his grand vizier, Kara Mustafa Pasha, to carry during the campaign.[2] Mehmed IV and his sons remained behind in the Serbian city, as the grand vizier and the sultan's preacher, Vani Mehmed, set off with the Ottoman army and their allies—the Crimean khan and Thököly's Hungarian army—to besiege the Habsburg capital over six hundred kilometres to the northwest. On 13 July, with an insufficient number of troops, lacking proper fodder, and with underfed horses incapable of mounting an attack, the Ottomans reached the place where Suleiman I had pitched his tent in 1529. A day later, they appeared before the well-fortified citadel of Vienna.

The fortress city was ringed by numerous palisades, bastions, and high walls, and a twenty-metre-wide ditch, defended by hundreds of pieces of heavy artillery. Even though the army lacked the requisite large cannons and enough firepower to take the citadel, Kara Mustafa Pasha offered the Viennese the choice between surrendering and converting to Islam, which would give them eternal salvation; surrendering without a fight and submitting to Islamic rule without conversion, which would guarantee them peace and prosperity; or fighting, in which case the victorious Ottomans would annihilate them and enslave their children, making them Muslims.[3] Vienna's defenders—'the herd of rabid pigs destined to burn in the eternal flames of Hell', as the Ottomans called them—chose to fight the 'gazis of Islam' rather than surrender or convert.[4]

No matter the high mindedness of the grand vizier, the two-month siege was a disaster for the Ottomans. Ottoman soldiers were lambasted by contemporary chroniclers for drinking wine and not giving up fornicating and pederasty, despite the fact that the siege occurred during the holy months of Rajab, Shaban, and Ramadan.[5] Bad omens abounded. Kara Mustafa Pasha's Istanbul palace burned to the ground in his absence. Mehmed IV's mother Hatice Turhan passed away. The Qur'anic verses that decorate her tomb warn of the horrible consequences for unbelievers in the afterlife and promise reward for those who heed the warning of the blazing fires of hell.[6] An encircled Vienna was supposed to be suffering such a fiery fate. Despite Ottoman sappers tunnelling below ground to explode mines to bring down its thick walls, the city would not fall, although its small number of defenders were starving, suffering from disease, and desperate for relief.

Sixty-thousand Christian relief forces arrived at Kahlenberg hill in the Vienna woods northwest of the city to save it, eventually outnumbering the deprived Ottoman forces at least two-to-one. On the sixtieth day of the siege, 12 September 1683, Kara Mustafa Pasha launched an attack on the relief army at the foot

of the hill. In the Ottoman view, the Christian soldiers seemed
to 'flow down upon them like black tar', covering everything in
the Muslim army's path. The enemy was like 'an immense herd of
furious boars that trampled and demolished them'.[7] Using misogynist language, chronicle writers thought the Ottomans were betrayed by their ally, the 'bitch' known as the Crimean khan, 'who
had less courage than a woman' and withdrew instead of covering the Ottoman troops, which were routed.[8] Under the leadership of the king of the Commonwealth of Poland-Lithuania, Jan
Sobieski III, winged Hussar cavalry—thus named due to the
metre-high 'wings' made of feathers attached to the back of their
armour—attacked the grand vizier's position. Knowing that he
would be executed for the defeat, the grand vizier intended to die
on the battlefield. But the cavalry commander and Vani Mehmed
begged him to withdraw, so they fled with Muhammad's banner while Ottoman troops were abandoned and cut to pieces.[9]
The grand vizier's sumptuous tent and precious cloaks, jewel-
encrusted daggers, and swords were seized by the victors.

At the forefront of military advances for centuries, the Ottomans had lost their onetime technological firepower advantage in
Central Europe, whose empires had now surpassed them. For two
decades, writers in Mehmed IV's service had boasted of his silencing of church bells and his replacement of them with the Islamic
call to prayer. But after the failed siege attempt of the Habsburg
imperial seat, captured Ottoman cannons would be remade into
the bell of Vienna's Saint Stephen's Cathedral.

Mehmed IV had the man who delivered the bad news executed
for bearing evil tidings. He ordered Grand Vizier Kara Mustafa's
execution in Belgrade as well. On Christmas Day 1683, the grand
vizier was stripped of the symbols of his office and as leader of
holy war: his imperial seal, the banner of Muhammad, and keys
to the Ka'ba in Mecca. Alerted to his fate while performing his af-
ternoon prayers in the citadel, Kara Mustafa dismissed his retainers and admonished them to remember him in their prayers. He

took off his turban. The executioner entered the room. He raised Kara Mustafa's beard and passed the noose around his neck, the doomed man telling him to tie it well. After two or three tugs, the former grand vizier took in his final breath. His body was taken out to an old tent and prepared for burial, then his head was cut off. The body was buried in the courtyard of a mosque in Belgrade opposite the citadel, but his head was saved, packed in straw, and sent to Edirne, to be set upon a gate at the entrance to the sultan's palace.[10]

MEHMED IV'S DOWNFALL

Following the disastrous rout at Vienna in 1683, the arguments for Islamic piety and gaza rang hollow. The sultan was pressured into returning to Istanbul and a sedentary life, urged to abandon the military campaign and his inordinate appetite for the hunt. Janissaries and jurists were incensed that the sultan ignored their demands and continued to go to the hunt either before daybreak, returning at night, or at night and returning the following night, seemingly indifferent to the fate of the empire. He neglected his army, his subjects, and his own religious obligations, especially prayer.[11] The sultan's preacher, Vani Mehmed, had made the connection between the Turks' conversion to Islam and their subsequent conquest and conversion of much of Eurasia by their pious descendants. He had taken an active role exhorting Ottoman troops in battle.[12] After the debacle at Vienna, he was blamed for impudently inciting the sultan to launch the campaign by reminding him of his gazi Oğuz forebears and was banished to Bursa, where he passed away.[13]

The failure at Vienna and the loss of Buda, which the Ottomans had held for over a century and a half, and then Belgrade to the Habsburgs in 1686 contributed to Mehmed IV's downfall. In the wake of these defeats, with the treasury nearly emptied, the grand vizier imposed an extraordinary tax on the restive religious class. It was taken by force, quarter by quarter, house by house, from all Muslim functionaries save the sheikhulislam.[14] In 1687, following another Ottoman defeat—this time by the Holy League of the Habsburgs, Poland-Lithuania, Venice, and the pope at Mohács, Hungary, the scene of a great Ottoman triumph the previous century—the forty-seven-year-old ruler faced revolt by jurists and Janissaries alike.

Executing the grand vizier did not placate them. Janissaries ignored orders to remain in Edirne and marched on the imperial capital.[15] Gathering in Hagia Sophia, Janissaries, jurists, and viziers declared it was canonically valid to dethrone a sultan who was occupied with the chase while the enemy attacked and occupied the lands of the empire. They blamed the sultan for having destroyed everything by trusting a few men of evil intention, which included his deceased preacher, Vani Mehmed.[16] They deposed Mehmed IV and confined him to house arrest, first in Topkapı Palace and then in Edirne. He asked his guards, 'Are you going to kill me?'[17] He had not forgotten the fate of his father, Ibrahim I, the second Ottoman ruler to be executed.

Mehmed IV's successor was to be Suleiman, his forty-five-year-old younger brother. But Suleiman, too, was terrified of being killed. He refused to come out of the harem. Breaking down from decades of anxiety about this moment, he asked whether the officials summoning him could understand what it was like to spend a life in terror, how 'it is better to die at once than to die a little each and every day', and began to cry.[18] He had nothing suitable to wear for the enthronement. The chief eunuch put his own sable over Suleiman's robe. Thus dressed, he became Suleiman II (reigned 1687–1691), as his brother Mehmed IV, his other brother Ahmed, and the two princes Ahmed and Mustafa were put under house arrest. Mehmed IV died of natural causes six years later.

The sedentary sultan had returned. When writing about Mehmed IV's death a generation after it occurred, an historian did not call him a pious gazi or mention gaza or jihad. Instead, he claimed that Mehmed IV died in the harem.[19] A man who had spent his life breaking free of the harem to establish himself as a manly warrior-sultan nevertheless ended his life in it. That was where he belonged, according to eighteenth-century demands on the sultanate.

At this point, the dynasty began another new phase. Beginning with Osman I and lasting for approximately three centuries, *devlet* had meant that fortune and power inhered in the sultan, who was coequal with the dynasty. By the time of the two enthronements and depositions of Mustafa I and the murder of Osman II, devlet had come to signify the dynasty and sultanate, as the person of the sultan was made distinct from the sultanate. Loyalty was due to the dynasty rather than to an individual. Beginning with the deposition of Mehmed IV and the decreased power of the sultanate attendant to it, devlet gradually came to have its modern definition: government (or state).[20] Obedience was not due to a man, or to an office, but to the administration. Less attention would be paid to the sultan, who had lost his cosmically imbued fortune. To compensate, future sultans would try to increase their Islamic legitimacy. Accordingly, the rest of the chapters of this book will mainly offer less of a personality- or family-dynasty-centred narrative and more of an administration-focused one, because that was the characteristic of the distinct regime that began in this period and lasted to the end of empire.

BURYING THE MEMORY OF THE GAZI SULTAN

Mehmed IV's successors chose to bury him not in the gazi abode of Edirne but in Istanbul, in his mother Hatice Turhan's tomb, behind her New Mosque in Eminönü.[21] On the explanatory panel in the mausoleum, Mehmed IV is referred to as 'the Hunter', not 'the Gazi'. Entering Hatice Turhan's mausoleum, one notices how many coffins fill the main room (the remains are buried under the tomb). Unlike the mausoleum of Suleiman I, with few coffins in the centre of the sanctuary, this tomb is chockablock with caskets of princes and sultans. The first large coffin is that of the mausoleum's patron and main guest, the valide sultan. One has to fully enter the main door before noticing Mehmed IV's turban-topped casket a little behind his mother's. In death, as in early life, he could not escape her shadow. Despite his years of independent action, he lies next to her in the earth beneath the tomb. The significance of his reign would be overshadowed by subsequent historical events.

The bureaucracy headed by the grand vizierate desired a sedentary, ceremonial sultan of no real significance in Istanbul, not a restless, virile warrior based in Edirne. In contrast to the previous two decades, after he was dethroned, Mehmed IV was no longer referred to as a gazi and his proclivity for hunting was thereafter widely criticised. After his reign, the term was used pejoratively, and by the nineteenth century he became known as 'the Hunter'—by that point a symbol of waste and extravagance, not war and manliness. In the Military Museum in Istanbul there is scant trace of Mehmed IV, other than a record of how far he could shoot an arrow, instead of how far he pushed the boundaries of the empire.

Located in an Ottoman-era military school, the massive Military Museum in the Harbiye district of Istanbul narrates the long history of the 'Turkish' army from its origins in Central Asia through to the Turkish Republic.[22] Like the Pavilion of the Holy Mantle and Holy Relics at Topkapı Palace, this museum, run by the Turkish military, displays 'sacred relics': Orhan's iron battle helmet, part of the chain that the Byzantines futilely stretched across the mouth of the Golden Horn in 1453 to keep the Ottomans at bay, Selim I's horse's armour. It thrills visitors with daily, boisterous, live performances of the Ottoman military band in its auditorium. But the museum tells a peculiar history of Turkish warfare. It celebrates Seljuk and Ottoman victories, from

Malazgirt (Manzikert) near Lake Van in 1071 to Mohács in 1526, but does not include any defeats.

The Ottomans rise at the Military Museum, but they do not fall. The Turkish displays exhibit no seventeenth-century Ottoman campaign tents. To see them, one has to visit the Museum of Military History in Vienna and its permanent exhibit *War Against the Ottomans*. There, children celebrate their birthdays in Ottoman tents captured at the failed 1683 siege.[23] At the Military Museum in Istanbul, the Ottoman period focuses on the rise of the Ottomans, the conquest of Constantinople, and the reigns of Mehmed II, Selim I, and Suleiman I. Missing is a statue or display of Mehmed IV, thanks to whose conquests the Ottoman Empire reached its greatest territorial extension in the Mediterranean (Crete) and Eastern Europe (Poland and Ukraine) but failed, once again, to take Vienna. Turning to Europe as manly conquering warrior, he also promoted widescale conversion of people and Islamisation of territory.

Mehmed IV's absence and the selective history telling of the Military Museum raise a host of questions. Should we concern ourselves with distinguishing between 'good' and 'bad' sultans? How accurate are the Ottoman leaders' reputations and the monikers given them? Ottoman chroniclers and moralists believed they did matter. They focused on character, praising or blaming sultans for the onset of historical processes (whether rise or decline) that had wider and more complicated causes. On the one hand, Suleiman I had been handed the world on a silver platter by his father, Selim I, who had doubled the empire's territory, taking the three Islamic holy cities of Mecca, Medina, and Jerusalem, and who identified his son as his successor, sparing him from having to engage in fratricide. Suleiman I also benefited from being born as the master of the auspicious conjunction, the tenth sultan at the dawn of the tenth century in the Islamic calendar, a moment when Muslims believed a well-omened ruler would arrive. With such advantages, it is difficult to imagine him not succeeding. On the other hand, it is doubtful that Mehmed IV's father, Ibrahim I, was as flawed as chroniclers depicted him. It is also hard to see how Mehmed IV, who tried to break with nearly a century of precedent of a sedentary sultanate, could not have failed.

Mehmed IV is notable for being the second-longest reigning Ottoman ruler and for having one of the worst reputations of any sultan. He presided over stunning military successes, including the conquest of the entire island of Crete in 1669. But he was also responsible for the failed final Ottoman siege of the Habsburg capital in 1683. Having sought a return to an earlier era of pious, manly, gazi sultans and a comparable historical legacy, he is remembered instead as a profligate hunter.

REVOLT

Mehmed IV's long reign, which ended in disgrace, was followed by the brief, undistinguished reigns of his brothers, Suleiman II and Ahmed II (reigned 1691–1695), and his son, Mustafa II (reigned 1695–1703). These rulers added religious meaning to their enthronements, utilising the symbols of the Sunni caliphate. Suleiman II was the first to wear the turban ascribed to the biblical Joseph and have descendants of Muhammad play a visible role at his accession. Ahmed II was the first to pray before the mantle of the Prophet as part of his accession rituals. Mustafa II was the first sultan to gird the sword of Muhammad, and not that of an illustrious Ottoman ancestor, at the mosque of Ayyub al-Ansari in Eyüp.[24] But these years were memorable more for Janissary rebellion and the 1699 Treaty of Karlowitz between the Ottomans and Habsburgs than anything else.

The failed siege of Vienna effectively ended the reign of Mehmed IV, the career of his preacher, Vani Mehmed, and the power of the puritanical Kadızadeli movement. Yet Vani Mehmed's son-in-law Feyzullah—son of Vani Mehmed's patron in

provincial Erzurum and preacher to Mustafa II—was soon blamed
for having inordinate influence over the administration and palace. Feyzullah was condemned for violating protocol, precedent,
and the expectations of deserved appointments. He engaged in
nepotism, appointing his sons to positions for which they were
not qualified. He made his son sheikhulislam designate. He was
seemingly too powerful, determining government appointments
and domestic and foreign policy decisions. But as conventional
notions of the time held, sheikhulislams were meant to be apolit-
ical and act as spiritual and moral checks to temporal power, not
wield it. Janissaries demanded that Feyzullah's power be limited.

Feyzullah Efendi did not offend only the Janissaries. He managed to unite almost the entire Muslim population against himself
and the sultan in spring and summer of 1702. He accomplished
this feat by attempting to impose Kadızadeli Islam, which emphasised 'enjoining the good and forbidding wrong', on the diverse
Muslims of the entire realm. He should have realised such austere
piety had been discredited since the fall of its main promoter, the
preacher Vani Mehmed, and his patron Sultan Mehmed IV after the failed siege of Vienna. Nevertheless, Feyzullah took the
Kadızadeli aim of creating a brotherhood of all believers a great
step further by promoting standardised beliefs taught to and confirmed by every Muslim.

He had the grand vizier issue an imperial decree in the sultan's name imposing religious tests on all Sunni Muslims and the
sending of agents to instruct and ensure right practice. The decree
ordered testing imams and preachers for their knowledge of Islam
and adherence to Sunnism. College and primary school teachers
were commanded to not deviate from teaching the Sunni curric-
ulum. Those religious functionaries who did not obey were to be
dismissed. As leader of the religious hierarchy, the sheikhulislam
was in control of the hiring and firing of such officials. But he
overstretched by targeting all Muslims from Bosnia to Basra, Belgrade to Beirut, Rûmeli, Anatolia, Syria, and Iraq. Urban dwellers,

villagers, and even nomads—'those who live in woolen tents'—
were to be instructed in the basic duties of the faith (praying, fasting, alms giving, pilgrimage), and compelled to attend communal
Friday prayers and to instruct their children in right Sunni Muslim practice as well. College students were to be assigned to make
sure people fulfilled their Muslim religious obligations. Magis-
trates were to admonish the people to discharge their moral duties.[25] Sweeping in its intentions, and violating the still-prevailing
laissez-faire attitude towards Muslim religious diversity, such an
order was guaranteed to be met with resistance not only from deviant dervishes but from most Muslims.

In 1703, with wide popular backing, soldiers demanding over-
due pay and merchants and Janissaries insisting the court move
back to Istanbul fomented rebellion against the sultan's preacher,
Feyzullah. The revolt was a backlash against the attempts to impose religious conformity and to resituate the sultan and his palace
school at the centre of power.[26] By then, client-patron relationships,
blood relationships, and ethnic ties had become the deciding factors by which elite men married to royal women established and
maintained their circles of power—known as households rivalling
the sultan's household—and had pushed aside sultanic power.[27]
Many of those who rebelled in 1703 sided with the grand vizier
and pasha households against the sultan and his sheikhulislam.
After this rebellion, their situation was confirmed.

The rebellion illustrated the struggle between a decaying Collection system, which had become much less important and ultimately fell into abeyance and then obsolescence as the empire
reached the limits of its expansion under Mehmed IV, and an
interest group that supported the grand vizier and pasha households. With the end of territorial enlargement, the empire needed
men with specialised experience. By the end of the seventeenth
century, half of all key administrative posts were staffed by men
trained in or attached to these households, rather than the palace. Mehmed IV had been deposed following a conflict with these

same interest groups. The 1703 rebellion was caused by Mustafa II's attempt to neutralise that competing power structure.

During the 1703 uprising, a Janissary rebel named 'Deranged' or 'Pockmarked' Ahmed demanded the overthrow of the dynasty and its replacement by a 'popular assembly', a Janissary oligarchy.[28] Rebel soldiers deposed Mustafa II. In 1703, the Janissaries replaced him with Mehmed IV's younger son, thirty-year-old Ahmed III (reigned 1703–1730), and arrested, tortured, and executed Feyzullah by beheading him. To make the public spectacle of his humiliation complete, they dismembered the corpse and forced Armenians and Greeks to parade his body through the streets of Edirne as they sang dirges and burned incense, as though the Muslim scholar and former sheikhulislam had been a Christian. The corpse's feet were tied to the head, the head impaled on a pole and paraded around. The corpse and head were then thrown in the Tunca river. Feyzullah's eldest son and Vani Mehmed's two sons were also executed.[29]

AHMED III: THE SWEET WATERS OF EUROPE

Following this brutal purge, Ahmed III presided over a new age, with Ottomans and Western Europeans again sharing cultural tastes. In eighteenth-century Europe, a culture of pleasure emerged, in which men and women gathered to enjoy themselves in the new gardens, promenades, public squares, and coffeehouses. In the early eighteenth-century Ottoman Empire, lifetime tax farms helped propel a Muslim elite to untold riches. Combined with expanded trade with Western Europe, these tax farms helped spawn a new consumer culture never before seen in the empire. As the Christian and Muslim elite built the first multistorey wooden waterside mansions on the Bosporus for which Istanbul is famous, Ahmed III promoted ostentatious displays as well, including lavish circumcision and wedding festivals. He had thirty daughters; thus there were many opportunities for such public events. The sultan, unlike his recent predecessors, who had viewed themselves as nearly godlike, made himself visible to the public. He took pleasure-boat trips along the Golden Horn and Bosporus.[30]

The nouveaux riches, especially royal and elite women, delighted in the new garden pavilions and pleasure gardens on the Bosporus and Golden Horn, many of which were built by the grand vizier, Damad (Son-in-Law) Ibrahim Pasha (in office 1718–1730), who raised the funds to pay for them by cutting the military payroll, purging soldiers from the ranks, and raising taxes. Men and women wore new, more revealing fashions and enjoyed new foods and drinks—such as coffee, which had been condemned a generation before—and sugar-based sweets. At their festivals they fawned over massive, towering, phallic floral constructions made of sugar, coloured paper, metal, and beeswax.[31]

Poet Enderunlu Fazıl Bey gives us insight into what went on at these parties. He advised his male reader to wear gold-embroidered robes, drink a couple of cups of wine, let a lock of hair fall jauntily down from his head covering, and recite an erotic poem: 'That one laughs from behind the veil / That one looks at the ground, blushing modestly / Those chuckles, that flirting, that glance / When she looks at you out of the corner of her eye, oh my!' The 'oh my' was soon to come: 'One of them starts to sing a song / So they might work their arts on you / One hastens to entice you / [Her] mantle falls from her back'. Two women sitting in a swing set among the cypresses, 'casually clad / One alluringly rocks the swing / The other recites lovely songs'. The poem becomes pornographic: 'As she swings her gown falls open / Showing every bit of her to you / To you she lets her trouser-tie be seen / To you, perhaps, her secret treasure'.[32]

This flirtatious scene took place in one of the gardens of Ahmed III's 'abode of felicity', Sa'dabad Palace in Eyüp, where the 'sweet waters of Europe' (Kağıthane stream) end in the Golden

Horn. The palace was similar to Louis XIV's Versailles and Peter the Great's Summer Palace and Gardens at Petrograd.[33]

As in contemporary London, Paris, Berlin, and Vienna, men and women in Istanbul gathered to stroll and sprawl, drink and smoke, sing and dance, feast and flirt, and be entertained in the new public spaces in the city, many featuring coffeehouses.[34] The elite loved 'splash and spectacle' and building ornate fountains around the city.[35] Near Topkapı Palace, Ahmed III built a glittering, gilded, turquoise-tiled domed fountain with overhanging wooden eaves between Hagia Sophia and the palace's Imperial Gate. Nearly as beautiful is the similar one in the port of Üsküdar on the Asian side of the city. The fountains are marked by floral motifs, especially the tulip, which is the symbol of the age: beautiful on the outside, but lacking utility. The elite collected and planted hundreds of thousands of these flowers for their pleasure gardens. The pleasure-seeking continued at night, as the same tulip beds were bedecked with lanterns.

In the rest of Europe, the Ottomans became associated with beauty, luxury, leisure, pleasure, romance, ostentation, and even intellectual output. Beauty was associated with the Ottoman Empire in the form of the tulip, and the flower was imported into Europe, first by Habsburg ambassador Ogier Ghiselin de Busbecq and the Fugger merchant family in Germany, and then through the Netherlands. The Netherlands experienced a tulip craze and is today the culture we associate more with the flower than the Ottoman.

Increased trade, travel, peaceful relations, and the first dispatch of more Ottoman ambassadors to Christian Europe (a practice begun at the end of the sixteenth century) led in the seventeenth and eighteenth centuries to the phenomenon of *Turquerie*, in which goods such as paintings and tapestries were imported from the Ottoman Empire to Central and Western Europe, while literature such as plays, operas, and novels were set against an Ottoman backdrop.[36] Especially following the Treaty of Karlowitz of 1699, which marked an end to the Ottoman-Habsburg conflict, Europeans, above all the French, emulated Ottoman fashions and tastes and expanded diplomatic and commercial contacts. The desire was reciprocated. During this period, the Ottoman court experienced a craze for everything French. This included Louis XV furniture: clocks, mirrors, and European-style chairs and sofas (the first the Ottomans had used, as they had formerly sat on divans, which were armless, backless cushioned seats). French craftsmen were commissioned to decorate interiors, such as Ahmed III's Chamber of Fruits dining room in the harem in Topkapı Palace. European fascination with the Ottomans and Ottoman openness to European culture allowed an exchange of art and luxuries together with new commercialisation, consumption, and sociability among elite European and Ottoman men and women. And the new sociability included a new way of thinking.

Western European guests, Greek-speaking Muslims, and Ottoman Turkish–speaking Greeks gathered at Ahmed III's court to discuss the natural sciences, including astronomy, the utility of knowledge, natural philosophy, and virtue.[37] No Ottoman court since that of the conqueror of Constantinople, Mehmed II, had seen such discussions of ancient and modern knowledge or witnessed such a predominance of Greeks—both those who had remained Christian and those who had converted to Islam.[38] The Greek-speaking Muslims included the sultan's (and former sultan Mustafa II's) Cretan convert mother, Rabia Gülnüş (valide sultan 1695–1715); the fellow Cretan convert and head of the privy physicians Nuh Efendi; Ioannina-native palace librarian Esad Efendi; and the historian and Chios native Hezarfen Hüseyin Efendi. The Ottoman-speaking Greeks included Alexander and Nicholas Mavrokordatos, the patriarch of Jerusalem Chrysanthos Notaras, and the historian Demetrius Cantemir.[39]

The host of this amiable, like-minded circle of thinkers and courtiers, Ahmed III, permitted the establishment of the first

Ottoman-language printing press. It boasted Esad Efendi as editor and a Hungarian convert to Islam, Ibrahim Müteferrika, as head. It mainly published histories, grammars, and dictionaries, as well as works on geography. The sultan authorised translations of a number of French, Greek, and Latin works into Arabic and Ottoman Turkish. Praising the ancients for having the courage to innovate, Müteferrika published the first work of Cartesian philosophy in Ottoman Turkish, a book on magnetism. Grand Vizier Damad Ibrahim Pasha ordered telescopes and microscopes from France and conducted physics experiments in the palace.[40]

Ottoman Greek thinkers' interest in translations and telescopes is considered part of the first phase of the 'Greek enlightenment', which connected Greek intellectuals in the Ottoman Empire to those in other parts of Europe including the Venetian Republic and Habsburg Vienna. But few scholars have considered the Greek enlightenment as a component of a broader 'Ottoman enlightenment'.[41] If we recognise the Ottomans as being part of Europe, however, there is nothing keeping us from using the phrase to at least describe the agnostic freedom of inquiry shared by Christian and Muslim intellectuals at Ahmed III's court.

What is remembered about Ahmed III's era is that Ottoman artists began to work directly for other Europeans, producing costume albums or illustrated erotic manuals. Europeans acquired Ottoman illustrated manuscripts, as well as their first Ottoman chronicles. European travellers also produced images based on their observations. All of these representations and new forms of knowledge circulated in Europe, often reinterpreted in the form of novels and plays set in Asia and the Ottoman Empire. Many European artists produced tragedies or operas about life in the empire. With its choruses of singing Janissaries, Wolfgang Amadeus Mozart's wildly popular *The Abduction from the Seraglio* (1782) demonstrated how Central Europeans imagined Ottomans at the time. Racy scenes of a Spanish hero rescuing his betrothed from slavery in the palace ('seraglio') harem of lusty Pasha Selim

(Sultan Selim I?) by outwitting the evil vizier Osmin (Osman?) gave audiences an impression of Ottoman wealth, sensuality, magnanimity, and sadistic violence.

Along with the tulip, another good that symbolised the cultural diffusion of leisure and pleasure was coffee, imported to the rest of Europe almost exclusively from the Ottoman Empire in the sixteenth and seventeenth centuries, but mainly from the Dutch colony of Java in Southeast Asia from the beginning of the eighteenth century.[42] As coffee shops sprouted across Europe, they inevitably added storefront signs of turbaned Ottomans. The Haus zum Arabischen Coffe Baum (1720) in Leipzig, Germany, for example, boasts a large figure of a reclining Turk giving a cup of coffee to Eros over its main door. This was the period when Johann Sebastian Bach composed his short comic opera dedicated to women coffee addicts, the *Coffee Cantata* (ca. 1735), for the Zimmerman coffeehouse in that same city.[43]

Just as they had done with tea obtained from China, the European elite made coffee consumption the central part of polite ceremonial. Some European coffeehouses even offered the same services as their Ottoman counterparts, including storytellers and poets, waiters in 'Ottoman dress', Turkish carpets, or the serving of coffee with sherbet and tobacco. Public baths in London offered coffee as refreshment.[44]

In some European countries, the Turquerie would prove so long-lasting as to be assimilated as a crucial element of the national culture. The 'national dish' of Sweden, *köttbullar*, or Swedish meatballs, are none other than Ottoman *köfte*. The Ottomans' ally against Russia, Swedish king Charles XII (reigned 1697–1718), fell in love with the little meatballs while in Ottoman Moldova. He returned with the recipe, but substituted pork for lamb. He also introduced stuffed cabbage and coffee to the Nordic land.[45]

Along with meatballs, coffee and coffeehouses, and tulips, Ottoman military music conquered Europe. The Ottoman military bands were the first in the world. European publics in the seventeenth and eighteenth centuries thrilled to the discordant sounds of the bands smashing their cymbals and playing their horns as they marched in battle and at diplomatic exchanges. Europeans created their own moustachioed, turbaned Ottoman bands, performing at carnivals and weddings. Three hundred 'Janissaries' played at the wedding of Prince Friedrich August II and Maria Josepha of Austria in Dresden in 1719.[46] European armies adopted the practice, and by the end of the eighteenth-century military bands across Europe boasted bass drums, cymbals, kettledrums, tambourines, and Turkish crescents (jingling Johnnies).[47]

First displayed onstage, Ottoman fabrics, furniture (the divan, the ottoman), and décor entered European homes. European elite women—even Empress Maria Theresa—were especially enamoured with ostentatious Ottoman clothing.[48] They admired the Ottomans' presumed hedonism. According to Lady Mary Wortley Montagu, who resided in Istanbul as the wife of the British ambassador in 1717 and 1718 and enjoyed the coffee served to her by Ottoman ladies, the Ottomans were not as unpolished as Christian Europeans represented them. She depicted them instead as true libertines. She declared they had 'a right notion of life; they consume it in music, gardens, wine, and delicate eating, while we are tormenting our brains with some scheme of politics or studying some science to which we can never attain. . . . Considering what short liv'd, weak animals men are, is there any study so beneficial as the study of present pleasure?'[49]

REVOLT AGAIN

For the first fifteen years of his reign, Ahmed III had been served by a dozen grand viziers. But in 1718, nepotism became the determining factor for the awarding of high positions of government. In 1717, Ahmed III married Nevşehirli Ibrahim Pasha to his daughter Fatma Sultan and the following year appointed him grand vizier. He became known as Damad (Son-in-Law) Ibrahim Pasha. Damad Ibrahim Pasha's son from his first marriage was married to Ahmed III's daughter Atike Sultan. The navy admiral Kaymak (Cream) Mustafa Pasha married Fatma Hanım, one of Damad Ibrahim Pasha's daughters from his first marriage.[50] The chief assistant to the grand vizier, Kethüdha Mehmed Pasha, who also came from Nevşehir, in central Anatolia, was married to Damad Ibrahim Pasha's other daughter from his first marriage, Hibetullah Hanım. Two of Damad Ibrahim Pasha's nephews were also married to daughters of Ahmed III. Two of his great-grandchildren (the offspring of Kaymak Mustafa Pasha's daughter and Kethüdha Mehmed Pasha's son) married each other.[51]

Between 1718 and 1730, the husbands of six of Ahmed III's daughters were viziers. So, too, were the husbands of four daughters of the sultan's predecessor, Mustafa II. Ahmed III's sister Hatice Sultan was married first to a boon companion of the sultan, then to a grand vizier, and finally, at the age of eighty, thirty years after her second husband had passed away, to another grand vizier. Jurists also tried to enter the elite through marriage ties with the dynasty and statesmen.[52]

What these intricate ties of nepotism illustrate is how power was held collectively. The dynasty allied with high officials connected through the sultan's daughters and sisters. Rather than the sultan alone, or even his family, it was as if nonroyal dignitaries ensured the continuity of the dynasty and empire. And to do so, these men displayed their wealth and generosity, as if they were members of the Ottoman house. Royal women had a share in this, as they built lovely waterside mansions on the Bosporus or Golden Horn where they and their husbands, who were viziers or other high administration officials, hosted lavish banquets, ostentatious displays of consumption. At the two-week princely circumcision and princess wedding festival in 1720, there was a significant change in protocol, as Ahmed III's imperial tent was set up alongside those of Damad Ibrahim Pasha, Kaymak Mustafa Pasha, and Kethüdha Mehmed Pasha, as if they together shared power. All four tents offered visitors pomp and circumstance, feasts, and gifts.[53]

Damad Ibrahim Pasha, Kaymak Mustafa Pasha, and Kethüdha Mehmed Pasha exhibited their blood affinity to the royal family, pretensions to being as wealthy as the dynasty, and generosity by conspicuously displaying their large collections of bejewelled, golden weapons; precious furs and fabrics; jewellery; thousands of pieces of silver, crystal, and Chinese porcelain and greenware (celadon) serving sets; enough bedding to furnish several palaces; and libraries' worth of precious Islamic manuscripts at their many waterside pavilions and mansions on the Bosporus and Golden Horn. Damad Ibrahim Pasha named three of the rooms in one of his waterside mansions after Mehmed II, Bayezid II, and Suleiman I. He possessed a gold sword inscribed 'Sultan Suleiman son of Sultan Selim Khan' and other priceless weapons bedecked in dozens of diamonds and hundreds of rubies and emeralds. He also obtained dynastic genealogies containing miniature portraits of sultans owned by previous sultans, gifted to him by Ahmed III.[54] Opposition to the dynasty sharing power, the concentration of power and wealth in the hands of this small group of relatives, and the policies they imposed led to revolt.

In the Ottoman domains the new wealth and ostentatious display of luxury grew alongside an expansion of the underclass. For every partying prince and smiling princess there were thousands of down-and-out commoners who did not receive taxpayer money with which to live a luxurious lifestyle and who resented those who did. As Ottoman military losses and shrinking borders in Southeastern Europe propelled people to travel to the imperial capital in search of homes and work, Istanbul was flooded with immigrants from former Ottoman territories. What they found were slums and poverty in an economically polarised city.[55] The regime was unable to control their movements. When the

Janissaries revolted in 1726, they were joined by members of this underclass, who even stoned Ahmed III's palace in Beşiktaş on the European shore of the Bosporus.[56] Worse was to come for the dynasty in 1730—and from a not unexpected quarter.

Janissary-connected, beardless Albanian youth who worked in public baths as shampooers and prostitutes pleasuring mature men bedevilled Ottoman authorities throughout the eighteenth century.[57] As the Collection fell into disuse, Janissary applicants as young as eight years old but most on the verge of puberty were permitted to live in the Janissary barracks and serve Janissaries until they grew facial hair. In private, they attended to their master's needs. In public, the young boys wore veils over their faces so that other men could not gaze upon their beardless faces and desire them.[58] Because they were not paid a salary, some of these Janissary interns worked in the public baths as shampooers and prostitutes in order to earn a living.[59] One such man led a revolt that toppled a sultan.

Patrona Halil was originally a beardless youth of Albanian origin who had worked as a shampooer in the Bayezid Bath in Istanbul.[60] In September 1730 when the city's elites were away planting tulip bulbs in a garden on the Dardanelles, Patrona Halil led a rebellion joined by artisans, the petty bourgeoisie, small-scale merchants, religious students, and scholars.[61] They blamed the Grand Vizier Damad Ibrahim Pasha, Kaymak Mustafa Pasha, and Kethüdha Mehmed Pasha for the situation they detested. They united around their distaste for the public picnicking and frolicking of Christians and Jews, and especially the newfound public presence of elite women. Women dared to wear their hair loose, show cleavage, and don light, transparent clothing—to the joy and ire of men. In the words of Ignatius Mouradgea d'Ohsson, an Istanbul Armenian and French Catholic historian who served as translator at the Swedish diplomatic mission and late in life settled in Paris, 'No woman covers her breast, especially in the summer, except with a blouse that is usually made of thin gauze'.[62] The rebels aimed to 'stop the regime that robbed them of their daily living' through extraordinary war taxes to finance campaigns in Iran after the Safavid dynasty had collapsed in 1722.[63] In contrast to the conspicuous consumption of the nouveaux riches, Patrona Halil wore simple clothes and went about barefoot like a radical Sufi, a deviant dervish. Perhaps he was a Bektaşi Sufi.

The second day of the rebellion was a Friday, the day when Muslim men gather for communal prayer.[64] It was the day when it was the norm to complain to the sultan about injustices after the communal prayer, either through petition or protest. Because of this timing, rebel ranks grew larger and began to include Janissaries, a menacing sign for the dynasty. The demonstrators refused to break up, instead demanding to speak to high officials, including Grand Vizier Damad Ibrahim Pasha, whom they blamed for their troubles. On the third day of rebellion, as the insurgents first blockaded and then attacked Topkapı Palace, the sultan decided to sacrifice his grand vizier as a scapegoat to end the dangerous uprising. The grand vizier was executed on the sultan's orders and his corpse given to the angry mob to desecrate. They claimed he was not a Muslim, but an Armenian or Greek, as proven by his allegedly being uncircumcised and having a tonsure.[65] After parading the corpse around the city, the rebels ripped it into pieces and dumped them in Ahmed III's babbling fountain outside Topkapı Palace. But even this did not curb the rising demands of the crowds who wanted the sultan's neck too. Realising he had to abdicate to protect the peace and save his own life, Ahmed III declared thirty-five-year-old Mahmud, son of his brother Mustafa II, his successor rather than either of his own eldest sons and gave up his throne.

The new sultan, Mahmud I (reigned 1730–1754), agreed to have the palace and gardens at Sa'dabad and those of his ministers burned to the ground.[66] Palace librarian, first printing-press editor, and Greek speaker Esad Efendi and Ottoman-speaking Greek patriarch Chrysanthos Notaras soon passed away, and the Müteferrika printing press ceased its operations. The Ottoman enlightenment proved short-lived (although the Greek enlightenment flourished again later in the century). Mahmud I also cancelled some of the grievous taxes established by the executed grand vizier and allowed thousands of rebels to register as the sultan's salaried troops. Their demands met, the popular rebels, who had even established a shadow cabinet and demanded the right to make administrative appointments, did not last long in power. A little over a week after he was enthroned, the sultan decided to wipe them out. He waited until he had the support of the Janissaries, who had had a falling out with these armed commoners after they murdered one of their own. The sultan arranged for Patrona Halil and his men to be called into the palace on the pretence of honouring them with government positions. Instead, they were murdered inside the Yerevan pleasure pavilion, built by Murad IV to celebrate his conquest of the fortress in Armenia from the Safavids in 1635.[67] After this massacre, Janissaries killed the rebels' supporters who tried to flee.

Coffeehouses and public baths favoured by Albanians were shut. Albanians were banished from the city. It became illegal to employ Albanian men as shampooers in the bathhouses.[68] But even these measures did not prevent another revolt in Istanbul the following year, fomented by rebels who had escaped the dragnet and returned to attack the Janissaries. It was quickly suppressed and accompanied by more measures to restrict migration to the imperial capital. Restrictions were also reimposed on male prostitutes. To uphold the gendered religious hierarchy of society, gender segregation was reinstated in public spaces. Because the norms delineating the clothing permitted to be worn by Muslim women and by all Christians and Jews had been openly flaunted by the nouveaux riches during Ahmed III's reign, sumptuary laws were also reintroduced.[69]

RUSSIA: THE RISE OF A NEW THREAT

Whereas once the Safavids were the main danger to the eastern frontier of the Ottoman realm, in the second half of the eighteenth century a new threat rose to replace that of the fallen Shi'i empire: Russia. The Ottoman sultans who first faced this new threat were less prepared to handle it, as seniority was the only reason they had ascended to the throne. When Mahmud I died in 1754, he was replaced by his fifty-five-year-old brother, Osman III (reigned 1754–1757). Osman III poisoned Ahmed III's forty-year-old son, Mehmed, in 1756, leading to the oldest remaining of Ahmed III's sons, Mustafa III (reigned 1757–1774), taking the throne after Osman III. He was replaced by Ahmed III's third and youngest son, the forty-eight-year-old Abdülhamid I (reigned 1774–1789).

One significant carryover from the era of Ahmed III was the emphasis on diplomacy with Western Europe, especially the courts of Maria Theresa (reigned 1740–1780) in Vienna and Frederick II (reigned 1740–1786) in Berlin. But relations with a newly powerful Russia under German-born empress Catherine II (reigned 1762–1796) were belligerent. Catherine II continued the military and naval expansion of Peter I (reigned 1696–1725), who had established a regular army provisioned with the latest artillery weapons and constructed a sizeable fleet. Russia aimed to attack the Ottoman Empire from Ukraine, to seize the Crimean peninsula and control the Black Sea, and to stir up Orthodox Christians in Southeastern Europe against the Ottomans. During these decades under Catherine II the Russians accomplished all these plans.

To block the Dardanelles and cut off Istanbul from the south, a Russian fleet launched from a naval base in Peter I's capital of Saint Petersburg on the Baltic Sea, travelled all the way around Europe, entered the Mediterranean, and arrived off the Aegean coast of Anatolia in 1770. Smaller in number yet better armed, the

Russian navy destroyed an Ottoman fleet in a surprise attack at Çeşme off the coast of İzmir, killing thousands of sailors, leading to Russian control of the Aegean. At the same time, a Russian army routed a much larger Ottoman-Tatar force on the Danube frontier. Russians instigated rebellion among Greeks in the Morea (the Peloponnese peninsula). The next year, Russia invaded the Crimea and extended its frontier to the Black Sea. The Ottoman vassal the Crimean khan sided with Russia, which granted him independence, although under Russian protection.[70] The Ottomans were compelled to agree to Russian territorial gains through the Treaty of Küçük Kaynarca in 1774, some of whose planks Russia interpreted as giving it the right to protect Orthodox Christians in the Ottoman Empire, by war if necessary. In 1783 Russia annexed the Crimea. When the last Crimean khan, Şahin Giray, seen as the puppet of Catherine II and a traitor, arrived an exile in the Ottoman Empire, Abdülhamid I had him executed.

From their new Black Sea bases, the Russians had moved their fleet to within two and a half days' sail from the Ottoman capital.[71] Catherine II quickly moved to annex half of Ukraine. In 1795, Russia, Prussia, and Austria partitioned the Commonwealth of Poland-Lithuania among themselves. In all of her newly won territories, the Russian ruler expelled Muslims and resettled Christians, especially Greeks from the Ottoman Empire, in their place.[72] Many of these Greeks became wealthy merchants connecting the overland but especially maritime trade of the Russian and Ottoman Empires with Central and Western Europe. Others entered Russian military and diplomatic service and would return to the Ottoman Empire in the future to play an important role in rebellions.[73] Catherine II called for the conquest of Istanbul, the reestablishment of the Byzantine Empire under Russian control, and the reconsecration of the Hagia Sophia as the main church of Christianity.[74] A new rival had arisen claiming the mantle of the Romans. The Ottomans had great reason to fear their northern neighbour.

FROM REVOLT TO REFORM

The deposition of Mehmed IV led to the return of a weak sultanate whose officeholder was manipulated by pashas and viziers and
deposed at will by Janissaries and jurists. The subsequent era of
cultural openness and exchange with Europe and intellectual innovation under Ahmed III, too, was undone by Janissary revolt, as
soldiers continued to have the final say over who sat on the throne.
Humiliating territorial losses, including that of the Crimean
khanate—the remnant of Genghis Khan's Mongol empire, which
had given liege to the Ottoman sultan for several centuries—to a
new enemy, Russia, whose strength rested on an army made up of
well-trained conscript soldiers, an expanded navy, and a class of
officers trained in war colleges, offered lessons to the Ottomans.
A cycle of opulence, rebellion, and military defeat propelled the
empire to an era of reform. In order to break this cycle, the dynasty had to do away once and for all with its greatest rival power
centre: the Janissaries.

The final six chapters of this book narrate the period from 1789
to 1922, the last 133 years of the Ottoman dynasty and empire.
This era was marked by diverse attempts by administrators, intellectuals, sultans, and military leaders to save the empire from its
own worst tendencies and dismemberment by foreign powers. As
the Ottomans became ever more connected to the rest of Europe,
for good and for ill, they sought to hold the empire together in the
face of internal rebellion and revolution. They grasped for new
ways to link the dynasty to its subjects, experimenting with ever
more radical and modern forms of governance, war, and violence.

17

REFORM
Breaking the Cycle of
Rebellion from Selim III to Abdülaziz I

A T THE END of the Crimean War in 1856, the concert of European states recognised the Ottoman Empire as an equal member. But by that point they were anything but equal. At the end of the eighteenth century the Ottoman elite realised that the dynasty and empire had fallen behind the military and economic levels of elsewhere in Europe and of Russia, whose armies encroached on their territory from without. Within the empire, subject peoples imbued with nationalism began to demand autonomy or independence. In response, eighteenth and nineteenth century sultans and elites launched reforms to strengthen the empire against occupation and colonisation from abroad and chaos within. In their view, they needed to modernise the empire, striking the right balance between adapting European innovations and strengthening their own traditions. Reforming sultans went so far as to wipe out the Janissaries, suppress the Bektaşi Sufi order with which the army was affiliated, and ostensibly abolish the hierarchical social order based on religious and class difference. Conversion to Islam was no longer a path to assimilation. But instead of saving the empire, these changes deepened the chasm between Ottoman Christians and Muslims. One of the reasons for this was that in this era, elite Muslims—while promoting the newly granted religious freedom, constitution, and parliamentary form of government—did not relinquish the idea of the superiority of Islam or the primacy of Islamic law. They exalted Ottoman Muslims and, for the first time, Turks, including the sultan caliph who was the head of government.

SELIM III: A BREAK WITH THE PAST

For the Ottoman Empire, the nineteenth century was a long one, for it began in 1789, the year that witnessed the French Revolution. Accompanied by massive bloodshed, French revolutionaries would abolish the monarchy, execute the king, disestablish the church, nationalise its revenue and property, and close churches and monasteries. They established a de-Christianised republic based on the principle of the equality of all citizens no matter their religion (but not their gender). The French established a system of rule based on the will of the people and freedom of speech. They unleashed nationalism and made devotion to the fatherland a guiding principle. They abolished the slave trade.

The French Revolution had been preceded by the American Revolution (1775–1783), during which thirteen British colonies in North America fought for and gained their political independence. The founding principles of the United States of America as articulated in the Constitution (1787) and Bill of Rights (1791) include the separation of powers and the prohibition of religious tests for officeholders. They also include individual liberty manifested in freedom of speech, religion, and the press, the right to assembly, to petition, to hold property (including African American slaves), and to impartial justice. The Ottoman dynasty closely monitored these developments with trepidation. In the early nineteenth century, some of the component elements of the empire, such as the Greeks and Serbs, would be inspired by these ideas,

including nationalist revolution. In the second half of the nineteenth century, influential Ottoman Muslim intellectuals and
statesmen would also promote patriotism, liberty, and separation
of powers.

Less revolutionary but nonetheless dramatic transformations
ensued in the Ottoman Empire with the rise of Selim III (reigned
1789–1807), the son of Mustafa III, who acceded to the throne
at the age of twenty-eight upon the death of his uncle, Abdülhamid I. Selim III was a sultan willing to change the administration
and the military root and branch, revising relations between ruler
and subjects and among subjects. The dynasty also renegotiated
its relation to various groups in society and to the new imperial
powers.

Acceding to the throne in the year of the French Revolution,
which would spark feelings of nationalism within the empire and
contribute to its shrinkage and then collapse, Selim III sought to
strengthen his realm. Coming to power in the midst of a losing
campaign against Russia—and keeping one eye on this nemesis,
with an ultimate goal to retake the Crimea—he incorporated into
his army the latest French, Prussian, and Russian advances in
the military sciences. Open to reforms yet hesitant to completely
revolutionise society, Selim III favoured Europe and European
advisors; when still a prince, he had corresponded with France's
Louis XVI (reigned 1774–1792). At the same time, Selim III was
keen to maintain the gendered religious hierarchy of Ottoman
society. As he launched his new order, Selim III enforced clothing restrictions on women, Christians, and Jews, marking them
as distinct. The centrepiece of his reform was a new army and
navy corps made up of Muslim recruits. The sultan revised the
aims of Osman II, who had been deposed and murdered for his
reforms nearly two centuries earlier. The new army was trained by
French military advisors at new academies and medical schools.
The Ottoman elite began to learn French. Selim III established the
first permanent Ottoman embassies in Berlin, London, Paris, and

Vienna, dispatching portraits of himself to such figures as Emperor Napoleon Bonaparte (reigned 1804–1814, 1815), who began his military and political career during the French Revolution.

Despite good relations with France, like the rest of the European continent including Russia, the Ottoman Empire suffered from Napoleon's militant expansion. During the Napoleonic Wars—which lasted from 1792 to 1815 and which partly played out on Ottoman territory—France invaded and occupied Egypt, which had been part of the Ottoman Empire since the early sixteenth century. The 1798 occupation was a reminder of the role that the Ottomans played in European history. Napoleon's aim in targeting Egypt was Britain, for he sought to control the route to India.

The arrival of the French demonstrated the weakened Ottoman condition in the face of the expanding military might of other European powers in the nineteenth century. In 1799, Napoleon and his army marched from Egypt to Syria, but returned to Egypt after failing to capture the coastal fortress of Acre, Palestine. It was defended by the semiautonomous governor of Sidon and Damascus—the Bosnian Cezzar (the Butcher) Ahmed Pasha—and a British fleet. To seize power in Paris, Napoleon returned to France that same year. It was only in 1801 that the Ottomans, relying on the British navy, forced the French army to quit Cairo and Alexandria. Nevertheless, the Ottomans again allied with France and went to war against Britain and Russia in 1806 as the Napoleonic Wars continued. In late 1806, the British fleet bombarded Istanbul.

While breaking new ground within the empire, the reformist sultan Selim III faced opposition from entrenched interests, especially the Janissaries, who were unhappy with the creation of a new corps. He was also opposed by the jurists, who were nervous about the French culture on display and were concerned about a revitalised sultanate that they had thought they had under their control. Tax farmers were outraged when their holdings were confiscated to pay for the new army. He also alienated provincial notables. In summer 1806, they blocked the new army from being set up in Thrace. The new order had been stopped.

In spring 1807, Janissaries in Istanbul rioted. They were joined by underclass militiamen led by a Turk named Mustafa, whose Albanian supporters demanded the abolition of the new corps. Thanks to a legal opinion issued by his own sheikhulislam, Selim III was deposed. The reason given was that he had introduced innovations allegedly contrary to Islamic law. He was murdered a year later while under house arrest. He suffered the same fate as Osman II, killed in 1622 in part for attempting to create a new army.

Conventional wisdom has long depicted a clash in late Ottoman society between those labelled as Westernisers, modernisers, reformers, and secularists versus Islamists, traditionalists, conservatives, and religious reactionaries.[1] But the categories were not exclusive. Modernising Islamist reformers initiated secularising processes, as in Selim III's reforms. But the Janissaries and jurists did their best to limit the power of the sultan. High points of radical change and reform would occur under Selim III's successors.

MAHMUD II: NEW ALLIANCES AS THE EMPIRE BEGINS TO BREAK APART

Twentysomething Mustafa IV, son of Abdülhamid I, had been put in power upon the deposition of his cousin Selim III in 1807. In July 1808 he ordered the murder of Selim III so as to put down a rebellion that was demanding the restoration of his predecessor, and his assassins attacked Selim III in his private quarters. In the words of the official chronicler, they 'defiled his corpse with blood and earth', dumped his body outside, covered it with a tarp, and left it.[2] Mustafa IV's young brother, the future Mahmud II, was hidden by servants until it was safe to appear.[3] But Mustafa IV lasted only a year in office before he, too, was deposed in a coup, in August 1808. From the point of view of the dynasty, something had to be done to prevent further humiliation.

Twenty-eight-year-old Mahmud II (reigned 1808–1839) was enthroned during the coup that deposed Mustafa IV, led by provincial notable Bayraktar Mustafa, who also was commander of the Ottoman Danubian army. Bayraktar was appointed grand vizier. In September 1808, he led an assembly in Istanbul made up of the heads of leading Anatolian and Rumelian notable families as well as members of the imperial council, chief military judges, and commanders of the Janissaries and the cavalry at the sultan's court. They and the sultan signed a contract, the Deed of Alliance (*sened-i ittifak*).[4]

The deed aimed to bring about unity and order in the realm. To accomplish this aim, the signatories agreed to protect the person of the sultan and the dynasty and to draft soldiers to create a new standing army (*sekban-ı cedid*, New Militia), deployed in camps in the provinces as an alternative to the Janissaries. They pledged to collectively punish anyone who attacked or betrayed the ruler and the sultanate or opposed the creation of the new army. They agreed to implement the decisions of the grand vizier as representative of the sultan and to punish those who opposed them, yet also to depose the grand vizier if he acted unlawfully. The signatories consented to the rule of provincial notables and their inviolable power in perpetuity in their respective regions. They outlawed arbitrary punishment of these notables if they were suspected of committing an offence. Should the Janissaries rebel in Istanbul, the signers of the deed pledged, the provincial notables would immediately send soldiers from the new standing army to put down the insurrection. The rebels would be executed after judicial investigation if found guilty of treason. The threat of the Janissaries as an autonomous political opposition in league with the populace hung over the document.

The signers of the deed intended for it to be maintained over the following generations, to be signed and affirmed by all future grand viziers and sheikhulislams. But within a couple of months, in November 1808, the Janissaries in Istanbul rebelled again. Thousands of people were killed in the imperial capital, including Bayraktar Mustafa and many of the deed's signatories. Bayraktar Mustafa had taken refuge in a powder magazine; when the Janissaries entered he blew himself up.[5]

Bayraktar Mustafa's deed, which had never been implemented or publicly announced, was effectively null and void. The standing army in the provinces could not arrive in Istanbul in time to save the regime. Memory of that agreement, however, would have long-lasting political effects. The deed was neither a constitutional nor a republican reform. It was not egalitarian, as it concerned only the Muslim elite running the empire. It did not set up a consultative assembly or diet. However, it envisioned government as a negotiated partnership, a coalition of elites. It was the first legal document limiting the power of the sultanate and the dynasty's ability to execute its servants and confiscate their wealth and property without judicial process.[6]

Mahmud II would have to wait to promote reform so that he could ensure stable sultanic rule. He had his predecessor, Mustafa IV, strangled as the Janissaries marched on the palace in November 1808.[7] Troops loyal to the sultan killed thousands of Janissaries. The navy even fired on the Janissary barracks from their ships in the Golden Horn.[8] But Mahmud II agreed to the Janissaries' demand to disband the New Militia. He remained the only living male heir of the Ottoman dynasty, his position still at the mercy of the Janissaries.

Facing insurrection from within the regime, Mahmud II also had to contend with the fact that Serbs, Greeks, and Egyptians gained measures of independence during his reign. Following sustained revolts, Serbia was granted semi-autonomy following the 1814–1815 Congress of Vienna, the peace conference that concluded the Napoleonic Wars. Controlled by Austria, Russia, Prussia, and Great Britain, the congress excluded the Ottoman

Empire, despite its role in the recent wars. The great powers omitted the empire from the idea and geography of Europe. Serbia was given full autonomy in 1830. Following a nearly decade-long uprising, Greece (consisting of what is today southern Greece as far north as Arta and Volos, midway on the mainland) was given autonomy in 1830 and independence in 1832. Greek independence was related to Egyptian secession. After decades of independent political and military action that threatened the Ottoman dynasty, an Egyptian rebel proclaimed independence in 1838 and two years later he and his heirs were granted rule over Egypt for perpetuity.

For Greeks, the movement began among diaspora intellectuals outside the Ottoman Empire who were inspired by the American and French revolutions. The most influential intellectual, Rigas Velestinlis—a native of Thessaly who was based in Vienna—reinterpreted the French *Declaration of the Rights of Man and of the Citizen* and promoted a revolution that would replace Ottoman rule with an independent, secular, democratic Greek republic modelled on Jacobin France.[9] The revolutionary, secret Philikí Etaireía (Friendly Society) was founded in 1814 in Odessa, Russia—the Black Sea port built by Catherine II and home to many wealthy Greek merchants as well as the new Greek bourgeoisie—and began to disseminate these ideas within the Ottoman Empire wherever Greeks lived, including Moldova, Wallachia, and the Peloponnese peninsula. Wealthy and influential Greeks including professionals, local notables, governors, priests, militiamen, members of the Istanbul secular elite, and Greek Russian military officers joined the organisation, which espoused violence to achieve the goal of freedom for Orthodox Christians.[10]

Southeastern Europe in the eighteenth and nineteenth century experienced that which seventeenth-century Anatolia had faced: the rise of provincial notables who amassed great fortunes in cash through lifetime grants of tax farming, which they used to employ large militias and purchase government office. Finding themselves with such regional power, they often rebelled against the central government. The difference with Anatolia was that the new local powerful men in Southeastern Europe were as likely to be Christian as Muslim. The British, French, Habsburgs, Ottomans, and Russians had all armed Greeks and used them as irregulars in the eastern Mediterranean and Southeastern Europe in the Napoleonic Wars. These were accompanied by high-ranking Greeks in the armies of the Christian empires as well. All of these men—provincial notables, irregulars, and officers—would join the 1821 rebellion.[11]

In late March of that year, Ottoman forces were engaged in a campaign to take back control from the forces of Tepedelenli Ali Pasha: an overly powerful, wayward provincial Muslim notable in mountainous Ioannina, in northwestern Greece, some of whose advisors were leading members of the Friendly Society. Seizing the opportunity, a Christian local notable, Petrobey Mavromihalis, came out in rebellion, which spread rapidly across the Peloponnese in a mass revolt joined by peasants who rose up against their landlords.[12] Within weeks, having massacred or expelled Muslims and Jews and pillaged their property, the rebels controlled most of the fortresses, garrisons, and towns of the peninsula.[13]

The Ottoman court chronicler records that Mahmud II was so enraged by the audacity of the rebels that he demanded that 'all of his Greek subjects be massacred'.[14] He decreed that the commander of the Janissaries begin carrying out the order in Istanbul and the surrounding region. Sheikhulislam Halil Efendi, supported by the grand vizier Seyyid Ali, asked the sultan to delay implementing this plan for several days so that he could investigate whether Islamic law permitted the intended massacres.[15] Thus buying time, the sheikhulislam and grand vizier alerted the Orthodox patriarch, Gregory V, and several metropolitans and urged them to declare their loyalty to the dynasty and to condemn the rebels. The Christian notables appeared before Mahmud II, trembling with fear as they begged for mercy because they had nothing to do with the uprising. As a result, the sultan ordered that those Greek subjects who were not guilty of rebelling would not be attacked.[16] A general massacre was thus averted.

Yet, not trusting his Christian subjects, Mahmud II ordered that all Greeks and Armenians residing in Istanbul (including the districts of Galata, Üsküdar, and Eyüp) surrender their firearms.[17] The sultan did not forgive the grand vizier and sheikhulislam for resisting his wishes. The grand vizier was stripped of his ministerial rank and exiled to Gallipoli. The sheikhulislam, who had refused to issue a fatwa allowing the mass murder of innocent Christians, was dismissed from office and exiled to Afyon-Karahisar.[18]

The new grand vizier, Benderli Ali Pasha, believed that the leader of the Greek church had advance knowledge of the rebellion. Spurred by Benderli Ali Pasha, Mahmud II reneged on his promise. He decreed that the patriarch, despite his declarations of innocence, his having had excommunicated the rebels, and his advanced age (over ninety years old according to the Ottoman chronicler), be hanged from the main gate of the patriarchate on 22 April, Easter Sunday.[19] After the corpse had remained on the gate three days, intended as a warning of what happens to those who dare rebel against the sultan, officials made sure the elderly Christian spiritual leader's humiliation was complete. They ordered Jews to take down the corpse, tie stones to it, and cast it in the sea so that Greeks could not bury their leader.[20]

By summer 1821 the Greek uprising had inflamed not only the Peloponnese, but also much of the Greek mainland and Macedonia, the Aegean islands, and the islands of Cyprus, Chios, and Crete. Although most of these revolts were soon crushed, at the end of the year the rebels still controlled central Greece and the Peloponnese. In December 1821, a national congress composed of all the rebel factions throughout Greece gathered in Epidavros in the Peloponnese, proclaimed a constitution, and declared the founding of an Orthodox Christian democratic republic.[21]

In early 1822, the Ottomans captured and executed the rebellious Muslim local notable Tepedelenli Ali Pasha and were able to turn their full attention to the Greek rebellion. But in summer the Ottoman force sent to retake the Peloponnese was routed and its commander committed suicide. A rebel Greek navy—formed from formerly Ottoman ships and their captains and sailors— ruled the coasts. But by the next year the different factions of Greek rebels soon turned to fighting each other. From 1824 to 1827 the Ottomans managed to take back control over most rebel areas. They did so with the help of the Albanian Mehmed Ali of the Aegean port of Kavala (today in Greece).

After being appointed Ottoman governor of Egypt in 1805 following the French and British withdrawal, Mehmed Ali had carved out a semi-independent kingdom by wiping out all opposition, massacring members of the Ottoman military class. The Ottomans could not remove him, and his power expanded first as head of a successful Ottoman effort between 1811 and 1818 to reassert control over Arabia. Mehmed Ali had a conscript army trained by French military advisors and the latest muskets at his disposal, as well as a well-armed navy. His forces suppressed the Greek rebellion on Cyprus and Crete in 1821.

In 1825 Mehmed Ali's son Ibrahim Pasha launched a successful sea and land assault from Crete on the rebel-held Peloponnese. As the Egyptians fought the rebels from the south, an Ottoman army descended from the north. Soon the Ottomans again controlled central Greece. But news of the atrocities committed during Ibrahim Pasha's capture of the town of Missolonghi in western Greece in April 1826—after a yearlong siege that had reduced the inhabitants to near starvation—where the surviving men were killed and the women and children sold into slavery, spurred intervention by foreign powers, which would prove decisive for the Greek struggle.[22]

MAKING REFORM PERMANENT

Janissary revolt, Greek rebellion, insurrectionary provincial notables, the inferiority of the Ottoman army, defeats at the hands of other Europeans, the forced reliance on superior European armies and navies: all of these factors forced Mahmud II to seek a radical solution to a question faced by the dynasty since repeated Janissary revolts and military defeats had begun in the seventeenth century. How to save the empire? One way was not merely to rein in the Janissaries, but to abolish their regiments and annihilate their men.

Rather than simply establish a new army alongside the Janissaries, as Selim III and Osman II had attempted—paying for it with their lives—Mahmud II sought to hollow the Janissaries out from within. In 1826, he ordered hundreds of men to be taken out of each unit and made into a new elite army corps based on new drills, tactics, training, uniforms, and weapons. In June, the Janissaries revolted in Istanbul, but the sultan had planned for their disobedience. Inspired by the sight of the symbol of the call to jihad, the Prophet Muhammad's banner at Sultan Ahmed I's mosque (the Blue Mosque), troops loyal to the sultan and armed men from across the city slaughtered most of the Janissaries who had gathered in the Hippodrome. Others set fire to their barracks, burning them alive.[23] An estimated six thousand Janissaries were massacred.[24] Having made up the elite backbone of the Ottoman military for five centuries, the Janissaries were wiped out in less than half an hour.[25] Surviving Janissaries fled, thousands of provincial Janissaries were hunted down, and the entire corps was abolished.

Since the seventeenth century, Western European observers had noted that rather than being a 'despotism', Ottoman government had been a type of 'limited monarchy', with the Janissaries and jurists serving as a check upon the sultan's power.[26] Sharing their view was Ottoman intellectual and poet Namık Kemal. A generation after the Janissaries' destruction, Kemal reflected on their political role over the previous two centuries. In his view, the jurists held the legislative power, the sultan and his ministers wielded the executive power, and the Janissaries restrained the executive branch.[27] But with their demise, others would have to arise to perform that function.

The Bektaşi Sufi order to which the Janissaries were attached was also viciously attacked during Mahmud II's reign. To survive, it was forced to become a clandestine movement. Throughout the empire, Bektaşi shrines and lodges were burned to the ground or handed over along with their assets to the regime-supporting Halveti, Mevlevi, and Nakşibendi orders. Bektaşi sheikhs were executed or banished. Even the Jewish quartermasters of the Janissaries—Çelebi Bekhor Isaac Carmona, Yehezkel Gabay of Baghdad, and Isaiah Aciman, among the most wealthy and influential Jews in the empire, who also served as money changers to the dynasty—were murdered as part of the collective punishment of all Janissaries. The immense fortunes of these bankers were confiscated by the sultan and the large debts he and others owed them were cancelled.[28]

As the Janissaries and Bektaşis and those connected to them were destroyed, the Mevlevi Sufi order continued to be influential, especially from its Istanbul lodge. The head of the order, the Mevlevi grand çelebi, a descendant of Rûmi, was the girder of the sword at the enthronement ceremonies of the sultan held in Eyüp outside the walls of Istanbul on the Golden Horn. Selim III had been a member of the order and had composed musical numbers for its whirling ceremonies. He had had a close relationship with the famous poet and sheikh of the Galata Mevlevi lodge, Mehmed Galip, who propagated the sultan's reforms. Mevlevis now supported the reforms of Mahmud II, who was also a member of the order and relied on Mevlevi confidants and courtiers, using them to overcome opposition from other members of the religious class.

But with their newfound, more reform-supporting turn, would the Mevlevis remain loyal?

After the bloodletting of 1826, the new Victorious Army of Muhammad replaced the Janissaries. Soldiers were dressed in Western-style uniforms and given the latest European weaponry, and the army was paired with a professional bureaucracy and massive investment in public works, notably roads and bridges. Professional colleges were opened to train a generation of administrators, architects, engineers, and military doctors. Censuses and means for more effective tax collection followed suit. Just like in other European states and empires, modernising nineteenth-century sultans would invest in conscription for a standing army, telegraph technology, and railways for the same reason: to centralise control and better govern the population.

To control the population, the government had to know what people thought. As in the rest of Europe, one new way of managing the population was to learn what gossip and rumours people were spreading at coffeehouses. In an unprecedented expansion of governmental surveillance, most likely begun during Mahmud II's reign after the destruction of the Janissaries (who had owned one-third of the coffeehouses in Istanbul), spies continuously fanned out across the imperial capital and systematically listened to the conversations of people, mainly in coffeehouses, but also in barbershops, at the mosque, on the streets, at markets, at public baths, and even in the privacy of homes. They reported what people said about the government and the sultan to officials who recorded and analysed the conversations. The grand vizier relayed these reports directly to the ruler, who used this knowledge of public opinion to shape his policies and undercut opposition, increasing his own popular legitimacy.[29]

In 1829, Mahmud II decreed that civilian men had to wear a fez and Western-style jacket and trousers. He was the first sultan to have a portrait of himself wearing a Western-style kit distributed across the empire, displayed in barracks, government offices, and schools. In the 1830s, Mahmud II became the first Ottoman ruler to take lengthy imperial excursions whose sole aim was to see his empire (Rûmeli and Anatolia) and come into contact with the population. The journeys were undertaken to shape public opinion in his favour, to draw the people closer to the sultan.[30]

THE EMPIRE CONTINUES TO BREAK UP

Having abolished the Janissaries and replaced them with a new, smart, elite army corps, Mahmud II still faced the imperial headache of the Greek rebellion, as well as further troubles. A British, French, and Russian fleet defeated an Ottoman-Egyptian fleet three times its size at the Bay of Navarino (Pylos) in the Ionian Sea in 1827.[31] By 1829 Ibrahim Pasha had evacuated Greece. That year, a Russian army invaded Southeastern Europe and took territory as near to Istanbul as the former Ottoman capital of Edirne, as another Russian army attacked from the Caucasus and conquered eastern Anatolia, including Erzurum and Trabzon. It seemed the Ottoman Empire was about to fall. The Russian advances compelled the Ottomans to agree to a peace treaty by which they gave autonomy to Serbia and Greece, as well as to Moldova and Wallachia under Russian oversight. The first king of Greece was Bavarian Catholic prince Otto (reigned 1832–1862). The seventeen-year-old son of King Ludwig I, he symbolised foreign, especially British, French, and Russian, intervention in Ottoman Southeastern Europe.

Independence was also pursued by Bulgarians, Macedonians, and others. Unlike rebels of the sixteenth and seventeenth centuries, who were looking to be rewarded with positions within the Ottoman system, these rebels wanted their liberty. Inspired by the American and French Revolutions, they wanted out, to go their own way, and they intended to take their entire nation with them, breaking away and establishing new states. These rebellions demanded different answers. The Ottomans could let them go, reframe the social contract, or try to crush them—which they did, with calamitous results, both in terms of the number of dead and the loss of Ottoman territory. The Ottomans were weak, and when subject peoples rebelled they had the backing of much stronger foreign empires. At times the Ottomans needed foreign powers to save the dynasty from rebels.

After the Ottoman-Egyptian fleet was destroyed in 1827 at Navarino, French advisors helped Mehmed Ali improve his personal military and navy again and in 1831 he launched a campaign by sea and land against Ottoman Syria. His forces under his son Ibrahim Pasha invaded Anatolia. The Ottoman army sent to oppose Ibrahim Pasha was defeated and its head, the grand vizier, was captured. By 1833 Ibrahim Pasha's army reached Kütahya, a town in the region of northwestern Anatolia where the Ottomans had first risen to power. The weak Ottoman dynasty could do nothing but reward Mehmed Ali and Ibrahim Pasha for their rebellion with governorships in Syria and the Hijaz—Arabia in addition to Egypt. Finally, in 1838, Mehmed Ali proclaimed his independence. An Ottoman army marched on Ibrahim Pasha's forces in 1839 but was defeated near Antep in southeastern Anatolia. Shortly thereafter Mahmud II died of tuberculosis and his son Abdülmecid (reigned 1839–1861) became ruler, just as the grand vizier defected to Mehmed Ali in Egypt and took the imperial navy with him.[32] It was only the diplomatic involvement of Austria, Britain, Prussia, and Russia that enabled the Ottomans to secure an agreement with the rebels to return the navy and withdraw to Egypt, where Mehmed Ali and his heirs were granted governorship in perpetuity the following year, reflecting the spirit of the never-implemented Deed of Alliance of 1808.

The Serbian, Greek, and Egyptian episodes during Mahmud II's reign illustrate 'the eastern question', which, from the point of view of the imperial powers, was how to balance their own interests with those of the emerging nation-states as they divided up the Ottoman Empire. Throughout the nineteenth century, Christian subjects would revolt, one or more foreign powers would intervene militarily or diplomatically on their behalf, and other foreign powers would seek a political settlement restoring the balance of power, benefiting the rebels to the detriment of the Ottomans.[33] The Ottomans, however, did not see themselves as moribund and about to collapse. But they did perceive the need for additional major changes.

ABDÜLMECID I: THE PERIOD OF REFORMS

Under Abdülmecid I, reform edicts in 1839 and 1856 instituted more thoroughgoing reforms, the last granting equality to all citizens of the empire, no matter their religion. The act intended to sweep away a nearly six-century-old social order, in which Ottoman society had been governed by distinct legal and social hierarchies favouring Muslims above Christians and Jews.

Abdülmecid I built the magnificent Dolmabahçe Palace in Beşiktaş on the European shore of the Bosporus, with a chandelier given by Queen Victoria. The new palace was designed and constructed by members of the Armenian Balyan family of architects to the dynasty, who had been educated in France and built numerous mosques and palaces in the imperial capital. Abdülmecid I's new home made concrete the move away from Topkapı Palace and all it represented. Located in the heart of the old city, Topkapı Palace had been built by Mehmed II after the conquest of the city from the Byzantines in 1453 as the centre of administration, a palace hidden by walls in the heart of the ancient city. Abdülmecid I built a palace architecturally modelled on Western European palaces and, like its counterparts elsewhere in Europe, visible to the public. He ushered in the Tanzimat (Period of Reforms, 1839–1876).

The 'empire's longest century' was marked by the creation of a new class of bureaucrats who aimed to guide the empire through a period of administrative and legal reorganisation and reform. The objective was to centralise the bureaucratic system and increase control through newly developed technologies and agency specialisation, including the establishment of new provincial and urban administrative bureaus.[34] This led to widened public control of administration, diffusion of authority, and the entrance of new people into the realm of administration.

The many edicts and laws issued by the sultan during this period introduced new state primary and secondary schools, open to all irrespective of religion. Prior to this, each religious community had been responsible for educating its children in its own religion and language. Law was also secularised. Formerly, Islamic law courts, which applied Islamic and secular law, had been supreme, but now secular courts were introduced, and as their jurists grew in prominence, Islamic jurists began to lose their power. The former Ottoman class system dividing tax-exempt elite from tax-paying commoners was abolished, making all male citizens equal and, for the first time, eligible to serve in the military, regardless of religion. The economy was liberalised, the right to private property protected.

The changes even affected the timeworn practice of slavery. Abdülmecid I closed the Istanbul slave market and ended the trade in African slaves, but without ever completely abolishing slavery. Circassian girls continued to stock the private homes of the Ottoman elite.

MORE RADICAL REFORMS

In 1839, Abdülmecid I promulgated the Decree of the Rose Garden. The decree guaranteed 'security for life, honour, and property' of all subjects, and a 'regular system of assessing taxes'.[35] Tax collection would no longer be based on tax farming, through which a tax farmer could abuse his grant to obtain taxes by demanding amounts greater than what he was required to submit to the central treasury. That practice was criticised in the words of the decree as 'handing over the financial and political affairs of a country to the whims of an ordinary man and perhaps to the grasp of force and oppression, for if the tax farmer is not of good character he will be interested only in his own profit and will behave oppressively'. The decree also called for an 'equally regular system for the conscription of requisite troops', which was meant to be universal conscription, what it referred to as 'the inescapable duty of all the people to provide soldiers for the defence of the fatherland'. Universal conscription was in fact never realised in that era. What was most radical about the decree was its affirmation that 'the Muslim and non-Muslim subjects of our lofty Sultanate shall, without exception, enjoy our imperial concessions'.

What is striking about the decree is the way it mixes Islamic and Western European elements. It begins with praise for the Qur'an and Muhammad and states the necessity of adherence to Islamic law, and then justifies the introduction of the basis of European statecraft, including regular taxation and universal conscription. On the one hand, the decree was meant for European, especially British, consumption. One of the aims of issuing it was to secure British aid to suppress Ottoman governor Mehmed Ali, who at that time had built a mini-empire in Egypt, Syria, and the Hijaz and was threatening Anatolia. The decree was published in Ottoman Turkish and in French. It was proclaimed in Gülhane Park adjacent to Topkapı Palace before European diplomats. On the other hand, it was the work of Ottoman reformers who realised that the empire needed to change its financial and political administration to survive. The most important of these was a former ambassador to Britain and France, Foreign Minister Mustafa Reşid Pasha, a man with close relations to the dynasty and whose family and network were primarily Mevlevi Sufis.[36]

Most significant, the Period of Reforms brought about changes in the religious hierarchy of the empire. For the first time, the religious hierarchy was being replaced by equality between different religious groups. The decree aimed to sap the strength of ethnic nationalism by increasing the patriotism of its subjects. By granting his Christian subjects equality, the sultan aimed to convince them to support his regime and not be persuaded to join nationalist movements.

The sultan wanted to create an Ottoman nation, promoting Ottomanism. Ottomanism was a new ideology that advocated the loyalty of all subject peoples, no matter their religion or ethnicity, to his person and to the empire. The sultan reportedly stated that he wanted to be able to distinguish the religious differences of his subjects only when they entered their houses of prayer, as in France, where all citizens were equal and Jews, for example, were referred to as 'French of Mosaic persuasion'.[37] This type of nationalism was based on voluntary consent rather than on blood or lineage, and on the belief in the possibility of integrating diverse peoples into a single nation. Whereas for nearly six centuries the singular path to integration as an Ottoman had been conversion to Islam, this new ideology was based on loyalty alone.

Equality meant that apostasy could no longer be punished. From the beginning, Muslims had been prohibited from converting to Christianity or Judaism, but the inverse was encouraged and facilitated through various Ottoman institutions such as the Collection, which had recruited hundreds of thousands of Christian boys for the administration and military, and the harem, which had brought tens of thousands of female slaves to the home of the royal family to serve as concubines or become wives. The last official beheading of an apostate—an Armenian shoemaker named Avakim who had converted to Islam and become Mehmed before reverting to Christianity—however, occurred in Istanbul in 1843. That he was executed wearing European dress was seen as especially provocative by foreign statesmen and journalists.[38] Under intense pressure from the British and French, Abdülmecid I promised foreign diplomats the following year that apostasy would no longer be punishable by a death sentence in the empire.

Because the issue was so sensitive for the dynasty and administration, provincial authorities were secretly informed of the sultan's wish, and they committed to not making the decision public and not trying offenders in local courts, but sending them instead to Istanbul.

The apostasy law was not abolished; the sultan had promised only to hinder future executions. With this arrangement, the sultan was able to gain credence in the rest of Europe and in Ottoman reformist circles but still not lose Islamic legitimacy in the eyes of the Muslim majority. But debates over the sentence illustrate how the Ottoman regime found itself floundering among competing demands. For the first time, conversion of Ottoman subjects had become an international issue. The dynasty found itself caught between foreign powers, Muslim public opinion, and its commitment to granting equal rights to Ottoman Christians and Jews. As part of the eastern question, foreign powers took upon themselves the role of protectors of Ottoman Christians. Beginning with the Treaty of Küçük Kaynarca in 1774, Russia had claimed to be the protector of Greeks and Armenians. The British declared themselves protectors of the Protestants, a group recognised in the Ottoman Empire only in 1847, and of Jews. The Ottoman regime feared internal disorder and external intervention. Contested conversions of obscure subjects brought it both. The French and German consuls in Salonica were lynched by a mob because they were blamed for the apostasy of a Christian Bulgarian girl who had converted to Islam.[39] The Ottoman government feared Muslims converting to a minority religion. That Catholic and Protestant missionaries from Europe and North America were now permitted to offer education in the empire and convert Ottoman subjects to Christianity only increased their anxiety.

The decree of 1839 was promulgated as the Ottomans faced a rising tide of nationalism that had begun to break the bonds between the sultan and millions of his subjects and had caused the loss of much precious territory in Southeastern Europe and the Middle East. But the decree did not succeed in its aims. The reforms only exacerbated the various nationalist movements and did not increase Ottoman patriotism. Less than two decades later, a new decree was promulgated. The Imperial Reform Edict of 18 February 1856 came at the end of the Crimean War.

THE CRIMEAN WAR AND THE GRANTING OF EQUALITY TO ALL OTTOMAN SUBJECTS

The Crimean War (1853–1856) was fought by the Ottomans, Britain, and France against Russia. It was another manifestation of the eastern question, as the war was sparked by Russia demanding to serve as protector of the millions of Orthodox Christians in the Ottoman Empire, as well as disputes between Russia and France over the control of the Church of the Nativity in Bethlehem and the Church of the Holy Sepulchre in Jerusalem, built on the spot where Christians believe Jesus was crucified. The first modern war, a dress rehearsal for the methods of destruction of the First World War, the Crimean War included new weapons and tactics—accurate, long-range rifles, steamships and armoured ships, sea mines, and trench warfare—the mass killing of soldiers and attendant civilian casualties, the application of new technologies—battlefield communication by telegraph and transporting of troops and heavy guns by rail—and reporting from the field by journalists accompanied by photographers. Telegraphs and steamships allowed news to travel faster. Extensive media coverage by the new war correspondents led to a high level of public interest. Public opinion influenced military decisions. In response to the catastrophic proportion of casualties caused by disease, the war launched modern military medicine as seen in the reforms of the Russians, who were the first to use anaesthesia in battlefield surgery and a system of triage to sort the wounded.[40]

The conflict began in autumn 1853 with a Russian invasion in Southeastern Europe. Eighty thousand troops crossed the Prut river into Moldova and Wallachia (Romania), hoping, unsuccessfully, to provoke a Christian uprising against Ottoman rule.[41] Pursuing an ongoing war in the region, the Ottomans attacked Russian forces in the Caucasus region of Georgia in coordination with the guerrillas of their local ally, Sheikh Shamil.[42] Russia destroyed the Ottoman fleet based at Sinope on the southern coast of the Black Sea and bombed the Muslim neighbourhoods of the town as well.[43] At the end of 1853, the British and French agreed to launch a large naval expedition to the Black Sea to defend the Ottoman Empire, push the Russian navy back to the Crimean Peninsula, and decrease Russia's power in Europe.[44] War was declared in spring 1854. That summer, British, Ottoman, and French troops—including many Algerians—pushed the Russian army north out of Bulgaria and back across the Danube into Wallachia. But the allied troops suffered tremendously from cholera in their camps in the port of Varna, and the soldiers threatened to mutiny. Nevertheless, the allies decided not to end the war—despite having already met the goal of expelling Russia troops from Southeastern Europe—but to expand it by sending their armies from Varna across the Black Sea to the Crimea.

Beginning in September, the allies besieged Sevastopol, located on the southwest corner of the peninsula, the base of the Russian Black Sea fleet. Over the course of nearly a year, millions of deafening bombs exploded along a hundred kilometres of trenches and over 125,000 Russians died defending the town.[45] Surveying piles of thousands of dead and wounded laying everywhere after one battle, a British war correspondent recorded the industrial carnage: 'Some had their heads taken off at the neck, as if with an axe; others their legs gone from the hips; others their arms, and others again who were hit in the chest or stomach, were literally as smashed as if they had been crushed in a machine'.[46] As at Varna, many more were felled by cholera.

Over the course of the Crimean War, as many as three-quarters of a million combatants were killed or died of disease.

Four hundred and fifty thousand of these were Russian.[47] The Russian defenders fell so fast and thick in the final battle for Sevastopol that the advancing French troops used the dead and wounded in a ghastly way as human sandbags.[48] The French lost one hundred thousand soldiers and the British gave up twenty thousand dead. The Ottomans lost 120,000 soldiers.[49] The Ottoman soldiers were beaten by their British allies, who treated them as little more than beasts of burden or slaves and used them mainly to dig trenches or haul loads. Many Ottoman soldiers died from malnutrition because they were not given enough to eat.[50] The Crimea was the place where, in the words of Russian writer Leo Tolstoy, one of the last defenders to leave Sevastopol, 'you will see war not as a beautiful, orderly, and gleaming formation, with music and beaten drums, streaming banners and generals on prancing horses, but war in its authentic expression—as blood, suffering and death'.[51] The war left Russia aching to take revenge on the Ottoman Empire.

Just prior to the war, Tsar Nicholas I (reigned 1825–1855)— who, like Catherine II, aimed to destroy the Ottoman Empire and replace it with a Christian kingdom united with Russia, with the Hagia Sophia again the centre of the Orthodox Church—had referred for the first time to the Ottoman Empire as 'the sick man of Europe'. He believed in its imminent collapse and had planned for its partition.[52] But the war ended instead with the Russian Black Sea fleet and its bases destroyed, Russia losing its protectorate over Moldova and Wallachia and having to withdraw from the eastern Anatolian town of Kars, which was seized in 1855 despite the efforts of the British general who commanded Ottoman forces. Instead of breaking apart, the Ottoman Empire was recognised for the first time in the Treaty of Paris (signed 30 March 1856) as an equal member of the concert of European states, states with whom the Ottomans had actually been intimately engaged since the fourteenth century.

One of the key issues that the other European powers, especially Britain, pressed upon the Ottomans after the war was the need to guarantee the protection and rights of Christian subjects, which the Ottomans saw as a pretext for foreign intervention in their internal affairs. The Russian tsar also demanded security for Christians in the Ottoman Empire, yet when he later regained the Crimea he expelled hundreds of thousands of Muslim Tatars—who relocated to the Ottoman Empire—and settled formerly Ottoman Christians, especially Greeks and Bulgarians, in their place.[53] He also drove hundreds of thousands of Muslims from the northern Caucasus, forcing them to seek refuge in the Ottoman Empire. It was in this context that, even before the delegates met in Paris for the peace conference, the most significant outcome of the war from the point of view of Ottoman subjects emerged.

The 1856 edict—issued by Abdülmecid I one week prior to the beginning of the peace talks—made that which had been implied by his 1839 decree explicit: complete religious freedom, no forced conversion, and genuine equality. The decree relinquished, at least in theory, the predominant role of Muslims. Not all the Muslim ruling elites were happy about this. According to intellectual and government minister Ahmed Cevdet Pasha, 'Many Muslims began to grumble: "Today we lost our sacred national rights which our ancestors gained with their blood. The Muslim community used to be the ruling community, but it has been deprived of this sacred right. This is a day of tears and mourning"' for Muslims.[54] As an expression of such sentiment, already in 1859 there was a coup attempt in Istanbul by a group of officers and Nakşibendi Sufis, but it was quickly suppressed.

The government declaration of religious freedom caused a convert alert.[55] Beginning at the end of the 1850s, tens of thousands of people the empire had considered Muslims because their ancestors had converted to Islam centuries before revealed themselves as Christians instead, protégés of Austria, Britain, France, Greece, or Russia.[56] The Kromlides Greek-speaking Muslims in the Pontus area of the eastern Black Sea, the Stavriotes in central Anatolia, and the Hemşinli Armenian-speaking Muslims along

Eighteenth-century depiction of the *valide sultan* (mother of the sultan) being offered a cup of coffee by her attendants in the palace
Credit: 'Dans le sérail', *Costumes turcs de la cour et de la ville de Constantinople*, pl. 4, Dessins exécutés par un artiste turc, 1720. BnF, département des Estampes et de la Photographie, OD-6-4 © Bibliothèque nationale de France

Portrait of Hürrem Sultan
Credit: Workshop of Titian, Italian, c. 1488–1576 *Portrait of a Woman*, ca. 1515–1520. Oil on canvas, 39 3/16 x 30 1/2 inches, SN58. Bequest of John Ringling, 1936, Collection of The John and Mable Ringling Museum of Art, the State Art Museum of Florida

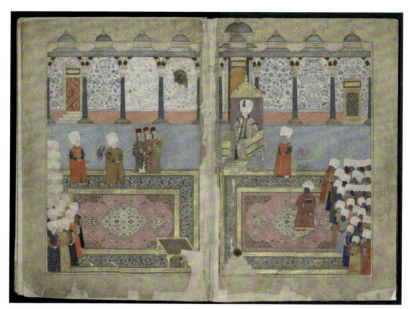

Osman II with the European eunuchs
of the Third Court and the African
eunuchs of the harem (1620)
Credit: Medhî, *Şâh-nâme*, an Ottoman
Turkish translation of the Persian epic,
Uppsala University Library, Sweden, Ms.
O Cels. 1, fols. 1b–2a, public domain

Miniature depicting male dancer
and musicians performing for
the sultan and public at princely
circumcision festival (1582–1583)
Credit: Lokman, *Surnâme-i Hümâyun*,
Topkapı Palace Museum, Istanbul,
Ms. Hazine 1344/Bridgeman Images

A women's party
Credit: Miniature from *Memorie Turchesche*, Cicogna Codex 1971, watercolour from the seventeenth-century Venetian school, Museo Correr, Venice, Italy/Bridgeman Images

Equestrian portrait of Osman II (1618), the first Ottoman sultan to be deposed and murdered
Credit: Topkapı Palace Museum, Istanbul, Ms. Hazine 2169, fol. 13a/Bridgeman Images

Painting of the arrival of the relief forces at Kahlenberg hill at the siege of Vienna (1683)

Mehmed IV as child sultan

Performers, including boys, dancing on tightrope and on a boat perform for Ahmed III at a nautical festival

Credit: Vehbi, *Surnâme* (1720) Topkapı Palace Museum, Istanbul, Ms. 3593/Bridgeman Images

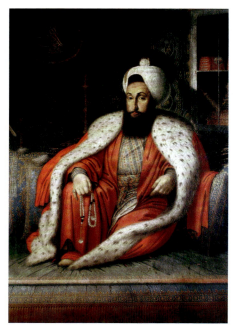

Portrait of Selim III

Credit: Constantin Kapıdağı, 'Sultan Selim III in Audience' (1803), Topkapı Palace Museum, Istanbul/ Bridegman Images

Portrait of Mahmud II
Credit: Topkapı Palace Museum, Istanbul/ Bridgeman Images

Allied sovereigns and commanders of the Crimean War including Queen Victoria and Abdülmecid I
Credit: George Baxter, colour lithograph/ Bridgeman Images

Portrait of a young Abdülhamid II
Credit: George Grantham Bain Collection/Library of Congress, Prints and Photographs Division, Washington, DC, Digital File Number: cph 3b24436/ Bridgeman Images

1908 postcard declaring 'Long live freedom, equality, brotherhood, and justice' in Armenian, Greek, Ottoman Turkish, French, and Judeo-Spanish
Credit: Isa Akbaş collection, in Edhem Eldem, *Pride and Privilege: A History of Ottoman Orders, Medals and Decorations* (Istanbul: Ottoman Bank and Archive Research Center, 2004), 369

Mehmed Talat Pasha (1915)
Credit: General Photographic Agency/Hulton Archive/ Getty Images, #52782735/Bridgeman Images

Starving Armenian orphans
Credit: Bridgeman Images

Mustafa Kemal Atatürk
Credit: Bridgeman Images

The last sultan Mehmed VI arrives in
Malta on a British warship, 9 December 1922
Credit: CSU Archives/Everett Collection/
Bridgeman Images

the Black Sea coast all declared that since their ancestors had converted they had never been truly Muslim but had secretly adhered to their former faith. Conversion and apostasy became more a question of political authority than of religion or theology. Loyalty was tied to religion, which became nationalised.[57] If a Muslim converted to Christianity, the regime assumed that the apostate would be a fifth column supporting foreign powers. The empire assumed that only Muslims could be loyal to the state, despite its claims to embrace all of its subjects as equals.

At the same time as it feared losing its own Muslims to apostasy, the Ottoman Empire eagerly accepted other empires' apostates. Following the Europe-wide 1848 revolutions, thousands of useful refugees—several thousand soldiers along with the leading politicians and generals from revolutionary Hungary, Italy, and Poland—were welcomed in the empire. Choosing to ignore the Forty-Eighters ideology—constitutional government, parliamentary rule, and national liberation—the Ottomans focused on the exiles' leadership experience and military abilities. Their arrival strengthened the Ottomans at the expense of the Habsburg Empire and Russia, which demanded that the rebels and their leaders—including Lajos Kossuth, the leader of Hungary's parliament, who proclaimed Hungarian autonomy from the Habsburg Empire and then fought for its independence during the revolution—be handed back. But the Ottomans instead gave them asylum, and many of these men became Muslims.[58] Conversion exempted them from expulsion by making them Ottoman subjects. In this way, the empire continued its old politics of conversion, using Islam as a means of integrating men into the elite military and administration of the empire.

Whereas once the Ottomans raised boys into men, now the men were already fully formed and experienced military experts. Whereas apostasy was a way to abandon Ottomanness, conversion remained a path to becoming and being Ottoman, to the Ottoman Way. General Józef Bem, hero of the Polish uprising against

Russia in 1830 and commander of Hungarian forces in Transylvania in 1848, died as a circumcised Ottoman Muslim named Murad Pasha, killed fighting the Druze in Lebanon in 1850.[59] The commander in chief of Ottoman forces during the Crimean War was a converted Croatian Serb and Orthodox Christian who received a military education in Austria, Ömer Lutfi Pasha.[60] Many Polish and Hungarian Forty-Eighters served in the defence of Kars in 1855.

Waiting for help to arrive from abroad would not be enough. During this period, the Ottomans established secular schools to train their own governing elite in the new sciences of war and administration. Most significant was the Galatasaray Imperial High School, built in 1868 on the grounds of a former palace for training Collection child recruits. Its imposing, gilded gates are the main feature of Galatasaray Square in Istanbul today. Galatasaray's main language of instruction was French. Despite regime apprehensions about the loyalty of its Christian subjects, the school aimed to educate members of all religions as civil servants. Unlike the Collection recruits of the past, these young men did not have to convert to Islam, be circumcised, and learn the Islamic languages of Arabic, Persian, and Turkish. They obtained high positions in many ministries, including the Foreign Ministry. Yet this centripetal effort faced off against a centrifugal one. The protégés, Ottoman subjects under the legal protection of foreign powers, exercised privileged commercial relations with their European sponsors, leading to the emergence of a wealthy and highly visible Christian and Jewish bourgeoisie in the empire. This group established its own schools and clubs and developed increasing nationalist sentiment—sentiment that, as seen in the Serbian and Greek cases, could lead to autonomy or independence. Within the empire, among Armenians and Greeks, the decrees of 1839 and 1856 led to the increased power of lay authorities at the expense of the religious leaders, the patriarchs. Ottoman Christians established their own lay assemblies and drafted their own constitutions for communal rule. Perhaps to hinder movements for autonomy and independence, an Ottoman citizenship law was issued by the sultan in 1869 that decoupled religion from citizenship.[61] It declared, 'All subjects of the empire are called Ottoman'. No longer would a convert to Islam automatically become an Ottoman subject. Islam was no longer a path to integration.

THE ROLE OF WOMEN IN SOCIETY

Beginning with the reform era, the issues of the veil, polygamy, arranged marriages, women's visibility in public, and their participation in social life were hotly contested.[62]

A lively public sphere in print emerged in nineteenth-century Istanbul and other cities of the empire. In their periodicals and books, leading Ottoman Muslim intellectuals grappled with the question of how much to adopt from Western Europe. Some believed the entirety of 'Western civilisation', including its morality and such features as romantic love, were universal values that had to be accepted in their entirety. For others, only the material innovations—new technologies, ways of administration and government, communications, and new forms of transportation such as the railway—needed to be utilised in order to become modern.

One of the main points of contention centred on women in the public sphere. Those who believed Western values were universal advocated an end to polygamy and promoted women's education. They claimed that society as a whole could not be modern until women were liberated. Those who rejected the nonmaterial aspects of Western society defended women staying within the private sphere of the home.[63] But all these writers accepted Islam as the dominant culture. They differed only in the extent to which they advanced what they considered a civilising project. The most radical aspect of civilising the empire was making all subjects, but not women, equal. On that they agreed. Where they disagreed was on the question of devlet, of governance.

THE FIRST OTTOMAN CONSTITUTION

The first constitution in the Ottoman Empire was granted to the Armenian community in the early 1860s. In 1860, the Armenian-language draft document of the new form of communal governance was entitled the 'Armenian National Constitution'. The 1863 official Ottoman Turkish text ratified by the government labelled it instead 'Regulations of the Armenian Patriarchate'.[64] The Ottoman Turkish name was logical, as the constitution privileged the centrality of the church and the Armenian patriarch as the head of the assembly and all the committees established by the constitution. The aim was to modernise the institution of the patriarchate.[65]

While the Armenian-language version of the constitution established a 'National General Assembly', the Ottoman Turkish version referred to a 'General Assembly'.[66] The final version also insisted that the phrase 'loyalty to the administration and dynasty' be added to the patriarch's oath of office. Befitting its name, the Armenian constitution established a representative administration, consisting of an elected general assembly of 140 men. With only twenty clergy members from Istanbul, the rest were lay members. Eighty seats were reserved for Istanbul Armenians.[67] The men elected to these posts were bureaucrats in the Ottoman government, merchants, and progressive intellectuals educated outside the empire. Despite its conservative nature—reserving a central place for the patriarch and the privilege of the Istanbul elite, who held almost three-quarters of the seats—it was a step towards a more secular, democratic form of governance over the Armenian ethno-religious community and its functionaries, churches, schools, monasteries, law courts, hospitals, wealth, and properties. The Armenian constitution had an indirect influence on the future empire-wide Ottoman constitution. Muslim intellectuals perceived Christian assemblies as a model for an Ottoman parliament.

THE YOUNG OTTOMANS:
ISLAMIST CONSTITUTIONALISTS

The Young Ottoman movement emerged in the 1860s among bureaucrats who had served in the imperial translation bureau and were well versed in the latest Western European, especially French, ideas, including nationalism. They burst into public consciousness with the first independent newspaper, *Tasvir-i efkâr* (Illustration of Opinion), edited by Ibrahim Şinasi, who fled to Paris in 1865 in the face of new censorship laws intended to silence his critical journal.[68] He left the newspaper in the hands of the articulate Namık Kemal. That same year, six men (including Kemal) founded a secret society, the Patriotic Alliance, modelled along the lines of the Carbonari in Italy.[69] In their private meetings with other disgruntled bureaucrats and members of the dynasty—including the crown prince, Murad—in their newspaper columns and pamphlets, and in their clandestine speeches in mosques, Islamic colleges, and coffeehouses, these and other intellectuals discussed how they could adopt American and French Revolutionary political concepts and forms of government while keeping true to the empire's Islamic values. They criticised the regime, especially the new bureaucratic elite and statesmen who had risen thanks to the reforms of Selim III and Mahmud II from the turn of the nineteenth century to midcentury, and who overshadowed Sultan Abdülaziz I (reigned 1861–1876), Abdülmecid I's successor.

The Young Ottomans accused these bureaucrats of concentrating power in their own hands, of being little more than a handful of self-appointed individuals administering the empire unchecked by the sultan, the military, or the jurists. They were concerned about the new bureaucratic elite being the first Ottomans to join foreign Masonic lodges. They criticised the secularisation of law and education in the empire. Worst of all, the Young Ottomans accused these new government ministers of being superficially Europeanised and of caring most about opening theatres, attending balls, looking the other way as their wives cheated on them, using European toilets, and allowing women to appear in public in low-necked tops.[70]

The Young Ottomans were supported by lower-level bureaucrats facing shrinking opportunities to rise in government, by jurists who had lost status in the face of the secularisation of administration and law, and by the military, which had lost power to the new bureaucracy and was now made up of lower-class recruits. Their efforts were funded by the disgruntled, extremely wealthy grandson of Mehmed Ali—the early nineteenth-century semi-independent ruler of Ottoman Egypt—Prince Mustafa Fazıl Pasha. Mustafa Fazıl Pasha had been passed over as hereditary governor of Egypt, despite it being his right, and sought revenge on the Ottomans from exile in France.[71]

The leading Young Ottoman ideologue was Namık Kemal, who came from a Bektaşi Sufi family, was son of the sultan's astrologer, and had travelled throughout Europe, residing for a time in England.[72] Working in the imperial translation bureau, Kemal was stimulated by the ideas of Jean-Jacques Rousseau, Montesquieu, Giuseppe Garibaldi, and Voltaire. Convinced by American and French revolutionary and Enlightenment writings on the necessity of a constitution, the separation of powers, checks on the executive branch, popular sovereignty, and representative government, Kemal was nevertheless keen to assert the supremacy of Islam. He favoured a government based on religious law and a constitution rooted in Islam but modelled on the French version—a parliamentary form of representative government with the sultan caliph, the leader of all Sunni Muslims, at its head. He believed both that the sultan's authority came from God and that it was the result of a contract between him and the people. It was a vision of government *for* the people, not government by the people, as in the United States and Western Europe.[73] The sultan, who would also be limited by the laws, would oversee a government where a council of state nominated by the sultan would prepare laws, an elected senate would approve or reject the laws, and an elected lower chamber would control the budget.[74]

As important, Kemal popularised the terms *hürriyet* (liberty) and *vatan* (fatherland) and gave them an emotional and religious intensity. In his words, 'One should love one's fatherland because the most precious gift God has bestowed on us, life, began with the breathing of the air of the fatherland'.[75] He promoted Ottomanism, a vision of the union of the constituent peoples of the empire in devotion to the fatherland and empire, no matter their ethnic or religious background. Yet at the same time he glorified Ottoman Muslims and the spirit of holy war, or gaza. He was a patriot who aimed to preserve the empire. He believed that equal political rights and representative government were the paths to that more perfect union of imperial citizens, but he still promoted a leading role for Muslims and Islam.

The regime was stung by the criticism of these civil servants and exiled them within the empire. They regrouped in Paris in 1867, where they began to call themselves the Young Ottoman Society.[76] Bankrolled by Mustafa Fazıl Pasha, they published journals in Paris, Geneva, and London, including Namık Kemal's *Hürriyet* (Liberty) after 1868, and were able to circulate them within the Ottoman Empire via Western European post offices.[77] When by 1871 their main targets of criticism, Fuat Pasha and Ali Pasha—who had for two decades held the offices of foreign minister and grand vizier interchangeably and were disciples of the author of the reform edict of 1839, Mustafa Reşid Pasha—had passed away, the Young Ottomans returned to advocate change within the empire. Along with writing for the pro–Young Ottoman newspaper *İbret* (Warning), Kemal in 1873 staged and published his popular, patriotic play, *Vatan yahut Silistre* (Fatherland, or Silistre—referring to a town on the bank of the Danube river on the Bulgaria-Romania frontier). The piece advocated self-sacrifice by both men and women on the battlefield to save the Ottoman Muslim homeland in Southeastern Europe from Russian attack. Its characters sing,

> *Wounds are medals on the brave's body.*
> *Martyrdom is the soldier's highest rank.*
> *The earth is the same, above and underneath.*
> *March, you brave ones, to defend the fatherland.*[78]

The patriotic sentiment of this play, along with the outspoken criticism of the regime by the Young Ottomans, increased the government's fear of a coup. It closed the Young Ottoman newspaper *İbret* and again exiled these ideologues and put them under house arrest that same year.[79]

Inspired by ideals of fatherland and liberty, and facing uprisings in Bosnia and Herzegovina and Bulgaria—where nationalism was stimulated by the Ottoman establishment in 1870 of a Bulgarian Orthodox church, the exarchate, separate from the Greek Orthodox patriarchate—and the threat of war with Russia, leading statesmen decided to act.[80] Midhat Pasha, a constitutionalist who had long been praised by the Young Ottomans as an ideal statesman, Minister of War Hüseyin Avni Pasha, and Sheikhulislam Hayrullah Efendi launched a coup and deposed Sultan Abdülaziz I on 30 May 1876.[81] They replaced him with his nephew Murad, a longtime supporter of the Young Ottomans and advocate of a constitution and parliament, who became Murad V. His first private secretary was one of the leading Young Ottomans, Ziya Pasha. Within two weeks of his accession, the former sultan Abdülaziz I committed suicide and an army captain killed Hüseyin Avni Pasha and other ministers at a cabinet meeting. The ministers decided to act quickly and have the sultan declare a constitution, but physicians determined that Murad V, suffering from alcoholism and a nervous breakdown, was unfit to rule. His response to suddenly being enthroned was like that of many princes since the seventeenth century: taken from the harem to be made sultan at a mature age, they believed they were being led to their execution. His younger brother Hamid refused to be appointed regent. He demanded to be sultan. He received the oath of allegiance as Abdülhamid II on 1 September 1876.[82]

A committee to draft a constitution began to meet in October 1876. Headed by the reformer and vizier Midhat Pasha, among its members were several Young Ottomans including Namık Kemal and Ziya Pasha.[83] Another member was Krikor Odyan, one of the architects of the 1860 Armenian constitution and close friend and advisor of Midhat Pasha.[84]

Within three months, the Ottomans promulgated their first constitution for all subjects of the empire. The Ottoman government system put forth in 1876 was based on the Belgian constitution of 1831 and the Prussian constitution of 1850. Belgium was established as a parliamentary monarchy with a separation between the legislative (a parliament made up of a house of representatives and senate), judicial (the courts), and executive powers (the king and his ministers). Prussia also established a bicameral legislature in 1850 along with a government based on separation of powers. However, the kaiser retained more power than the king in Belgium. In Prussia, the king granted some of his subjects the right to a share in governance yet retained full authority. The Ottoman constitutional system more resembled that of Prussia than of Belgium. One could also add a local source of inspiration: the constitution granted to the Armenians a little more than a dozen years earlier. Elections were held for parliamentary representatives in December and January 1877. The Ottoman parliament first met in Istanbul in March 1877.

The Young Ottomans were successful. Thanks in part to the spread of their modern ideas, by 1877 the Ottomans boasted their own parliament and constitution and had enshrined the principles of equality and universal subjecthood. The constitution declared that while Islam was the religion of the Ottoman Empire, 'the practice of all recognised religions in Ottoman dominions is free on the condition that they do not disturb public order and general propriety. The rights granted to various creeds are all under the guarantee of the state'.[85] The question was how long those newfound rights would be maintained.

18

REPRESSION
A Modern Caliph, Abdülhamid II

C HEERED ON BY the West, Abülhamid II (reigned 1876–1909) started out as a liberal reformer. In 1876, at the beginning of his reign, he promulgated a constitution, and in 1877 he opened parliament, carrying out the reforms the Young Ottomans had demanded. But in the wake of the most devastating war with Russia yet, he turned into a dictator one year later, suspending the constitution, murdering its author, dissolving parliament, arresting the opposition including members of parliament, jailing journalists, and exercising personal control over the empire. Faced with intense foreign pressure, debilitating power struggles among the elite, and an inability to obtain the financial resources to meet his goals, the sultan sought a way to strengthen and save the empire. He chose to do so through modern strategies infused with religious meaning, promoting himself as caliph in charge of a modernised Islam and an Islamised empire, and converting sectarian groups. He became a ruler who was as much a modernist who opposed the West as an Islamist who emphasised secular technical education.[1] A champagne-tippling French speaker who played piano and loved Western classical music and comic opera—and built a theatre in his palace where they could be performed—Abdülhamid II was a sincere Muslim who sought to save the empire in his own modern, Islamist way.[2] Chasing the opposition from the empire, he unwittingly sparked the formation of a group of revolutionaries called the Young Turks who would be the undoing of the empire.

THE WAR OF 1877–1878

After announcing the constitution and ushering in the first elected parliament in 1877, the empire suffered from the cataclysmic war of 1877–1878 with archenemy Russia. To understand the context and importance of this war, we need to bear in mind that the Ottomans and an ever-expanding Russian Empire had already fought seven wars since the eighteenth century. The most recent was the Crimean War of 1853–1856, which saved the territory of the empire but compelled the Ottoman regime to take out large loans from British and French banks, to which it became financially subservient. Along with interest on the loans, the Ottoman treasury had to pay back twice the amount borrowed.[3] More important, the Crimean War ended with Russia humiliated and seeking revenge. Russia aimed to seize the Bosporus straits and liberate Orthodox-Christian-majority regions of Southeastern Europe from Ottoman rule.

It was the last Russo-Ottoman war, which took place from 1877 to 1878, that was the most consequential. It nearly ended the centuries-old Ottoman presence in Southeastern Europe. It caused a mass exodus of Muslims, traumatised by war, from the region into the remaining territories of the Ottoman Empire. Most important, it induced a psychological shift among Ottoman elites, opening their eyes to the reality that the empire was vulnerable to foreign occupation of its core Roman provinces, which could lead to the downfall of the dynasty.

The war of 1877–1878 occurred amid rebellion and political uncertainty in the Ottoman Empire. Nationalist uprisings broke out in Bosnia, Herzegovina, Montenegro, and Bulgaria in 1875. These were accompanied by the massacres of many Muslims, including new immigrant populations of Crimean Tatars and Circassians displaced by the Crimean War. In reprisal, Ottoman Circassian irregulars slaughtered tens of thousands of Bulgarians in April 1876. The massacres contributed to the loss of the Ottomans' British ally. Reflecting Renaissance humanists' depictions of the 'barbarian Turks', Britain's Liberal prime minister William Gladstone published a best-selling pamphlet that year entitled *Bulgarian Horrors*. In it he argued that the Turks were 'from the black day when they first entered Europe, the one great anti-human specimen of humanity. Wherever they went, a broad line of blood marked the trail behind them; and as far as their dominion reached, civilisation disappeared from view'.[4] His political opponent, the pro-Ottoman Sephardic Jewish–born Conservative leader Benjamin Disraeli, who was also disparaged in the pamphlet, argued against such sentiment to little avail.

As already related, a coup deposed Sultan Abdülaziz I in May 1876. Humiliated, he committed suicide and was replaced by his alcoholic nephew Murad V, who had close relations with the Young Ottomans but who had a nervous breakdown and was declared mentally unfit and replaced by his brother Abdülhamid II in September. Abdülhamid II promulgated a new constitution in December, aimed in part at dampening demands for independence or autonomy and foreign oversight of Southeastern European Ottoman territories.

In April 1877, Russia declared war after the Ottomans refused their demands for Bulgarian autonomy. The Ottomans remembered it as the War of '93, as it was the year 1293 in the Muslim calendar. As with previous Russo-Ottoman wars, this conflict was fought on two fronts, at either end of the Black Sea in eastern Anatolia and in Southeastern Europe. On the eastern front, 55,000 Ottoman soldiers faced a Russian force twice that size, while on the western front the Ottomans outnumbered their opponents 180,000 to 160,000.[5] No matter the number of forces at their disposal, the Ottomans faced defeat on both fronts. Their forces

were spread across a wide theatre, there was a lack of communication between military commanders, the battles were directed
from Istanbul rather than the fronts, soldiers lacked provisions
and munitions, and the Ottoman Black Sea fleet was nowhere to
be found.[6]

On the western front, the Russians crossed the Danube into
Romania and with their Bulgarian allies chalked up many victo-
ries, committing atrocities against Muslim villagers and towns-
people and forcing a mass exodus of hundreds of thousands of
Muslims from Southeastern Europe who were then resettled in
Anatolia. After a seven-month siege, the Russians finally took
Plevna in Bulgaria in December. Thereafter the Russians marched
unhindered through Thrace, taking Edirne in January 1878. By
March Russian troops had reached San Stefano, twelve kilometres
from Istanbul (today's Yeşilköy, the location of Atatürk Airport).
The Ottomans had to agree to an armistice to stop the Russians
from marching on Istanbul, destroying the dynasty, and reestab-
lishing an Orthodox empire in its place.

The Treaty of San Stefano, signed on 3 March 1878, gave Serbia,
Romania, and Montenegro independence, provided autonomy
to Bosnia and Herzegovina, which were occupied by Austria-
Hungary (which the Habsburg Empire was renamed in 1867),
and created a large, Russian-occupied Bulgaria stretching from
the Black Sea to the Aegean and including Macedonia and Salonica. Hundreds of thousands of Muslims were expelled from
Bulgaria. In the wake of the war and over the course of the next
three decades nearly one million Muslim migrants fled the Balkans for the Ottoman Empire.[7] The Russians had recouped their
losses from the Crimean War. The fate of the Ottoman Empire,
the eastern question, was the common concern of all European
states, especially those opposed to Russian expansion. Alarmed
by the Russian gains contained in the treaty, Britain and Austria-
Hungary compelled Russia to accept in July 1878 the Treaty of

Berlin instead, whereby Russia's military-political gains from the war were restricted. As a price for its diplomatic intervention, Britain demanded Cyprus from the Ottomans. Russia remained in control of much of northeastern Anatolia, where Sultan Abdülhamid II agreed to undertake reforms ameliorating the condition of Armenians. Half of Bulgaria, including Macedonia, was returned to the Ottomans. But the Ottomans had lost one-third of their territory.

The outcome of the war was especially detrimental to the Ottoman claim over Southeastern Europe. As the Southeastern European provinces gained autonomy or independence and half a million Muslim refugees immediately resettled in the remaining Ottoman domains, the empire's territory became less European and less Christian. The refugees' new ruler would promote their bond to him as Muslim leader.

ABDÜLHAMID II: REINVIGORATING THE CALIPHATE, MODERNISING ISLAM, ISLAMISING THE EMPIRE

In the aftermath of the war with Russia, Abdülhamid II suspended the constitution and parliament. This action was met with two armed coup attempts—one fomented by Young Ottomans, the other by Freemasons—attempting to replace the sultan with his now sober, calm predecessor, Murad V. Both failed. In 1881 Abdülhamid II arrested leading reformers, including the author of the constitution, Midhat Pasha, and sentenced them to death for the murder of Sultan Abdülaziz I, who had committed suicide. The sultan commuted their punishment to life imprisonment in the Hijaz, Arabia, but had them murdered soon after.[8]

Abdülhamid II then replaced liberal reforms with a completely new formula for saving the empire: proto-Muslim nationalism. The sultan sought to reinvigorate the institution of the caliphate and thereby unite all world Muslims under his authority. He emphasised his status as caliph rather than as mere sultan, something not seen since the sixteenth century, when Suleiman I was the first sultan to adopt the title.

Reflecting Islamic piety by forbidding the display of Abdülhamid II's likeness, his regime promoted Islamic symbols related to the sacredness of the sultan caliph in public spaces, especially by having the imperial monogram appear on public buildings across the empire.[9] This was part of a process to build loyal subjects through the proselytization of what it deemed the correct interpretation of Islam. Imperial Islamic generosity and greatness included guaranteeing the security of the pilgrimage to Mecca for all Muslims, assisted by the Ottoman Hijazi railway that ran from Damascus to Medina and the Hijazi fleet that protected the coast of western Arabia. The efforts were intended to demonstrate that Abdülhamid II was a pious sultan who was protector of pilgrims and custodian of the holy shrines.[10] He sent emissaries to distant Muslims in Africa and China. He made references to the first generations of Muslims, such as through the acquisition and display of holy relics and the calligraphic rendering of Muhammad's and the first caliphs' names in the ancient Hagia Sophia, once the greatest church in Christendom and now the largest Friday mosque in Istanbul.[11]

Abdülhamid II sought to modernise Islam. The Hanafi school of Sunni Islamic law, one of four main interpretations of Sunni law that had exclusive doctrines and practices, was emphasised as the 'official belief'. This was no coincidence, for Hanafism recognised the legitimacy of a strong and able ruler who protected Islam and upheld Islamic law, as Abdülhamid II styled himself, rather than believing that legitimacy was via descent from Muhammad's Quraysh tribe.[12] Ottoman sultans' only claim to legitimacy was by might and rendering justice, not through genealogy. The empire standardised and regularised Islamic legal rulings, publishing a codification and disseminating it across the empire.

The effort met with resistance in areas such as Iraq and Yemen, where scholars favoured other legal schools or had different local legal customs.[13] The regime also sought to monopolise and control sacred script, such as by distributing its own version of the Qur'an. It prevented the publication and importation of Qur'ans from Iran and Russia, whose Muslims were not seen as loyal to the Ottoman caliph.[14]

The regime engaged in what it considered a modernising and civilising mission against peripheral populations.[15] It aimed to settle, integrate, control, and make useful tribal groups while ensuring religious conformity, targeting rural Albanians, Kurds, and the Bedouin, the nomads of the desert. The sultan wished to enlighten by converting to his understanding of Sunni Islam religious groups deemed heretical, such as Yazidis, Shi'is, and Alevis—the descendants of the Red Heads and the supporters of the Safavids in the sixteenth century. The Alevis did not strictly adhere to Islamic law, did not place primary emphasis on the Qur'an, and did not fast during Ramadan but during the Shi'i holy month of Muharram. They did not take the pilgrimage to Mecca but to their own saint shrines in Anatolia and Iraq.[16] The effort to convert people—who believed in a saintly, divine Ali and the revolutionary ideas of Ibn Arabi and Sheikh Bedreddin—to a different version of Islam was often accompanied by violence, including massacres.[17] The regime's actions were similar to the Americanisation of Native Americans and their settlement and conversion in the American West in the same era. There was also an increase in the conversion of Ottoman Christians to Islam.[18]

The sultan sent out preachers who acted as missionaries and built schools and mosques in Albania, Anatolia, Iraq, Syria, and Yemen where tribal Albanians, Arabs, Bedouin, or Kurds, and Alevis, Yazidis, or Shi'is predominated. Alongside modern sciences, the new Hamidian schools emphasised religious curricula focused on Hanafi Sunnism. The regime educated the sons of leading families in new schools in Istanbul, such as the Imperial

School for Tribes, and sent them back to their home regions, hoping they would compel their compatriots to be civilised, loyal Ottomans and Hanafi Sunnis, as they themselves had become.[19] But these policies targeting socially or religiously marginal groups were largely unsuccessful.[20]

Women's public role remained at the centre of debates about modernisation. The Hamidian regime was conservative and modern. The late nineteenth century witnessed calls from men and women to improve women's status in society, especially in education and employment rights. The way was led by men such as Namık Kemal and Şemseddin Sami, author of *Women* (1882). Sami envisioned societal progress as being dependent on the education and training of women.[21] Yet these writers advocated liberty only within the limits allowed by Islam. There may not yet have been any Ottoman suffragettes. But there were patriarchal feminists—including the Hamidian regime, which opened teachers' colleges for women and primary, secondary, and technical schools for girls. There were also women who advocated better education and more opportunities for themselves.

These Ottoman feminists' views were expressed in women's newspapers and magazines. The *Ladies' Own Gazette*, published between 1895 and 1909, boasted editors and writers who were almost all women. There was also a journal for adolescents, and a publishing house that produced monographs on gender issues.[22] The earliest writers were women of the Ottoman elite, mostly daughters of government officials educated at home or in the palace, such as the first Ottoman woman novelist, Fatma Aliye. Within a few years the writers included schoolteachers and businesswomen from the new women's fashion industry and recognised pedagogues such as Ayşe Sıdıka, author of *The Principles of Education* (1899). The sultan served as patron of the *Ladies' Own Gazette*, which promoted women's education in order to support the conservative aims of making women into better mothers, better wives, better Muslims, and loyal Ottoman subjects. The journal accordingly displayed anti-European and anti-Christian attitudes.

Not only did Ottoman Muslim women launch a women's movement, but so, too, did Kurdish and Armenian women.

MOBILISING THE KURDS

The Armenians who lived in the same eastern Anatolian region (called by Armenians western Armenia) as the Kurds (who called it northern Kurdistan) had the misfortune to demand autonomy with foreign oversight.[23] They complained of depredation, double taxation, land confiscations, and insecurity. When he signed the 1878 Treaty of Berlin, the sultan agreed to reforms to improve their condition. His aim was to solve the eastern question by avoiding a pretext for further foreign intervention. On the ground, Armenians continued to face violence from Kurds. The Kurds, because they stood at the frontier with the rival Safavid and then Qajar empire in neighbouring Iran, had for centuries been largely tolerated and given autonomy by the empire. Local chiefs and princes had been granted authority to rule so long as they recognised the sultan as sovereign and contributed their armed forces to his military campaigns. Left largely to their own devices, the Kurds were dominated by autonomous princes, ruling landlord families, their peasant clients (tribes or confederations), and religious leaders (Sufi sheikhs). Yet the Kurds were also subject to forced settlement, taxation, and oppression by the Ottomans. Proposed supervision of the Armenians by the British and the Russians during Abdülhamid II's reign, coupled with Armenian demands for autonomy, rankled the sensitivities of Ottoman statesmen and made them turn to the Kurds.

Abdülhamid II aimed to exercise better control over his empire. One area of especial concern was the eastern frontier with Russia. As a result of the war of 1877–1878, Russia occupied the former Ottoman provinces of Ardahan, Batum, Doğubayezid, and Kars.

Northeastern and southeastern Anatolia were sensitive regions for the imperial centre. In the mid-nineteenth century, the Ottomans had settled tribes and nomads and decreased the power of and then eliminated Kurdish chiefs and provincial notables on the frontier, such as in northern Iraq and near Diyar Bakir.

In the late nineteenth century, the Ottomans suppressed the established Kurdish ruling princes. This led to direct Ottoman rule in these areas for the first time but also to more upheaval in the countryside. The old established chiefs and princes had maintained law and order in their respective regions. Now there was a free-for-all, as other tribal groupings fought over control of villages, agricultural land, and pastures. This had major implications for the people of the region, including the Armenians and Assyrians, which in turn encouraged Russian, British, and later American intervention.

In the absence of the princes, sheikhs grew in political influence as mediators among Kurds. Many were affiliated with Sufi orders, whether Bektaşi or Nakşibendi. Especially during the reign of Abdülhamid II, the Ottomans viewed the Kurds as a force for suppressing Armenian nationalists. Armenians outside the empire founded nationalist organisations: the Social-Democratic Party of the Bell (Hnchakian, founded in Geneva, Switzerland, 1887) and the Armenian Revolutionary Federation (Dashnaktsutyun, founded in Tbilisi, Georgia, 1890), which agitated for autonomy or independence through their newspapers, education, and propaganda, and for armed struggle including assassinations, revolts, and terrorism.[24] The Ottomans supported the Nakşibendi sheikh Ubaydallah of Nihri (near Hakkari, in southeastern Anatolia) in his military campaigns in the east against the Russians, against Iran, and against local Christians in the 1870s and 1880s. Ubaydallah's declarations have caused scholars to label him the first Kurdish nationalist. He had told the British that 'the Kurdish nation . . . is a people apart' and the Kurds 'want our affairs to be in our own hands'.[25] Yet he also declared loyalty to the sultan, who supported him in attacking his enemies.

As part of this effort to improve control of the Ottoman east, in 1890 Abdülhamid II instituted the Hamidiye light cavalry regiments made up of Kurdish troops. Their mission was to suppress dissent, whether by Kurds or Armenian nationalists, in Kurdistan, the term the Ottomans used for the region of Anatolia, Syria, and Iraq where Kurdish people predominated. The establishment of the Hamidiye was also meant to boost Kurdish loyalty to the sultan, in part by increasing the religious ties between Turks and Kurds.[26] The sultan emphasised that they were Muslim brothers, despite their historic, linguistic, national, and social differences.

Modelled on the Cossacks of the Russian Empire, the Hamidiye officers were sent for training in St. Petersburg, which was remarkable, considering how Russia was their enemy. The aim was to transform the Kurds, a local power challenging imperial control, into an arm of royal authority. The effort was envisaged as a civilising project, a way to settle and command barbaric tribes that had only recently revolted against the empire. It was supposed to be an effective way to govern, tax, and conscript members of this parallel state in a region long autonomous from central control and then use them to manage the other dangers.

Crimes against property were part and parcel of ethnic cleansing. Pastoral Kurds were settled by authorising them to usurp the lands of Armenian farmers and villagers, often by force.[27] The process deprived Armenians of their means of subsistence, forcing them to migrate. Subject to expropriations, hundreds of thousands of Armenians fled the region for the cities of western Anatolia. In the context of Armenian revolts in southeastern Anatolia in Sasun (1894), Zeytun (1895–1896), and Van (1896), several hundred thousand other Armenians were massacred from 1894 to 1896 as a form of collective punishment by local Kurds, Hamidiye units, and regular Ottoman troops in the six eastern provinces of

Bitlis, Diyar Bakir, Erzurum, Mamüretülaziz, Sivas, and Van.[28] Forced migration and massacres in eastern Anatolia contributed to an Ottoman project of demographic engineering, replacing Christians with Muslims. Tens of thousands of Muslim Circassian refugees who had been expelled from their own homelands by Russia were settled in the region amid the remaining Armenians, further Islamising it.

These policies put material resources into the hands of Muslim refugees and the local Kurds, buying their loyalty. It was effective in stamping out Kurdish rebellion and in co-opting the local power-holding Kurdish nobles and sheikhs. But the creation of the regiments and the arming of Kurds dispossessed Armenians of their lands. It increased tensions between Kurds and other Muslims and between Kurds and Armenians and other local Christians such as the Assyrians, leading to tragic consequences then and in later decades.

During these massacres of Armenians, mass conversions took place. Both the massacre of Ottoman Christian subjects and their rapid mass conversion to Islam under such circumstances were unprecedented in Ottoman history. Thousands of Armenians converted to Islam to save their lives because they were afraid of the Kurds, especially the Hamidiye cavalry.[29] Government officials in the provinces blamed 'savage' Kurds for the violence that compelled the conversions. Most of these Armenians converted back to Christianity after the violence subsided in 1897. Apostasy was no longer a capital offence. Yet for the many abducted Armenian children and young girls who were raped and married off, there was no going back. They became part of the Kurdish population.

MANAGING THE DYNASTY'S BRAND

For the deaths of his Christian subjects and for his dictatorship, Abdülhamid II became a bogeyman in the rest of Europe and the empire. His paternalism and piety, however, compared to those of his Austro-Hungarian and Russian contemporaries, and the Ottoman Empire was not the only place experiencing unrest. Russia was also plagued by riots and pogroms against an ethno-religious minority, in this case Jews, in the same era.

When Abdülhamid II suspended the parliament in 1878, he chased the opposition from the empire. They coalesced in Paris as the Young Turks. Like the Carbonari in Italy, they were members of a secret society promoting revolution and constitutionalism. In 1884, the regime was responsible for the murder of the author of the constitution that the sultan had promulgated and then abolished, Midhat Pasha. News of such atrocities was amplified by the sultan's own exiled Ottoman critics in the major Western and Central European capitals.

Outrage in Europe also fed on the fact that Abdülhamid II proved a strong sultan, something not seen in centuries. He promoted an image of himself as a descendant of nomadic, warrior sultans. He emphasised the dynasty's Turco-Mongol and nomadic-warrior origins and promoted its alleged descent from the Oğuz tribe. He restored the tombs of the first two sultans, Osman and Orhan, in Bursa, and rebuilt the tomb of Osman's father, Ertuğrul, in Söğüt.[30] At an annual ceremony, Turks dressed like Turco-Mongol nomads rode into Söğüt, singing, 'We are soldiers of the Ertuğrul regiment', and then played Mongolian polo.

Facing sustained negative publicity, the Hamidian regime engaged in image management in Europe and North America.[31] The telegram, rail, and printing press, and the presence of so many foreigners in the empire—journalists, diplomats, businessmen, travellers, and missionaries—made events and developments well-known to the outside world, for good or bad. The image-obsessed Abdülhamid II was well aware of this fact and sought to change his image in world opinion. He did so by engaging in damage control and positive brand projection.

Ottoman embassies bribed the authors of newspaper articles, theatre plays, and operas to change how they wrote about the

Ottomans. They paid other authors to write positive accounts and ghostwrote fluff pieces.[32] They published a journal depicting the West as violent and degenerate, covering lynchings and poverty in the United States and Englishmen murdering their mistresses.[33] The sultan amassed a huge collection of news clippings, keeping an eye on everything written about him in the foreign press and seeking revenge on those who had written supposed slights. Abdülhamid II sought to rebrand the Ottoman Empire through propaganda efforts, not by changing its practices or stopping the massacres. Protecting the human rights of his subjects rather than violating them would have been a surer path to changing his regime's image. Nevertheless, forgotten is the fact that some of the most ardent supporters of Abdülhamid II's propaganda efforts were Jews.

JEWS RALLY BEHIND THE SULTANATE YET AGAIN

While relations between the dynasty and Ottoman Christians worsened despite the Christians' newfound rights, Jews demonstrated anew their devotion to the sultanate. In the fifteenth and sixteenth centuries, Jewish chroniclers and intellectuals had engaged in an internal dialogue, praising the sultan in messianic terms for having defeated the Jews' enemies and oppressors, the Byzantines and Catholics, for having conquered Jerusalem, and for having gathered Jews in the Holy Land. They saw these as signs of the arrival of the messianic age. After the messianic movement of Sabbatai Zevi in the mid-seventeenth century, they ceased referring to the sultan as the messiah. In the nineteenth century, they revived the old trope and made their praise of the sultan public for different reasons.[34]

Yet Jews now faced a momentous decision. The nineteenth century had witnessed the execution of the heads of the three leading Jewish families, largely because of their connections to the Janissaries. The same epoch saw Greek independence, the rise of Greek and Armenian nationalist movements within the empire, the independence of Southeastern European states, and the nationalist sentiments of Jews in the Ottoman Empire. The Jews could either turn to their own nationalist movement—Zionism, which few Ottoman Jews supported—or choose to forget the still-lamented trauma of the unjust murders of their leaders in 1826, seek reconciliation with the dynasty, and side with the empire to become allies against Christians. The Jewish leadership took the latter path. Numerically smaller, economically weaker, and with a worse public image than that of the Armenians or Greeks, Ottoman Jews sought a way to make themselves appear useful, loyal, relevant, and reliable to the sultan.[35] Their investment in positive patriotism meant publicly declaring their loyalty to the empire and condemning Ottoman Christians as traitors.

In 1892, on the four hundredth anniversary of the arrival of Jews expelled from Spain, Ottoman Jewry planned their first public ceremony celebrating the 'welcome' given them by Ottoman sultans and expressing their gratefulness for Ottoman Muslim 'tolerance'.[36] Unlike their medieval predecessors, the nineteenth-century Jews did not focus on the sultan, who was seen as a tool of the divine plan and not actually possessing any human agency to act. Instead, they presented all Ottoman Muslims (Turks), and not merely the sultan, as tolerant. It was to be a public performance of patriotism, of fealty to the empire and the ruler. In the end, it consisted not of empire-wide public processions, however, but the reciting of special prayers in synagogues and the sending of telegrams to the sultan.[37] Nonetheless, it was a public declaration that the Ottoman Jews had turned over their services to the state, openly siding with Abdülhamid II against his enemies, the Greeks and Armenians of the empire.

In 1892, the leaders of the Ottoman Jewish community presented its members as loyal and useful. Reflecting the long-held utopian view, they argued that the Ottoman Empire was the first 'open land to receive all the oppressed who desired tranquillity'.[38]

The empire was a 'refuge' where Jews 'benefited from the freedom of religion'. The Jews were 'true citizens' capable of 'making
the country flourish'. These leaders proclaimed that all Jews, all
around the world, were indebted to the Ottoman dynasty, which
was the first to 'love' them. They urged world Jewry to 'forever
recognise' the Ottoman Empire and 'express the most profound
respect for everything bearing the name "Ottoman"'.[39] Aron de
Joseph Hazan, a community leader from İzmir, promoted the 1892
quadricentennial commemorating the arrival of Iberian Jews. He
proclaimed that the Ottoman dynasty had given Jews refuge from
'the tyranny of the Spanish government and European barbarism', obliging Jews to declare their gratitude publicly.[40] According to Hazan, doing so would offer 'absolute proof of the profound
gratitude we feel towards the Ottoman government' and serve as
a retort to Ottoman Muslim 'anti-Semites who accuse us of being
ingrates and who claim that we are not true patriots'.[41]

Jews were put to the test only four years later. First, anti-Jewish
racism was voiced by Muslims in print. Then on 26 August 1896
several dozen members of the Armenian Revolutionary Federation armed with bombs and revolvers, desperate to avenge the
recent massacres and to bring the plight of Ottoman Armenians
to the attention of the whole of Europe, stormed and occupied
the Ottoman Bank in Galata, Istanbul. While after fourteen hours
the surviving revolutionaries were allowed safe passage out of the
country, Istanbul Armenians were not so fortunate. What ensued
was a massacre of thousands of Armenians by Kurds and Turks.[42]
Jews responded as a model minority with claims of affinity with
Muslims. Some Jews participated in the violence against Armenians, attacking them and looting their homes or assisting the
mobs in finding victims.[43] Other Jews saved Armenians by giving
them prayer books and prayer shawls so they could pass as Jews.[44]
Jewish leaders in Istanbul considered publicising the fact that Jews
had endangered their own lives to save Armenians. But the Jewish leadership decided to suppress reports of this aid, worrying

about what it would mean for their alliance with Muslims against a common enemy, Ottoman Christians.

Ottoman Jews' propaganda efforts were echoed by those of Theodor Herzl in Vienna, the founder of political Zionism. The leaders of the Zionist movement wished to gain Abdülhamid II's support for establishing a Jewish homeland in Ottoman Palestine. Herzl believed that if the Zionists assisted the sultan on the Armenian issue, the sultan would support the Zionists. In 1896, believing in conspiracy theories about alleged Jewish control of the media, the sultan suggested to Herzl that he marshal 'Jewish power' on the Ottoman Empire's behalf so as to dampen international outrage regarding the massacres. As he related in his diary, Herzl responded, 'Excellent!'[45]

Abdülhamid II had demanded that Herzl convince the European press 'to present the Armenian question in a fashion friendly' to the Ottoman Empire.[46] Fearing that the massacre of Armenians in Istanbul would lead to the deposition of the sultan, which would mean the end of the Zionist dream, Herzl used all his contacts, as Zionist leader and as journalist, to try to turn the public relations tide in the Ottomans' favour in Europe.

In Western Europe, Abdülhamid II was labelled the 'red sultan' on account of the massacres. He was usually depicted with a hooked nose and bloodstained hands in political cartoons in the Western press. Despite the atrocities, Herzl sought to rouse public opinion to support the sultan.[47] He also aimed to counter Western European Islamophobic stereotypes about Muslims and the Ottomans, as Abdülhamid II was considered abroad as an indolent debaucher, a sexualised Oriental despot lording over his harem. A widely circulated cartoon of the sultan portrayed him smoking a water pipe, his face a composite of nude women.[48]

These drawings of a bloody or sexualised Abdülhamid II are widely known. They reflected the fanciful depictions of the Ottomans that had been circulated in the rest of Europe for centuries. But it is important to pause the chronological narrative of the story of the Ottoman dynasty to see how Ottoman images of themselves and the people they ruled, and other European representations of the Ottomans, had changed. For what is little known is that, like other European colonialists at this point in history, the Ottoman ruling elite harboured prejudiced and racialised views of the various populations they oversaw, especially nomads, Kurds, and Arabs.

LOOKING WITHIN
The Ottoman Orient

B y the nineteenth century, Christian Europeans had begun to perceive of the Ottomans as a dynasty corrupted by
luxury and decadence. In their view, the empire was the 'sick man
of Europe'. As Central and Western European powers grew in
global dominance and prestige opposite the empire, they no longer admired what they had earlier feared, and they began to view
the Ottomans as inferior. From the fourteenth century through
the seventeenth century, Central and Western Europe had generally dreaded ascendant Ottoman military power. As the Ottoman
military threat to Central Europe waned by the eighteenth century, Christian Europeans viewed the Ottomans as paragons of
culture and refinement and as patrons of magnificence and the
arts. But by the nineteenth century, which corresponded to the
rise of Western European colonial strength and dominance over
parts of the Middle East, the Christian Europeans had begun to
view themselves as preferable in every way.

The Western European approach to Muslim-majority regions
such as the Ottoman Empire has been labelled as Orientalism,
a proto-Islamophobia. Orientalism was Christian Europe's con-
trasting image of the Eastern 'other', based on the comparison
made between the allegedly superior colonising Occident and the

supposedly backward colonised Orient. The Eastern other was everything the Western 'self' imagined itself not to be: lazy, ignorant, obscurantist, and religiously fanatic, yet sensuous and erotic. In many popular Orientalist paintings, the male artists—many of whom had never been to the Middle East or who used English women as models—represented the Ottoman Empire as an exotic, romantic fantasyland full of oppressed, veiled, yet nude women, where life had not changed since biblical times. Tied to the way Western Europeans imagined the empire was the way the West dealt with the East. As Westerners began to rule over former parts of the Ottoman Empire such as Algeria and Egypt, Orientalism expressed increasing Western European dominance and authority over the region.[1]

In the nineteenth century, across the European empires, rigid rules against mixing between groups, enforcement of social hierarchies based on race, and policies centred on the civilising mission predominated. The Ottoman Empire partook in this global trend. The Ottoman elite adopted a similar approach as other European empires to its own subject peoples in the age of imperialism. Just as Western Europeans made the distinction between Ottomans and Europeans more firmly at this time, so, too, did the Ottomans internalise Orientalist views and draw sharper lines between themselves and the people they ruled. The Ottoman elite became obsessed with their exotic image in the West and denigrated those groups that contributed to it.

In the nineteenth century, Western imperialists did not have a monopoly on prejudiced and racialised views of the governed. Ottomans sent to rule outlying provinces could be just as Orientalist as their Western counterparts. Already in the sixteenth century Ottoman Muslim intellectuals such as the disgruntled historian Mustafa Ali—who had diagnosed the decline of the empire as caused by a turn away from staffing the administration with Ottoman Rûmis—disparaged Kurds and Turks. He described them as unfit to rule themselves or others, depicting them as simpletons easily won over by flattery and gifts of uniforms, horses, and weapons, yet also untrustworthy, potentially disloyal, and morally bankrupt. In the nineteenth century, Ottoman Muslim travel writers and administrators sent from Istanbul to the Albanian and Arabophone peripheries of the empire depicted Albanians, Arabs, Bedouin, and nomads inhabiting such regions as Arabia, Lebanon, Libya, Transjordan, and Yemen similarly to how Europeans described Muslims and Ottomans or settlers in the United States viewed Native Americans.[2] Abdülhamid II compared the Kurds and nomads in eastern Anatolia to the 'savage tribes in America'.[3]

Reading these Ottoman Orientalists' accounts, one discovers that there were many regions competing to be the Ottoman Wild West. The Ottoman Turkish elite serving the sultan in these provinces or travelling there for other reasons saw the people living there as 'wild', 'violent', 'primitive', 'uncivilised savages' in need of enlightenment so as to be brought into the modern world. As many of these groups were already Muslim, Islam was not the sole marker of civilisation. The people in the provinces were encouraged to abandon nomadism and settle in urban areas, trade ignorance for education in newly built schools, and relinquish sloth and poverty for industriousness. They were to exchange a diseased body for one improved by hygiene and modern medicine, measure their day by twenty-four-hour clock time assisted by the construction of prominent clock towers, and dress in Westernised late-Ottoman fashion. They were supposed to discontinue what were perceived as crude manners, lax morals, and odd customs.

Orientalism was one of the factors that helped unravel the empire of conversion. Moving away from Islam and conversion as the principal glue of society and towards a civilising mission as the thing that bound the elite together, these Ottoman Turkish elites saw themselves as shouldering the 'Ottoman man's burden' in relation to the Albanians, Arabs, and Islamic sectarians of the empire, such as the Druze. Sometimes they viewed people in places like Arabia or Lebanon with such disdain that they referred to them as nonhuman, as 'insects'.[4]

Ottoman administrators in Arab provinces such as Yemen and Ottoman Muslim travellers within the empire or in Africa expressed as much antipathy towards their subjects as British and French colonial administrators did. Wealthy Ottomans travelling into the outback of the empire frequently displayed Orientalist attitudes: they judged local peoples by what they considered civilised Ottoman culture, found them lacking, and dismissed them as 'backward', 'savage', and not 'modern'.[5] They viewed them as the other, displaying feelings of innate superiority even when the people in question were also Muslims or subjects of the same sultan. Just as Christian Europeans viewed people who were not Christians as the least civilised, Ottoman elites viewed Africans and people who were not Muslims as lower on the scale of civilisation.

Mehmed Emin, a servant of the sultan travelling to Central Asia in the mid-1870s, viewed Ottoman culture as superior and 'the Turkish race' as better than others. He imagined the reason for Ottoman success as being racial: 'Because the Turks who were the origin of our Ottoman nationhood came under the leadership' of the Oğuz tribe 'from such a progressive, civilised and prosperous area' they were able to establish 'a world-conquering state which unified so many nations and showed the world the model of a new civilisation'.[6]

According to the man of letters Ahmed Midhat Efendi, writing in 1878, the Ottomans had much to learn from Western Europe, just as Muslim-majority societies had much to learn from the Ottomans. While Europe had progressed 'with many inventions and modernised with new laws of civilisation' and had 'really amazed the human mind', Muslim-majority societies need 'our guidance in matters of progress and innovation'.[7] The Ottomans, he argued, should embark on a civilising mission to the Arab world.

An Ottoman translator and diplomat from the 1870s noted that the Sudan was uncivilised and culturally backward. He looked down on the 'half-naked' inhabitants and disparaged 'the ridiculous customs of the negroes in Central and South Africa who are still pagan'. Taking a page out of the racist views of white Southerners in the United States, he added, 'They have an innate inclination towards play and dance which are the amusements the negro races love most'.[8]

Ottomans wrote as colonialists. The Treaty of Berlin of 1878, despite causing the Ottomans to lose one-third of their territory in Europe in the wake of the 1877–1878 war with Russia, gave the Ottomans the chance to participate in the scramble for Africa. The last Ottoman holdings in Africa were in Libya, which became a focus of Abdülhamid II in the final decades of his reign. At the 1884–1885 Berlin Conference, also known as the Congo Conference, which legitimated foreign colonialism in Africa, the Ottoman delegation referred to its holdings of Tripoli, Benghazi, and Ghat in Libya as colonies. Writing in 1908, an Ottoman administrator and parliamentarian criticised Ottoman neglect of North Africa and advocated a revitalised Ottoman commitment to Tripoli. His reason was explicitly imperial. Controlling Tripoli allowed 'the fastest civilised connecting link' between Europe and the markets of Central Africa.[9] In his 1909 travelogue of the Sudan, a diplomat bemoaned the fact that the Ottomans had not acted in time to colonise that country, ceding it to another colonial power, the British.

The Ottoman elite had internalised Western European Orientalist views of themselves. They expressed their own Orientalism regarding the people they ruled. Ottoman Orientalism was ingrained in elite visions of how to reform the empire and make it modern. More significant is the fact that the degrading sentiment was pervasive. These elites wished to transform their own 'Orient': they centralised the empire, took control of administration of the provinces directly without local mediators (the notables upon whom they had formerly relied), and constructed railways, roads, primary, secondary, and military schools, barracks, mosques, and government buildings. They sought to convert those groups they perceived as not being modern—Arabs, Bedouin, nomads, Kurds, lower classes, and women—and who hindered the progress they wished to make into useful populations so as to save the empire. The Ottoman elite conceived of themselves from the mid-nineteenth century as a civilised and civilising force, as did other European Orientalists. The elite articulated not the white man's burden, but what one Turkish scholar has labelled 'the white man's burden wearing a fez'.[10] They saw themselves as being enlightened and therefore charged with uplifting stagnant peoples and groups, rejuvenating the empire's east, and bringing about a renaissance.

In the view of another imperial translator, who referred to the areas south of Ottoman Libya in his work *New Africa* (1890), colonialism was a positive good in which 'a civilised state sends settlers out to lands where people still live in a state of nomadism and savagery, developing these areas, and causing them to be a market for its goods'.[11] Ottoman provincial governors' views of the Bedouin were as paternalistic as those of British, French, and German colonial officials. The comments of their wives about Arabs were similar to European women travellers' views of the same peoples in that era.

Artist Naciye Neyyal, who accompanied her husband, Tevfik Bey, to Jerusalem, where he was governor between 1897 and 1901, noted that their life there was like that of 'a prince and princess ruling a faraway kingdom'.[12] She also wrote in a patronising way of the Bedouin: 'I sensed that they liked us because, although they are savage, and live so far from civilisation, they appreciate goodwill and know how to be thankful'.[13] It was no accident that thirty-four of the final thirty-nine Ottoman grand viziers were Turks.[14] The elite was becoming more Turkish and less tolerant of others, even when those others were fellow Muslims.

ORIENTALISM, GENDER, AND SEXUALITY

Western armchair and in-person visitors to the empire were more concerned with Ottoman women than any other topic. A central element in Orientalist representations of Ottoman otherness was the harem—the private quarters of a Muslim home, not something only the sultan had—which they depicted as a sexualised fantasy zone. European men and women portrayed themselves as 'liberators' of Ottoman women, whom they sought to unveil (and disrobe), while being titillated by the idea of secluded women and polygamy. The English painter John Frederick Lewis resided in Cairo for a decade in the middle of the nineteenth century, 'going native' by living among Arabs in a palatial home in an old quarter and dressing like them in robes and turban. He entertained visitors with coffee and hookah pipes like an Ottoman gentleman and was considered the main British authority on the harem, despite never having entered one.[15] He relied upon women travellers' accounts for his knowledge. He used his English wife, Marian, as his model, including as the sleeping 'Cairene' woman depicted in his *Siesta* (1876), part of Tate Britain's permanent exhibition, *Walk Through British Art*.[16] Likewise, he labelled his own self-portrait as *Portrait of a Memlook* (Mamluk) *Bey.*

These fanciful conceits notwithstanding, his voyeuristic painting *The Harem* (1849) gained him fame in Britain.[17] It depicts a turbaned Mamluk bey with bejewelled dagger lounging on a luxurious sofa with a young woman, with two other women at his feet—his three Georgian, Greek, or Circassian concubines or wives—in his harem in Cairo. None of these women are veiled. Next to them stands a smiling African servant woman. They are watching a very dark-skinned, tall, grinning African eunuch display an embarrassed, seminude East African slave woman clutching what remains of her garment. Another African slave holds a water pipe. A gazelle sits on the divan. Another wanders across the room. Despite its preposterousness, this image was taken as a realistic ethnographic study. The painting was hailed by art critics as 'one of the most remarkable productions of this age of English art' and 'the most extraordinary production that has ever been executed in water-colour'.[18]

Upper-class European women gained actual access to harems, beginning in the eighteenth century with Lady Mary Wortley Montagu, who recorded her knowledge in the well-known *Turkish Embassy Letters*. Having witnessed firsthand the lifesaving effects of variolation (an early form of immunisation against smallpox) in Istanbul, she promoted it to England. More and more British women visited the empire in the nineteenth century. Despite their relationships with harem women and their knowledge of the harem as a family quarter rather than as a sexual playground, they tended to repeat Orientalist stereotypes of harems as exotic places of fantasy—lesbian or feminine rather than masculine—and sites of mystery and intrigue, comparing them to *The Thousand and One Nights* and seeing them as dens of timeless luxury, sensuality, and beauty.[19]

Ottoman women from the harem sometimes sought to subvert such narratives. One response is found in Ottoman art and literature. Elite Ottoman women commissioned portraits, carefully choosing how they would be depicted so as to have some manner of control over how the West viewed them. Reformer sultan Abdülmecid I's daughter Fatma, at that time in her late teens, invited British traveller Mary Adelaide Walker to enter her harem to paint her portrait around the same time as Lewis was painting *The Harem*.[20] Walker resided in Istanbul for thirty years. She painted Sultan Abdülaziz I's portrait for the Ottoman exhibition at the 1867 Universal Exposition in Paris, which he visited. Abdülaziz I spent six weeks in France, and visited Austria, Belgium, England, Germany, and Hungary, the first and only sultan to travel outside the imperial domains not at the head of an army, and the first sultan to visit Western Europe.[21] In London he commissioned

Englishman Charles Fuller to cast a bronze equestrian statue of him, which he displayed in his new Beylerbeyi Palace on the Asian side of Istanbul.[22]

Over the course of six months, as Walker painted her, Fatma chose her dress, a combination of Western European and Ottoman fashion, and her pose.[23] The portrait is staid and formal. It depicts the princess wearing a white French-silk outfit, a European-style bodice beneath a loose robe with Ottoman baggy trousers, as well as a diamond-covered girdle and a small portrait of her father.[24] Fatma prohibited the portrait from being circulated outside the palace, so that her figure would not be gazed upon by strangers. Her father Abdülmecid I's 1857 portrait by Armenian painter Ruben Manas was sent to the queen of Sweden, Sophia of Nassau, as a gift and is still exhibited today at Drottningholm Palace in Stockholm. It depicts a nineteenth-century European ruler in a headdress meant to distinguish him both from other rulers and from his turbaned predecessors, including Selim III: a red fez. His daughter's portrait is known only from Walker's notebooks.[25] Unlike the male fantasy works such as those by Lewis, works such as Walker's are still relatively unknown in the canon of Orientalist art.

The imagined divide between the Western self and the Eastern other assumed political significance as support of Greek culture and Greek independence spread in Western Europe. In this context, Orientalist painters depicted Turks and Muslims in stereotypes. One was as bloodthirsty tyrants and religious fanatics. A well-known example is Eugène Delacroix's *The Massacre at Chios* (1824), based on the 1822 Ottoman massacre and enslavement of many thousands of Greek civilians during the Greek rebellion. *The Massacre at Chios* is painted in gory and shocking detail, with suggestions of rape—nude and emaciated Christ-like men, elderly women, and children. One babe tries to suckle at the breast of its nude, dead mother. Another stereotype is Alexandre-Gabriel

Decamps's *The Turkish Patrol* (1830). In it, fierce and fearsome armed men race through a deserted street, veiled women looking on from the shadows.

Another main theme in Orientalist painting is that Muslims are lustful and paedophiles. Jean-Léon Gérôme's *The Snake Charmer* (1880) shows a nude young boy with his back to the viewer. Facing his audience of leering men, the boy holds an erect snake aloft. One man wears a classical Janissary helmet. They sit with their backs to a brilliant blue-tiled building reminiscent of the circumcision chamber in Topkapı Palace.[26] The same painter's *Arab Girl in a Doorway* (1873) presents the viewer a veiled young girl, perhaps a prostitute, beckoning from an alleyway with breasts exposed. Jean-Auguste-Dominique Ingres's *The Turkish Bath* (1862–1863) fills the tableau with an impossible scenario of countless, fully nude, blonde or red-haired women lounging in the harem bath, two in intimate embrace, an erotic fantasy that was everything the actual harem was not.

The first Western-trained Ottoman artist, Osman Hamdi Bey, the founder of Istanbul's Academy of Fine Arts (1882) and Archaeology Museum (1891) was schooled in these offensive depictions. Osman Hamdi's obituary referred to him as 'the most Parisian of the Ottomans—the most Ottoman of the Parisians'. He lived many years in France, was married to French women, and painted Orientalist works that were lent 'authenticity' because the artist was an Ottoman.[27] His work illustrates how the Ottoman elite incorporated Orientalist discourse about the Ottomans and deployed it against their own people.

Osman Hamdi's Greek father was a survivor of the Ottoman massacre at Chios during the Greek rebellion that led to independence. He was subsequently purchased as a slave by the Ottoman admiral of the navy, who sent him to be educated in France. Like his father, Osman Hamdi also studied in Paris. His painting master was none other than the Orientalist Gérôme—painter of *The Snake Charmer*—with whom he maintained a lifelong friendship. Osman Hamdi was an Ottoman Orientalist who used the same components of Orientalist paintings—women, Islam, Topkapı Palace tiles, prayer rugs, incense holders, and sixteenth-century Janissary helmets—and sometimes gave them shocking new meaning.

Osman Hamdi's paintings, which were exhibited in Western Europe and North America rather than in Istanbul, most often depict a thick-bearded 'Oriental' male, using himself as model, wearing typical 'Oriental' dress in a representative location, such as a mosque, surrounded by 'Oriental' artifacts.[28] These works reflect the Orientalist aim to civilise the exotic Arabs and nomads he encountered when he spent two years as an administrator in Ottoman Iraq.[29] His views and depictions of Muslims and Arabs are hard to distinguish from those of Western European Orientalists. Yet one of his most shocking paintings went much further than other Orientalist artists for its blasphemous depiction. With his daughter as the likely model, *Genesis* (1901), exhibited in Berlin and London, depicts a young, pregnant woman wearing a bold, sunflower-coloured décolleté dress sitting in a mosque. What is astonishing about her is that she is perched on a Qur'an stand with her back to the *mihrab* (prayer niche) and trampling on open Qur'an manuscripts, perhaps signifying female emancipation from Islam.[30] The work was never displayed in the Ottoman Empire.

Genesis celebrates women's reproductive power. As illustrated by this painting, Osman Hamdi's art is testimony to another cultural change. As Europe, including the Ottoman Empire, transformed over the course of the eighteenth and nineteenth centuries and began to find the man-boy love of pederasty to be inappropriate, so, too, did the Ottoman elite begin to disapprove of such practices and become ashamed of them. This led to denial and silencing of such 'embarrassment'.[31] Once normal, same-sex relations became frowned upon and deemed offensive, such that today they are barely remembered or remarked upon, despite their

obvious presence in the Ottoman literature of the premodern era.
Already in the Period of Reforms of the mid-nineteenth century,
Ottoman reformists aimed to crack down on such practices.

For centuries it was deemed acceptable for older men to desire
young men. But in the nineteenth century, Western Europeans began to look at Ottoman sex and sexuality as depraved, deformed,
libidinous, and licentious. Reflecting on their sexual practices, Ottomans also began to feel a sense of disgrace. They presented their
morality as based on rigidly defined gender roles, the seclusion
of women, and a heterosexual ethic. In the oft-cited, self-serving,
perhaps disingenuous words of nineteenth-century historian and
conservative reformist statesman Ahmed Cevdet Pasha, in the
mid-nineteenth century Ottoman men ceased loving boys: 'With
the increase of women lovers the number of boy-beloveds decreased and the sodomites seem to have disappeared off the face
of the earth. Ever since then the well-known love for and relationships with the young men of Istanbul was transferred to young
women as the natural order of things', a transformation caused in
part by the 'disapproval of [Western European] foreigners'.[32]

Thus began the journey to suppress established sexual dis-
courses, silence them, and replace them with other sanitised
genres. And this is the legacy we have today. Ubiquitous sixteenth-
century works such as those by Crazy Brother (Deli Birader)
Gazali, which promote sex with boys as superior to sex with
women, are not seen as part of the Ottoman literary canon. Modern Turks have used such texts to disparage both Ottoman court
literature and the Ottoman dynasty and elite as 'perverse', seemingly unaware that they are mimicking the arguments of nineteenth-century Western Europeans who portrayed the Ottomans
as decadent.[33] They have criticised Ottoman court poetry as 'per-
verted' and thus unworthy of study in Turkey. They take expressions of desire to be merely metaphorical, rather than reflecting
any actual sexual relations.

Modern Westerners have also generally avoided including homoeroticism in their description and analysis of their own culture and history, as well as that of the Ottoman Empire and Middle East. This is due in part to a desire not to offend their Middle Eastern or Turkish colleagues and audiences, or perhaps because they accept the argument that such homoerotic love poetry was merely spiritual, or that it was an imitation of earlier Persian poetry. It supposedly had nothing to do with anything worldly, with actual love. We forget that once men did not glorify married love with women but love with boys. It was deemed normal. The fact that rape was a criminal offence and that the only legally sanctioned sexual intercourse was between a man and his wife and between a master (male) and his slave (female) did not hinder the flourishing of an elite Ottoman male culture of pederasty. Such elite male pederasty had also flourished in the rest of contemporary Europe. As sixteenth-century Ottoman thinker Mustafa Ali wrote of his own inclinations, until the age of thirty he alternated between desiring pretty girls and beautiful boys.[34]

By the era of Abdülhamid II, however, the Ottoman elite had become consumed by their exotic image in the rest of Europe, hypersensitive to what they perceived as slights and slurs. They did all they could to reject their own society's 'backwardness' and change it to a 'civilised' one based on Western European values.[35] To accomplish this aim, some radicals based in Salonica demanded the overthrow of the old regime and all the values for which it stood. One of them was named Enver Bey, the red-fez-capped, handlebar-moustachioed, modern-military-uniform-wearing subject of Osman Hamdi Bey's last major portrait.[36] Enver Bey and like-minded militants were called the Young Turks. They were influenced by the Young Ottomans but turned away from the Islamic content of their predecessors' aims. Islam had served for centuries to make Ottoman Muslims religious equals, as conversion had been a pathway to such equality. When the Ottoman elite internalised Western views of Muslims and adapted them as an Ottoman Orientalism, they undermined the role of Islam in uniting its citizens and weakened the bonds that formed the framework for the empire of conversion. Promoting revolution, war, and genocide, the Young Turk power grab in 1913 would lead to dictatorship and the end of the dynasty in the following decade.

20

SAVING THE DYNASTY
FROM ITSELF
Young Turks

FOR CENTURIES, THE Ottomans had been open to receiving every type of person as a Muslim, no matter his or her language or background, whether a slave, commoner, or member of the elite. When faced with losing power to the ascendant Western European empires and brand-new Southeastern European nations, the Ottomans began to turn away from the Ottoman Way of incorporating diversity of Islam and conversion to it. In an effort to restore the empire to its once dominant position, certain activists among the Ottoman elites sought to remake it into a 'civilised' Ottoman Muslim nation-empire on par with the West. No longer an empire of conversion, it was to be made into an empire of Muslim Turks. The Ottoman elites' Orientalist view of their own society and the peoples they governed was channelled into new forms of ethno- and ethno-religious nationalism. When compounded by coups, revolutions, counterrevolutions, and war, the consequence was that tolerance was replaced by ethnic cleansing and genocide, leading ultimately to the dynasty's demise.

From the 1880s to 1913, the Young Turks would promote revolution and two wars but face counterrevolution and resistance.

Working together with Sufis, Freemasons, and other esoteric groups in Ottoman Salonica—the port city in Macedonia that is today Thessaloniki, Greece—these Muslim officers and bureaucrats of varied backgrounds spearheaded opposition to Abdülhamid II. At first they demanded only restoration of the constitution and parliament, but their demands soon evolved to overthrow the sultan. In a short period of time, the ideology of these elitist, militarist, anti-Christian imperialists evolved from Ottoman Muslim nationalism to Turkish nationalism.

THE RISE OF NEW POLITICAL ACTORS

In every age of Ottoman history, deviant dervishes posed a potential threat to the dynasty. One group that became important in the Period of Reforms (1839–1876) and after were the descendants of the followers of the Jewish 'deviant dervish' Sabbatai Zevi, who had converted to Islam in the seventeenth century and primarily resided in Salonica. In the Ottoman telling, Sultan Mehmed IV converted Sabbatai Zevi to Islam in 1666. But according to letters the self-proclaimed messiah wrote after the conversion, Sabbatai Zevi changed religion because that was what the 'true' God, whom he 'alone has known', wanted him to do.[1] He claimed to have converted neither while in a manic or depressive state nor while under duress by the sultan. He did it of his own volition, he declared, 'thanks to the great power and strength of truth and faith'.[2] He called on other Jews to follow suit, urging those who followed him into Islam to bury their belief in him as the messiah in their hearts and to live it secretly.[3] That underground faith reemerged in tandem with the progressive reforms of the second half of the nineteenth century, as his followers worked first to enact social change and then conspired with the Young Turks to foment revolution, with explosive results for the dynasty.

Legally Muslims, Sabbatai Zevi's followers secretly continued to adhere to the beliefs and practices of him and his successors, in whom they believed Sabbatai Zevi's soul had been reborn. Trans-migration of souls had been a common theme in deviant dervish theology. But most elements of their theology and rituals placed them beyond the pale of Islam and Judaism alike. Unlike Jews, they ostensibly followed the requirements of Islam such as fasting during Ramadan. Unlike Muslims, they maintained belief in Sabbatai Zevi's messianism. They called themselves 'the Believers', but outsiders referred to them as the Dönme, 'the Converts'.[4]

The Dönme benefited from the establishment of a locally selected mayoralty, municipal council, and other local political bodies, and late nineteenth-century Western European capitalism as well.[5] Dönme politicians and international merchants formed a conspicuous, significant part of the new elite.

From the fifteenth century to the mid-seventeenth century, Salonica had been the centre of the Ottoman Empire's woolen cloth and textile industry. Having founded the industry, Jews predominated in it, supplying the market and receiving a monopoly to furnish uniforms for the Janissaries. The expanding ranks of the Janissary corps over the sixteenth century benefited Salonican Jews. In the seventeenth century, however, treaties allowed Western Europeans to export their textiles to the Ottoman Empire. Competition from English, Dutch, and French suppliers, the rising price of raw materials, and fiscal crises weakened the Ottoman textile industry.

One of those affected was Sabbatai Zevi's father, Mordecai, who like many other Salonican Jews sought his fortunes instead in the boomtown of İzmir, the port city on the Aegean coast of Anatolia. As brokers and agents for English merchants, Mordecai and his two eldest sons made enough of a fortune to allow Sabbatai Zevi to study Jewish law with famous rabbis who were also drawn to the city by its wealth. As fortunes were being made and heresies hatched in İzmir, Salonica's wool manufacturing declined and became merely a military supply industry, continuing only due to the need to supply the Janissaries. By the eighteenth century, trade between Salonica and Western Europe had increased greatly, but as is the case in a multicultural, plural empire, when one ethno-religious group declines, it presents an opportunity for another group to rise and take its place. Salonican Jewish merchants and manufacturers had been largely replaced by other groups, including Italian Jews who were protected by foreign consuls. The abolition of the Janissaries in 1826 led to the demise of woolen cloth manufacturing by Jews.

The decline of most Salonican Jews afforded an opportunity to many Dönme, who stepped into Jews' former role and became the leading textile merchants. New economic possibilities were also seized upon by the Dönme, who soon became wealthy and significant economic players. This wealth, combined with being ostensibly Muslim, speaking both Turkish and French, and fluency in Ottoman culture, allowed them to take advantage of their legal position as Muslims. They easily rose in a city in which Jews predominated.

The Period of Reforms introduced new political positions, which Dönme promptly filled, expanding their power, wealth, and influence in the city. The best example is Salonican mayor Hamdi Bey (in office 1893–1902), who was an urban reformer, international businessman, and leader of one of the three Dönme sects.[6] He changed the face of the city, hiring the Italian architect Vitaliano Poselli to plan and build most of Salonica's new public buildings. Poselli designed the eclectic Dönme mosque (1904), the last Ottoman mosque built in the city. Hamdi Bey put an Ottoman stamp on modernity. He made public fountains run red with sour cherry juice, the favoured Ottoman drink. And he furthered the interests of the Dönme, ensuring they served in local politics without suspicion or interference from officials sent from Istanbul. The prevalence of members of his sect of Dönme in municipal offices—recognisable by their shaved heads, like deviant dervishes—caused at least one governor to take notice. Şemsi Efendi, a famous Dönme educator, opened a school just two blocks east of the governor's building. The proximity of Dönme schools to the seat of the governor was symbolic of the heavy proportion of Dönme in city governance.

While helpful in introducing modernising administrative, architectural, and educational reforms, as well as embracing global capitalism for industrialising the empire, the Dönme became a dangerous threat to the palace when they joined forces with revolutionary, underground opposition groups in Salonica.

OPPOSITION TO ABDÜLHAMID II

Salonica was a site of great political agitation. It was the birthplace of the Young Turk revolutionary movement as well as assorted socialist organisations.[7] It had the highest concentration of factory labour in the empire, particularly in the tobacco industry. Headed by Bulgarian Jew Avram Benaroya, the city's Workers' Solidarity Federation was considered by the Second International—the global federation of socialist parties and trade unions—to be the spark of the proletarian struggle in the East. Salonica was also a centre of Masonic activity and the main domicile of the Dönme. Salonica was one of the Ottoman cities best supplied with schools, including a law faculty, and army headquarters, both of which were open to new currents of thought. Professionals and civil servants who shared a progressive outlook—especially employees of the Post and Telegraph Department such as Mehmed Talat (later promoted to pasha) and members of the Third Army such as Enver Bey (later promoted to pasha)—made up the majority of the revolutionaries. The heart of the struggle was Salonica.

Abdülhamid II had his supporters, as all dictators do. They included the top military brass and the members of the religious class that supported his Islamisation campaign. But more legion were his enemies, who opposed his closing of the parliament, suspension of the constitution, and authoritarian reign.

Opposition to Abdülhamid II was launched by the Committee of Union and Progress (İttihat ve Terakki Cemiyeti, CUP), first initiated as a secret society (with a slightly different name, the Committee of Progress and Union) in 1889 by students at the Royal Military Medical Academy in Istanbul. They were heavily influenced by biological materialist ideology. Biological materialism promoted science in place of religion to cure all of society's ills. The CUP supporters later spread to Paris, Geneva, and Cairo, and then to cities throughout the Ottoman Empire, including Salonica. Following a failed coup attempt in 1896, opponents of Abdülhamid II's autocratic rule who had operated underground in the empire in the 1890s were forced to move overseas. The constitutionalists operated mainly abroad for a decade. In 1907, they reemerged in strength in the empire as a political organisation. By that time, the CUP was a merger of the decades-old, Paris-based Committee of Progress and Union and the new Salonica-based Ottoman Freedom Society. The guiding figures of the Committee of Progress and Union included Dr. Bahaettin Şakir and Dr. Nazım, the director of the modern municipal hospital in Salonica.[8] He would become one of the two leading Young Turk ideologues. The Ottoman Freedom Society had been founded in 1906. One founder was Mehmed Talat, born in the Hasköy district of today's Bulgaria, who knew Ottoman Turkish, Greek, and French and had been exiled to Salonica, where he ran the Telegraph and Post Office.[9] Another was Enver Bey.[10]

These men, who in wishing to save the empire paved the way for its end, shared common characteristics. They were part of a new generation of elite, highly educated, young, urban Muslim men. Most were Rûmis, as they came from Southeastern Europe, northwestern Anatolia including Istanbul, and the Aegean. They received higher education in the new medical and military colleges. Despite calling themselves Young Turks, the four students who founded the organisation at the Royal Military Medical Academy that would later become the CUP were not Turks. They were Ibrahim Temo (an Albanian), Abdullah Cevdet (a Kurd), Mehmed Reşid (a Circassian), and İshak Sükûti (a Kurd).[11]

Sufi brotherhoods and Freemasons also played a role in opposition politics in the Hamidian era, supporting the CUP and favouring the assassination or overthrow of Abdülhamid II. Although that sultan had been close to a sheikh from the Nakşibendi order named Gümüşhanevi, the Bektaşi and Mevlevi Sufi orders opposed him.[12] Ruthlessly suppressed in 1826 because of their affiliation with the Janissaries, the Bektaşis had made a comeback by the beginning of Abdülhamid II's reign in 1876 and were the strongest Sufi order opposing the regime.[13] The Young Turks were sympathetic to the Bektaşis because they considered the Sufi order to be liberal, and a number of Young Turks were Bektaşi. The radical tendencies of the Bektaşis matched the progressive ideas of the Young Turks, and Bektaşis were affiliated with Freemasons, who let the CUP use their lodges after 1906.

The CUP also had a relationship with Rûmi's Mevlevi order. Mevlevi lodges distributed CUP propaganda, and Mevlevi sheikhs hosted CUP meetings in their homes. Other sheikhs were exiled together with Young Turks for their political activism. Sultan Abdülmecid I had supported the Mevlevis, and his successor, Sultan Abdülaziz I, had been a member of the Mevlevi order, as was Sultan Abdülhamid II's brother Mehmed Reşad in Galata.[14] But during Abdülhamid II's reign, the Mevlevi order had abandoned its traditional quietism, and the CUP tried to install Mehmed Reşad as sultan in a failed coup in 1896. In the last decade of Abdülhamid II's rule, the Mevlevi sheikhs in Istanbul, İzmir, and Konya aligned with the CUP, and some were arrested and exiled. The grand çelebi even asked the British for asylum.[15]

The Sufi role in revolutionary politics was significant, but until 1895 it was the Freemasons who were more important in opposition politics. The Freemason Murad V, envisioned as an enlightened sultan who would unite Turks and Greeks, had come to power in a coup d'état aided by Freemasons in 1876. The nucleus of the Young Turks emerged from the members of a Masonic lodge established by those who had brought that sultan to the throne.

Until 1902, because they were forbidden in the empire, Ottoman Freemasons had organised their own political organisations under other names and distributed political tracts on liberty and freedom across Europe. Thereafter they supported the Paris-based Committee of Progress and Union (which with the Ottoman Freedom Society became the CUP in 1907), whose leader, Ahmed Rıza, included in his inner circle many prominent Freemason leaders. All the founding members but one of the Ottoman Freedom Society in Salonica were Freemasons or became Freemasons. They were members of either the Italian Obedience of Macedonia Risorta or the French Obedience of Véritas (Truth). After the merger of the Committee of Progress and Union and the Ottoman Freedom Society as the CUP, the CUP was based in Salonican Masonic lodges.[16] In a society not ready to abandon hierarchies of religion, and in which sectarianism had become a problem—leading to massacres of Armenians in Anatolia and Maronite Christians in Syria—Christians, Jews, and Muslims could meet in Masonic lodges as equals, united in secrecy. Freemasons benefited from social egalitarianism, which allowed them to accommodate their religious differences and promote societal change. At Masonic lodges, strangers were transformed into brothers seeking the same political goal. Murad V's successor, Abdülhamid II, recognised the threat and suppressed the Freemasons. His government labelled them a constant source of treason.

There were close links between secret societies of Freemasons and the diverse members of the CUP, a secret society imitating Masonic practices and meeting in Masonic lodges. In a dictatorship, secrecy afforded political organisation. The Jewish attorney Emmanuel Carasso, one of the leaders of the CUP in Salonica and in the hierarchy of the entire organisation, received medals of honour from the very sultan he worked to overthrow. He also headed the Italian rite Macedonia Risorta, whose lodge was the site of secret CUP meetings and the place where CUP archives and records were kept. The Masonic order counted among its members the majority of the leaders of the Salonican branch of the CUP. Freemasonry was important for the CUP. Masonic lodges were crucial channels through which oppositional politics could germinate.

Many prominent Dönme were Freemasons as well as Sufis, which facilitated their entry into the CUP. Dönme were among the founders of the French Obedience of Véritas, established in 1904, and sat on its supreme council. That order counted two future grand viziers, Ali Rıza Pasha and Hussein Hilmi Pasha. Jews and Dönme were prominent in the clubs of Freemasons where the CUP met in Salonica.[17] Mason and dervish lodges where many Dönme participated in Sufi rituals sided with the CUP against the sultan, in part because Freemasons and some Sufi sects promoted equality and brotherhood. Conveniently, given Salonica's secret CUP cells, Masonic membership, and revolutionary cells in the Third Army, ancient underground storage spaces located in the main Dönme neighbourhoods allowed passage undetected from house to house and even from neighbourhood to neighbourhood. When police raided homes, people on the run and the secret documents they carried could easily disappear in these spaces.

Dönme played an important founding and supporting role in the revolutionary movement.[18] The banker, textile merchant, director of one of the largest banking and commercial houses in the city, and head of the chamber of commerce Mehmed Kapancı used his wealth to fund the CUP. Wealthy merchants such as Kapancı supported the revolution because they were Freemasons who believed that the sultan was stifling society. These were men who supported progressive schools that promoted critical thinking, especially the Dönme schools the Feyziye (Excellence) and Terakki (Progress), considered centres of revolution.

Some Dönme became so committed to the political ideas discussed in secret CUP meetings at the city's Masonic lodges that they were considered the revolutionary vanguard. Dönme intellectuals and civil servants played a crucial revolutionary role. Their history and religion had caused them to evolve more and more into an association of freethinkers, separate from Muslims and Jews yet placed in a position to be a progressive factor in the city.

Dönme, Freemasons, Bektaşi and Mevlevi Sufis, students at the new medical and military colleges, young army officers, wealthy capitalists, liberal professionals, and bureaucrats all conspired to compel Abdülhamid II to reinstate the constitution and parliament.

REVOLUTION

Determined to save the empire from itself and its ever more dictatorial ruler, the CUP, led by Muslim men of diverse background (Albanian, Caucasian, Circassian, Dönme, Kurdish, and Turkish) launched the events of June and July 1908 known as the constitutional revolution. What transpired was actually not very impressive, but it achieved the CUP's aim. The revolutionaries considered their event on par with the other significant events that occurred in July, the French Revolution and the American Declaration of Independence.[19] But there was no storming of the Bastille as in France, and the sultan was left formally in power. More like an armed revolt, it did not seem to be a revolution at all. The CUP forced Abdülhamid II to reinstate the abrogated 1876 constitution and reconvene the parliament. This was no mass uprising. Nor was it a toppling of the political and social system.

The revolution of 1908 was triggered by the secret CUP central committee in Salonica when it decided to reveal itself by publicly rejecting British and Russian efforts to make Ottoman Macedonia an autonomous region under foreign oversight.[20] Macedonia was claimed by Greek, Bulgarian, Macedonian, and Serbian nationalists. As the Ottomans had steadfastly refused to offer autonomy, the diverse Southeastern European Christian nationalists had

proselytised national consciousness among their people through
their churches and schools, used violence against Ottoman authorities (who responded in kind), and appealed for foreign intervention to achieve their political aims.[21]

The self-outing of the CUP caused the Ottoman government
to investigate it. The CUP shot the man charged with this task,
Nazım Bey, brother-in-law of Major Enver Bey of the Ottoman
Third Army. The CUP ordered its branches throughout Macedonia to start an insurgency and to form guerrilla bands on the
model of those of the Bulgarians, Greeks, Macedonians, and Serbs
already operating in the region to fight both the Christian guerrillas and Ottoman forces that opposed them. Enver Bey, leader of
the CUP branch in Monastir, western Macedonia, headed to the
hills. He established a band of guerrillas outside Salonica. Battalion commander Adjutant Major Niyazi Bey, an Albanian, formed
a guerrilla band in Macedonia.

Other CUP branches in other Ottoman cities and their leaders
sent telegrams to the sultan demanding the restoration of the constitution and parliament. Şemsi Pasha, the Ottoman general sent
after them, was murdered by the CUP. Enver and Niyazi traversed
the Macedonian countryside with their bands. They rallied Muslims behind them by playing on their fears of attacks by Christian guerrillas supported by the Russian army. They made little
use of the soldiers under their command, who they assumed were
loyal to the sultan. They appealed instead to Muslims—Albanians,
self-sacrificing volunteers, brigands and outlaws, and CUP men—
rather than Christian villagers. They planned to march on Istanbul.
When they captured Monastir and its significant garrison, they
declared that the constitution was back in force. Abdülhamid II
agreed to reconvene the prorogued parliament of 1878. Urban-
based junior officers educated in the new military academies had
gone to the mountains of Macedonia with irregular forces and had
compelled the sultan to act. The constitutional revolution was over.

In their proclamation to the public, read out in city squares across the empire to jubilant crowds, the constitutional revolutionaries declared that 'the basis for the constitution will be respect for the predominance of the national will'.[22] The will of the people, and not the whims of the sultan, was to be the governing force of empire. They offered universal suffrage to men, permitted political parties, freed the press, gave more rights to women, and confirmed that 'every citizen will enjoy complete liberty and equality, regardless of nationality or religion'. All Ottomans were 'equal before the law as regards rights and duties relative to the state' and were 'eligible for government posts, according to their individual capacity and their education'. They confirmed that Christians and Jews were liable for military service. In fact, between 1908 and 1914, to an extent not seen even after the reform decrees of 1839 and 1856—which promised legal equality to all subjects of the sultan—Armenians, Greeks, and Jews entered political office and military service.

When the revolution was announced, speeches were made on the balcony of the Dönme-owned Olympos Hotel on Plateia Eleftherias (formerly Olympos Square) in Salonica. Among the speakers was Moiz Kohen (who later adopted the Turkish name Tekinalp), a Turkish nationalist of Jewish background. He shouted, 'We want brotherhood between all peoples. We are all one without regard to religion or sect. Long live the fatherland! Long live freedom! There are no Greeks, Jews, or Bulgarians, there are only Ottomans'.[23] Postcards printed to mark the event travelled the globe, depicting the diverse Ottoman peoples uniting behind 'freedom, equality, brotherhood, and justice', the words translated into Armenian, Greek, Ottoman Turkish, French, and Judeo-Spanish.

Dönme journalists played a decisive role in the events of July 1908. Journalist Ahmet Emin Yalman, a Dönme member of the Véritas lodge and leading CUP activist and publicist, was put in charge of organising the movement's propaganda in Salonica. He penned patriotic poems and articles welcoming the new freedoms and propagating the movement's excitement about the beginning of a new era. He held street demonstrations and organised writers and a press association. In 1914, Yalman would become the news editor of the CUP's main publication, *Echo*. Yalman's alma mater, the Dönme school Terakki—whose name, 'Progress', was the same as that used in the title of the CUP—boasted that it raised freedom-loving, constitution-supporting youths, and that those who announced the second constitutional government were Terakki graduates.[24] The Dönme Feyziye school was proud of its former administrator, the new finance minister Mehmed Cavid, and praised the revolution.

The revolution ushered in a renaissance for the Bektaşi Sufi order and Masonic lodges favoured or founded by the CUP. Revolutionary officers visited Bektaşi lodges to pay tribute, and Bektaşi publications were again permitted. Newspapers attacking the Bektaşis were closed. New Bektaşi lodges were opened.[25] Freemasons declared themselves 'the main force' behind the 1908 revolution, supported the CUP in power, and thrived. The CUP established its own exclusive Masonic lodge in 1909, Le Grand Orient Ottoman, to reduce the power of foreign-affiliated lodges.[26] Its first grand master was none other than Young Turk leader Mehmed Talat.

Elections were held in October and November. CUP-backed candidates won 287 of the 288 seats in parliament. The lone opposition parliamentarian was a member of the Liberal Party. The bicameral legislature opened in December.[27]

The CUP held sway in parliament and in the provinces with its local party bosses. Yet the real centre of CUP power was not its parliamentarians, but its secretive central committee in Salonica, which numbered fewer than two dozen members. Members included Mehmed Talat, Enver Bey, Dr. Bahaettin Şakir, and Dr. Nazım. The central committee was the real power holder in the empire. The members of the central committee we know about averaged around thirty-five years of age, all had college educations, and nearly half originated in Southeastern Europe, with most of the rest coming from Istanbul and the Aegean region.[28] These demographics displayed the continued relevance of Rûminess, of being Roman.

The CUP—its junior officers and civil servants—did not formally take power. It was influential behind the scenes in the newly elected parliament and was able to have a grand vizier appointed that was to its liking. But it faced much opposition and responded in brutal fashion. The CUP was blamed for the assassination of the leading Liberal opposition newspaper editor Hasan Fehmi in 1909. His assassination galvanised massive anti-CUP opposition, organised by the Liberal Party, Nakşibendi Sufi sheikhs, and students of religious colleges, as well as a group calling itself the Muslim Union. Members of the Muslim Union were especially worried by the new societal role of women. In 1908, just as Armenian women fought for women's rights, self-proclaimed Muslim feminists had published half a dozen journals and founded organisations, such as the Ottoman Association for the Protection of the Rights of Women, demanding legal reforms including the end to polygamy and expanded access to education and employment outside the home.[29]

WOMEN'S RIGHTS

Beginning in 1908, there was a renewed clash of two cultural visions, a central feature of which was the role of women in society. One group called for equality between men and women and making women visible in the public sphere. It perceived Islam as a hindrance to modernity and civilisation. If women were veiled and not participating in political life, then the empire would never become modern or civilised and would surely fall. For the opposing group, such exposure of women corrupted society, which needed to adhere to a model in which women's roles were well-defined and women's bodies invisible. In this vision, if women

were unveiled and participated in societal roles formerly the preserve of men, then the empire would come to ruin. Both groups
looked at women's bodies and saw the future of the empire—for
good or ill.

Radicals advocated for the human rights of women, arguing
for the necessity of seeing women as human beings rather than
as females limited to roles as wives and mothers.[30] They argued
against the practice of veiling. Only when women were unveiled
and participating fully in the life of society would they become
human beings, individuals. In this view, free individuals were the
building blocks of a modern society. Once women were treated as
individuals, Ottoman society would become civilised.

Their opponents, the Muslim Union, countered that unveiling
women and thrusting them from the private to the public sphere
would cause moral and political decline. They claimed that what
the radicals advocated was not freedom, but a turning away from
religion towards anarchy and chaos, thereby ruining the family,
the true building block of society. They proposed a correlation between the abandoning of the veil and the opening of taverns and
whorehouses.[31] And they opposed the new freedoms granted by
the constitution and fomented rebellion to replace it.

COUNTERREVOLUTION AND THE
DEPOSITION OF ABDÜLHAMID II

Much more dramatic than the constitutional revolution of 1908
was the counterrevolution of April 1909. The counterrevolution
witnessed a mass uprising and its ruthless suppression, massacres
of Armenians, and the deposition of Abdülhamid II.

In April 1909, an armed uprising broke out in Istanbul. The
mutinous troops and the religious students who joined the mob
marched to the palatial parliament building located adjacent to
the Hagia Sophia (designed by an Italian architect, the parliament
building burned down in a fire in 1933). The counterrevolutionaries

demanded the dismissal of a number of government ministers, including the grand vizier, the banishment of some CUP parliamentarians, and restoration of Islam and Islamic law.[32] Although Islamic law was still in effect in the empire, Western European secular law was increasingly practised, in part due to the opening of the empire to capitalism and world trade. Gathering at the Hippodrome, where they were joined by more soldiers and lower-ranking religious scholars, the protestors quickly took over Istanbul. The grand vizier resigned, and the counterrevolutionaries attacked and even killed CUP parliamentarians and destroyed the offices of their newspapers. The CUP was driven out of Istanbul or forced underground.

From their base in Macedonia, troops loyal to the CUP organised themselves as the Action Army. It was led by Mahmut Şevket Pasha, the hero of the revolution of 1908, and included mainly Albanian volunteers along with Turks, Armenians, Bulgarians, Greeks, and a Jewish battalion from Salonica. The army was sent by train to Istanbul to defend the constitution, shed blood in the name of brotherhood, and suppress the insurrection. It accomplished all of these aims in less than two weeks. With the rebels holed up in the artillery barracks in what is today Gezi Park in Taksim Square, the Action Army bombed the barracks and partly destroyed them before the rebels surrendered.[33] Jewish volunteers suffered dozens of casualties taking the neighbourhood from the counterrevolutionaries.

Meanwhile, news of the counterrevolution had incited Turks, Kurds, Circassians, and Muslim refugees in the southern Anatolian city of Adana to express their anti-CUP feelings by massacring tens of thousands of Armenians with the complicity of local governmental and army officials.[34] Local notables and religious students in Adana and the surrounding region opposed the new visibility of Armenian political parties and cultural institutions, which they blamed on the reinstitution of the constitution and parliament. Despite the complete destruction of the Armenian quarter of the city and many adjacent Armenian villages, the CUP responded leniently towards the main culprits, not wishing to exacerbate hostility against itself. Nevertheless, in the wake of the massacres in Adana and surrounding region, on 20 August 1909 the newly appointed interior minister Mehmed Talat and the CUP signed an accord with the Armenian Revolutionary Federation to cooperate 'to save the Ottoman fatherland from separation and division' and to defend the constitution against reactionaries.[35]

The CUP was deeply shaken by the counterrevolution and used it as a pretext to restrict the freedoms granted by the constitution, thereby strengthening the party's grip over the empire. The counterrevolution confirmed CUP leaders' belief that Muslim 'reactionaries' were among their greatest enemies. Within days of the surrender of the rebels, the parliament—representing the nation, the will of the people—deposed Abdülhamid II. It sent the last of the strong sultans and caliphs to house arrest in Salonica, the city from whence the CUP had launched its own coup. It replaced Abdülhamid II with his younger brother, the Mevlevi Sufi Mehmed Reşad, who became Mehmed V (reigned 1909–1918). Blaming the counterrevolution on the Muslim Union—the organisation of religious extremists that had protested against women's rights and in favour of Islamic law—the army, ruling under martial law, executed its leader, the Nakşibendi sheikh Dervish Vahdeti.

Alongside religious Muslim opposition to the CUP, several other factors had been at work to spark the counterrevolution. They included tensions between the young officers and revolutionaries trained in the new academies and the undereducated officers and soldiers loyal to the sultan who had been hurt by the CUP's mass purge of their ranks. The Liberal opposition party in parliament also played a major role in the revolt. But this pragmatic alliance between secularists and Islamists instigating revolt instead brought about military rule under the CUP. In the view of the CUP in 1909, however, this was a war between themselves—the representatives of enlightenment and progress—and the forces of reaction, represented by Sultan Abdülhamid II and the Muslim Union.

Abdülhamid II was placed under house arrest in a Jewish villa built by the architect Vitaliano Poselli.[36] Mehmed Cavid was part of the delegation that relayed to Abdülhamid II the news of his downfall. This Freemason and former Feyziye school principal was the most influential Dönme government minister who came to power after the sultan was deposed.[37]

After the revolution, the Dönme Cavid served in the new parliament from 1908 to 1918 and was one of the leaders of the CUP in 1916 and 1917. He was finance minister between 1909 and 1912, and again in 1917 and 1918. Although influential, Cavid was overshadowed by his fellow Salonicans Mehmed Talat and Enver Bey, who were not of Dönme origins.[38]

The overrepresentation of Dönme in the CUP allowed conspiracy theorists to believe the revolution of 1908 was a Dönme or Jewish plot, even though most of the new elite was not Dönme, most Dönme were not members of the new elite, and the Dönme were distinct from Jews. Revolutionaries who had Jewish background but did not consider themselves Jewish played down their origins. So, too, did others who were falsely considered Jewish, such as the radical Mustafa Kemal. Although Mustafa Kemal did not have Jewish ancestors, he was accused of acting on behalf of 'secret Jews'.[39]

Mustafa Kemal was born in Ottoman Salonica in 1881. Salonica boasted a Francophone Muslim and Dönme elite who incorporated the latest pedagogical methods in their schools. Mustafa Kemal benefited from the 'new type of education', which combined Ottoman and modern French schooling courses and methods. Although the family lived in a Muslim rather than a Dönme neighbourhood, Mustafa Kemal's progressive father enrolled him in the exclusive primary school of Dönme leader Şemsi Efendi. This fact has stoked the fire of conspiracy theories about his identity, as has the fact that 'Dönme' in Turkish slang means 'passive homosexual'. Mustafa Kemal's conservative mother had first insisted he go to the local religious Muslim school instead.[40] But after a few days at the Muslim school, he switched to the Dönme school, which was attacked repeatedly by conservative Muslims. Şemsi Efendi's school taught Dönme and Muslim religious principles, not secularism. Mustafa Kemal lost his father when he was seven, and one could argue he spent the subsequent years searching for a replacement father. One day he would claim to be the father of all Turks, calling himself Atatürk.

Mustafa Kemal founded the Fatherland and Freedom Society in Damascus in 1905, and had come to Salonica to open a branch in that city. While he may or may not have actually opened one, he was in contact with other opposition politicians. In the end, the Fatherland and Freedom Society became the Ottoman Freedom Society, established by Mehmed Talat and Enver. All of the members of this group were Freemasons, and one was a leading Sufi; it merged with the CUP in 1907. Mustafa Kemal was a member of that generation of revolutionaries who would bring down the Ottoman dynasty.

A CHANGED IDEOLOGY AT
THE CENTRE OF POWER

The Young Turks shared a worldview. They were Muslim men of diverse background born between 1875 and 1885, most Rûmis. They were educated in the new leading institutions of the empire, including the new military medical colleges. They formed an elite of military officers and bureaucrats who shaped the politics of the last decades of the empire.[41] They saw the rising Christian middle class as a threat. They conceived of a future empire without Christians, whom they began to equate with foreigners, while at the same time perceiving European bourgeois culture as a model to be adopted and adapted.[42] Tellingly, they banned Christians and Jews from membership in the Ottoman Freedom Society in Salonica when it was founded in 1906.

Having been educated in the new science-oriented colleges, they shared a belief in rationality, progress, and enlightenment and were heavily influenced by French and German thinkers.[43] Contrary to traditional Ottoman attitudes, they also believed that authority did not come from age. In their view, it arose from education. The Young Turks were no peaceniks. From the beginning, they used violence to achieve their aims and take power. These young men believed that the future was theirs to shape. The fact that they were able to topple the elderly, seemingly all-powerful Abdülhamid II, whose spies and police were everywhere, gave them an unbreakable confidence in their own potential. Seeing themselves as saviours of the empire, they were haunted by the fear that Muslim opponents could undo their enlightening mission, such as occurred with the counterrevolution of 1909. Referring to their opponents as 'reactionaries', they despised religious leaders and were jealous of their ability to whip up the masses with accusations of alleged Young Turk atheism and desecration of holy places. Their religious opponents spread rumours of their wine drinking and alleged entering of mosques with their shoes on.

Most of these Young Turks served with the Ottoman army in Southeastern Europe fighting guerrilla warfare against paramilitary bands of Bulgarian, Greek, Macedonian, and Serbian revolutionaries. The fight was especially vicious in Macedonia. A terrorist group known as the Internal Macedonian Revolutionary Organisation, formed by schoolteachers in Salonica in 1893, bombed banks, post offices, and cafés, assassinated and kidnapped government officials, robbed and murdered local notables, burned government buildings, and fomented uprisings to gain national independence.[44] Violence was not an outgrowth of nationalism, but a force that helped create it.[45] The Young Turks' experiences strengthened their view that a life-and-death struggle between nations was taking place, a view that caused them to consider all Christians as terrorists supported by foreign powers.[46] They adopted the nationalism and military tactics of their enemy. Enver Bey, Mustafa Kemal, and others would organise guerrilla resistance against the invading Italians in Libya after 1911. Again and again, CUP officers and self-sacrificing volunteers (suicide squadrons) used violent guerrilla tactics.

The revolution of 1908 and the counterrevolution a year later confirmed for the Young Turk leadership that they faced two life-and-death struggles. One was between Ottoman Christians and foreigners on the one side, and Muslim Turks on the other. The other was an all-important internal battle between Muslims. The Young Turks claimed to be civilised, enlightened, modern, progressive, revolutionary Muslims facing off against religious, reactionary, traditional Muslims.[47]

They also had an imperial view. They were on a mission to save the empire. As an intellectual elite, they saw themselves as the vanguard, steamrolling change in society. This entitled them to lead top-down, radical changes. For them, the empire was more important than the individual, who was expected to sacrifice his or her life if need be.[48] For this reason, after the revolution of 1908 they violently suppressed labour unrest, banned trade unions, and made industrial action nearly impossible.[49] Between 1909 and 1912 the CUP-dominated parliament passed legislation limiting free speech, a free press, and the right to assembly and to form associations.

The Young Turks were militarists who believed in social Darwinism as taught to them by their German military instructors.[50] Darwinism is the scientific theory that evolution favours those organisms that fit their environment and their time, those with inherited traits that best allow them to survive and reproduce. Social Darwinism was an imperialist, colonialist theory of a struggle for survival waged between races or nations. It was war on a global scale. The Prussian general Colmar von der Goltz had taught the Young Turks at the Ottoman Royal Military Academy that the only way for the Turkish nation to 'earn its right to live' among other nations was by making the Turks into 'a nation in arms' at the expense of those other nations.[51] This belief promoted the sentiment that 'every Turk is born a soldier' and every man is called upon to die for his fatherland. Instilled with the conviction that the empire must be a military nation led by army officers, the Young Turks conceived of the world in terms that propelled them to kill rather than be killed.

The CUP leadership was also anti-religion.[52] These secularists and atheists used Islam consciously as a tool, treating religion as the stimulant, not the opiate, of the masses. Like the sultans who preceded them, they used Islam to propagate loyalty to themselves, to increase the bonds among their followers, and to inspire and mobilise them against their enemies. At the same time, they presented their enemies as reactionaries and obscurantists who hindered the progress of the nation.

Echoing the Ottoman 'science' of reading the fate written on one's forehead to determine who is most fit for palace service— used for centuries in the selection of Collection recruits—the CUP promoted phrenology to prove theories about the hierarchies of races. Phrenology is the disgraced pseudoscience that links the form of the skull to intellectual abilities and moral character. As proponents of the view that science could solve all social problems, the Young Turks absorbed Western European ideas about race. These included the Frenchman Gustave Le Bon's obsession with protecting the superior race—in his case, white Europeans—and Edmond Demolins's inquiry into the alleged superiority of the Anglo-Saxons. The Young Turks simply replaced the Anglo-Saxons or white races with the Turks. After Japan's victory over Russia in 1905, leading thinkers such as Russian Turk Yusuf Akçura promoted Turkish nationalism based on race.

Akçura's article 'Three Kinds of Policy' played a role in the advancement of Turkism similar to that played by Friedrich Engels and Karl Marx's *The Communist Manifesto* in the spread of communism. In the article, Akçura argued that the best choice among Ottomanism, Islamism, and Turkism was the latter.[53] Akçura had been educated at the Ottoman Royal Military Academy in Istanbul. An opponent of Abdülhamid II, he had been exiled and ended up in Paris, where he studied at the École Libre des Sciences Politiques (today Sciences Po). He returned to Istanbul in 1908 following the revolution. He promoted Turkist idealism by editing the journal *Turkish Homeland* and serving as a professor of political history.

'Three Kinds of Policy' was published in 1904 in Cairo in the extreme nationalist Young Turk journal *Türk*. It was published again in Istanbul as a pamphlet in 1912. In this work, Akçura argued that the political project of Ottomanism—to create an Ottoman nation based on a union of the empire's diverse peoples through loyalty to the dynasty—had failed in part due to the rise of nationalism.[54]

Pan-Islamism, the political unification of all Muslims through loyalty to the caliph sultan, was an impossibility, he claimed. The Ottomans did not rule over all Muslims, who were divided among competing empires. He concluded that the only viable political strategy was the 'creation of a Turkish political nation based on race' and the unification of the primarily Muslim Turkic peoples, including those beyond the Ottoman borders in the Caucasus and Russia. Nationalism would be the determining force of the future.

Casting aside the Arabs and Christians of the empire, Akçura argued that Turkism, an idea still in its infancy, held the most advantages. Since ethno-religious bonds were stronger than religious bonds alone, Ottoman Turks would be strongly united, joined by Muslim elements that were already Turkified. He added ominously that other elements would be Turkified by force.[55]

In his racialised fantasy, he envisioned the unification of all Eurasian Turkic peoples, from East Asia to Southeastern Europe and Africa, with the Ottoman Empire at its centre. The Turkish world would join the 'white' and 'yellow' races in a middle position, and the Ottoman Empire would assume the duty in Turkic-majority Eurasia that Japan sought as leader of East Asian states.

For Akçura, Turkism comprised not only the great sultans and intellectuals of Ottoman history, but also the Oğuz (the Central

Asian people to whom the Ottomans traced their origins), Genghis Khan, and Timur Lenk (Tamerlane). Akçura's way of thinking was revolutionary. But his prediction of the rise of Turkism was an omen for the unravelling of the empire of conversion and the separation and decimation of some of its component peoples.

NATIONALISM, THE BALKAN WARS, AND A COUP

After the 1908 revolution, Austria annexed Bosnia and Herzegovina. Bulgaria declared independence. The large island of Crete proclaimed union with Greece. The Cretans had supported the 1821 Greek rebellion and engaged in several insurrections against the Ottomans from the 1860s to the 1890s. Following the 1889 revolt and further violence in 1896, including massacres of Cretan Christians and Muslims, the Ottomans had offered Crete autonomy, appointment of a Christian governor, and the election of an assembly, two-thirds of whose members would be Christians. But Greece sent troops to the island and declared Crete part of Greece. In 1897, Greece and the Ottoman Empire fought a thirty-day war in Epirus, in northwestern Greece, and Thessaly, in eastern Greece, to settle the Cretan question. The Ottoman army, whose officers were trained by German advisors and whose soldiers were equipped with the latest German rifles and field artillery, was victorious.[56] After receiving a large war indemnity from Greece, the Ottomans conceded to make Crete an autonomous part of the empire with a high commissioner chosen by Britain, France, and Russia, who selected a Greek prince. Ottoman troops left the island accompanied by a mass exodus of Cretan Muslims.[57] A decade later when Cretans again declared they had joined Greece, the Ottomans could do nothing to stop them. In 1911, Italy invaded Libya, then took the Dodecanese islands, including Rhodes—an island within sight of the Anatolian coast conquered by Suleiman I in 1522.

Worst of all for the Ottomans were the two Balkan Wars. In October 1912, an alliance of former Ottoman provinces, now the independent states of Bulgaria, Greece—which had rearmed and reformed its army and navy with assistance from Britain, France, and Germany—Montenegro, and Serbia, declared war on the empire in order to seize its few remaining European provinces including Macedonia. Macedonia was a rich agricultural region and home to Salonica, one of the Ottoman Empire's largest, most industrialised port cities best connected by rail, and the birthplace of the Young Turks. This was the First Balkan War.

Attacked on multiple fronts, the unprepared Ottoman army was quickly defeated by the Bulgarians at Kırkkilise ('Forty Churches', now Kırklareli, 'The Place of the Forty') and Lüleburgaz, in Thrace; by the Serbs moving south into Kosovo, Skopje, and Lake Ohrid in Macedonia; by the Serbs and Montenegrins besieging Durazzo, Albania, on the Adriatic coast; and by the Greeks who besieged Ioannina in northwestern Greece. The Ottomans worried Salonica would fall and sent deposed sultan Abdülhamid II to the imperial capital, where he would pass away six years later. Ottoman forces withdrew to within fifty kilometres of Istanbul. By November the Bulgarian army besieged Edirne, the second Ottoman seat of the dynasty, from 1369 to 1453. On 8 November, as Bulgarian forces also drew near, the Ottomans surrendered Salonica—first captured in 1430 and the hometown of the CUP's leaders—to the Greek army. This led to the mass expulsion of Southeastern European Muslims to the empire and compelled the Ottomans to demand a cease-fire. According to the armistice signed in December 1912, the Ottomans granted independence to Albania. The Western powers wanted the Ottomans to give up Edirne as well.

It seemed the government would accede to this plan. Political opposition had grown to the CUP hold on power since 1909. In spring 1912, the CUP seemed on the verge of losing its dominance to a new party that united conservatives and liberals. The CUP contrived to dissolve parliament and engineered new elections, accompanied by much violence, making sure its candidates won. But an anti-CUP group of officers demanded the government resign or face insurrection. That summer the government was replaced by a unity cabinet that was as opposed to the role of the military in politics as it was to the CUP. It dominated parliament, dissolved the CUP, and began to exile or arrest leading members of that organisation. It was this anti-CUP government that was in power during the First Balkan War.

The decision to surrender Edirne caused the CUP to seize direct power by the barrel of a gun. On 23 January 1913, Mehmed Talat and Enver Bey along with a few CUP officers stormed a cabinet meeting and killed the grand vizier's guards and the minister of war. Enver Bey put his pistol to the head of Grand Vizier Kâmil Pasha, forcing his resignation.[58] Sensing a weakness at the Ottoman centre, the Balkan states relaunched their attacks. In March 1913, the Ottomans surrendered Ioannina to Greece and Edirne fell to the Bulgarians. A new armistice and peace treaty in April confirmed the loss of the latter city, the former Ottoman capital, the hearth of the gazis. The CUP had failed in its primary aim.

But fortunately for the Ottomans, the Second Balkan War broke out in June and the Balkan states turned on each other. Each wanted to maximise its territorial gains at the expense of the others. All sides attacked Bulgaria. Enver seized the chance and led forces to retake Edirne in July. Despite this victory, the greatest consequence of the Balkan Wars was the loss of almost all remaining Ottoman territory in Europe, including some of the empire's oldest provinces—Albania, Macedonia, and western Thrace—acquired as early as the fourteenth century.

The wars exacerbated anti-Christian sentiment in the empire. Efforts began in 1912 during the Balkan Wars to create a 'national economy' by organising boycotts of Christian (whether Ottoman or foreign) merchants and businesses. As a result of the two Balkan Wars, nearly 350,000 Muslims from Southeastern Europe migrated to the empire, almost half settling in the western coastal regions of Anatolia.[59] In 1914, the Ottomans abrogated the capitulations—the trade privileges and concessions granted to European Christian powers since the Renaissance—through which the class of Ottoman subjects protected by those foreign powers had grown exponentially over the course of the nineteenth century. The CUP aimed to replace the rising Ottoman Christian, Jewish, and European merchant class with a Muslim Turkish bourgeoisie. What they envisioned was a massive transfer of wealth and property. As part of these efforts, in June 1914 Mehmed Talat ordered the expulsion of over 150,000 Greeks, half from the area where the largest number of Balkan migrants had settled on the Aegean coast. By his own calculations, Mehmed Talat determined that the Greeks had to abandon over one million *dunum* of valuable arable fields, vineyards, gardens, orchards, and olive groves, thousands of farm animals, and tens of thousands of homes, stores, and windmills—all of which were redistributed to Muslims.[60]

Traumatised by the massacres of Muslims in Southeastern Europe, humiliated on the battlefield, and having lost their homelands, the CUP leaders sought revenge on perceived enemies. They had surrendered their ancestral Southeastern Europe and Aegean islands, controlled by the Ottomans for half a millennium, so they turned to Anatolia, adopting it as the new fatherland, the final place to make their stand. Other peoples who stood in their way would be damned, leading to population expulsions, ethnic cleansing, forcible assimilation, massacre, deportation, and genocide.[61] Nationalist movements within the empire—Arab, Greek, Jewish (Zionist), and Kurdish—had gained supporters. But in the CUP's conspiratorial, paranoid view, one group in particular stood in their way of saving the empire: the Armenians.

21

THE GENOCIDE OF THE ARMENIANS AND THE FIRST WORLD WAR

Talat Pasha

W HEN THE CUP came to power in the constitutional revolution of 1908, a mass was held in Istanbul at the Holy
Trinity Armenian Church. It was attended by Ottoman officials and members of all religious communities, including the
sheikhulislam, the supreme Muslim religious authority in the
empire. After the ceremony, the crowd went to Taksim Garden,
where thousands celebrated Turkish-Armenian brotherhood.[1]
One of the main hopes of the revolution was that it would bring
about brotherhood and equal citizenship in the empire, uniting
its diverse peoples behind Ottomanism, which transcended ethno-religious difference. But it failed.

A year later, the CUP faced a countercoup by mutinous soldiers and religious students, which caused its leaders to see hidden
conspiracies everywhere, allowing them to justify their militarist
rule and martial law. That same year witnessed the massacre of
tens of thousands of Armenians in and around Adana, victims of
opponents of the CUP who viewed Armenians as CUP supporters
who benefited from newfound freedoms. Constitutionalism did
not bring about equal rights, as the CUP and the leaders of the

constituent peoples of the empire did not want to give up their place in the order of things; Ottoman Muslims did not intend to relinquish their position as the empire's ruling element. The CUP's leaders were not committed to constitutionalism but used it as a means to their end of centralising the empire behind their party's rule, assimilating difference, privileging Ottoman Turks, and doing away with the rights granted to others by the former social and political order.

For their part, the leaders of the various ethno-religious communities were intent on preserving the privileges, power, and authority granted to them over the previous six centuries. Yet their constituents were intent on overthrowing the old leadership and embarking on more democratic, often secular, forms of internal communal rule, including national assemblies to elect their own leadership, administrative decentralisation, and multilingualism. The new freedoms, including freedom of the press, and political democratisation in the empire and within communities meant more, not less, emphasis on separate culture and nationalism. Politicians and community leaders exiled or jailed by Sultan Abdül-hamid II had returned from abroad or were released.

Kurdish intellectuals who supported the CUP had begun producing journals in exile, and, after 1908, in the empire, such as *Kurdistan*. Yet at the same time, many of the Kurdish *aghas* (large landlords) and sheikhs opposed the CUP. From 1909 onward there were numerous rebellions in southeastern Anatolia, northern Syria, and northern Iraq promoting regional autonomy. Outlawed underground political groups became political parties, advocating for political autonomy for their ethno-national group. Armenian parties were among them.

As part of the Period of Reforms, since 1863, Ottoman Armenians had had a national constitution that defined the powers of the patriarch within the empire, as well as an Armenian National Assembly. Since the second half of the nineteenth century, they had witnessed the rise of an Armenian merchant class, an explosion in the number of Armenian periodicals, and new educational institutions that spread literacy and promoted Armenian cultural and national consciousness. At the turn of the twentieth century, they demanded either political autonomy for Armenian-majority regions or complete equality for Armenians.

Following the coup of 1913, with Sultan Abdülhamid II's successor Sultan Mehmed V now irrelevant, the empire was in the hands of Enver Pasha as minister of war, Mehmed Talat Pasha as interior minister, and Cemal Pasha as minister of the navy, commander of the Fourth Army, and military governor of Syria. The path was opened to implement their ideology of social Darwinism, or survival of the fittest, for saving the empire. It included turning fully away from an empire that recognised and tolerated difference.

In 1913, these men established a single-party dictatorship, a militarist regime headed by a conspiratorial revolutionary committee. In the crucible of war, they would promote a Muslim empire that was to be achieved through violent demographic engineering.[2] Ripping up the Ottoman social contract, they promoted the interests of Muslims and Turks at the expense of other elements of society, considering them no longer compatriots or citizens but enemies. This began during the Balkan Wars of 1912–1913 with anti-Christian boycotts and the ethnic cleansing tactic known as 'population exchanges', with which the Balkan countries expelled hundreds of thousands of Muslims and the Ottomans drove an equal number of Christians out of western Anatolia and their remaining European territories. Soon the regime turned to bloodshed.[3]

The ruling pashas adopted CUP central committee member Ziya Gökalp's vision that 'the people are the garden, we are the gardeners', entrusted to enact 'purifying' social engineering of the homeland.[4] From 1913 they implemented a strict state of emergency in the empire lasting five years—which they justified with the threat of domestic uprising and foreign invasion—and used violence, intimidation, coercion, corruption, and lawlessness. The parliament that was elected in winter 1913–1914 was controlled by the CUP. Acting like the secretive, irredentist Christian guerrilla armies (Bulgarian, Greek, Macedonian, Serbian) of Southeastern Europe they admired, yet with the reins of an empire at their command, the CUP leaders promoted perpetual war at home and abroad. They would stifle all dissent and kill all their enemies, real and imagined, including former allies, journalists, civilians, women, children, and lawmakers from 1913 to 1918.

In June 1915, Ottoman Armenian member of parliament Krikor Zohrab, once on close terms with Mehmed Talat Pasha— they used to play backgammon together—asked for an explanation for why the regime was targeting Armenians. After all, the CUP had made an alliance with the Armenian Revolutionary Federation while in opposition in Paris in 1907. The two groups had made another accord in Istanbul after the countercoup of 1909. The Armenian Revolutionary Federation had been a member of the CUP-led parliamentary bloc, and Zohrab had been a member of the CUP-led coalition in parliament. Nevertheless, he was arrested on orders of Interior Minister Talat Pasha and assassinated while being transferred to prison.[5] In Talat Pasha's view, Armenians stood in the way of the establishment of a secure empire based in Anatolia.

Other options for saving the empire were available. The CUP could have chosen peace, liberalism, constitutionalism, equality, parliamentarianism, reform, partnership, and cooperation with the Ottoman Liberal Party and Armenian political groups, especially the Armenian Revolutionary Federation. They could have strengthened the remaining, smaller territory in their control. But in attempting to maximise their territory, the regime leaders chose war, bloodshed, dictatorship, and genocide. They did not want Anatolia to be like Macedonia, their homeland, now lost to the empire.[6] As a result, the CUP's legacy is fearsome: military coups and states of emergency; an uncompromising nationalism, militarism, and quest for centralised control; and cycles of collective violence and denial of violence with no accountability for the perpetrators.[7]

ENTERING THE FIRST WORLD WAR AND CARRYING OUT THE GENOCIDE

When Serbian militants assassinated Archduke Franz Ferdinand, the presumptive heir to the throne of Austria-Hungary, in Sarajevo in June 1914, the Ottoman regime first sought an anti-Serbian alliance with England and France, which was rebuffed, and then with Germany, which was supported by Kaiser Wilhelm II (reigned 1888–1918). Germany and members of the Ottoman regime, including Enver Pasha and Mehmed Talat Pasha, signed a secret agreement in August in which the Ottomans pledged to join the war on Germany's side against Russia. Germany promised to play a leading military role within the Ottoman Empire and defend its territory. Together with their German allies, Ottoman leaders believed, a call to jihad by the Ottoman sheikhulislam would help the war effort by inspiring insurrection among colonised Muslims around the world and incite Muslims in the empire to mobilise to fight. Britain, with its hundreds of millions of Muslim subjects, especially in South Asia, was one target, and France, which ruled over tens of millions of Muslims, mainly in Africa, was the other. But the CUP quickly moved to sideline the sheikhulislam, removing him from the cabinet in 1916 and limiting his jurisdiction, as well as bringing the Islamic law courts under the control of the Ministry of Justice and the Islamic colleges under the purview of the Ministry of Education.[8] The call to jihad was nothing more than war propaganda.

Germany would help the Ottomans avenge their enemies. Following the losses in the Balkan Wars, a humiliated Enver Pasha wrote, 'Our hatred is intensifying: revenge, revenge, revenge, there is nothing else'.[9] Since the 1878 Treaty of Berlin, Germany and the Ottoman Empire had had close economic relations, of which the Berlin-Baghdad railway is most famous. Even closer were diplomatic and especially military relations. Kaiser Wilhelm II made official visits to Istanbul in 1889 and 1898, bestowing an ornate fountain on the Hippodrome two years later. Ottoman cadets were routinely sent to Potsdam to train at the German war academy, emerging as officers in the German army. The Ottoman military academy had been reformed and was run by German officers. Enver Pasha had served as military attaché at the Ottoman embassy in Berlin from 1909 to 1911, where he was a media star, the face of the renewed, post–Abdülhamid II Ottoman Empire. Enver Bey brand cigarettes were advertised ubiquitously in the German capital.[10] More ominously, imperial Germany's chancellor Otto von Bismarck had urged the Ottomans to avoid implementing reforms that would ameliorate the Armenians' condition in the eastern provinces. Other German officials had justified the Ottoman massacres of Armenians from 1894 to 1896, blaming the victims for having provoked their punishment and giving full support to Sultan Abdülhamid II and his view that 'the Armenians are rebels who attack with sword and dynamite'.[11]

Thanks to these ties, the Ottomans entered the First World War on the side of Germany in autumn 1914. Hundreds of German officers and tens of thousands of German soldiers aided the Ottoman war effort. Bronsart von Schellendorf was chief of general staff. Otto Liman von Sanders served as head of the German military mission from 1913 to the end of the war in 1918, as well as commander of the Ottoman Fifth Army. The seventy-year-old Colmar von der Goltz, who had taught the Young Turks about social Darwinism at the Ottoman Royal Military Academy, headed the Ottoman Sixth Army. The German chief of general staff, General Erich von Falkenhayn, was given command of the Palestine front. Rudolf Höss, future commandant of the Nazi death camp Auschwitz, killed men for the first time while fighting for the Ottomans on the Iraqi front.[12]

A key reason for the Ottomans joining the First World War allied with Germany was the opportunity to fight against archenemy Russia. Russia was long seen as having meddled in Ottoman affairs on behalf of the Armenians. That some Ottoman Armenians joined the Russians during the war was enough to confirm to the Ottoman regime that all Armenians were traitors. In fact, many more Ottoman Armenians enlisted in the Ottoman army and battled against Russia.[13] In October 1914, the Ottoman navy began attacking the Russian fleet in the Black Sea. By November, the Ottomans were at war with Russia's Triple Entente allies Britain and France as well.

Seeing the Ottoman Empire as a European power changes the conventional narration of the war. The focus has generally been on Britain, France, and Germany, with less attention paid to the Ottomans and Russians. But rather than focusing on the trenches on the western front, we turn to the battles in the East, where major campaigns were fought from 1914 to 1918, revealing once again that the events and developments of European history are best depicted on a broad canvas stretching from London to Baghdad and beyond.

Thinking they would quickly defeat the Ottomans and thereby accelerate the war's end, the leaders of the Triple Entente found instead that they were mired in costly campaigns in Ottoman territories that lengthened the war.[14] Great Britain sent two and a half million troops to the Ottoman fronts; at one point, one quarter of its armed forces was deployed there. Twenty percent of Russian troops were engaged against the Ottomans in 1916, the year before the Bolshevik Revolution.[15] Moreover, war gave the Ottoman regime the opportunity to annihilate the Armenians, whom they blamed for their failures.

The regime began to turn against the Armenians after the Battle of Sarıkamış, on the Caucasus frontier, against Russia (December 1914–January 1915). Enver Pasha took command of the one hundred thousand troops of the Ottoman Third Army to attack

Russia on the mountainous eastern frontier. In late December 1914, he launched a surprise attack on the Russian Caucasus army, hoping to capture the town of Sarıkamış and retake the provinces in eastern Anatolia lost in the 1878 war. But it was the middle of winter, when the region is blanketed by freezing cold and heavy snow. Facing blizzards, lacking adequate provisions, tents, winter shoes, and cold-weather garments, and carrying only light weapons, the Ottoman Third Army was decimated, losing more than eighty thousand soldiers, most of whom froze to death. Enver Pasha's chief of staff reported seeing a soldier by the side of the road stuffing handfuls of snow into his mouth as he screamed. He 'had gone insane. In this way we left 10,000 men behind under the snow in just one day'.[16] Thousands more were lost to friendly fire, as in thick fog one Ottoman regiment mistook another for Russians. Only one-fifth of the Third Army survived.[17] The disaster left the eastern borderlands exposed to depredation, as Russian troops massacred Muslim villagers.

During the Sarıkamış campaign, some Ottoman Armenian soldiers had crossed over to the Russian side. Ottoman Muslim soldiers began to turn on the Armenians in their ranks, shooting their fellow soldiers, blaming them for giving information about their movements to the Russians. Their actions were reflected by views at the top, as Enver Pasha blamed the disaster on the Armenians, not on his own arrogance and terrible planning. Only months earlier the CUP had proposed an alliance with the two main Armenian political parties—the Social-Democratic Party of the Bell and the Armenian Revolutionary Federation—promising autonomy and Armenian administration in part of eastern Anatolia. Furious at Russian meddling in their empire, they had hypocritically urged Armenian anti-Russian activity across the border. When Ottoman Armenian political leaders refused to stir up trouble in Russia, the proposal was abandoned.

In the middle of January 1915, soon after the failed Ottoman attack on the Russians at Sarıkamış, Cemal Pasha led a campaign against the British in the Sinai at the Suez Canal. Like Enver Pasha, Cemal Pasha also believed in the impossible, that he could take the enemy by surprise and defeat it with inadequate numbers of men and insufficient matériel. The Sinai was as hostile for an army as the Caucasus. Cemal Pasha's Fourth Army had only twenty-five thousand Arab, Bedouin, Druze, Kurdish, and Ottoman soldiers with which to defeat at least fifty thousand better-armed British, Egyptian, Indian, Australian, and New Zealander soldiers and their impressive arsenal, including warships defending the strategic canal.[18] The Ottomans were repelled and unable to take the waterway. Cemal Pasha retreated. Unlike Enver Pasha, he managed not to lose most of his army.

Following these two defeats, the Ottomans faced the Gallipoli campaign. The British and the French sent their warships to take the Dardanelles, the strait that leads from the Aegean to the Sea of Marmara and Istanbul, with the aim of compelling the Ottomans to surrender and thereby hastening the end of the war. The first attacks caused panic in Istanbul and plans to relocate the dynasty, government, and gold reserves to Eskişehir in Anatolia.[19] The regime sought a scapegoat for these setbacks, which they feared would lead to a Russian or British occupation of Istanbul. They found it in the Armenians. Deluded by conspiracy theories about the Armenians, they could not grasp that the most dangerous internal enemies conspiring with foreign powers were the Christian and Muslim Arabs who were plotting with the British and French to divide up the empire in a postwar settlement.

Serving as governor-general of Syria and commander of the Fourth Army during the war, Cemal Pasha acted brutally towards any hint of disloyalty. He used the long-practised Ottoman policy of deportation, exiling tens of thousands of rebellious Arabs, and ordered the public hangings of scores of Arab separatists. The execution sites in Beirut and Damascus are still known as Martyrs' Square. Cemal Pasha initiated a surprising shift in Ottoman policy, considering the overall close relations between the CUP regime and Ottoman Jewish leadership and the fact that the Jewish press in the Ottoman Empire and Central Europe continued to give the Ottomans positive coverage. He deported thousands of Jews from Jaffa, Palestine, perceiving them to be dangerous separatists, until ally Germany and Mehmed Talat Pasha intervened to stop him. But what Jews faced in Palestine from Cemal Pasha was nothing like Talat Pasha's policies directed against the Armenians in Anatolia.[20]

In hindsight, the Ottomans should have paid more attention to the Arabs. The Arab Revolt of 1916 and 1917 and the British campaign in Sinai and Palestine in 1917 would end four hundred years of Ottoman rule of the Islamic holy cities of Mecca, Medina, and Jerusalem. The loss of these regions would lead to the collapse of the Ottoman war effort and ultimately contribute to the downfall of the dynasty. It was not Armenians conspiring with Russians that posed the gravest threat to the empire, but Arabs plotting with the British.

Hussein, the sharif of Mecca, an Arab descendant of Muhammad, and thus a man with religious legitimacy among Muslims, and an opponent of the CUP's centralising measures, had refused to back the Ottoman call for jihad. He decided instead to take advantage of the First World War and rebel, and he was strongly backed by the British. The rebellion began in summer 1916 in the Hijaz region of western Arabia, with the Arabs at war with the Ottomans. Shells from an Ottoman hilltop garrison in Mecca hit the Great Mosque, set fire to the canopy over the Ka'ba (the shrine that is Muslims' holiest place), and destroyed the name of seventh-century caliph Uthman on the mosque's façade. The defenders took the latter as an omen that the dynasty would fall: the Turkish equivalent of 'Uthman' is 'Osman'.[21]

Although the Ottomans' machine guns and cannons gave them a military advantage against Sharif Hussein's Bedouin cavalry, British warships, airplanes, and artillery eventually tipped the balance in favour of the rebels and the Ottomans lost the Hijaz. It was when the Arab Revolt was placed under British command in 1917 that the Ottomans lost the Sinai, Baghdad, and Jerusalem— in short, the Middle East.[22] After 401 years of Ottoman rule, Jerusalem became British prime minister David Lloyd George's 'Christmas present for the British nation'.[23] The white bedsheet that the Ottomans used to signal their surrender of the city is now held in the Imperial War Museum London.[24]

Major campaigns on the Ottoman front in the Middle East played a critical role in the history of the First World War. But at a secret meeting in Istanbul in January 1915, seeing the Armenian bogeyman everywhere, Talat Pasha, Enver Pasha, Cemal Pasha, Dr. Nazım, and Dr. Bahaettin Şakir decided to annihilate the Armenian population. According to Dr. Nazım, the war gave them the opportunity to attack 'blameless Armenian women, children and populace'. Even though this would be savagery, he asked, 'Wasn't war itself savagery?'[25]

In February and March 1915, after the Ottomans failed to take the Suez Canal from the British and just as the Triple Entente began its naval campaign in the Dardanelles, Enver Pasha ordered tens of thousands of Armenian men serving in the Ottoman military in central and eastern Anatolia to turn in their weapons. Put into labour battalions, they would suffer a high death rate. Those who were not worked to death or killed en masse in 1915 were murdered in 1916.[26] These policies provoked rebellion by Armenians.

In March 1915, a minor rebellion served as an excuse to deport the entire Armenian population of the town of Zeytun in the southern Anatolian region of Cilicia, which had been an Armenian kingdom before the ancestors of the Ottomans had arrived in the region. Zeytun had seen an influx of Muslim refugees from the Balkans—some of whom were appointed governor, district governor, and police chief—contributing to tensions with Christians in the area. Britain, France, and Armenian organisations in Europe had considered an invasion of the Cilician coast in 1915 to open a new front in the war, but nothing came of these plans. Zeytun was made a conscription centre for the army, bringing more Muslims into the district and inciting Armenian men to flee to avoid recruitment into labour battalions. Armenian deserters and violent bandits caused further tension. In February, some young revolutionaries planned a rebellion, which was opposed by local church leaders and Armenian notables, who informed Muslim officials of their plans. Several dozen Armenians attacked Muslim soldiers and gendarmes and were joined by over a hundred supporters who took refuge in a local monastery at the beginning of March. They cut the telegraph wires, took several Muslim officials as hostages, and demanded that they be given the barracks and government building. Ottoman authorities used Armenian notables as go-betweens to secure the release of the hostages. The notables, merchants, landowners, church leaders, and majority of the Zeytun Armenian population opposed the rebellion and did not join.

At the end of March, the Ottoman army began its assault on the rebels in the monastery using German weapons including a Krupp cannon, but the rebels had fled to the mountains. The army seized the monastery and burned it to the ground. Over the next two weeks, they arrested all Armenians of military age in the vicinity and imprisoned the Zeytun notables who had helped them. They were later hanged. On the orders of Talat Pasha, by June the army had confiscated all the possessions of the Armenians of Zeytun and deported them without provision to an area in Konya known for its harsh climate. Of the twenty thousand Armenians sent to Konya, many died of starvation and disease. In August, the survivors were deported to Ras al-Ayn and Deir ez-Zor in the Syrian desert. Along the way many more died from lack of food and water. In these two Syrian locales, the Armenians were massacred. In Zeytun, their homes were given to Macedonian Muslims. The government renamed the town Süleymanlı in honour of a gendarme commander killed by Armenian rebels.[27]

Also in March 1915, Enver Pasha's brother-in-law Cevdet Bey was appointed governor of the eastern Anatolian province of Van, which had the largest concentration of Armenians in the empire.[28] Cevdet Bey's Kurdish and Circassian irregulars had engaged in massacres of Armenians in Iranian Azerbaijan, and they began to do the same in the Armenian villages outside the city of Van. In April they attacked Aigestan, the Armenian quarter of Van, where thousands of armed Armenians had barricaded themselves. The walled city was reduced to rubble. In May, Ottoman forces ended their siege and fled westward as the Russian army approached from the east. The Russians estimated their path was littered with over fifty thousand Armenian corpses, half the Armenian population of the region. On 18 May a detachment of Armenian soldiers fighting for Russia entered Van first. The Russians took over the city and citadel and appointed as governor Aram Manukian from the Armenian Revolutionary Federation. It was the first time in over five hundred years that an Armenian had ruled Van. Armenians and Russians took revenge on the Muslims who remained, massacring Kurds. The Russian advance into Anatolia was stopped by Cevdet Bey at Bitlis in July and the Russians decided to withdraw from Van, taking tens of thousands of Armenians with them. But before reaching safety in the Caucasus, one-third were killed in attacks by Kurds. The Ottomans retook Van. Van had been the CUP leaders' worst nightmare come true: Armenian rebellion leading to foreign occupation.[29]

In the midst of this event, on 24 April 1915, Interior Minister Mehmed Talat Pasha sent a telegram to twenty-five governors in Thrace, Anatolia, and Syria referring to what he perceived as the existential danger to the empire posed by the rebellions at Zeytun and especially Van, where 'traitorous' Ottoman Armenians conspired with Russian Armenians and the Russian army to attack the imperial domains, 'stabbing the Ottoman army in the back'. He ordered the governors to immediately close all branches of the two major Armenian political parties, confiscate their documents, arrest their party leaders and officers and any other Armenians deemed traitorous, and send them to suitable locations where they would be prosecuted in courts-martial.[30]

That night, the day before the Allied landing at Gallipoli, Talat Pasha ordered up to three hundred Armenian political leaders, educators, writers, clergy, and dignitaries in Istanbul jailed and tortured in Ibrahim Pasha's sixteenth-century palace on the Hippodrome. These men and at least one woman—the writer Zabel Yessayan, who managed to escape—were then taken to the Haydarpasha Train Station (a gift from Kaiser Wilhelm II, on the Asian side of the city), and shipped to Ankara and Kastamonu province, where they were hanged or shot.[31]

With German general Otto Liman von Sanders as commander in chief of the defence of the Dardanelles, the Ottomans were bogged down defending the straits over the ensuing eight and a half months. What had begun as a naval campaign had turned into a ground war. It became a squalid stalemate, waged by close-quarter trench warfare, just as on the western front. Thousands of men perished pointlessly for each hundred metres gained. Soldiers died by machine gun, artillery blast, exploding mines, bayonet blades, brush fire, and disease. The Gallipoli peninsula filled with corpses—on both sides the dead lay unburied, decomposing in the stifling heat. As one British soldier wrote,

> *The flies! Oh, God, the flies*
> *That soiled the sacred dead.*
> *To see them swarm from dead men's eyes*
> *And share the soldiers' bread.*
> *Nor think I now forget*
> *The filth and stench of war,*
> *The corpses on the parapet*
> *The maggots on the floor.*[32]

The Ottoman forces and their hero Colonel Mustafa Kemal defended the peninsula valiantly, managing to hold the high ground
while suffering a staggering casualty rate, as did the attacking
Allied forces. Divided evenly between the Allies (Australian,
British, French, Indian, and New Zealander forces) and the Ottomans, more than five hundred thousand of the eight hundred
thousand men who fought there between the Allied landing on
25 April 1915 and the Allies' final evacuation on 9 January 1916
were killed, taken prisoner, or wounded.[33] For the Ottomans, this
costly victory was well worth the price, for they were able to prevent the conquest of Istanbul. For the Triple Entente powers, who
thought they would quickly defeat the Ottomans and speed up the
end of the war, the result was the opposite. The Ottomans and the
Germans would continue to battle the British and French across
the Middle East in Iraq and Syria.

The Ottomans went on to defeat a British-Indian expeditionary
force at Kut in Iraq in April 1916, after which they employed the
prisoners of war in forced labour, but this was the last Ottoman
victory. After that battle, the Ottoman army could barely hold its
own in the Middle East. The army was devastated by hunger and
disease, including cholera, malaria, and typhus. Its soldiers were
poorly equipped and dressed in rags. It suffered a high desertion
rate—jihad or not—and lacked in transportation. Yet in 1915 it
was used to annihilate its fellow citizens.

ANNIHILATING THE ARMENIANS THROUGH
DEPORTATION AND MASSACRE

Having cut off the head of the Armenian nation by murdering
the top three hundred intellectual, religious, and cultural leaders
arrested on 24 April, the CUP regime went for the body under the
cover of war. Interior Minister Mehmed Talat Pasha authored the
provisional Deportation Law of 27 May, issued by the cabinet and
signed by Minister of War Enver Pasha, Grand Vizier Said Halim

Pasha (who resigned in 1917 and was replaced by Talat Pasha), and Sultan Mehmed V. Chilling for the latitude given to the military, the law authorised the army to 'deport individually or collectively, and to resettle elsewhere, the inhabitants of villages and towns suspected of treason or espionage, or according to military necessity'. The army was 'permitted and compelled to immediately punish in the most severe manner, or attack and annihilate in the event of [armed] resistance, those who in any manner opposed the carrying out of government decrees, or acts for the defense of the homeland and the establishment of public order'.[34]

From May until the end of summer, Talat Pasha issued further written orders, usually sent as telegrams from his personal telegraph machine in his home.[35] These telegrams sent to provincial governors in central and eastern Anatolia ordered them to use the army to deport Armenian men, women, and children to Ras al-Ayn and Deir ez-Zor in the Syrian desert and other camps along the Euphrates, under the oversight of the Interior Ministry.

At the same time, acting on secret, oral orders from CUP central committee members including Dr. Nazım and Dr. Bahaettin Şakir—the son of refugees from Bulgaria and head of the Special Organisation, formed from self-sacrificing CUP volunteers—the Special Organisation outfitted, paid, and commanded armed gangs made up of Southeastern European and Caucasian migrants, Turks, and Kurds to annihilate the caravans as they moved out of the towns.[36] According to the memoir of a former CUP central committee member, the gendarmerie received orders to turn deported Armenians over to bands of Special Organisation irregulars who were waiting for them at prearranged locations 'like vultures'. These caravans 'were dispatched like herds of sheep to the slaughterhouse'.[37]

The Armenian woman Pailadzo Captanian of the Black Sea port of Samsun survived the deportation. Her three- and five-year-old sons also lived because she gave them to a Greek family for safekeeping at the beginning of the forced journey. Her husband, however, did not survive, because at the beginning of the forced marches, men were often separated from women and children, tied together with ropes in small groups, taken to the outskirts of their towns, and shot dead, axed, or bayoneted. Pailadzo Captanian kept a diary recording the gruesome events that unfolded.[38]

At the beginning of July 1915, the Armenians of Samsun began their thousand-kilometre forced march by way of Aleppo to Deir ez-Zor in the Syrian desert, a wasteland not suitable for sustaining the lives of thousands of survivors weakened by a harrowing journey. As the convoy passed through Armenian villages, Captanian saw houses with broken windows and open doors, the furniture scattered outside, and a church treated likewise, its Bibles torn to shreds and ritual objects thrown on the floor.[39] When the convoy reached the village of Tonuz (today Şarkışla), five hours from Sivas, the men, including her husband, were separated from the rest of the caravan and forced into a stable.[40] The women screamed at the gendarmes to release their men. Despite the women's cries of despair, the soldiers forced them to continue their journey without the men.

When the convoy reached the village of Hasançelebi in Malatya province to rest, Captanian witnessed how deported young men and old Armenian men from Amasya, Sivas, and other places were crammed into a large building guarded by soldiers and farmers armed with axes.[41] She and the other women and children were then forced to march out of the village. Two hours later, the soldiers and villagers returned without their captives. Many were carrying the clothes of the missing men and youths.[42] One of the Turks confided to them that he had witnessed how all were shot. But his news was not even necessary, as there was no doubt about what had happened.

One evening, Captanian's convoy rested in Hekimhan. As they slept, many of the young women were taken away and raped, or they were kidnapped, never to return.[43] The others gathered money to bribe the guards to protect them. They also were attacked by Kurds who stole their luggage, clothing, mattresses, and bedcovers.[44] From then on, the nightly attacks were repeated. Over the following days the remaining refugees rested in Kırkgöz along with thousands of other Armenian deportees from every social class. In the whole area there was only one well, near which many ill and dying people lay. Corpses began to putrefy, 'which befouled the air and poisoned the living'.[45] The next morning the journey continued on foot. The first thing Captanian saw was a wagon full of children, rounded up by the municipality of Malatya. Thousands of orphans were gathered in the city, without care, emaciated.[46] They died like flies.[47]

A month after having left Samsun, Captanian's marching column reached the mountainous Fırıncılar region south of Malatya. It would take it two months to go through the mountains to Suruç. As the refugees climbed through the Taurus Mountains, they felt like they were walking through a desecrated cemetery because, with every step, they trod on decayed corpses. The ghoulish situation making the deportees into living corpses, she recalled: 'How terrifying the victims looked! Wide open mouths gaping in emaciated faces'.[48]

The women from Tokat and Sivas were part of a caravan that followed the same path Captanian's caravan took, but rather than halting in Suruç it went by way of Urfa to Ras al-Ayn. Of seven hundred women, hardly sixty reached the final destination.[49] The women were stripped by their Kurdish guards and forced to march naked. Nude, they walked for days in the burning sun. With one hand they protected their heads from the heat, with the other they tried to protect their modesty, as the local people they passed mocked them. They were burned, covered with blisters, beaten by their guards. The humiliated caravan was called 'the column of the naked'.[50] It was turned into a slave market. According to Captanian, 'They were sold off like cows, some for a fixed price, others auctioned off to men'.[51]

Worse, if it can be imagined, was the situation of mothers in her caravan, who carried their children in sacks on their backs.

None of the mothers reached the final station, dying along the way of exhaustion, hunger, and thirst.[52] Only some of the children survived. Captanian recalls the numerous children left by the wayside. One of them she could not forget—a five-year-old boy. Next to him lay the still-warm corpse of his mother. As he saw Captanian's caravan, the boy stood up, stretched out his arms, and begged to be taken. When asked where his mother was, he responded by pointing to the corpse, telling them he did not know why she did not wake up.[53]

Captanian describes thirst as being crueller than hunger. Despite her thirst, she kept herself from drinking from any suspicious bodies of standing water, as there were usually corpses in them. Most drank regardless. Thirst made her drink from the Euphrates, although dozens of bodies floated before her very eyes.[54] Captanian also recalled the monotonous sound of the caravan—like a swarm of bees, it was made up of the weeping, sobbing, and wailing of the deported.[55] It was the terrible sound of her dying people, echoing in the valleys and mountains.

Captanian asked one of the Turkish donkey drovers why they drove them from one place to another. To where were they being led? He responded, 'Your journey will end where you croak. That is the truth'.[56] Captanian agreed with the drover: 'The authorities led the deportees on the longest possible journey to systematically decimate them through exhaustion, hunger, thirst, murder and [sexual] assault' before they even reached their destination.[57]

After three months, the deportees reached Aleppo in Syria. By the end of the summer of 1915, eastern Anatolia had been cleared of Armenians. Then, over the next year, Mehmed Talat Pasha ordered the deportation of Armenians from western Anatolia, including areas that were not a theatre of war. Talat Pasha was a fastidious recordkeeper. In his private notebook compiled at the end of 1916 or beginning of 1917, he calculated that he had deported 924,158 of the one and a half million Ottoman Armenians living in the empire in 1914.[58] According to his figures, Captanian was but one of 34,500 Armenians deported from the province of Trabzon from a prewar population of 37,549. Talat Pasha determined that only 350,000 to 400,000 Armenians remained alive in the empire in 1916.[59] He listed no Armenians in Trabzon, nor in the other eastern provinces of Erzurum, Bitlis, Van, Diyar Bakir, and Elazığ (previously called Mamüretülaziz). Those who survived the deportations and reached the camps suffered a very high death rate there. The inmates wasted away from disease, thirst, and starvation, and were raped and murdered by their own guards.

A German soldier, posted to the ambulance service of the Ottoman Sixth Army, led by Field Marshall Colmar von der Goltz, reported from Ras al-Ayn in November 1915 how the camp was filled with hunger, death, illness, and despair, the smell of excrement and putrefaction.[60] All of this misery was surpassed by the awful sight of the ever increasing number of orphaned children, who sat on the ground, neglected, starving, bereft of the slightest amount of human concern, freezing in the cold of the desert night, their faces caked with dirt and dried tears.[61]

The horror was not just in Ras al-Ayn and Deir ez-Zor, but in the valleys and on the banks of rivers there were, in the words of the same German soldier and eyewitness, such 'camps of misery'.[62] The 'mighty stream of an exiled nation, the hundreds of thousands of the damned' that diminished in the mountains finally petered out in the desert. Deportation was 'a journey of no return'.[63]

Those who had not succumbed to the policy of death on the marches or to deliberate starvation and death in the camps by summer 1916 were burned alive, drowned, or massacred in a final rampage east of Deir ez-Zor.[64] To understand the utter destruction of the Armenians, it is useful to look at the motivations of some of the major perpetrators.

Dr. Mehmed Reşid was governor of Diyar Bakir in 1915 and 1916. Reşid was a Circassian refugee from the Caucasus and Bulgaria, a graduate of the Royal Military Medical Academy, and a founder of the CUP. He had been governor of Karesi in the Marmara region, from which he had expelled Ottoman Greeks in 1913 and 1914. Obsessed with modern scientific ideas, social Darwinism, and conspiracy theories, he believed it was necessary 'to liquidate' the Armenians before they 'eliminated' the Ottoman Muslims. Furiously scribbling his defence at the end of the war and before he committed suicide in 1919, he declared, 'The fatherland was about to be lost, therefore, I proceeded eyes closed and without consideration, convinced that I was acting for the welfare of the nation'. In his view, 'the Armenian bandits were a load of harmful microbes that had afflicted the body of the fatherland. Was it not the duty of the doctor to kill the microbes?'[65] He was responsible for the death of 120,000 Armenians and Assyrians, along with four Ottoman governors or district governors whom he ordered murdered for opposing his genocidal plans.[66]

Interior Minister Mehmed Talat Pasha sent a telegram to Governor Mehmed Reşid dated 12 July 1915 concerning the governor's unauthorised organisation of massacres of Armenians and Christians 'without distinction as to sect' within the province he governed. In Mardin, for example, 'seven hundred people from among the Armenians and other Christian inhabitants were recently taken outside of the city at night and without due authorisation, slaughtered like sheep', and that 'the total of those killed to date in these massacres is estimated at two thousand persons'.[67] Alarmed by the indiscriminate killing of Christians, Talat Pasha scolded Reşid for applying to Assyrian Christians the same measures 'intended for the Armenians'. The governor had been ordered to target only Armenians. Talat Pasha sent telegrams in August to governors of the eastern provinces commanding them not to deport Armenian Catholics and Protestants.[68] Members of the Armenian national church were the sole group Talat Pasha intended to destroy. In his eyes, they were the Armenians making common cause with their scheming Christian brethren in Russia.

Some Armenians managed to escape murder and deportation. A couple hundred thousand fled abroad to Russia and elsewhere. An estimated one hundred thousand Armenians, in situations of duress, converted to Islam to save their lives. Tens of thousands of Armenian girls and women were raped and subjected to sexual violence, taken into Muslim families as daughters or brides, and converted to Islam and taught Kurdish or Turkish, thereby escaping deportation. While in becoming Muslim some managed to physically survive, in doing so they were stripped of their Armenian identity, language, and religion. Although some Armenians deemed useful to the army and railway escaped in 1915, many were deported to their deaths within a year. The same was true of men who converted to Islam—for many, the change of faith saved their lives only temporarily. Armenians in the major western cities, especially Istanbul, also survived. So did those with personal relations with people in a position to save them, those who could offer artisanal skills or bribes, those from denominations other than the national Armenian church, and those protected by foreigners. The Armenians of the eastern province of Dersim found shelter among their Alevi Kurd neighbours, with whom they shared an affinity.[69] We can estimate that out of a population of one and a half million Armenians in the Ottoman Empire in 1914, 650,000 to 800,000 had been annihilated by 1916.[70]

Referring to the sporadic massacres of hundreds of thousands of Armenians during the reign of Abdülhamid II (1894–1896 and 1909), in July 1915 Mehmed Talat Pasha boasted that he had 'accomplished more in three months about crushing the Armenians than Abdülhamid II could do in thirty-seven years'.[71] At the end of August 1915, he told the German ambassador that 'the Armenian question no longer exists'.[72] At the same time he wrote in a telegraph to authorities in Ankara that because 'the Armenian question' had been resolved, 'there's no need to sully the nation and the government with further atrocities'.

Cabinet minister Mehmed Cavid recorded in his diary in summer 1915 that he was horrified by the most 'monstrous murder and enormous dimension of brutality that Ottoman history had ever known'. He accused the central committee of the CUP of having managed 'to destroy not only the political existence, but the life itself of a whole people [the Armenians]'. In committing these acts, they 'put an inextinguishable stain' on the administration.[73]

Sheikh Faiz al-Hussein, former district governor of Mamüretülaziz in southeast Anatolia (present-day Elazığ, Turkey), asked whether it was right that the CUP, which proclaimed itself the defender of Islam, the caliphate, and of Muslims, 'should transgress the command of God, transgress the Qur'an, the traditions of the Prophet, and humanity?' For they committed acts 'at which Islam is revolted, as well as all Muslims and all peoples of the earth, be they Muslims, Christians, Jews, or idolaters'.[74]

Other ethno-religious groups were also subject to destruction by the Ottomans during the First World War. Primary among them were the Assyrians, an ancient Christian people who lived in eastern Anatolia and western Iran. Massacred along with Armenians from 1894 to 1896 and in 1909, Assyrian civilians were also repeatedly subjected to forced expulsions and massacres by the Ottoman army, the Special Organisation, and the Kurdish Hamidiye cavalry from 1914 to 1916. They were especially targeted in eastern Anatolia in Hakkari, where they were accused of siding with the Armenians and the British. They were attacked along the Ottoman-Persian border near Van and in the Iranian Azerbaijan city of Urmia, invaded and occupied by the Ottomans, where they were accused of disloyalty and collaboration with the Russians.[75] In the latter case, Iran's foreign minister formally protested to the Ottoman government about the 'atrocities committed by the Ottoman troops' and Kurdish cavalry, noting that Christian villagers were 'mercilessly massacred'.[76] At the Paris Peace Conference in 1919, a delegation of Assyrians would claim that a quarter of a million people, nearly half their original population, had been killed by the Ottomans. While Assyrians formed resistance and self-defence units in Hakkari and Urmia, nothing could justify Ottoman mass expulsions and murder of civilian noncombatants.

EXPLAINING THE GENOCIDE

How could it have come to this? Why would the Ottoman regime turn on its own citizens? Why would an empire that had allowed different groups of people to live together with little violence for so many centuries turn to a policy of annihilating one of the constituent peoples? The Armenian genocide is a part of European history, not only because many of the Young Turks emerged as militants in Paris and Geneva, or because they borrowed their ideas from Western Europe, or even because German generals and government officials were complicit in mass murder, justifying genocide as 'military necessity'.[77] Although the first genocide committed by a European empire in Europe began in Istanbul, it was not motivated by Islam or Turkic ethno-nationalism. Nor was it a civil war between Turks and Armenians or the result of class tensions. It was not an inevitable event predestined to occur due to some innate quality of the empire or its rulers. The genocide was rather a contingency resulting from many actors and factors, one that could have occurred only during the perceived exigencies of world war.

Some have suggested that religion played a key role in the genocide. After all, Muslims (Turks and Kurds) targeted a Christian population (Armenians). As many as one hundred thousand Christian girls and women converted to Islam when they were taken in by Muslim families as servants and brides, thereby sparing their lives during the massacres. The Ottomans had converted Christians for centuries. This was the last great wave of religious conversion in the empire.

But if Islam was a primary motivation, why had the Ottomans never attempted to wipe out the empire's Christians prior to 1915?

From the days of Osman at the turn of the fourteenth century, Muslims had ruled over Christians, but had never before sought their annihilation. The Ottomans targeted Armenians in 1915, with Assyrian Christians also suffering great losses. The Ottomans made clear distinctions between these groups and Greeks, Catholics, and Protestants. Greeks were deported but not massacred. If the perpetrators were motivated by Islam, why were Armenians and Assyrians, not all Christians, singled out?

This was not a clash between Islam and Christianity. Armenians who had converted to Islam but had not disappeared into Muslim homes were not spared deportation to their death. The aim was to destroy the Armenian people. The regime was driven by a relentless desire to wipe out the Armenians and Assyrians, paying no heed to Islamic precepts that prohibited such actions. But Islamic piety served for some Muslims as a reason to save the Christians targeted by the regime.[78] Citing Islamic protection of Christians, a number of local officials refused the orders to deport Armenians—the governors of Adana and Ankara and a local official in Mardin among them. But they were either replaced or assassinated for resisting orders. If Islam was the motivating factor, then why did the regime not target all people who were not Muslims, such as Jews? The people who ordered the massacres were not Muslim religious fanatics, but atheists who used religion as a tool to save the empire, despite their personal anti-religious convictions.

It might appear that Turkish ethno-nationalism caused the perpetrators to become murderers. Again, this claim is undermined by the fact that Albanians, Bulgarians, Circassians, Dönme, Kurds, and Turks all contributed to the murderous effort, and not Turks alone. Kurds especially could not have been motivated by Turkish nationalism to assault their Armenian neighbours. The CUP was not made up of Turkish ethno-nationalists. To claim that they were overlooks the diverse backgrounds of the leadership.

This was not an ethnic conflict, or a civil war fought between Turks and Armenians. Ottoman Muslims and the CUP were not pursuing the establishment of an ethno-national Turkish state at that time, but were aiming to save the Muslim empire. Until the Ottoman Empire entered the First World War in November 1914, the Ottoman Armenian political parties held similar views. They promoted reform within the empire, an amelioration of oppression, and some form of political autonomy, not separation. Such reforms included the Armenian Reform Agreement, signed by the Ottomans and other European powers in early 1914, which entailed the creation of two provinces in eastern Anatolia to serve as an autonomous Armenia under the supervision of European inspectors- or governors-general based in Erzurum and Van. They were to work to ameliorate the conditions of the Armenians, especially the seizure of their agrarian landholdings by Kurds.[79] The CUP abrogated the agreement when the Ottoman Empire entered the war later that same year.[80] But all reforms, especially those permitting foreign oversight and intervention, were viewed by the CUP as a lethal threat to the empire's national security and territorial integrity.

Was the genocide the result of class tensions? In eastern Anatolia there was competition and strife between Kurdish landlords and Armenian peasants, exacerbated by the ever deeper reach of the more powerful, centralising policies of Sultan Abdülhamid II. In the cities, especially Istanbul, Muslims resented the rise of the Armenian bourgeoisie. Yet such an explanation cannot clarify why the Armenians bore the primary brunt of Kurdish and Muslim envy and resentment. The Greeks of western Anatolia, whether peasants or part of the rising middle class, were not deported to their death in the desert. Nor were Jews of similar class stature.

The genocide of 1915 was in fact a contingent event. It was not the culmination of a purported preexisting Turkish or Muslim genocidal impulse, previously manifested in the turn-of-the-century Abdülhamid II–era massacres. The oldest extant narrative account of the Ottoman dynasty depicts the early Ottoman rulers as annihilating every last enemy man and boy and enslaving all women and girls. In the first centuries of Ottoman rule, the Ottomans had used the Collection to forcibly transfer hundreds of thousands of Christian children for their administration and military. But such views and practices of rule did not point inevitably to this. Without the First World War, there would not have been all-out genocide. The CUP leadership was a revolutionary cadre seeking the radical transformation of state and society in order to save the empire. Driven by existential fear of being massacred by their enemies, and in need of an 'enemy of the people' to rally the elements deemed to form the empire's core, the CUP leaders were suddenly thrust into the context of world war. It is in that situation that they carried out the annihilation of a people blamed for their condition.

During the First World War, the CUP regime faced Russian political and material support for the Armenians of Anatolia, Armenian revolutionaries slaughtering Muslim soldiers and civilians in eastern Anatolia, and an Armenian uprising in Van that led to the Russian army occupying the region and appointing an Armenian governor. This is not to blame the victims for their own destruction, but to point out how events fit the mindset of the perpetrators.[81] Uprisings in eastern Anatolia cannot justify the mass deportation and murder of unarmed civilians far from the battle zones, such as in Bursa. Nor can they justify the destruction of visible traces of those people, the demolition of their churches, and the plundering of their wealth and property. Such practices point to a cultural genocide, the annihilation of Armenians' historical presence after their murder as a people. The only explanation for that is to be found in how the leaders of the regime viewed them: as a dangerous, disloyal population conspiring with foreign enemies.

An historical parallel presents itself. When the Polish Jewish teenager Herschel Grynszpan assassinated a Nazi diplomat in France in 1938 in revenge for Nazi treatment of his parents, the Nazis used the event as a pretext to launch the 9–10 November pogrom known as Kristallnacht. It was the beginning of the Holocaust. Historians would not rationalise or justify the Holocaust on this single act. Why, then, do we do so with the Ottomans?

PUNISHING THE PERPETRATORS

Germany and the other Central powers, including the Ottoman Empire, were defeated. November 1918 witnessed the armistice ending the war and the abolition of the monarchies in Germany and Austria-Hungary. Among the Triple Entente powers, Russia had undergone the Bolshevik revolution, with the last tsar, Nicholas II, having been executed four months earlier. The Ottoman dynasty could read the writing on the wall.

On 31 October 1918, the Ottoman minister of the navy signed an armistice with the commander of the British Black Sea fleet at Mudros on the island of Lemnos. The British pledged that their forces would advance no further north from Syria and Iraq. The Ottomans agreed to military occupation of the Bosporus, gave up control over the railways, ports, and telegraph lines, demobilised and disarmed their troops, surrendered all Arab-majority provinces, and gave the Allied powers the right to send their militaries to occupy any Ottoman territory. In November, as their planes flew overhead, their battleships steamed into the city, and their flags decorated major streets, fifty thousand British, French, Greek, and Italian troops took over Istanbul, although the official occupation did not begin for another year and a half. The CUP may have lost the war, but it had succeeded in its battle. By 1918, Anatolia was largely bereft of Armenians.

As soon as the Ottoman-British armistice was signed, the leaders of the Ottoman regime—Mehmed Talat Pasha, Enver Pasha,

Cemal Pasha, Dr. Bahaettin Şakir, and others—fled to Germany, where they were offered asylum. Britain, France, and the United States demanded that Germany send the members of the regime home to stand trial. The requests were denied.

The dynasty—led by pro-British, anti-CUP sultan Mehmed VI, who had replaced his brother Mehmed V, who had died in July 1918—members of the Liberal Party, the occupying Allied powers, and the remaining CUP members all competed for power after the CUP leadership left. The sultan appointed an anti-CUP grand vizier on 11 November. The next governments through late 1919 were also led by anti-CUP grand viziers who were close to the palace.

The postwar Liberal, anti-CUP governments acknowledged what had happened to the Armenians and acted to punish the perpetrators. In 1919, as the victorious Allies continued to occupy Istanbul, courts-martial were empowered to arrest and try CUP members, military officers, and government officials including grand viziers and cabinet ministers. There were several dozen trials, the extensive evidence for which was made up exclusively of the testimony, telegrams, memorandums, communications, and letters of Ottoman army officers, government officials, and CUP members. According to the indictment pronounced on 12 April 1919 and the supplementary indictment of 22 May, the CUP was a criminal organisation operating under the guise of a political party. CUP central committee members were charged with having illegally seized the machinery of government, violated the empire's laws and constitution, and used violence to fulfil their hidden aims, which included the annihilation of the Armenians.

Nearly two dozen members of the CUP leadership, cabinet, central committee, and Special Organisation were declared legally responsible for carrying out clandestine aims under cover of war through violence, 'tyranny and oppression', including the planned 'looting of money and property, the burning of houses and corpses, the massacre of the population, rape, torture and

oppression'. A 'sizeable portion of the victimised' was Armenian.[82] These massacres were 'carried out under the express orders
and with the knowledge of Talat, Enver and Cemal' Pasha.[83] According to the supplementary indictment of 22 May, the express
orders included attacking convoys of deported Armenians with
gangs formed by the Special Organisation for this purpose. As a
consequence, 'the Armenians were annihilated and their goods
and possessions looted and plundered'.[84] The government, rather
than protecting the Armenians, removed from office anyone who
objected to their treatment. Mehmed Talat Pasha, Enver Pasha,
Cemal Pasha, and Dr. Nazım were found guilty on 26 May and
sentenced to death (in absentia) on 19 July 1919.[85] In a trial held
on 13 January 1920, Dr. Bahaettin Şakir was sentenced to death
(in absentia) for atrocities committed by his Special Organisation,
'which had been formed for the purpose of destroying and annihilating the Armenians'.[86]

Of the eighteen perpetrators sentenced to death, because fifteen
had fled the empire, only three were hanged. One was Mehmed
Kemal, the lieutenant governor of Yozgat in central Anatolia. His
funeral turned into a demonstration, as he was seen as a hero and
martyr by Muslims. From 1919 to 1922, as the trials were under-
way, the world's first memorial to the Armenian genocide stood
in the heart of occupied Istanbul, in Taksim Square. But the weak
Ottoman government and the British eventually gave up on the
prosecution. Most defendants were set free.

In 1921 and 1922, members of the Armenian Revolutionary
Federation assassinated the members of the genocidal regime who
had taken refuge outside the Ottoman Empire. In Berlin, they
killed forty-seven-year-old Mehmed Talat Pasha, Dr. Bahaettin
Şakir, and Cemal Azmi, the former governor of Trabzon province.
Azmi had been sentenced to death (in absentia) by the postwar
Ottoman courts-martial for implementing 'the plans necessary
for the actual massacre and annihilation of the Armenians under the guise of implementing the Deportation Law', including

by having his men ferry women and children in boats deep into Black Sea waters and then throwing them overboard.[87] Armenian assassins shot fifty-year-old Cemal Pasha in Tbilisi, Georgia. The widows and family members of those CUP leaders assassinated by Armenians after the war in revenge killings were given pensions by the Grand National Assembly of what was now the new Turkish Republic. Their children were given free education and Armenian property.[88] Mehmed Talat Pasha's widow was awarded an Armenian mansion. The bloodstained shirt that he was wearing the day he was assassinated would later be placed on display in the Military Museum in Istanbul.

Following Talat Pasha's assassination in broad daylight on a busy street in Berlin in 1921, his young Armenian killer, Soghomon Tehlirian, was acquitted. The grounds for his release were that he had been avenging the murder of his family and the Armenians of his hometown of Erzurum. A young Polish Jewish law student named Raphael Lemkin attended the sensational trial, which changed his life. He was troubled by the fact that while Tehlirian's murder of one man was deemed a crime, the murdered man's annihilation of one million people was not.[89] It was through this trial that he realised that the principle of state sovereignty allowed governments to commit crimes against their own citizens with impunity. Twenty years later, during the Second World War, when he saw it happening to his own family, Lemkin coined the term 'genocide'. The Ottoman regime engaged in all five acts enumerated in Article II of the Genocide Convention.[90]

22

THE END
Gazi Mustafa Kemal

A T THE END of the First World War, the Ottoman Empire was devastated and most of its territory occupied. Anatolia's population had been decimated and impoverished, and the countryside and many cities were in ruins as a result of war, genocide, migration, famine, and epidemics. Eight hundred thousand Ottoman soldiers—one out of every four enlisted men—had been killed or died from disease; an equal number had been wounded. As many as four million civilians had died or were killed, from a prewar population of twenty million. Civilians in the Ottoman Empire suffered a much higher mortality rate—calculated as proportion of the population rather than absolute numbers—than most other belligerents.[1] In some eastern provinces, half the population had died or been killed. One quarter had been displaced.[2]

As foreign troops arrived in Istanbul in 1918, the League of Nations awarded Britain a mandate—a commission to administer the government and military affairs—of Palestine, Transjordan, and Iraq. France was given a mandate over Syria and Lebanon. The Allied powers partitioned Anatolia, placing the Aegean region including İzmir under Greek control and dividing the Mediterranean region (as far inland as the city of Konya in central Anatolia) between France and Italy. What remained independent Ottoman territory was central Anatolia and a small section of the Black Sea coast. To humiliate the Ottomans, the French general who was occupation commander rode into Istanbul on a white horse, imitating Mehmed II's entry in the same city in 1453.[3]

It was in this postwar era that the last remaining subject peoples of the sultan, especially the Kurds and Armenians, had their best chance at obtaining autonomy or independence. Although instrumental in the carrying out of the Armenian genocide, the Kurds had also been subject to the CUP regime's harsh policies of resettlement from 1913 to 1918. The regime had intended to assimilate Kurds among Turks by forcibly resettling hundreds of thousands of them in the west, so that they would not constitute a majority anywhere in the empire. The First World War devastated Kurdistan. Warfare, genocide, massacre, starvation, disease, and famine caused staggering losses to Arabs, Armenians, Assyrians, Kurds, and Turks.

The victorious Allies, especially the British and the Americans, led by President Woodrow Wilson—whose 'Fourteen Points' programme outlined what was hoped to be a long-lasting peace at the end of the First World War—promoted creating an Armenian and a Kurdish mandate in eastern Anatolia. These plans were never realised. Instead, defeat in war and the Europeanising impulses begun in the nineteenth century ultimately brought down the dynasty. The man who ensured its demise was an Ottoman First World War hero.

Blond and blue-eyed, the Salonican-born military officer Mustafa Kemal (1881–1938), a Young Turk, CUP member, and veteran of the 1908 revolution, the 1909 Action Army, and the First World War, was sent by the Ottoman government to Samsun on the Black Sea coast as military inspector of the Third Army in May 1919. He began instead to organise all remaining Ottoman army units and guerrilla bands. Ordered to defend the empire, the sultan, and the caliphate, he would soon turn against all but the first. He began to lead the CUP's regional resistance committee—the Defence of

Popular Rights societies—whose interests differed from those of the government in Allied-occupied Istanbul.[4] When the Ottoman government ordered his arrest, the army refused, choosing to follow Mustafa Kemal as leader. By April 1920, he had established a shadow parliament in Ankara. Defeat in war would lead to the overthrow of the dynasty by this Ottoman army officer.

From 1918 to 1922, the Young Turks were not guided by Ottomanism, Islamism, or Turkism. Their leading light was again Ottoman Muslim nationalism, as it had been a decade earlier. The CUP revamped the Special Organisation and other irregulars as armed guerrilla groups in Anatolia. The political organisation, the Defence of Popular Rights societies, was for the Muslim peoples of Anatolia alone, especially Turks and Kurds. The exclusion of Christians was made explicit at the congress of Erzurum in 1919, which gathered the resistance groups from the seven eastern provinces. It declared that its goal was 'to defend the historic and national rights of the Muslim population'. Muslims 'form one nation, consisting of Turks and Kurds'.[5] That same year, the western Anatolian Defence of Popular Rights societies promoted Muslim nationalism and faced off against Ottoman Christians and European powers.

The Sivas Congress, convened by Mustafa Kemal in 1919 after the congress at Erzerum, dedicated itself to the battle to preserve 'our state which belongs to the Muslims'. This was Ottoman Muslim nationalism and territorialism, explicitly excluding the Arabophone regions. Mustafa Kemal defined the fatherland as the area of Anatolia peopled by Kurds and Turks where the Ottoman army was in charge. This was a small area, as much of Anatolia was occupied by European powers.

There was no room in this new polity for the remaining Christians of Anatolia. In December 1919, Mustafa Kemal accused the Armenians of having a 'genocidal policy' against Muslims.[6] He praised Ottoman tolerance and declared that what had happened to the Armenians and Greeks during the war was the consequence of their separatist nationalism, which 'they pursued in a savage manner, when they allowed themselves to be made tools of foreign intrigues and abused their privileges'. Christian Europe, he argued, had committed far worse crimes than the massacres committed by the Ottomans. He blamed the victims, belittled the severity of the violence, and accused others of having committed far worse assaults.

Elections held in autumn 1919 brought a Muslim nationalist parliament to power in winter 1920. The parliament adopted the National Pact of January 1920, which articulated all the sentiments of the Erzurum and Sivas congresses. The National Pact supported the right of only Muslims to the land. It rejected the occupation and partition of the areas of Anatolia inhabited by an Ottoman Muslim majority. It gave up any claims to Arab-majority regions. The Ottoman Empire in this vision was to be an Anatolian, Turkish-Kurdish polity.

The last Ottoman sultan, Mehmed VI (reigned 1918–1922)—who could see a flotilla of Allied warships from the windows of his residence, Dolmabahçe Palace—and the Ottoman government in Istanbul in 1918 and 1919, however, pursued an anti-CUP, pro-British policy and complied with the demands of the occupying Allied powers. In March 1920, when the official occupation of the city began, the British and their thirty thousand troops put an end to legal political activity.

The last Ottoman parliament prorogued itself in protest in April. On 23 April, parliamentarians who were able to escape arrest by the occupying powers along with delegates elected from among the Anatolian Defence of Popular Rights committees assembled in rebel-controlled Ankara at the first meeting of a shadow government, the Grand National Assembly, which still recognised the sultan caliph as supreme leader. Allied high commissioners administered the capital, which was beset by sky-high inflation, lack of basic food and fuel, a large refugee population, and a housing shortage.

In April, the Ottoman government charged Mustafa Kemal with treason and sentenced him to death in absentia. The sheikhulislam gave a fatwa, a legal opinion, that the resistance groups led by Mustafa Kemal were traitors, whom Muslims should kill. For his part, Mustafa Kemal had the mufti of Ankara, the leading specialist in Islamic law in the city, declare in a legal opinion that the members of the government were traitors. He emphasised that his struggle was for the sake of the empire, sultanate, and caliphate. It was a Muslim (Turkish and Kurdish) resistance movement supported by Sunni dignitaries, Alevis, and Bektaşi Sufis. Most Kurds believed Mustafa Kemal's rhetoric that Turks and Kurds were brothers and supported his campaigns to save the presumably Muslim empire and caliphate from foreigners and local Christians.

On 10 August 1920, a delegation from the sultan's government signed the Treaty of Sèvres with the Allied powers outside Paris. The treaty left very little territory in the hands of Ottoman Muslims. It created an independent Armenia in eastern Anatolia, gave Greece eastern Thrace and İzmir, internationalised the Bosporus, presented France with a sphere of influence in southern Anatolia, let Italy control southwestern Anatolia, and gave the Kurds autonomy in much of northern Kurdistan, with the right to vote for independence one year later and unite with southern Kurdistan in today's Iraq (which was controlled by Britain). The Grand National Assembly in Ankara refused to accept these terms or comply with its orders.

The Allied powers, the British in particular, gave Greece the right to enforce the Treaty of Sèvres. Several years of warfare ensued, waged mainly between the Anatolian Muslim resistance and foreign occupying powers and their local Christian allies, but also between soldiers of the Istanbul government and Mustafa Kemal's forces. Defeating the army of the short-lived independent Republic of Armenia—established in 1918 and led by members of the Armenian Revolutionary Federation—in autumn 1919 and

signing a treaty of friendship with the Soviet Union in early 1921
allowed the Anatolian fighters to focus on western and northwestern Anatolia. Greek armies, after having been given the green light
by the British to occupy İzmir in 1919, conquered much territory
in the region throughout 1920 and 1921. The Greeks were stopped
by the forces under the command of Mustafa Kemal at the Battle of the Sakarya, only eighty kilometres southwest of Ankara,
during a nearly three-week struggle in September 1921. Mustafa
Kemal's men had changed the situation on the ground and had
become the de facto government of the Muslim rump state, driving foreign armies out of much of Anatolia, defeating the French
in southern Anatolia, and threatening to take southern Kurdistan
(northern Iraq) from the British.

In August and September 1922, in their last great offensive
following the Battle of the Sakarya, Mustafa Kemal's forces, the
Ottoman Muslim nationalists, routed the Greek army south of
Afyon-Karahisar, capturing its commander in chief and driving
its surviving troops and the Greek population of western Anatolia all the way back to İzmir on the Aegean coast. The Muslim
nationalists burned the city to the ground, targeting first the Armenian quarter and then the Greek Orthodox neighbourhoods,
sparing only the Muslim and Jewish districts.[7] Thousands of desperate Greeks fled to İzmir's harbour and then onto waiting ships,
which took them to Greece, never to return.

Mustafa Kemal crushed or outmanoeuvred left-wing, right-
wing, and Islamist rivals, including Enver Pasha—who was based
alternately in Berlin, Baku, and Moscow and tried unsuccessfully
to rally former CUP and Special Organisation members to join
his own Muslim army entering Anatolia from the east. He served
as political leader and commander in chief of the political and
military battles between 1919 and 1922, which were reframed afterward as Turkey's successful war for independence.[8] Brooking
no resistance, Mustafa Kemal's followers assassinated or lynched

politicians and journalists who opposed them.[9] The shadow-government Grand National Assembly in Ankara promoted Mustafa Kemal to field marshal, conferring upon him the messianic title of 'saviour' and the old Ottoman title of gazi, holy warrior.

Turning his back on Ottoman Muslim nationalism, as well as on his connection to the Ottoman past, Mustafa Kemal adopted the title of gazi, which harkened back to what the Ottomans had argued was the crucial factor in their rise. At the same time, he began to promote the ideology of secular Turkish nationalism in its place. On 1 November 1922, the Grand National Assembly separated the caliphate from the sultanate, named Mehmed VI's cousin Abdülmecid II, the eldest Ottoman male heir, as caliph, and abolished the sultanate. The last Ottoman cabinet resigned. Only the Ankara government would represent the empire. Fearing for his life, a little over two weeks later the last sultan, Mehmed VI—escorted by the commander in chief of Allied forces occupying the Ottoman Empire, British general Charles Harington—left Yıldız Palace. Mehmed VI boarded the British warship *Malaya* and sailed to Malta. With British backing, he attempted to gain recognition as the caliph in Mecca. Failing in his efforts in the first half of 1923, he retired to the Italian Riviera.[10]

On 29 October 1923, the Turkish Republic was declared in Ankara. The Ottoman Empire was replaced by a constitutional-ist republic that abrogated the caliphate. In 1924 the last caliph, Abdülmecid II, and the remaining members of the dynasty were expelled from Turkey and forbidden from returning. Abdül-mecid II took refuge in Switzerland and then France.[11] The last sultan, Mehmed VI, passed away on 16 May 1926 in San Remo. He was buried in Damascus a month and a half later. After more than six hundred years in power, the rule of the Ottoman family had ended.

The 1923 Treaty of Lausanne replaced the Treaty of Sèvres. It was negotiated between Britain, France, Italy, and Greece on one side, and Mustafa Kemal's government in Ankara—where the Defence of Popular Rights committees had been reestablished as a single political party, the Republican People's Party—on the other. The Treaty of Lausanne recognised the establishment of the independent Turkish Republic. All foreign troops were ordered to leave. But so were some religious minorities. Based on the principle that nation-states should have homogenous populations, the treaty mandated a compulsory, irreversible 'population exchange' of Greek Orthodox Christians in Turkey and Muslims in Greece.[12] The approximately 200,000 Greek Orthodox and 350,000 Muslims who were 'exchanged' were forbidden to return.[13] Approximately one million Greek Orthodox had already fled from western Anatolia to Greece after Greek forces were routed in 1922. The Greek Orthodox in Istanbul and two islands in the Dardanelles were exempt, as were Muslims in western Thrace. Along with war, genocide, famine, epidemics, and forced migration, this internationally sanctioned ethnic cleansing contributed to Anatolia's Christian population decreasing from one in five inhabitants (20 percent) in 1913 to one in forty (2 percent) in 1923.[14]

The Treaty of Lausanne gave neither Armenians nor Kurds autonomy. Both had been promised autonomy in the Treaty of Sèvres in 1920, but neither Armenia nor Kurdistan was even mentioned in the new agreement. The Turkish Republic ceased mentioning Kurds and Kurdistan, and Turkish place names replaced Kurdish, Armenian, and Greek ones. Turning its back on a decade of Ottoman Muslim nationalism—when Islam was used to build loyalty to the leaders and especially to link Turks and Kurds in common cause to wage war against perceived enemies—the new republic would be one for the Turks alone.

Mustafa Kemal fashioned a new nation from the ashes of the Ottoman Empire. To do so he chose to jettison the past, to obliterate any and all connections with what had come before. According to a Turkish scholar, the Turkish Republic 'was originally based on forgetting'.[15] Already in 1922, Mustafa Kemal—who would be given the name Atatürk, the father of the Turks, by the Grand National Assembly in 1934 and would lead the Turkish Republic from its founding until his death in 1938—declared, 'The new Turkey has absolutely no relation with the old Turkey. The Ottoman state has gone down in history. Now, a new Turkey is born'.[16]

CONCLUSION
The Ottoman Past Endures

I N MANY WAYS, in the republic's early decades the nationalists who followed Atatürk in both outlook and strategy carried the outcome of the Ottoman centuries to one extreme: they managed to convert Turkey's population into Western-leaning Europhiles. Mustafa Kemal Atatürk and his revolutionary cadre established a westward-looking, secular, nationalist republic, a 'Turkey for the Turks' based in Ankara in Anatolia. In turning their backs on the Ottoman Empire and dynasty, on the Greeks and Armenians, the Kurds and Arabs, they also turned their backs on the Ottoman Way, incorporating others through religious conversion and tiered tolerance, ethno-religious plurality, and gendered social strata. In 1924 and 1925, Turkey disestablished the religious class and confiscated their endowments, abolished the office of the sheikhulislam, closed Sufi lodges and Muslim schools, banned Sufi orders, and outlawed religious dress. To cut the next generation off completely from its Ottoman, Islamic past, in 1928 and 1929 the republic educated the nation in a new language: modern Turkish, expunged of Arabic and Persian vocabulary and written in Latin rather than modified Arabic script. The books of the fathers became illegible to the children of the republic. Even the call to prayer was recited in Turkish, rather than Arabic. Legal equality between the sexes and the equal rights of all citizens regardless of religious or ethnic background were also instituted by the abolishment of Sharia courts in 1924 and the incorporation of a new civil code modelled on that of Switzerland in 1926. Compulsory co-ed national education was established, and in 1934 women were allowed to vote and be elected to public office.

But new social hierarchies prevailed. In 1933, on the tenth anniversary of the founding of the republic, Atatürk declared that the Turkish nation was 'great', of 'excellent character', 'intelligent', enlightened, an 'exalted human community', devoted to science, and 'civilised'.[1] These adjectives were everything that he and his cohort of secularist Turkish nationalists believed the Ottoman Empire was not. Such declarations carried one meaning to those who considered themselves and were accepted as Turks. What it meant for those who were excluded, including Armenians, Dönme, Greeks, Jews, Kurds, and religious Muslims, was another matter.

Despite Atatürk's efforts at expunging it, the past would not go away in Turkey. Alleged political conspiracies by former CUP allies and a series of uprisings by religious Muslims and Kurds belied the claim that everyone in the country was happy to call himself a secular Turk, devoted to Atatürk's single-party, ethnonationalist state. Atatürk had the two most influential surviving members of the CUP central committee, Dr. Nazım and Mehmed Cavid, hanged after a show trial in 1926. Scores of Muslims who refused to wear a brimmed hat, which hindered praying, were executed. When Sufis calling for the return of Sharia and the caliphate murdered a soldier at Menemen near İzmir in 1930, nearly three dozen religious Muslims were hanged as punishment and the officer became a martyr for the new secular republic. An Armenian priest told a Kurd, 'We were the breakfast for them, you will be the lunch. Don't forget'.[2]

Indeed, only a decade after the Armenian genocide, Kurdish uprisings such as that of Sheikh Said in 1925 were mercilessly suppressed. In 1930 during a Kurdish rebellion, Justice Minister

Mahmut Esat declared, 'The Turk is the master of this country. All those who are not pure Turks have only one right in the Turkish homeland: the right to be servants, the right to be slaves'.[3] One of Atatürk's half dozen adopted orphan daughters, the Armenian Sabiha Gökçen, Turkey's first female pilot and the world's first female fighter pilot, bombed Kurdish civilians from the sky during the massacre of tens of thousands of Kurds at Dersim (renamed Tunceli, meaning 'bronze hand') in 1938, the year of Atatürk's death.[4]

Continuing the Orientalist, civilising mission of the late Ottoman Empire, the Turkish Republic viewed Kurds as savages, 'mountain Turks' in need of civilising. This time that 'civilisation' was secularist Turkish nationalism. The Kurds were especially affected by the 1934 Settlement Law, which entailed mass deportations of Kurds, moving them from predominantly Kurdish-populated eastern regions to the west and their replacement by Turkish immigrants. The state outlawed all dialects of the Kurdish language. When the adoption of surnames was made mandatory, Turkey prohibited using letters necessary for forming Kurdish names. In fact, the letter X was not included in the new Turkish alphabet for this reason. Turkey made mention of 'Kurds', 'Kurdish', and 'Kurdistan' a crime.[5] To this day, southeastern Anatolia—Kurdistan—is at war; Kurdish guerrillas are refusing to submit to Turkification. The fires lit in 1915 have yet to be extinguished.

INHERITING THE OTTOMANS

Although headed by Muslims, the Ottoman Empire was very much a European empire. Centuries of conversion, Islamisation, and incorporation of Christians and Jews into the empire meant that the Ottoman legacy was and is still seen and felt across Europe, Turkey, and the Middle East today. It is present in the physical landscape and urban layout, the historical memory, and popular culture. Cities from Hungary to Egypt are sprinkled with Ottoman bathhouses, cemeteries and tombs, city walls, fountains, fortresses, houses, inns, marketplaces, mosques, palaces, and ornate villas. The dome of the tomb of sixteenth-century Bektaşi Sufi Gül Baba is visible as one crosses the Danube from Pest to Buda in the Hungarian capital. The symbol of Thessaloniki, Greece, is the White Tower, built by the Ottomans in the fifteenth century. A pink-domed Ottoman mosque, shorn of its minaret and used as an art gallery, graces the 'Venetian' harbour of Chania, Crete. Suleiman I built the famous walls of the Old City of Jerusalem. The skyline of the peninsula of Istanbul looks much as it did during the Ottoman era. So do those of many towns in Southeastern Europe, such as Plovdiv in Bulgaria, or the Old Town of Sarajevo, Bosnia, which still boasts an enormous Ottoman cemetery rising to the top of a large hillside. The presence of Muslim and Turkish-speaking populations in Europe and the Balkans and the paucity of Christians in today's Turkey are also outcomes of the Ottoman centuries. The Old Town of Rhodes, considered the largest intact medieval city in Europe, is actually an Ottoman ghost town now chockablock with tourists. One can still pray in the Ottoman-era Shalom synagogue built in the sixteenth century.

Even cities never besieged or captured by the Ottomans bear traces of the fear of that eventuality. A horrifying early eighteenth-century statue on the Charles Bridge in Prague depicts a corpulent, turbaned, horseshoe-moustachioed Turk with a large, curved sword and barking dog guarding three nude, shackled, wailing Christian male captives. Crowds of tourists admire another 'Turkish' figure on the oldest astronomical clock in Europe near the bridge in Prague's Old Town; that figure, positioned next to a skeleton representing death, symbolises vice and pleasure. Another turbaned, horseshoe-moustachioed caricature, this time of a 'Turkish dwarf', amuses visitors at the reconstructed late seventeenth-century 'dwarf garden' at the Baroque Mirabell Palace in Salzburg. He is unsuccessfully straining with all his tiny might to break a tree trunk, symbolizing the successful resistance in 1683 of the last failed Ottoman siege of Vienna. At the other end of Europe, a life-size, turbaned, ornately costumed Ottoman ambassador greets visitors at the display of the eighteenth-century Vauxhall Pleasure Gardens at the Museum of London.

The legacy of Ottoman history is not only Muslim. In Istanbul, surviving Ottoman-era Christian or Jewish cemeteries, churches, and synagogues speak to a vanished past. How many passersby wonder why modern Turkey contains the fifteenth-century Ahrida Synagogue, which boasts a boat-shaped pulpit in commemoration of the welcome given Jews from Spain; the Church of Saint George, the seat of the Orthodox patriarchate since the seventeenth century; and the nineteenth-century Bulgarian Saint Stephen Church? One comes across ruins of Armenian and Assyrian churches in Turkey, not only in eastern Anatolia but in Istanbul as well, the shattered remains of their genocides at the beginning of the twentieth century.

European museums boast captured Ottoman tents, weaponry, and even the skulls of grand viziers, such as that of Kara Mustafa Pasha, the leader of the failed siege of 1683, preserved in the Vienna Museum. At the Museum of Military History in Vienna, children celebrate their birthday in Ottoman tents captured at that siege. Vienna's Saint Stephen's Cathedral has a bell made of melted Ottoman siege cannons. As Ottoman armies overran vast stretches of European territory, they gave rise to *Türkenfurcht*, fear of the Turk, which was manifested especially in Austria. In the Austrian city of Graz, 1480 was remembered as the year of the 'plagues of God'. Memorialised in a large fresco painted in 1485 on the south wall of the cathedral in the centre of the city, the three plagues were locusts, Black Death, and Turks.

In Central Europe one comes across menacing 'Turks' carved in wood and stone, as well as images of Turks as bearers of coffee and pleasure. 'Turkish' coffee—known officially in Greece as 'Greek' coffee since the military junta of 1967–1974 and as Arab,

Armenian, Bosnian, or 'traditional Serbian' coffee elsewhere—is enjoyed with Turkish delight and baklava across a wide region. Ottoman and Turkish terms appear in many languages. Ottoman-language manuscripts and archival documents are found in many libraries of Europe and the Middle East, be they in Zagreb, Skopje, or Cairo. Sofia's national library boasts the second-largest collection of Ottoman documents in the world. Ottoman-era land deeds are still used in several regions, including Greece, Lebanon, and Israel, where one finds Ottoman-language inscriptions carved into stone and the sultan's *tughra*, his imperial cipher, on gates. The Ottomans live again in best-selling novels set in the Ottoman past written in languages as diverse as Arabic, French, German, Greek, Serbian, and Turkish, and in Turkish television series reimagining the exploits of Osman's father Ertuğrul, Suleiman I, or Abdülhamid II, which are popular from Brazil to Indonesia. While nostalgia sells, painful aspects of the Ottoman past remain and have proven more difficult to confront.

REVISITING *THE WHITE CASTLE*

What has happened in the past has an impact on the present. The past, whether in Turkey or Greece, or any other former part of the Ottoman Empire, is anything but dead. The question is what to do with the memories. The descendants of the Ottomans and their former subjects are now debating how the sorrows of previous generations have affected them, how they should speak of and commemorate the past, and how the problems bequeathed to them can be overcome. Many are freeing their minds from the chains of official history, facing difficult truths about what their ancestors did, and coming to terms with the prejudices they hold against the people with whom they share, or once shared, a homeland.[6]

Towards the end of Orhan Pamuk's novel *The White Castle*, Hoja and his Italian slave accompany the sultan on his hunts and military campaigns in Southeastern Europe. Hoja has the sultan's soldiers force Christian and Muslim villagers alike to confess their faults, as the slave had made him do. This process of self-awareness, undertaken on a much larger scale and with more coercion and violence than the experiment endured at home, produces the same results: people make the same confessions about having committed the same transgressions, no matter their religion.[7] Since people are the same everywhere, they should recognise themselves in others. After all, they are capable of committing the same crimes.

Pamuk poses the question 'Why am I what I am?'[8] At the beginning of the novel, Hoja is unwilling to engage in any self-reflection. Instead of writing about himself, he writes about why others are the way they are. He declares with an exaggerated self-confidence that the other is inferior.[9] But what makes him superior? What makes us and them, self and other, East and West, Muslim, Christian, and Jew any different? By narrating history to establish a connection to the past and to ourselves, we find the answer.

The Ottoman story is an inseparable part of Europe's story. As much as they were Asian, as much as they had a unique political organisation, the Ottomans were the inheritors of Rome. When the European past is broadened to include the Ottoman dynasty and its Eurasian empire, it expands our definition of so many historical phenomena, including tolerance and genocide, which are otherwise impossible to understand. Our ancestors breathe through us. Because our lives have been shaped by their actions, their entangled histories are worth discovering and placing in the right context, especially if such histories are unfamiliar yet closer to us than we realised.

ACKNOWLEDGMENTS

I never would have imagined writing this book were it not for Adam Gauntlett, who, after realising that I was the only professor in the United Kingdom teaching Ottoman history from beginning to end, convinced me to write a complete history of the dynasty. I would like to thank dear friend Theresa Truax, who saved this book at a crucial stage. I am grateful for the wise counsel of Joe Zigmond at John Murray and Brian Distelberg at Basic Books, who offered invaluable criticism on many book drafts. I am indebted to Roger Labrie for asking important questions, which compelled me to rewrite the manuscript until it was clearer. I would like to express my gratitude to Yorgo Dedes, Ceyda Karamürsel, Chris Markiewicz, Esra Özyürek, Christine Philliou, Elyse Semerdjian, Gagan Sood, Bedross Der Matossian, and Taylor Sherman, who graciously commented on all or sections of the manuscript in the midst of a plague year. I am thankful that the International History Department at the London School of Economics and Political Science granted sabbatical leave, which enabled me to finish writing this book. My debt to my teachers, Carl Petry, Rudi Lindner, Fatma Müge Göçek, Ronald Grigor Suny, Robert Dankoff, and Cornell Fleischer, who taught me to look critically at Ottoman history from different perspectives, will be evident to all specialist readers of this work.

LIST OF OTTOMAN RULERS
AND THEIR REIGNS

Osman I	ca. 1288–ca. 1324
Orhan I	ca. 1324–1362
Murad I (assassinated)	1362–1389
Bayezid I (death in captivity)	1389–1402
Interregnum	1402–1413
Mehmed I	1413–1421
Murad II (abdicated)	1421–1444
Mehmed II	1444–1446
Murad II	1446–1451
Mehmed II	1451–1481
Bayezid II (deposed, likely poisoned)	1481–1512
Selim I	1512–1520
Suleiman I	1520–1566
Selim II	1566–1574
Murad III	1574–1595
Mehmed III	1595–1603
Ahmed I	1603–1617
Mustafa I (deposed)	1617–1618
Osman II (deposed, murdered)	1618–1622
Mustafa I (deposed)	1622–1623
Murad IV	1623–1640

Ibrahim I (deposed, executed)	1640–1648
Mehmed IV (deposed)	1648–1687
Suleiman II	1687–1691
Ahmed II	1691–1695
Mustafa II (deposed)	1695–1703
Ahmed III (deposed)	1703–1730
Mahmud I	1730–1754
Osman III	1754–1757
Mustafa III	1757–1774
Abdülhamid I	1774–1789
Selim III (deposed, murdered)	1789–1807
Mustafa IV (deposed, murdered)	1807–1808
Mahmud II	1808–1839
Abdülmecid I	1839–1861
Abdülaziz I (deposed, suicide)	1861–1876
Murad V (deposed)	1876
Abdülhamid II (deposed)	1876–1909
Mehmed V	1909–1918
Mehmed VI (sultanate abolished)	1918–1922
Abdülmecid II (caliph)	1922–1924

NOTES

To cut down on the number of notes, I have not cited basic reference tools every time I have used them for factual details. These include articles on individuals and historical events in the various editions of the *Encyclopaedia Iranica*, *Encyclopaedia of Islam*, *Encyclopaedia Judaica*, and the Turkish version of the *Encyclopaedia of Islam*, the *İslam Ansiklopedisi*, and its continuation as *Türkiye Diyanet Vakfı İslam Ansiklopedisi*. I have relied on Caroline Finkel, *Osman's Dream: The Story of the Ottoman Empire, 1300–1923* (London: John Murray, 2005) and Erik J. Zürcher, *Turkey: A Modern History*, 4th revised ed. (London: I.B. Tauris, 2017) for the basic outline and chronology of Ottoman history.

INTRODUCTION: THE WHITE CASTLE

1. Amos Oz, *A Tale of Love and Darkness*, trans. Nicholas de Lange (London: Chatto & Windus, 2004), 47.

2. Orhan Pamuk, *The White Castle: A Novel*, trans. Victoria Holbrook (New York: Vintage, 1998). The novel was originally published in Turkish as *Beyaz Kale* (Istanbul: Can, 1985). The quote in this paragraph is found on page 58.

3. Pamuk, *The White Castle*, 62, 65, 67, 69–70, 82.

4. Pamuk, *The White Castle*, 143, 151.

5. Pamuk, *The White Castle*, 155.

6. Those interested in this topic can read Noel Malcolm, *Useful Enemies: Islam and the Ottoman Empire in Western Political Thought, 1450–1750* (Oxford: Oxford University Press, 2019).

7. Franco Cardini, *Europe and Islam*, trans. Caroline Beamish (New York: Blackwell, 2001), 122, 136. Originally published in Italian in 1999 with the subtitle *History of a Misunderstanding*, the book was simultaneously published in translation in English, French, German, and Spanish two years later.

8. *The Ottomans: Europe's Muslim Emperors*, directed by Gillian Bancroft, narrated by Rageh Omar (London: BBC Two, 2013); Albert Hourani, 'How Should We Write the History of the Middle East?' *International Journal of Middle East Studies* 23 (1991): 130.

9. Paolo Giovio, writing about Suleiman I in his *Commentario* addressed to Charles V in 1532, quoted in Malcolm, *Useful Enemies*, 28.

10. My understanding of the tropes of Byzantine historiography come from Averil Cameron, *Byzantine Matters* (Princeton, NJ: Princeton University Press, 2014).

11. Cemal Kafadar, 'A Rome of One's Own: Reflections on Cultural Geography and Identity in the Lands of Rum', *Muqarnas* 24 (2007): 7–25, here 9.

12. Benjamin J. Kaplan, *Divided by Faith: Religious Conflict and the Practice of Toleration in Early Modern Europe* (Cambridge, MA: Belknap Press, 2007), 4.

13. Kaplan, *Divided by Faith*, 10.

14. Francis Osborne, *Political Reflections upon the Government of the Turks*, 1656, cited in Malcolm, *Useful Enemies*, 302.

15. Marc Baer and Ussama Makdisi, 'Tolerance and Conversion in the Ottoman Empire: A Conversation with Marc Baer and Ussama Makdisi', *Comparative Studies in Society & History* 51, no. 4 (October 2009): 927–940.

16. Kaplan, *Divided by Faith*, 8.

17. 'Tolerance and Conversion in the Ottoman Empire', 930.

18. Sir Paul Rycaut, *The History of the Present State of the Ottoman Empire*, 4th ed. (London: Printed for John Starkey and Henry Brome, 1675), 147–148.

19. Kaplan, *Divided by Faith*, 9.

CHAPTER 1: THE BEGINNING: GAZI OSMAN AND ORHAN

1. David Morgan, *Medieval Persia, 1040–1797* (Harlow, UK: Longman, 1988), 64–65.

2. Marshall G. S. Hodgson, *The Venture of Islam*, vol. 2, *The Expansion of Islam in the Middle Periods* (Chicago: University of Chicago Press, 1977), 415.

3. 'Part 2', *Islam: Empire of Faith*, directed by Robert Gardner (Arlington, VA: PBS, 2001); Hodgson, *The Venture of Islam*, 2:405.

4. *The Travels of Ibn Battuta: A.D., 1325–1354*, trans. and ed. C. Defremery, B. R. Sanguinetti, and H. A. R. Gibb, vol. 2 (Cambridge: Cambridge University Press, 1962), 446.

5. Aşıkpaşazade, *Tevārīh-i Āl-i Osmān, Aşıkpaşazade Tarihi* (Istanbul: Matba'a-i Āmire, 1332AH/1913–1914), 3–4.

6. Rudi Paul Lindner, *Explorations in Ottoman Prehistory* (Ann Arbor: University of Michigan Press, 2007), 15–34.

7. Aşıkpaşazade, *Tevārīh-i Āl-i Osmān*, 4.

8. Rudi Paul Lindner, *Nomads and Ottomans in Medieval Anatolia* (Bloomington: Indiana University Press, 1983), 4.

9. Rudi Paul Lindner, 'How Mongol Were the Early Ottomans?', in *The Mongol Empire and Its Legacy*, ed. Reuven Amitai-Preiss and David Morgan (Leiden, The Netherlands: Brill, 2000), 282–289.

10. Aşıkpaşazade, *Tevārīh-i Āl-i Osmān*, 9. For an analysis of this story, see Baki Tezcan, 'The Memory of the Mongols in Early Ottoman Historiography', in *Writing History at the Ottoman Court: Editing the Past, Fashioning the Future*, ed. H. Erdem Çıpa and Emine Fetvacı (Bloomington: Indiana University Press, 2013), 23–38.

11. Lindner, *Nomads and Ottomans in Medieval Anatolia*, 1–38.

12. A tenth-century Arab traveller gave a firsthand account of how the Oğuz Turkic women were so carefree they did not even worry about being nude in the presence of strangers. Ibn Fadlān, *Ibn Fadlān and the Land of Darkness: Arab Travellers in the Far North*, trans. Paul Lunde and Caroline Stone (London: Penguin, 2012), 12.

13. *The Adventures of Ibn Battuta: A Muslim Traveler of the 14th Century*, ed. Ross E. Dunn (Berkeley: University of California Press, 1986), 168.

14. Colin Imber, *The Ottoman Empire, 1300–1650: The Structure of Power* (London: Palgrave Macmillan, 2002), 252–253.

15. Hodgson, *The Venture of Islam*, 2:207, 211–214.

16. Hodgson, *The Venture of Islam*, 2:239.

17. This paragraph is based on Claude Addas, *Quest for the Red Sulphur: The Life of Ibn 'Arabī*, trans. Peter Kingsley (New York: Islamic Texts Society, 1993), 65–66, 98; Alexander D. Knysh, *Ibn 'Arabi in the Later Islamic Tradition: The Making of a Polemical Image in Medieval Islam* (Albany: State University of New York Press, 1999), 13, 110; Hodgson, *The Venture of Islam*, 2:227–230, 239–241; and Michael Chodkiewicz, *Seal of the Saints: Prophethood and Sainthood in the Doctrine of Ibn 'Arabi*, trans. Liadain Sherrard (Cambridge: The Islamic Texts Society, 1993).

18. Ahmet Yaşar Ocak, '*Kutb* ve isyan: Osmanlı Mehdici (Mesiyanik) hareketlerinin ideolojik arkaplanı üzerine bazi düşünceler', *Toplum ve Bilim* 83, *Osmanlı: Muktedirler ve Mâdunlar* (Kış 1999–2000): 48–56.

19. Andrew Peacock, 'Sufis and the Seljuk Court in Mongol Anatolia: Politics and Patronage in the Works of Jalal al-Din Rumi and Sultan Walad', in *The Seljuks of Anatolia: Court and Society in the Medieval Middle East*, ed. A. C. S. Peacock and Sara Nur Yıldız (London: I.B. Tauris, 2012), 206–226.

20. Franklin D. Lewis, *Rumi: Past and Present, East and West—The Life, Teachings, and Poetry of Jalâl al-Din Rûmi* (London: Oneworld, 2000), 168.

21. Quoted in Lewis, *Rumi*, 406.

22. My understanding of the deviant dervishes in this period is largely based on Ahmet T. Karamustafa, *God's Unruly Friends: Dervish Groups in*

the Islamic Middle Period, 1200–1550 (Salt Lake City: University of Utah Press, 1994).

23. Lewis, *Rumi*, 149–151.

24. Hodgson, *The Venture of Islam*, 2:498.

25. *Encyclopaedia of Islam, THREE*, s.v. 'Baba Ilyas-i Horasani', by Ahmet Yaşar Ocak, first published online 2015, http://dx.doi.org/10.1163/1573-3912_ei3_COM_24265.

26. *Encyclopaedia of Islam, THREE*, s.v. 'Bektaş, Hacı', by Thierry Zarcone, first published online 2012, http://dx.doi.org/10.1163/1573-3912_ei3_COM_24009.

27. *Velâyetnâme*, ed. H. Duran, Ankara, 2007, 282–290 (fols. 58a–60a), cited in Zeynep Yürekli, *Architecture and Hagiography in the Ottoman Empire: The Politics of Bektashi Shrines in the Classical Age* (London: Routledge, 2012), 32.

28. Yürekli, *Architecture and Hagiography in the Ottoman Empire*, 107.

29. *Vilâyet-nâme: Manâkıb-ı Hünkâr Hacı Bektâş-ı Velî*, ed. Abdülbaki Gölpınarlı (Istanbul, 1958), 71–75, cited in Cemal Kafadar, *Between Two Worlds: The Construction of the Ottoman State* (Berkeley: University of California Press, 1995), 30.

30. Aşıkpaşazade, *Tevārīh-i Āl-i Osmān*, 6.

31. *The Book of Dede Korkut*, trans. Geoffrey Lewis (New York: Penguin, 1972), 40–41.

32. Lindner, *Nomads and Ottomans in Medieval Anatolia*, 37–38.

33. Kemal Silay, 'Introduction', in *Tac'd-Din Ibrahim Bin Hizir Ahmedi, History of the Kings of the Ottoman Lineage and Their Holy Raids* [Ghaza] *Against the Infidels*, trans. Kemal Silay, ed. Şinasi Tekin and Gönül Alpay Tekin (Cambridge, MA: Harvard University Press, 2004), vii–xix.

34. Ahmedi, *History of the Kings of the Ottoman Lineage*, 1; Quoted in Pál Fodor, 'Ahmedî's *Dāsitān* as a Source of Early Ottoman History', *Acta Orientalia Academiae Scientiarum Hung.* XXXVIII, no. 1–2 (1984): 41–54, here 47.

35. Ahmedi, *History of the Kings of the Ottoman Lineage*, 3–4.

36. Ahmedi, *History of the Kings of the Ottoman Lineage*, 4.

37. Kafadar, *Between Two Worlds*, 76–78.

38. Mehmed Neşri, *Kitab-i cihan-nüma, Neşri tarihi*, ed. Faik Reşat Unat and Mehmed Köymen (Ankara: Türk Tarih Kurumu, 1949), 78–79 and 92–95.

39. Aşıkpaşazade, *Tevārīh-i Āl-i Osmān*, 11, 12, 23–25.

40. Kafadar, *Between Two Worlds*, 85.

41. Halil Inalcik, 'Timariotes chrétiens en Albanie au XV siècle d'après un registre de timars Ottoman', *Mitteilungen des Österreichischen Staatsarchivs* 4 (1952): 118–138; Halil Inalcik, 'Stefan Duşan'dan Osmanlı İmparatorluğuna: XV. asırda Rumeli'de hıristiyan sipahiler ve menşeleri', in *Mélanges Fuad Köprülü* (Ankara: Dil ve Tarih Coğrafya Fakültesi, 1953):

67–108; Halil Inalcik, 'Ottoman Methods of Conquest', *Studia Islamica* II (1954): 104–129; Ahmet Yaşar Ocak, 'Social, Cultural and Intellectual Life, 1071–1453', in *The Cambridge History of Turkey*, vol. 1, *Byzantium to Turkey, 1071–1453*, ed. Kate Fleet (Cambridge: Cambridge University Press, 2009), 353–422, here 364.

42. William Shakespeare, *Henry V*, act 4, scene 3.

43. Aşıkpaşazade, *Tevārīh-i Āl-i Osmān*, 13.

44. Aşıkpaşazade, *Tevārīh-i Āl-i Osmān*, 4–5.

45. Aşıkpaşazade, *Tevārīh-i Āl-i Osmān*, 15–17; Leslie Peirce, *The Imperial Harem: Women and Sovereignty in the Ottoman Empire* (Oxford: Oxford University Press, 1993), 34–35.

46. Imber, *The Ottoman Empire, 1300–1650*, 254–255.

47. Caroline Finkel, *Osman's Dream: The History of the Ottoman Empire* (London: John Murray, 2005), 7.

48. Tezcan, 'The Memory of the Mongols', 28.

49. Ahmedi, *History of the Kings of the Ottoman Lineage*, 6.

50. The quotes in this paragraph are from *The Adventures of Ibn Battuta*, 151–152.

51. G. Georgiades Arnakis, 'Gregory Palamas Among the Turks and Documents of His Captivity as Historical Sources', *Speculum: A Journal of Mediaeval Studies* 26, no. 1 (January 1951): 104–118, here 106.

52. Arnakis, 'Gregory Palamas Among the Turks', 108.

53. Aşıkpaşazade, *Tevārīh-i Āl-i Osmān*, 36.

54. Lindner, *Explorations in Ottoman Prehistory*, 35–56.

55. Aşıkpaşazade, *Tevārīh-i Āl-i Osmān*, 36.

CHAPTER 2: THE SULTAN AND HIS CONVERTED SLAVES: MURAD I

1. Kafadar, *Between Two Worlds*, 126.

2. Uli Schamiloglu, 'The Rise of the Ottoman Empire: The Black Death in Medieval Anatolia and Its Impact on Turkish Civilization', in *Views from the Edge: Essays in Honor of Richard W. Bulliet*, ed. Neguin Yavari, Lawrence G. Potter, and Jean-Marc Oppenheim (New York: Columbia University Press, 2004), 271.

3. Rudi Paul Lindner, 'Seljuk Mints and Silver Mines', *Turcica* 41 (2009): 363–371.

4. Lindner, *Explorations in Ottoman Prehistory*, 102–116.

5. Kafadar, *Between Two Worlds*, 131.

6. Hodgson, *The Venture of Islam*, 2:416.

7. Kafadar, *Between Two Worlds*, 136–137.

8. Aşıkpaşazade, *Tevārīh-i Āl-i Osmān*, 36–37. We do not know what happened to Osman's other sons.

9. Gagan Sood, 'Knowledge of the Art of Governance: The Mughal and Ottoman Empires in the Early Seventeenth Century', *Journal of the Royal Asiatic Society* 30, no. 2 (2020): 253–282.

10. Heath W. Lowry, 'Impropriety and Impiety Among the Early Ottoman Sultans (135–1451)', *The Turkish Studies Association Journal* 26, no. 2 (2002): 29–38, here 31.

11. Rudi Paul Lindner, 'Bapheus and Pelekanon', *International Journal of Turkish Studies* 13, no. 1–2 (2007): 7–26.

12. Doukas, *Decline and Fall of Byzantium to the Ottoman Turks: An Annotated Translation of "Historia Turco-Byzantina"*, trans. Harry J. Magoulias (Detroit: Wayne State University Press, 1975), 73.

13. Judith Herrin, *Unrivalled Influence: Women and Empire in Byzantium* (Princeton, NJ: Princeton University Press, 2013), 314.

14. Speros Vryonis Jr., *The Decline of Medieval Hellenism in Anatolia and the Process of Islamization from the Eleventh to the Fifteenth Century* (Berkeley: University of California Press, 1971), 288–402, especially 348–350 and 402.

15. F. W. Hasluck, *Christianity and Islam Under the Sultans*, ed. Margaret Hasluck, 2 vols. (New York: Octagon Books, 1973); V. L. Ménage, 'The Islamization of Anatolia', in *Conversion to Islam*, ed. Nehemia Levtzion (New York: Holmes & Meier, 1979), 52–67; David Shankland, ed., *Archaeology, Anthropology and Heritage in the Balkans and Anatolia: The Life and Times of F.W. Hasluck*, 2 vols. (Istanbul: Isis, 2013).

16. The deed was first cited in İsmail Hakkı Uzunçarşılı, 'Gazi Orhan Bey vakfıyesi, 724 Rebiülevvel-1324 Mart', *Belleten* V (1941): 277–288. For more recent discussions of its significance, see Kafadar, *Between Two Worlds*, 61; and Finkel, *Osman's Dream*, 10.

17. Nikephorus Gregoras, *Byzantina Historia*, vol. 3, 202.12–203.4, cited in Rustam Shukurov, 'Byzantine Appropriation of the Orient: Notes on its Principles and Patterns', in *Islam and Christianity in Medieval Anatolia*, ed. A. C. S. Peacock, Bruno de Nicola, and Sara Yıldız (London: Routledge, 2015), 180.

18. Tom Papademetriou, *Render unto the Sultan: Power, Authority, and the Greek Orthodox Church in the Early Ottoman Centuries* (Oxford: Oxford University Press, 2015).

19. Schamiloglu, 'The Rise of the Ottoman Empire', 272.

20. Doukas, *Decline and Fall of Byzantium to the Ottoman Turks*, 135.

21. Celia Kerslake, 'A Critical Edition and Translation of the Introductory Sections and the First Thirteen Chapters of the "Selīmnāme" of Celālzāde Mustafā Çelebi' (PhD diss., University of Oxford, 1975), 46b.

22. Imber, *The Ottoman Empire, 1300–1650*, 135.

23. 'Kavanin-i Yeniçeriyan-i Dergah-ı Ali' (The Laws of the Janissaries), in *Osmanlı Kanunnameleri* 9 (Istanbul, 1996), ed. Ahmed Akgündüz, quoted in Imber, *The Ottoman Empire, 1300–1650*, 136.

24. Inalcik, 'Timariotes chrétiens en Albanie au XV siècle'; Inalcik, 'Stefan Duşan'dan Osmanlı İmparatorluğuna'; and Inalcik, 'Ottoman Methods of Conquest'.

25. Metin Kunt, 'Transformation of *Zimmi* into *Askeri*', in *Christians and Jews in the Ottoman Empire: The Functioning of a Plural Society*, ed. Benjamin Braude and Bernard Lewis (New York: Holmes & Meier, 1982), 1:59.

26. Alexander Lopasic, 'Islamisation of the Balkans with Special Reference to Bosnia', *Journal of Islamic Studies* 5, no. 2 (1994): 163–186.

27. *Encyclopaedia of Islam, THREE*, s.v. 'Booty', by Rudolph Peters, first published online 2015, http://dx.doi.org/10.1163/1573-3912_ei3_COM_25367.

28. Muhammed b. Mahmûd-i Sirvânî, *Tuhfe-i Murâdî*, ed. Mustafa Argunsah (Ankara, 1999), 73, quoted in Kafadar, 'A Rome of One's Own', 13–14.

29. Konstantin Mihailović, *Memoirs of a Janissary*, trans. Benjamin Stolz, historical commentary and notes by Svat Soucek (Ann Arbor: University of Michigan Press, 1975).

30. Sadeddin, *Tacü't-Tevarih* (Istanbul, 1279/1862–1863), 1:41.

31. Halil Inalcik, *The Ottoman Empire: The Classical Age, 1300–1600* (London: Weidenfeld & Nicolson, 1973), 78.

32. Speros Vryonis, 'Isidore Glabas and the Turkish Devshirme', *Speculum* 31, no. 3 (July 1956): 433–443.

33. The text is available on the website of the United Nations Human Rights Office of the High Commissioner: UN General Assembly, Resolution 260 A, Convention on the Prevention and Punishment of the Crime of Genocide, December 9, 1948, www.ohchr.org/en/professionalinterest/pages/crimeofgenocide.aspx.

34. Ahmet Akgündüz, *Osmanlı kanunnâmeleri ve hukukî tahlilleri*, vol. 1, *Osmanlı hukukuna giriş ve Fatih devri kanunnameleri* (Istanbul: Fey, 1990), 341.

35. Cemal Kafadar, 'The Question of Ottoman Decline', *Harvard Middle Eastern and Islamic Review* 4, no. 1–2 (1997–1998): 30–75, here 39.

36. Kemalpaşazade, *Tevârîh-i Âl-i Osmân*, cited in Ahmet Uğur, *The Reign of Sultan Selīm I in the Light of the Selīm-nāme Literature*, Islamkundliche Untersuchungen, Bd. 109 (Berlin: Klaus Schwarz, 1985), 354–356.

37. Nicolas Vatin and Gilles Veinstein, *Le Sérail ébranlé: Essai sur les morts, dépositions et avènements des sultans ottomans XIVe-XIXe siècle* (Paris: Fayard, 2003), 170.

38. Aşıkpaşazade, *Tevārīh-i Āl-i Osmān*, 63–64.

39. Doukas, *Decline and Fall of Byzantium to the Ottoman Turks*, 83.

40. Imber, *The Ottoman Empire, 1300–1650*, 255.

41. Doukas, *Decline and Fall of Byzantium to the Ottoman Turks*, 84.

CHAPTER 3: RESURRECTING THE DYNASTY: BAYEZID I, MEHMED I, AND MURAD II

1. Lowry, 'Impropriety and Impiety', 30.

2. Lowry, 'Impropriety and Impiety', 31.

3. Hodgson, *The Venture of Islam*, 2:433–434.

4. Johann Schiltberger, *The Bondage and Travels of Johann Schiltburger, a Native of Bavaria, in Europe, Asia and Africa, 1396–1427*, reprint of Hakluyt edition of 1879 (Frankfurt, 1995), cited in Finkel, *Osman's Dream*, 29.

5. The histories include anonymous *Chronicles of the Ottoman Dynasty* and those written by Aşıkpaşazade, Oruç b. Adil, Mehmed Neşri, Şehnameci Lokman, and Şukrullah. Mehmet Fuad Koprülü, 'Yıldırım Beyazıd'ın esareti ve intiharı hakkında', *Belleten* 1, no. 2 (1937): 591–603. Several years later, Bayezid I's remains were transferred for burial in his mosque-dervish lodge complex in Bursa.

6. Jerry Brotton, *This Orient Isle: Elizabethan England and the Islamic World* (London: Allen Lane, 2016), 162–163.

7. For the most recent production of the Royal Shakespeare Company, see 'Synopsis', *Tamburlaine*, Royal Shakespeare Company, www.rsc.org.uk/tamburlaine/the-plot.

8. Marlowe's work was but one of many commemorations in woodcut, painting, tapestry, and opera illustrating Bayezid I's humiliating treatment, and that of his wife, allegedly forced to serve Timur and his guests at a banquet in the nude. These works include Jean Magnon, *Le Gran Tamerlan et Bejezet* (1648); the paintings at Eggenberg Palace near Graz, Austria (1670s); Nicholas Rowe, *Tamerlane* (1702); George Frideric Handel, *Tamerlano* (1725); and Antonio Vivaldi, *Bajazet* (1735).

9. Halîl bin İsmâil bin Şeyh Bedrüddîn Mahmûd, *Simavna Kadısıoğlu Şeyh Bedreddin manâkıbı*, ed. Abdülbâki Gölpınarlı and İsmet Sungurbey (Istanbul: Eti, 1967).

10. The complete text of Abdülvasi Çelebi, *Halilname* (1414), is translated in Dimitris J. Kastritsis, *The Sons of Bayezid: Empire Building and Representation in the Ottoman Civil War of 1402–13* (Leiden, The Netherlands: Brill, 2007), 221–232.

11. Doukas, *Decline and Fall of Byzantium to the Ottoman Turks*, 119–120.

12. Doukas, *Decline and Fall of Byzantium to the Ottoman Turks*, 121.

13. Doukas, *Decline and Fall of Byzantium to the Ottoman Turks*, 121.

14. Doukas, *Decline and Fall of Byzantium to the Ottoman Turks*, 121.

15. Shukrullah ibn Shahabeddin, *Bahjat al-tavârîkh* (1456–1468), quoted in Mehmed Şerefeddin Yaltkaya, *Simavne Kadısı oğlu Bedreddin* (Istanbul: Evkafı İslâmiye, 1924), 85–86.

16. Nâzım Hikmet, 'Simavne Kadısı Oğlu Şeyh Bedreddin Destanı' (1936), in Nâzım Hikmet, *Bütün Şiirleri* (Istanbul: Yapı Kredi, 2017), 503.

17. Gülru Necipoğlu-Kafadar, 'The Süleymaniye Complex in Istanbul: An Interpretation', *Muqarnas* 3 (1985): 92–117, here 110.

18. Aşıkpaşazade, *Tevārīh-i Āl-i Osmān*, 93.

19. Hikmet, 'Simavne Kadısı Oğlu Şeyh Bedreddin Destanı', 516.

20. Hikmet, 'Simavne Kadısı Oğlu Şeyh Bedreddin Destanı', 510.

21. Neşri, *Kitab-i cihan-nüma*.

22. Aşıkpaşazade, *Tevārīh-i Āl-i Osmān*, 92.

23. Aşıkpaşazade, *Tevārīh-i Āl-i Osmān*, 93.

24. Oruç b. Adil, *Tevarih-i Al-i Osman*, ed. Franz Babinger (Hannover, 1925), 43–45, here 44.

25. Idris Bitlisi, *Heşt behişt* (Eight Paradises, 1502), British Library Persian Mss Add 7746 and 7747, 229b–230a.

26. Hikmet, 'Simavne Kadısı Oğlu Şeyh Bedreddin Destanı', 498.

27. Michel Balivet, *Islam mystique et révolution armée dans les Balkans ottomans: Vie du Cheikh Bedreddîn, 'le Hallâj des Turcs' (1358/59–1416)* (Istanbul: Isis, 1995); Ahmet Yaşar Ocak, *Osmanlı toplumunda zındıklar ve mülhidler (15.–17. yüzyıllar)* (Istanbul: Tarih Vakfı, 1998), 136–202.

28. Morgan, *Medieval Persia, 1040–1797*, 92; William H. McNeill, 'The Age of Gunpowder Empires, 1450–1800', in *Islamic & European Expansion: The Forging of a Global Order*, ed. Michael Adas (Philadelphia: Temple University Press, 1993), 103–139; William H. McNeill, *The Pursuit of Power: Technology, Armed Force, and Society Since A.D. 1000* (Chicago: University of Chicago Press, 1983).

29. Aşıkpaşazade, *Tevārīh-i Āl-i Osmān*, 95, and Mehmed Neşri, *Kitâb-ı cihân-nümâ*, ed. F. R. Unat and M. A. Köymen (Ankara: Türk Tarih Kurumu, 1987), 2:552–554.

30. Aşıkpaşazade, *Tevārīh-i Āl-i Osmān*, 96.

31. Anonymous, *Gazavât-i Sultân Murâd b. Mehemmed Hân. Izladi ve Varna Savaşları Üzerinde Anonim Gazavâtnâme*, ed. Halil Inalcik and Mevlud Oğuz (Ankara: Türk Tarih Kurumu, 1989), translated in Colin Imber, *The Crusade of Varna, 1443–45*, Crusade Texts in Translation 14 (Farnham, UK: Ashgate 2006), 50.

32. Anonymous, *Gazavât-i Sultân Murâd b. Mehemmed Hân*, 60.

33. Anonymous, *Gazavât-i Sultân Murâd b. Mehemmed Hân*, 70.

34. Anonymous, *Gazavât-i Sultân Murâd b. Mehemmed Hân*, 71.

35. Anonymous, *Gazavât-i Sultân Murâd b. Mehemmed Hân*, 73.

36. Anonymous, *Gazavât-i Sultân Murâd b. Mehemmed Hân*, 74.

37. Vatin and Veinstein, *Le Sérail ébranlé*, 309.

38. Lowry, 'Impropriety and Impiety', 36–37.

39. Anonymous, *Gazavât-i Sultân Murâd b. Mehemmed Hân*, 77–78.

40. Anonymous, *Gazavât-i Sultân Murâd b. Mehemmed Hân*, 79.

41. Anonymous, *Gazavât-i Sultân Murâd b. Mehemmed Hân*, 79–80.

42. Gasparo Zancaruolo, *Cronaca Zancaruola*, unpublished, excerpt in Franz Babinger, 'Von Amurath zu Amurath: Vor- und Nachspiel der

Schlacht bei Warna (1444)', *Oriens* 3 (1950): 595–596, translated in Imber, *The Crusade of Varna*, 186.

43. Anonymous, *Gazavât-i Sultân Murâd b. Mehemmed Hân*, 83.
44. Anonymous, *Gazavât-i Sultân Murâd b. Mehemmed Hân*, 84.
45. Anonymous, *Gazavât-i Sultân Murâd b. Mehemmed Hân*, 85.
46. Anonymous, *Gazavât-i Sultân Murâd b. Mehemmed Hân*, 86.
47. Anonymous, *Gazavât-i Sultân Murâd b. Mehemmed Hân*, 89.
48. Michel Beheim, 'Türkenschlacht bei Warna', in Hans Gille and Ingeborg Spriewald, *Die Gedichte des Michel Beheim* (Berlin: Akademie-Verlag, 1968), vol. 1, no. 104, 328–356, translated in Imber, *The Crusade of Varna*, 176.
49. Anonymous, *Gazavât-i Sultân Murâd b. Mehemmed Hân*, 60.
50. Anonymous, *Gazavât-i Sultân Murâd b. Mehemmed Hân*, 92.
51. Beheim, 'Türkenschlacht bei Warna', 177.
52. Anonymous, *Gazavât-i Sultân Murâd b. Mehemmed Hân*, 96–98.
53. Anonymous, *Gazavât-i Sultân Murâd b. Mehemmed Hân*, 100.
54. Peter Schreiner, *Die byzantinischen Kleinchroniken* (Vienna: Verlag der Österreichischen Akademie der Wissenschaften, 1975), I, chronicle 54, 13, 389, translated in Imber, *The Crusade of Varna*, 187.
55. Anonymous, *Gazavât-i Sultân Murâd b. Mehemmed Hân*, 100.
56. Aşıkpaşazade, *Tevârîh-i Âl-i Osmân*, ed. Nihal Atsız (Istanbul: Türkiye, 1949), 183–185, translated in Imber, *The Crusade of Varna*, 185.
57. Anonymous, *Gazavât-i Sultân Murâd b. Mehemmed Hân*, 100.
58. Anonymous, *Gazavât-i Sultân Murâd b. Mehemmed Hân*, 102.
59. Anonymous, *Gazavât-i Sultân Murâd b. Mehemmed Hân*, 102.
60. Beheim, 'Türkenschlacht bei Warna', 179.
61. Al-Sakhāwī, *Al-Tibr al-Mabsûk fî Dhayl al-Sulûk* (Cairo, n.d.), 98–99, translated in Imber, *The Crusade of Varna*, 187.
62. Al-Sakhāwī, *Al-Tibr al-Mabsûk fî Dhayl al-Sulûk*, 188.
63. Aşıkpaşazade, *Tevârîh-i Âl-i Osmân*, 264.
64. Aşıkpaşazade, *Tevārīh-i Âl-i Osmān*, 139–140.
65. Kemalpaşazade, *Tevârîh-i âl-i Osmân*, ed. Ş. Turan (Ankara: Türk Tarih Kurumu, 1954), 7:9–10.

CHAPTER 4: CONQUERING THE SECOND ROME: MEHMED II

1. Gülru Necipoğlu, *Architecture, Ceremonial, and Power: The Topkapı Palace in the Fifteenth and Sixteenth Centuries* (Cambridge, MA: Harvard University Press, 1991), 249.
2. Halil Inalcık, 'The Policy of Mehmed II Toward the Greek Population of Istanbul and the Byzantine Buildings of the City', *Dumbarton Oaks Papers* 23/24 (1969/1970): 231–249; *Encyclopaedia of Islam 2*, s.v., 'Istanbul', by Halil Inalcik.
3. Doukas, *Decline and Fall of Byzantium to the Ottoman Turks*, 194.

4. Doukas, *Decline and Fall of Byzantium to the Ottoman Turks*, 196.

5. Doukas, *Decline and Fall of Byzantium to the Ottoman Turks*, 200–201.

6. Kritovoulos, *History of Mehmed the Conqueror*, trans. Charles T. Riggs (Princeton, NJ: Princeton University Press, 1954), 56.

7. Kritovoulos, *History of Mehmed the Conqueror*, 58–59.

8. Doukas, *Decline and Fall of Byzantium to the Ottoman Turks*, 200–201.

9. Doukas, *Decline and Fall of Byzantium to the Ottoman Turks*, 201.

10. Kritovoulos, *History of Mehmed the Conqueror*, 73.

11. Kritovoulos, *History of Mehmed the Conqueror*, 74.

12. I modified the passage quoted in Bernard Lewis, *Istanbul and the Civilization of the Ottoman Empire* (Norman: University of Oklahoma Press, 1963), 8, by comparing it with the text of Friedrich Giese, ed., *Die altosmanische Chronik des 'Āşıkpaşazāde* (Leipzig, Germany: Otto Harrassowitz, 1929), 132.

13. Tursun Bey, *Târîh-i Ebü'l-Feth*, ed. Mertol Tulun (Istanbul: Baha, 1977), 62.

14. Doukas, *Decline and Fall of Byzantium to the Ottoman Turks*, 225–226.

15. Doukas, *Decline and Fall of Byzantium to the Ottoman Turks*, 227.

16. Kritovoulos, *History of Mehmed the Conqueror*, 77.

17. Tursun Bey, *Târîh-i Ebü'l-Feth*, 63.

18. Quoted in Lewis, *Istanbul and the Civilization of the Ottoman Empire*, 7–8.

19. Walter G. Andrews and Mehmet Kalpaklı, *The Age of Beloveds: Love and the Beloved in Early-Modern Ottoman and European Culture and Society* (Durham, NC: Duke University Press, 2005), 1–8.

20. Doukas, *Decline and Fall of Byzantium to the Ottoman Turks*, 235.

21. Kritovoulos, *History of Mehmed the Conqueror*, 82.

22. Kritovoulos, *History of Mehmed the Conqueror*, 85–86.

23. Lowry, 'Impropriety and Impiety', 33–34.

24. Doukas, *Decline and Fall of Byzantium to the Ottoman Turks*, 233–235.

25. Amiroutzes writing to Mehmed II in 1466, quoted in Inalcik, 'The Policy of Mehmed II Toward the Greek Population of Istanbul', 233.

26. Kritovoulos, *History of Mehmed the Conqueror*, 3.

27. Kritovoulos, *History of Mehmed the Conqueror*, 14.

28. Kritovoulos, *History of Mehmed the Conqueror*, 4.

29. Kritovoulos, *History of Mehmed the Conqueror*, 14.

30. Giacomo de' Languschi, quoted in Franz Babinger, *Mehmed the Conqueror and His Time*, trans. Ralph Manheim, ed. William C. Hickman, Bollingen Series XCVI (Princeton, NJ: Princeton University Press, 1978), 112.

31. Mehmed Neşri, *Kitâb-ı cihân-nümâ*, ed. F. R. Unat and M. A. Köymen (Ankara: Türk Tarih Kurumu, 1987), 2:711, 713.

32. Tursun Bey, *Târîh-i Ebü'l-Feth*, 75.

33. Tursun Bey, *Târîh-i Ebü'l-Feth*, 65–76.

34. Tursun Bey, *Târîh-i Ebü'l-Feth*, 67–68.

35. Molly Greene, *The Edinburgh History of the Greeks, 1453 to 1768: The Ottoman Empire* (Edinburgh: Edinburgh University Press, 2015), 4, 25.

36. Kritovoulos, *History of Mehmed the Conqueror*, 93.

37. *Encyclopaedia of Islam 2*, s.v. 'Istanbul', by Halil Inalcik.

38. Halil Inalcik, 'Ottoman Galata, 1453–1553', in *Essays in Ottoman History* (Istanbul: Eren, 1998), 275–376.

39. Mark Epstein, 'The Leadership of the Ottoman Jews', in *Christians and Jews in the Ottoman Empire*, 1:101–115.

40. Kevork Bardakjian, 'The Rise of the Armenian Patriarchate of Constantinople', in *Christians and Jews in the Ottoman Empire*, 1:89–100.

41. Benjamin Braude, 'Foundation Myths of the *Millet* System', in *Christians and Jews in the Ottoman Empire*, 1:69–88.

42. Greene, *The Edinburgh History of the Greeks*, 183, referring to an eighteenth-century imperial order solicited by the patriarch.

43. Greene, *The Edinburgh History of the Greeks*, 29–31.

44. Greene, *The Edinburgh History of the Greeks*, 29, 64.

45. Greene, *The Edinburgh History of the Greeks*, 64–65.

46. Necipoğlu, *Architecture, Ceremonial, and Power*, 4.

47. Necipoğlu, *Architecture, Ceremonial, and Power*, 12, 248.

48. Necipoğlu, *Architecture, Ceremonial, and Power*, 20, 86, 94.

49. Necipoğlu, *Architecture, Ceremonial, and Power*, 242, 247–248.

50. Vatin and Veinstein, *Le Sérail ébranlé*, 272–273.

51. Inalcik, *The Ottoman Empire*, 61–62.

52. Eleazar Birnbaum, 'Hekim Yakub, Physician to Sultan Mehemmed the Conqueror', *Harofe Haivri: The Hebrew Medical Journal* 1 (1961): 222–250.

53. Imperial decree issued by Bayezid II, quoted in Imber, *The Ottoman Empire, 1300–1650*, 133. Imber provides no page number to his reference.

54. Mustafa Ali, *Künh ül-ahbar* (Istanbul, 1277AH/1861), 1:14–15.

55. Ali, *Künh ül-ahbar*, 1:14–15.

56. Ali, *Künh ül-ahbar*, 1:14–15.

57. Kafadar, *Between Two Worlds*, 146.

58. Necipoğlu, *Architecture, Ceremonial, and Power*, 90.

59. Greene, *The Edinburgh History of the Greeks*, 28.

60. Karen Barkey, *Empire of Difference: The Ottomans in Comparative Perspective* (Cambridge: Cambridge University Press, 2008), 80.

61. Greene, *The Edinburgh History of the Greeks*, 62–63.

62. Halil Inalcik, 'Mehmed the Conqueror and His Time', *Speculum* 35 (1960): 408–427.

63. Kafadar, *Between Two Worlds*, 147.

64. Greene, *The Edinburgh History of the Greeks*, 27.

65. Aşıkpaşazade, *Tevārīh-i Āl-i Osmān*, 143.

66. Halil Inalcik, 'Ahmed 'Âşıkî ('Âşık Paşa-zâde) on the Conqueror's Policy to Repopulate Istanbul', in Halil Inalcik, *The Survey of Istanbul 1455: The Text, English Translation, Analysis of the Text, Documents* (Istanbul: Türkiye İş Bankası Kültür Yayınları, 2012), 586–587; Tursun Bey, *Târîh-i Ebü'l-Feth*, 67–69.

67. Aşıkpaşazade, *Tevārīh-i Āl-i Osmān*, 191–192.

68. Oruç, *Tevārīh-i Āl-i Osmān, Die frühosmanischen Jahrbücher des Urudsch*, ed. F. Babinger (Hannover: Orient-Buchhandlung Heinz Lafaire, 1925), 131.

69. Kafadar, *Between Two Worlds*, 146–147.

70. Halil Inalcik, 'The Socio-Political Effects of the Diffusion of Firearms in the Middle East', in *War, Technology and Society in the Middle East*, ed. V. J. Parry and Malcolm Yapp (Oxford: Oxford University Press, 1975), 195–217, here 207.

71. Juvainî, *The History of the World Conqueror*, in *The Islamic World*, ed. William H. McNeill and Marilyn Robinson Waldman (Chicago: University of Chicago Press, 1973), 254–255.

72. Hodgson, *The Venture of Islam*, 2:406.

73. Juvainî, *The History of the World Conqueror*, 256.

74. Rustam Shukurov, 'Harem Christianity: The Byzantine Identity of Seljuk Princes', in *The Seljuks of Anatolia*, 115–150.

75. Greene, *The Edinburgh History of the Greeks*, 36–37.

76. Inalcik, 'The Policy of Mehmed II Toward the Greek Population of Istanbul'.

CHAPTER 5: A RENAISSANCE PRINCE: MEHMED II

1. For example, Inalcik, *The Ottoman Empire*, 30.

2. Lindner, *Nomads and Ottomans in Medieval Anatolia*, 1.

3. J. Michael Rogers, 'Mehmed the Conqueror: Between East and West', in *Bellini and the East*, ed. Caroline Campbell, Alan Chong, Deborah Howard, and J. Michael Rogers (London: National Gallery, 2005), 80–97, here 82.

4. Rogers, 'Mehmed the Conqueror: Between East and West', 83.

5. Greene, *The Edinburgh History of the Greeks*, 28.

6. On the Islamisation of Trabzon, see Heath Lowry, *The Islamization and Turkification of the City of Trabzon (Trebizond), 1461–1583* (Istanbul: Isis, 2009).

7. Kritovoulos, *History of Mehmed the Conqueror*, 177.

8. Kritovoulos, *History of Mehmed the Conqueror*, 209–210.

9. Rogers, 'Mehmed the Conqueror: Between East and West', 83.

10. Rogers, 'Mehmed the Conqueror: Between East and West', 95, 92.

11. Rogers, 'Mehmed the Conqueror: Between East and West', 89.

12. Marshall G. S. Hodgson, 'Cultural Patterning in Islamdom and the Occident', in *Rethinking World History: Essays on Europe, Islam, and World History*, ed. Edmund Burke III (Cambridge: Cambridge University Press, 1993), 164.

13. Edmund Burke III, 'Introduction: Marshall G. S. Hodgson and World History', in Hodgson, *Rethinking World History*, xix.

14. Nancy Bisaha, *Creating East and West: Renaissance Humanists and the Ottoman Turks* (Philadelphia: University of Pennsylvania Press, 2006), 94.

15. Bisaha, *Creating East and West*, 58–60.

16. Bisaha, *Creating East and West*, 62.

17. Bisaha, *Creating East and West*, 46.

18. Aeneas Silvius Piccolomini (Pope Pius II), quoted in Bisaha, *Creating East and West*, 68.

19. Erasmus, *Consultatio de bello Turcis inferendo* (1530), quoted in Bisaha, *Creating East and West*, 175.

20. Kritovoulos, *History of Mehmed the Conqueror*, 181–182.

21. Lucette Valensi, *The Birth of the Despot: Venice and the Sublime Porte*, trans. Arthur Denner (Ithaca, NY: Cornell University Press, 1993), 23.

22. Dandolo's report of 1562, quoted in Valensi, *The Birth of the Despot*, 28.

23. Valensi, *The Birth of the Despot*, 35.

24. Morosini's report of 1585, quoted in Valensi, *The Birth of the Despot*, 73.

25. Malcolm, *Useful Enemies*, 202.

26. 'The Conquest of Tunis Series', Tapices flamencos en España, Carlos de Amberes Foundation and Grupo Enciclo, http://tapestries.flandesen hispania.org/The_Conquest_of_Tunis_series.

27. Malcolm, *Useful Enemies*, 159.

28. Scipione Ammirato, who wrote for the Medici family in Florence, analysed in Malcolm, *Useful Enemies*, 182–183.

29. Niccolò Machiavelli, *The Prince*, trans. Ninian Hill Thomson (Digireads.com, 2015), 10.

30. Quoted in John J. Saunders, ed., *The Muslim World on the Eve of Europe's Expansion* (Englewood Cliffs, NJ: Prentice Hall, 1966), 25.

31. Brotton, *This Orient Isle*, 176.

32. William Shakespeare, *Richard II*, 2.1.40–50.

33. Brotton, *This Orient Isle*, 1–7, 287.

34. Brotton, *This Orient Isle*, 287.

35. Daniel Vitkus, *Turning Turk: English Theater and the Multicultural Mediterranean, 1570–1630* (New York: Palgrave Macmillan, 2003), chapter 4.

36. Nabil Matar, 'Britons and Muslims in the Early Modern Period: From Prejudice to (a Theory of) Toleration', *Patterns of Prejudice* 43 (2009): 213–231.

37. Christine Isom-Verhaaren, *Allies with the Infidel: The Ottoman and French Alliance in the Sixteenth Century* (London: I.B. Tauris, 2011).

38. Brotton, *This Orient Isle*, 5.

39. Quoted in Susan Skilliter, 'Three Letters from the Ottoman "Sultana" Safiye to Queen Elizabeth I', in *Documents from Islamic Chanceries*, ed. S. M. Stern (Cambridge, MA: Harvard University Press, 1965), 119–157, here 131.

40. Quoted in Skilliter, 'Three Letters from the Ottoman "Sultana" Safiye to Queen Elizabeth I', 139, note 57.

41. Brotton, *This Orient Isle*, 8.

42. Marcus Gheeraerts the Younger, *Portrait of an Unknown Woman*, c. 1590–1600, oil on canvas, 216.2 x 135.5 cm, Hampton Court Palace, www.rct.uk/collection/406024/portrait-of-an-unknown-woman#/referer /682722/682750.

43. For an exploration of their lives see Nabil Matar, *Islam in Britain, 1558–1665* (Cambridge: Cambridge University Press, 1998); Nabil Matar, *Turks, Moors, and Englishmen in the Age of Discovery* (New York: Columbia University Press, 1999).

44. Matar, *Turks, Moors, and Englishmen in the Age of Discovery*, 33.

45. Linda T. Darling, 'The Renaissance and the Middle East' in *A Companion to the Worlds of the Renaissance*, ed. Guido Ruggiero (Oxford: Oxford University Press, 2002), 55–69.

46. Morgan, *Medieval Persia, 1040–1797*, 77–78. Compare 'Soltaniyeh', World Heritage Centre, UNESCO, https://whc.unesco.org/en/list/1188; Tom Mueller, 'Brunelleschi's Dome', *National Geographic*, February 2014, www.nationalgeographic.com/magazine/2014/02/Il-Duomo.

47. Finkel, *Osman's Dream*, 82.

48. Rogers, 'Mehmed the Conqueror: Between East and West', 95.

CHAPTER 6: A PIOUS LEADER FACES ENEMIES AT HOME AND ABROAD: BAYEZID II

1. Nicolas Vatin, 'On Süleyman the Magnificent's Death and Burials', in *The Battle for Central Europe: The Siege of Szigetvár and the Death of Süleyman the Magnificent and Nicholas Zrínyi (1566)*, ed. Pál Fodor (Leiden, The Netherlands: Brill, 2019), 433, 437.

2. Imber, *The Ottoman Empire, 1300–1650*, 116.

3. *Encyclopaedia of Islam 2*, s.v. 'Djem', by Halil Inalcik.

4. Isom-Verhaaren, *Allies with the Infidel*, 64–67.

5. Isom-Verhaaren, *Allies with the Infidel*, 88.

6. Isom-Verhaaren, *Allies with the Infidel*, 89.

7. Shai Har-el, *Struggle for Domination in the Middle East: Ottoman-Mamluk War, 1485–1491* (Leiden, The Netherlands: Brill, 1995).

8. Karamustafa, *God's Unruly Friends*, 1–2.

9. Inalcik, *The Ottoman Empire*, 187.

10. Karamustafa, *God's Unruly Friends*, 63.

11. Ahmet Yaşar Ocak, 'Bektaşi menakıbnamelerinde tenasüh inancı', in *II. Milletlerarası Türk Folklor Kongresi Bildirileri* (Ankara, 1982), 4:397–408; Karamustafa, *God's Unruly Friends*, 47–48.

12. Karamustafa, *God's Unruly Friends*, 48.

13. Vladimir Minorsky, 'The Poetry of Shah Ismail I', *Bulletin of the School of Oriental and African Studies* 10 (1942): 1006–1053.

14. Ahmet Yaşar Ocak, 'Ideologie officielle et reaction populaire', in *Soliman le Magnifique et son temps: Actes du Colloque de Paris, Galeries nationales du Grand Palais, 7–10 mars 1990*, ed. Gilles Veinstein (Paris: La documentation française, 1992), 185–192.

15. *Encyclopaedia of Islam, THREE*, s.v., 'Alevīs', by Markus Dressler, first published online 2012, http://dx.doi.org/10.1163/1573-3912_ei3_COM_0167.

16. Ismail E. Erünsal, 'II. Bayezid devrine ait bir inamat defteri', *Istanbul Edebiyat Fakültesi, Tarih Enstitu Dergisi* 10–11 (1981): 303–341, here 314.

17. Pál Fodor, 'Ahmedī's *Dāsitān* as a Source of Early Ottoman History', *Acta Orientalia Academiae Scientiarum Hungaricae* 38, no. 1–2 (1984): 41–54, here 45, 48.

18. Geoffrey Lewis, 'Introduction', in *The Book of Dede Korkut*, trans. Geoffrey Lewis (New York: Penguin, 1972), 9–23.

19. *The Book of Dede Korkut*, 60, 62.

20. *The Book of Dede Korkut*, 65.

21. *The Book of Dede Korkut*, 198.

22. *The Book of Dede Korkut*, 70.

23. Imber, *The Ottoman Empire, 1300–1650*, 123.

24. Halil Inalcik, 'The Rise of Ottoman Historiography', in *Historians of the Middle East*, ed. Bernard Lewis and P. M. Holt (Oxford: Oxford University Press, 1962), 164–165; Ruhi, *Tevarih-i Al-i Osman* (1511), quoted in Inalcik, 'The Rise of Ottoman Historiography', 165.

25. Idris Bitlisi, *Heşt behişt* (Eight Paradises, 1502), quoted in Inalcik, 'The Rise of Ottoman Historiography', 166.

26. Inalcik, 'The Rise of Ottoman Historiography', 165–166.

27. Bitlisi, *Heşt behişt*, 229b–230a.

28. Kerslake, 'A Critical Edition and Translation', 49b.

29. *Encyclopaedia of Islam, THREE*, s.v., 'Crimea', by Dariusz Kołodziejczyk, first published online 2012, http://dx.doi.org/10.1163/1573-3912_ei3_COM_24419.

30. Kerslake, 'A Critical Edition and Translation', 58b.

31. Kerslake, 'A Critical Edition and Translation', 24b, 26b, 27a.

32. Kerslake, 'A Critical Edition and Translation', 76b, 78a-b.

33. Vatin and Veinstein, *Le Sérail ébranlé*, 57–60.

34. Quoted in Uğur, *The Reign of Sultan Selīm I*.

CHAPTER 7: MAGNIFICENCE:
FROM SELIM I TO THE FIRST
OTTOMAN CALIPH, SULEIMAN I

1. Letter from Selim to Ismail, ca. 1514, in McNeill and Waldman, *The Islamic World*, 338–342.

2. Letter from Ismail to Selim, 342–344.

3. Minorsky, 'The Poetry of Shah Ismail I'.

4. Irène Mélikoff, 'Le problème kizilbas', *Turcica* 6 (1975): 49–67; I. Mélikoff, 'La divinisation de 'Alî chez les Bektachis-Alevis', in *From History to Theology: Ali in Islamic Beliefs*, ed. Ahmet Yaşar Ocak (Ankara: Türk Tarih Kurumu, 2005), 83–110.

5. McNeill and Waldman, *The Islamic World*, 337.

6. Çağatay Uluçay, 'Yavuz Sultan Selim nasıl padişah oldu?' *Tarih Dergisi* 6 (1954): 53–90; 7 (1954): 117–142; 8 (1956): 185–200.

7. Elke Eberhard, *Osmanische Polemik gegen die Safawiden im 16. Jahrhundert nach arabischen Handschriften* (Freiburg, Germany: Klaus Schwarz, 1970).

8. *Türkiye Diyanet Vakfı İslam Ansiklopedisi*, s.v. 'Sarıgörez Nûreddin Efendi', by Mehmet İpşirli, https://islamansiklopedisi.org.tr/sarigorez -nureddin-efendi.

9. Celalzade Mustafa, *Selim-nâme*, ed. Ahmed Uğur and Mustafa Çuhadar (Ankara, 1990), 137–138, cited in Yürekli, *Architecture and Hagiography in the Ottoman Empire*, 98.

10. M. C. Şehabettin Tekindağ, 'Yeni kaynak ve vesikaların ışığı altında Yazuv Selim'in Iran Seferi', *Tarih Dergisi* 17 (1967), 56.

11. The description of the muskets is from Kerslake, 'A Critical Edition and Translation', 82a.

12. Sadeddin Efendi, *Selimname*, 75r, cited in Peirce, *The Imperial Harem*, 37.

13. *Türkiye Diyanet Vakfı İslam Ansiklopedisi*, s.v. 'Diyarbakır', by Nejat Göyünç, https://islamansiklopedisi.org.tr/diyarbakir. Note that the author does not use the word 'Kurdish'.

14. Michael Winter, 'The Ottoman Occupation', in *The Cambridge History of Egypt*, ed. Carl Petry, vol. 1, *640–1517* (Cambridge: Cambridge University Press, 1998), 495.

15. An account of the army is given in Selim I's victory proclamation, summarised in Imber, *The Ottoman Empire, 1300–1650*, 277. Imber gives no citation to the original source, however.

16. Winter, 'The Ottoman Occupation', 498.

17. Inalcik, 'The Socio-Political Effects of the Diffusion of Fire-arms in the Middle East', 202.

18. *Encyclopaedia of Islam 2*, s.v. 'Selīm I', by Halil Inalcik.

19. Winter, 'The Ottoman Occupation', 503.

20. Carl Petry, 'The Military Institution and Innovation in the Late Mamlūk Period', in *The Cambridge History of Egypt*, ed. Carl Petry, vol. 1, *640–1517* (Cambridge: Cambridge University Press, 1998), 479–480.

21. Finkel, *Osman's Dream*, 110.

22. Inalcik, *The Ottoman Empire*, 34.

23. Ibn Iyas, cited in Michael Winter, *Egyptian Society Under Ottoman Rule, 1517–1798* (London: Routledge, 1992), 7–8.

24. Winter, *Egyptian Society Under Ottoman Rule*, 9.

25. Winter, *Egyptian Society Under Ottoman Rule*, 10.

26. Both the Ottomans and Habsburgs collected 'unicorn horns', which were, in fact, narwhal tusks. One is on display today at the Imperial Treasury at the Hofburg Palace in Vienna.

27. Sanjay Subrahmanyam, 'Turning the Stones Over: Sixteenth-Century Millenarianism from the Tagus to the Ganges', *Indian Economic and Social History Review* 40, no. 2 (2003): 129–161.

28. Cornell H. Fleischer, 'The Lawgiver as Messiah: The Making of the Imperial Image in the Reign of Süleimân', in *Soliman le Magnifique et son temps*, 162–163.

29. Lutfi Pasha, *Tevārīh-i Āl-i Osmān* (ca. 1550s), cited in Fleischer, 'The Lawgiver as Messiah', 163.

30. Fleischer, 'The Lawgiver as Messiah', 164.

31. Addas, *Quest for the Red Sulphur*, 263.

32. Addas, *Quest for the Red Sulphur*, 277–278; Knysh, *Ibn 'Arabi in the Later Islamic Tradition*, 15.

33. Sadeddin, *Tacü't-Tevarih*, 2:397.

34. Vatin and Veinstein, *Le Sérail ébranlé*, 123.

35. 'Part 3', *Islam: Empire of Faith*, directed by Robert Gardner (Arlington, VA: PBS, 2001).

36. Ebru Turan, 'The Sultan's Favorite: İbrahim Pasha and the Making of the Ottoman Universal Sovereignty in the Reign of Sultan Süleyman (1516–1526)' (PhD diss., University of Chicago, 2007), 83.

37. For an account of the siege, see Nicolas Vatin, 'La conquête de Rhodes', in *Soliman le Magnifique et son temps*, 435–454.

38. Vatin, 'La conquête de Rhodes', 447–448.

39. Vatin, 'La conquête de Rhodes', 437–438.

40. Turan, 'The Sultan's Favorite', 96–97.

41. Vatin, 'La conquête de Rhodes', 438–439.

42. Vatin, 'La conquête de Rhodes', 439, 445; *Encyclopaedia of Islam THREE* , s.v. 'Rodos', by S. Soucek, first published online 2012, http://dx .doi.org/10.1163/1573-3912_islam_SIM_6309.

43. Snjezana Buzov, 'The Lawgiver and His Lawmakers: The Role of Legal Discourse in the Change of Ottoman Imperial Culture' (PhD diss., University of Chicago, 2005), 35. Buzov translates the preamble on pp. 196–232. For example: 'While he is not a prophet, to that distinguished

creature / The Creator gave all moral qualities of the prophets / All saints recognised his saintly power / If that shah [emperor] is called 'holy', that suits the notion of holiness'. Preamble to the Law Code of Egypt (1525), translated in Buzov, 'The Lawgiver and His Lawmakers', 211.

44. Finkel, *Osman's Dream*, 121–122.

45. Turan, 'The Sultan's Favorite', 240.

46. Turan, 'The Sultan's Favorite', 243.

47. Turan, 'The Sultan's Favorite', 244.

48. V. J. Parry, 'The Reign of Sulaimān the Magnificent, 1520–66', in *A History of the Ottoman Empire to 1730: Chapters from 'The Cambridge History of Islam' and 'The New Cambridge Modern History'*, by V. J. Parry, H. Inalcik, A. N. Kurat, and J. S. Bromley, ed. M. A. Cook (Cambridge: Cambridge University Press, 1976), 79–102, here 83–84.

49. McNeill and Waldman, *The Islamic World*, 311.

50. Mevlana Isa, *Cāmiʿüʾl-meknūnāt* (Collector of the Concealed), composed between 1529 and 1543.

51. Barbara Flemming, *'Der Gâmi' ül-meknûnât*: Eine Quelle Âli's aus der Zeit Sultan Süleymans', in *Studien zur Geschichte und Kultur des vorderen Orients. Festschrift für Bertold Spuler zum 70. Geburtstag* (Leiden, The Netherlands: Brill, 1981), 79–92; Barbara Flemming, 'Sâhib-kirân und Mahdi: Türkische Endzeiterwartungen im ersten Jahrzehnt der Regierung Süleymâns', in *Between the Danube and the Caucasus*, ed. Gyorgy Kara (Budapest: Akadémiai Kiadó, 1987), 43–62; Barbara Flemming, 'Public Opinion Under Sultan Süleymân', in *Suleyman the Second and His Time*, ed. Cemal Kafadar and Halil Inalcik (Istanbul: Isis, 1993), 49–57, here 50, 53; Fleischer, 'The Lawgiver as Messiah', 165.

52. Flemming, 'Public Opinion Under Sultan Süleymân', 56–57.

53. Cornell H. Fleischer, 'Shadows of Shadows: Prophecy in Politics in 1530s Istanbul', *International Journal of Turkish Studies* 13 (2007): 51–62.

54. Abd al-Rahman al-Bistami, *Miftāh al-jafr al-jāmiʿ* (Key to the Comprehensive Prognosticon), composed in the early fifteenth century.

55. Cornell H. Fleischer, 'Shadow of Shadows: Prophecy in Politics in 1530s Istanbul', in *Identity and Identity Formation in the Ottoman World: A Volume of Essays in Honor of Norman Itzkowitz*, ed. Baki Tezcan and Karl Barbir (Madison, WI: University of Wisconsin Press, 2007), 51–62, here 59–60.

56. Fleischer, 'The Lawgiver as Messiah', 170.

57. Levhi, cited in Fleischer, 'The Lawgiver as Messiah', 169.

58. Otto Kurz, 'A Gold Helmet Made in Venice for Sultan Sulayman the Magnificent', *Gazette des beaux-arts* 74 (1969): 249–258; Gülru Necipoğlu, 'Süleyman the Magnificent and the Representation of Power in the Context of the Ottoman-Habsburg-Papal Rivalry', *Art Bulletin* 71, no. 3 (September, 1989): 401–427.

59. Necipoğlu, 'Süleyman the Magnificent and the Representation of Power', 401.

60. Necipoğlu, 'Süleyman the Magnificent and the Representation of Power', 407.

61. Necipoğlu, 'Süleyman the Magnificent and the Representation of Power', 409.

62. Necipoğlu, 'Süleyman the Magnificent and the Representation of Power', 411.

63. Jean Bodin, *Methodus* (1566), 292, quoted in Malcolm, *Useful Enemies*, 74.

64. Cardini, *Europe and Islam*, 146.

65. Cardini, *Europe and Islam*, 147; Malcolm, *Useful Enemies*, 77–78.

66. Malcolm, *Useful Enemies*, 79.

67. Andrew Hess, 'The Moriscos, an Ottoman Fifth Column in Sixteenth-Century Spain', *American Historical Review* 74, no.1 (1968), 20.

68. Cardini, *Europe and Islam*, 147.

69. Stephen A. Fischer-Galati, *Ottoman Imperialism and German Protestantism, 1521–1555* (Cambridge, MA: Harvard University Press, 1959; New York: Octagon Books, 1972), 117.

70. Carl Max Kortepeter, *Ottoman Imperialism During the Reformation: Europe and the Caucasus*, New York University Studies in Near Eastern Civilization 5 (New York: New York University Press, 1972), 209, note 107.

71. Kortepeter, *Ottoman Imperialism During the Reformation*, 241.

72. Quoted in Çetin Yetkin, *Türk halk hareketleri ve devrimler* (Istanbul: Milliyet, 1980), 77–78, cited in Yürekli, *Architecture and Hagiography in the Ottoman Empire*, 35.

73. Ocak, 'Ideologie officielle et reaction populaire', 188.

74. Colin Imber, 'A Note on "Christian" Preachers in the Ottoman Empire', *Osmanlı Araştırmaları* 10 (1990): 59–67.

75. Victoria Holbrook, 'Ibn ʿArabi and Ottoman Dervish Traditions: The Melâmi Supra-Order (Part One)', *Journal of the Muhyiddin Ibn ʿArabi Society* 9 (1991): 18–35, here 24.

76. Ocak, 'Ideologie officielle et reaction populaire', 188–189.

77. The source is Ottoman historian Idris Bitlisi, *Selim-nâme*, cited in Vladimir Minorsky, 'Shaykh Bālī-Effendi on the Safavids', in *Medieval Iran and its Neighbours* (London: Varorium Reprints, 1982), 441; see also Colin Imber, 'The Persecution of the Ottoman Shīʿites According to the Mühimme Defterleri, 1565–1585', *Der Islam* 56 (1979): 245–273.

CHAPTER 8: SULTANIC SAVIOURS

1. Marc David Baer, 'Sultans as Saviors', in *Sultanic Saviors and Tolerant Turks: Writing Ottoman Jewish History, Denying the Armenian Genocide* (Bloomington: Indiana University Press, 2020), 30–52.

2. Benjamin Arbel, *Trading Nations: Jews and Venetians in the Early Modern Eastern Mediterranean* (Leiden, The Netherlands: Brill, 1995), 77–94.

3. Eliyahu Capsali, *Seder Eliyahu zuta: Toldot ha-'Ot'omanim u-Venit-si'ah ve korot 'am Yisrael be-mamlekhot Turki'yah, Sefarad u-Venitsi'ah* (History of the Ottomans and Venice, and the Jews in Turkey, Spain, and Venice), 1523, ed. Aryeh Shmuelevitz, Shlomo Simonsohn, and Meier Benayahu (Jerusalem: Mekhon Ben-Tsvi, 1975–1983).

4. Doukas, *Decline and Fall of Byzantium to the Ottoman Turks*, 172.

5. Aryeh Shmuelevitz, 'Capsali as a Source for Ottoman History 1450–1523', *International Journal of Middle East Studies* 9 (1978): 339–344, here 339–340.

6. Capsali, *Seder Eliyahu zuta*, 1:43.

7. Capsali, *Seder Eliyahu zuta*, 1:10.

8. Capsali, *Seder Eliyahu zuta*, 1:10. The original text in Isaiah reads, 'Assyria, rod of My anger, in whose hand, as a staff, is My fury! I send him against a people that provokes Me, to take its spoil and to seize its booty and to make it a thing trampled like the mire of the streets'.

9. Henriette-Rika Benveniste, 'The Idea of Exile: Jewish Accounts and the Historiography of Salonika Revisited', in *Jewish Communities Between the East and West, 15th–20th Centuries: Economy, Society, Politics, Culture*, ed. L. Papastefanaki and A. Machaira (Ioannina: Isnafi, 2016), 31–53, here 39.

10. Capsali, *Seder Eliyahu zuta*, 2:7.

11. Heinrich Graetz, *History of the Jews*, trans. B. Löwy (Philadelphia: Jewish Publication Society of America, 1891–1898), 4:559–561.

12. Yosef Hayim Yerushalmi, *Zakhor: Jewish History and Jewish Memory* (Seattle: University of Washington Press, 1982), 64.

13. *Consolação ás tribulações de Israel* (Consolation of the Tribulations of Israel [i.e., the Jewish people]) (1553).

14. Samuel Usque, *Samuel Usque's Consolation for the Tribulations of Israel (Consolaçam ás tribulaçoens de Israel)*, trans. Martin A. Cohen (Philadelphia: Jewish Publication Society of America, 1964), 231.

15. *Sefer divre ha-yamim le-malkhey Tzarefat u-malkhey beyt Ottoman ha-Togar* (History of the Kings of France and the Kings of the Dynasty of Othman, the Turk) (1554–1577).

16. Joseph Ha-Kohen, *The Chronicles of Rabbi Joseph ben Joshua ben Meir the Sephardi*, trans. C. H. F. Bialloblotzky (London, 1835), 273.

17. Cecil Roth, *Doña Gracia of the House of Nasi: A Jewish Renaissance Woman* (Philadelphia: Jewish Publication Society of America, 1948), 180.

18. Roth, *Doña Gracia of the House of Nasi*, 116.

19. Roth, *Doña Gracia of the House of Nasi*, 117.

CHAPTER 9: THE OTTOMAN AGE OF DISCOVERY

1. Giancarlo Casale, *The Ottoman Age of Exploration* (Oxford: Oxford University Press, 2010), 4–8.

2. Andrew C. Hess, 'The Evolution of the Ottoman Seaborne Empire in the Age of the Oceanic Discoveries, 1453–1525', *American Historical Review* 75, no. 7 (December 1970): 1892–1919, here 1892.

3. Just over two decades ago, there were no books that included the Ottomans as one of the maritime powers of the Mediterranean and Asia. John Wills Jr., 'Maritime Asia, 1500–1800: The Interactive Emergence of European Domination', *American Historical Review* 98 (1993): 83–105.

4. Seydi Ali Reis, *Mirror of Countries*, in *The Sacred Books and Early Literature of the East*, vol. 6, *329–395*, ed. Charles F. Horne (New York: Parke, Austin, and Lipscomb, 1917), available online in *Internet Medieval Sourcebook*, https://sourcebooks.fordham.edu/source/16CSidi1.asp.

5. David Arnold, *The Age of Discovery, 1400–1600*, 2nd ed. (London: Routledge, 2002), xi.

6. Arnold, *The Age of Discovery*, 10.

7. Casale, *The Ottoman Age of Exploration*, 5–6.

8. Salih Özbaran, 'Osmanlı İmparatorluğu ve Hindistan Yolu: Onaltıncı yüzyılda ticaret yolları üzerinde Türk-Portekiz rekabet ve ilişkileri', *Tarih Dergisi* 31 (March 1977): 66–146.

9. Casale, *The Ottoman Age of Exploration*, 20.

10. Hess, 'The Evolution of the Ottoman Seaborne Empire', 1905.

11. Sadeddin, *Tacü't-Tevarih*, 2:86, quoted in Palmira Brummett, *Ottoman Seapower and Levantine Diplomacy in the Age of Discovery* (Albany: State University of New York Press, 1994), 90.

12. Hess, 'The Evolution of the Ottoman Seaborne Empire', 1906.

13. Brummett, *Ottoman Seapower and Levantine Diplomacy*, 91–92.

14. Casale, *The Ottoman Age of Exploration*, 13.

15. Casale, *The Ottoman Age of Exploration*, 22–23.

16. Brummett, *Ottoman Seapower and Levantine Diplomacy*, 120.

17. One such stuffed falcon—along with Ottoman cannonballs from the siege of Rhodes, Ottoman chain mail and battle helmets, and an oxidised bronze cannon Henry VIII gave the Knights Hospitaller to defend Malta—is on display at the Museum of the Order of Saint John in London, located in the remaining Tudor-era tower gate of the English headquarters of the order.

18. Isom-Verhaaren, *Allies with the Infidel*, 3–5.

19. Jean de Monluc, quoted in Isom-Verhaaren, *Allies with the Infidel*, 1.

20. Blaise de Monluc, French diplomat and ambassador to Venice, quoted in Isom-Verhaaren, *Allies with the Infidel*, 161.

21. Isom-Verhaaren, *Allies with the Infidel*, 35–36.

22. Isom-Verhaaren, *Allies with the Infidel*, 35–36.

23. Isom-Verhaaren, *Allies with the Infidel*, 72, 115.

24. Isom-Verhaaren, *Allies with the Infidel*, 117–119.

25. Isom-Verhaaren, *Allies with the Infidel*, 126.

26. 'Stèle en mémoire de Catherine Ségurane', Nice Côte d'Azur Metropolitan Convention and Visitors Bureau, http://en.nicetourisme.com/nice/51142-stele-en-memoire-de-catherine-segurane.

27. Isom-Verhaaren, *Allies with the Infidel*, 133.

28. Isom-Verhaaren, *Allies with the Infidel*, 164.

29. Isom-Verhaaren, *Allies with the Infidel*, 129.

30. Isom-Verhaaren, *Allies with the Infidel*, 137–138.

31. Isom-Verhaaren, *Allies with the Infidel*, 43–44.

32. Isom-Verhaaren, *Allies with the Infidel*, 44.

33. Hess, 'The Moriscos'.

34. Malcolm, *Useful Enemies*, 100.

35. Malcolm, *Useful Enemies*, 101.

36. Hess, 'The Evolution of the Ottoman Seaborne Empire', 1908.

37. Salih Özbaran, 'The Ottoman Turks and the Portuguese in the Persian Gulf, 1534–1581', *Journal of Asian History* 6 (1972): 56–74.

38. Casale, *The Ottoman Age of Exploration*, 37.

39. Casale, *The Ottoman Age of Exploration*, 59.

40. Brummett, *Ottoman Seapower and Levantine Diplomacy*, 120.

41. Casale, *The Ottoman Age of Exploration*, 75.

42. Casale, *The Ottoman Age of Exploration*, 95–98.

43. Casale, *The Ottoman Age of Exploration*, 119.

44. Casale, *The Ottoman Age of Exploration*, 129.

45. Casale, *The Ottoman Age of Exploration*, 131.

46. Casale, *The Ottoman Age of Exploration*, 137.

47. Inalcik, *The Ottoman Empire*, 39–40.

48. Casale, *The Ottoman Age of Exploration*, 160–163.

49. Casale, *The Ottoman Age of Exploration*, 137.

50. Finkel, *Osman's Dream*, 159.

51. Finkel, *Osman's Dream*, 161.

52. Inalcik, *The Ottoman Empire*, 51.

53. Quoted in *Encyclopaedia of Islam 1*, s.v. 'Sokolli', by J. H. Kramers.

54. The painting includes the detail of rows of distraught-looking, shirtless, horseshoe-moustachioed, and shaved-headed Janissaries and North Africans taken into captivity aboard the Christians' vessels.

55. The final Ottoman attempt to conquer Mombasa, and with it the entire Swahili coast, was defeated by the surprise appearance of a large army of African warriors in 1589. Fleeing from the Africans and surrendering to the Portuguese, the Ottoman commander Mir Ali lived out the rest of his life in Portugal, where he converted to Christianity. Casale, *The Ottoman Age of Exploration*, 176.

56. Marshall G. S. Hodgson, 'The Role of Islam in World History', in *Rethinking World History*, 99.

57. Giancarlo Casale, 'Did Alexander the Great Discover America? Debating Space and Time in Renaissance Istanbul', *Renaissance Quarterly* 72 (2019), 884, 886–887.

58. Inalcik, *The Ottoman Empire*, 52.

59. Inalcik, *The Ottoman Empire*, 179.

60. Bernard Lewis, 'The Muslim Discovery of Europe', *Bulletin of the School of Oriental and African Studies* 20, no. 1/3 (1957): 409–416, here 416.

61. Bernard Lewis, *Islam and the West* (Oxford: Oxford University Press, 1993), 15.

62. Bernard Lewis, *The Muslim Discovery of Europe* (New York: George J. Mcleod, 1982), 297.

63. Lewis, 'The Muslim Discovery of Europe', 415.

64. Cemal Kafadar, 'A Death in Venice (1575): Anatolian Muslim Merchants Trading in the Serenissima', *Journal of Turkish Studies* 10 (1986): 191–218, here 202.

65. Kaplan, *Divided by Faith*, 303–305.

66. Kafadar, 'A Death in Venice (1575)'.

67. *Encyclopaedia of Islam, THREE*, s.v. 'Coffee and Coffeehouses, Ottoman', by Michel Tuchscherer, first published online, 2012, http://dx.doi.org/10.1163/1573-3912_ei3_COM_24410.

68. *Gazavāt-ı Hayreddīn Paşa*, trans. and ed. Mustafa Yıldız (Aachen, Germany: Shaker, 1993), 243, quoted in Cemal Kafadar, 'How Dark Is the History of the Night, How Black the Story of Coffee, How Bitter the Tale of Love: The Changing Measure of Leisure and Pleasure in Early Modern Istanbul', in *Medieval and Early Modern Performance in the Eastern Mediterranean*, ed. Arzu Öztürkmen and Evelyn Birge Vitz (Turnhout, Belgium: Brepols, 2014), 248.

69. 'Vasco da Gama: Round Africa to India, 1497–1498 CE', *Internet Modern History Sourcebook*, https://sourcebooks.fordham.edu/mod/1497degama.asp.

70. 'Christopher Columbus: Extracts from Journal', *Internet Medieval Sourcebook*, https://sourcebooks.fordham.edu/source/columbus1.asp.

71. Abbas Hamdani, 'Columbus and the Recovery of Jerusalem', *Journal of the American Oriental Society* 99, no. 1 (1979): 39–48.

72. Miguel Cervantes, *Don Quixote*, trans. John Rutherford (London: Penguin, 2000), 74–75.

73. Casale, *The Ottoman Age of Exploration*, 11–12.

74. Salih Özbaran, *Ottoman Expansion Towards the Indian Ocean in the 16th Century* (Istanbul: Bilgi University Press, 2009).

75. Hess, 'The Evolution of the Ottoman Seaborne Empire', 1915–1916.

76. Seydi Ali Reis, *Mirror of Countries*.

CHAPTER 10: NO WAY LIKE THE 'OTTOMAN WAY'

1. I am grateful to the staff of the British Museum for having allowed me to view the object. The tughra was featured in former museum director Neil MacGregor's *A History of the World in 100 Objects* and broadcast on BBC Radio 4: Neil MacGregor, 'Tughra of Suleiman the Magnificent',

14 September 2010, in *A History of the World in 100 Objects*, produced by Anthony Denselow, podcast, MP3 audio, 13:50, www.bbc.co.uk /programmes/b00tn9vc

2. Barkey, *Empire of Difference*.

3. Ogier Ghiselin de Busbecq, 'Turkish Letters', in McNeill and Waldman, *The Islamic World*, 346.

4. Busbecq, 'Turkish Letters', 347.

5. Metin Ibrahim Kunt, 'Ethnic-Regional (Cins) Solidarity in the Seventeenth-Century Ottoman Establishment', *International Journal of Middle East Studies* 5, no. 3 (June 1974): 233–239.

6. Greene, *The Edinburgh History of the Greeks*, 39. The independent Serbian patriarchate would be abolished and joined to the Greek Orthodox patriarchate in the eighteenth century. Greene, *The Edinburgh History of the Greeks*,182–183.

7. Cornell H. Fleischer, *Bureaucrat and Intellectual in the Ottoman Empire: The Historian Mustafa Âli (1541–1600)* (Princeton, NJ: Princeton University Press, 1986), 164.

8. Ömer Lütfi Barkan, 'Essai sur les données statistiques des registres de recensement dans l'Empire ottoman aux Xve et XVIe siècles', *Journal of the Economic and Social History of the Orient* 1 (1957): 9–36.

9. Inalcik, 'Ottoman Galata, 1453–1553', 324–327.

10. Robert Mantran, 'Un document sur la cizye à Istanbul à la fin du XVIIe siècle', *Journal of Turkish Studies* 11 (1987): 11–15.

11. Jon Mandaville, 'Usurious Piety: The Cash Waqf Controversy in the Ottoman Empire', *International Journal of Middle East Studies* 10, no. 3 (1979): 289–308.

12. Mehmet Ertuğrul Düzdağ, *Şeyhülislam Ebussuud Efendi fetvaları ışığında 16. asır Türk hayatı* (Istanbul: Enderun Kitabevi, 1972), 109–117. Christians, Jews and Muslims were considered 'believers'.

13. Fleischer, *Bureaucrat and Intellectual in the Ottoman Empire*, 93.

14. Necipoğlu, 'Süleyman the Magnificent and the Representation of Power', 422.

15. Busbecq, 'Turkish Letters', 345.

16. Imber, *The Ottoman Empire, 1300–1650*, 116.

17. 'Part 2', *Islam: Empire of Faith*.

18. Necipoğlu-Kafadar, 'The Süleymaniye Complex in Istanbul', 100–101.

19. Necipoğlu-Kafadar, 'The Süleymaniye Complex in Istanbul', 103.

20. Necipoğlu-Kafadar, 'The Süleymaniye Complex in Istanbul', 106.

21. Necipoğlu-Kafadar, 'The Süleymaniye Complex in Istanbul', 111.

22. Yürekli, *Architecture and Hagiography in the Ottoman Empire*, 98.

23. Matrakçı Nasuh, *Süleymânnâme*, Ms. Marburg, Staatsbibliothek Hs. Or. Oct. 95, fol. 19a, quoted in Yürekli, *Architecture and Hagiography in the Ottoman Empire*, 43.

24. M. Tayyib Gökbilgin, 'Rüstem Paşa ve hakkındaki ithamlar', *Istanbul Üniversitesi Edebiyat Fakültesi Tarih Dergisi* 8 (1955), 46–50, quoted in Yürekli, *Architecture and Hagiography in the Ottoman Empire*, 47.

25. Karamustafa, *God's Unruly Friends*, 83.

26. Karamustafa, *God's Unruly Friends*, 84.

27. Phillippe du Fresne-Canaye, quoted in Necipoğlu-Kafadar, 'The Süleymaniye Complex in Istanbul', 115, note 24.

28. Busbecq, 'Turkish Letters', 351.

CHAPTER 11: HAREM MEANS HOME

1. 'Part 2', *Islam: Empire of Faith*.

2. Leslie Peirce, 'Part I: The Politics of Reproduction', in *The Imperial Harem*.

3. Peirce, *The Imperial Harem*, 59.

4. Marc Baer, 'Islamic Conversion Narratives of Women: Social Change and Gendered Religious Hierarchy in Early Modern Ottoman Istanbul', *Gender & History* 16, no. 2 (August 2004): 425–458.

5. Cihangir, born a hunchback in 1531, was not considered fit either for a princely governate or to compete with his brothers for the sultanate. He died at the age of twenty-three, most likely from complications arising from his congenital spinal condition.

6. Peirce, *The Imperial Harem*, 62.

7. This is a main argument of Andrews and Kalpaklı, *The Age of Beloveds*.

8. *Encyclopaedia of Islam, Second Edition*, s.v. 'Ibrāhīm Pasha', by M. Tayyib Gökbilgin, accessed 8 May 2020, first published online 2012, http://dx.doi.org/10.1163/1573-3912_islam_SIM_3457; Turan, 'The Sultan's Favorite'.

9. Report of Pietro Zen, Venetian ambassador to the Ottoman Empire, 1523, 109, quoted in Turan, 'The Sultan's Favorite', 139.

10. Turan, 'The Sultan's Favorite', 139–140.

11. Turan, 'The Sultan's Favorite', 170–171, 210–223.

12. Crazy Brother (Deli Birader) Gazali, quoted in Andrews and Kalpaklı, *The Age of Beloveds*, 239.

13. Peirce, *The Imperial Harem*, 75.

14. Buzov, 'The Lawgiver and His Lawmakers', 30–34.

15. Preamble to the Law Code of Egypt (1525), translated in Buzov, 'The Lawgiver and His Lawmakers', 221.

16. Buzov, 'The Lawgiver and His Lawmakers', 38.

17. Piero Bragadin, Venetian ambassador to the Otoman Empire, 1526, 103, quoted in Turan, 'The Sultan's Favorite', 144.

18. Fleischer, 'Shadow of Shadows', 62.

19. Quoted in Leslie Peirce, *Empress of the East: How a European Slave Girl Became Queen of the Ottoman Empire* (New York: Basic Books, 2017), 168.

20. Andrews and Kalpaklı, *The Age of Beloveds*, 248.

21. Vatin, 'On Süleyman the Magnificent's Death and Burials', 435.

22. Vatin and Veinstein, *Le Sérail ébranlé*, 135.

23. Imber, *The Ottoman Empire, 1300–1650*, 116.

24. Vatin and Veinstein, *Le Sérail ébranlé*, 307–308.

25. Selânikî Mustafa Efendi, quoted in Finkel, *Osman's Dream*, 152.

26. Ismail Hakkı Uzunçarşılı, *Osmanlı tarihi*, vol. 3 (Ankara: Türk Tarih Kurumu, 1983), 1, 41.

27. Fleischer, *Bureaucrat and Intellectual in the Ottoman Empire*, 53.

28. Gülru Necipoğlu, *The Age of Sinan: Architectural Culture in the Ottoman Empire* (London: Reaktion Books, 2005), 233.

29. Judith Herrin, *Unrivalled Influence: Women and Empire in Byzantium* (Princeton, NJ: Princeton University Press, 2013), 3.

30. Judith Herrin, *Byzantium: The Surprising Life of a Medieval Empire* (London: Allen Lane, 2007), 185, 191.

31. Herrin, *Unrivalled Influence*.

32. Herrin, *Unrivalled Influence*, 8.

33. Herrin, *Unrivalled Influence*, 314.

34. Herrin, *Unrivalled Influence*, 315.

35. Rashid al-Din Fazlullah, *The Compendium of Histories*, quoted in George Qingzhi Zhao, *Marriage as Political Strategy and Cultural Expression: Mongolian Royal Marriages from World Empire to Yuan Dynasty* (New York: Peter Lang, 2008), 10.

36. 'Ibn Battuta: Travels in Asia and Africa 1325–1354', *Internet Medieval Sourcebook*, https://sourcebooks.fordham.edu/source/1354-ibnbattuta.asp

37. Ibn Battuta's account of Anatolia can be found in *The Travels of Ibn Battuta A.D. 1325–1354*, trans. H. A. R. Gibb (Cambridge: Cambridge University Press, 1962), 2:412–469.

38. Quoted in Andrews and Kalpaklı, *The Age of Beloveds*, 151.

39. Quoted in Skilliter, 'Three Letters from the Ottoman "Sultana" Safiye to Queen Elizabeth I', 139.

40. Quoted in Skilliter, 'Three Letters from the Ottoman "Sultana" Safiye to Queen Elizabeth I', 142.

41. Quoted in Skilliter, 'Three Letters from the Ottoman "Sultana" Safiye to Queen Elizabeth I', 143.

42. James Shapiro, *Shakespeare and the Jews* (New York: Columbia University Press, 1996), 73.

43. Selânikî Mustafa Efendi, *Tarih-i Selânikî*, ed. Mehmed İpşirli (Istanbul: Istanbul Üniversitesi Edebiyat Fakültesi, 1989), 2:854. See also Mehmed İpşirli, 'Mustafa Selânikî and His History', *Tarih Enstitüsü Dergisi* 9 (January 1978): 417–472.

44. Selânikî Mustafa Efendi, *Tarih-i Selânikî*, 2:854.

45. Selânikî Mustafa Efendi, *Tarih-i Selânikî*, 2:855.

46. Na'ima, *Tarîh-i Naîmâ* (Istanbul: 1281-1283AH), 1:231, 247; Naîmâ Mustafa Efendi, *Târih-i Na'îmâ (Ravzatü'l-Hüseyn fî hulâsati ahbâri'l-hâfikayn)*, ed. Mehmed İpşirli (Ankara: Türk Tarih Kurumu, 2007), 1:162–163.

47. John Sanderson, *The Travels in the Levant (1564–1602), with His Autobiography and Selections from His Correspondance*, new ed., W. Forster, 85f, quoted in Salo Wittmayer Baron, *A Social and Religious History of the Jews*, 2nd revised ed. (New York: Columbia University Press, 1952–1983), 18:133–134.

48. Selânikî Mustafa Efendi, *Tarih-i Selânikî*, 2:855.

49. Selânikî Mustafa Efendi, *Tarih-i Selânikî*, 2:856.

50. Selânikî Mustafa Efendi, *Tarih-i Selânikî*, 2:856–857.

51. Selânikî Mustafa Efendi, *Tarih-i Selânikî*, 2:864; quoted in İpşirli, 'Mustafa Selaniki and His History', lxv.

52. Selânikî Mustafa Efendi, *Tarih-i Selânikî*, 2:856. Hezarfen Hüseyin Efendi (d. 1676) also mentions the subsequent imposition of sumptuary restrictions following the killing of the lady-in-waiting in his work completed in 1672–1673, *Telhîsü'l-beyân fî kavânîn-i Âl-i Osmân*, ed. Sevim İlgürel (Ankara: Türk Tarih Kurumu, 1998), 55.

53. Nev'izade 'Ata'i, *Hada'iku'l-haka'ik fi tekmileti'ş-şaka'ik*, 2:197, in *Şakaik-ı nu'maniye ve zeyilleri*, ed. Abdülkadir Özcan, 5 vols. (Istanbul, 1989), referenced in Baki Tezcan, 'The "Kânûnnâme of Mehmed II": A Different Perspective', in *The Great Ottoman-Turkish Civilisation*, ed. Kemal Çiçek, et al. (Ankara: Yeni Türkiye, 2000), 3:657–665, here 664, note 38. Tezcan does not translate the quote into English.

54. Jane Hathaway, *Beshir Agha: Chief Eunuch of the Ottoman Imperial Harem* (Oxford: Oneworld, 2005), 13.

55. Hathaway, *Beshir Agha*, 19.

56. Hathaway, *Beshir Agha*, 20.

57. Hathaway, *Beshir Agha*, 21.

58. Jane Hathaway, *The Chief Harem Eunuch of the Ottoman Empire: From African Slave to Power-Broker* (Cambridge: Cambridge University Press, 2018), 2, 9–10, 53. When Murad III passed away, he was even buried in the burial shroud of the chief harem eunuch. Eager to hide the sultan's corpse until his oldest son could arrive to claim the throne, Murad III's harem attendants neglected to render him funeral care, which was postponed until later. They had no linen cloth with which to wrap the deceased, but as it was too dangerous to risk obtaining one from outside the palace, which would attract attention, they used the shroud that the chief harem agha had prepared for his own burial. Vatin and Veinstein, *Le Sérail ébranlé*, 125.

59. Hathaway, *Beshir Agha*, 26.

CHAPTER 12: BEARDED MEN
AND BEARDLESS YOUTHS

1. Marc David Baer, *German, Jew, Muslim, Gay: The Life and Times of Hugo Marcus* (New York: Columbia University Press, 2020), 19.

2. Quoted in Andrews and Kalpaklı, *The Age of Beloveds*, 3–4.

3. The quotes in this paragraph are from Lewis, *Rumi*, 169, 193, and 196.

4. Hodgson, *The Venture of Islam*, 2:245.

5. Andrews and Kalpaklı, *The Age of Beloveds*, 128.

6. A number of studies appearing around the same time make these arguments: along with Andrews and Kalpaklı, *The Age of Beloveds*, see Afsaneh Najmabadi, *Women with Mustaches and Men Without Beards: Gender and Sexual Anxieties of Iranian Modernity* (Berkeley: University of California Press, 2005); Khaled el-Rouayheb, *Before Homosexuality in the Arab-Islamic World, 1500–1800* (Chicago: University of Chicago Press, 2005); Dror Ze'evi, *Producing Desire: Changing Sexual Discourse in the Ottoman Middle East, 1500–1900* (Berkeley: University of California Press, 2006); and Kathryn Babayan and Afsaneh Najmabadi, eds., *Islamicate Sexualities: Translations Across Temporal Geographies of Desire* (Cambridge, MA: Harvard University Press, 2008).

7. Quoted in Andrews and Kalpaklı, *The Age of Beloveds*, 45.

8. Najmabadi, *Women with Mustaches and Men Without Beards*, 11.

9. Poet Crazy Brother (Deli Birader) Gazali, quoted in Andrews and Kalpaklı, *The Age of Beloveds*, 177.

10. Quoted in Andrews and Kalpaklı, *The Age of Beloveds*, 44.

11. The poet Latifi, quoted in Andrews and Kalpaklı, *The Age of Beloveds*, 64–65.

12. The poet Revani, quoted in Andrews and Kalpaklı, *The Age of Beloveds*, 65.

13. Ze'evi, *Producing Desire*, 22–23.

14. Ze'evi, *Producing Desire*, 31, 35.

15. Quoted in Andrews and Kalpaklı, *The Age of Beloveds*, 171.

16. Fleischer, *Bureaucrat and Intellectual in the Ottoman Empire*, 55.

17. Ze'evi, *Producing Desire*, 138–147.

18. Selim Kuru, 'Sex in the Text: Deli Birader's *Dâfi'ü 'l-gumûm ve Râfi'ü 'l-humûm* and the Ottoman Literary Canon', *Middle Eastern Literatures* 10, no. 2 (2007), 157, 164–165.

19. Kuru, 'Sex in the Text', 162.

20. Kuru, 'Sex in the Text', 163.

21. Fleischer, *Bureaucrat and Intellectual in the Ottoman Empire*, 170.

22. Quoted in Andrews and Kalpaklı, *The Age of Beloveds*, 137–138.

23. Quoted in Andrews and Kalpaklı, *The Age of Beloveds*, 138.

24. Quoted in Kuru, 'Sex in the Text', 167.

25. Quoted in Andrews and Kalpaklı, *The Age of Beloveds*, 257.

26. Quoted in Andrews and Kalpaklı, *The Age of Beloveds*, 143.

CHAPTER 13: BEING OTTOMAN, BEING ROMAN: FROM MURAD III TO OSMAN II

1. Vatin and Veinstein, *Le Sérail ébranlé*, 125.

2. Vatin and Veinstein, *Le Sérail ébranlé*, 132.

3. Hodgson, 'The Role of Islam in World History', 97–98.

4. Fleischer, *Bureaucrat and Intellectual in the Ottoman Empire*, 13–17.

5. Fleischer, *Bureaucrat and Intellectual in the Ottoman Empire*, 254.

6. Fleischer, *Bureaucrat and Intellectual in the Ottoman Empire*, 16–17, 255–256.

7. Norman Itzkowitz, *Ottoman Empire and Islamic Tradition* (Chicago: University of Chicago Press, 1972), 34.

8. Kafadar, 'A Rome of One's Own', 15.

9. Mustafā Ali, *Mustafā Ali's Counsel for Sultans of 1581*, trans. and ed. Andreas Tietze (Vienna: Verlag der Österreichischen Akademie der Wissenschaften, 1979–1982), 1:63.

10. Fleischer, *Bureaucrat and Intellectual in the Ottoman Empire*, 315–318.

11. Mustafa Ali, quoted in Casale, *The Ottoman Age of Exploration*, 184–185.

12. Fleischer, *Bureaucrat and Intellectual in the Ottoman Empire*, 135.

13. Mustafa Ali, *Künh ül-ahbar*, Suleimaniye Library, Istanbul, MS Nuruosmaniye 3409, fol. 424b, quoted in Fleischer, *Bureaucrat and Intellectual in the Ottoman Empire*, 154.

14. Fleischer, *Bureaucrat and Intellectual in the Ottoman Empire*, 155–158.

15. Sanjay Subrahmanyam, 'A Tale of Three Empires: Mughals, Ottomans, and Habsburgs in a Comparative Context', *Common Knowledge* 12, no. 1 (2006), 73.

16. Tietze, *Mustafā Ali's Counsel for Sultans of 1581*, 1:41.

17. Marc David Baer, 'Manliness, Male Virtue and History Writing at the Seventeenth-Century Ottoman Court', *Gender & History* 20, no. 1 (April 2008): 128–148, here 132.

18. Kafadar, *Between Two Worlds*, 146, 152.

19. According to Hungarian-origin historian Ibrahim Peçevi (d. 1650), quoted in Imber, *The Ottoman Empire, 1300–1650*, 109. Imber does not provide any page references to this quote.

20. Selânikî Mustafa Efendi, *Tarih-i Selânikî*, 2:436.

21. Ozgen Felek, 'Displaying Manhood and Masculinity at the Imperial Circumcision Festivity of 1582', *Journal of the Ottoman and Turkish Studies Association* 6, no. 1 (Spring 2019), 142.

22. Mustafa Ali, cited in Fleischer, *Bureaucrat and Intellectual in the Ottoman Empire*, 154, note 40.

23. Inalcik, *The Ottoman Empire*, 61–62.

24. Baki Tezcan, *The Second Ottoman Empire: Political and Social Trans-formation in the Early Modern World* (Cambridge: Cambridge University Press, 2012), 115.

25. Müneccimbaşı, *Sahâ'ifü-l-ahbâr* (Istanbul, 1285H), 618, cited in Vatin and Veinstein, *Le Sérail ébranlé*, 310–311.

26. Tezcan, *The Second Ottoman Empire*, 46–47.

27. According to a Venetian report quoted in Finkel, *Osman's Dream*, 184–185.

28. Finkel, *Osman's Dream*, 195.

29. Baer, 'Manliness, Male Virtue and History Writing', 133.

30. Inalcik, 'The Socio-Political Effects of the Diffusion of Fire-arms in the Middle East', 199–200; Halil Inalcik, 'Military and Fiscal Transformation in the Ottoman Empire, 1600–1700', *Archivum Ottomanicum* 6 (1980): 283–337.

31. Mustafa Akdağ, *Celâlî isyanları, 1550–1603* (Ankara: Ankara Üniversitesi, 1963); Inalcik, 'The Socio-Political Effects of the Diffusion of Fire-arms in the Middle East', 201; William Griswold, *The Great Anatolian Rebellion, 1000–1020/1591–1611*, Islamkundliche Untersuchungen Bd. 83 (Freiburg, Germany: Klaus Schwarz, 1983).

32. Tezcan, *The Second Ottoman Empire*, 141–142.

33. Tezcan, *The Second Ottoman Empire*, 143, 150.

34. Karen Barkey, *Bandits and Bureaucrats: The Ottoman Route to State Centralization* (Ithaca, NY: Cornell University Press, 1993).

35. Tezcan, *The Second Ottoman Empire*, 146.

36. Silahdar Fındıklılı Mehmed Ağa, *Tarih-i Silahdar* (Istanbul: Devlet, 1928), 2:263.

37. Sam White, *The Climate of Rebellion in the Early Modern Ottoman Empire* (Cambridge: Cambridge University Press, 2013).

38. Molly Greene, *A Shared World: Christians and Muslims in the Early Modern Mediterranean* (Princeton, NJ: Princeton University Press, 2000), 39–44; Michael Meeker, *A Nation of Empire: The Ottoman Legacy of Turkish Modernity* (Berkeley: University of California Press, 2002), 162–176.

39. Greene, *The Edinburgh History of the Greeks*, 184.

40. Inalcik, 'Military and Fiscal Transformation in the Ottoman Empire'.

41. Daniel Goffman, *Izmir and the Levantine World, 1550–1650* (Seattle: University of Washington Press, 1990).

42. Inalcik, 'Military and Fiscal Transformation in the Ottoman Empire'.

43. Inalcik, *The Ottoman Empire*, 41.

44. Bernard Lewis, 'Ottoman Observers of Ottoman Decline', *Islamic Studies* 1, no. 1 (March 1962): 71–87.

45. Cornell H. Fleischer, 'Between the Lines: Realities of Scribal Life in the Sixteenth Century', in *Studies in Honour of Professor V.L. Ménage*, ed. Colin Heywood and Colin Imber (Istanbul: Isis, 1994), 45–61.

46. Rifa'at 'Ali Abou-El-Haj, *Formation of the Modern State: The Ottoman Empire, Sixteenth to Eighteenth Centuries* (Albany, NY: State University of New York Press, 1991), 24–25.

47. Fleischer, *Bureaucrat and Intellectual in the Ottoman Empire*, 8.

48. Fleischer, 'Between the Lines'.

49. Cemal Kafadar, 'The Myth of the Golden Age', in *Süleymân the Second [sic, the First] and His Time*, ed. Halil Inalcik and Cemal Kafadar (Istanbul: Isis, 1993), 37–48.

50. Üveysi, *Nasîhat-ı İslâmbol* (Admonition to Islambol) (ca. 1620s or 1630s), quoted in Baki Tezcan, 'From Veysî (d. 1628) to Üveysî (fl. ca. 1630): Ottoman Advice Literature and Its Discontents', in *Reforming Early Modern Monarchies: The Castilian Arbitristas in Comparative European Perspectives*, ed. Sina Rauschenbach and Christian Windler, Wolfenbütteler Forschungen 143 (Wiesbaden, Germany: Harrassowitz, 2016), 141–156, here 153.

51. Üveysi, *Nasîhat-ı İslâmbol*, 153.

52. Koçu Bey, advisor to Murad IV, writing in 1631, quoted in Lewis, 'Ottoman Observers of Ottoman Decline', 76.

53. Katib Çelebi, *Destûr ul-amel li islah il-halel* (Guide to Practice for the Rectification of Defects, 1653) and *Mizan ul-hakk* (Balance of Truth, 1656).

54. Kafadar, 'The Question of Ottoman Decline', 43.

55. Tezcan, *The Second Ottoman Empire*, 113–114.

56. Katip Çelebi, *Fezleke* (Istanbul: Ceride-i Havadis Matbaası, 1287 AH/1871 CE), 1:390.

57. Tezcan, *The Second Ottoman Empire*, 115. He was also born to the youngest sultan to become a father in history, the fourteen-year-old Ahmed I.

58. Tezcan, *The Second Ottoman Empire*, 118–119.

59. Tezcan, *The Second Ottoman Empire*, 115.

60. Vatin and Veinstein, *Le Sérail ébranlé*, 158–159.

61. Baki Tezcan, 'Khotin 1621, or How the Poles Changed the Course of Ottoman History', *Acta Orientalia Academiae Scientiarum Hungaricae* 62 (2009): 185–198.

62. Tezcan, *The Second Ottoman Empire*, 151–152.

63. Tezcan, *The Second Ottoman Empire*, 163–164.

64. *Anonim bir ibranîce kroniğe göre 1622–1624 yıllarında Osmanlı devleti ve Istanbul*, trans. Nuh Arslantaş and Yaron ben Naeh (Ankara: Türk Tarih Kurumu, 2013), 32.

65. *Anonim bir ibranîce kroniğe göre 1622–1624 yıllarında Osmanlı devleti ve Istanbul*, 33.

66. Nicolas Vatin, 'Le corps du sultan ottoman', *Revue des mondes musulmans et de la Méditerranée* 113–114 (2006): 213–227.

67. *Anonim bir ibranîce kroniğe göre 1622–1624 yıllarında Osmanlı devleti ve Istanbul*, 36.

68. *Anonim bir ibranîce kroniğe göre 1622–1624 yıllarında Osmanlı devleti ve Istanbul*, 37.

69. Katib Çelebi, *Fezleke*, 2:22.

70. Katib Çelebi, *Fezleke*, 2:23.

71. The event is discussed in Vatin and Veinstein, *Le Sérail ébranlé*, 238–239.

72. *Anonim bir Ibranîce kroniğe göre 1622–1624 yıllarında Osmanlı devleti ve Istanbul*, 49–51.

73. Vatin and Veinstein, *Le Sérail ébranlé*, 78–79.

74. Kafadar, 'The Question of Ottoman Decline', especially 55, 60–61; Cemal Kafadar, 'Janissaries and Other Riffraff of Ottoman Istanbul: Rebels Without a Cause?' in *Identity and Identity Formation in the Ottoman World*, 113–134, although the author provides no citations of his sources, perhaps because the article is actually the text of a talk delivered in 1991; Tezcan, *The Second Ottoman Empire*.

75. Tezcan, *The Second Ottoman Empire*, 236.

76. Quoted in Malcolm, *Useful Enemies*, 370.

77. Quoted in Tezcan, *The Second Ottoman Empire*, 7, and Malcolm, *Useful Enemies*, 371.

78. Andrews and Kalpaklı, *The Age of Beloveds*, 322–323.

79. Rifa'at Ali Abou-El-Haj, *The 1703 Rebellion and the Structure of Ottoman Politics* (Leiden: Nederlands Instituut voor het Nabije Oosten, 1984), 28.

80. Lewis V. Thomas, *A Study of Naima*, ed. Norman Itzkowitz, New York University Studies in Near Eastern Civilization 4 (New York: New York University Press, 1972).

81. Cornell H. Fleischer, 'Royal Authority, Dynastic Cyclism, and "Ibn Khaldûnism" in Sixteenth-Century Ottoman Letters', *Journal of Asian and African Studies* 18, no. 3–4 (July 1983): 198–220.

82. *Ahlak-ı Ala'i* (Ala'id Ethics), quoted in Fleischer, 'Royal Authority, Dynastic Cyclism, and "Ibn Khaldûnism"', 201.

CHAPTER 14: RETURN OF THE GAZI: MEHMED IV

1. Baer, 'Manliness, Male Virtue and History Writing', 130.

2. Vatin and Veinstein, *Le Sérail ébranlé*, 159, 194–195.

3. *Türkiye Diyanet Vakfı İslam Ansiklopedisi*, s.v. 'Murad IV', by Ziya Yılmazer, https://islamansiklopedisi.org.tr/murad-iv.

4. Naima, cited in Vatin and Veinstein, *Le Sérail ébranlé*, 195.

5. Baer, 'Manliness, Male Virtue and History Writing', 134.

6. Baer, 'Manliness, Male Virtue and History Writing', 135.

7. Evliya Çelebi, *Seyahatname*, quoted in Robert Dankoff, *An Ottoman Mentality: The World of Evliya Çelebi* (Leiden, The Netherlands: Brill, 2004), 103–104.

8. Katip Çelebi, cited in Baer, 'Manliness, Male Virtue and History Writing', 135.

9. Katip Çelebi, *Fezleke*, 2:309, 339–340.

10. Katip Çelebi, *Fezleke*, 2:310.

11. Karaçelebizade Abdülaziz Efendi, *Ravzatü'l-ebrâr zeyli (Tahlîl ve Metin) 1732*, ed. Nevzat Kaya (Ankara: Türk Tarih Kurumu Basımevi, 2003), 9.

12. Mehmed Hemdani Solakzade, *Tarih-i Al-i Osman*, Topkapı Palace Museum Library, Ahmed III 3078, fols. 466a–b; Vecihi Hasan Çelebi, *Tarih-i Vecihi*, Topkapı Palace Museum Library, MS. Revan 1153, fol. 45b.

13. Solakzade, *Tarih-i Al-i Osman*, fol. 466b; Vecihi Hasan Çelebi, *Tarih-i Vecihi*, fol. 45b.

14. Katip Çelebi, *Fezleke*, 2:329.

15. Karaçelebizade, *Ravzatü'l-ebrâr zeyli*, 4.

16. Karaçelebizade, *Ravzatü'l-ebrâr zeyli*, 6.

17. Katip Çelebi, *Fezleke*, 2:337.

18. Mehmed Halife, *Tarih-i Gilmani*, Topkapı Palace Museum Library, Revan 1306, fol. 18b.

19. Katip Çelebi, *Fezleke*, 2:329–330.

20. Karaçelebizade, *Ravzatü'l-ebrâr zeyli*, 12–13.

21. Naima, *Tarih-i Naima* (Istanbul: 1281–1283 AH), 4:332.

22. Solakzade, *Tarihi-i Al-i Osman*, fol. 467b.

23. Baer, 'Manliness, Male Virtue and History Writing at the Seventeenth-Century Ottoman Court', 133.

24. Naima, *Tarih-i Naima*, 4:397; Naima, *Tarih-i Naima*, 5:304.

25. Topkapı Palace Museum Archive, Arzlar, E. 7002/1 to E. 7002/86.

26. Naima, *Tarih-i Naima*, 5:420.

27. Marc David Baer, 'The Great Fire of 1660 and the Islamization of Christian and Jewish Space in Istanbul', *International Journal of Middle East Studies* 36, no. 2 (May 2004): 159–181.

28. Lucienne Thys-Şenocak, *Ottoman Women Builders: The Architectural Patronage of Hadice Turhan Sultan* (Farnham, UK: Ashgate, 2006), 107–188.

29. Baer, 'Manliness, Male Virtue and History Writing', 139.

30. Baer, 'Manliness, Male Virtue and History Writing', 140.

31. Baer, 'Manliness, Male Virtue and History Writing', 138.

32. Hasan Ağa, *Cevahir et-Tarih*, Topkapı Palace Museum Library, Revan 1307, fols. 1b–2a.

33. Hasan Ağa, *Cevahir et-Tarih*, fol. 156a.

34. Hasan Ağa, *Cevahir et-Tarih*, fol. 159a, fol. 170b.

35. Hasan Ağa, *Cevahir et-Tarih*, fol. 179a.

36. Dankoff, *An Ottoman Mentality*, 49.

37. Abdurrahman Abdi Paşa, *Vekāyināme*, Köprülü Library, Istanbul, 216, fols. 334a–b. Abdi Pasha was Mehmed IV's chronicler and confidant.

38. Yusuf Nabi, *Fethname-i Kamaniça*, Topkapı Palace Museum Library, MS. Hazine 1629, fol. 3b.

39. Yusuf Nabi, *Fethname-i Kamaniça*, fol. 61a.

40. Yusuf Nabi, *Fethname-i Kamaniça*, fol. 6a.

41. Yusuf Nabi, *Fethname-i Kamaniça*, fols. 33b, 51a; fol. 38b.

42. Yusuf Nabi, *Fethname-i Kamaniça*, fol. 28a.

43. Yusuf Nabi, *Fethname-i Kamaniça*, fol. 38b.

44. Marc David Baer, *Honored by the Glory of Islam: Conversion and Conquest in Ottoman Europe* (New York: Oxford University Press, 2008), 184.

45. John Covel, 'Dr. Covel's Diary', in *Early Voyages and Travels in the Levant*, ed. J. Theodore Bent (London: Hakluyt Society, 1893), 209–210.

46. Baer, *Honored by the Glory of Islam*, 191.

47. Baer, 'The Great Fire of 1660'.

48. The fire is narrated in Baer, *Honored by the Glory of Islam*, 82–85.

49. Abdi Pasha, *Vekāyi'nāme*, fols. 128b–129b.

50. Mehmed Halife, *Tarih-i Gilmani*, Topkapı Palace Museum Library, Revan 1306, fols. 62b, 63a.

51. The view of Mehmed Halife, *Tarih-i Gilmani*, 61a.

52. Baer, *Honored by the Glory of Islam*, 85–91.

53. Office of the Istanbul Mufti, Islamic Law Court Records Archive, Istanbul Şer'iye Sicilleri 10, fol. 156b, May 9, 1662, translated in Baer, *Honored by the Glory of Islam*, 98–99.

54. Baer, *Honored by the Glory of Islam*, 93.

55. Kürd Hatib Mustafa, *Risāle-i Kürd Hatīb*, Topkapı Palace Museum Library, MS. Eski Hazine 1400, 18a.

56. Baer, *Honored by the Glory of Islam*, 132–134.

57. Baer, *Honored by the Glory of Islam*, 122.

58. Baer, *Honored by the Glory of Islam*, 138.

59. These Christians amassed more power and wealth than Jews ever had in the empire because they were a crucial cog in Ottoman governance. Operating like vizier or pasha households, or provincial notables whose patronage network reached the capital, Phanariots possessed the offices of translator for the imperial navy, translator for the imperial council, and governor of the Danubian principalities of Moldova and Wallachia (Romania). Christine Philliou, 'Communities on the Verge: Unraveling the Phanariot Ascendancy in Ottoman Governance', *Comparative Studies in Society & History* 51, no. 1 (2009): 151–181.

CHAPTER 15: A JEWISH MESSIAH IN THE OTTOMAN PALACE

1. Madeline Zilfi, *The Politics of Piety: The Ottoman Ulema in the Postclassical Age (1600–1800)* (Minneapolis: Bibliotheca Islamica, 1988), 136.

2. Amin Ahmad Razi, *Haft Iqlim*, ed. Javad Fazil (Tehran: 'Ali Akbar 'Ilmi, 1961), 3:499, quoted in Sunil Sharma, 'The City of Beauties in Indo-Persian Poetic Landscape', *Comparative Studies of South Asia, Africa and the Middle East* 24, no. 2 (August 2004), 81.

3. Mehmed Halife, *Tarih-i Gilmani*, fol. 7b.

4. Zilfi, *The Politics of Piety*, 149.

5. Marc David Baer, 'Death in the Hippodrome: Sexual Politics and Legal Culture in the Reign of Mehmet IV', *Past & Present* 210, no. 1 (February 2011): 61–91.

6. Silahdar, *Tarih-i Silahdar*, 1:732.

7. Baer, *Honored by the Glory of Islam*, 121.

8. Baer, *Honored by the Glory of Islam*, 122.

9. Baer, *Honored by the Glory of Islam*, 123.

10. Baer, *Honored by the Glory of Islam*, 124.

11. Gershom Scholem, *Sabbatai Sevi: The Mystical Messiah, 1626–1676*, trans. R. J. Zwi Werblowsky (Princeton, NJ: Princeton University Press, 1973), 174.

12. Scholem, *Sabbatai Sevi*, 212–213.

13. 'Nathan of Gaza, A Letter to Raphael Joseph', trans. David Halperin, in Paweł Maciejko, ed., *Sabbatian Heresy: Writings on Mysticism, Messianism, and the Origins of Jewish Modernity* (Waltham, MA: Brandeis University Press, 2017), 6.

14. Ada Rapoport-Albert, *Women and the Messianic Heresy of Sabbatai Zevi 1666–1816*, trans. Deborah Greniman (Oxford: Littman Library of Jewish Civilization, 2011), 22–26.

15. Renée Levine Melammed, *Heretics or Daughters of Israel? The Crypto-Jewish Women of Castile* (Oxford: Oxford University Press, 1999).

16. Rapoport-Albert, *Women and the Messianic Heresy of Sabbatai Zevi*.

17. Rapoport-Albert, *Women and the Messianic Heresy of Sabbatai Zevi*, 107.

18. Rapoport-Albert, *Women and the Messianic Heresy of Sabbatai Zevi*, 108.

19. Rapoport-Albert, *Women and the Messianic Heresy of Sabbatai Zevi*, 141.

20. Rapoport-Albert, *Women and the Messianic Heresy of Sabbatai Zevi*, 258–259.

21. Rapoport-Albert, *Women and the Messianic Heresy of Sabbatai Zevi*, 261.

22. Baer, *Honored by the Glory of Islam*, 124–125.

23. Scholem, *Sabbatai Sevi*, 403; Rapoport-Albert, *Women and the Messianic Heresy of Sabbatai Zevi*, 137–138.

24. Baer, *Honored by the Glory of Islam*, 125.

25. Baer, 'The Great Fire of 1660'.

26. Baer, *Honored by the Glory of Islam*, 125.

27. Silahdar, *Tarih-i Silahdar*, 1:393.

28. *The Memoirs of Glückel of Hameln*, trans. Marvin Lowenthal (New York: Harper, 1932; New York: Schocken, 1977), 46.

29. Baer, *Honored by the Glory of Islam*, 126.

30. Baer, *Honored by the Glory of Islam*, 126.

31. *The Memoirs of Glückel of Hameln*, 45.

32. Baer, *Honored by the Glory of Islam*, 126.

33. Minkarizade Yahya ibn Ömer, *Fetāvā-i Minkarizade Efendi*, Suleimaniye Library, Istanbul, Hamidiye 610, fol. 34a.

34. Abdi Paşa, *Vekāyi'nāme*, fols. 224a–b.

35. Baer, *Honored by the Glory of Islam*, 131.

36. Scholem, *Sabbatai Sevi*, 859.

37. Scholem, *Sabbatai Sevi*, 729, 847.

CHAPTER 16: THE SECOND SIEGE OF VIENNA AND THE SWEET WATERS OF EUROPE: FROM MEHMED IV TO AHMED III

1. Baer, *Honored by the Glory of Islam*, 212.

2. Baer, *Honored by the Glory of Islam*, 214.

3. Cited in Baer, *Honored by the Glory of Islam*, 215.

4. Richard Kreutel, ed., *Kara Mustafa vor Wien: Das türkische Tagebuch der Belagerung Wiens 1683, verfasst vom Zeremonienmeister der Hohen Pforte* (Munich: Deutscher Taschenbuch, 1967), 20–21, 31–32.

5. Silahdar, *Tarih-i Silahdar*, 2:91–92.

6. Cited in Baer, *Honored by the Glory of Islam*, 218.

7. Kreutel, *Kara Mustafa vor Wien*, 76.

8. Kreutel, *Kara Mustafa vor Wien*, 79–80.

9. Baer, *Honored by the Glory of Islam*, 220.

10. Baer, *Honored by the Glory of Islam*, 223–224.

11. Silahdar, *Tarih-i Silahdar*, 2:245–246.

12. Baer, 'Manliness, Male Virtue and History Writing', 134.

13. Baer, *Honored by the Glory of Islam*, 208–209, 226.

14. Silahdar, *Tarih-i Silahdar*, 2:262–263.

15. Silahdar, *Tarih-i Silahdar*, 2:290.

16. Silahdar, *Tarih-i Silahdar*, 2:291.

17. Silahdar, *Tarih-i Silahdar*, 2:298.

18. Silahdar, *Tarih-i Silahdar*, 2:297.

19. Silahdar, *Tarih-i Silahdar*, 2:690–691.

20. Abou-El-Haj, *Formation of the Modern State*, 19.

21. Baer, *Honored by the Glory of Islam*, 253.

22. The museum's website is https://askerimuze.msb.gov.tr.

23. The museum's website is Heeresgeschichtliches Museum, Militärhistorisches Institut, https://www.hgm.at/en.html.

24. Vatin and Veinstein, *Le Sérail ébranlé*, 293, 295.

25. The decree is translated in Abou-El-Haj, *Formation of the Modern State*, 113–119.

26. Abou-El-Haj, *The 1703 Rebellion and the Structure of Ottoman Politics*.

27. Kortepeter, *Ottoman Imperialism During the Reformation*, 243.

28. Quoted in Kafadar, 'Janissaries and Other Riffraff of Ottoman Istanbul', 133.

29. Silahdar Fındıklılı Mehmed Ağa, as told in Finkel, *Osman's Dream*, 331–332.

30. Ahmed III was onto something. Nothing is as enjoyable in Istanbul as sitting outside on the upper deck of a slow-moving commuter ferry travelling from the European to the Asian side, sipping piping-hot tea from a tulip-shaped glass after having popped in two white sugar cubes that sizzle as they dissolve and tossing pieces of sesame ring to screeching seagulls suspended effortlessly in midair, the silhouettes of the domes and minarets of the city set against the background of a sky lit up by a pink and purple sunset. Tea, however, was not yet consumed in eighteenth-century Istanbul.

31. Ariel Salzmann, 'The Age of Tulips: Confluence and Conflict in Early Modern Consumer Culture (1550–1730)', in *Consumption Studies and the History of the Ottoman Empire, 1550-1922*, ed. Donald Quataert (Albany: State University of New York Press, 2000), 83–106, here 92.

32. Quoted in Shirine Hamadeh, 'Public Spaces and the Garden Culture of Istanbul in the Eighteenth Century', in *The Early Modern Ottomans: Remapping the Empire*, ed. Virginia Aksan and Daniel Goffman (Cambridge: Cambridge University Press, 2007), 277–312, here 277–278.

33. Finkel, *Osman's Dream*, 345.

34. Hamadeh, 'Public Spaces and the Garden Culture of Istanbul', 278.

35. Shirine Hamadeh, 'Splash and Spectacle: The Obsession with Fountains in Eighteenth-Century Istanbul', *Muqarnas* 19 (2002): 123–148. One can get a sense for what this must have been like in the eighteenth century by visiting one of the many cafés in Tophane in Istanbul, where you can smoke a water pipe in the shade on a summer day, the original eighteenth-century fountain, now dry, peering over your shoulder.

36. Alexander Bevilacqua and Helen Pfeifer, 'Turquerie: Culture in Motion, 1650–1750', *Past & Present* 221, no. 1 (2013): 75–118.

37. This section is based on Greene, *The Edinburgh History of the Greeks*, 192–215.

38. Greene, *The Edinburgh History of the Greeks*, 203.

39. Bekir Harun Küçük, 'Natural Philosophy and Politics in the Eighteenth Century: Esad of Ioannina and Greek Aristotelianism at the Ottoman Court', *Osmanlı Araştırmaları/Journal of Ottoman Studies* 41 (2013): 125–158.

40. Bekir Harun Küçük, 'Early Enlightenment in Istanbul' (PhD diss., University of California, San Diego, 2012), 164, 172; Greene, *The Edinburgh History of the Greeks*, 199.

41. The main proponent of this view is Küçük, 'Early Enlightenment in Istanbul'.

42. Steven Topik, 'The Integration of the World Coffee Market', in *The Global Coffee Economy in Africa, Asia and Latin America, 1500–1989*, ed. William Gervase Clarence-Smith and Steven Topik (Cambridge: Cambridge University Press, 2003), 28–29.

43. The lyrics of 'Schweigt stille, plaudert nicht—Kaffeekantate' can be found at www.bach-cantatas.com/Texts/BWV211-Eng3P.htm.

44. Bevilacqua and Pfeifer, 'Turquerie', 96.

45. Ceylan Yeginsu, 'Swedish Meatballs Are Turkish? "My Whole Life Has Been a Lie"', *New York Times*, 2 May 2018, www.nytimes.com/2018/05/02/world/europe/swedish-meatballs-turkey.html.

46. Bevilacqua and Pfeifer, 'Turquerie', 75.

47. Bevilacqua and Pfeifer, 'Turquerie', 98–101.

48. Bevilacqua and Pfeifer, 'Turquerie', 107.

49. Lady Mary Wortley Montagu, *The Letters and Works of Lady Mary Wortley Montagu*, ed. Lord Wharncliffe and William Moy Thomas (Cambridge: Cambridge University Press, 2011), 1:369–370.

50. The nickname might refer to his skin tone, or his not having a beard.

51. Tülay Artan, '18. yüzyıl başlarında yönetici elitin saltanatın meşruiyet arayışına katılımı', *Toplum ve Bilim* 83, *Osmanlı: Muktedirler ve Mâdunlar* (Kış 1999–2000), 294–296.

52. Artan, '18. yüzyıl başlarında yönetici elitin saltanatın meşruiyet arayışına katılımı', 296–297.

53. Artan, '18. yüzyıl başlarında yönetici elitin saltanatın meşruiyet arayışına katılımı', 302–303.

54. Artan, '18. yüzyıl başlarında yönetici elitin saltanatın meşruiyet arayışına katılımı', 306–313.

55. Fariba Zarinebaf, *Crime and Punishment in Istanbul 1700–1800* (Berkeley: University of California Press, 2010), 34–35.

56. Finkel, *Osman's Dream*, 350.

57. Serkan Delice, 'The Janissaries and Their Bedfellows: Masculinity and Male Homosexuality in Early Modern Ottoman Istanbul, 1500–1826' (PhD diss., London College of Fashion, University of the Arts London, 2015), chapter four.

58. Delice, 'The Janissaries and Their Bedfellows', 174–175.

59. Delice, 'The Janissaries and Their Bedfellows', 178.

60. Delice, 'The Janissaries and Their Bedfellows', 162.

61. Salzmann, 'The Age of Tulips', 94.

62. Quoted in Hamadeh, 'Public Spaces and the Garden Culture of Istanbul', 305.

63. Barkey, *Empire of Difference*, 213–214.

64. This account of the rebellion follows that of Finkel, *Osman's Dream*, 353–357, which is based on original Ottoman and foreign accounts.

65. Faik Reşit Unat, *1730 Patrona ihtilâli hakkında bir eser, Abdi Tarihi* (Ankara: Türk Tarih kurumu, 1943), 39–40, cited in Vatin and Veinstein, *Le Sérail ébranlé*, 253.

66. Salzmann, 'The Age of Tulips', 97.

67. *Türkiye Diyanet Vakfı İslam Ansiklopedisi*, s.v. 'Bağdat Köşkü', by Semavi Eyice, https://islamansiklopedisi.org.tr/bagdat-kosku.

68. Zarinebaf, *Crime and Punishment in Istanbul*, 60–61.

69. Hamadeh, 'Public Spaces and the Garden Culture of Istanbul', 302–304.

70. Alan Fisher, *The Russian Annexation of the Crimea, 1772–1783* (Cambridge: Cambridge University Press, 1970).

71. Finkel, *Osman's Dream*, 381.

72. Orlando Figes, *Crimea: The Last Crusade* (London: Allen Lane, 2010), 18.

73. Thomas Gallant, *The Edinburgh History of the Greeks, 1768 to 1913: The Long Nineteenth Century* (Edinburgh: Edinburgh University Press, 2015), 19–21, 25.

74. Figes, *Crimea*, 12–13, 25–26.

CHAPTER 17: REFORM: BREAKING THE CYCLE OF REBELLION FROM SELIM III TO ABDÜLAZIZ I

1. Engin Akarlı, 'The Problems of External Pressures, Power Struggles, and Budgetary Deficits in Ottoman Politics Under Abdulhamid II (1876-1909): Origins and Solutions' (PhD diss., Princeton University, 1976), 2.

2. Mütercim Ahmed Asım, *Tarih*, 2:204, quoted in Vatin and Veinstein, *Le Sérail ébranlé*, 67.

3. Vatin and Veinstein, *Le Sérail ébranlé*, 161.

4. The document is translated into English in Ali Yaycioglu, *Partners of the Empire: The Crisis of the Ottoman Order in the Age of Revolutions* (Stanford: Stanford University Press, 2016), 205–220.

5. Erik J. Zürcher, *Turkey: A Modern History*, 4th revised ed. (London: I.B. Tauris, 2017), 23.

6. Yaycioglu, *Partners of the Empire*, 234.

7. Mütercim Ahmed Asım, *Tarih*, 2:255, cited in Vatin and Veinstein, *Le Sérail ébranlé*, 161.

8. Finkel, *Osman's Dream*, 423.

9. Gallant, *The Edinburgh History of the Greeks*, 43–44.

10. Gallant, *The Edinburgh History of the Greeks*, 62.

11. Gallant, *The Edinburgh History of the Greeks*, 49–50.

12. Gallant, *The Edinburgh History of the Greeks*, 65, 74.

13. Gallant, *The Edinburgh History of the Greeks*, 73.

14. Şanizade Mehmed Ataullah Efendi, *Şanizade Tarihi (1223–1237/ 1808–1821)*, ed. Ziya Yılmazer (Istanbul: Çamlıca, 2008), 2:1072. Although this transliterated version of the text is printed in two volumes, the original nineteenth-century text was published in four volumes. The pages quoted here are in the third volume of the original.

15. Şanizade, *Şanizade Tarihi*, 2:1073.

16. Şanizade, *Şanizade Tarihi*, 2:1074.

17. Şanizade, *Şanizade Tarihi*, 2:1078–1079.

18. Şanizade, *Şanizade Tarihi*, 2:1080. In Bursa, his wife Hâcce was accused of witchcraft, murdered, and her naked corpse left exposed for one

or two days in public. A distraught Halil Efendi died soon after. Şanizade, *Şanizade Tarihi*, 2:1224–1226. The latter pages are in the fourth volume of the original.

19. Şanizade, *Şanizade Tarihi*, 2:1121. These pages are in the fourth volume of the original. The patriarch was actually seventy-four years old. Benderli Ali Pasha was soon dismissed and executed. The street in front of the patriarchate was named Grand Vizier (Sadrazam) Ali Pasha in the 1920s. It was renamed in the 1990s.

20. Şanizade, *Şanizade Tarihi*, 2:1123–1124. Several metropolitans from Anatolia were also hanged in Istanbul.

21. Gallant, *The Edinburgh History of the Greeks*, 86.

22. Gallant, *The Edinburgh History of the Greeks*, 95–96. Among the fatalities at Missolonghi was the British Romantic poet and satirist George Gordon, Lord Byron.

23. Howard Reed, 'The Destruction of the Janissaries by Mahmud II in June 1826' (PhD diss., Princeton University, 1951), cited in Finkel, *Osman's Dream*, 434–436.

24. Reed, 'The Destruction of the Janissaries', 236–237, cited in Finkel, *Osman's Dream*, 435.

25. Şirvânlı Fatih Efendi, *Gülzâr-i Fütûhât*, 13, cited in Finkel, *Osman's Dream*, 435.

26. Sir James Porter, late eighteenth-century British ambassador in Istanbul, quoted in Tezcan, *The Second Ottoman Empire*, 8.

27. Cited in Şerif Mardin, *The Genesis of Young Ottoman Thought: A Study in the Modernization of Turkish Political Ideas* (Princeton, NJ: Princeton University Press, 1962), 310.

28. Abraham Galanté, *Histoire des Juifs d'Istanbul* (Istanbul: Imprimerie Husnutabiat, 1941), 27–28.

29. Cengiz Kırlı, 'Kahvehaneler ve hafiyeler: 19. yüzyıl ortalarında Osmanlı'da sosyal kontrol', *Toplum ve Bilim* 83, *Osmanlı: Muktedirler ve Mâdunlar* (Kış 1999–2000): 58–77.

30. Abdülkadir Özcan, 'II. Mahmud'un memleket gezileri', *Prof. Dr. Bekir Kütükoğlu'na Armağan*, Istanbul Üniversitesi Edebiyat Fakültesi Tarih Araştırma Merkezi (Istanbul: Edebiyat Fakültesi, 1991), 361–379.

31. Gallant, *The Edinburgh History of the Greeks*, 99–100.

32. Finkel, *Osman's Dream*, 445.

33. Zürcher, *Turkey*, 49.

34. İlber Ortaylı, *İmparatorluğun en uzun yüzyıl*, 3rd ed. (Istanbul: Hil, 1995), 77–150.

35. 'The Gülhane Decree and the Beginning of the Tanzimat Reform Era in the Ottoman Empire, 1839', trans. Halil Inalcik, in *The Middle East and North Africa in World Politics: A Documentary Record*, vol. 1, *European Expansion, 1535–1914*, ed. J. C. Hurewitz (New Haven, CT: Yale University Press, 1975).

36. Yener Bayar, 'The Life and Work of Mustafa Reshid Pasha, Nineteenth-Century Ottoman Reformer' (PhD diss., London School of Economics and Political Science, in progress).

37. Galanté, *Histoire des Juifs d'Istanbul*, 26.

38. Selim Deringil, *Conversion and Apostasy in the Late Ottoman Empire* (Cambridge: Cambridge University Press, 2012), 69, 75.

39. Deringil, *Conversion and Apostasy in the Late Ottoman Empire*, 98–105.

40. Figes, *Crimea*, 295–296.

41. Figes, *Crimea*, 118.

42. Figes, *Crimea*, 141.

43. Figes, *Crimea*, 142.

44. Figes, *Crimea*, 147.

45. Figes, *Crimea*, xvii, xx.

46. Nicholas Woods, quoted in Figes, *Crimea*, 269.

47. Figes, *Crimea*, xix, 489.

48. Figes, *Crimea*, 389.

49. Figes, *Crimea*, 483.

50. Figes, *Crimea*, 253.

51. Leo Tolstoy, *The Sebastopol Sketches*, trans. D. McDuff (London, 1986), 44, 47–48, quoted in Figes, *Crimea*, 298.

52. Figes, *Crimea*, 105, 323. Nicolas I was buried with a silver cross bearing an image of the Hagia Sophia as a church.

53. Alan Fisher, 'Emigration of Muslims from the Russian Empire in the Years After the Crimean War', *Jahrbücher für Geschichte Osteuropas* 35, no. 3 (1987): 356–371.

54. (Ahmed) Cevdet Paşa, *Tezâkir*, ed. Cavid Baysun (Ankara: Türk Tarih Kurumu, 1953–1967), 1:68, quoted in Mardin, *The Genesis of Young Ottoman Thought*, 18, and Finkel, *Osman's Dream*, 459.

55. Esra Özyürek, 'Convert Alert: German Muslims and Turkish Christians as Threats to Security in the New Europe', *Comparative Studies in Society and History* 51, no. 1 (2009): 91–116.

56. Deringil, *Conversion and Apostasy in the Late Ottoman Empire*, 111–112.

57. Deringil, *Conversion and Apostasy in the Late Ottoman Empire*, 115.

58. Deringil, *Conversion and Apostasy in the Late Ottoman Empire*, 162.

59. Deringil, *Conversion and Apostasy in the Late Ottoman Empire*, 159–160.

60. Deringil, *Conversion and Apostasy in the Late Ottoman Empire*, 192.

61. Deringil, *Conversion and Apostasy in the Late Ottoman Empire*, 157.

62. Nilüfer Göle, *The Forbidden Modern: Civilization and Veiling* (Ann Arbor: University of Michigan Press, 1996), 30–33.

63. Göle, *The Forbidden Modern*, 31–32.

64. Arus Yumul, 'Osmanlı'nın ilk anayasası', *Toplum ve Bilim* 83, *Osmanlı: Muktedirler ve Mâdunlar* (Kış 1999–2000), 346.

65. The Greek Orthodox patriarchate received its 'Regulations' in 1862, and the chief rabbinate received its own in 1865.

66. Yumul, 'Osmanlı'nın ilk anayasası', 347.

67. Yumul, 'Osmanlı'nın ilk anayasası', 343.

68. Zürcher, *Turkey*, 62.

69. Mardin, *The Genesis of Young Ottoman Thought*, 21.

70. Namık Kemal, cited in Mardin, *The Genesis of Young Ottoman Thought*, 115.

71. Zürcher, *Turkey*, 63–64.

72. Mardin, *The Genesis of Young Ottoman Thought*, 288.

73. Mardin, *The Genesis of Young Ottoman Thought*, 399.

74. Mardin, *The Genesis of Young Ottoman Thought*, 311–313.

75. Namık Kemal, 'Vatan', *İbret*, 12 March 1873, quoted in Mardin, *The Genesis of Young Ottoman Thought*, 327.

76. Mardin, *The Genesis of Young Ottoman Thought*, 44–45.

77. Zürcher, *Turkey*, 64.

78. Namık Kemal, *Vatan şiiri* (Fatherland poem), quoted in Kemal Karpat, *The Politicization of Islam: Reconstructing Identity, State, Faith, and Community in the Late Ottoman State* (Oxford: Oxford University Press, 2001), 334.

79. Mardin, *The Genesis of Young Ottoman Thought*, 67.

80. İpek Yosmaoğlu, *Blood Ties: Religion, Violence, and the Politics of Nationhood in Ottoman Macedonia, 1878–1908* (Ithaca, NY: Cornell University Press, 2014), 53–60. Nationalism was diffused to the wider Bulgarian population in the exarchate churches and its new schools.

81. Mardin, *The Genesis of Young Ottoman Thought*, 70.

82. Zürcher, *Turkey*, 67–68.

83. Mardin, *The Genesis of Young Ottoman Thought*, 73.

84. Yumul, 'Osmanlı'nın ilk anayasası', 349.

85. Quoted in Deringil, *Conversion and Apostasy in the Late Ottoman Empire*, 64.

CHAPTER 18: REPRESSION: A MODERN CALIPH, ABDÜLHAMID II

1. Akarlı, 'The Problems of External Pressures', 3.

2. Benjamin Fortna, 'The Reign of Abdülhamid II', in *The Cambridge History of Turkey*, ed. Reşat Kasaba, vol. 4, *Turkey in the Modern World* (Cambridge: Cambridge University Press, 2008), 41.

3. Zürcher, *Turkey*, 59.

4. William Ewart Gladstone, *Bulgarian Horrors and the Question of the East* (London: John Murray, 1876), 9.

5. *Türkiye Diyanet Vakfı İslam Ansiklopedisi*, s.v. 'Doksanüç Harbi: 1877–1878 Osmanlı-Rus savaşı', by Mahir Aydın, https://islamansiklopedisi.org.tr/doksanuc-harbi.

6. *Türkiye Diyanet Vakfı İslam Ansiklopedisi*, s.v. 'Doksanüç Harbi'.

7. Murat Bardakçı, ed., *Talât Paşa'nın evrak-ı metrûkesi: Sadrazam Talât Paşa'nın özel arşivinde bulunan Ermeni tehciri konusundaki belgeler ve hususî yazışmalar* (Istanbul: Everest, 2013), 35.

8. Finkel, *Osman's Dream*, 500–501.

9. Selim Deringil, *The Well-Protected Domains: Ideology and the Legitimation of Power in the Late Ottoman Empire, 1876–1909* (London: I.B. Tauris, 1998), 22, 26, 29.

10. Deringil, *The Well-Protected Domains*, 60–61.

11. Deringil, *The Well-Protected Domains*, 37–39.

12. Deringil, *The Well-Protected Domains*, 48.

13. Deringil, *The Well-Protected Domains*, 50.

14. Deringil, *The Well-Protected Domains*, 53.

15. Selçuk Akşin Somel, 'Osmanlı modernleşme döneminde periferik nüfus grupları', *Toplum ve Bilim* 83, *Osmanlı: Muktedirler ve Mâdunlar* (Kış 1999–2000): 178–199.

16. *Encyclopaedia of Islam, THREE*, s.v., 'Alevīs', by Markus Dressler.

17. Deringil, *The Well-Protected Domains*, 68–75.

18. Deringil, *The Well-Protected Domains*, 85.

19. Eugene Rogan, 'Aşiret Mektebi: Abdülhamid II's School for Tribes (1892–1907)', *International Journal of Middle East Studies* 28, no. 1 (February 1996): 83–107; Deringil, *The Well-Protected Domains*, 99–104.

20. Somel, 'Osmanlı modernleşme döneminde periferik nüfus grupları', 197–198.

21. Göle, *The Forbidden Modern*, 32.

22. Elizabeth Frierson, 'Unimagined Communities: Women and Education in the Late-Ottoman Empire, 1876–1909', *Critical Matrix* 9, no. 2 (1995): 55–90.

23. David Leupold, *Embattled Dreamlands: The Politics of Contesting Armenian, Kurdish and Turkish Memory* (London: Routledge, 2020), 108, 111, 153.

24. Ronald Grigor Suny, *"They Can Live in the Desert but Nowhere Else": A History of the Armenian Genocide* (Princeton, NJ: Princeton University Press, 2015), 86–87.

25. Quoted in David McDowall, *A Modern History of the Kurds*, 3rd rev. ed. (London: I.B. Tauris, 2004), 53.

26. Janet Klein, *The Margins of Empire: Kurdish Militias in the Ottoman Tribal Zone* (Stanford, CA: Stanford University Press, 2011).

27. Stephan Astourian, 'The Silence of the Land: Agrarian Relations, Ethnicity, and Power', in *A Question of Genocide: Armenians and Turks at the End of the Ottoman Empire*, ed. Ronald Grigor Suny, Fatma Müge Göçek, and Norman Naimark (Oxford: Oxford University Press, 2011), 55–81.

28. Suny, *"They Can Live in the Desert but Nowhere Else"*, 105–123.

29. Deringil, *Conversion and Apostasy in the Late Ottoman Empire*, 203.

30. Deringil, *The Well-Protected Domains*, 27, 31–32.

31. Deringil, *The Well-Protected Domains*, 135–149.

32. Deringil, *The Well-Protected Domains*, 137.

33. Deringil, *The Well-Protected Domains*, 149.

34. Baer, *Sultanic Saviors and Tolerant Turks*, 53–72.

35. Julia Phillips Cohen, *Becoming Ottomans: Sephardi Jews and Imperial Citizenship in the Modern Era* (Oxford: Oxford University Press, 2014), 6, 8.

36. Cohen, *Becoming Ottomans*, 49.

37. Cohen, *Becoming Ottomans*, 59.

38. Teacher Mercado Joseph Covo (d. 1940), quoted in Devin Naar, 'Fashioning the "Mother of Israel": The Ottoman Jewish Historical Narrative and the Image of Jewish Salonica', *Jewish History* 28, no. 3 (2014): 337–372, here 363.

39. Covo, quoted in Naar, 'Fashioning the "Mother of Israel"', 366.

40. Quoted in Cohen, *Becoming Ottomans*, 49.

41. Quoted in Cohen, *Becoming Ottomans*, 54.

42. Suny, *"They Can Live in the Desert but Nowhere Else"*, 123–125.

43. Cohen, *Becoming Ottomans*, 75–76.

44. 'Eyewitness to Massacres of Armenians in Istanbul (1896)', in *Sephardi Lives: A Documentary History, 1700–1950*, ed. Sarah Abrevaya Stein and Julia Phillips Cohen (Stanford, CA: Stanford University Press, 2014), 134–139.

45. Margaret Lavinia Anderson, '"Down in Turkey, Far Away": Human Rights, the Armenian Massacres, and Orientalism in Wilhelmine Germany', *Journal of Modern History* 79, no. 1 (March 2007): 80–111, here 87.

46. Quoted in Yair Auron, *The Banality of Indifference: Zionism and the Armenian Genocide* (London: Transaction, 2000), 116.

47. Auron, *The Banality of Indifference*, 119.

48. Irvin Cemil Schick, 'Sultan Abdülhamid II from the Pen of His Detractors: Oriental Despotism and the Sexualization of the Ancien Régime', *Journal of the Ottoman and Turkish Studies Association* 5, no. 2 (Fall 2018): 47–73.

CHAPTER 19: LOOKING WITHIN: THE OTTOMAN ORIENT

1. Edward Said, *Orientalism* (London: Routledge, 1978), 1–3.

2. Eugene Rogan, *Frontiers of the State in the Late Ottoman Empire: Transjordan, 1850–1921* (Cambridge: Cambridge University Press, 1999), 151; Maurus Reinkowski, *Die Dinge der Ordnung: Eine vergleichende Untersuchung über die osmanische Reformpolitik im 19. Jahrhundert* (Munich: R. Oldenbourg, 2005), 249–253.

3. Quoted in Deringil, *The Well-Protected Domains*, 41.

4. Reinkowski, *Die Dinge der Ordnung*, 245.

5. Christoph Herzog and Raoul Motika, 'Orientalism "alla turca"', *Die Welt des Islams* 40, no. 2 (2000): 141–195.

6. Quoted in Herzog and Motika, 'Orientalism "alla turca"' 185–186.

7. Quoted in Herzog and Motika, 'Orientalism "alla turca"', 142.

8. Quoted in Herzog and Motika, 'Orientalism "alla turca"', 191.

9. Quoted in Herzog and Motika, 'Orientalism "alla turca"', 168.

10. Selim Deringil, '"They Live in a State of Nomadism and Savagery": The Late Ottoman Empire and Post-Colonial Debate', *Comparative Studies in Society and History* 45, no. 2 (2003), 312.

11. Deringil, 'They Live in a State of Nomadism and Savagery', 312.

12. Deringil, 'They Live in a State of Nomadism and Savagery', 334.

13. Deringil, 'They Live in a State of Nomadism and Savagery', 334.

14. Deringil, 'They Live in a State of Nomadism and Savagery', 338.

15. Mary Roberts, *Intimate Outsiders: The Harem in Ottoman and Orientalist Art and Travel Literature* (Durham, NC: Duke University Press, 2007), 21.

16. Roberts, *Intimate Outsiders*, 39. One can view the painting on Tate Britain's website: www.tate.org.uk/art/artworks/lewis-the-siesta-n03594.

17. Roberts, *Intimate Outsiders*, 33.

18. Roberts, *Intimate Outsiders*, 21, 31.

19. Roberts, *Intimate Outsiders*, 60–61.

20. Roberts, *Intimate Outsiders*, 109.

21. Finkel, *Osman's Dream*, 471–472.

22. Finkel, *Osman's Dream*, 473–474.

23. Roberts, *Intimate Outsiders*, 111.

24. Roberts, *Intimate Outsiders*, 112.

25. Roberts, *Intimate Outsiders*, 114.

26. The Palestinian literary critic Edward Said chose the painting to grace the cover of the first edition of his 1978 classic, *Orientalism*.

27. Edhem Eldem, 'Making Sense of Osman Hamdi Bey and His Paintings', *Muqarnas* 29 (2012), 374.

28. Eldem, 'Making Sense of Osman Hamdi Bey', 371.

29. Edhem Eldem, ed., *Un Ottoman en Orient: Osman Hamdi Bey en Irak, 1869–1871* (Paris: Actes Sud, 2010).

30. Eldem, 'Making Sense of Osman Hamdi Bey', 355–363.

31. Najmabadi, *Women with Mustaches and Men Without Beards*; Ze'evi, *Producing Desire*; and Kuru, 'Sex in the Text'.

32. Quoted in Ze'evi, *Producing Desire*, 164.

33. Kuru, 'Sex in the Text', 159.

34. Mustafa Ali, cited in Fleischer, *Bureaucrat and Intellectual in the Ottoman Empire*, 23.

35. Deringil, *The Well-Protected Domains*, 150–151, 171–172.

36. Eldem, 'Making Sense of Osman Hamdi Bey', 376–377.

CHAPTER 20: SAVING THE DYNASTY
FROM ITSELF: YOUNG TURKS

1. 'Sabbatai Tsevi, A Letter on Conversion', trans. Paweł Maciejko, in Maciejko, *Sabbatian Heresy*, 34.

2. 'Sabbatai Tsevi, A Letter on Conversion', 35.

3. 'Sabbatai Tsevi, Bury My Faith!', trans. David Halperin, in Maciejko, *Sabbatian Heresy*, 37.

4. Marc David Baer, *The Dönme: Jewish Converts, Muslim Revolutionaries, and Secular Turks* (Stanford, CA: Stanford University Press, 2010).

5. Baer, *The Dönme*, 86–87.

6. Baer, *The Dönme*, 89.

7. Baer, *The Dönme*, 90.

8. Baer, *The Dönme*, 91.

9. His identity papers are found in Bardakçı, *Talât Paşa'nın evrak-ı metrûkesi*, 235.

10. Hans-Lukas Kieser, *Talaat Pasha: Father of Modern Turkey, Architect of Genocide* (Princeton, NJ: Princeton University Press, 2018), 49.

11. Erik J. Zürcher, 'Who Were the Young Turks?', in *The Young Turk Legacy and Nation Building: From the Ottoman Empire to Atatürk's Turkey* (London: I.B. Tauris, 2010), 97–98.

12. Karpat, *The Politicization of Islam*, 112; Baer, *The Dönme*, 92.

13. Baer, *The Dönme*, 93.

14. Lewis, *Rumi*, 452.

15. Lewis, *Rumi*, 452–453.

16. Baer, *The Dönme*, 94.

17. Baer, *The Dönme*, 95.

18. Baer, *The Dönme*, 96.

19. Şükrü Hanioğlu, 'The Second Constitutional Period, 1908–1918', in *The Cambridge History of Turkey*, 4:62.

20. Erik J. Zürcher, 'The Historiography of the Constitutional Revolution: Broad Consensus, Some Disagreement and a Missed Opportunity', in *The Young Turk Legacy and Nation Building*, 26–40.

21. Yosmaoğlu, *Blood Ties*, 2.

22. 'The Young Turks', trans. A. Sarrou, in *Civilization Since Waterloo*, ed. Rondo Cameron (Paris, 1912), 40–42.

23. Baer, *The Dönme*, 97.

24. Mehmet Ö. Alkan, *İmparatorluk'tan Cumhuriyet'e Selânik'ten İstanbul'a Terakki Vakfı ve Terakki Okulları, 1877–2000* (Istanbul: Terakki Vakfı, 2003), 94.

25. Baer, *The Dönme*, 93.

26. Baer, *The Dönme*, 94.

27. Zürcher, *Turkey*, 93.

28. Zürcher, 'Who Were the Young Turks?', 102–104.

29. Yeşim Arat, 'Contestation and Collaboration: Women's Struggles for Empowerment in Turkey', in *The Cambridge History of Turkey*, 4:389–390.

30. Göle, *The Forbidden Modern*, 38.

31. Göle, *The Forbidden Modern*, 43.

32. Erik J. Zürcher, 'The Ides of April: A Fundamentalist Uprising in Istanbul in 1909?', in *The Young Turk Legacy and Nation Building*, 73–83.

33. Asena Günal and Murat Çelikkan, *Hatırlayan şehir: Taksim'den Sultanahmet'e mekân ve hafıza/A City That Remembers: Space and Memory from Taksim to Sultanahmet* (Istanbul: Truth Justice Memory Center, 2019), 208–209.

34. Bedross Der Matossian, 'From Bloodless Revolution to a Bloody Counterrevolution: The Adana Massacres of 1909', *Genocide Studies and Prevention: An International Journal* 6, no. 2 (2011): 152–173.

35. Kieser, *Talaat Pasha*, 76–79.

36. Baer, *The Dönme*, 98.

37. Baer, *The Dönme*, 99.

38. Baer, *The Dönme*, 100.

39. Baer, *The Dönme*, 110.

40. Ahmet Emin Yalman, *Yakın tarihte gördüklerim ve geçirdiklerim*, ed. Erol Şadi Erdinç, 2nd ed. (Istanbul: Pera Turizm ve Ticaret, 1997), 1:700–701; Baer, *The Dönme*, 45–46.

41. Erik J. Zürcher, 'The Young Turk Mindset', in *The Young Turk Legacy and Nation Building*, 110–123.

42. Zürcher, 'The Young Turk Mindset', 110–112.

43. Zürcher, 'The Young Turk Mindset', 112–114.

44. Yosmaoğlu, *Blood Ties*, 25–36, 78.

45. Yosmaoğlu, *Blood Ties*, 5.

46. Zürcher, 'The Young Turk Mindset', 114–115.

47. Zürcher, 'The Young Turk Mindset', 116.

48. Zürcher, 'The Young Turk Mindset', 117.

49. Zürcher, *Turkey*, 91–92.

50. Zürcher, 'The Young Turk Mindset', 117–118.

51. M. Şükrü Hanioğlu, *Atatürk: An Intellectual Biography* (Princeton, NJ: Princeton University Press, 2011), 33–35.

52. Baer, *The Dönme*, 92.

53. Yusuf Akçura and Ismail Fehmi, 'Yusuf Akçura's Üç Tarz—ı Siyaset ("Three Kinds of Policy")', *Oriente Moderno* 61, no. 1/12 (January–December 1981): 1–20.

54. Akçura and Fehmi, 'Yusuf Akçura's Üç Tarz—ı Siyaset ("Three Kinds of Policy")', 5.

55. Akçura and Fehmi, 'Yusuf Akçura's Üç Tarz—ı Siyaset ("Three Kinds of Policy")', 18.

56. Gallant, *The Edinburgh History of the Greeks*, 294–299.

57. Gallant, *The Edinburgh History of the Greeks*, 300.

58. Kieser, *Talaat Pasha*, 133–136.

59. Bardakçı, *Talât Paşa'nın evrak-ı metrûkesi*, 39.
60. Bardakçı, *Talât Paşa'nın evrak-ı metrûkesi*, 79–81.
61. Zürcher, 'The Young Turk Mindset', 118–121.

CHAPTER 21: THE GENOCIDE OF THE ARMENIANS AND THE FIRST WORLD WAR: TALAT PASHA

1. Bedross Der Matossian, *Shattered Dreams of Revolution: From Liberty to Violence in the Late Ottoman Empire* (Stanford, CA: Stanford University Press, 2014), 23–24.
2. Kieser, *Talaat Pasha*, 25.
3. Eyal Ginio, *The Ottoman Culture of Defeat: The Balkan Wars and Their Aftermath* (Oxford: Oxford University Press, 2016).
4. Ziya Gökalp, 'Kızılelma', *Türk Yurdu* 2, no. 31 (January 1913), quoted in Kieser, *Talaat Pasha*, 101.
5. Kieser, *Talaat Pasha*, 18–19.
6. Kieser, *Talaat Pasha*, 109, 159.
7. Fatma Müge Göçek, *Denial of Violence: Ottoman Past, Turkish Present, and Collective Violence Against the Armenians, 1789–2009* (Oxford: Oxford University Press, 2015).
8. Zürcher, *Turkey*, 121.
9. Quoted in Mustafa Aksakal, *The Ottoman Road to War in 1914: The Ottoman Empire and the First World War* (Cambridge: Cambridge University Press, 2008), 38.
10. Stefan Ihrig, *Atatürk in the Nazi Imagination* (Cambridge, MA: Belknap Press, 2014), 1–2.
11. Stefan Ihrig, *Justifying Genocide: Germany and the Armenians from Bismarck to Hitler* (Cambridge, MA: Harvard University Press, 2016), 27, 34, 40; Sultan Abdülhamit, *Siyasî hatıratım* (Istanbul: Dergah, 1987), 133, quoted in Fortna, 'The Reign of Abdülhamid II', 56.
12. Ihrig, *Atatürk in the Nazi Imagination*, 4–5.
13. Suny, *"They Can Live in the Desert but Nowhere Else"*, 231.
14. Eugene Rogan, *The Fall of the Ottomans: The Great War in the Middle East* (New York: Basic Books, 2015), xvii.
15. Hanioğlu, 'The Second Constitutional Period, 1908–1918', 94.
16. Quoted in Rogan, *The Fall of the Ottomans*, 111.
17. Rogan, *The Fall of the Ottomans*, 114.
18. Rogan, *The Fall of the Ottomans*, 115.
19. Rogan, *The Fall of the Ottomans*, 135.
20. Kieser, *Talaat Pasha*, 295–314.
21. Rogan, *The Fall of the Ottomans*, 298.
22. Rogan, *The Fall of the Ottomans*, 309, 353.
23. Rogan, *The Fall of the Ottomans*, 351.
24. One can view the object on the website of the Imperial War Museum London: 'Flag, Military, White, Surrender of Jerusalem by Turks',

catalogue no. FLA 553, Imperial War Museum, www.iwm.org.uk/collections/item/object/30016591.

25. Doctor Nazım, quoted in the 1929 memoir of Kurdish journalist and former CUP Central Committee member Rıfat Mevlanzade, *Ittihat Terakki iktidarı ve Türk inkılabın içyüzü* (Istanbul: Yedi Iklim, 1993), 125, quoted in Göçek, *Denial of Violence*, 202.

26. Suny, *"They Can Live in the Desert but Nowhere Else"*, 248–249.

27. Aram Arkun, 'Zeytun and the Commencement of the Armenian Genocide', in *A Question of Genocide*, 221–243.

28. Leupold, *Embattled Dreamlands*, 125.

29. Suny, *"They Can Live in the Desert but Nowhere Else"*, 253–263.

30. Bardakçı, *Talât Paşa'nın evrak-ı metrûkesi*, 23–24.

31. Günal and Çelikkan, *Hatırlayan şehir*, 334–335.

32. A. P. Herbert, 'Flies', written at Gallipoli in 1915, quoted in Rogan, *The Fall of the Ottomans*, 196.

33. Rogan, *The Fall of the Ottomans*, 214.

34. Bardakçı, *Talât Paşa'nın evrak-ı metrûkesi*, 25–26.

35. 'Talât Paşa'nın eşi Hayriye Talât Hanım (Bafralı) ile mülâkat (Ekim 1982)', in Bardakçı, *Talât Paşa'nın evrak-ı metrûkesi*, 211.

36. *Takvîm-i Vekâyi'* #3540 (28 Nisan 1335), 4-14 (Karârnâme), translated in Vahakn Dadrian and Taner Akçam, *Judgment at Istanbul: The Armenian Genocide Trials* (Oxford: Berghahn Books, 2011), 280.

37. Mevlanzade, *Ittihat Terakki iktidarı ve Türk inkılabın içyüzü*, 126–127, quoted in Göçek, *Denial of Violence*, 202.

38. Madame P. Captanian, *Mémoires d'une déportée arménienne* (Paris: M. Flinikowski, 1919). The work was translated into Turkish in the 2010s.

39. Captanian, *Mémoires d'une déportée arménienne*, 20.

40. Captanian, *Mémoires d'une déportée arménienne*, 23–24.

41. Captanian, *Mémoires d'une déportée arménienne*, 30.

42. Captanian, *Mémoires d'une déportée arménienne*, 31.

43. Captanian, *Mémoires d'une déportée arménienne*, 35.

44. Captanian, *Mémoires d'une déportée arménienne*, 36.

45. Captanian, *Mémoires d'une déportée arménienne*, 40.

46. Captanian, *Mémoires d'une déportée arménienne*, 46.

47. Captanian, *Mémoires d'une déportée arménienne*, 47.

48. Captanian, *Mémoires d'une déportée arménienne*, 67.

49. Captanian, *Mémoires d'une déportée arménienne*, 130.

50. Captanian, *Mémoires d'une déportée arménienne*, 130.

51. Captanian, *Mémoires d'une déportée arménienne*, 131.

52. Captanian, *Mémoires d'une déportée arménienne*, 68.

53. Captanian, *Mémoires d'une déportée arménienne*, 68.

54. Captanian, *Mémoires d'une déportée arménienne*, 72.

55. Captanian, *Mémoires d'une déportée arménienne*, 87.

56. Captanian, *Mémoires d'une déportée arménienne*, 95.

57. Captanian, *Mémoires d'une déportée arménienne*, 96.

58. Bardakçı, *Talât Paşa'nın evrak-ı metrûkesi*, 77, 109. Talat Pasha wrote that although the Armenian population was tabulated as reaching only 1,256,403 in 1914, because not all were counted, the actual figure was as high as 1,500,000.

59. Bardakçı, *Talât Paşa'nın evrak-ı metrûkesi*, 109. He noted that although he counted only 284,157 Armenians living in the empire after the deportations, one-third of whom were in Istanbul, it was necessary to add 30 percent to the figure to arrive at what he considered the true number remaining, which was between 350,000 and 400,000 people.

60. Armin T. Wegner, *Der Weg ohne Heimkehr. Ein Martyrium in Briefen* (Berlin: Fleischel, 1919), reprinted in *Wege ohne Heimkehr: Die Armenier, der Erste Weltkrieg und die Folgen*, ed. Corry Guttstadt (Hamburg: Assoziation A, 2014), 121.

61. Wegner, *Der Weg ohne Heimkehr*, 122.

62. Wegner, *Der Weg ohne Heimkehr*, 122.

63. Wegner, *Der Weg ohne Heimkehr*, 122.

64. Kieser, *Talaat Pasha*, 262.

65. Quoted in Hans-Lukas Kieser, 'From "Patriotism" to Mass Murder: Dr. Mehmed Reşid (1873–1919)', in *A Question of Genocide*, 137.

66. Göçek, *Denial of Violence*, 227.

67. Quoted in Suny, *"They Can Live in the Desert but Nowhere Else"*, 294.

68. Suny, *"They Can Live in the Desert but Nowhere Else"*, 295.

69. Suny, *"They Can Live in the Desert but Nowhere Else"*, 321–323.

70. See the discussion of Talat Pasha's figures in Fuat Dündar, 'Talât Paşa'nın evrak-ı metrûkesi'ni "okumak"', *Toplumsal Tarih* 196 (Nisan 2010): 92–96.

71. Quoted in Kieser, *Talaat Pasha*, 232.

72. Kieser, *Talaat Pasha*, 234.

73. Mehmed Cavid Bey, *Meşrutiyet Rûznamesi* (Ankara: Türk Tarih Kurumu, 2014–2015), 3:135–136, quoted in Kieser, *Talaat Pasha*, 22–23.

74. Faiz al-Huseyin, Bedouin notable of Damascus, *Martyred Armenia*, translated from the original Arabic (New York: George H. Doran, 1918), quoted in Kieser, *Talaat Pasha*, 275, 277.

75. David Gaunt, 'The Ottoman Treatment of the Assyrians', in *A Question of Genocide*, 244–259.

76. Quoted in Gaunt, 'The Ottoman Treatment of the Assyrians', 253–254.

77. Eric Weitz, 'Germany and the Young Turks: Revolutionaries into Statesmen', in *A Question of Genocide*, 175–198.

78. George N. Shirinian, 'Turks Who Saved Armenians: Righteous Muslims During the Armenian Genocide', *Genocide Studies International* 9, no. 2 (Fall 2015): 208–227.

79. Kieser, *Talaat Pasha*, 163–164.

80. Kieser, *Talaat Pasha*, 184.

81. Robert Melson, *Revolution and Genocide: On the Origins of the Armenian Genocide and the Holocaust* (Chicago: University of Chicago Press, 1992), 49–52.

82. *Takvîm-i Vekâyi'* #3540 (28 Nisan 1335), 4-14 (Karârnâme), translated in Dadrian and Akçam, *Judgment at Istanbul*, 272–273.

83. *Takvîm-i Vekâyi'* #3540, 277.

84. *Takvîm-i Vekâyi'* #3571, 127–140 (Iddi'ânâme ve Karârnâme), translated in Dadrian and Akçam, *Judgment at Istanbul*, 284.

85. *Takvîm-i Vekâyi'* #3604, 217–220 (Karar Sureti), translated in Dadrian and Akçam, *Judgment at Istanbul*, 330.

86. *Takvîm-i Vekâyi'* #3771, 1–2 Ma'muretü'l'aziz Taktîl Muhâkemeleri (Karar Sureti), translated in Dadrian and Akçam, *Judgment at Istanbul*, 300.

87. *Takvîm-i Vekâyi'* #3616, 1–3 Trabzon Tehcîr ve Taktîli Muhâkemesi (Karar Sureti), translated in Dadrian and Akçam, *Judgment at Istanbul*, 294–295.

88. Göçek, *Denial of Violence*, 382.

89. Philippe Sands, *East West Street: On the Origin of "Genocide" and "Crimes Against Humanity"* (London: Weidenfeld & Nicolson, 2016), 149.

90. The text is available on the website of the United Nations Human Rights Office of the High Commissioner: UN General Assembly, Resolution 260 A, Convention on the Prevention and Punishment of the Crime of Genocide, December 9, 1948, www.ohchr.org/en/professionalinterest/pages/crimeofgenocide.aspx.

CHAPTER 22: THE END: GAZI MUSTAFA KEMAL

1. Hasan Kayalı, 'The Ottoman Experience of World War I: Historiographical Problems and Trends', *Journal of Modern History* 89 (December 2017), 880–881.

2. Zürcher, *Turkey*, 164.

3. Hasan Kayalı, 'The Struggle for Independence', in *The Cambridge History of Turkey*, 4:116–117.

4. Kayalı, 'The Struggle for Independence', 122.

5. Quoted in Erik J. Zürcher, 'Young Turks, Ottoman Muslims and Turkish Nationalists: Identity Politics 1908–38', in *The Young Turk Legacy and Nation Building*, 223–224.

6. Suny, *"They Can Live in the Desert but Nowhere Else"*, 339.

7. Hervé Georgelin, *La fin de Smyrne. Du cosmopolitisme aux nationalismes* (Paris: CNRS Éditions, 2005), 199–225.

8. A forty-one-year-old Enver Pasha was killed by the Soviet Army in Turkestan (today Tajikistan), Central Asia, in 1922.

9. Among them was Ali Kemal, great-grandfather of Boris Johnson, British prime minister (2019–). 'Boris Johnson - How We Did It', *Who Do You Think You Are?*, BBC One, www.bbc.co.uk/whodoyouthinkyouare/new-stories/boris-johnson/how-we-did-it_1.shtml.

10. *Türkiye Diyanet Vakfı İslam Ansiklopedisi*, s.v. 'Mehmed VI', by Cevdet Küçük, https://islamansiklopedisi.org.tr/mehmed-vi.

11. Spending the last twenty years of his life devoted to prayer, painting, and music, he passed away in Paris on 23 August 1944, two days before the city was liberated from the Nazis. His corpse remained in the Grand Mosque of Paris for a decade before it was given permission for burial in Medina, Saudi Arabia. *Türkiye Diyanet Vakfı İslam Ansiklopedisi*, s.v. 'Abdülmecid Efendi', by Cevdet Küçük, https://islamansiklopedisi.org.tr /abdulmecid-efendi.

12. League of Nations, Treaty Series, No. 807, Convention Concerning the Exchange of Greek and Turkish Populations and Protocol, signed at Lausanne, January 30, 1923, article 1.

13. Renée Hirschon, 'The Consequences of the Lausanne Convention: An Overview', in *Crossing the Aegean: An Appraisal of the 1923 Compulsory Population Exchange Between Greece and Turkey*, ed. Renée Hirschon (Oxford: Berghahn Books, 2003), 14.

14. Çağlar Keyder, *State and Class in Turkey: A Study in Capitalist Development* (London: Verso, 1987), 79.

15. Esra Özyürek, 'Introduction', in *The Politics of Public Memory in Turkey*, ed. Esra Özyürek (Syracuse, NY: Syracuse University Press, 2007), 1–15, here 3.

16. Quoted in Uğur Ümit Üngör, *The Making of Modern Turkey: Nation and State in Eastern Anatolia, 1913–1950* (Oxford: Oxford University Press, 2012), 224.

CONCLUSION: THE OTTOMAN PAST ENDURES

1. 'Atatürk's Speech at the 10th Anniversary of the Turkish Republic', October 29, 1933, Atatürk Society of America, ataturksociety.org.

2. Quoted in Raffi Khatchadourian, 'A Century of Silence', *New Yorker*, 5 January 2015, 32–53, here 36.

3. Quoted in Baer, *The Dönme*, 250.

4. On Gökçen's role as a pilot during the Dersim rebellion, and a photo of her in uniform, see Hanioğlu, *Atatürk*, 210–211; on the massacres in Dersim and Gökçen's Armenian background, see Göçek, *Denial of Violence*, 347–348, 420, and 598 note 69, as well as Hrant Dink, 'Sabiha-Hatun'un sırrı', *Agos* 6 (February 2004): 1.

5. Zürcher, 'Young Turks, Ottoman Muslims and Turkish Nationalists', 232.

6. Fethiye Çetin, 'Hikâyelerden köprüler kurmak', in Ayşe Gül Altınay and Fethiye Çetin, *Torunlar* (Istanbul: Metis, 2009), 20.

7. Pamuk, *The White Castle*, 135.

8. Pamuk, *The White Castle*, 58.

9. Pamuk, *The White Castle*, 64, 74–75.

INDEX

Basic Books UK is a dynamic new imprint from John Murray Press that seeks to inform, challenge and inspire its readers. It brings together authoritative and original voices from around the world to make a culturally rich and broad range of ideas accessible to everyone. Drawing on the most innovative thinking in the worlds of politics, history, economics, science, and literature, Basic Books explores the interconnectedness of ideas and institutions that determine how we live, work and feel and reflects the key issues that affect us as individuals and as a society.

PUBLISHED BY BASIC BOOKS UK

Mediocre by Ijeoma Oluo

Survival of the City by Edward Glaeser and David Cutler

Life is Simple by Johnjoe McFadden

Rule of the Robots by Martin Ford

Making Darkness Light by Joe Moshenska

The Ottomans by Marc David Baer

A Natural History of the Future by Rob Dunn

The Nowhere Office by Julia Hobsbawm

Free Speech by Jacob Mchangama

Hidden Games by Moshe Hoffman and Erez Yoeli

The Ceiling Outside by Noga Arikha

Before We Were Trans by Kit Heyam

Slouching Towards Utopia by J. Bradford DeLong

African Europeans by Olivette Otele

How to Be Good by Massimo Pigliucci

The Mongol Storm by Nicholas Morton

For Profit by William Magnuson

Escape from Model Land by Erica Thompson